S0-AEP-248

FIBERGLASS BOATBUILDING
FOR AMATEURS

by

KEN HANKINSON, NAVAL ARCHITECT

PUBLISHED BY
GLEN-L MARINE DESIGNS

OTHER PRACTICAL "HOW-TO" BOATING BOOKS
PUBLISHED BY GLEN-L:

"BOATBUILDING WITH PLYWOOD"
"INBOARD MOTOR INSTALLATIONS"
"HOW TO BUILD BOAT TRAILERS"
"HOW TO FIBERGLASS BOATS"

FOR BOOK LITERATURE, WRITE TO:
GLEN-L MARINE DESIGNS
9152 Rosecrans
Bellflower, CA 90706

AUTHOR'S NOTE: The author does not necessarily approve of, or condone all of the building procedures, practices, or methods that may be shown in the photos or illustrations, especially from a safety standpoint. The figure numbers designating illustrations and photos refer to chapter number and the respective sequence. For example, Fig. 16-1 refers to the first illustration in Chapter 16.

COPYRIGHT 1982
GLEN-L, Bellflower, California
LIBRARY OF CONGRESS
CATALOG CARD NUMBER
82-80253
ISBN 0-939070-05-7

ALL RIGHTS RESERVED
PRINTED IN THE U.S.A.

No part of this book may be reproduced in any form without permission in writing from the publisher.

TABLE OF CONTENTS

acknowledgements

As is often said in other books in this section, no book is the product of a single person, and this book is no exception. The subject of fiberglass boatbuilding, even as it applies to the amateur alone, is simply too broad for a single person to know ALL about ALL aspects. On a subject like this, the author's job is to not only articulate his own knowledge, but to sort and sift through the body of information available on the subject, and then put it down in a form that the neophyte can understand and use. To do this, he must call on the resources of others having the latest data and intimate involvement with the current developments in the field, working closely with them in order to spread the word. Thus, there are several people that I wish to thank who took the time to put up with numerous phone calls and personal interviews, and who reviewed certain portions of the text for accuracy and clarity. Without their help, this book would not have been possible.

First, there is Thomas J. Johannsen, President of Torin, Inc., the North American distributor for AIREX foam. Tom is not only an expert on the applications of foam cores in fiberglass boat construction, but a product representative of the highest integrity. Tom's experience with both the factory producer and the amateur "one-off" boatbuilder using foam cores probably surpasses that of any other person.

Second, there is William Seemann, President of Seemann Fiberglass. As the inventor and developer of C-FLEX fiberglass planking, Bill, more than any one person, has put fiberglass boatbuilding within the reach of the amateur. As far as down-to-earth practical information is concerned, there is probably no more knowledgeable expert.

Then there is Keith R. Walton, Director of Marine Products for the BALTEK Corporation, manufacturers of "CONTOUR-KORE" END-GRAIN BALSA core. Keith, who is also a naval architect, was invaluable as a source expert on the use of balsa core in fiberglass boatbuilding.

I am also grateful to Craig Riley, Product Manager from ORCON Corporation, for his ambitious help and interest in the book with regard to the applications of high modulus materials. With representatives such as Craig, amateur boatbuilders everywhere will be able to practically use the boatbuilding materials of tomorrow sooner than would be the case ordinarily. Mr. George Bush, representative of KNYTEX Corp., also helped corroborate much of the information on high modulus materials.

Special thanks is given to Mr. Dick Seward whose boat is shown under construction in Chapter 22, for his willingness to experiment with new construction methods and materials. Dick, along with Greg Nichols, the boat's designer, are the type of builders willing to experiment with new methods that help pave the way for other amateurs everywhere who want to keep up with the latest advances in technology.

I also want to thank Christopher G. Hart and David J. Reed of AMERICAN KLEGE-CELL Corporation for their assistance with regard to using foams in fiberglass boatbuilding, and Platt Monfort for providing information on his FERRO-GLASS system which deserves more interest from the amateur builder.

I should also mention various colleagues

in the field of design and construction who contributed their feedback, illustrations, and opinions, including Robert Steward, naval architect and former president of Huckins Yacht Corporation; Ted Brewer, noted naval architect; Norman Cross, well-known multihull designer; Ken Austin of South Bay Multihulls, and Joe Conboy of Joseph Conboy, Ltd.

Finally, and perhaps most important, I am indebted to the numerous amateur builders who, over the years, have provided a wealth of information by describing their problems and asking questions. When added up, they have helped perfect the fiberglass boatbuilding process and have made it easier and simpler for amateur boatbuilders in the future. To these builders I say, keep those cards and letters coming!

introduction

An introduction to a book gives the author a chance to define the scope of what is to follow and tell the reader generally what is going to be discussed. It's also a place where the author can delimit the text, or in other words, tell the reader what he will NOT read and why.

What's the goal of this book? Quite simply, it is to provide a ready reference that will cover as comprehensively as possible all aspects of building a boat from so-called "fiberglass" materials from the standpoint of the amateur builder. In the process, the author assumes that the reader/builder has NO PREVIOUS EXPERIENCE OR KNOWLEDGE of fiberglass materials and procedures. On the other hand, however, certain assumptions must be made, mainly that anyone who would attempt to undertake a boatbuilding project has reasonable "do-it-yourself" abilities, a reasonable amount of manual dexterity, a modicum of common sense, and a desire to learn and follow certain procedures and instructions. If you can't respond positively to these criteria, you may read the book, but you should probably not try to build a fiberglass boat.

The approach in writing the book has been to emphasize methods that are within the realm of the amateur builder. Just what does the "realm" include? With most amateurs, budgets are perhaps most important. The boatbuilding project shouldn't send one to the poor house. While there are many materials and methods that can be used to build a "fiberglass" boat, some are quite expensive, especially in relation to other materials and methods. Then too, the methods should be suitable for the typical novice. Generally, this means that methods requiring critical "do-or-die" procedures, or those that are labor intensive, or those that require highly trained skills, are best left to the factory. Luckily, and surprisingly to most novices, fiberglass boatbuilding need not fall into these categories as we'll explain later. Finally, the amateur builder should be assured of a reasonable degree of success with his project. Hence, "guinea pig" methods should be left to others.

While some amateurs are "experimenters" by nature and often pave the way to new and better methods, the typical amateur can't waste his hard-earned bucks on something that will offer questionable results. Thus, the text may not describe the ONLY way to build a fiberglass boat, or ALL the ways to build a fiberglass boat, or even the BEST way to build a fiberglass boat (however one may wish to define the word, "best"). But it WILL describe the PRACTICAL ways for the majority of amateurs to build a boat from fiberglass. We will, however, include some new approaches using some more advanced materials that hold promise for the amateur who is the more "experimental" type.

We will attempt to cover these boatbuilding procedures in three ways; first by written text, then by photos, and finally with illustrations. Over the years working with amateurs, the author has found one major problem with many amateur builders, and this is that many DON'T want to read; they just want to "DO" and get on with the project. While a picture may be worth a thousand words, the field of fiberglass technology is too complex to tell by pictures alone. You MUST be willing to read and learn about this field, even if for your own personal safety alone. Unless you have the luxury of a private "teacher" who will take you by the hand and guide you through all aspects from the bottom to the top, please invest the brief period of time it will take to read this book BEFORE venturing forth into the world of fiberglass boatbuilding. Doing so will no doubt save a lot of wasted time, effort, and most important, MONEY.

Because the field of fiberglass and plastics (not to mention boatbuilding and design in general) is rapidly changing, a book on these subjects can at best only reflect the state of the art at the time it is written. Naturally, it takes quite a while to gather all the information and actually get it to the printed page. Thus, in this fast-changing world of high technology, one can only hope that the information which follows will remain topical for as long as possible. That's why it is risky to make a statement that if any materials or methods have been left out, they have probably been considered as unproven, or too costly, or not readily available, or otherwise not within the scope of the average amateur.

In other words, while the text is as "up-to-date" as it can be, it is not necessarily the last word on the subject. The materials and processes used to make boats are constantly changing, not only because of changes in technology, but because of the changing needs and desires of people who build and use boats. These changes occur due to the world economy, inflationary pressures, fuel and material shortages, fashion, and the like. There is no question that boats in the future will have to be more economical to build and use. This means more sophisticated designs using stronger materials to make lighter boats. Although the future is always a bit frightening, there is no need to feel at this time that these needs can't or won't be fulfilled in the amateur-built boat. In fact, as will be shown, many of the materials used today to build fiberglass boats were yesterday's "high-technology" ma-

terials. They have proven to be as well suited to the professional builder as they have been to the amateur builder. It's all a process of education and experience that simply requires a little time.

Building a boat probably develops a higher sense of pride and accomplishment than any other endeavor. It's a hobby that the entire family can participate in. Boatbuilding results in a product that can provide years of enjoyment while retaining a certain amount of value that can usually be recouped when the boat is no longer needed. In short, it can be a good investment in many ways. Whether you want to build a small boat or a large one, whether it be a power boat or a sailboat, whether of round bilge form or hard-chine, if the reader follows the text, there is no reason why his boat cannot equal or exceed the quality of a comparable factory-built fiberglass boat.

At the beginning of this introduction, it was noted that there were some limitations. In other words, there are certain things that will NOT be covered, some of which ARE normally included in the typical "boatbuilding" text. For example, the subject of lofting (that is, redrawing the lines of the hull to full size) has been omitted. Also omitted are the topics of joinery, engine installations, electrical, plumbing, hardware, equipment, spars and rigging, and outfitting EXCEPT as these subjects relate specifically to the fiberglass structure (hull and deck primarily).

There are a couple of reasons for not including these subjects. First, books are expensive, and the bigger they are, the more costly they become to the ultimate buyer. Secondly, the author has already written books which include some of these topics, or in other cases, excellent texts already exist on the respective subjects. Highly recommended texts have been listed in the Bibliography, with a brief description of their contents so the reader can be better informed to see if they meet his needs.

Finally, the book is not a fiberglass repair

manual. This is a subject that could fill an entire book. However, for those looking for such a book, probably the best place to start is with the suppliers of fiberglass materials themselves. Since they are interested in selling the materials, many have published informative manuals that cover fiberglass repair procedures. But for the person who first builds his own fiberglass boat, if a repair is ever needed, he will be miles ahead of the game, and will no doubt be able to repair or maintain his own boat with little further education.

CHAPTER 1

The terminology "fiberglass" has practically become a household word over the past decade. Everyone THINKS they know what fiberglass is, but do they really? Many people think of fiberglass as a single homogeneous material such as wood, steel, or other plastics. To add to the confusion, there is an abundance of names for fiberglass which, quite simply, refer to the same thing.

For example, depending on the geographical area where you might be, or who may be doing the talking, you might hear terms like "glass fibre", or "glass reinforced plastic" (frequently abbreviated as "GRP"), all terms which are commonly used by the British. Or in this country, the terms "fiberglass reinforced plastic" (often abbreviated "FRP"), or "glass fiber", or simply "fiberglass" are commonly used. Whichever is the case, they all refer to the same generic product.

For our purposes in order to keep things simple, throughout this book we'll call this form of plastic boatbuilding technology "fiberglass", since this is what most people call it. But later in the text, we'll be exploring other materials used in a similar fashion to build boats which are NOT actually a form of REAL fiberglass. Because these other materials can be used in conjunction with fiberglass materials, the correct terminology in these instances should be "reinforced plastics", with the boats that result being referred to as "plastic" boats. However, these materials are so similar to fiberglass in the finished product that the generic "handle" will no doubt stick in most people's minds even though the boat may not be "100% fiberglass". The word "plastic" still carries a derogatory connotation in the minds of many regardless of how good or suitable the material may be for a given purpose.

So, what exactly is fiberglass? Regardless of the generic muddle, fiberglass, as we'll use the term, means a wide variety of laminated materials made up into the form of a composite usually consisting of relatively low strength plastic resins combined with relatively high strength reinforcements made from glass or other materials to form an end product, or "laminate". The materials are used this way because they have much improved characteristics when used in combination than if used individually. In other words, the components work in co-operation for a greater effect than the sum of their parts. In technical terms, we call this a "synergistic" material.

Yet although this fiberglass material is great for building boats, there probably is no such thing as an "all-fiberglass" boat (except perhaps for some small mass produced plastic dinghies), and there is no reason why there should be. Fiberglass boats are usually a combination of materials that use the best qualities of the materials involved, forming a true "composite" structure. As we'll see, fiberglass boats can include true fiberglass reinforcing fabrics, various types of resins, numerous forms of core materials including wood and plastic foams, wire meshes, and other organic and synthetic fiber reinforcements.

We have referred to the composition of the various materials and how in fiberglass boatbuilding a laminate is formed from them. In other words, a structure is formed by applying layers of the various materials

FIG. 1-1 — The 11' "FEATHER" daysailer is an ideal fiberglass boatbuilding project for the beginner. Photos of the
construction of this boat are shown in Chapter 16. This
"one-off" male molded design from GLEN-L uses the
C-FLEX fiberglass planking method.

1 what is a fiberglass boat?

together with a liquid resin that saturates and bonds them all together. This is similar to how a sheet of plywood is made. The thin wood veneers can be likened to the various layers of fiber reinforcement, with the glue being the liquid resin which bonds the layers together, making the laminate a serviceable structural component. This combination of materials when used in fiberglass structures is commonly referred to as the "layup", and the process of saturating them with resin is called "wetting out". We will use variations of these two terms frequently.

Once the reader accepts the definition of fiberglass and the possibility of using the materials for boatbuilding, the next question is usually, how is it done? When one considers that it is conceivable to take a free flowing sticky liquid like resin, and combine it with a limp, floppy fabric like fiberglass, and form an incredibly tough, rigid, structure, certainly some magic must be involved, and there is. One form of the magic is chemical, while the other form of the magic is not magic at all, but is quite physical in its requirement.

We'll discuss both the chemical and physical "magic" in more detail in later chapters. But to introduce the reader to the entire concept in simple terms, the physical requirement is basically a surface against which the laminate can be applied. It follows that by shaping this surface, we can make up a laminate into just about any form or shape desired.

The surface used to shape a boat hull, or any other part, is called the "mold". In fiberglass boatbuilding, there are basically two types of mold, which can best be described with the comparison to a bowl. If we layup the laminate on the inside of the bowl, the mold is referred to as a "female" mold. Conversely, if we layup the laminate on the outside of the bowl, the mold is referred to as a "male" mold. In purely structural terms, it makes absolutely no difference technically whether our laminate is laid up on the outside or the inside of the bowl, or mold. However, a unique quality of fiberglass boat construction is that whatever the surface quality of the mold is, it is transferred IN EVERY DETAIL directly to the surface of the molded part that is against the surface of the mold. Since it is possible to build a mold with extremely fine, smooth surfaces, it stands to reason that we would want this surface transferred to the surface of our boat's hull, and indeed this is exactly what takes place in production fiberglass boatbuilding.

However, there is one catch, and this is that it is extremely tedious and costly to build such a "female" mold in the first place. In order for the effort and cost to be worth it, many hulls have to be built to amortize the cost of the mold. Furthermore, in order to build the female mold, another part must first exist called the "plug". This plug can be an actual boat hull or part, but it is usually a rather elaborate "mock-up" over which the female mold is made, in effect, being the "male" part. In short, it takes the production builder three major steps (the "plug", the "mold", and the molded hull or part) before he has his first actual boat to sell. We'll discuss the entire process in more detail in Chapter 15.

In the early days of fiberglass technology, it took years to perfect the female mold procedures that are now commonplace. While this production technology eventually brought boating within the reach of millions by lowering the cost to both buy and keep a boat, it also made things difficult for the amateur who just wanted to build a single fiberglass boat. In boatbuilding, the terminology, "one-off", is used to describe the building of a single boat, or perhaps a few boats, and because of the expense and work, the female mold process usually rules it out for "one-off" work.

Furthermore, the equipment and methods involved are usually beyond the skills and budgets of most amateurs. This is not to say that there are not techniques available to build female molds easily and cheaply; there are and one such approach will be discussed in Chapter 15. However, female molded boats are usually not as practical for the amateur. What works in the factory does not necessarily apply to the person building his own boat even though the materials used by either are basically the same.

Nevertheless, numerous attempts have been made along the evolutionary trail of fiberglass boatbuilding to provide a means by which it is easy and practical to build just a single "one-off" fiberglass boat, including variations with both female and male mold methods. Only in the recent past, however, with the development and refinement of the materials and methods featured in this book, has it been practical for the amateur to build his own fiberglass boat, AND with quality of structure and finish that equals or even surpasses that of factory production methods. It is with these methods and materials on which we will focus the major attention of this text.

CHAPTER 2   can you build your own fiberglass boat?

Can you build your own fiberglass boat? Sure, why not? But this is more than simply a rhetorical question. What we are talking about are the skills and abilities and even personal character traits required to carry off the project successfully. We all know that some people succeed while others do not. But what makes the difference?

To best answer our chapter heading question, one must keep in mind that boats built in the past, before the invention of fiberglass, required highly skilled workmen who fabricated special parts and assembled them under highly labor intensive conditions that did not lend themselves to mass production techniques. This made boats expensive, relatively speaking, and kept them from being as common as they are today. It was possible for an amateur to build his own boat in order to save costs, but he still required greater skills and abilities than the average person, as well as a large assortment of tools with which to do the work. Hence, amateur boatbuilders were a rare breed, with the majority of "home-built" boats being rather simple, inexpensive craft relegated to the smaller sizes for the most part.

The invention of fiberglass reinforcements together with polyester and other plastic resins changed all the past premises and limitations, and made the mass production of boats inevitable. Although the process of tooling up for a production boat was and is costly, and a gamble, this expense can be quickly amortized and recouped after a certain number of hulls have been sold. Although certain operations in the production of fiberglass boats require some specially trained workers, by and large the molding processes use basically unskilled workers compared to the skilled labor required in the past. Hence, labor costs have dropped, production has increased, and boat prices have dropped, relatively speaking.

The key point to keep in mind in deciding whether you can build your own fiberglass boat is that basically unskilled labor is required for the construction of the hull, and perhaps the other major components such as the cabin and deck. This is especially so using the materials and methods we will concentrate upon. In other words, fiberglass boatbuilding is suitable for ANYONE. What skills ARE required can be learned quickly, and are really more in the form of special "techniques" rather than actual skills in the usual sense. Furthermore, mistakes in fiberglass work which may occur can usually be readily corrected so that it is rather difficult to botch up a project completely, such as could occur, for example, in welding up a steel hull in the improper sequence causing not only a poor "oil can" surface, but even a hull distorted completely out of shape and not correctable.

However, there are other factors to consider and other questions to ask yourself if you want to have a successful project. First, start off with a project that is within your means size-wise, cost-wise, and time-wise. More boatbuilding project are aborted midstream because a builder bit off more than he could chew than for any other reason.

If you are not sure of your abilities or your desire to work in fiberglass, then build a smaller boat first, using the material or method you would like to work with on the bigger project. This way, if you change your mind, you won't be out much in either time, work, or money. But more importantly, you'll gain experience quickly, together with the necessary confidence, as well as getting a "feel" for the boatbuilding process. Although this "crawl-before-you-walk" approach of starting with a small boat first is advocated, it must be admitted that many people who have never built a boat before often jump in head first and successfully build a much bigger boat than would be advisable.

Another way to guarantee a successful project is to start off with a good set of plans. This is covered in more detail in Chapter 9, but suffice it to say now, don't try to go "creative" and design your own boat. The value of a good set of plans will be repaid many times over by the savings in time and work that they will provide. Carefully consider the type of boat you want or need to suit your requirements, and once the plans have been selected, stick to them. Follow the recommendations of the designer as closely as possible. The chief cause of an inferior "home-built" boat is usually failing to follow the design, and branching out on your own.

While making minor changes is one of the main reasons for building your own boat, always check with the designer first to make sure that modifications are feasible and will not cause any structural damage to the boat which could affect its performance or safety. And if you do get into rather extensive modifications, be willing to pay for his services. A naval architect is a professional just like a doctor or a lawyer. He survives because of what he knows. The plans that he prepares are more than pieces of paper; they are valuable information that took time and ability, and if changes are desired, it should be realized that more of his time will be required, the same as if you consulted with your doctor or lawyer.

Probably the most important quality determining the successful outcome of your project, however, is not skill, ability, or money. Instead, it is the quality of *perseverance*. The person who can stick with the project through thick and thin, who plods ahead even if ever so slowly, and who has the patience to do things the "right" way instead of the "quick-and-dirty" way, will turn out a far superior craft than the impatient, slap-dash worker bent on short-cutting his way through.

Many people are afraid that they don't have the ability to handle tools and do the manual labor required in boatbuilding. But quite frankly, virtually none of the tools required takes any special skill that cannot be quickly learned. In fact, the skills or techniques can be quickly learned once you get a feel for what has to be done. Anyone who has average "do-it-yourself" abilities can build a fiberglass boat. Furthermore, the tools used are common types readily available, and you will not need to invest much for them. In fact, the few power tools that are absolutely necessary can either be rented or purchased. If they won't be needed in the future, they can always be resold so that much of your investment can be recouped.

There is one final quality that will definitely prove of service in the boatbuilding project, and this is what is best called "scrounging" ability. The person who can really organize himself, and who can really "bird dog" for tools, supplies, and equipment, will really save on his boatbuilding project. However, not everyone has this ability, even with the resources that are available to us all today. Planning ahead is NOT a quality that all of us have, yet it is vital in a boatbuilding project that may go on for a considerable period of time. For example, the shrewed "scrounger" realizes that boating is a seasonal activity, and the best prices and buys can be had in the off-season. Another aspect of this ability is that one can often trade or barter for goods and services with others looking for similar deals. The "scrounger" is the type that often "kills two birds with a single stone", taking care to conserve his resources and not waste time. Not only does this person seem the happiest during the boatbuilding project, he is also the one who saves the most money.

FIG. 2-1 — The 9' "FOAMEE" hull is built using a PVC foam sandwich core with thin fiberglass skins on each side. The result is a strong, lightweight sailing dinghy ideal as a starter project for the amateur. Photos of this GLEN-L design under construction are shown in Chapter 19.

CHAPTER 3

why build a fiberglass boat?

Part of the reason for this chapter is to reconfirm some of the facts about fiberglass as a boatbuilding material and to dispell some of the myths. As most people realize, there are many materials that can be used to build boats, whether they be factory built or built by the amateur. Not very long ago, there was a time when it seemed that EVERYONE wanted a fiberglass boat. In the early days of fiberglass boats, the material was, at the least, "oversold" by over-zealous salespeople and the boating press, who no doubt saw a goldmine in advertising dollars from the jillions of up-and-coming fiberglass boatbuilding firms.

We were told that fiberglass boats were "maintenance-free", were lighter in weight, were faster and stronger, and would last virtually forever. And when oil was cheap, fiberglass boats were also cheaper than those made from other materials for the most part, or at least highly competitive with regard to price. Because it was easy for a person to become a fiberglass boatbuilder (all you had to do was go get a competitor's boat, tip it upsidedown, take a mold right from it, and you were in business), fiberglass boatbuilding firms sprung up overnight in every corner imaginable.

But now that fiberglass boats have been with us for quite a period of time, and taking into consideration the horrendous rise in oil prices in the past several years, a degree of "normalcy" (for want of a better term) has been restored in the boatbuilding field. As the storm blew over, boaters who had different needs and requirements realized that, lo and behold, there indeed were other materials that could be used to build a boat, and in many cases, more suitably so than with

fiberglass. Thus there has been a revived interest in boats built from all sorts of materials, such as plywood, wood, steel, and aluminum, all of which took somewhat of a "back seat" when fiberglass hit the scene. The point is that more and more people have come to realize the real advantages and shortcomings of fiberglass, so the material must stand on its REAL merits, and not those dreamed up by advertising copywriters. Let's look into the purported advantages of fiberglass boats and maybe we'll help decide why YOU as an amateur builder REALLY want to build and own a fiberglass boat.

FIBERGLASS BOATS ARE "MAINTENANCE FREE"

Over the years this has probably been the most touted reason to have a fiberglass boat. However, this aspect has also been the most highly oversold. First and foremost, there is no such thing as a "maintenance-free" boat, and there probably never will be. Boats are like any other mechanized object; they all require some sort of maintenance.

It IS true, however, that fiberglass boats, at least with regard to those portions of the boat (especially the hull) that are built out of fiberglass, do require FAR LESS maintenance than just about any other boatbuilding material. However, one need only take a walk through any good sized marina and see what happens to fiberglass boats that are neglected by their owners. While there may be no suffering from "dry rot" (that old malady of wood boats usually blown all out of proportion to its actual damaging effects), one can see fiberglass boats suffering from cracked and crazed gel coats (the exposed exterior surface on fiberglass moldings), pockmarked surfaces (called "osmosis"), faded and discolored surfaces, and even evidence of structural problems which will be discussed in further detail in following chapters.

The difference in maintenance compared to boats built from other materials, then, is one of degree. Those shiny bright, slick surfaces of fiberglass boats eventually must have attention, either by a thorough waxing and polishing, or they must be painted just like any boat. It is often argued that while a wood boat, for example, may require a fresh coat of paint each and every season, as long as the job is not skipped, it may actually be easier to apply a coat of paint than it is to do a waxing and polishing job on a fiberglass boat, at least in terms of pure elbow grease. Think about it!

While most factory-built fiberglass boats depend on special gel coat resins for the durability of their external surfaces, more than one fiberglass boat manufacturer has converted to applying paint OVER these gel coated hulls for added durability and better appearance. If the boat is to remain in the water, a fiberglass boat needs a coat of bottom paint just like any other boat that will remain in the water for long periods.

FIBERGLASS BOATS ARE LIGHTER

It is a common misconception that fiberglass is a "lightweight" material. While it is true that one can build a lightweight fiberglass boat, consider this: Fiberglass laminates weigh more than an equal weight of water, and therefore, they will NOT float. As we all know by comparison, most woods DO float. So which is lighter? Obviously wood is. This is one of the reasons why factory-built fiberglass boats often include large volumes of flotation material; they will NOT float on their own if the hull is punctured below the waterline.

But please don't misconstrue what we are saying. While fiberglass (meaning fiberglass reinforcements and polyester resin in a laminate) are not particularly light in weight, it does NOT mean that they cannot be used to build boats that are NOT light in weight, especially when used in a "composite" such as we'll discuss in this book.

The fact is that in the future, boats are going to have to be lighter in weight regardless of the material used in their construction in order to be economical to buy, operate, and transport as energy costs continue to escalate. And fiberglass will no doubt play an important part in the search for lighter, stronger structures. But its use will also include other materials as well, which have more favorable strength-to-weight factors. Some of these strong, lightweight materials will be discussed in later chapters.

FIBERGLASS BOATS ARE STRONGER

Actually, fiberglass with resin is a very flimsy sort of material quite lacking in stiffness, although in common parlance it is quite "tough". Just like other materials, however, one can build a boat from fiberglass that may be weak or strong; it all depends on how it is done. With fiberglass, great care is necessary in the design and construction to assure that proper stiffening is incorporated into the structure, and because of the nature of the material, no weak spots or areas of concentrated stresses are built in.

Other materials, such as steel and plywood, are much more forgiving with regard to structural oversights. With fiberglass, where the builder is dealing with chemical considerations as well as physical properties, some care is required in the building process to assure that the boat is strong enough. In the past, when a production fiberglass boat was found to have marginal strength, the builder merely slopped on a few more layers of fiberglass laminate in the given areas, in effect, increasing the hull thickness. However, today with the high price of resin and the need for ever-lighter boats, this is an outdated practice and emphasizes the need for more sophisticated use of materials.

The truth of the matter is that when fiberglass boatbuilding was a new technology, fiberglass boats were often severely lacking in strength. Early fiberglass boats frequently suffered structural shortcomings, even in boats built by major producers. Bulkheads popping out, hulls cracking, leaking hull-to-deck joints, stress concentrations causing hull failures or distortions, and other horror stories were unfortunately all too often true. As with any new technology, it takes time to work the "bugs" out, and such was the case with fiberglass. Luckily, these sorts of problems are seldom heard any longer now that builders and designers know more about what they are doing.

FIBERGLASS BOATS ARE FASTER

With the exception of heavy materials like steel, there are fast boats built out of a wide range of materials. The argument continues as to just what is the "best" material for so-called "fast" boats.

If one is talking in terms of competition type craft, whether power or sailboats, it is easy to find boats winning racing events built out of many different materials. While speed directly benefits from less weight, there is absolutely no reason why a fiberglass boat would be any faster than a boat built from another material if the boats were to the same design of similar power or speed potential, and the same weight.

Just consider that some of the record holding powerboats, such as the racing hydros, are built from plywood. Yet most of the ocean powerboat racers have been built

of fiberglass. On the other hand, many of the race-winning sailboats in the larger sizes have been built from aluminum or from the new "high modulus" sandwich core composites like those mentioned later in this book.

FIBERGLASS BOATS ARE WORTH MORE

This sweeping generalization may or may not be true, depending on many variables. Resale value in particular is a very fickle element which varies with locale, the current state of the economy, fashion, the quality of construction or maintenance of any given craft under consideration, and the degree of equipment that may be included in the evaluation.

While it is true that the population has generally been "hypnotized" by the advertising copywriters and much of the boating press into believing that fiberglass is the "only" boatbuilding material, the actual facts have been coming to surface. Whereas only a few years ago we found only fiberglass boatbuilders advertising in the many boating magazines, we now see advertising for wood boatbuilders, steel boatbuilders, aluminum boatbuilders, and others. In fact, the magazines themselves are now devoting more editorial content to many more hull construction materials and methods than they once did, mainly because different materials are better for different boats in different places.

All this has had a big effect on the value of boats, whether new or used. Where fiberglass boats may be the only type that can be sold in one area, only wood boats, for example, would fetch a good price in another area. In other words, the value of any boat will vary.

As far as the amateur-built boat is concerned, one often hears that they have inherently poorer resale value. However it is the author's experience that this certainly need not be the case, and often an amateur-built boat may actually be worth more. Part of this problem is one of semantics. When one runs across a superbly constructed amateur-built boat that sells for a good price, it is usually listed or referred to as "custom-built". On the other hand, when one sees a botched job by an amateur, we hear the negative connotation, "home-made".

As a designer who has dealt with amateur builders for many years, I am convinced that if you follow the plans and do a conscientious job throughout your building project, there is no reason why your boat can't be good enough to be called "custom-built" as opposed to just "home-made". It all depends on YOU, the builder. Of course, if you simply don't care about these matters, then don't complain at the time the boat is sold about getting a poor price for it if you chose not to take the necessary care during the construction. If you go "creative" and build a monstrosity that is a "white elephant", it's nobody's fault but your own.

Another element which goes hand-in-hand with the valuation problem is one of insurance. Some amateur builders have had bad experiences in insuring their vessels, and in many cases with good reason. If you create such a monstrosity that nobody else wants it but yourself (in other words, a "valueless" boat), how can an insurance underwriter be expected to issue insurance on such a boat? It probably is NOT because the boat is "home-made", but rather because a value cannot be established since none exists! On the other hand, if your boat features the "custom-built" approach we mentioned previously, then it's usually just a matter of determining the true insurable value of the boat in question, and this is usually accomplished by survey. Thus, while you may not like paying the premium, or you may feel that the valuation determined by the survey is not high enough, there is no reason why your boat

should not be insurable.

THE COST CONSIDERATION

Fiberglass is NOT the cheapest material with which to build a boat, especially for the amateur builder. But then, boats are not cheap either, and probably never will be. We've made a cost comparison to other materials that might be used by the amateur boatbuilder in the Appendix, but this is purely on a materials cost per square foot basis, and does not consider many unknowns.

While determining the cost early in the construction IS an important factor for most amateurs, let it be stated at the outset that anyone who tells you how much it is going to cost to build YOUR boat is simply a liar! Unfortunately, there are a few rather unscrupulous firms in the profession selling boat plans who will tell prospective amateur builders anything they want to hear. This includes giving unrealistic cost figures when, quite simply, the costs are undeterminable, even by experts.

Determining how much a boat will cost to build is a lot like buying a new car. First, there's the "sticker" price, and then you start adding on all the "goodies" desired in order to get the actual price. With a boat, it's even harder, and the bigger and more complex the boat becomes, the harder it gets. You, as the builder and owner, must first make some decisions. How you wish to equip and outfit your boat is strictly a matter of personal preference. For example, your boat may require an engine of a given rating for power. But there are many different brands of engines, and for a given horse-power, prices may vary considerably. Again taking the automobile analogy, a Chevrolet and a Cadillac may both be cars, but they sure don't cost the same. This comparison can be applied to just about everything used in building a boat. There are so many choices in materials and equipment that it is possible for a given boat to be twice as costly as its identical twin EVEN IF EQUIPPED WITH COMPARABLE EQUIPMENT, but purchased from different suppliers at different times. Of course, "ball park" estimates are possible, and it is here that some progress can be made in determining, perhaps not how much you will spend, but how much you are likely to save by building your own boat.

The problem with fiberglass boats is that as they get smaller, it becomes more difficult to justify building one yourself. In the smaller sizes, and by this we are talking about boats LESS than 20' in length, mass production techniques and competition are such that smaller boats can be purchased ready-made for quite favorable prices. This is NOT to say that you may not still want to build your own fiberglass boat in the smaller sizes, but merely to point out the truth that you will have a harder and harder time saving any money the smaller the boat becomes.

However, as the size of the boat increases, so too does the chance to realize ever-greater cost savings. Because the larger boats are more labor intensive (both with regard to production boats as well as to amateur-built boats), the labor becomes a bigger "chunk" of the total cost. And because you will be providing your own labor "free" so to speak, you'll save on this big portion of the cost.

Other savings by the amateur include things like dealer mark-ups, sales commissions, costs of advertising, transportation, and the typical items of "overhead" which are a part of production boatbuilding that will not be applicable to the person building his own boat. While it's hard to make any definite statements, probably the best that can be said about cost savings (considering our break in boat size being in the 20' category as the bottom line for any appreciable savings to occur) is that most amateurs will be able to save about 1/3 over the cost of a COMPARABLE production boat, and in the

case of those "scroungers" we dicussed earlier, some may be fortunate to save up to around 50%. Note that this assumes comparable boats, and by this, we mean a boat of as nearly the same size, type, and degree of equipment as will be the boat you undertake to build. But there are NO guarantees. If you are not careful, are a poor planner, waste time and materials, buy at the wrong times from the wrong sources, make mistakes, and otherwise go at the project in the wrong way, there is a chance that you won't save a dime. In fact, you may spend more than what it would cost for a comparable production boat.

But then again, building a boat yourself is not always done to save money. In fact, while many amateurs begin work on this pretense, many become boatbuilding fanatics, enjoying the hobby so much that the end use of the boat becomes secondary to the construction. Some even sell their boats as soon as they are done, and start again with another. Don't be surprised if it happens to you; boatbuilding is a contagious hobby, but a wholesome one as well.

Getting back to the discussion on costs, about the only element of the project that can be narrowed down to any degree early in the planning stages is the actual cost of the hull construction materials alone. Here there is not as much room for deviation, even though there may be several options all using fiberglass in one form or another. A boat will take so much resin and so much fiberglass, and not much else of any great magnitude. The problem with determining the exact amount of materials that will be required, however, is not how much is used, but instead, how much is lost. If more resin is mixed than can be used, or fiberglass materials are cut without considering waste, or any number of other variables that could occur during the construction procedures, you could spend and use much more than may actually be required.

As far as depending on the designer to tell you how much it will cost for hull materials alone, remember that while he may be able to tell how much it costs in his area, you may be many hundreds or even thousands of miles away from him. Costs for supplies will vary considerably depending on the area in which the hull will be built. Inflationary pressures and energy problems don't help the situation either. The cost one day may not be the cost on the next day, because materials used in fiberglass boatbuilding, especially resins, have a record of price volatility, as well as availability problems. In fact, these problems with fiberglass boatbuilding materials have been some of the reasons why there has been a renewed interest in other boatbuilding materials; in many cases other materials have proven both cheaper and easier to get.

IS A FACTORY-BUILT BOAT BETTER THAN ONE BUILT BY AN AMATEUR?

This is surely a legitimate question to pose, for if the amateur cannot build a boat that will at least be the equal of a factory-built boat in terms of quality, it would be folly to waste time with the project. However, it is perhaps presumptuous to consider that ALL factory-built boats are automatically superior craft of high quality. Such is surely not the case; some boats built by factories feature very high quality, while others do not. Yet the materials used by either boatbuilder are probably virtually the same type, and as far as the amateur is concerned, he will be using the same materials also. So as long as the design is sound and the quality of workmanship is good, there really is no reason why the amateur-built boat cannot equal a factory-built boat, at least in terms of quality of materials.

But what about appearance and structural integrity and quality of workmanship? Obviously, these are all variables. For example, the ability of each amateur will vary just as it will with the factory worker. Yet, if the amateur can follow instructions,

grasp the reading of a blueprint, and have some manual ability, there is certainly nothing difficult about emulating a worker in the factory situation. In fact, the basic, simple nature of handling fiberglass materials is not only what has made factory fiberglass boat production possible, but has made fiberglass hobbycraft so widely popular with the masses.

Of course, the actual appearance of the boat has as much to do with the designer as with the worker, so half the battle is whether or not a good looking design done by a professional is chosen. It is your job to interpret and carry out the design as the designer intended, and if questions arise about how to do it, contact the designer personally and ask him what his thoughts and intentions were.

As far as structural integrity of the boat is concerned, assuming that the design is sound, and proper practices as described in this book are followed, there is no reason why your boat should be inferior in terms of the actual structural integrity. In fact, there is every reason to believe that the person building his own boat will take more care than would some indifferent factory worker who has no personal stake in the boat he builds.

Quality control is one of the main problems in the factory situation, and when building your own boat, who is better qualified than YOU to assure that all steps are adhered to, that all laminates are installed as specified, and that the proper materials have been used throughout? Since the amateur is not working to a timeclock and it's his life on the line when at sea, building your own boat can give much peace of mind.

WHAT'S THE DIFFERENCE IN A PRODUCTION BOAT AND AN AMATEUR "ONE-OFF"?

If it is assumed that both boats are built in

a female mold, as can be done in some cases practically by the amateur, there need be no difference between the factory-built boat and one built by an amateur. In fact, many production builders were once amateurs who started out in business in exactly this manner.

However, what we are getting at here is just what the difference is between those boats built IN a female mold on an assembly line, and those boats built OVER a male mold using "one-off" processes. In this latter instance there IS a difference, but only ONE difference.

As noted earlier, the boat built in a female mold is a three-part process, with the hull being made in a mold which imparts the mold surface directly to the molded part, in our case, the hull of the boat or perhaps the boat's superstructure as well. In female mold work, the hull is literally built from the outside to the inside, with the first layer of the laminate being applied against the mold surface.

On the other hand, in male mold "one-off" hulls, the hull is built up over the male mold formwork from the inside to the outside, so there is no mold surface as such involved. As a result, in order to develop a surface quality similar to that imparted to the surface of the hull molded in a female mold, some work is required sanding and filling, with this then being followed with a coating system or "paint".

If the procedures discussed in this book are followed, and the hull painted properly using one of the modern coating systems, there is virtually no way to tell the difference between boats built with either method. Before the perfection of the several "one-off" materials and new finishing procedures, such was not the case. However, there is nothing unusual today about "one-off" male molded fiberglass boats, and there are numerous professionals who build boats day in and day out using the very same methods and materials that are described in this text. The best part is that these methods and materials are ideally suited to the amateur builder also.

In short, the female molded boat usually has a gel coat surface because this is the first product applied against the surface of the mold, while the male molded "one-off" boat does not, simply because it is not required and not applicable. The color of the female molded boat can be provided in the gel coat (although female molded boats may also be painted, as is sometimes the case), while the color on the outside of the male molded "one-off" boat must be provided by paint since there is no gel coat. Whether a boat has a gel coat or not makes no difference otherwise, and a boat built by one method is not necessarily superior nor inferior to one built by the other method.

CHAPTER 4

The tools and equipment used in amateur fiberglass boatbuilding will vary somewhat depending on the size, type, and complexity of the boat being built. For example, a small open dinghy may have little in the way of internal structure or fittings, in effect being a glorified plastic "bowl" in simplicity of form. A boat like this could be built with only a minimum of fiberglass tools. On the other hand, a large sail or power yacht would not only require a larger selection of fiberglass tools, but probably a large assortment of woodworking tools as well as mechanic's tools. While a distinction can be made for those tools used for fiberglass work as opposed to those used in other aspects of the project, the uses to which tools can be put sometimes overlap. For example, many tools used in fiberglass work are also used for woodworking, so there really is no clear-cut distinction in tool usage.

With a couple of notable exceptions, the tools used in fiberglass boatbuilding are similar whether the boat is being built in a female mold or over a male mold using a "one-off" process. Compared to other forms of boatbuilding using other materials, most tools used for fiberglass boat construction are simple and inexpensive, with nothing special or unique being required, at least for the amateur. Some of these tools will be shown in use in photos throughout the text.

As far as selecting the tools to use, our recommendations include certain things that are absolutely necessary to the boatbuilding operation, some things that are commonly used, and in many cases, items that will be optional depending on the builder's desires. Tools are a matter of personal preference often based on experience.

What's right for one builder may not be right for another. Furthermore, tools are changing all the time, and what may be state-of-the-art one day may be surpassed the next day by some new ingenious "labor saver". So don't feel that this chapter is arbitrary; if you feel that some other tool is better, by all means use it or at least give it a try. Perhaps it's one that is not known, and if this is the case, see to it that the word gets out if it succeeds.

Experience, like so many things in life, is always the best teacher. So use our recommendation only as a general guide, varying the listing to match the project as well as your needs and experiences. Just make sure that what is used is SAFE!

POWER TOOLS

The selection of power tools required can be limited, and such tools that would not be used frequently can be rented. However, rental costs can add up quickly, and it may be cheaper to buy and later resell the tool if it is no longer needed. For the most part, power tools should be of the portable type that can be taken to the work site, since you won't be able to bring the boat to the equipment because of its size.

For power tools, either the electric or pneumatic types can be used. Although one can scrounge around for used power tools, such as at swap meets, flea markets, and auctions, unless you are an expert in their evaluation, or can repair them when needed, it is probably wiser for the novice to buy new equipment.

While some may disagree (feeling that it

is best to buy cheap and wear it out, then buy cheap again), buy the most rugged power equipment affordable. If available, get the double insulated type or else provide a positive ground if they are electric tools. Working on a boat often involves working around water, moisture, damp ground, and the like, so this safety element should always be considered.

Most power tool makers usually have several lines of tools varying from cheap to expensive, and from handyman quality to commercial duty. Usually the more expensive a tool is, the better and longer it will last, AND the cheaper it will be in the long run in all probability. The lightweight, cheap equipment frequently featured by discounters just won't stand up to the arduous continuous-duty use required in boatbuilding work. Before purchasing power tools, especially sanders and grinders, check if possible with the instruction manual or the guarantee for any provisions AGAINST using the tool in fiberglass work. In some cases, tool makers void the warranty if used with fiberglass because the grinding dust from fiberglass can be extremely hard on electric motors. So whenever possible, search out "commercial quality" or "heavy duty" equipment; it will last longer, need fewer repairs, be more dependable, and if you decide to sell it later on, will probably be worth more money. As a personal opinion, good equipment is NOT an expense, but rather an investment! Good quality power equipment will ALWAYS be in demand, whether new or used, so buy the best you can afford.

Although most fiberglass boatbuilding requires a minimum of power equipment, there may be those who have had little experience handling such equipment. If you feel reluctant about using power tools, read through the listing of the tools to be used and get some experience with them. Sign up for a night school class in woodworking, or if you want to learn to use a disc sander, a good way would be to take an auto body

repair class. Mastery of this tool will go a long way in making your project a success. Using the power tools in our list does not require any special skills or unique coordination, just a little practice. While some of the work done with power tools in fiberglass boatbuilding can be tedious, there is certainly nothing required that an individual with average "hand-eye" coordination cannot accomplish with a bit of practice.

SANDERS

If building a fiberglass boat by a male mold method, your most important tool will be a power disc sander or grinder. On the other hand, if building a boat from a female mold, it is possible that there will be little need for this tool. The reason is that the disc sander will be your primary hull finishing tool with male mold methods, but in female mold work where the hull surface is formed by the smooth surface of the female mold, there is virtually little if any finish work required (assuming that you already possess the mold). Even in female mold work, however, you might still have a need for the disc sander for making your mold.

In any case, for those using male mold methods, let's talk about sanders a bit. Power sanders come in basically three types; belt sanders, disc sanders, and finish sanders, all either electric or air driven. Of course, with air driven tools you must have a compressor, and these can come in quite handy for many other tasks.

Finish sanders remove little material and are slow. For this reason, finish sanders can be used with a heavy hand without fear of damaging the surface. The primary purpose for finish sanders, however, is for final finish work prior to painting and for use between coats of paints in some cases.

Belt sanders may be used to a limited degree, and some actually prefer them. Both the belt sander and the disc sander take a bit of practice to prevent gouging and digging in, but once these skills are mastered, you'll find yourself operating these tools with a deft hand. With belt sanders, a heavy machine is preferable so that it won't "skip" around, letting the weight of the machine bear down on the surface so that the sanding belt can do the job without the operator bearing down tediously. Work the belt sander back and forth in long, even strokes as opposed to side-to-side motions, keeping the sanding surface as level as possible.

With disc sanders, select a dual-speed unit with a 7" to 9" diameter disc, turning from about 4500 to 6000 RPM, and with a low speed setting of from 1500 to 3000 RPM. This will be ideal for both sanding work and finishing or polishing. Otherwise, you should have two sanders, one to each specification. Numerous attachments are available for these machines, including different backing pads, polishing pads, grinding wheels, etc. For hull finish work, a plastic or rubber backed foam disc pad (see Chapter 13) gives a soft, resilient backing to the sanding disc. These pads are available in several densities and sizes, and their flexibility prevents or minimizes gouging and digging in when surface sanding. As a word of warning, however, be careful NOT to exceed the RPM rating of the pads you buy. Many of these pads use a disc adhesive to attach the sanding disc to the pad, although self-adhesive discs are available.

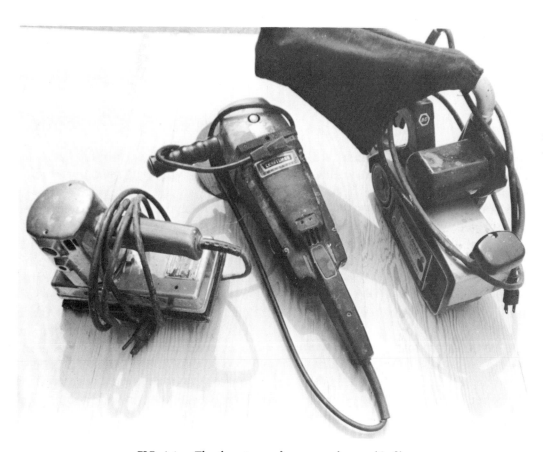

FIG. 4-1 — The three types of power sanders used in fiberglass boatbuilding as described in the text. Commercial duty tools are preferable for the rigorous use to which they will be subjected.

DRILLS

Probably the next most useful power tool will be a good power drill, preferably one that is of the variable speed type and reversible. A 3/8" is a handy size that will serve for both drilling and driving of screws. Have a good assortment of high quality drill bits since fiberglass is hard on tool edges. In most boat work, you'll need a good set of countersink bits and probably hole saws in several sizes. The variable speed drill also makes a good resin mixer. You can buy mixing attachments or make your own. For added convenience, a couple of these drills is desirable; one for drilling pilot holes, and another fitted with a screwdriver bit ready for driving screws so you don't have to keep changing bits constantly. Since these tools are relatively inexpensive and will come in handy forever, having two is an affordable luxury for most.

SAWS

Next on the list of power equipment will be saws. The extent that power saws will be necessary, however, will vary with the boat being built. Yet it is difficult to imagine any boatbuilding project that cannot benefit from both a portable jig saw or saber saw, and a portable circular saw. On larger projects, a power table saw or radial arm saw, not to mention a band saw, will definitely come in handy. Stationary saws will also allow a savings to be made on materials since you'll be able to resaw your own lumber to size. Even though the boat may be built primarily of fiberglass, a good amount of lumber will be used in most projects, if only for the building form and mold members.

With jig saws, there are all sorts of special blades that will come in handy with fiberglass work, including metal cutting blades, plywood blades, and blades unaffected by the abrasion caused by sawing through fiberglass. For the portable circular saw, an abrasive cut-off disc can be used for cutting C-FLEX fiberglass planking, either in the raw state or once it has been coated with resin.

The best blades to use on saws at the present state of technology are the carbide-tipped types. While they seem expensive in first cost, they last so much longer without resharpening, and cut so much more smoothly and faster, that they not only make the work more pleasurable, but safer as well. Of course, for rough work on the fiberglass itself, if you think that you may ruin a blade, use a cheaper expendable type if you wish. Note that the table or radial arm saws are stationary tools primarily used for woodworking operations, and may not necessarily be required or desired on the project that you are working on. This is a personal decision that each worker will have to make on his own.

OTHER POWER & EQUIPMENT

Other power equipment tools are largely optional types, the need for which will vary with working conditions, size of project, etc. For example, if conditions do not insure a positive flow of ventilation, a fan or two should be used, preferably of the large, slow speed type that will not set up noticeable drafts. Another handy piece of equipment is a large capacity power vacuum. As noted earlier, an air compressor is quite handy. Air driven tools eliminate any shock hazard, can be used in areas where electricity may not be available, and they tend to have more power and greater reliability. An air compressor via an air hose can be used to help keep the work area clean and for applying paints and finishes for those skilled with the use of spray guns. A heater may be necessary in colder areas to bring up ambient temperatures. But such a heater must not have an exposed flame that could ignite volatile fumes that will be present at the work site.

HAND TOOLS

Hand tools, like power tools, may be used exclusively for fiberglass work, or may serve a combination of purposes, including woodworking. Most of the tools used for fiberglass work are simple and inexpensive, and you can even make some of them yourself. Again the list will vary with the scope of the project, the builder's desires and experiences, his budget, etc.

For most projects, a good assortment of woodworking tools will still be required. These will be used for the basic formwork, hull supporting structure, interior, etc. The typical do-it-yourselfer will already have a good assortment of these, so this will save on expenses. Such tools as various types of clamps, a spirit level, a framing square, a plumb bob, hammers, planes, chisels, a good vise, screwdrivers, measuring tapes, wrenches, mechanic's tools, awls, a utility knife, sanding block, nail sets, sliding T-bevel, pliers, tin snips (used also for cutting lengths of C-FLEX), handsaws, hacksaws, and the like come in handy for most

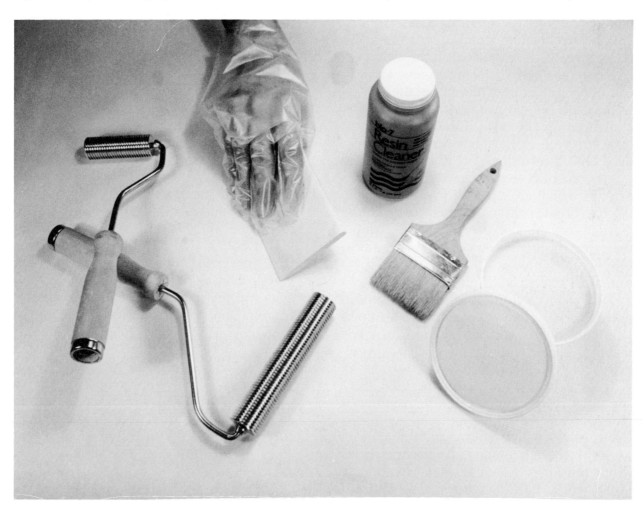

FIG. 4-2 — Hand tools used for doing fiberglass laminating work are simple and inexpensive. This photo shows the basic tools required, including metal mat rollers with unpainted wood handles with sockets for extensions, a vinyl rubber type of squeegee, and a natural bristle brush also with an unpainted wood handle. The clear plastic gloves, resin cleaner, and barrier cream (right) make cleanup easy and protect the worker from resin and solvents.

boatbuilding projects.

The tools used for the fiberglass boat-building phases are, for the most part, even simpler and cheaper. These tools are used for the application of the basic fiberglass laminate, and also include the equipment and supplies which aid this operation, including the finishing of the hull if building with male mold methods.

To begin with, you'll need basic fiberglass application tools like brushes, rollers, and squeegees. In these three categories, there are many sizes and types of each available, so here are some guidelines to use for selection.

When buying brushes, make sure the handles are BARE UNPAINTED wood. Painted handles are attacked by resin and bits of paint will get tracked all through the laminate and resin, causing a mess. Don't use old paint brushes either, as the resin will attack the old paint within the brush and mess up the resin. Use new brushes only, or well-cleaned brushes previously used ONLY in resin.

All brushes should have NATURAL bristles which are fairly stiff (you can clip off the bristles in some cases to make a "stiffer" brush). Don't worry about getting high quality bristles since they tend to be too flexible anyway, and after using the brush awhile, you'll probably throw it away. In short, get the cheapest fairly short natural bristle brushes available with unpainted handles. A brush width of 3" to 4" is usually ideal, with perhaps a narrower brush for close quarters.

Many types of rollers can be used for applying resin, but the most common mohair paint rollers are entirely suitable. Use the ones which have a cardboard core; most of these are solvent resistant and won't fall apart. Use a short-nap type for finish work and a long-nap (¾" to 1") for laminating work or for working the initial coat of resin on C-FLEX fiberglass planking.

In selecting rollers, consider those that can be fitted with an extension handle (most seem to have this feature today) for working on large areas or where you can't reach far enough without one. Some rollers have plastic parts which may be softened by resin and other solvents, but there will probably be no way of knowing this beforehand. Like brushes, look for rollers with unpainted wood handles. Buy several rollers so that a fresh one is ready to go while one is being cleaned in solvent. It is also a good idea to have a good assortment (say a couple of each) of wide, medium, and narrow widths, and perhaps an inside corner and outside corner type for the project with a lot of angles and corners.

Another type of roller is used for applying fiberglass mat and is called a mat roller. These are essential for any boat using mat in the layup. The ordinary paint roller, brushes, and squeegees can't practically be used to wet out mat and remove entrapped air since these tools just tend to pull the mat apart. The serrated mat rollers overcome these problems, and although a bit expensive, they are worth the money. Most come with durable handles and can be fitted with extensions. Several sizes and types are available, both for flat surfaces, and for use on inside and outside corners. Narrower width rollers with extensions are sometimes necessary for rolling out mat in tight places, such as on the inside of keel appendages and the like. Mat rollers are available in metal and plastic types, with the former preferable since any hardened resin that sticks can be burned off instead of using more expensive solvents. If you don't want to buy mat rollers, you can make your own by using a series of alternating large and small washers (say ⅝" and 1" in diameter) threaded onto a rod and retained, then bent to shape to form a roller and handle (see Fig. 4-3).

Squeegees come in many sizes and are made from many different materials. Those used for fiberglass work must be made from a material that is not affected by resin or ketone solvents such as acetone. For general laminating work, a size at least 6″ wide will suffice. Squeegees come in different flexibilities and it is hard to define what the ideal degree of stiffness should be since it will vary. However, a lot of pressure must be exerted when working the squeegee, so beware of anything that is too flexible or resilient. The semi-flexible types with a tapered edge made from vinyl-rubber are quite versatile and inexpensive.

Tools that are similar to squeegees are the various trowels and screeds usually used for applying the final fill coats of resin, but which can be used on larger projects for general laminating work also. These tools are usually steel blades and can be purchased ready-made under several names, such as drywall knives, putty knives, and troweling knives. Or make your own from old saw blades, scraps of sheet metal, etc. Widths will vary with what is comfortable for you, how much work needs to be done, the general hull contours, etc. For hulls that change shape quickly, especially in smaller boats, a narrow screed will be called for, and possibly one with more flexibility. On the other hand, working large flat areas may require a stiffer, longer tool. In some cases (as will be noted in Chapter 13 on finishing), a notched trowel may be used, similar to those used for spreading linoleum adhesive.

An old saw blade sometimes works well in this case.

Another group of tools can best be classified as "shaping" tools. In fiberglass boat-building, there are many instances where an area will have to be shaped or "sculpted", especially in working with resin putty fillers, as well as in shaping wood members. For woodworking these can include wood rasps, files, and planes. Some of the best tools are the surface forming tools (under the brand name, "Surfoam") which come in many types. The plane-type and rasp-type versions of these tools will shape and remove a lot of material rapidly. An ordinary putty knife will also come in handy, and several things can be used to form fillets of varying radii, including tin can lids, plastic tops, or even the back side of a spoon. Most builders will be able to think up more of these shaping devices as the occasion arises.

If the project is any size at all, it is a good idea to have a measuring and layout table so that lengths of fiberglass reinforcing materials can be rolled out as required (see Fig. 4-4). This will help keep the materials clean also. Rolls of fiberglass materials are rolled around a tube through which a length of heavy pipe can be inserted, that when supported on the ends, forms a roller to make unrolling the heavy materials easier. Make a permanent measuring scale along an edge of the table so you'll know how much material to reel off without using a measuring tape each time. For cutting material to length, use an old pair of shears, or with mat, it is just as easy to tear off a length, leaving a rough edge. Don't use a good pair of shears since they will dull quickly, and it's easy to damage them with resin.

Although plastic buckets abound and are quite reasonable in cost, it is just as easy to make your own resin containers by cutting off the tops of old plastic bleach and ammonia bottles. Most of these are not affected by resin or solvents, and can be used over and over again. If the leftover resin

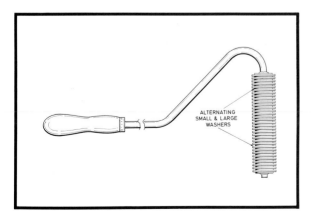

FIG. 4-3 — Mat rollers can be made by using alternating small and large washers threaded onto a bent rod and retained.

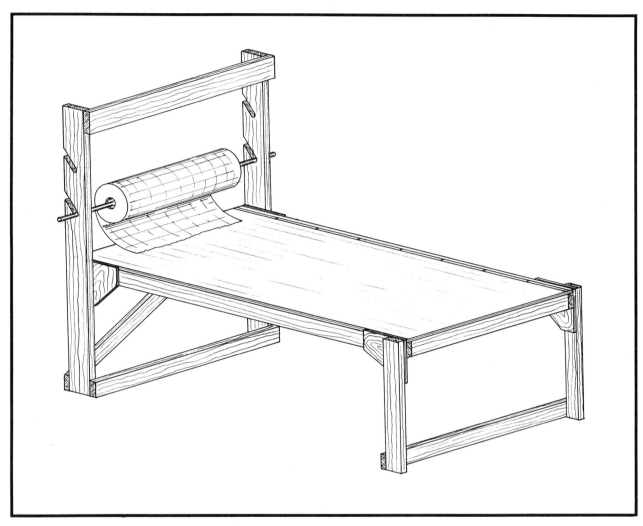

FIG. 4-4 — This simple measuring and layout table can be made from scrap lumber and a sheet of hardboard for the top. Since rolls of fiberglass material are heavy, the table should be strong. This table has space for two rolls of material for convenience when using conventional laminates. One space can be used for mat and the other for woven roving. A length of heavy pipe holds the rolls in place. A measuring tape is located along the edge.

cures hard in these, it will break free from the container after it gets hard and shrinks a bit, leaving the inside clean for the next batch of resin.

Of course, if too much resin is left over in these plastic containers, the heat generated from setting up might melt the plastic, so it is a good idea to pour the leftover resin out over an area where it will do no harm rather than setting up a condition where heat will build up. By all means do NOT use "Styrofoam" or other styrene plastic containers for mixing resin as these plastics are attacked and dissolved by the resin, and the resin will just fall out through the bottom. In any case, have plenty of empty containers available, preferably in the half-gallon to one gallon size.

If using rollers, use the standard paint trays available for applying resin. If the trays are metal, there are standard plastic liners available (check to see first if these liners are attacked by the resin, however), or line your own trays with plastic wrap or aluminum foil. Have plenty of stirring sticks (make your own from wood) available for mixing resin, being sure to throw each away after mixing up a batch to prevent adding any partially catalyzed resin from batch to batch.

If the catalyst being used comes from containers that do not have measuring scales, mark the container in increments suitable to each measurement of resin to be used by placing a divided, marked length of masking tape onto the catalyst container. Another method is to buy small plastic squeeze bottles commonly available and use these as catalyst dispensers. A kitchen scale that will measure up to 10 lbs. with small increments between is good for measuring out volumes of resin and other materials.

Other material handling aids include a hand truck for moving around large items such as rolls of reinforcing (which commonly exceed 100 lbs. each), a drum rack or barrel stand for resin drums (remember, these weigh over 500 lbs. each!), a drum spout or resin gate, or a resin pump if the drum sets upright on the floor, and plenty of newspapers and rags. Not to be overlooked, have at least one Class "B" fire extinguisher of large capacity AND a telephone with the local fire department number handy as a safety precaution. Also have a source of running water and facilities for emergency eye washing. This latter facility is required in EVERY commercial situation for safety, and should be a part of your boatbuilding facility as well.

Other items needed include masking tape, parting film or mold release (we'll talk more about these later), thumb tacks, a caulking gun, staples, and a staple gun. If working with C-FLEX fiberglass planking, you can apply this material with the staple gun, or you can use ice picks ideally, if you can find them, or you can make your own ice picks (see Chapter 16).

For finish work, have a good supply and selection of various abrasive products (see later in the chapter for more information), as well as sanding masks or other respirator devices for dust protection when sanding and grinding. Also have goggles or other eye

protection devices for use when mixing resin and handling catalyst, as well as for working with power tools, AND USE THEM!

While some people don't like gloves because they lose some of the "feel" for working with the materials, there are numerous types of disposable thin plastic gloves that are worthwhile. These gloves can be peeled off from rolls as required and discarded, all the while keeping hands clean and reducing the need for solvents and cleaners which are generally expensive, with most not particularly desirable. The use of barrier cream also protects exposed skin and makes clean-up a lot easier and faster.

While acetone has traditionally been used for clean-up purposes, it has become so expensive that in many cases it is cheaper to throw a tool away rather than to clean it up. This is a personal judgement each builder will have to make, but rather large quantities are required for clean-up because the acetone is so volatile it evaporates rapidly. Because of its volatility, acetone is a VERY dangerous product and should always be stored in closed metal containers.

Some feel that lacquer thinner is a better alternative to acetone. While it is just as costly, it does not evaporate as rapidly. However, neither of these solvents is recommended for skin contact and their use should be avoided for cleaning up resin from exposed skin. A better solution is to use one of the many resin cleaner products available. While these are also expensive, they do not require much to do the job. Many are suitable for direct use on the skin as well as for cleaning tools. They save money in the long run and are not so dangerous to use. In addition to solvents or cleaners, also keep a bucket of water around with ordinary detergent to wash up hands and tools after cleaning in solvent or cleaner.

When working with all things fiberglass, always wear protective clothing, gloves, and/or barrier cream. Don't wear any clothing or shoes when working with resin that you won't mind throwing away since the resin on clothing and shoes simply cannot be removed. Protect floors you care about with scrap pieces of hardboard, plywood, plastic tarps, or stiff cardboard. With hardboard or plywood on the floor, bind these together to prevent them from moving by using scrap pieces of woven roving saturated with resin over the butt joints between the pieces of plywood or hardboard. On concrete floors, this is a good approach not only because it is almost impossible to remove resin from concrete, but in the event that you drop sharp tools, they will be protected from damage.

ABRASIVES

When building a fiberglass boat using male mold methods, quite a bit of final fairing and finish work (sanding and grinding) will be required. Thus, you will use a lot of "sandpaper" or abrasive products. These abrasive products come in a wide range of types, including discs of various diameters to suit disc sanders, continuous belts for belt sanders, and in sheet stock for hand work and finish sanders. There is also another product often used called "Foamglas", a brand name for a product made by Pittsburg Corning Corp., which will be discussed later.

There are several materials used to make abrasive products, but only a couple that should be considered. Ordinary flint paper (sometimes sold in grocery stores in "handy pack" packages) is virtually worthless for any boatbuilding use, so avoid it. The tan color of flint paper is easy to spot in the event that it is not so designated. The reddish-brown garnet paper is acceptable for woodworking purposes and finish work in joinerywork, but it will wear out quickly when used on fiberglass.

Silicon carbide, tungsten carbide, and aluminum oxide abrasives are the most suitable abrasives for fiberglass boatbuild-ing purposes. Most abrasive manufacturers state the type of abrasive used on the back of the product for easy identification. The better abrasive papers, while quite expensive initially, will hold their grit much longer and not load up so fast, making them probably more economical in the long run. Furthermore, with many of the sanding discs as they load up, it is possible to clean them in acetone if they are the resin bonded type, thus extending their life even longer. To minimize loading and filling of the paper, always use what is called "open coat" products (which is about all that you'll probably find anyway).

The question of what degree of grit (coarseness of fineness) of abrasive paper to get, as well as how much, can vary with the job, the quality of finish desired, personal preferences, etc. In buying sandpaper, there's a number on the back telling the degree of grit of the product. The larger this number, the finer the grit. For example, a #24 paper is quite coarse, while a #600 is quite fine. Another variation is with those abrasive products called "wet-or-dry". These products are usually used for final finish work such as wet sanding with water, and are usually quite fine grit.

In selecting the degree of grit of the abrasives needed, if your final finish is quite poor and rough, start out with a #24 to a #36 grit disc, working up to perhaps a #50 grit for a relatively smooth finish. For smoother surfaces, a #80 and even a #120 might be used. For hand and finish sanders, have a good selection of papers ranging in grit from about a #40 on up to a #220. And for final wet-or-dry finishing and polishing work, use a #400 to #600 type.

For initial fairing and sanding of resin putty filler coats which are described in detail in Chapter 13, a product like "Foamglas" is ideal. This product is a pumice-like rigid insulation material that can be cut into blocks of a size and shape to suit. The material works extremely well to smooth down the filler coats or fairing compounds since it acts like a self-cleaning abrasive, and is rigid enough to span low areas while reducing high spots. Although a rigid material, the blocks usually have enough flexibility to shape themselves to the contours of the hull. If this material is not available, one can make up sanding blocks or boards using long narrow wood strips, say 3' to 5' long, to which strips or cut belts of heavy grit abrasive paper are glued or tacked. However, such boards tend to be flat and relatively inflexible in more than one direction so that their use is mostly limited to larger, flatter surfaces.

TOOLS & EQUIPMENT LISTINGS

The tools and equipment required to build a fiberglass boat will vary as previously noted depending on many factors. Tools divide quite neatly between hand and power types, but not quite so neatly between those used EXCLUSIVELY for fiberglass purposes as opposed to other types of construction, particularly woodworking. As noted, most fiberglass boats will require some woodworking tools and equipment, and the larger the boat, the greater this need will be. And as the boat increases in size, the greater will be the need for power tools in order to save work, time, and money.

The attempt has been made to break down the listings with several categories so that the builder can select what is best to suit his needs. Categories 1-A and 2-A show tools and equipment, both hand and power, that are VIRTUAL NECESSITIES if you wish to build a fiberglass boat. These categories could also be considered as the "minimum" requirements if one is working on a shoestring budget where cost is the overriding factor.

Category 1-B lists power tools which are considered as a highly desirable addition to the minimum power tool requirements if the budget can stand it. These additional tools will save a lot of labor, but are not absolutely essential, especially for the smaller project.

Category 1-C lists power tools primarily of the woodworking type and would be suitable for large boatbuilding projects which will involve a lot of woodworking in addition to fiberglass work. This portion of the listing also reflects the "ultimate" in power equipment, and is applicable where the budget is not as critical. Many of the items in this category could be rented or perhaps borrowed as needed for the short duration that they may be required.

Category 2-B is an extension of Category 2-A, and primarily includes the tools and equipment that are required for building the larger fiberglass boat. This listing reflects the need for working with larger volumes of materials in larger structures.

Category 3-A includes tools and equipment that, while not directly applicable to fiberglass work as such, ARE required in just about any boatbuilding operation, especially in the early stages of setting up and building the formwork, for example. Most of these tools are quite common, simple, and inexpensive.

Category 3-B is an extension of Category 3-A, and again does NOT relate directly to fiberglass work, but does include those hand tools that would get used on the larger project where considerable woodworking would be required.

Use the listing as a general guide to select and organize your boatbuilding project, adding or deleting those items deemed suitable to your conditions. Note that the listings are not meant to be totally comprehensive; there's perhaps something that's been omitted, especially a new tool that we have not even heard of, but should be listed. The listing, however, provides the beginner with something to go on and get his project organized for the work at hand.

TOOL & EQUIPMENT LISTINGS

CATEGORY 1-A — POWER TOOLS
(Those which are a virtual necessity)
Disc sander/polisher — 7″ dual-speed or comparable type
Saber or jig saw
Drill — 3/8″ variable speed reversible or comparable type

CATEGORY 1-B — POWER TOOLS
(Those which are highly desirable)
All the above, PLUS:
Portable circular saw — 7″ approximate
Belt sander — heavy
Finish sander — orbital/straight-line type

CATEGORY 1-C — POWER TOOLS
(For larger projects where budget is not critical)
All the above, PLUS:
Drill — 3/8″ (a second "back-up")
Shop vacuum
Table or radial arm saw — 8″ (10″ is better) (*)
Band saw — 12″ (16″ is better) (*)
Drill press
Router with attachments
Shaper
Spray paint outfit with compressor
Jointer — 6″ or larger
Power plane
Bench grinder (for sharpening tools, buffing, etc.)
Stationary disc sander
Thickness planer or surfacer (*)
Ventilation fans — large diameter, slow speed

(*) These tools are desirable where boatbuilding woods are not
available to size, or where the builder desires to cut his own
lumber to size to save money or to suit building conditions.

CATEGORY 2-A — HAND TOOLS & EQUIPMENT
(Those which are a virtual necessity for fiberglass work)
Brushes — natural bristle with bare wood handles, 3″ – 4″
Rollers — mohair paint type with long and short nap
Rollers — serrated mat type (metal preferred)
Squeegees
Mixing buckets
Stirring sticks — unpainted wood, one for each resin batch
Trowels or screeds
Abrasive papers and discs
Sanding blocks
Dust mask or respirator
Goggles or face mask
Putty knives
Barrier cream or disposable gloves
Protective clothing and tarps
Surface forming tools
Detergent with water bucket
Resin cleaner/solvent
Shears
Utility knife
Masking tape and thumb tacks
Newspapers
Fire extinguisher

CATEGORY 2-B — HAND TOOLS & EQUIPMENT
(Optional added items desirable for larger fiberglass projects)
All of the above, PLUS:
Extension handles for rollers
Paint trays for resin with liners
Staple gun with staples
Ice picks (optional, for applying C-FLEX)
Abrasive fairing products (such as "Foamglas")
Scale — 10 lb. capacity
Abrasive cut-off disc for circular saw
Measuring and layout table
Hand truck
Drum stand and spigot, or drum pump

CATEGORY 3-A — HAND TOOLS & EQUIPMENT
(Those NOT directly related to fiberglass work, but which ARE a
necessity in a boatbuilding project)
Measuring tape
Builder's or framing square
Plumb bob
Chalk line
Spirit level
"C" clamps or comparable type (as many as possible)
Hammer, claw-type
Drill bits — 1/16″ to 3/8″ — set
Screwdriver set or bits for power drill (or similar tools)

CATEGORY 3-B — HAND TOOLS & EQUIPMENT
(Those NOT directly related to fiberglass work, but HELPFUL in
larger, more complex projects)
All of the above, PLUS:
Hammers — ball-peen, short-handled sledge
Saws — rip, cross-cut, back, keyhole, coping, hacksaw
Miter box
Planes — block, jack, and smooth types
Awl
Chisels — wood type, 1/4″ to 1″ — set
Nail set
Wood rasp
Try-square or combination square
Mallet
Files — half-round, bastard, round, and flat types
Expansive bit
Countersink bits — set
Plug cutters
Spade or wood boring bits — 1/4″ – 1″ set
Punch set
Caulking gun
Vise — woodworkers and bench types
Hole saws — set for power drill
Sliding T-bevel
Clamps — pipe or bar type (as many as possible)
Pliers — slip-joint, adjustable, vise grip, needlenose types
Cold chisel set
Diagonal or wire cutters and strippers
Mechanic's wrenches — box-end, open-end, and socket sets

CHAPTER 5

fiberglass materials

WHAT IS FIBERGLASS?

The conventional fiberglass boat, if there is such a thing, basically consists of laminates made up of various fiberglass reinforcements and resin, which is usually of the polyester type. Basically, the true fiberglass reinforcing materials are made from glass filaments using virtually the same ingredients as those used in ordinary window glass, namely silica or sand. These glass filaments can be made in different ways to have differing qualities of strength, abrasion resistance, flexibility, chemical stability, and so forth.

The different types of glass are designated by a letter identifying code such as "E", "A", or "S". For example, the common fiberglass filament used to make up the conventional fiberglass boatbuilding reinforcing materials is called "E"-type glass, with the "E" standing for electrical grade. This type of glass has a tensile strength of around 500,000 p.s.i., with the actual glass being a lime-alumina borosilicate glass of low alkali content. It has high chemical stability and high moisture resistance making it well suited to marine conditions.

The "E"-type glass is considered of medium strength and high rigidity, but more important, the main reason this type is so common is low cost. While maybe not the highest strength glass available, it does have all the strength that is normally necessary for most conventional boat work, and this is balanced by its favorable cost. There are other types of glass that are stronger, such as the "S"-type glass described in Chapter 21, but these are usually more costly on a weight basis. Then too, other types of glass may be better suited for more specialized purposes, such as the "T"-type used for storage tanks, and the "A"-type, which is not alkali-free.

THE MAKING OF FIBERGLASS REINFORCEMENTS

The fiberglass filaments are made into materials that we ordinarily refer to as "fiberglass", such as rovings, yarns, cloths, mats, and woven rovings, many of which we'll be discussing shortly.

In the process of making the materials, the strands of filaments must be coated with a sizing material. There are various types of sizings, but their purposes are similar: (1) to bind the monofilaments together into a more easily handled fiber, which is the actual strand; (2) to lubricate the filaments so that they won't abrade and break each other, causing a reduction in filament strength; and (3) to increase surface contact between the fibers and resin; that is, to increase the quality of the fibers to soak up resin rapidly. This latter quality is called "wettability".

Since the sizing materials are incompatible with the resins which will be used with the fiberglass materials to form laminates, the sizing must be cleaned or specially "finished" so the resin will saturate and bond to the fiberglass. There are many cleaning processes or "finishes" used, but for boatbuilding materials, the two common types are known as "chrome" and "silane". These finishes give the fiberglass materials their characteristic "white translucent" appearance. This leads us to a tip for the unwary: If you are offered fiberglass materials which do NOT have this "white translucent" quality, or are otherwise "dirty" or "greasy" in appearance, DON'T BUY THEM NO MATTER HOW CHEAP THEY MAY BE! Such material has not been cleaned or finished, and will not bond with resin.

While all this technical background information may seem a little confusing to the beginner, if material is bought from a reputable firm, especially one dealing directly with the marine field, there will be little need for concern that you are getting the proper material. Just beware of claims for "special" treatments or "unique" finishes. While some weavers try to dazzle one with fancy labels to camouflage their supposedly "secret" processes, this just adds to the confusion. So don't approach your supplier and ask for materials with "special name" finishes; he'll probably not know what you are talking about. Just make sure that what you get is "marine grade" (with that white translucent quality) AND clean.

The fiberglass materials discussed below do not represent a comprehensive overview of all the various reinforcement products that are available. Instead, we have limited the discussion to those fiberglass materials which may be considered as conventional types that are readily available at reasonable prices, or those of most importance to the majority of people who will be building their own fiberglass boats. Many other specialty reinforcement materials that are available and would be used in an amateur-built fiberglass boat are discussed in other chapters as they are applicable. But at this early stage in the text, there is no need to add to the confusion of the beginner. Also, those reinforcement products which are really only suited to special uses in production situations using highly trained workers are not discussed in this book even though you may come across them in your travels. Part of the problem in attempting to be totally comprehensive is that technology is advancing rapidly, and there is a great deal of experimentation going on. The main purpose of this book is not an overview of developing technologies, but rather a manual based upon materials and methods suited to amateurs building fiberglass boats.

ROVINGS

Fiberglass rovings might be considered the basic "stuff" of which other fiberglass materials are made, and they are used by themselves as well. A roving consists of strands of glass fibers grouped together to form an untwisted yarn. Our primary interest in rovings is that they are used to make woven roving, described later. However, in production work these rovings, which are in endless strands rolled into long coils on spools, are usually fed through machines called "chopper guns" that cut up the rovings into short pieces, shoot them out to-

FIG. 5-1 — Rovings are a basic fiberglass material. Endless strands of glass fibers are grouped together to form an untwisted yarn, or roving. The roving is used to make woven roving and also fed through machines called "chopper guns" in the "sprayup" process.

gether with catalyzed resin, and deposit them onto a mold surface, usually a female mold.

Once on the mold surface, the end product is much like a mat, which is also discussed later. The chopper gun is usually held by hand by an operator and the method of building up a laminate in this manner is called the "spray-up" process. Because this equipment is quite elaborate and expensive, and a rather high degree of skill and experience is required to properly operate the gun, plus the fact that most knowledgeable people consider the process inferior at least for structural components, it is seldom used in amateur fiberglass boatbuilding. Thus we will not discuss it further.

MAT

Fiberglass mat is a reinforcing material made of glass fibers about 1" to 2" in length, or in continuous strands arranged in a random swirl pattern held together with a resinous binder. It resembles a felt material. The type most often used in boat work is commonly referred to as "chopped strand mat" or abbreviated as "CSM". It is categorized by weight PER SQUARE FOOT (note the emphasis here for this is something you should remember). Weights vary ordinarily from a light ¾ ounce to a heavier 3 ounce per square foot. Most commonly used weights are the 1 ounce, 1½ ounce, and 2 ounce varieties.

Mat is comparatively low in cost and is commonly used in fiberglass laminates because it is easy to wet out; it absorbs resin readily. Mat also gives good bonding between layers of woven materials like cloth and woven roving, as will be discussed in more detail later. Mat also builds up thickness quickly and can be molded into complex shapes easily. Mat, however, is not as strong as cloth or woven roving, and if used alone, will provide a laminate that is brittle because the resin content will be too high in proportion to the glass content.

Mat comes in rolls (38" and 50" wide being common widths) and is sold in bulk by the pound, or by the lineal measurement in smaller quantities. If buying mat in bulk, your dealer will probably give a good price if you buy roll quantities. The only problem with this is that there is often no such thing

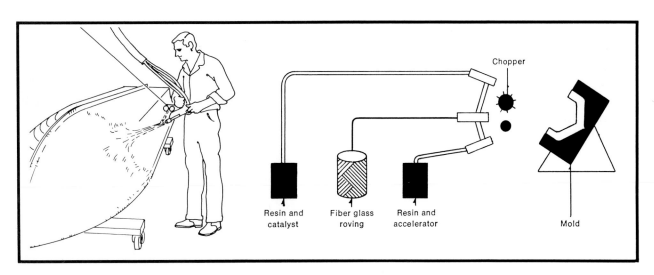

FIG. 5-2 — In the "sprayup" process, rovings are fed through the "chopper gun" and deposited onto the mold surface along with catalyzed and promoted resin. The elaborate and costly equipment, plus skill required by the operator, makes this method unsuitable for most amateurs. For structural components, the process is also considered inferior to hand layup methods.

as "standard length" rolls; they vary considerably, which means that you could get much more than you need, or maybe much less. A lot of mat will be used in most fiberglass boatbuilding projects.

WOVEN ROVING

Woven roving is just what it says it is, a coarse, open weave, heavy fabric made from rovings. The square-weave type is commonly used. The rovings are arranged into a latticework weave with edges usually unselvedged but often lightly stitched to prevent unraveling. Woven roving is categorized by weight PER SQUARE YARD (unlike mat, please note), ranging from approximately 14 ounces to 40 ounces per square yard. However, the most common weights for our purposes will be the 18, 24, and 27 ounce varieties usually available in widths of 38" to 50". Woven roving is commonly abbreviated as "WR". Lighter weight materials are easier to wet out and are often specified for the amateur for this reason.

Woven roving gives high strength to a laminate at a reasonable cost, which makes it an important structural element in the laminate. However, because of its coarse weave, it is not used where surface appearance is important, as the weave cannot be concealed without an excessive build-up of resin. Woven roving is more difficult to wet out than mat or cloth, but it builds up thickness and strength rapidly. Like mat, woven roving is purchased by the pound in bulk, with varying lengths of rolls, or by lineal measurement in smaller quantities. A lot of woven roving will be used in most fiberglass boatbuilding.

CLOTH

Fiberglass cloth is woven from fine yarns of various twist and ply construction into a wide range of types, weights, and widths.

FIG. 5-3 — Mat is formed from randomly oriented strands of glass fibers held together with a resinous binder forming a bulky felt-like material.

FIG. 5-4 — A close-up shot of mat clearly shows the random fiber orientation of this material.

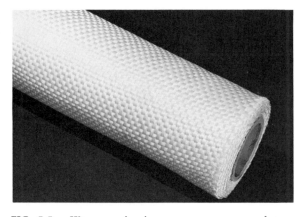

FIG. 5-5 — Woven roving is a coarse, open weave heavy fabric made from rovings. The rovings are commonly arranged in a square latticework weave with unselveged edges.

Cloth is categorized by weight PER SQUARE YARD (just like woven roving, so do take note), ranging approximately from 2 ounces (very light) to 40 ounces (very heavy) per square yard. The most commonly used weights in boat work range from 6 ounce to 10 ounce material. Cloth is usually sold by the running yard from rolls that are 38", 44", 50", or 60" in width. The most common type is classed as a plain square open-weave type, and is easy to work and wet out. Unlike most woven roving, cloth is woven with selvedged edges to keep the fabric from unraveling.

Because fiberglass cloth must be woven by a rather elaborate process just like any other fabric, this drives the cost up considerably above mat or woven roving on a weight basis. And because of the light-weight nature of the material, it takes a lot of it to build up thickness and strength, which can be more easily achieved with greater economy by the use of mat and woven roving. Hence it is not used much in fiberglass boatbuilding as a structural laminate material except in smaller boats or where thin laminates are required. Its primary use is as a sheathing material (such as over plywood) for increased durability, reduced maintenance, added abrasion resistance, and where joint reinforcement is

desired.

A variation of fiberglass cloth is fiberglass tape. Fiberglass tapes are actually narrow rolls of cloth, from about 2" to 12" in width and with selvedged edges. Such tapes are convenient to use in tight spaces, such as at inside corners, and to reinforce joints or to make joints watertight. They are also used in repair work. Cloth tapes are usually sold by the lineal measurement.

COMBINATION MAT/WOVEN ROVING

To speed production, there are materials available that are a combination of mat and woven roving in one material. These are available under various trade names (such as "Fabmat"). Common types have the equivalent of a combination of 18 ounce woven roving together with 1 ounce chopped strand mat, or 24 ounce woven roving together with 1½ ounce chopped strand mat.

The only drawback with these materials is that they are primarily intended for production operations where plenty of labor is available to wet out the material. For the amateur working alone or short-handed, or who is otherwise inexperienced, these materials may be more work and worry than

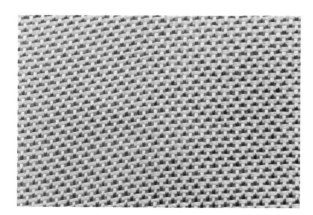

FIG. 5-6 — Cloth is a woven fabric with selvedged edges made from fine yarns. The common plain square open-weave type is shown.

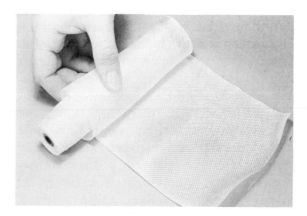

FIG. 5-7 — Fiberglass cloth tape is a narrower form of fiberglass cloth and has selvedged edges.

using mat and woven roving separately. Simply put, they are more difficult to wet out. Most are available in the same widths as mat or woven roving, and are sold by the pound in bulk, or lineally in smaller amounts.

OTHER FIBERGLASS MATERIALS

These include several of the more complex and sophisticated materials, including the "high modulus" materials discussed in Chapter 21. For example, there are the unidirectionals, the bi-axials, and the tri-axials that, while they can be made from fiberglass yarns, are also available in other types of reinforcements such as Kevlar and carbon fiber.

The main difference in these specialty materials as compared to conventional woven rovings is that the fibers are usually non-woven with strands oriented into distinct and specific directions within the fabric instead of in the latticework orientation of the typical woven roving. The reason that this is done is to build in strength properties in specific directions so that thinner, lighter, and stronger laminates can be made.

While these materials can accomplish this purpose, at the present time they are more expensive, not as readily available, and require more deft handling and knowledge in their application. While still in their developmental stages of use in fiberglass boatbuilding, these materials will no doubt become more common in fiberglass boats built both by factories and by amateurs. This, in turn, will no doubt lower the cost, and as the word gets out on how they are to be used properly, their use will become more "second nature", much the same way that the conventional mat and woven roving materials are thought of today. We'll discuss the uses of some of these materials in more detail later. However, at this point, the typical amateur need not be too concerned with these often so-called "exotic"

materials until he acquires more knowledge and experience. There is still a question as to whether all of these materials are suitable for the first-time builder. This is further complicated by the fact that there are few designs available for the amateur which incorporate these more-advanced materials, and little in the way of proven data to allow conversion of more conventional laminates to those using these materials.

A

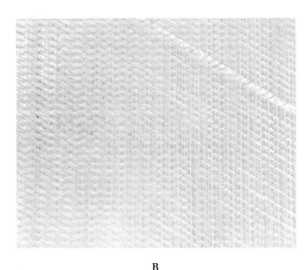

B

FIG. 5-8 — Some of the specialty fiberglass materials include bi-axial (A) and tri-axial (B) fabrics. These materials are not woven; the fibers are stitched into position, with the fibers oriented into distinct and specific directions.

MECHANICAL & PHYSICAL PROPERTIES
OF FIBERGLASS MATERIALS (*)

	MAT	WOVEN ROVING	CLOTH
Flexural strength (p.s.i.)	16−28,000	30−65,000	26−30,000
Flexural modulus (p.s.i.)	800,000	1,500,000	1,200,000−2,000,000
Tensile strength (p.s.i.)	9−18,000	30−55,000	14−24,000
Specific gravity	1.4−1.6	1.5−1.7	1.5−1.7

(*)Owens-Corning Fiberglas Corp.

FIG. 5-9 — Several properties of common fiberglass materials used in conventional laminates are shown. Reviewing the figures shows why a high balance of woven roving is preferred in relation to mat in the conventional laminate.

Cloth, while it is stronger than mat, is also more costly than either mat or woven roving. Thus it is seldom used in fiberglass laminates, except in smaller boats where thinner skins are desired.

WARP & WEFT

Because a large percentage of fiberglass materials are woven much like other fabrics, one may frequently be confronted with the terms "warp" and "weft" (or sometimes called "fill" or "woof"). The terminologies are often mentioned in discussions regarding the strength of various materials with regard to their orientation in a laminate, for example. Since the terms can be a little confusing, let's clear up any misunderstanding now. Quite simply, warp means in the longitudinal direction of a fabric, or lengthwise. Weft (fill or woof) means across the width of the fabric at right angles. Going across the fabric on a diagonal at 45 degrees to the warp and weft is said to be on the bias. In fiberglass, whether a material is actually woven or not, warp means lengthwise and weft means across the width of the material.

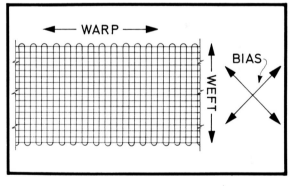

FIG. 5-10 — Warp, weft, and bias are terms commonly used to describe fiber orientation in fabrics.

As noted previously, fiberglass laminates consist of two materials which work together to develop characteristics that are better than if one of the materials was used separately. One of these materials, the fiberglass reinforcement, has already been discussed. The other material in the composition is the resin. The science of plastics has given the world so many different kinds of resins, it is a wonder that chemists can keep matters straight! However, in fiberglass boatbuilding we're only concerned with a couple of types.

The two types of resin most commonly used in boatbuilding are the epoxy and polyester types. We'll discuss the epoxy types first because their use is limited. The so-called "unsaturated" polyesters form the bulk of the resins used in most fiberglass boatbuilding, whether being done by the factory or by the amateur builder. Hence, it is the type that warrants the most comprehensive discussion.

Both the epoxy and polyester type resins are classed as "thermosetting" resins. This means that they cure by internally generated heat and cannot be melted or liquified again by the application of heat like a "thermoplastic" resin can. These thermosetting resins are sticky, syrup-like fluids of varying viscosities, and they have their own peculiar characteristics which we'll describe in enough detail to allow you to make an informed selection for your purposes.

EPOXY RESINS

Epoxy resins are not commonly used in fiberglass boatbuilding primarily because they are too expensive. This situation could change, of course, given the vagaries of the world energy supply situation. However, it is unlikely that they will supersede polyester types for several other reasons which will become apparent as we progress, mainly that polyesters perform more than adequately in most cases, making epoxies unnecessary.

Epoxy resins consist of two parts that, when mixed together, activate and cure. The curing agent is ordinarily called the "hardener", and unlike polyester resins with their small amount of added catalyst, such hardeners make up a large portion of the final "brew". The ratios of resin to hardener can vary dramatically from formulation to formulation. For example, some epoxy resins have a one-to-one mix, while others may have a five-to-one mix. Add to this an incredible array of both resins and hardeners available and the average novice will walk away in a daze!

By varying the combinations of resins and hardeners, the clever chemist can come up with epoxy formulations offering many different characteristics, some suitable for our uses, but many others that are not. Hence, in order to select a suitable boatbuilding combination, one requires either a lot of knowledge and experience, or a lot of trust about what's on the label and who is doing the selling.

Why would anyone consider using epoxy resins in the first place? In general, epoxy resins have greater bonding strength (which makes them ideal as a glue or adhesive), less shrinkage, absorb less water in the cured state, offer superior abrasion resistance, and have better physical characteristics. Through the infinite variations in combinations available, the formulators can come up with products for special purposes that could never be fulfilled with the polyester types.

However, these advantages usually don't offset the disadvantages of epoxy resins when it comes to using them in a laminate, especially the additional cost. Epoxy resins require more care in handling (although some may argue this point after they learn of the hazards involved with polyester resins). The epoxies also cure more slowly, which slows down the builder's progress (one of the main reasons why production outfits avoid the stuff), and they are more difficult to finish, especially in male mold construction, mainly because of the slow-cure properties.

Another problem with epoxies is that there is a tendency for the resins to lose viscosity as the heat of cure or exotherm increases, making the resin difficult to work on vertical or inclined surfaces. Compounded by the slow cure properties, this quality makes the laminator's job a tedious one in these situations. While epoxy resins can be used for bonding woven materials to core materials such as foam, for example, most epoxy formulations are generally not practical for wetting out mat since the mat soaks up large quantities of the resin, making the conventional laminate much more costly than one made from polyester resin. It can be argued that the superior bond made possible by epoxy resins makes the use of mat between layers of woven materials unnecessary, resulting in perhaps a more "efficient" laminate. However, for most boats, the extra gain in efficiency is not worth the extra cost and trouble. Although bonding qualities may be superior, epoxy resins do not contribute proportionally higher laminate strengths.

Nevertheless, there are occasions where epoxy resins are ideal to use, and while their use IS limited in fiberglass boatbuilding, they CAN come in handy in many situa-

tions, especially as an adhesive. In application over the following materials, or for bonding, epoxy resins or adhesives are highly recommended, or a "must" if you want something that will stick forever. These include bonding to aluminum, steel, teak, oak, redwood, Western red cedar, cypress, and non-porous surfaces. In short, the epoxies are excellent glues whereas the polyesters are not.

A wet epoxy can be applied over a cured polyester, and vice versa; however, the two should NEVER be mixed in the uncured or wet state. The first resin must be fully cured. Note that while epoxies will stick well to cured polyesters, polyesters will not stick well to cured epoxies. Furthermore, if bonding to epoxies must be subsequently done, the cured epoxy surface should be lightly sanded, or at least wiped with a solvent wash to assure as good a bond as possible.

With glued fittings applied to polyester surfaces using epoxies (or any other superior adhesive for that matter), there is always a danger of delamination of the fiberglass laminate or gel coat. Stresses or loads onto a glued part should not be applied in the direction which would pull away from the polyester surface, because the strength of the glue will be greater than the strength of the polyester resin bonding the layers of laminate together. The result could be a damaged and weakened laminate, and this is why it is always better to mechanically attach to fiberglass whenever possible, using methods prescribed later in the text.

While epoxy resins CAN be used for woven laminates where added bonding strength is important, or where the service will be severe, their high cost usually rules them out for extensive layups. If you plan on using epoxy resins, take EXTREME care in their use, especially if using amine hardeners. Many epoxy formulations can cause severe dermatitis, skin burns, and respiratory problems, even to those who are naive enough to think they are immune! I have run across a number of builders who did not heed this advice because they had been using epoxy with their bare hands for years with no problems. Then all of a sudden, with no apparent warning, they broke out in severe rashes and dermatitis, sometimes to the point where a hospital visit was required. So always wear protective clothing, gloves, and barrier cream when working with epoxy resins, as well as eye protection and face masks when sanding. Also make sure a good supply of fresh air circulates in the work area. If epoxy resin gets on bare skin, wash it off immediately with soap and water or denatured alcohol.

POLYESTER RESINS

By far the most common resin used in fiberglass boatbuilding is the polyester type. The mechanical properties of polyester resins are somewhat less than the epoxies, and their caustic chemical resistance is also less. However, these are not highly critical factors in boatbuilding, and are more than offset by the relatively low cost, rapid room temperature curing capabilities, and ease of fabrication and handling. The long-term chemical resistance and durability of polyester resins is amply satisfactory for most boats.

Polyesters are petro-chemical based products which begin life in the oil refining process. The following, while perhaps a bit technical, gives some background of the manufacturing process. In making the resin, various anhydrides, polybasic acids, glycols, and styrene are made by reaction processes from benzene, propylene, and ethylene, which the resin manufacturer "mixes" together and "cooks" in large kettles to form a "base" resin.

At a point in the cooking process, the base resin is thinned with styrene, which makes up a large percentage of the resin (from about a third to a half of the final product is

styrene). Once thinned with styrene, the resin is ready to be sold, except for the addition of various ingredients to make a given resin more suited to a specific purpose. Naturally, a resin manufacturer can "formulate" his resins in certain ways, and also add various fillers, promotors or accelerators, and other modifying additives to the point that polyesters are not all the same. Much has to do with the end use for which the products will be used, as we shall see.

If the resin cooking process just mentioned was carried through, the resin would harden completely. But since the process is in effect halted part-way through, the resin is said to be "pre-polymerized", or partially hardened. However, because the resin has been sent on its way to hardening, the "cooking" process causes a lasting effect on the resin, and it will still eventually harden over an extended period of time on its own. This is why resin should be "fresh" when purchased and used, as old resin will not function properly because it will be farther along on its way to eventual curing. Most resin manufacturers do a good job in assuring that they and their distributors maintain fresh stock. Normal shelf life is usually an easy six months, with a year or even two not being unusual when properly stored. It is even possible to prolong these times if the resin can be refrigerated (but NOT frozen). Resin should be stored in a cool, dry place NOT in direct sunlight where temperatures will not exceed much over 70°F.

ACCELERATORS & CATALYSTS

When working with the resin, however, one can't wait forever for the resin to harden on its own. So to fully polymerize ("cook" or cure) the resin in use, two additional ingredients are required. One is called the "accelerator" (sometimes called a promotor or activator; they're all the same thing), and the other is called the "catalyst" (sometimes called the "hardener").

These two elements work as a "team" to help the resin speed up its final job of hardening. In effect, the catalyst is what internally generates the heat required to make the resin set up hard, or "cure", while the accelerator is what makes this cure happen at ordinary working temperatures without the use of externally applied heat. There are no by-products resulting from this curing process. The proportion of these two ingredients is what effects the curing cycle (better known as the "gel time"), or the time it takes to reach the cured state.

Catalysts and accelerators are chemicals which work only in certain combinations or systems, several combinations of which will work in polyester resins. However, for most boat work the typical accelerator is technically known as cobalt napthanate (a purple-colored fluid commonly referred to as "cobalt"), while the usual catalyst is methyl ethyl ketone peroxide. You'll sometimes hear people refer to this catalyst as "M-E-K" which is NOT correct; methy ethyl ketone ("M-E-K" without the "P" for the peroxide) is actually a solvent in the acetone family, and NOT a catalyst. So to refer to the catalyst properly, call it "M-E-K peroxide".

The heat these two materials set up when mixed in the resin is the result of rapid oxidation, the speed of which is determined by the amount and proportion of these ingredients (only a very slight amount of both is required), as well as the ambient temperature where the curing takes place (plus a couple of other minor factors which will be mentioned along the way). The catalyst is too explosive in its pure form; it is normally in solution with a non-reactive solvent and hydrogen peroxide. Because ratios vary with catalyst manufacturers, some differences in cure characteristics may occur. Thus, if catalyst suppliers are changed, check a test batch prior to use for performance and cure time.

Some time ago, polyester resins were sold without the accelerator mixed in the resin (or "unpromoted"). This had to be added by the user, as well as the user also adding the catalyst. However, serious problems sometimes occurred since it was violently discovered that when cobalt napthanate and M-E-K peroxide were mixed into the resin AT THE SAME TIME, or together, they could explode and catch fire due to the immediate, rapid, uncontrollable release of oxygen created by the coming together of the two materials.

As a result, resin manufacturers now usually mix the cobalt (.05 to .5% by weight) into the resin by itself at the factory (calling it "pre-promoted" resin), with the catalyst packed separately for final addition by the user. Yet because both of these items can still be purchased separately and used by the ultimate user, an important safety rule should be emphasized:

WARNING: DO NOT MIX COBALT NAPTHANATE AND METHYL ETHYL KETONE PEROXIDE TOGETHER OR AT THE SAME TIME AS A VIOLENT REACTION, FIRE, OR EXPLOSION WILL OCCUR.

The final addition of the catalyst to the pre-promoted resin will make the resin cure or get hard by the heat reaction. The speed of this reaction varies with the ambient temperature and the amount of catalyst added as mentioned, but other things may effect the cure also.

For example, high humidity tends to slow down the cure, while low humidity speeds curing. Catalysts lose their strength with age, so more may be required for comparable gel times if it is not fresh. Resin will also cure more rapidly in a compact mass, but more slowly when dispersed over a wide, shallow area (you can prolong the pot life or time that the resin can be worked by using long, wide, shallow pans or paint trays as opposed to cylindrical pots or containers). Another trick used to increase the pot life is to keep the catalyzed resin under refrigeration or on ice, or with the container set into a bucket of cold water while not in use.

The average amount of catalyst used is about 1% to 2% by weight, but variations of from 0.5% to 5% will have little ill effect on the completed laminate if this range is necessary to your conditions. It is probably better to put in a little too much catalyst than not enough, at least until you get the "hang" of it. While much is written about precise measurements of catalyst, you'll probably soon find yourself squirting in the proper amounts largely by "feel" once a little experience is gained in your working climate.

While general ambient temperatures for fiberglass work should be 70 degrees F. or better, there are times when some will have to work in colder climes. In VERY cold conditions (and in fiberglass work, this means from about 40 degrees to 60 degrees F.), it may be necessary to purchase "cold weather" resin or add extra cobalt napthanate, as well as somewhat more catalyst. If resin does not set up in a few hours, there is the danger that your laminate could absorb moisture and perhaps cause a serious loss of strength or other physical characteristics.

At temperatures below 60 degrees there is also the danger of an incomplete cure, which could lead to disastrous results. Unless provisions are made to keep ambient temperatures, as well as temperatures of the laminating products themselves and the actual molding surfaces, at least 60 degrees F. or higher, cure times may be abnormally disrupted.

For example, gel time will INCREASE by 3 to 5 minutes for every degree of temperature reduction. If you had been working at 70 degrees F. one day, and the next day the temperature dropped to 60 degrees F., gel time could increase perhaps 30 to 50 minutes. Consequently, it is highly recommended to NEVER do fiberglass boatbuilding where ambient temperatures cannot be kept at least at 60 degrees F. And if your conditions approach this temperature, you should probably consider using resin with

added cobalt as a precaution. The added cobalt will shorten storage stability to a minor degree, but for long shelf life, always keep resin at or below 70 degrees F. and in a dry place.

C.		F.	C.		F.
−17.8	**0**	32	10.6	**51**	123.8
−17.2	**1**	33.8	11.1	**52**	125.6
−16.7	**2**	35.6	11.7	**53**	127.4
−16.1	**3**	37.4	12.2	**54**	129.2
−15.6	**4**	39.2	12.8	**55**	131.0
−15.0	**5**	41.0	13.3	**56**	132.8
−14.4	**6**	42.8	13.9	**57**	134.6
−13.9	**7**	44.6	14.4	**58**	136.4
−13.3	**8**	46.4	15.0	**59**	138.2
−12.8	**9**	48.2	15.6	**60**	140.0
−12.2	**10**	50.0	16.1	**61**	141.8
−11.7	**11**	51.8	16.7	**62**	143.6
−11.1	**12**	53.6	17.2	**63**	145.4
−10.6	**13**	55.4	17.8	**64**	147.2
−10.0	**14**	57.2	18.3	**65**	149.0
− 9.44	**15**	59.0	18.9	**66**	150.8
− 8.89	**16**	60.8	19.4	**67**	152.6
− 8.33	**17**	62.6	20.0	**68**	154.4
− 7.78	**18**	64.4	20.6	**69**	156.2
− 7.22	**19**	66.2	21.1	**70**	158.0
− 6.67	**20**	68.0	21.7	**71**	159.8
− 6.11	**21**	69.8	22.2	**72**	161.6
− 5.56	**22**	71.6	22.8	**73**	163.4
− 5.00	**23**	73.4	23.3	**74**	165.2
− 4.44	**24**	75.2	23.9	**75**	167.0
− 3.89	**25**	77.0	24.4	**76**	168.8
− 3.33	**26**	78.8	25.0	**77**	170.6
− 2.78	**27**	80.6	25.6	**78**	172.4
− 2.22	**28**	82.4	26.1	**79**	174.2
− 1.67	**29**	84.2	26.7	**80**	176.0
− 1.11	**30**	86.0	27.2	**81**	177.8
− 0.56	**31**	87.8	27.8	**82**	179.6
0	**32**	89.6	28.3	**83**	181.4
0.56	**33**	91.4	28.9	**84**	183.2
1.11	**34**	93.2	29.4	**85**	185.0
1.67	**35**	95.0	30.0	**86**	186.8
2.22	**36**	96.8	30.6	**87**	188.6
2.78	**37**	98.6	31.1	**88**	190.4
3.33	**38**	100.4	31.7	**89**	192.2
3.89	**39**	102.2	32.2	**90**	194.0
4.44	**40**	104.0	32.8	**91**	195.8
5.00	**41**	105.8	33.3	**92**	197.6
5.56	**42**	107.6	33.9	**93**	199.4
6.11	**43**	109.4	34.4	**94**	201.2
6.67	**44**	111.2	35.0	**95**	203.0
7.22	**45**	113.0	35.6	**96**	204.8
7.78	**46**	114.8	36.1	**97**	206.6
8.33	**47**	116.6	36.7	**98**	208.4
8.89	**48**	118.4	37.2	**99**	210.2
9.44	**49**	120.2	37.8	**100**	212.0
10.0	**50**	122.0			

FIG. 6-1 — This chart allows temperature conversions from Fahrenheit to Celsius, and vice versa. To convert from Celsius to Fahrenheit, find the Celsius degrees in the center column and read the equivalent Fahrenheit degrees in the right hand column. To convert from Fahrenheit to Celsius, find the Fahrenheit degrees in the center column and read the equivalent Celsius degrees in the left hand column.

Two final points about catalysts: Don't try to substitute any other type of catalyst for the one you should be using, and DON'T FORGET TO PUT CATALYST INTO EACH BATCH! If you forget the catalyst, the resin will probably NEVER set. If this happens on an INNER layer of your laminate, you'll have to remove the outer layers on top and start the area over again, which may be impossible if you have catalyzed these outer layers, and difficult at the very least. Attempting to brush on or spray on catalyst afterwards will never set up more than a thin shell, and handling the catalyst in this manner is hazardous.

LAMINATING & FINISHING RESINS

Polyester resin is called an "air-inhibited" resin; that is, the surface exposed to the air will not cure (at least completely) in the presence of air; it will exhibit a surface tackiness even though the resin will NOT be in a fluid state. In order for the resin surface to cure completely and overcome this tackiness, it must be sealed off from the air. This can be done in two ways.

The ordinary way is to purchase a resin that contains a non-air inhibiter which is usually a wax additive. Once the resin has been applied, the wax will "float" to the surface as a result of the exotherm (heat given off as the resin sets up), thereby sealing out the air and allowing the resin to cure. Such a polyester resin which contains this wax additive is referred to as a "finishing" resin because it is usually used as the final coat prior to finish work. We'll tell you how to make your own finishing resin in a little bit.

The other way to cure the resin is to seal the surface from the air AFTER the resin has been applied by applying a surface coating over the resin. This can be done by using a sheet material such as cellophane or "Mylar" (both are called parting films), or with a spray application of a product such as polyvinyl alcohol (commonly known as "P-V-A"), a form of release agent. These methods of sealing out the air, however, are usually limited to smaller areas, such as in repair work, and most amateurs will use a resin containing the wax additive for curing of the final coat.

Resins which do not contain the wax additive, as do the finishing resins previously noted, are referred to as "laminating" resin. Therefore, we have a simple breakdown of the two types of polyester resins usually used in fiberglass boatbuilding, which are:

LAMINATING RESIN (AIR INHIBITED, CONTAINS NO WAX)

FINISHING RESIN (NON-AIR INHIBITED, CONTAINS WAX)

Laminating resin should be used throughout the fiberglass boatbuilding process with the exception of final coats. The reason for this is that a fiberglass laminate is not a homogeneous material as the uninformed often thinks. Instead, fiberglass is a combination of layers of fiberglass reinforcements each saturated and bonded together, similar in configuration to a sheet of plywood with its plies bonded together with glue.

The surfaces of layers in a laminate saturated with laminating resin remain tacky as the laminate is built up to assure a sound bond for the application of subsequent layers of material. This bond is referred to as an "interlaminar" bond. If finish resin were used for laminating purposes, the wax in the resin which floats to the surface would have to be removed before applying additional laminates in order for bonding to take place, and there are only two ways this can be done.

First, you can attempt to wash or wipe down the surface with a solvent such as acetone. But the problem with this technique, at least over large areas, is that it tends to just "push" the wax around as it builds up. The other and most effective way to remove the wax is by sanding. This is tedious work in laminating, since each layer would have to be done before subsequent layers could be applied. So the best advice is to use laminating resin in the first place, so that laminating can be done without interruption. In this manner you'll be assured of a sound interlaminar bond, which would always be suspect if a finishing resin were used instead. Resin simply won't stick well to a wax-coated surface.

MAKING YOUR OWN FINISHING RESIN

To simplify the resin buying situation, you can purchase just one kind of laminating resin for the entire project and make your own finishing resin as required by using the laminating resin and adding the wax additive, or "surfacing agent" as it is called.

First, let's explain how the resin manufacturer makes his finishing resin. When the resin is being "cooked", and therefore heated, wax can be added at this time and readily dispersed throughout the resin batch. This way the resin manufacturer is assured that a complete surface cure will be effected once the resin is used.

On the other hand, when adding your own wax or "surfacing agent" (a mix of paraffin in a solution of styrene), it will usually be done at room temperature. If it is too cold, you will not get an even mix. Don't attempt to "heat" the resin as the manufacturer's do; this is dangerous! But do try to have the resin at normal room temperature or higher, preferably not less than 65 degrees F., with 70 degrees F. or more being preferable. The surfacing agent should be at this minimum temperature or above also. In cold weather, the surfacing agent may appear cloudy or a clear solid may form on the surface of the solution in the container. If this happens, warm the container of surfacing agent to about 90 degrees F. by placing it in a container of warm TAP water. DO NOT HEAT THE SURFACING AGENT OVER OR NEAR AN OPEN FLAME OR

ELECTRIC HEATER! Also, do not allow water to enter the container. If the resin itself is not up to these temperatures, it can be warmed in a similar manner as it will affect the dispersion of the surfacing agent within the resin as well.

The amount of surfacing agent to use can vary between 1% and 5% BY WEIGHT OF RESIN, although 2% to 3% seems best. (If using surfacing agent with vinylester resins, make a test sample first; a higher concentration of wax may be required to set this type of resin up tack-free.) In other words, for each gallon of resin which usually weighs about 9 lbs., add approximately 2 to 4 ounces of surfacing agent, or as noted in the instructions if provided with the product. Add surfacing agent BEFORE the catalyst and stir it in well, but NOT so vigorously that a lot of air bubbles get into the resin. Thorough mixing IS important! You'll be able to "see" the surfacing agent in the resin since it appears as a silky "film" and this filmy appearance should be well dispersed in the resin batch. Hence it is a good idea to stir frequently during use also.

If too much surfacing agent is added, the resin viscosity can change and become too thin because of the styrene portion of the additive, which is a primary ingredient of the resin as well as a thinner. If not enough surfacing agent is added, the resin surface will not cure completely "tack-free" in all areas, and at worst, the surface will have to be sanded and another coat with more surfacing agent (plus perhaps a larger amount of catalyst making what is called a "hot" coat) applied so it will cure. But experience has shown that there is usually enough latitude with the products so that problems are far and few between. The biggest problem is that people do not mix the ingredients enough, and that the temperatures are frequently too low for proper mixing.

Take care when using surfacing agent as the material is harmful if inhaled or swallowed, and may irritate the skin, eyes, nose, and throat. Keep it out of the reach of children, avoid breathing a spray mist, and use only with adequate ventilation. Keep the container closed when not in use, and if any gets on your clothing, wash them before wearing them again.

THIXOTROPY

A term which frequently confuses the novice with regard to resin is "thixotropic". Many people think that thixotropic resins are those which are "thick", which is a misconception. Others read advertising claims from resin merchants that their resin is thixotropic and "won't run or sag". But the real definition of thixotropic is the quality of a resin to thicken at rest, but become fluid again on agitation and stirring.

What this rather confusing definition from the plastic engineers means in plain words is that the tendency for a resin to run or sag in use is MINIMIZED by the quality of thixotropy. The myth that there are some resins in boat work which will NOT run or sag should be dispelled. ALL polyester resins will run or sag on vertical or inclined surfaces to some degree. While it IS possible to formulate a resin that would not run, such a resin would be virtually impossible to use in boatbuilding since it would not wet out the fiberglass reinforcement in time without curing first. In other words, it would not be a workable resin.

The quality of thixotropy, then, is a variable one, with some resins more or less thixotropic than others. Beware of resins which tend to brag about the quality of thixotropy since it may be harder to wet out than a less thixotropic resin, and shrink too much. The fillers added to resin to make it thixotropic, if overdone, will affect the qualities of the resin unduly. The qualities of thixotropy can be a mixed bag, having both good as well as bad features, depending on the ultimate use of the resin.

In general laminating work, thixotropic qualities are not necessary to a high degree.

In certain cases, such as the initial wetting out of the C-FLEX material, as will be explained in Chapter 16, a completely nonthixotropic resin is called for to obtain satisfactory results. Resins are usually made thixotropic by the addition of fillers such as silicon dioxide, a product made from sand.

Thixotropy should not be confused with resin viscosity, or the ability of a resin to resist flow. Resins are available in many different viscosities similar to that of motor oils, with varying viscosities to suit varying requirements of use. Whether a resin is rated as low, medium, or high in viscosity, however, it may contain varying degrees of thixotropic qualities as well.

For example, a high viscosity resin could have low thixotropic value (little or no filler added), while a low viscosity resin may include thixotropic additives, and vice versa. Viscosity is the result of the chemical manufacturing process, while thixotropic qualities usually are provided by the addition of thixotropic agents or fillers AFTER the resin is made. These added fillers do contribute to the resin's viscosity.

RESIN FLEXIBILITY

Resins are classified as rigid, semi-rigid, and flexible, with the terms all being relative to one another. As noted, a wide variation in properties can be obtained by the resin manufacturer by the use of basic ingredients and proportions, even though all polyester resins are similar.

The quality of flexibility in a resin actually refers to the percentage of elongation of the cured resin at rupture under tensile (pulling) stress. However, whether a resin is rigid, semi-rigid, or flexible also has some bearing on other characteristics. The following describes the qualitative parameters of flexibility and some of these characteristics:

RIGID RESINS: Rigid resins have higher physical strength properties than more flexible types, but they are more brittle and have less impact resistance. This type of resin is suitable for small boats having little or no framing, or for larger boats with substantial framing (framing meaning internal structural members). Elongation is between 0.5% and 3.0% before rupture.

SEMI-RIGID RESINS: These resins are compounded to have greater resiliency and impact resistance than rigid types. These resins also have somewhat better aging resistance, and are suited to larger hulls having some internal structure. Elongation at rupture is from 3% to 10%.

FLEXIBLE RESINS: These resins are not suitable for use in boat hulls alone, but are often mixed with rigid resins to form semi-rigid resins (by the manufacturer usually). This type of resin is considered both flexible and elastic, having elongation exceeding 10%.

While it may seem that the flexible and especially the semi-rigid resins may offer potential advantages in increasing a hull's resistance to impact loads, most experts feel that such resins offer little advantage to the primary hull structure due to an increase in hull flexibility. Hence, rigid resins of the "general purpose" type are commonly used in boats, with a supporting internal structure in the hull as required. An exception is that in boats produced in female molds, the gel coats used against the mold surface require the qualities found in a semi-rigid or flexible type resin, although the balance of the laminate would include resins of a more rigid type.

ORTHO, ISO, & VINYLESTER RESINS

Just when you thought you knew everything about resin and hadn't even asked, here's another wrinkle we'll throw at you about resins. Sooner or later along your travels through the polyester resin "jungle", you'll hear mention of the terms "ortho", "iso", and "vinylester" resins. Just

what are these resins? And are the terms important to your boatbuilding knowledge?

Well, don't despair, because they are all variations on the polyester type. In other words, they are sub-categories. The main difference, at least chemically, is that each is made a little bit differently, but essentially the same, varying only in molecular weight and structure. Again the reasons for these variations have to do with the final qualities desired in a laminate and the conditions it will be subjected to.

Ortho resins (technically called "orthophthalic resins") and iso resins (technically known as "isophthalic resins") refer to differences in the acid base of the resin. The ortho resins are less complex from a molecular standpoint than iso resins, while the vinylester types are more complex molecularly than either the iso or ortho types. But they are ALL polyester types. To simplify things at the outset of this section, by an overwhelming majority, the resins most used in fiberglass boatbuilding, especially those that would be used by the amateur, are of the ortho type. Why? Because of lower cost primarily, and because the qualities offered by either the iso or vinylester types are usually not needed in the majority of boats being built, although the use of iso resins is on the increase.

Why, then, would anyone want to use either the iso or vinylester resins over the ortho type? Both iso resin and the vinylesters have higher physical properties and impart improved characteristics to a laminate. For example, iso resins have better corrosion and solvent resistance over ortho resins, and are also tougher and have more impact strength. This is why iso resins are commonly used for gel coat resins. Iso and vinylester resins are also reputed to have better bonding qualities.

The vinylester resins are even better than iso resins with regard to chemical and corrosion resistance, while retaining their higher strength properties at higher temperatures, a quality which has proven valuable in the aerospace field. Their high resistance to chemical and corrosive elements makes the vinylesters important in the field of storage tank fabrication and for various industrial applications.

The vinylester resins also have an inherent elongation flexibility that gives laminates made from this resin an improvement where certain high stresses cannot be eliminated in the design process, such as mechanical cycling and vibration. An application where this quality could be important might be in the construction of high-speed ocean racing powerboats, for example.

Yet many fiberglass materials experts and resin chemists are surprised at the interest shown in vinylester resins for boatbuilding, stating that really adequate strength and other physical properties can be achieved with general purpose ortho and iso resins using proper laminates and fabricating practices. Their argument is that unless the higher strength properties at elevated temperatures and high resistance to chemical and other corrosive elements offered by the vinylesters are necessary, there is no need to pay the premium price for vinylester resins. We'll discuss the uses of all these resins in more detail where applicable.

Other problems also exist with vinylester resins. Shelf life is frequently much less than regular polyesters. Many are sold as unpromoted resins requiring the ultimate user to add the promotor. Further complicating this is the fact that different and more complex promotor systems are used, such as the usual cobalt, plus another one called dimethylanaline (or "DMA"), which is an extremely dangerous product and a carcinogen.

Because two promotors may be required as well as the addition of the catalyst, the vinylester resins can be more difficult to work regarding gel times and curing procedures because of varying proportions of the three ingredients. This can be tricky for the amateur and lead to problems and question-

able results. Because of this AND the potential safety and health hazards, some resin experts feel that final mixing of the promotors with vinylester resins should NOT be left with the ultimate user. Regardless of whether the vinylester is pre-promoted or not, the user is advised to contact the resin manufacturer or supplier in all cases for their recommendations regarding the ultimate use to which the resin will be applied as well as proper handling procedures.

The question is, then, are vinylesters worth it? Many of the custom "high performance" builders who build competition craft think so, especially those using the high modulus reinforcements noted in Chapter 21. Their argument is that the performance of any composite has to do not only with the reinforcement materials and their combination as well as orientation in a laminate, but also with the type of resin used. It is believed that vinylesters provide better impact resistance, improved abrasion resistance, better water resistance, and greater flexibility, especially where the high modulus materials are involved.

Yet there is not much testing going on to support these claims, and many experts feel that fashion has been dictating much of the use of vinylesters as opposed to the other polyesters. However, the author has observed empirical results with foam cores using vinylester resins with thin, high modulus skins as opposed to those comparable laminates using general purpose polyesters that show both better bonding of the skins to the cores and higher impact resistance. But even still, for the majority of boats that would be built by an amateur, the alleged and proven superior qualities of vinylester resins simply do not warrant the additional cost and trouble. The ortho resins are usually good enough, and if you want something a bit better, then use an iso resin. While currently iso resins cost about 10% more than ortho resins, the vinylesters cost nearly TWICE as much. For most amateurs, this alone will rule out the use of vinylester resins.

FIRE—RETARDANT RESINS

Cured polyester resins will burn gloriously when ignited, and will continue to burn until extinguished, or until they run out of combustible material. Naturally, this can make a boat owner nervous, but then just about any boat could have a fire aboard at some point regardless of the material it is built from. To make resin less vulnerable it would seem that it would be desirable to make it "fireproof", since the fiberglass reinforcement part of the laminate can't burn.

While no resin is completely FIRE-PROOF, there ARE resins which are FIRE-RETARDANT; that is, they may discolor, smoke, and char in the presence of extreme heat, but they will self-extinguish once the flame source is removed.

Fire-retardant resins can be formulated by the manufacturer by the addition of several different ingredients, such as small amounts of antimony trioxide, alumina trihydrate, or chlorinated paraffins (waxes), or fire-retardancy may be formed as an integral part of the chemical structure of the resin. It would seem that the use of fire-retardant resins would be recommended practice in fiberglass boat construction, especially in engine spaces, around fuel tanks, in galley areas, or anywhere where there is a high fire hazard. Indeed, the U. S. Government commonly specifies this type of resin for U. S. Navy and Coast Guard vessels when they are made from fiberglass. Yet why is it that most production fiberglass boats do not use this resin?

One's first reaction would be that manufacturers probably don't use fire-retardant resins because they cost more, and indeed they do! However, the additional cost could no doubt be justified in most cases. For example, insurance premiums could conceivably be reduced. But there are problems to overcome with respect to fire-retardant resins. For example, some self-extinguishing resins have a higher viscosity, which makes them harder to work with, especially for the amateur. In some cases, the compounds added which are not chemically bound in the resin may reduce the physical properties of the resin, such as decreasing its weather resistance, and leech out upon exposure, diminishing the fire-retardant value.

These resins give off dense smoke and fumes during combustion (as do regular polyester resins) which make their fire-retardant qualities a mixed blessing. Another problem is that fire-retardant resins take longer to cure. The ratio or percentage of catalyst is more critical in fire-retardant resins. Resin chemists recommend nothing less than 1% of catalyst per volume or else the completed part may be too flexible. Also, because cure time can vary with ambient temperatures, one must be very accurate in judging the amount of catalyst required for proper cure using fire-retardant resins.

It is easy to see that where government vessels are involved, the extra cost and trouble required for the use of fire-retardant resin may not be important, since the taxpayer foots the bill. But for the average amateur on a budget and having enough problems sorting his way through the job first time out, the mixed benefits of fire-retardant resins may not be worth the trouble. Perhaps a partial solution to the problem would be to use regular resins in the laminate with the exception of the outermost coats, finishing off with the fire-retardant type, or to use this approach only in areas where fire danger is greatest. This may not, however, be totally successful, and perhaps the best solution is to invest in a good fire protection system if the boat is of any size.

THINNING & SPRAYING RESIN

Generally, thinning of resin (or thickening resin for that matter) is not recommended, at least for general laminating work. Resin should never be thinned with the idea of "stretching out" the resin in the hopes of saving money. Doing so will adversely affect the properties of the resin and make the resulting laminate of questionable strength and durability. Resin can be thinned (if absolutely necessary) for spraying purposes up to about 5% by weight with acetone, but should NOT be thinned with acetone for any other purpose. In fact, even for spraying, adding acetone is highly questionable. The acetone does not participate in the curing process of the resin, and actually tends to lower the temperature of the resin since it volatizes so rapidly, thereby affecting the cure time. When being sprayed, there is a tendency for the acetone to "trap" in the resin, and because it evaporates so rapidly, the acetone tends to leave "pinholes" in the surface. Also, in curing, the acetone can cause cracking, shrinking, and a surface glaze due to rapid evaporation.

A better thinner is the liquid styrene monomer because the resin already contains it and is therefore compatible with it. For spraying, the amount of styrene varies depending on the viscosity of the resin. Up to 15% of styrene by weight can be added in certain cases, but the usual proportions are about 5%. Resins with low viscosity require less thinning than more viscous resins or those with a higher degree of thixotropy. Spraying of resin is usually done only for final or finish coats, or for gel coat application inside female molds. It is NOT practical nor recommended for the amateur to spray resin for general laminating work, and for most who will be building using male mold methods, there will be little if any need for spraying or spray equipment. The information provided is simply for those who are interested or who may have a need at some point for spraying resin.

When spraying resin, a pressure-feed spray gun should be used to apply the resin as opposed to a siphon-feed type due to the viscosity of the resin. Use acetone to clean the gun BEFORE the resin sets up hard or else the spray gun will be ruined. A batch of resin can usually be sprayed through a gun in about three minutes, but the resin should be catalyzed for a pot life of from 15 to 20 minutes. If flaws or thick areas build up, a brush can be used to smooth out these areas before the resin gels.

The technique used to spray resin is otherwise similar spraying paint, so that anyone familiar with paint spraying should have no problems adapting to resin. But practice is required. Repeated coats of finishing resin can be sprayed on as long as the surface does not set up. If a delay occurs or the resin does set up, the surface should be sanded before applying additional coats.

Spraying resin puts lots of fumes and spray mist into the air which can be dangerous. Spray only with adequate ventilation, wear a respirator, and avoid any open flames, heat sources, or smoking in the area. If thinning with styrene, be VERY careful when using this product and use eye protection in its presence. If using styrene in the vicinity of gel coated molds, take care to avoid drops of styrene from falling onto the mold since it can soften the gel coat and leave marks.

PIGMENTING RESIN

Many resin suppliers sell pigments that can be added to resin to color them. However, adding pigments to resin in fiberglass boatbuilding (at least for general laminating purposes) is NOT recommended. The main reason is that pigments impair the visual inspection of the layup as it progresses, making it difficult to spot defects, such as resin-rich or resin-starved areas, air entrapment, and the like. Secondly, pigments are simply not needed so why spend the money? Mixing in pigments is more work, and it is difficult to control the mixing proportions.

Pigmented resins do, however, have some limited applications in fiberglass boatbuilding. Fiberglass laminates in the ordinary state are largely transparent or translucent; you can see a lot of light through them. In production boatbuilding using female molds, pigmented gel coats are applied against the mold surface not only for cosmetic and appearance reasons, but for adding the necessary opacity to prevent this translucent quality.

Another use for pigmented resin is sometimes used in male mold boatbuilding of the type discussed in this text. Instead of depending just on a final paint covering for durability and appearance, some prefer to mix pigments into the final resin coating or filler coats to match closely the color of paint that will be used on the exterior. Then if there is a mar or scratch to the painted surface in use, it will not be so obvious (see Chapter 13 for more information on finishing methods).

If you wish to use pigments, they should be added BEFORE the catalyst. If using surfacing agent, this should be added before the pigment so the surfacing agent can be seen while mixing. While pigments do vary, some pigment containers include no instructions on how to use them. In most cases, liquid pigments are usually mixed in a ratio of 4 ounces of pigment to each gallon of resin unless otherwise stipulated. If paste-type pigment is used, follow the instructions provided with the product. In order to get good depth of color, more pigment than would seem necessary is often required, and should be mixed into all finish coats. Excessive pigmentation, however, will slow gel time, retard cure, and cause surface tackiness, so don't use too much. Don't be surprised if the brilliant colored pigment suddenly turns murky and muddy when mixed in the resin and the final color comes out less brilliant than you would

like; this is just one of the problems in attempting to color resins and why they have little use in amateur fiberglass boatbuilding except for use in gel coats.

GEL COATS

Gel coats are pigmented polyester resins usually of a flexible or semi-flexible type that are the first step in female mold fiberglass boat construction. Gel coats can be ortho, iso, or neopentylglycol (neo) based resins, however, the iso or neo types are preferred for gel coats for increased strength and durability. Gel coats formulated from epoxy resins are seldom seen in the boating field; polyester laminates used against a cured epoxy surface result in a poor bond. The gel coat is usually sprayed against the mold surface and becomes the exterior of the completed boat for boats build in this manner.

A wide variety of colors are available for gel coats, yet they should not be confused with paints. Gel coats are generally formulated for production boatbuilders using female mold construction methods and factory conditions. As a result, they are really not well suited to the novice since in almost all cases, they are primarily intended for spray application using rather special equipment and techniques. However, for the person who wishes to build a boat in a female mold, this does not mean that he cannot use gel coats. He can either acquire the necessary spray application equipment and learn how, or he can apply the gel coat by brush, a technique not highly recommended. In either case, it is recommended that the person who wishes to take this approach contact and work closely with the gel coat supplier, who can provide the necessary technical advice which is too extensive to explore completely in this text (although the subject is discussed in some detail in Chapter 15). Suffice to say that gel coats are NOT paints, and whether they are sprayed OR brushed, they will NOT behave like paints; they need special techniques, and even under the best of conditions, are subject to many problems that are best resolved between the gel coat maker and the user.

In male mold fiberglass boat construction, the use of gel coats is not preferred for many reasons. When building a boat in this manner, one is literally building from the inside out, with the exterior coating being the last coat or layer as opposed to female mold work where the exterior coating is the first coat against the mold surface.

Most gel coat resins are air-inhibited types which depend on this mold surface to "lockout" the air so they can cure against the mold surface, yet retain a tacky surface for the application of subsequent layers of fiberglass on the inside of the mold for a positive interlaminar bond. While one could use a final gel coat with wax or surfacing agent added on the exterior of a male molded boat, or cover the surface coat with PVA agent or a film covering such as cellophane or "Mylar", such practice is usually limited to small areas like those found in repair work. More information on the use of gel coats in finish work is provided in Chapter 13.

In addition to the numerous exterior gel coat formulations available, there are many other gel coats for specialized purposes. For example, there are interior gel coats or polyester enamels, or "flow coats" as they are sometimes called, which are used on the inside of fiberglass hulls to give them a more finished and attractive appearance. This type of coating contains wax so that it will cure hard (since it is NOT sprayed against the mold surface). These interior gel coats are often a low-gloss or non-gloss finish which is usually sprayed on (although most can be rolled on also but brushing is usually not advised), and can have "spatter" effects added to minimize hull interior flaws. Since appearance on the inside is not as critical as that on the outside, the use of

interior gel coats is perhaps better suited to the amateur, but their application should not be considered other than a cosmetic coating, and therefore optional with the builder.

Another type of gel coat is the flame-retardant type. However, unless a fire-retardant resin is used throughout a laminate, this type of resin will not be completely effective, as was noted earlier. The burning rate of a laminate made with fire-retardant resin is virtually unaffected whether the gel coat is a standard or a flame retardant grade. The primary reason that flame-retardant gel coats are made is to meet military or other prescribed regulations.

Still another type of gel coat is tooling gel coat used for making molds and plugs for female mold construction. These are special formulations with unique qualities suited to these usages, and have little place in most amateur boatbuilding projects using male mold methods. As can be seen, the choices for gel coats are many and varied. If you think that you may have an application requiring the use of a gel coat, it is recommended that you contact one of the manufacturers which specialize in this field for their advice (also see Bibliography).

A POLYESTER RESIN SCENARIO

Up to this point we've talked a lot about resins, their characteristics, types available, and various related aspects. But there may be many who have never been around polyester resins or who have never had an occasion to use them. This section, then, is specifiically for these people. We'll describe what's supposed to happen in use and what to expect. We'll even give some tips to help out with problems, and follow up with some important safety aspects so trouble can be avoided.

First, let's get rid of any apprehensions at the outset. My feeling is that ANYONE can learn to work with resins, and with very little effort, acquire acceptable skills quickly. After all, one of the main reasons for the proliferation of fiberglass products has been that they can be produced with what amounts to unskilled labor. This fact alone makes fiberglass boatbuilding an ideal method for the beginner. While mistakes can be made, 90% of these can be corrected or avoided without detriment to the final product AS LONG AS CARE IS EXERCISED AND YOU ARE ORGANIZED! Fiberglass work can be a messy, sticky job, but it surely does not require any unique skills; just a little prior information, and that's what this book is for.

While polyester resins will cure either by the addition of the catalyst to provide internally generated heat, or by externally applied heat, the latter method is far too expensive and difficult for something as large as a boat hull. So into our first batch of resin we'll use MEK peroxide to send the resin on its way to final cure.

In most cases, the resin supplier will provide a little chart that tells how much catalyst is required to catalyze the resin when at a certain ambient temperature. At least for the first batch, follow the directions. As more experience is gained in handling the resin, and you see how it reacts to the catalyst and temperature, you'll find that you can probably gauge the amount required closely enough "by feel".

Since only so much resin at a time can be worked, catalyze only enough to do a certain part of the job. If you don't know how much this may be, start off with a quart or less, increasing the amount somewhat as work continues if you find later that more can be used at a time. Because catalyst is such an extremely dangerous product with regard to eye damage, it is always advisable to wear eye protection when mixing the catalyst into the resin (although you'll rarely see this done in most production shops even though they know better!)

Mix in the catalyst, stirring the resin thoroughly, but not vigorously, as this can cause too many air bubbles in the resin which may have to be worked out of the laminate. Minor bubbles, however, have little effect, so don't be too concerned with them. Stir the resin for about two minutes to assure even dispersion of the catalyst (if you don't, the cure will not be even).

For quite a while after the catalyst has been stirred in, it will seem as though nothing is taking place. Don't add more catalyst! And don't sit down and have a cup of coffee or jawbone with the neighbors. Once that resin is catalyzed it won't stop for anything on its way to curing!

Shortly after the resin has been catalyzed, it will start changing color from perhaps a pretty blue or pinkish color (depending on the brand of resin, since tints vary), to a more muddy or brownish character. Of course, by this time you should have applied a lot of this batch of resin to the job at hand. But if you haven't, the container may be starting to get a little warm. This is the exothermic reaction taking place, and as it continues, you had better use the resin a bit faster. Of if you want to slow down the exothermic reaction a little, place the container in a bucket of ice or cold water, or put it in a refrigerator (one without food stuffs inside), or pour the resin into a flatter, shallower container. If none of these steps are taken, or the resin is not used up, you'll notice the resin starting to resemble a gelatin dessert that hasn't set up fully in the refrigerator.

The amount of time that has transpired from stirring in the catalyst to this "gelatin" point is called the "pot life", or time available for using the resin. The pot life of a resin, as we have noted, depends on several things, including the amount of catalyst used, the ambient temperature, the freshness of the resin, etc. A "normal" pot life (if there is such a thing) can be from 15 to 60 minutes, but a more workable range is from 30 to 45 minutes. While there may be occasions where you'll want the resin to "kickoff" in 15 minutes or less, this short time can cause undue shrinkage and heat build-up in certain cases, and most will not be able to work the resin so quickly.

Pot life of resin is similar to the terminology, "gel time". The difference is that gel time is the time available to work the resin ONCE IT HAS BEEN APPLIED TO THE SURFACE, since surface application allows the resin to be spread out over a larger area where the heat is automatically reduced. Resins therefore will have a somewhat longer gel time than they do a pot life. The moral of the story, then, is to get the resin applied to the working surface as soon as possible, both to minimize waste and to have a longer time to work the resin.

Now let's presume that a container of resin has started to gel and you have not had a chance to use it all. What do you do? Throw it away! It should not be used after this point has been reached. But don't just throw it into the trash can. Why? It's possible for the heat being generated during exotherm to start a fire! As we noted before, a concentrated mass of resin builds up more heat than a well dispersed batch, and if the amount in the mass is large enough, and ambient temperatures are high, or there has been perhaps too much catalyst used, then there is definitely a chance for a fire to start. So when discarding catalyzed resin that cannot be used, do so over a broad area to prevent heat build-up, and do so only where there are no combustible materials.

Throughout this resin scenario from the addition of the catalyst to the resin setting up hard, you'll be able to check on catalyzation, gelling, and curing effects by subtle color changes in the resin. Remember not to set up the resin too fast, since this can cause undue shrinkage of the part and lead to distortion, difficulty in removing the part from the mold, and stress concentrations. But also remember to catalyze EACH AND EVERY batch of resin.

Work in ideal temperatures whenever possible. While laminates can be built up in ambient temperatures down to 60 degrees F. and up to about 100 degrees F., a range of from 70 to 85 degrees F. is ideal as long as you do NOT work in direct sunlight or in the rain.

Once the resin has been applied to the surface and worked, and the resin begins to gel, it should not be tampered with further until it has cured (there are some slight exceptions to this rule, as will be explained in Chapter 12 where we discuss laminating procedures). Cure time refers to the time required for the resin to set up hard enough so that other work can be performed on it, or more technically, the time required for the resin to reach a "polymerized" state once the catalyst has been added.

While much depends on the ambient temperature, cure times of between one and three hours are typical. Anything a little longer than this is acceptable within reason as long as there is no danger of high humidity (rainfall, fog, mist, etc.) in the vicinity that could dimish the physical properties of the resin and layup.

Note that cure time does NOT mean that the resin has fully cured; this will take a considerably longer time, perhaps several days. During this time the fiberglass hull or part will still have some degree of flexibility, and if holding the hull or part to the intended shape is important (as it is in a boat hull, for example), one must take care to prevent distortion from occurring until the part is rigid enough, or has this rigidity instilled by the addition of structural members BEFORE removing it from its mold. This statement applies whether the hull or part is made IN a female mold or OVER a male mold. The fiberglass part will still continue to cure until final strength is realized some considerable length of time after fabrication. While a specific time for this to occur cannot be given, periods up to several days to a week or more are not unusual.

How will you know how long curing will take in your case? Is there a way you can tell if the part has cured long enough? Or has cured properly in any case? In production work they often use what is called a Barcol hardness tester which can be used after the application of each laminate to check the degree of cure. Just in case you have the necessary Barcol hardness testing device, a Barcol reading of 40 is typical. Another test to determine cure state is called the acetone sensitivity test. This is simple for anyone to perform. Just apply a small amount of acetone on the resin surface and rub lightly until the acetone evaporates. If the surface softens or becomes tacky, the resin has not set up completely (although it may still be hard enough to perform subsequent work). Generally, however, cure state will usually be obvious and testing, as such, will seldom be necessary in the amateur-built boat.

CATALYST RATIOS PER QUART OF RESIN

MEKP %	APPROX. CC	APPROX. TEASPOON	APPROX. LIQUID OZ.
1.0	9	2	1/3
1.5	13	2-3/4	1/2
2.0	18	3-3/4	7/10

FIG. 6-2

RESIN SAFETY ASPECTS

Now that you know how resin reacts once you catalyze it and work with it, let's talk a little about how to treat it, especially with regard to safety. First, let me state that nobody really knows with certainty what the long-term hazards are of working with polyester resins, mainly because they have not been around long enough to fully assess the ill effects. But we DO know that the stuff isn't going to increase our longevity, and in fact, many of the constituents of resin are especially hazardous if NOT treated with care and respect.

For example, styrene (the main component in resin and also a part of surfacing agent) is an irritant to both the eyes and to the respiratory system at about 400 PPM (parts per million) or over, and at 10,000 PPM may be fatal. However, in most situations styrene vapor (which is what you are mainly smelling when you smell that pungent "sweet" odor of resin) rarely exceeds 200 PPM. At higher concentrations, styrene vapors have a somewhat anaesthetic or narcotic effect (like being a little bit drunk). If overexposure to fumes results, remove the victim from exposure to a well-ventilated area, use oxygen or artificial respiration as required, and make him comfortably warm but not hot.

As noted, eye protection is EXTREMELY important when working with resins AND ESPECIALLY MEK PEROXIDE CATALYST. In case of eye contact with styrene or catalyst, flush promptly with copius amounts of water for 15 minutes AND SEEK MEDICAL ATTENTION IMMEDIATELY, especially if direct catalyst is involved. This product can cause severe skin burn and permanent blindness, so avoid contact with eyes and mucous membranes as well. If swallowed, give large quantities of water or milk, and get immediate medical attention, being sure to tell medical personnel the products involved. Children and those unfamiliar with resin products should be kept away from them at all times, especially if they are unsupervised.

If resin gets on your clothing, especially a large batch, the clothing is no doubt ruined. Remove the saturated clothing promptly, however, and wash the affected skin areas with soap and water. Numerous resin cleaner products are also available for direct use on the skin in lieu of soap and water, but are more costly.

If spilled on the ground or floor area, be sure that all sources of ignition are out (remember that water heater or other appliance nearby that may have a pilot light!). Ventilate the area, remembering that styrene vapor is heavier than air so it will settle low. Scoop up the spilled material or absorb it with inert materials like vermiculite or sand, and dispose into a closed non-combustible container. Wash the contaminated area with trisodium phosphate and water. Resin, catalyst, and surfacing agents are ALL flammable products, so avoid heat sources, open flames, and smoking around these products. Don't store catalyst at over 100 degrees F., and don't thin or mix MEK peroxide with acetone. Don't ship or send MEK peroxide catalyst on an airplane, either, as it is classed as "organic peroxide" which is not allowed aboard commercial aircraft. It will oxidize many metals, including steel, copper, and brass.

In the event of fire, DON'T fight it with water! Treat it like an oil or fuel fire using foam, carbon dioxide, dry chemical, sand, or CLASS "B" extinguisher. Note that styrene will polymerize readily at elevated temperatures in a closed container, so keep heat away from containers to prevent a violent rupture.

Do NOT expose catalysts to any form of heat or direct sunlight. Catalysts should never be diluted with acetone; an explosion may result. If using spray guns, these should also be grounded and all worn parts should be replaced before use. Such equipment should be explosion proof.

Finally, DO take care with resin products and treat them with the respect they deserve. If you do, you will have few problems.

CHAPTER 7

There are numerous fillers added to resins by the resin manufacturer as well as by the ultimate user. Fillers may be added for a wide variety of reasons. For example, a resin manufacturer may add fillers to give the resin thixotropic or fire retardant properties. Or the ultimate user may add fillers in order to make putties or filler coats that make finishing and sanding easier. In fiberglass boatbuilding, especially if building with one of the male mold processes, there will be many occasions to work with resin/filler combinations, particularly with filler coats more fully described in Chapter 13. What follows is a general description of various filler products, why they are used, and general handling procedures.

Probably the most common filler added by resin manufacturers is silica in various forms (silicon dioxide, colloidal silica, fumed silica, etc.) to give the resin thixotropic qualities. Silica fillers are available under several brand names such as "Cabosil" and "Aerosil". While up to about 3% by weight of this filler can be added to resin to prevent it from draining from vertical or inclined surfaces, the usual range is from 1% to 2%. Whenever possible, it is preferable to buy resins with these fillers already added by the manufacturer, although you can add your own silica if necessary. The reason is that the manufacturer has better control to assure the proper proportion and dispersion. Too much silica can make a resin difficult or even impossible to handle and use, and it tends to make the resin brittle. Yet when added to a recommended level, this filler increases the hardness of the resin and improves abrasion resistance.

Silica (as well as other types of fillers) are often added to gel coat resins for several reasons, such as for better workability, denser colors, minimizing crazing, reducing shrinkage, improving the surface finish, and increasing abrasion resistance. But too much filler can impair weather resistance, cause surface crazing, cause a loss of strength, and result in a poor finish. This is why for best results, use gel coats from firms which specialize in these products and get their recommendations as to which of their products to use for a given application.

The following is a brief listing of some various types of fillers and some of the qualities they impart to the resin (although most will have little need for them in ordinary fiberglass boatbuilding work).

Asbestos fillers can be added to improve heat resistance, and increase strength, rigidity, and moldability. Note, however, that asbestos is dangerous for the amateur to handle and work with, especially when sanding. Carbon black can be added to resin to increase weather resistance, while improving moldability, electrical conductivity, and lubricity. Fluorocarbons can be added to reduce friction and increase impact strength. Graphite can also be added to reduce friction. Chopped glass fibers can be added to increase impact strength and decrease shrinkage. Ceramic powders improve dimensional stability, compressive properties, wear resistance, and bearing properties. Wood flours and ground pecan or walnut shells also increase impact strength, reduce cost, and decrease shrinkage.

Other fillers, as previously noted, are added to make fire-retardant resins. However, alkaline fillers like calcium carbonate should not be used in laminates where fire-retardant properties are required. Fillers should not be used in laminates forming tanks either. Because fillers can add to the opacity of resins, they should be avoided in general laminating work since it makes it difficult to detect flaws and defects in the laminate, such as air bubbles and air en-

FIG. 7-1 — Microsphere products come in several forms and types. The tiny gas-filled bubbles have the consistency of fine-grained sand, flour, or dust, and are very light in weight.

trapment. Note that fillers are sometimes used in combinations for a balance of improved properties, as well as singly.

In spite of this wide array of fillers, the average amateur boatbuilder will make do with a much smaller number of types. The primary use for fillers in boatbuilding, as was emphasized, is for exterior surface or "fill" coats when building with male mold methods, and to make putties that are used to form fillets, fill holes and gaps, and for bonding purposes. While many filler formulations can be bought (both epoxy and polyester based) ready to use and readily available, there is no reason why you can't make your own when needed, AND at a much lower cost. There are several materials that can be used by the amateur, and we'll discuss these so you'll know what's best suited to your specific application.

For the filling of large areas, voids, or for core inserts where high density and weight are acceptable, calcium carbonate, silica, or talc (magnesium silicates) can be used. These will extend the resin for economy, but are heavy and change the viscosity quickly (see Fig. 7-2). Milled glass fibers can be mixed with resin for filling and forming fillets, however, this combination is difficult to sand and finish. Asbestos fibers provide a putty with strength, hardness, and scuff resistance, but it is dangerous to breathe and hence it is not recommended where sanding of the cured product is required.

Ordinary sawdust or wood flour also makes a suitable filler for filling voids or for core inserts. This is a cheap and readily available filler material. Properties of the cured filler vary depending on the type of wood used and the consistency. The finer the dust, the denser and less porous the filler will be when cured. It will be necessary to experiment with resin/catalyst ratios since the sawdust tends to inhibit or retard cure times, but over-catalyzing should be avoided or else the mix may smoke or burn, especially in a dense mass.

Add catalyst BEFORE adding the sawdust for an even cure, but stir in the saw dust immediately after the catalyst has been mixed so the mix does not set up prematurely. Don't use wet saw dust from wood that has not been dried. Experiment to determine how much sawdust to use; this varies with the consistency of the sawdust, the type of wood, and the viscosity desired.

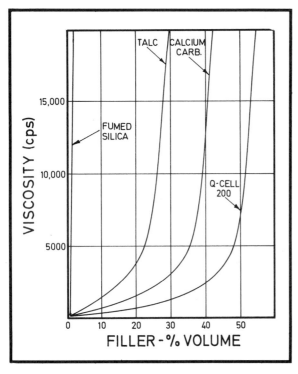

FIG. 7-2 — The effect on viscosity of adding several common filler materials to a typical polyester laminating resin is shown in the graph. It is apparent that only small additions of silica build viscosity very quickly. Also, moderate amounts of either talc or calcium carbonate build relatively high viscosities. The microsphere filler (in this case, Q-CEL 200, a registered trademark of the Philadelphia Quartz Company) has much less of an effect on viscosity because of their uniform spherical shape. This allows for a much greater resin displacement while remaining at a workable viscosity level. Other microsphere fillers react in a similar fashion. In other words, the addition of the microspheres makes the resin go farther. Adding microspheres is a lot like adding "air" to the resin, whereas the other types of fillers add weight and increase density. Resin extension is the main criterion in evaluating the cost of various types of fillers. While the cost of such a filler may be high on a weight basis, a little bit goes a long way, thereby reducing the cost per unit volume.

MICROSPHERES

None of the foregoing fillers ideally suit all the requirements for finishing use in the male mold boatbuilding project. What is most needed is a filler material that can reduce the density of the resin, one that is easy to apply and finish, one that has good physical properties, and one that is reasonable in cost. Some advocate an all-talc filler in resin. Although talc does give abrasion resistance and is cheap, it should NOT be built up more than a fraction of an inch without added reinforcement since it tends to be brittle, making it of questionable durability as a surface filler coat on male molded hulls.

A better solution to the filler problem and that of making putties is to use one of the microsphere products combined with resin to form what is called a "syntactic foam", a resin which has been "stretched out", made into a lower density, and made lighter in weight. In addition, this type of filler improves the strength-to-weight ratio of the resin, improves its rigidity, provides increased compressive strength, and makes a surface that is easier to sand and finish. These types of fillers are largely responsible for relieving the tedious sanding and finishing required on male molded hulls to get them to look like those hulls that come out of female molds. The amateur builder thus has a good chance of having a hull that looks like it was built by a professional.

Microspheres is a generic term for numerous types of lightweight, hollow, gas-filled beads or spheres that have the consistency of VERY fine-grained sand. Adding them to the resin is a lot like adding particles of air, and a little bit goes a long way. Microspheres are available under many different trade names, each having their good and not-so-good features. Some are made in the form of glass spheres while others are a phenolic plastic balloon. Some behave differently than others, both in application and in finishing qualities. For example, some may be easier to sand than others, while some may provide better feathering ability and shaping qualities than others. These types of fillers are a part of a rapidly changing technology, and many new microsphere products seem to hit the market each year, so it is difficult to generalize about them. Thus, what follows should be tempered with the foregoing comments.

Mixing up a batch of filler using microspheres is pretty much guesswork. About the best that can be said is that fillers used to make resin putty fillers are added and mixed until they feel and handle "right"! While one microsphere manufacturer suggests that a 5% concentration BY WEIGHT is trowelable, and that a 10% concentration is "very viscous", when working with small amounts, trying to figure out 5% or 10% of the filler material by weight requires VERY accurate scales capable of measuring in small increments because the fillers are so light and bulky. Experience has shown, however, that measuring accuracy is not so critical. Just add a little at a time, and practice will quickly give you a "feel" for the proper proportions best suited to your work. Just don't mix up more than can be used at any given time.

There is some disagreement about how to mix up microsphere fillers, especially as to whether the catalyst should be added before OR after the filler. This could vary with some fillers the author is not familiar with, but from a practical standpoint, the catalyst should be mixed in AFTER adding the filler, mixing up small batches at a time that can be conveniently mixed and used. The density of the mix may have some bearing on the situation. Furthermore, fillers may tend to either retard OR accelerate the cure time, so some experimentation with a small batch is always advisable when working with an unfamiliar product. If a filler inhibits the cure, more catalyst may need to be added.

Those who advocate mixing in the catalyst BEFORE the filler state that the problem with mixing in the catalyst AFTER the filler is that there may be a danger of not mixing the catalyst sufficiently with thicker putties, resulting in an incomplete cure. However, on the other hand, once the resin has been catalyzed, it can take some time to mix in the filler so it is to the proper consistency, free of lumps and smooth. In the meantime, the catalyst is sending the resin on its way to curing, thereby reducing the time available to work the mixture, perhaps reducing the time to an impractical limit if the weather is warm.

To assure that the filler is well mixed into the resin, there is a little "trick" that can be used if there is any doubt. Add a bit of pigment into the resin, and when the color change is even, the filler will also be evenly mixed in. If the catalyst has already been

FIG. 7-3 — One way to mix up a batch of resin filler is to use a kitchen whisk fitted to a drill press and mix at a fairly low speed. Many microsphere products must be carefully mixed so that the spheres do not collapse or fracture, thereby diminishing their filling ability and other physical properties.

mixed into the resin, you can tell if there is an even mix with most resins since the catalyst will cause the resin to change color somewhat. When the color is even, both the filler and resin (and the pigment as well, if also added) can be considered thoroughly mixed. As a precautionary note, most microsphere fillers are somewhat fragile. If mixed improperly, they can collapse and/or fracture, causing them to lose their filling properties. Hence, many filler companies advise using "low shear" mixing tools; in other words, don't mix vigorously with tools that damage the fillers. Using spatula-like tools by hand or low speed power mixers seems to work fine for most. A power drill or drill press fitted with a paint mixing attachment, kitchen wisk (see Fig. 7-3), or similar device can be used as well, as long as the mixture is not too stiff.

If the area being filled is large and deep, it is advisable to make more than one application to prevent too much heat build-up and shrinkage. In this case, use a laminating resin. However, if the surface to which the filler is being applied will require sanding and finishing, add surfacing agent to the resin prior to the catalyst or the filler, following the same instructions as if using the resin alone with regard to mixing and temperature requirements for the surfacing agent.

When using any of the filler materials, there can be quite a bit of "dust" in the air. Consequently, ALWAYS wear a dust mask when mixing or handling these products. Because the microsphere products are somewhat costly (at least by weight), a suitable resin putty filler can be made that works well for surface finishing of hulls built with male mold methods where light weight is not important by using a 50-50 mix of talc and microspheres added to the resin. This combination gives a good balance of low cost, good physical properties, and easy workability. The various applications and uses of fillers mixed with resins are shown in numerous places throughout the text.

CHAPTER 8 hull construction principles

In this chapter, the basic concepts of fiberglass boat construction and many of the various approaches that are possible will be discussed. In later chapters, the actual construction procedures as they relate to these various approaches will be described. In other words, this chapter will set the theoretical base for the technical material that follows.

Basically, there are two ways that a fiberglass boat can be built, and we have touched upon these to a certain extent already. First there is the female mold method used by the majority of production builders. We will illustrate the procedures used in the female mold process and include one variation of this method that is feasible for amateurs in Chapter 15. Second, there is the male mold method, which for the majority of amateurs will prove the most viable method for building a fiberglass boat. We will show several methods in following chapters which can be used to build male mold fiberglass boats.

In addition to these two basic methods of building fiberglass boats, the hull can be built in either of two concepts (see Fig. 8-1). The first and most basic is the single skin approach, and over the past years, this has been the most popular method for building fiberglass hulls, especially for production boats built in female molds. With male mold boats, single skin fiberglass boats can be built using materials such as C-FLEX fiberglass planking and FERRO-GLASS, which are both explained in separate chapters. Basically, a single skin fiberglass boat is just what it says, a hull that consists of a solid fiberglass laminate.

The other approach is the sandwich core method. This method results in a hull that has somewhat thin skins of fiberglass laminates on either side of a lightweight but comparatively thick core. The sandwich core method can be used in both female and male mold methods. Some typical core materials include various types of structural foams and balsa wood, and these also will be explained in following chapters.

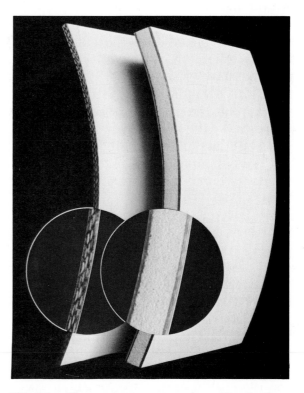

FIG. 8-1 — The two common approaches to fiberglass boat construction include solid fiberglass single-skin laminates (left) and sandwich core laminates (right) which include a thick but lightweight core material (such as the AIREX foam core shown) covered each side with thin solid fiberglass skins.

HOW DO YOU CHOOSE ONE METHOD OVER ANOTHER?

The primary factor determining the manner in which a fiberglass boat will be built depends on how many of a given type will be made, or in other words, whether you will undertake series production or not. It all has to do with total costs, plus perhaps convenience, the amount of labor involved, the quality of labor available, and other minor factors.

If one plans to build many boats of a given type, then a method suitable to series production should be chosen, preferably the female mold method. If a single boat is desired, then a method that is practical and economical for the construction of one craft should be selected. In most cases, this would involve one of the male mold or "one-off" processes. If the number of boats to be built are few, or the quantity unknown, then the choices in building methods have to be weighed more carefully, since the advantages and disadvantages of the various systems are not as clear-cut.

Basically, the choice between the fiberglass building methods boil down to either series production or "one-off" methods, and whether a female mold or male mold will be used.

FEMALE MOLD METHOD

The female mold method is the common industry-wide method for building series production boats. The novice often asks why he cannot make his own fiberglass boat just like those turned out by the factory. Most beginners seldom understand, at least completely, the entire process of how mass-produced boats are made, and why the process is not usually practical for building just a single boat. While it is true that the job can be done with largely unskilled labor, the big problem is the cost and effort involved to turn out just a single hull.

In building just one fiberglass boat using the female mold process as a factory would do it, the builder must literally build THREE "hulls" before having one that is complete enough to call a boat. It was pointed out earlier that the first of these "hulls" in the fiberglass boat manufacturing process is the "plug". From this plug, the next "hull" is made over it and this is called the "mold". And from inside this completed mold, the first complete hull (our third step) is built. While this triple-stepped process (see Fig 8-2) is not entirely universal in the industry, it is by far the most common method used for series production. The following will describe the process in more detail so the prospective builder can make a judgement if it is worth the trouble and expense to build a fiberglass boat in this manner.

THE "PLUG"

As noted, the factory-produced fiberglass boat is literally made from the outside in, which is virtually the opposite of the process of building most boats made from other materials. The fiberglass boat hull is made inside a "female" mold which has been formed over the plug which serves as the "male" part. The plug is an exact replica of the finished hull, and indeed it might be an actual boat hull.

Many an existing hull (often begged, borrowed, or stolen) has been used to form the plug, and this is one way (although surely an unethical, if not illegal way) to reduce tooling costs considerably. When a builder uses this technique to "short cut" the moldmaking process, it is called "splashing" a mold. Some unscrupulous builders who want to cash in quickly on another's success by not taking the time to design their own hulls and go through the trouble and expense of making their own plug, will simply purchase the other manufacturer's boat, tip it upsidedown, and "splash" a mold off of it.

To disguise the fact, a common trick is to make a few subtle or not-so-subtle changes to some area of the hull to make it at least appear a little different from the original. This practice has become so prevalent that some states, such as California where there are numerous fiberglass boatbuilders, have passed laws with stringent penalties for those caught in the act, but the effectiveness of such laws is debatable.

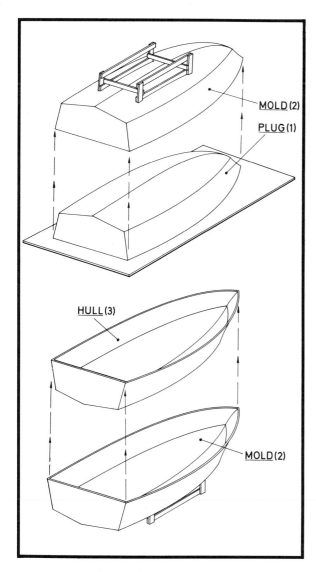

FIG. 8-2 — Production fiberglass boatbuilders use a three-step building process consisting of building a plug (1) over which a female mold (2) is made, with the hull (3) being built inside this mold. Such a process is usually prohibitive for the amateur building just a single "one-off" boat.

The legitimate builder, however, will have his boat designed first, either by his own staff or by a reputable firm of naval architects. Then the plug will be built from the designer's plans. In many cases where the hull design is an unproven or unusual type, prototype testing may be desirable, and in this instance, the plug can be made into an actual boat for testing purposes. At this stage, it is easy to make changes or corrections which can later be incorporated into the mold and reflected into the completed hulls once production begins.

In other cases, the plug will be built upsidedown in the factory in a stationary position. While the plug can be made from many different materials, it is imperative that it be perfect, without flaws, and that the surface has a super smooth glossy surface. The reason is that the surface of the plug will be transferred EXACTLY to the surface of the mold, which in turn is transferred EXACTLY to the surface of the final hull built inside the mold. The careful builder will take considerable time and care in the plug-making process since this largely determines the success of the resulting quality of the hull.

THE MOLD

After the plug is made, the surface is finished and waxed to a high gloss. This not only provides a high-gloss surface that is imparted to the mold surface, but it makes it easy to separate the mold from the plug afte the mold has been laid up over the plug. After waxing, a parting or release agent is applied to the plug surface, usually in the form of a sprayed coating of polyvinyl alcohol (PVA), which is a water soluble liquid. While some builders depend on just the waxed surface to guarantee release of the two parts, the use of PVA is more reliable, at least for the first few hulls.

The mold is made directly over the plug in much the same way as building the actual fiberglass boat. However, for series production where the mold may be used many times, it must be both strong and rigid. To increase rigidity and to make the mold mobile, a steel pipe framework is usually made integral with the mold. This framework is usually fitted with casters, and sometimes with rotational devices so that the mold can be "tipped" or angled for the worker's convenience in laying up the hull (see Fig. 8-3). On smaller hulls, the supporting mold framework can be wood. On boats which require it, either due to the shape of the hull or to surmount other molding difficulties, it is not uncommon for the mold to be made in two halves, or to

include mold inserts as aids in removing the hull from the mold (see Fig. 8-4).

With all the foregoing in mind, it is hoped that the amateur who may want just a single hull will see why it is generally impractical or uneconomical to go to the trouble of building a fiberglass boat by the female mold process. There are some exceptions, however, where it is relatively simple and easy to make a female mold, and this will be explained in Chapter 15. However, there are limitations, and for the most part, it is more practical and economical for the amateur to select one of the male mold or "one-off" methods.

FIG. 8-3 — A typical female mold used in production boatbuilding is shown. Note the husky framework reinforcing this mold and the "rotisserie" device that allows rotating or tilting the mold for easy access by the workers.

"ONE-OFF" CONSTRUCTION

The novice is frequently confused by the term "one-off", but it is quite basic. It means that only one boat of a given design will be built at a time. In other words, it means a "custom-built" boat. The term also loosely refers to limited production boats in which the basic hull forming members are used to build only a few boats at most. The builder would realize that it would not be economical to "tool up" for series production as is commonly done for factory-built boats.

Although a "one-off" boat can be built from any suitable material, this book is concerned only with those that are built from fiberglass or related materials. Both professional yards and amateur builders can use any of the "one-off" methods and materials to build boats, and they do. While it is conceivable that a fiberglass "one-off" boat can be built in a female mold, this procedure is usually too expensive for just a sin-

FIG. 8-4 — A split female mold is sometimes used to overcome molding problems and make removal of the molded part easier. The transom will be installed as a mold insert later. Note the balsa core sandwich structure with solid fiberglass laminate along the keel (see Chapter 20).

gle boat or if the hull form is too complex to make a simple, cheap mold. Hence, there is a need for methods which will allow a fiberglass "one-off" boat to be built at a reasonable cost within a reasonable period of time, and with results that can be comparable to boats built in female molds. This is where male mold methods enter the picture.

MALE MOLDS

What is a male mold? In "one-off" construction it is much the same as the plug used in series production. The main difference is that instead of making a mold off the plug, and then making the hull from the mold, the hull is built DIRECTLY over the male mold. Although the male mold can be a "full surface" mold (which is one method that can be used to build a "one-off" boat as

is described in Chapter 22), it is quite a bit more work to make a male mold in the manner that is used to make the plug used in female mold work. A simpler way is to make what can best be described as an "open" male mold, or a mold consisting of some transverse frames spanned lengthwise by longitudinal battens, which together emulate the shape of the hull (several of these "open battened" molds are illustrated in following chapers).

The problem with such a male mold, however, is that if conventional fiberglass materials are used for building up the laminate, such as mat and woven roving, the materials would not have adequate support like that provided by the surfaces of a female mold. Instead, the materials would dip and fall into the voids between the battens and frames, making it impossible to build the hull (see Fig. 8-5). Hence, the need

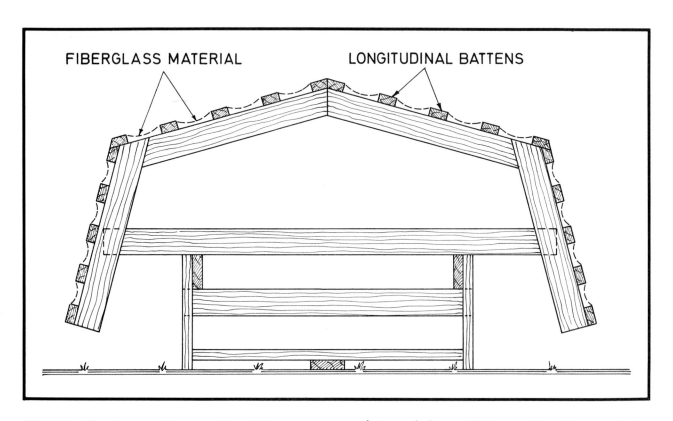

FIG. 8-5 — Fiberglass materials cannot be applied to an open battened male mold without some sort of surface covering or else the materials will simply droop and fall between the battens. This is one of the main reasons for the existence of the "one-off" construction materials and processes described in the text.

for some sort of a material that can be used over the open male mold with enough rigidity to allow a hull to be built from fiberglass becomes obvious. This is where materials like C-FLEX, FERRO-GLASS, and the various sandwich core materials come into the picture, and largely why many of these materials were invented or devised in the first place.

The big disadvantage with the male mold methods is that the hull is shaped OVER the male mold formwork, with the hull being built from the inside out instead of from the outside in like the female mold process. Thus since the hull is NOT laid up against the super smooth and glossy surface of the mold, additional work is required to achieve an exterior hull surface that will equal that which is produced in the female mold. But because so much experience has been gained in finishing procedures, plus the development of new resins and filler systems, not to mention improved techniques and tools, this work is much easier and more straightforward than it once was.

While some may argue that a fiberglass boat built OVER a male mold is inferior to one built INSIDE a female mold, such is NOT the case. In fact, there is no reason whatsoever that the male molded fiberglass boat cannot be every bit the equal of the female molded boat. It is actually possible to build a BETTER boat this way; one that is lighter in weight, and for a given weight, much stronger. Proof of this is evident by the numerous competition boats (both power and sail) that sweep up the trophies each and every year which have been built with the very same materials, and by the same male mold methods that are detailed in this book.

SINGLE SKIN & SANDWICH CORE CONCEPTS

A fiberglass boat can be built either in a single skin configuration, or with a sand-wich core method, whether it is built in a female mold or over a male mold, and whether it will be a "one-off" or a production boat. In some cases, a given boat may incorporate both approaches, depending on the area of the hull. In addition to fiberglass skins, other materials may be incorporated to make the fiberglass skin a "composite" consisting of perhaps several materials instead of "pure" fiberglass. In effect, there are many combinations of materials that can be used to form a laminate, and there are advocates with convincing arguments for all the single skin and sandwich core methods and materials. Which is the best approach is open to speculation, however, and the selection of the laminate configuration can be based on many factors.

For example, single skin construction, which has been the "conventional" method used by the majority of production boatbuilders, requires just a combination of fiberglass materials and one type of resin in order to build the hull (not counting the gel coat used in female molded hulls). This is simple and straightforward. But to get adequate hull strength in all but the smallest of boats without resorting to a complex interior supporting framework or "skeleton", a thick and heavy laminate must be used, or more expensive high-strength materials, such as the high-modulus materials described in Chapter 21.

Otherwise, an extensive inner framework of reinforcing members is required, much like framework on wood boats from the past, except in fiberglass boats, the frames would not typically be wood. Naturally, such a framework intrudes upon the space and accommodations in the boat, and the larger the boat becomes, the more extensive such a framework has to be. Single skin fiberglass boats with little inner supporting structure, then, must have thick hulls, or include sufficient structural members inside for strength. Either approach results in a boat that may tend to be heavier than is desirable. On the other hand, if high strength materials are used to gain strength with less weight, this adds to the cost. In either situation, the hulls will cost more, in the first case because more resin and reinforcing materials are required, and in the second case, because high strength materials cost more than conventional reinforcing materials.

Another problem with single skin boats is that they tend to "sweat" on the inside from condensation, and they tend to be noisy. Both of these problems, however, can be largely overcome with the installation of insulation material on the inside, such as with one of the foam materials, either of the structural or non-structural type. However, this does add to the cost and perhaps complexity.

Strengthwise, there is no reason why a single skin fiberglass boat can't be as strong as another, plus there are no chances of any problems occurring like those sometimes associated with sandwich core methods such as core shear, delaminating, etc., which will be discussed in later chapters.

Sandwich core laminates are distinctly different in principle from single skin laminates. The strength of the single skin fiberglass boat is mainly derived from the strength of the entire laminate and any internal framing members or skeletal gridwork. Sandwich structures, however, are a composite structure with relatively thin high-strength skins bonded to and separated by relatively thick low-strength core materials. Sandwich construction has so much integral strength that complex internal reinforcement or framing is largely eliminated. Furthermore, the skins need not be so thick and heavy as in the single skin boat, which reduces the amount of reinforcement and resin required, and makes for a potentially lighter hull. Sandwich cores also insulate against both sound and heat transfer, making a hull that does not sweat and operates more quietly.

However, core materials which are suitable for use in structural laminates tend to be costly, require more care in the construction, and add to the complexity of construction. In female mold construction, core materials must be of a type that will conform to all hull contours without forming air pockets between the skins and core. The use of cores also requires more design work on the part of the designer, as well as planning on the part of the builder. Core materials are not without their problems, as will be pointed out in later chapters.

LAMINATING METHODS

There are basically two ways to build up a fiberglass laminate. These include the hand "layup" process and the "sprayup" process. The sprayup process is primarily used in production facilities using a chopper gun tool that was described in Chapter 5, and is really not suited to use by the amateur, or for use over male molds. In boat hulls, however, the sprayup technique is considered inferior, although this need not be the case in all instances. Because quality control is directly dependent on operator control and skill, there is always the chance that an even layup with equal properties throughout will not result. Instead, the danger of resin-rich or resin-starved areas, or those with too much or too little reinforcement, may occur. This means a loss of strength in the completed part, and possibly a part that is too heavy. However, for production work where many smaller parts may be required, the chopper gun technique is commonly used, especially where an all-mat laminate offers sufficient strength. Most boat hulls, however, require greater strength than that offered in a chopper gun laminate, and because of the special equipment and skill required, this technique has little application for the amateur boatbuilder.

Consequently, most amateurs will build up fiberglass laminates by the hand layup method, which at first may sound a bit primitive to the novice. However, in fiberglass work, even under production conditions, this is actually the superior method at the present time simply because of greater control. The worker applies layer upon layer of reinforcement to build up the laminate, wetting it out with resin until a strong composite of fiberglass or related reinforcing materials and resin results. This process can result in a virtually defect-free laminate of high structural integrity and strength that simply cannot be equalled in the sprayup process. While perhaps a bit more labor intensive, the process does not require high worker skill and is still much faster than other materials that are used to build something as large as a boat hull.

LAMINATE CONFIGURATIONS

As pointed out before, a fiberglass boat made up of fiberglass laminates is not a homogenous single material such as, for example, steel. Instead, a laminate consists of many layers of material all bonded together with the resin. The resin wets out the fiberglass and bonds the layers together, making a structure that is much stronger than if using the materials individually.

In this book many different laminate configurations will be discussed using both conventional fiberglass materials and resin, as well as other materials such as sandwich cores and high-strength reinforcements. However, over the period of years that fiberglass has been used as a boatbuilding material, a laminate configuration has developed that has become so common and practical that it is referred to as the "conventional" layup (see Fig. 8-6). This conventional layup is applicable to boats built in female molds as well as to boats built over male molds, and also applies to boats using single skin hulls and those using sandwich cores.

The conventional layup consists of alternating layers of mat and woven roving, with variations made for different sizes of boats in the number of layers of each that are

used, as well as varying weights of materials in the alternating layers. While this type of laminate is not very sophisticated, it is simple and inexpensive, while offering a good balance in physical properties adequate for most boats. This conventional laminate is also said to be very "forgiving", which makes it well suited to the beginner. In other words, such a laminate has a wide latitude for accepting minor errors and defects that may inadvertently be worked in by the laminator, and yet, the results will not probably cause problems or lead to any catastrophies. Such is not always the case with other, more sophisticated, layups, as will be seen later. Hence, this type of layup is quite popular and trusted.

The conventional laminate, however, is not especially light in weight, nor is glass content (a measure of strength potential) as high as in other laminate configurations. For example, an all-woven roving layup without the use of any mat results in a higher glass content, and this is one reason why the military, for example, specifies this configuration. However, an all-woven rov-

FIG. 8-6 — The "conventional" laminate frequently discussed in the text consists of alternating layers of fiberglass chopped strand mat and woven roving.

ing laminate should be done in a single continuous operation to assure a positive bond between layers of reinforcement, and this is usually not practical for the amateur. Hence, a thin "blotter" layer of mat is usually used between the layers of woven roving to assure a positive interlaminar bond between all layers of reinforcement to negate any structural loss that may result from conditions where a laminate cannot be applied at one time.

A laminate that cannot be built up at one time, and is allowed to harden before subsequent layers are later applied over the cured surface, results in what is called a secondary bonding situation. This condition occurs frequently not only in building up a hull laminate, but also where other parts may be bonded to parts that are already cured. In the conventional layup however, the mat layer between woven roving layers provides a "bedding" layer, so to speak, that compresses enough between the interstices of the square weave woven roving pattern to provide a continuous reinforcing bond between layers of woven roving that would not exist if a layer of woven roving were first allowed to cure, and then another layer of woven roving were applied over this WITHOUT first applying a mat layer. In other words, the mat insures a positive interlaminar bond, and not only is it used in this situation, but also as the first layer between a cured part and one being applied over or to it.

In addition to providing a sound bond in a non-continuous bonding situation, mat also builds up stiffness. On the other hand, woven roving builds up strength, and the two together give a balance of characteristics in a laminate that usually provides all the strength necessary without being overly heavy. This simple, straightforward combination of materials makes it hard for the amateur to make a mistake in the layup sequence, since there are just two types of very obviously different materials, making it simple to tell which has been applied and

which is next. Add to this the fact that these materials are readily available at low cost, and it is easy to see why it is an ideal combination for the amateur working on a budget. Although there are other combinations of materials that can be used, both to make a laminate that is lighter and perhaps technically stronger, they require more expensive materials that are harder to find and possibly more difficult to work with. Further in this text these more sophisticated materials will be discussed plus the features of each evaluated in more detail.

LAMINATE DESIGN — FIBER ORIENTATION

Once the concept of warp, weft, and bias is understood, as was explained in Chapter 5, it does not take much to understand that the strength of a material is greatest in the direction that the fibers are oriented. Fiberglass materials are thus referred to as either isotropic or non-isotropic. An isotropic material is one where the strength properties are about equal in all directions, such as in chopped strand mat, where the fibers are laid in a random, but approximately equal, pattern in regards to fiber orientation.

A non-isotropic material is one where the fibers are oriented in certain directions, such as woven roving which has the fibers oriented lengthwise (along the warp) and crosswise (along the weft). Thus it is simple to realize that the greatest strength in this fabric will be along the length of the fabric, and with the next best strength going directly across the fabric at right angles.

However, if the material is pulled diagonally or on the bias, the fibers will tend to slide over each other and the piece of fabric will distort into a parallelogram relatively easily. This occurs simply because there are no fibers in this direction, and hence much less strength. In contrast, isotropic materials such as mat have equal strength in all directions because of fiber orientation (although in actuality the mat is not strong in comparison to woven roving). It should be added at this point that the discussion of fiber orientation is strictly theoretical, considering just one aspect of the reinforcing fibers themselves, and does NOT consider the total laminate once wetted out and bonded together with resin, which will change the actual performance characteristics dramatically.

In addition to isotropic and non-isotropic materials, there are those materials where the fibers work only in one direction, and these are said to be orthotropic. Such materials include the unidirectional types described in Chapter 21 where the strength in the weft direction is quite low and normally not considered any stronger than the resin with which it is held.

While all the foregoing may seem to be superfluous information, the orientation of materials with respect to warp, weft, and bias does have a bearing on the strength of the laminate and will help explain why a designer may specify a certain laminate sequence or schedule, as well as orientation of the materials in that laminate. The ability to orient fiber strength with the directions of principal stresses is one of the advantages of fiberglass structures as opposed to other boatbuilding materials which are isotropic materials, such as steel. In boats, the stresses are never in a single direction and never uniform in all directions. In fiberglass construction, the strength of the laminate is determined not only by the glass content, but also the direction of fiber orientation. There must be enough fibers oriented in the proper directions in order for the laminate to have enough strength (see Fig. 8-7).

A "balanced" reinforcement material (such as woven roving) will have less strength and stiffness in the warp direction than an orthotropic material with all the strength in the warp direction, because half of the fibers will be at right angles to the load and therefore largely ineffective. Con-

versely, in an orthotropic, uni-directional material, there will be very low strength in the weft direction perpendicular to the load. Thus, in the case of a laminate of woven roving, layers of mat added between (remember, the mat is isotropic with strength in ALL directions) the layers of woven roving will help regain some of the strength lost because of fiber orientation going the wrong way, so to speak, in the woven roving.

With a uni-directional material, layers in a laminate, can be applied in any direction necessary in order to counteract the stresses anticipated, all without the need for any

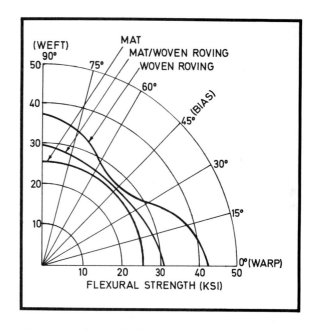

FIG. 8-7 — This graph shows the directional strength properties of common fiberglass laminates. For mat, note that strength properties are nearly uniform in all directions, but not as high in strength as woven roving, especially in the warp and weft directions. The mat is isotropic; that is, the fibers are oriented in all directions. Woven roving is considerably stronger in the warp (lengthwise) direction and also quite strong across the fabric, or in the weft direction, but only somewhat stronger than mat on the bias. This is due to the fact that the fibers in the woven roving run only in the warp and weft directions; not on the bias. The conventional mat-woven roving laminate is not as strong as an all-woven roving laminate, but is considerably stronger than an all-mat laminate. While the all-woven roving laminate is theoretically stronger, the mat-woven roving laminate is desirable for the amateur for reasons detailed in the text, and usually provides all the strength necessary.

wasted fibers. These "one way" strength characteristics can also be supplemented by using such reinforcements as the bi-axial and tri-axial materials, so that fiber strength, particularly along the bias, can be built into the laminate. The results with these more sophisticated and more costly materials may be lighter, thinner, and stronger laminates compared to conventional laminates.

However, what is true technically is not without blemishes in the practical world, and other factors enter into the picture. For example, overall performance and strength qualities of a laminate are directly affected by the skill of the laminator and the care taken, the ambient temperatures and rates of humidity at the work site, the rate of cure, and perhaps most importantly, the resin content. This last factor is perhaps most difficult to control, and in the high modulus materials, has a much more dramatic effect on the physical properties of the laminate than is the case with conventional laminates, if only because skin thickness is so much less.

Thus, the more sophisticated the technology becomes, the greater the quality control necessary to realize the promises held by the use of the more advanced materials and methods. Mistakes made in the more "exotic" materials can be expensive and serious, and for this reason, the beginner is advised to stick with the more conventional materials because they are safer and cheaper; there is not as much at stake. If the beginner does want to use the more sophisticated materials and methods, then he should realize that he is venturing into an area that may still be considered experimental in nature and as yet unproven over time.

VARYING MATERIALS IN A LAMINATE

In designing a boat, the naval architect goes through a lot of trouble in figuring out what combination of fiberglass reinforcing materials should be used in making the various structural components, especially with regard to the hull. While thickness of a laminate is a consideration, many people put too much emphasis on this quality alone, without considering what is in the laminate in the way of reinforcement, or without considering the structural members on the inside which provide added reinforcement, or without considering the orientation of the reinforcing materials in the actual laminate.

The hull thickness question will be discussed shortly, but many prospective builders want to "improve" on a designer's work, with the idea being that the thicker the laminate, the better! They reason, why not add some MORE material and really make the boat stronger!

While such an addition of laminate might technically add to the strength, this begs the question, how strong is strong enough? The problem is that after the boat is built with all the "improvements" of added laminate, and the boat sinks down perhaps several inches below its "marks" (the original designed waterline), it's the designer who suffers the blame. So if you think that you can "improve" upon the designer's work, why not contact him first and find out his opinion? Perhaps he had a reason for doing things the way they were done. In any case, ask his advice before making any substantial additions to specified fiberglass laminates.

THE HULL THICKNESS QUESTION

The preceding serves as an introduction of sorts to this subject. So much emphasis has been put on the thickness of fiberglass hulls as the ONLY measure of hull strength and quality that it causes many problems for the designer. Both the boating press (in the form of "boat tests" and feature articles), as well as advertising copywriters for the nation's boatbuilders, love to talk about laminate thicknesses and how much thickness it takes to make a boat. A favorite ploy at the typical boat show is for a manufacturer to have a plug cut out from one of his hulls showing just how thick (with the inference, how strong) his boat's hull REALLY is. Consequently, the typical person has begun to equate strength with hull thickness, and this can drive a naval architect nuts!

There are several reasons for discussing this subject. First, designers are frequently confronted by the novice who wants to convert the design of a boat intended for construction from another material (such as wood, plywood, aluminum, or steel) into fiberglass. The first question asked is, how thick should the hull be? Fig 8-13 gives one method of converting from several materials to fiberglass considering different types of strength factors. But laminate thickness alone may not guarantee adequate hull strength.

While most experienced designers may be able to give an educated "guess" for a hull thickness, it should be emphasized that in the range of sizes of boats under discussion being built in the conventional single skin method, hull thickness only amounts to fractions of an inch in most cases. Even the biggest fiberglass boats aren't as thick as most people think. A boat hull may require one area to be much thinner or thicker than another area for structural reasons. Or as often happens simply because of the nature of the application of materials, an area may be much thicker than another area even if it is NOT required that it be so. The main point is, thickness is just ONE element among many concerning hull laminates. Hull thickness does not always have a connection with "strength", however one may wish to define this much abused term. There are several different ways to measure and define strength, including bending strength, tensile strength, and stiffness. Also, there are many other

LAMINATE	NORMAL RANGE OF VARIATION (*)	
	% REINFORCEMENT	% RESIN
ALL-MAT	25/35	75/65
ALL-WR	40/50	60/50
ALL-CLOTH	45/55	55/45
MAT/CLOTH	30/40	70/60
MAT/WR	30/40	70/60

(*)By weight. Within these ranges, there will usually be no significant effect on total strength of the hull or part.

FIG. 8-8 — RESIN/GLASS CONTENT

The ratio of reinforcing fiberglass material and resin in a laminate (better known as "glass content") is important because the relationship will vary certain strength or physical properties. The amount of resin that will be used in a laminate can be easily determined if the weight of the fiberglass materials to be used is known. For example, if a laminate requires 33-1/3% glass content, this means that the resin content will have to be 66-2/3% of the laminate. In other words, for each pound of fiberglass, two pounds of resin should be used.

Laboratory tests are often done to check that the glass content is up to specifications by using what is called a "burn test". A sample of the laminate is first weighed, and then the resin is burned away leaving the glass portion remaining. The glass is then weighed and compared to the original weight. The ratio can then be readily determined.

The range of variations in glass content with most combinations of conventional laminates allows for quite a bit of latitude. For example, while mechanical properties will decrease with decreasing glass content, the thickness per ply in the laminate increases. This results in greater inertia and section modulus. However, for tension members such as stiffeners and the skins of sandwich panels, the reduction in tensile strength with decreasing glass content is not offset by the greater thickness. But for structures subject to flexure and compression, the load carrying capacity and overall stiffness of a low glass content laminate is somewhat higher than that of a high glass content laminate of the same number of plies.

Note that while laminates may have comparable glass contents, this does NOT mean that they will have comparable strength properties, unless they have the same composition of fiberglass materials. An all-mat laminate at 35% glass content will not be as strong as an all-woven roving laminate at 35% glass content, for example. However, an all-mat laminate at 35% glass content would be stronger than an all-mat laminate with a 20% glass content.

In effect, variations in glass content tend to balance out, at least in the conventional laminate. However, the ratio of resin-to-glass is more critical with sandwich skins or in thin high modulus skins. It should be kept in mind that if too much resin is used in a laminate, it will weigh more, cost more, and probably not be as durable due to brittleness. Thus it is always best to strive for as high a glass content as is practically possible, even though the hull or part will not suffer greatly if there are variations within the noted range at different areas in the laminate.

factors that help determine the various strength properties of a laminate other than thickness alone.

For example, glass/resin ratio (see Fig. 8-8) is something that is important, and generally the higher the percentage of glass, the stronger the laminate (assuming enough resin is used to make the glass rigid). Unfortunately, mat laminates, which build up thickness quite rapidly, have less glass content than any other, so that a THICK all-mat laminate would be MUCH weaker in tensile strength than say, a woven roving laminate of high glass content that was thinner.

The type of reinforcement or combination of reinforcements are important in laminate strength. For example, one laminate may be made from higher strength glass reinforcements than another of the same thickness and hence, be stronger. Or a laminate may include fiberglass reinforcements together with one or more of the high modulus materials, resulting in perhaps a quite thin laminate, but one that would have superior strength properties. Then too, the type of resin used can play a part, since strength properties do vary somewhat depending on the type of resin used. And these factors do not even include those factors which have already been discussed that can vary laminate quality and the resulting strength properties such as temperature, humidity, laminator skill and care, resin/catalyst mix, and so forth.

Thus, it should be clearer why a designer may hesitate in giving a straight and direct answer as to just how thick a laminate should be. There's a lot more to fiberglass hull laminate design than just thickness, especially when converting from one hull material to another. And as a precautionary note, beware of the person who willingly ventures to tell you just how thick is "thick

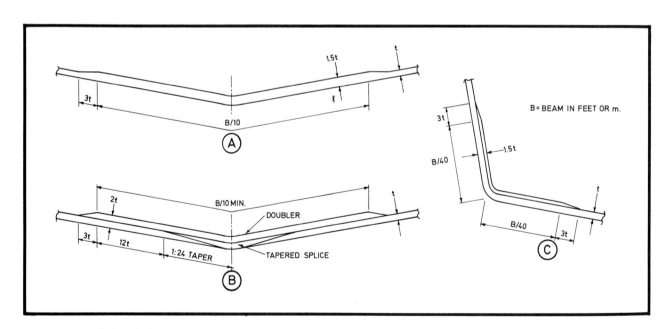

FIG. 8-9 — Hull skin thickness in the single skin fiberglass boat is not uniform at all points. Additional reinforcement may be required at many areas, such as along the keel centerline, chine junctions, and transom corners as shown by sections through these areas. Recommendations are from the A.B.S. rules and can be used as guidelines. In 'A', a section through the keel shows thickness at the centerline is built up to 1.5 times the hull thickness for an athwartship width equal to the beam of the boat divided by 10. Note the tapers equal to a distance of 3 times the hull thickness to prevent a "hard spot" from forming. In 'B', the section shows recommendations for joining hulls built in two halves (such as in a split mold). At chine and transom corners ('C'), the section shows hull thickness is built up an additional 50% for a distance either side of the corner equal to the beam of the boat divided by 40.

enough" for a fiberglass laminate. He may be the person whom designers often discuss in their own circles as the type who has too much information and too little knowledge. Or he may be just trying to give you a quick answer in order to get you off his back.

But you may ask, aren't there some "guidelines", some "rules-of-thumb", or foundation on which to figure the thickness of a laminate for a fiberglass hull, especially if NOT converting from another material? Yes, there are, but remember, what follows are just that, "rules-of-thumb", or "guesstimates". Note that these guidelines are NOT specific categorical recommendations for any and all vessels. Most are based on practical experience in the industry accumulated over the years using conventional mat and woven roving laminates only.

Two "rules-of-thumb" are often used to determine hull thickness of the single skin fiberglass pleasure boat. These are not based on engineering calculations, and do not consider any other factor than hull thickness. If you apply them to a boat, remember that most boats will still require some internal structural members such as bulkheads, floors, and localized reinforcements. Unless you are an expert in these matters, this is what naval architects are for.

The first guideline in the following chart shows the hull bottom thickness based on the waterline length of the boat:

BOAT WATERLINE LENGTH	HULL BOTTOM THICKNESS
20'	.25"
30'	.30"
40'	.40"
50'	.45"
60'	.55"

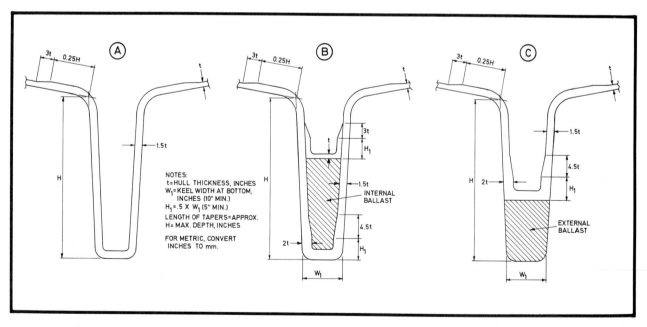

NOTES:
t=HULL THICKNESS, INCHES
W₁=KEEL WIDTH AT BOTTOM, INCHES (10" MIN.)
H₁=.5 X W₁ (5" MIN.)
LENGTH OF TAPERS=APPROX.
H= MAX. DEPTH, INCHES

FOR METRIC, CONVERT INCHES TO mm.

FIG. 8-10 — Hull thickness also varies in the single skin fiberglass boat having deep keel appendages. Recommendations from the A.B.S. rules again can serve as guidelines as shown by typical sections through these areas. In 'A', a section through a deep skeg shows this area built up to 1.5 times the hull thickness; this additional thickness is carried over onto the hull bottom for a distance equal to 25% of the height or depth of the skeg as shown. For sailboats with internal ballast, the thickness buildup is as shown by section 'B'. Note the laminate on the inside encapsulating the ballast which is equal to the hull thickness. For sailboats with external cast ballast, additional laminate can be provided as shown by section 'C'. In all cases, note the tapers and their degree which prevents "hard spots".

To determine the thickness of the hull side, multiply the bottom thickness figure by .75. Boats used for heavier duty use may require somewhat more thickness, say an increase of 10% to 20% additional. While more specific recommendations follow regarding the thickness of hulls using AIREX and END-GRAIN BALSA sandwich, some in the industry multiply the hull bottom thickness by a factor of .6 for the outer skin of sandwich panels, and by .4 for the inner skin.

Another guideline is based on a simple formula which says:

LENGTH OF BOAT OVERALL IN INCHES DIVIDED BY 1000 = THE SINGLE SKIN THICKNESS.

For example, if you had a boat 20' overall, this would be 20' x 12" = 240" divided by 1000 = .24", or about ¼" thick total. Note that NO consideration has been made whether the boat is a high-speed powerboat, multihull sailboat, monohull sailboat, workboat, or whatever.

For those who want to use an AIREX sandwich core structure, there is a "rule-of-thumb" often used also based on practical experience. Note in this case that the "formula" is NOT based on established sandwich construction formulae. Because an AIREX laminate (as will be discussed in more detail later) can yield without failure and return to its original configuration, application of standard formulae (which equate even a small amount of deflection with failure) would result in core and skin thicknesses that would EXCEED what is accepted industry practice and what has proven out in practice to work.

With AIREX, the "formula" assumes the hull to be a self-supporting shell without framing and/or stiffener sections (except in a powerboat or one with a large powerplant, one would have to consider the addition of engine stringers). To figure core and skin thickness if using AIREX as the construction material in a sandwich core method:

STRENGTH & STIFFNESS COMPARISON OF VARIOUS BOATBUILDING MATERIALS

	FIBERGLASS MAT	FIBERGLASS WOVEN ROVING	FIBERGLASS UNIDIREC-TIONAL	OAK	DOUGLAS FIR	STEEL	MARINE ALUMINUM
Specific Gravity	1.5	1.6	1.6	.85	.55	7.8	2.65
Tensile Strength (p.s.i.)	10,400	31,000	53,000	6,700	6,800	64,000	38,000
Crossbreaking strength (p.s.i.)	16,000	31,500	64,000	6,700	6,800	64,000	38,000
Modulus of elasticity (p.s.i.)	630,000	1,500,000	3,000,000	1,210,000	1,040,000	30,000,000	10,000,000
Glass content (%)	28	45	50	–	–	–	–

FIG. 8-11 — The strength and stiffness of various boatbuilding materials are compared to several types of fiberglass materials. Note that the modulus of elasticity ("stiffness") of oak and fir (representative of several types of wood used in boatbuilding) is fairly comparable to that of woven roving, and would be nearly the same in the typical mat/woven roving laminate. Because wood is cheaper and lighter in weight, with comparable stiffness, it is often encapsulated in fiberglass instead of using more expensive and heavier build-ups of solid fiberglass laminate to arrive at comparable stiffness. Note that the strength of unidirectional fiberglass is virtually as strong as steel, but only 10% as stiff.

STEP #1: Figure the single skin thickness as noted just previously.

STEP #2: Figure core and skin thickness as follows:

Core thickness = Multiply single skin by 1.5

Outer skin thickness = Multiply single skin by .4

Inner skin thickness = Multiply single skin by .3

In the previous example using a boat 20′ overall, it was determined that the single skin fiberglass thickness was .24″. With the sandwich core laminate using the above formula, to determine the core, multiply: 1.5 × .24″ = .36″. To determine the outer skin, multiply .4 × .24″ = .096″. And to determine the inner skin, multiply .3 × .24″ = .072″. Since the core material is available in ⅛″ increments approximately, select a ⅜″ thick foam (.375″). To figure what materials would be required for skins of these thicknesses, use the chart provided by Fig. 8-14. Using mat and woven roving in alter-

nating layers, determine how many layers of each would be required to get skins of the thicknesses determined in the formula (NOTE: In smaller boats, because skins may be quite thin, cloth is often substituted for woven roving).

Note that in the above case, the fiberglass used amounts to about 70% of the materials that would have been used in the single skin fiberglass laminate. Also note that while a basic premise of sandwich construction theory is that both skins should be equal in thickness, and of equal strength qualities, it is customary in boat use for the outer skin to be somewhat thicker for practical reasons. This extra thickness on the outside provides an added margin of safety to take the bumps and scrapes that boats are often subjected to.

It is also common to vary skin thickness in certain areas of a hull. For example, in powerboats of the hard-chine form, the bottom may be thicker than the topsides, or in a sailboat, the area around the keel will frequently have the core omitted, using a

COMPARISON OF VARIOUS BOATBUILDING MATERIALS AT EQUAL WEIGHT

	FIBERGLASS MAT	FIBERGLASS WOVEN ROVING	FIBERGLASS SANDWICH (AIREX)	STEEL	ALUMINUM	OAK	DOUGLAS FIR
Tensile Strength	100	280	254	119	208	115	179
Crossbreaking strength	100	173	384	15	77	131	317
Stiffness	100	193	2005	34	287	1060	3150

FIG. 8-12 — Strength factors on a POUND-FOR-POUND basis of several types of fiberglass laminates are compared to other common boatbuilding materials, using an all-mat laminate as a reference base. Note that while tensile strength in the fiberglass sandwich is about 10% less than an all-woven roving laminate, crossbreaking strength is more than double and stiffness increases more than ten times. However, Douglas fir is still more than 150% stiffer than the fiberglass sandwich, with the next highest percent-

age of crossbreaking strength, and much higher tensile strength than either oak, steel, or the all-mat laminate. Aluminum, a material often used for lightweight boats, has less crossbreaking strength per weight than any of the materials except for steel, and is less than 150% stiffer than the all-woven roving laminate. This comparison points out that where weight AND strength together are important, construction materials must be carefully chosen.

thicker all-glass laminate in this area, with perhaps a thinner sandwich laminate in the topsides. On the other hand, for a workboat, a heavier laminate may be desirable. In other words, the formula is for general use only, subject to many variables with no guarantees. So if in doubt, it is best to seek professional help.

What if you want to use a balsa core sandwich? There ARE some general con-

siderations which are different with balsa in terms of other core materials, and some "rules-of-thumb" which can be used as guidelines in figuring both core thickness and skin thickness, assuming conventional mat and woven roving layups.

First, the material that follows is based on "ordinary" boats in the smaller sizes, or in other words, pleasure boats of the range that most amateurs will be building. It is recom-

---

CONVERSION FACTORS OF COMMON BOATBUILDING MATERIALS FOR DETERMINING FIBERGLASS SKIN THICKNESS(*)

	WEIGHT LB.CU.IN.	BENDING STRENGTH FACTOR	STIFFNESS FACTOR	TENSILE STRENGTH FACTOR
Mat/Woven Roving Laminate	.055	.093	.223	.036
Aluminum	.098	.158	.126	.083
Steel	.238	.103	.087	.036
Plywood	.022	.389	.232	.526

NOTE: Thickness of comparative skin must be known. Then, primary factor must be determined, either bending strength, stiffness, or tensile strength (if prime factor NOT known, calculate for all three factors and choose thickest laminate).

EXAMPLE: Assume an existing aluminum panel ¼" thick, or .25".

FORMULA: Thickness of comparative material $\times \dfrac{\text{Factor for Mat/WR laminate}}{\text{Factor for comparative material}} =$ Fiberglass Skin Thickness

FOR EQUAL BENDING STRENGTH: $.25" \times .093 \div .158 = .147"$

FOR EQUAL STIFFNESS: $.25" \times .223 \div .126 = .442"$

FOR EQUAL TENSILE STRENGTH: $.25" \times .036 \div .083 = .108"$

Assuming stiffness is the most critical factor, how would the weight compare between the two per sq. ft.?

ALUMINUM: $12" \times 12" \times .25" \times .098$ (weight per cu. in.) = 3.53 lbs. per sq. ft.

FIBERGLASS: $12" \times 12" \times .442 \times .055$ = 3.5 lbs. per sq. ft.

(*) Factors do NOT consider additional reinforcing structures that may be provided or necessary.

FIG. 8-13 — If an existing panel thickness of plywood, steel, or aluminum is known, the nominal thickness of a conventional fiberglass laminate using mat and woven roving can be determined from the information provided. Once the thickness of laminate is determined, Fig. 8-14 can be used to determine the composition of the laminate to arrive at this thickness. Note that no consideration has been given to any additional structural members or stiffeners that may be a part of the comparative structure, or that may be required in the resulting fiberglass laminate to provide comparable strength properties in the completed part.

mended that balsa core thickness be NO LESS than ⅜" thick, even though thinner balsa core material is available. The cost difference between, say ¼" and ⅜" balsa is very slight, yet the increase in stiffness between these two is 50%! Therefore, leave the thinner stuff to incidental components such as hatch covers, motor boxes, controls consoles, and the like.

As a rough "rule-of-thumb" (and this is based on many years of past experience in the industry, and NOT on engineering calculations), core thicknesses for boats up to about 30' should be ⅜" thick. For boats up to about 40', use ½" to ⅝" thick balsa. For boats up to about 50', use ⅝" to ¾" balsa, and for boats in the 60' range, a 1" balsa core would be used.

WEIGHT, THICKNESS, & RESIN REQUIREMENTS FOR COMMON FIBERGLASS MATERIALS

MATERIAL	DRY WEIGHT LBS/SQ.FT. (*)	GLASS/RESIN RATIO	RESIN RQD. LBS/SQ.FT. (*)	WEIGHT TOTAL LBS/SQ.FT. (*)	NOM. THICKNESS PER PLY — INCHES (*)
¾ oz. CSM	.047	30/70	.110	.157	.023
1 oz. CSM	.062	30/70	.145	.207	.030
1½ oz. CSM	.094	30/70	.219	.313	.045
2 oz. CSM	.124	30/70	.289	.413	.060
7½ oz. CLOTH	.052	50/50	.052	.104	.013
10 oz. CLOTH	.070	50/50	.070	.140	.017
18 oz. WR	.125	50/50	.125	.250	.029
24 oz. WR	.167	50/50	.167	.334	.038
C-FLEX CF-39 (**)	.350	50/50	.280	.630	.080
C-FLEX CF-65 (**)	.510	50/50	.400	.920	.125

(*) Average nominal figures per layer; may vary slightly when combined with other materials in a laminate, as well as with differing glass/resin ratios.
(**) For initial coating, figure 40-50 sq. ft. per gal with CF-39, 25-30 sq. ft. with CF-65.

NOMINAL WEIGHT IN LBS. PER SQ. FT. OF VARIOUS TYPES OF SANDWICH CORE MATERIALS

THICKNESS	KLEGECELL TYPE 45 (3.0 LB.)	KLEGECELL TYPE 75 (4.5 LB.)	AIREX R62.80 (5 LB.)	END-GRAIN BALSA 6 LB.	END-GRAIN BALSA 9 LB.
¼"	.063	.094	.104	.125	.188
⅜"	.094	.141	.156	.188	.281
½"	.125	.188	.208	.25	.375
⅝"	.156	.234	.26	.313	.469
¾"	.188	.281	.312	.375	.563
1"	.25	.375	.417	.5	.75

FIG. 8-14 — This chart can be used to determine the weight, thickness, and amount of resin required for different materials used in fiberglass laminates. Use Fig. 8-15 for converting decimal inches to fractions of an inch.

DECIMAL CHART

FRACTIONAL INCHES CONVERTED TO DECIMAL INCHES AND MILLIMETERS

Fraction of Inch	Decimal of Inch	Decimal Millimeters	Fraction of Inch	Decimal of Inch	Decimal Millimeters
1/64	.015625	0.39688	33/64 ...	.515625	13.09690
1/32	.03125	0.79375	17/32	.53125	13.49378
	.03937	**1.**	35/64 ...	.546875	13.89065
3/64	.046875	1.19063		.55118	**14.**
1/16	.0625	1.58750	9/16	.5625	14.28753
5/64	.078125	1.98438	37/64 ...	.578125	14.68440
	.07874	**2.**		.59055	**15.**
3/32	.09375	2.38125	19/32	.59375	15.08128
7/64	.109375	2.77813	39/64 ...	.609375	15.47816
	.11811	**3.**	5/8	.625	15.87503
1/8	.125	3.17501		.62992	**16.**
9/64	.140625	3.57188	41/64 ...	.640625	16.27191
5/32	.15625	3.96876	21/32	.65625	16.66878
	.15748	**4.**		.66929	**17.**
11/64 ...	.171875	4.36563	43/64 ...	.671875	17.06566
3/16	.1875	4.76251	11/16	.6875	17.46253
	.19685	**5.**	45/64 ...	.703125	17.85941
13/64 ...	.203125	5.15939		.70866	**18.**
7/32	.21875	5.55626	23/32	.71875	18.25629
15/64 ...	.234375	5.95314	47/64 ...	.734375	18.65316
	.23622	**6.**		.74803	**19.**
1/4	.25	6.35001	3/4	.75	19.05004
17/64 ...	.265625	6.74689	49/64 ...	.765625	19.44691
	.27559	**7.**	25/32	.78125	19.84379
9/32	.28125	7.14376		.7874	**20.**
19/64 ...	.296875	7.54064	51/64 ...	.796875	20.24067
5/16	.3125	7.93752	13/16	.8125	20.63754
	.31496	**8.**		.82677	**21.**
21/64 ...	.328125	8.33439	53/64 ...	.828125	21.03442
11/32	.34375	8.73127	27/32	.84375	21.43129
	.35433	**9.**	55/64 ...	.859375	21.82817
23/64 ...	.359375	9.12814		.86614	**22.**
3/8	.375	9.52502	7/8	.875	22.22504
25/64 ...	.390625	9.92189	57/64 ...	.890625	22.62192
	.3937	**10.**		.90551	**23.**
13/32	.40625	10.31877	29/32	.90625	23.01880
27/64 ...	.421875	10.71565	59/64 ...	.921875	23.41567
	.43307	**11.**	15/16	.9375	23.81255
7/16	.4375	11.11252		.94488	**24.**
29/64 ...	.453125	11.50940	61/64 ...	.953125	24.20942
15/32	.46875	11.90627	31/32	.96875	24.60630
	.47244	**12.**		.98425	**25.**
31/64 ...	.484375	12.30315	63/64 ...	.984375	25.00318
1/2	.5	12.70003	1	1.	25.40005
	.5118	**13.**			

FIG. 8-15

While it is not practical to give a skin thickness for each thickness of core, a "rule-of-thumb" applying to conventional mat and woven roving laminates would be that the outer skin should be about 1/6 the thickness of the core, with the inner skin perhaps not quite so thick. Using a ⅜" core then, the skins would be about ¹⁄₁₆" thick (.0625"), while if using a ¾" core, the skins would be about ⅛" thick (.125"). Note, however, that in some parts of the hull, additional fiberglass reinforcing may be required, and this is again best determined by a professional.

In all the foregoing, it should be emphasized that the design of a structural sandwich core laminate is a problem that should be left up to experts, especially as the boat size increases, in order to make the most efficient structure. By efficiency, in engineering terms, this means a structure offering the optimum in strength and physical properties to fulfill the requirements of the intended service, all at the lowest cost, lowest weight, and in some cases, by the most practical fabrication methods.

CHAPTER 9

A WORD ABOUT BOAT PLANS

Before starting out with the actual construction procedures, a few words should be given on the subject of boat plans, full-size patterns, and lofting procedures. Regardless of the size or type of boat that will be built out of fiberglass, start off with a good set of plans from a known designer or design firm. Don't attempt to design your own boat, or attempt to build without plans, or attempt to build by the "seat-of-your-pants" approach. The value of a good set of plans will be repaid many times over by the savings in time and work that they will provide. Don't take a chance on questionable results when you are going to put in your own labor and hard-earned bucks in such an extensive project. The results could be disastrous!

There are numerous stock plans available for fiberglass boats, or if you can't find exactly what you want, a designer can always be commissioned to create a custom design. The advantage of stock plans, of course, is that they are usually much cheaper than a custom design and readily available; you won't have to wait for the designer to complete your plans as would be the case with a custom design. While there can be no generalizations made with regard to how much a custom design can cost, don't be surprised if the fees involved are 10 to 20 times the price of stock plans. The reason is that you are paying for a professional's time, and it can take a month's full-time work, or even longer, to custom design a boat from start to finish. However, with stock plans, the designer can amortize his costs over numerous sets of plans he expects to sell, and as a result, the cost of

the plans can be much lower.

Thus, the majority of people try to select a stock design. But as a designer, I want to emphasize one point: Don't be fooled in believing that the more you pay for a stock set of plans, the more you will receive, or the more complete that design will be. Some stock plans are incredibly cheap, yet VERY complete, including many details and in some cases, very comprehensive instructions. On the other hand, some stock plans can be quite costly, especially from some of the more well-known design firms who specialize in custom design work. Yet in many cases, stock plans from these firms are NOT specifically aimed at the amateur builder, and as such you'll be expected to have certain abilities and knowledge beyond what is normal for the average novice; details may be sketchy at best, and a set of written instructions is commonly NOT included. The point is that just because a set of stock plans may be available, it does not necessarily follow that they are intended for the beginner.

If a design is found that you are interested in, a set of study plans, if available, will usually tell a lot about the design beforehand, and if it is suited to your skills and abilities. In selecting a stock set of plans, be sure that they are specifically designed for the materials or methods that will be used to build the boat. As will be shown in this book, there are many ways to build a boat using fiberglass, and just because a given design can be built in "fiberglass", it does NOT mean that it is specifically intended for construction using the materials and processes that you may want to use.

Don't try to improvise from a design that

was originally intended for construction using another material either. Unfortunately, there are some designers and plans brokers who will tell you that their design can be built from virtually ANY material, or a wide variety of materials from the same set of plans. There have been some designers who have sold a single stock design that could supposedly be built from wood, plywood, steel, aluminum, ferro-cement, AND fiberglass! But beware of plans like this. Looked at logically, how could a designer include ALL the necessary details for ALL of these construction methods and materials at a reasonable price? The answer is that he probably can't. Not only will the details probably be lacking, but the final vessel (assuming that one could be completed from the information provided) may not perform satisfactorily, since the design criteria for such a wide selection of building materials cannot be uniformly applied to all.

On the other hand, if the plans purchased are intended for construction in a material OTHER than fiberglass, beware of changing it to fiberglass. While such a change may be possible or practical, always contact the designer first for his advice. If he thinks that such a change is practical, he will advise so, and if supplementary information is needed from him, be willing to pay for making such changes.

I am always astounded by people who are willing to pay thousands of dollars for materials and equipment to build a boat, yet when it comes to buying a set of plans or making changes to a design requiring some "extra" time from the designer, they are reluctant to pay for these perhaps intangible, but professional, services. Remember that the cost of a stock set of plans, as well as the fees for any additional professional services, are usually only a tiny fraction of the total cost of the boat, and will no doubt be repaid many times over in assuring that your boat will perform in a safe and satisfactory manner.

The main point is, stick to your plans as closely as possible, and once you have them, read and review them thoroughly BEFORE starting the project OR buying any materials. Quite often builders want to jump the gun and purchase materials BEFORE obtaining the plans. The problem with this approach is that most plans will include options or variables that could vary the amount, type, or usage of materials. Then too, the types, sizes, or costs of materials can vary considerably between different parts of the country. You could wind up spending more or even getting the wrong material. So always check to the plans for options and variables that may be applicable to your project and locale FIRST before buying materials.

LOFTING THE LINES

Lofting means redrawing the lines of the hull of the boat to full size to correct for any deviations from the scaled lines drawing provided with the plans. The table of offsets often provided with the lines drawing gives dimensions that have been scaled from the lines plans. These are used, together with the lines drawing, to carry out the lofting process. It is easy to realize that the designer or his drafter, when laying out and fairing the lines to scale, cannot fair them precisely to the fraction of an inch, since the width of a pencil line may be ¼" or more to the scale of the drawing. Hence, the lofting process is used to not only resolve these irregularities, but to provide the full size patterns or templates necessary to build the hull.

The lines drawing and the table of offsets often provided with the plans will vary in accuracy from designer to designer, depending on many variables such as the designer's eyesight, drafting ability, whether or not he "expands" his lines initially, and so forth. The resulting table of offsets therefore will vary in accuracy also. Thus, the amount of work that will be required to do the lofting and fairing of the lines could be a pleasure or result in a tedious and frustrating exercise.

The subject of lofting is one that often scares the pants off the typical beginner, and indeed it can be a tedious job that is hard on your knees. To carry out the lofting process properly, you should have a flat area (such as a garage floor) that is at least as long as the actual boat, and as high in profile, and equal in width to the half-beam. You'll need paper to match, along with fairing splines (long thin strips of wood, also called battens, that you can rip yourself on a table saw), and a way to hold the spline in place. The professional loftsman uses special weights called spline weights, or "ducks", to hold the splines in place, but if working on a wood floor, you can use nails. Some builders use several sheets of plywood as a loft floor, painting these with a glossy white enamel that allows the pencil lines to be erased, yet easily seen; the lines are then not drawn on paper.

We won't go further into the mechanics of lofting here since the subject has been covered both by the author in other texts, and by other authors numerous times. Lofting is an involved subject that could fill an entire book. Refer to the Bibliography for books on this subject if you need to pursue the subject further.

FULL SIZE PATTERNS

If you are fortunate, the plans may include full size patterns already. Some of the design firms which specialize in stock plans for amateurs include the option of buying full size patterns with many, if not all, the designs they make available. If this is the case in your situation, you may be able to dispense with the lofting task entirely, and the table of offsets as well.

Full size patterns can save a tremendous amount of time and work AS LONG AS THEY ARE ACCURATE! As a designer who has dealt in full size patterns for many

years, there are certain things to take note of if full size patterns are provided. While there are full size patterns of several types, such as blueprinted types, cut paper patterns, and those drawn out on paper, be careful of those types which are NOT made on a single sheet of paper. I have seen some full size patterns that consisted of many sheets that had to be lined up and joined together to form a single member, and this can cause problems.

Regardless of the paper used, there will always be a certain amount of expansion and contraction with the paper. If the pattern is on just a single piece of paper, this movement can largely be ignored with respect to the final accuracy of the completed boat; any deviations are distributed fairly equally and proportionately. Experience shows that most workers cannot, or do not, work so closely when cutting out their framing members to make these small, uniform deviations critical.

However, if you have to use full size patterns that consist of several sheets, and must align these to make a completed pattern for certain members, this can be difficult and sometimes frustrating due to conflicting line intersections. If the deviations are too great, you'll have to make compromises that will have to be faired out on the hull framework. It is even possible that you may not be able to work with some patterns. Some builders give up with these types of patterns, resorting to lofting the lines to compensate for the problem. Remember, however, that minor deviations can be expected and are usually acceptable in fiberglass boat construction.

But part of the problem is sometimes brought on by the builder himself, and this is because they do not treat the patterns with care. Since the patterns are just paper, they must be protected to a reasonable degree from the elements. Keep them out of the rain or away from extremely humid or dry conditions, and keep them out of the sun. Blueprinted patterns (and plans for that matter) will quickly fade in sunlight. Although you may receive patterns which have been folded for mailing purposes, and it may seem that this folding affects the accuracy, this has actually not proven to be a problem in practical use. Designers send the plans and patterns in this manner mainly because, strange as it may seem, mailing tubes often get severely damaged in transit under current postal handling practices.

HULL SKIN DEDUCTIONS

The lines of the hull shown on the lines drawing, or loftings, or full size patterns are usually taken to the OUTSIDE of the hull skin. If building by the female mold method, the mold would be a mirror image of these lines and could be built directly to these contours. However, if building a plug for female mold work, or building a hull using one of the male mold methods, there is the consideration of the hull skin thickness in order to arrive at the contours for the mold form or frame members (see Fig. 9-2). Whether or not a deduction will be made for the skin thickness will vary with several factors.

For example, if the boat is a competitive-type and built to a measurement rule, or a class boat where certain dimensional restrictions apply and must be verified, it is absolutely imperative that a deduction be made for skin thickness. For ultimate accuracy, such deductions should be made directly on the loftings, and this does require more skill and work on the part of the loftsman to assure that the final hull skin re-

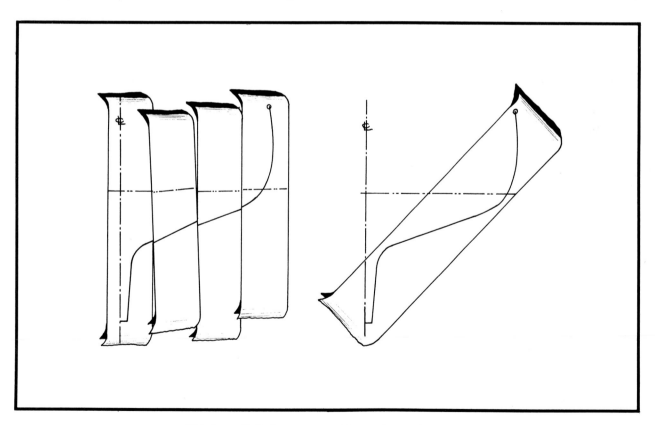

FIG. 9-1 — Full size patterns with members laid out onto several pieces of paper are more difficult to align and piece together than those where member contours are laid out on a single piece of paper.

flects the hull lines as designed. The exact thickness of a hull laminate must allow for some deviation since finished net thickness in fiberglass is at best an average. The more layers in a laminate, and the more varied the types of products in the laminate, the greater chance there is for a deviation in net laminate thickness.

Another situation is if the boat will be built using a core material. As a designer, I feel that at least the thickness of the core, together with the longitudinal battens, should be deducted, if not the outer skin laminate. This total extra thickness will be quite thick in comparison to a single skin fiberglass laminate. If this thickness is NOT deducted, and the male mold is built to the OUTSIDE lines of the hull, the effect is to completely revise the designer's work, including the displacement, coefficients of comparison, stability calculations, and more.

Admittedly, this change in characteristics may be only to a minor degree, but it could make for questionable results. So at the least, deduct the thickness of the core material and the longitudinal battens from the full size patterns or from the lofted body

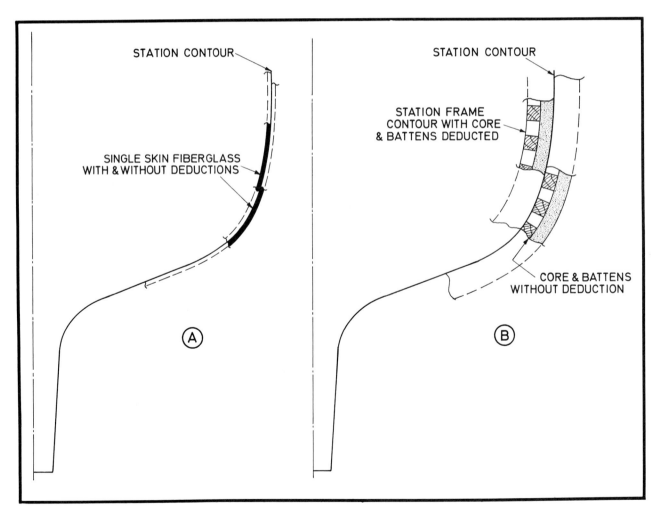

FIG. 9-2 — The effects of deducting or not deducting for the hull skin from the mold frame pattern contours are shown in exaggerated form for both single skin fiberglass ('A') and sandwich core hulls ('B'). With single-skin hulls, the differences are not as dramatic as with sandwich cored hulls. However, the choice can be based on several factors as noted in the text.

plan. This is easily done when transferring the patterns by using a small block of wood or dividers set to equal the thickness of the core material and battens, and using it as a marking gauge to mark along the block's inside edge while guiding the marking gauge along the contour of the patterns (see Fig. 9-3).

For single skin fiberglass boats, such as those using C-FLEX, it is probably acceptable to omit deducting for the skin thickness, using the body plan or pattern contours as given. But if using battens, such as

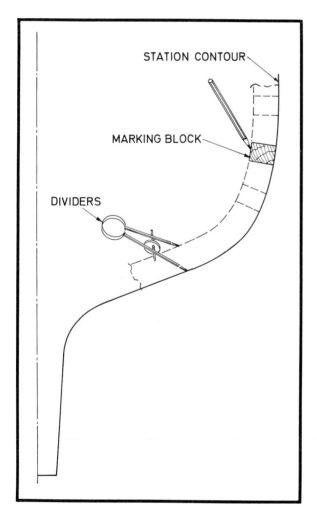

FIG. 9-3 — Hull skin deductions can be easily made from the full size mold frame pattern contours by using a marking block equal to the skin thickness (plus battens if these are used), or by setting dividers to match the thickness, and marking along the new inside contour accordingly.

the transverse batten method (see Chapter 16) to build your C-FLEX hull, you should technically deduct for these from the contours. Otherwise ignore the slight thickness of the hull skin since it will usually not be of any consequence, although the skin thickness can be deducted if desired.

One caution should be made about using full size patterns as opposed to lofting the lines to full size from a table of offsets. If the design includes BOTH a table of offsets AND full size patterns, do NOT attempt to scale the patterns and check the dimensions to the table of offsets. While the scaled dimensions MAY correspond to the dimensions noted in the table of offsets, it is NOT necessary that they do.

Remember that a table of offsets is a table of dimensions that the designer or his drafter has measured TO SCALE on a rather small working drawing; they have NOT necessarily been lofted or "verified" to full size; this is what the builder is supposed to do in the lofting process. So don't try to "second guess" the designer; if the full size patterns have been provided, use them! Otherwise, lay out the lines to full size by lofting.

Also, do NOT attempt to lay out frame members DIRECTLY from the dimensions given in the table of offsets WITHOUT lofting, as some builders attempt to do in order to "short cut" the operation. An unfair framework can result which will require perhaps laborious fairing work that should have been taken care of in the lofting process on the loft floor. While in some cases certain designers may use "corrected" offsets (either from proving the accuracy of the dimensions in the table of offsets from previously built vessels, or by actually lofting the lines), the lines should STILL be lofted if not using patterns, since minor variations can occur.

LAYING OUT FOR THE FRAMES

Once the boat has been lofted, or if working from patterns, you are ready to lay out for the frames. Whether working from patterns or full size loftings, the procedures are similar. The first step is to transfer the lines of the body plan or athwartship members to a plywood base, whether using full size patterns or loftings. This plywood base has to be at least as large as the largest section, considering BOTH halves of the boat, although patterns or loftings need be for only one-half the hull since virtually all boats are symmetrical about the centerline. There's no need to have both halves since you can simply flip the pattern or lofting over for the opposite side.

However, if the lines have been lofted directly onto a plywood base or wood floor you will already have the body plan drawn onto this base and can delete the preceding step. But, BOTH HALVES will still have to be drawn onto the base for laying out for the frame members, and you will have to be ACCURATE so that both sides are identical.

Regardless of the method used to obtain the full size contours, there are several methods that can be used to transfer the contours on paper or from the wood floor to the framing material that will be used to make your frames. We'll discuss a few that are quite easy and work well for the amateur.

First, consider that for reference purposes both a vertical and a horizontal plane will be required, one usually being the centerline of the hull for vertical reference, and another at 90 degrees or right angles to the centerline, such as the waterline (sometimes denoted as "DWL"), or other horizontal reference plane that may be called a "set-up level" or "baseline", or similar plane. NOTE THAT THESE TWO PLANES OF REFERENCE WILL BE USED THROUGHOUT THE CONSTRUCTION, so make sure they are transferred to any and all members which will be used to determine the hull shape, location of bulkheads and interior structure, cabin configuration, etc. BE ACCURATE AND NOTE THESE POINTS TO ALL MEMBERS THAT WILL BE USED TO FORM THE HULL!

In using full size patterns or paper loftings, they will be used for a two-fold purpose. First, they are used to transfer the station or section contours to the plywood base over which the frame members will be assembled. Secondly, they will be used to determine the contours of the frame members themselves, so treat them with care.

If using full size patterns and these are of the cut-paper type, mark a series of dashed lines around the pattern extremity to the plywood base or to the frame members. If the patterns are of the drawn, printed, or blueprinted type, several different methods can be used to transfer through from the pattern to the base or actual frame members underneath. These methods include using a dressmaker's pattern tracing wheel, punching through with a sharp pointed object such as an awl, or using carbon paper underneath and tracing over the pattern with a pencil. Use carbon paper facing down as well as up, or double-sided carbon paper, so the lines will be transferred to the underside of the pattern as well. Thus, when the pattern is flipped over, the lines will be visible on the reverse side of the pattern.

However, do NOT cut out printed or blueprinted paper patterns. Doing so can cause the patterns to distort and become inaccurate, so keep the entire sheet intact. Regardless of the method used, the dashed lines or marks transferred through are spaced about ½" apart. For athwartship members like frames, bulkheads, and transoms, where only half a pattern may be given, simply flip the pattern over and repeat the procedure to get the opposite side.

Another way to transfer the lines to the members (called "picking up and taking off" in lofting parlance) is the old loftsman's

trick of using nails laid flat (see Fig. 9-4).
This system is used where the lines are
drawn directly onto the wood floor. Any
type of nail will do as long as the heads are
thin with sharp edges. Simply lay the nails
on the lofted body plan lines, or on the lines
of any member you want to pick off, with
the nail heads along the line. Tap the heads
half way into the wood base with a hammer.
Space the nails about ½" apart where curves
are pronounced, and farther apart where
lines are straighter. Then set the material to
be used for the frame members over the
nails and stamp it down with your foot or
use a mallet to hammer it down onto the
nail heads so that marks are transferred to
the wood, duplicating the contour to the

part.

Since frames are usually symmetrical
about the centerline, and duplicate parts
(one for each side for each frame member
will usually be needed), nail another board
to the one pressed against the nail heads,
and cut them both together at the same
time to make duplicate parts. Be sure that
all reference marks are also transferred to
all members as applicable.

After cutting all frame members, using
any of the foregoing methods to determine
the contours from the loftings or full size
patterns, the frame members can be assembled, a frame at a time. The various members which are used to make a complete
frame are tacked to the plywood base (or

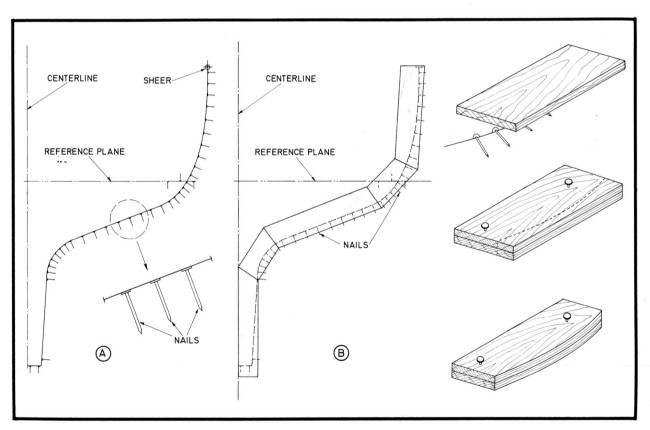

FIG. 9-4 — One way to transfer or "pick up" the contours to
the framing material with the lines on a wood floor or
plywood base is to use nails set partially into the wood along
the contours ('A'). The framing material is then set over
these nails as in 'B' and either stepped on or hit with a mallet
to transfer the contour to the framing members. Since most

frames are symmetrical about the centerline, thereby requiring duplicate members, nail another member together
with the nails set high for easy removal later, and cut the
two at once to form two identical members. Be sure reference lines show.

over the loftings or full size patterns) temporarily to prevent movement, and must be accurately aligned to the respective contour.

In addition to frames or similar athwart-ship members, most boats will also include stem form members, perhaps transoms, and other members which can be directly laid out from the patterns to the material that will be used for the member, and cut out. The preceeding assembly sequence noted for the frames is not required in this case. More details on the actual configuration of the frame members is given in Chapter 11.

CHAPTER 10

the building site

We've all heard the story of the man who built a boat in his basement and couldn't get it out. If such a story were actually true, no doubt we would scoff at the man for his lack of forethought and planning. Yet, getting yourself into a similar situation might be easier than you think, especially if you underestimate the size of your boat. Hence, careful planning and selection of the building site must be done BEFORE building your boat.

Is there such a thing as an "ideal" building site? Probably not. We've all no doubt come across a boat being built in the most unlikely of spots, wondering how the builder would ever hope to get the boat to the water. Yet as long as certain criteria are met, there are any number of areas where a boat can be built. The problem today is that because of the high demand for housing, and the rapidly growing population, and the high concentrations of population in urban areas, especially along the coastal and inland waterways used by boaters, good boatbuilding sites are becoming scarce and costly. New homes frequently have little, if any, yard space, and even the standard garage may not be available. Another problem is that local restrictions may prevent the building of a boat in your own residence if it is too large. But where there's a will, there's usually a way!

First, if the boat is not too large, it may be built in the garage, and for most, this is probably the ideal spot. More boats have no doubt been built in garages than in any other spot. While the length of a single car garage will be the determining factor of just how long the boat may be, if you have a double garage, or even a triple garage, you can turn the hull in a diagonal direction and increase the available length quite a bit, letting you build perhaps a longer boat than you might have thought possible. For example, assuming a standard 20' × 20' double garage, by turning the hull diagonally, you can probably build a boat in the trailerable category that is about 23' long, with reasonable access to all sides, and yet still be able to close the garage door (see Fig. 10-1). But take note that if building in the garage, check carefully to see that you can get the boat out when it is completed, or you may have to build up to a certain point, then move the boat outside for completion.

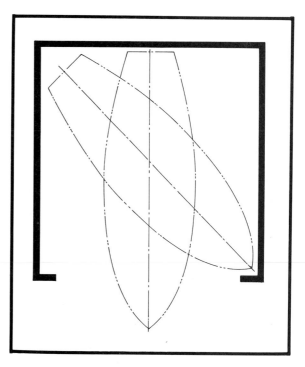

FIG. 10-1 — Turning the hull diagonally in the standard double garage will allow a longer boat to be built, while still being able to close the door.

Other common building sites can include the driveway, a patio area, or the yard, and of course, the proverbial basement as long as you can get the boat out at some point in the construction, whether completed or partially completed.

The size of the building area should allow complete access around the hull, although you can work in much more restricted quarters than you might think. Depending on the method used to right the hull, you can build in an area equal to the length and beam of the hull, with a foot or two around the sides and ends, but the more room the better. While there are methods to right a hull in virtually a space equal to its own width, if the hull is taller than it is wide while upsidedown on the building form, this will be the critical dimension that will have to be allowed for clearance when you flip the hull right side up.

If your residence is such that there is no way to build a boat there, you will have to seek other alternatives. There are plenty of solutions which have cropped up over the years, and here are a few. Old buildings, sheds, and barns that can be rented cheaply are commonly available if a little time is spent looking. In many boating areas, there are so-called "builder's co-ops" which offer space to amateur boatbuilders and even specialize in this sort of thing, providing the power and other facilities that will be required. Such a situation is ideal for the first-time builder as he will be with others in a similar situation where thoughts and ideas can be swapped at will.

You may wish to find a vacant lot somewhere and erect your own building shelter. The author has even come across builders who have had the boatbuilding "bug" so bad that they have rented or actually purchased houses which had suitable boatbuilding sites. In one case, a man had just retired and wanted to build a boat to live aboard. So he bought a house which had a large yard, then built his boat over a two year period, and sold the house at a profit when he was done!

In other cases, builders have purchased travel trailers and set these on vacant land, erecting a temporary shelter to house their boatbuilding project. When the boat was finished, they sold the trailer and vacated the property. As one can see, the possibilities and solutions are virtually unlimited.

Regardless of where you build the boat, it must be convenient and easily accessible. You will be spending a lot of time there, so it should be near your base of daily operation. Consider also how you will remove the boat from the site and transport it to the water. Of course, on smaller boats or those that are trailerable, this is not much of a problem. But with larger boats which will require special transport, plan the route carefully to avoid low bridges, power lines, congested streets, and the like. If special permits are required to move the boat, such as wide load permits and the like, these should be checked into BEFORE construction to make sure that it is possible to adhere to any special preconditions.

Just as in building a boat in the basement, if building in the back yard, there must be a way to get the boat out. In many cases, side yard access is too narrow. In this case it is not uncommon to hire a crane and actually lift the boat right out of the yard and over the roof of the house. This operation will no doubt draw a crowd, but the operation is usually quick and simple. Although crane rentals are not cheap, their use is limited to a brief period of time, usually entailing only a minimum fee.

The building site should have certain facilities available. For example, electrical power is almost a "must", although there are gasoline-powered motors to drive air compressors which could make it conceivable to use air-driven tools instead. Also, a portable generator can be used to provide electricity if municipal lines are not available. There should be a water source nearby as well as a telephone (if only for emergency use). While boats can be built in quite remote sites, it is always preferable to have emergency facilities, such as a medical facility and fire department, available.

Don't build your fiberglass boat out in the open without some sort of weather protection. At the least, erect a simple wood frame structure covered with heavy, inexpensive clear plastic sheet. Make sure that such a structure is adequately braced, and if the roof will be used for any other supporting structure or scaffolding, make it strong enough. One such structure is shown in Fig. 10-2. Direct exposure to the elements, such as the sun and rain, are not good for the resin and other materials such as foam cores. A shelter gives protection from these elements and protects the work area from dirt and drastic fluctuations in temperature and weather conditions that occur in many areas.

If possible, arrange the building site or shelter in consideration of prevailing winds, natural light, the effects of weather (like snowdrifts, tornadoes, hurricanes, etc.), and other conditions that could effect the results of your building efforts or impede progress. If possible, avoid building on a steep slope, or where water could settle, or where snow could bank up and damage the project. Arrange for a natural flow of ventilation, but try to put a check on winds that could cause drafts that may effect the curing properties of the resin or stir up annoying dust that could lead to bonding problems. In colder areas, plan for heating of the workspace, and provide artificial lighting as required. If you are working around electricity (as most will be), be sure that the electrical source has a secure ground to

FIG. 10-2 — Some sort of weather protection or "building shed" is advisable when building the fiberglass boat. The photos show an excellent, but somewhat elaborate, structure raised off the ground with a plywood floor. However, a simpler structure built on the ground will serve equally well, as long as it is braced adequately. Scrap lumber is all that is required for the framework, and heavy plastic sheeting can be draped over this to close in the sides and roof. Use battens over the plastic to keep it from blowing off.

earth for safety in the use of power tools.

Wherever you decide to build your boat, consider the neighbors and don't violate any local ordinances or laws. In many locales, it may be unlawful to build a boat in your yard, or may be done only under limited conditions, or a temporary permit or variance may be required. A check with local authorities is always desirable beforehand to find out just where you will stand.

As a last precaution, consider the security of the work area. Unfortunately today, there are people who will steal anything and everything, regardless of the value to them. Since there will be a considerable inventory of tools and supplies resulting from your hard-earned bucks, be vigilant to the surroundings. Also take note that if outside help is hired for any portion of the work, you may be responsible for their safety and well-being. A check with an attorney concerning any liability, as well as with your insurance agent for your own protection and security, may be desirable. Finally, arrange the work area so that those who do NOT belong there (children, stray animals, and people who don't know the dangers of the products being used) can be kept out, or at least controlled.

CHAPTER 11

male mold construction

INTRODUCTION

In forthcoming chapters, the various male mold methods and materials used to build fiberglass boats will be described separately. While each of the materials used in the various male mold methods is somewhat different as far as construction procedures are concerned, they all require a male mold or "form" over which the hull is built. This male mold, in turn, must be erected over a sub-structure that supports the male mold, which we call the building form. With all the materials used to build male molded hulls, the male mold as well as the building form are quite similar in configuration. Hence we will describe both the building form and the male mold in this chapter. Our description will be applicable to hulls being built from C-FLEX fiberglass planking, FERRO-GLASS, and any of the sandwich core materials, such as AIREX, KLEGECELL, or END-GRAIN BALSA using what is called an "open battened" mold.

THE BUILDING FORM

By definition, building a boat by a male mold method means that the hull will be built upsidedown. In order for the boat to be built in this position, the members making up the male mold have to be erected and supported onto a sub-structure which we refer to as the building form. This sub-structure is also sometimes called a "jig", "strongback", "building berth", or other names; they all mean the same thing, and they may all differ somewhat in the manner in which they are built. The building form

shown in Fig. 11-1 is NOT the ONLY way that it can be done, but it has proven to work well for a wide variety of boat types in a wide variety of building form situations, and it is cheap and easy to make. However, it may not necessarily adapt, at least completely, to the type of boat you are building. If the plans you are using show a different type of building form, by all means use what is specified. Note, however, that the general principles that will be described will still apply.

It will be assumed that you have already picked out the building site, using information and criteria from the previous chapter to make the selection. With the type of form shown it makes no difference if the ground is ordinary earth, a wood floor, asphalt pavement, concrete, or whatever. Furthermore, with this form, the site need NOT be level; some have built boats using this type of form on the side of hills! The only requirement is that the set-up members (those members which run fore and aft, and parallel with one another supporting the male mold frame members) must be level both lengthwise and athwartships. They should also be as far apart as practical. The floor or ground can deviate any which way.

The building form can be made from just about any scrap lumber as long as it is strong enough to support the load of the hull until it is completed. Furthermore, long lengths of lumber are not absolutely necessary; shorter members can usually be butt-joined, with the butt joint being backed by a long butt block of similarly sized stock or with scabs of plywood. Again, the only stipulation is that the set-up mem-

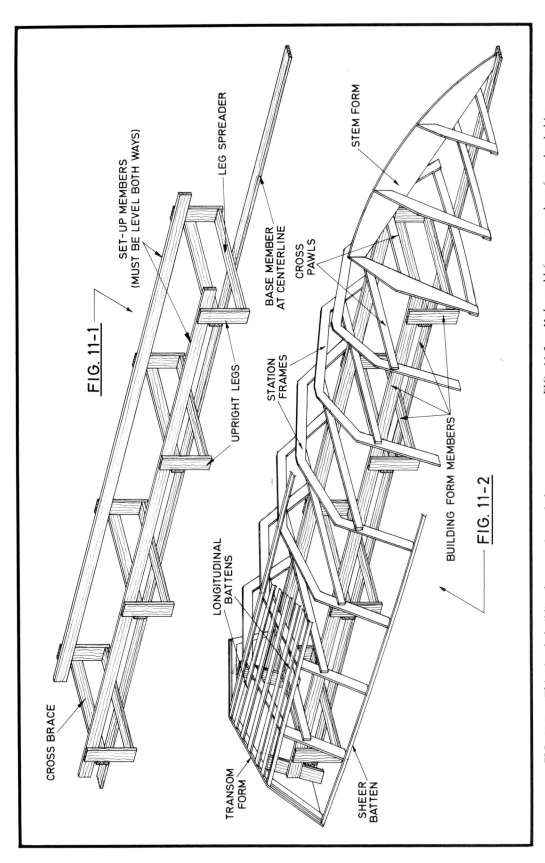

FIG. 11-1

CROSS BRACE

SET-UP MEMBERS (MUST BE LEVEL BOTH WAYS)

LEG SPREADER

UPRIGHT LEGS

BASE MEMBER AT CENTERLINE

STATION FRAMES

CROSS PAWLS

STEM FORM

LONGITUDINAL BATTENS

TRANSOM FORM

SHEER BATTEN

BUILDING FORM MEMBERS

FIG. 11-2

FIG. 11-1 — This simple building form can be made from scrap lumber and adapts to just about any ground surface, whether it is level or not. The important point is that the set-up members be level both lengthwise and athwartships.

FIG. 11-2 — Male mold frame members for a hard-chine hull are erected onto the building form shown in Fig. 11-1. Frames are fitted with cross pawls which support the frames on the set-up members. Note that the stem form, which provides the stem contour in profile view, is used to support several frames in the forward area. Although not shown, bracing members will usually be added as required between various frame and building form members to prevent movement.

bers be level in both directions. If the stock used for the set-up members warps and winds all over the place, you may have trouble getting and keeping the building form in alignment.

When setting up for building the hull of your boat, some mention is usually made about a reference plane or line. As noted previously, there are two of these reference planes in just about all boats; one being a vertical reference plane provided most often by the centerline of the boat, and the other a horizontal reference plane that can be the designed waterline, or any other designated horizontal plane. These two reference planes are used throughout the construction to true-up the hull and to plot dimensions used in the construction process. Keep them in mind at all times and transfer marks as required to keep them handy. A taut line or wire is often used to project the centerline of the hull.

With the building form shown, the first deviation will occur if the boat is being built in a dirt area. If this is the case, the base member is not needed to anchor the form to the ground. Instead, drive the upright legs directly into the ground as long as the earth is a fairly firm, stable type, or bury them in concrete. In all other areas, the base member is anchored to the floor. If it is a wood floor, it can be fastened directly into the floor. For asphalt or concrete, use lag bolts with lead expansion shields to hold the base member in place. Note that this base member is generally run coincidentally with the centerline of the boat, and is frequently used to support the end of the stem form forward or transom bracing aft. (See Fig. 11-2).

The width or spacing between the set-up members, together with their lengths, may be given on your plans. If not, then plot how far apart these members can be and how far fore and aft they can run without interfering with, or running out, into the hull contours. If not given, this is usually easily determined from the lines drawing body plan. It is not necessary for the set-up members to go completely fore and aft along the entire hull distance. Where the hull lines come together forward, for example, the set-up members can stop several frames aft of the bow, with the stem form being used to pick up and support perhaps several of these forward frame members (see Fig. 11-2).

The building form, even though it may be made from "junk" materials, is an important part of the boat's construction. All of the time and effort spent in lofting or accurately building the frames that will be used to build your hull will be wasted if the building form framework is not accurately located and precisely held in position. Do not use a haphazard form, or one that will spring out of shape as soon as members are spring around the hull form. Many beginners do not appreciate the forces that can be generated in building a hull mold and how these forces, if not checked, can distort the final shape of the hull. Remember that you will be leaning, pushing, shoving, pulling, and in some cases, forcing members in place, and these stresses are ultimately transferred to the building form. Don't be bashful about adding members to the building form whenever required to prevent movement, especially diagonal bracing to any area of the form which does not seem to have the necessary strength; this is common and expected.

The members making up the building form can be fastened or held by various methods. Ordinary nails are common, while some prefer the scaffolding type nail since they are easy to remove. Still others use screws or bolts, and in some cases, some members can be held in place with clamps which do allow for easy adjustments. If possible, the building form should be left in one spot until the hull is completed. But in many cases, this is not always possible. If the form must be moved with the hull in a semi-finished state, it must be realigned and re-leveled before continuing on with the construction. Hopefully this won't occur, especially in the middle of applying the laminate, which could be a disaster.

MALE MOLD CONSTRUCTION

The procedures for building the male mold will be similar, regardless of the type of material that will be used to build the hull of the boat. Specific deviations will be noted where it is necessary to suit the material in question. Note that the male mold is a by-product of the construction and will not remain in the completed boat, with perhaps a minor exception where permanent bulkheads that may sometimes be a part of the form also remain in the completed hull. But to avoid confusing things at this early stage, consider that basically the male mold is expendable.

To add to the confusion and inconsistency of common boatbuilding terms, the male mold is sometimes also referred to as the "form", "jig", or simply the "mold". But in this book, we'll always call it the male mold to distinguish it from the building form and female molds. Basically, the male mold construction consists of transverse members that we call frames, although sometimes these are called "mold frames", "formers", "forms", or other similar sounding terms.

The frames are erected onto the building form. For simplicity, the frames are usually located at stations coinciding with those stations shown on the lines drawing, but this may vary with the design. The contours for the frames are determined from the loftings or full-size patterns as has been discussed. In addition to these frames, other hull forming members may be required in order to fully determine the male mold contours, such as a longitudinal member called a stem form used to determine the stem contour, a transom form member, and perhaps a form for the keel on sailboats (see photos this chapter for several variations).

The frame and forming members used to make the male mold can be made from a variety of inexpensive materials, such as particleboard, plywood, or any scrap lumber such as pine or fir. However, the use of nominal 1" or thicker solid lumber is desirable because this material will hold the fastenings used to secure the various longitudinal battens, as well as the staples used to hold the C-FLEX (if using this material) better into the edge than will plywood or particleboard.

The size or widths of the lumber members used to make these frames and forming members matters little since smaller pieces can be joined to form completed members. In most boats, each of the frames will usually consist of several pieces. For ex-

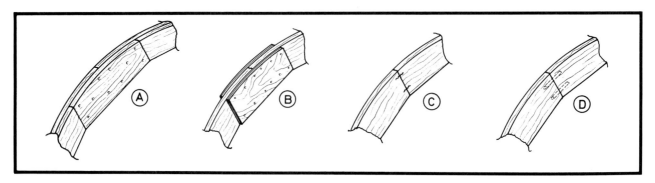

FIG. 11-3 — The male mold frames usually consist of several members which can be joined together by various methods to form a complete frame. In 'A', a double thickness member with lapped junctions is shown. In 'B', two members are joined with lapped plywood gussets on either side. In 'C', corrugated fasteners are used to join two joining members together. In 'D', two butt joining members are held together with glued dowelled joints.

ample, a hard-chine boat may have two bottom members and two side members per frame, while a round bilge boat may have frames made up of several pieces in order to suit the contour of the station. These members can be joined by several methods, including backing pieces or gussets made from wood or plywood, or fastened together with corrugated fasteners, or edge joined with glue and dowels (see Fig. 11-3). Although inexpensive scrap material can be used for the frame members, try to use material that is as true and flat as possible, free from warping or cupping that could distort the frame and make it difficult to true-up on the building form.

The methods used to transfer the lines to the frame members have been explained in

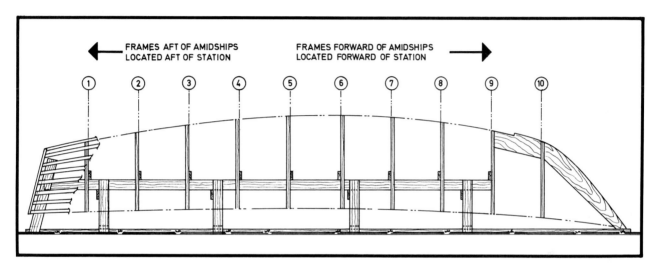

FIG. 11-4 — On male molds of the open battened type, frames forward of amidships are usually located to the forward side of the station, while frames abaft amidships are usually located to the aft side of the station. This provides adequate material for bevels where the battens land on a frame as opposed to resting just on corners.

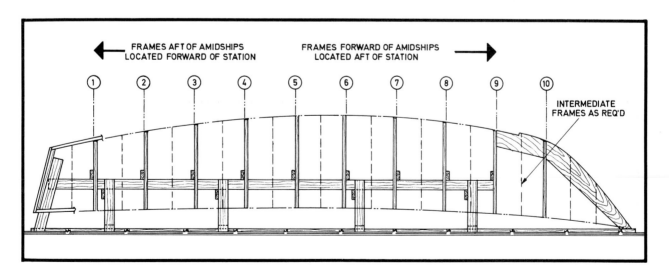

FIG. 11-5 — On male molds without battens, such as those sometimes used with C-FLEX hulls, frames are positioned exactly opposite that shown in Fig. 11-4. Those frames forward of amidships are located abaft the station points, while those frames abaft amidships are located forward of the station; virtually no fairing of the frame edges is required. The C-FLEX will bear only on the edges of the frames.

Chapter 9. After making all the frame members, they can be erected onto the building form. Use the spacing for the frame members as noted on the plans (which usually corresponds to the station spacing). Note that the transverse frames will be located either on the forward or after side of this station reference point. Notwithstanding any special instructions to the contrary provided on your plans, if building an open battened mold (we'll discuss longitudinal battens shortly), the frames are usually located to the FORWARD side of the station on those stations located FORWARD of amidships, and to the AFT side of the station on those stations located AFT of amidships (see Fig. 11-4).

On the other hand, if building a male mold without battens for C-FLEX, for example, using only closely spaced frames (say 14" to 18" apart), the frames are located exactly opposite; that is, with the frames to the AFT side of the station for the portion FORWARD of amidships, and to the FORWARD side of the station for those frames AFT of amidships (see Fig. 11-5). In this case, little, if any, fairing of the frames will be required. However, in the previous situation, some fairing of at least the notches or landing points for the longitudinal battens will be necessary so that battens will not just rest on corners of the frames.

TRANSOM FORMS

A few words should be mentioned regarding transoms and how they are formed when making fiberglass boats using male mold methods. First, it is possible that your boat may not even have a transom, in which case, it will be a double-ender. In this case, there is no transom form required. Instead, a longitudinal form just like that used for the stem is used in order to determine the contour of this area in profile view.

However, if the boat does have a transom, it can be made in many different ways, both

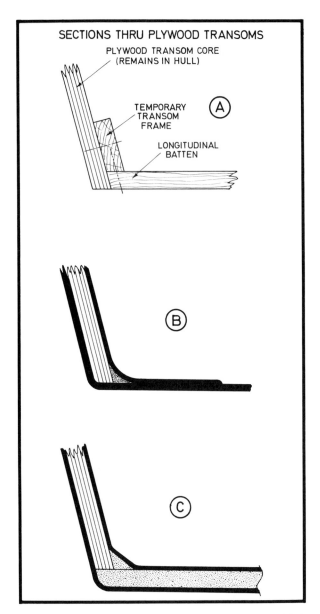

FIG. 11-6 — Plywood transom cores which will be molded into the boat and serve as a male mold member can have longitudinal battens fastened to temporary removable framing members on the inside ('A'). Bevel the transom edges as required. On C-FLEX hulls, the C-FLEX planking will land on the transom edge, with the laminate applied around onto the outer transom surface as in 'B'. After the hull is righted, a resin putty filler fillet can be applied at the inside transom corner and additional laminate applied over this area, encapsulating the plywood transom in place. In other cases, such as with sandwich cored hulls, battens will be used as in 'A', with the core lapping the plywood transom edge as in 'C'. After the outer skin is applied and the hull righted, the battens and transom frame are removed, and the inside corner is fitted with a cant strip or resin putty filler fillet. The inner laminate is then applied, lapping onto the transom and encapsulating it with fiberglass.

to suit the builder's desires, and to suit the design. There are vertical transoms, flat transoms, curved transoms, and those that are inclined either forward or aft. The methods used to form the transom will have some bearing on its configuration. The configuration for the transom may be determined from the loftings, or given as a full-size pattern, or it may be picked up directly from the work.

Probably the simplest transom is the flat-type which can be easily made from sheet plywood. Your plans should state if this is the case. If making a plywood transom that will remain in the boat, it will probably require bevels along the edges so that the fiberglass skin will mate flat along the edges. Use temporary wood framing on the inside surface of the plywood transom core to secure any longitudinal battens. These will be removed after the hull has been righted, prior to glassing the plywood transom in place on the inside (see Fig. 11-6).

In some cases, if working with full size patterns, a pattern for the transom may not be provided; instead, the contour will be taken directly from the work. There are a couple of ways that this may be done (see Fig. 11-7 and 11-8). First a false or temporary frame may be erected aft BEYOND the transom; offsets or a pattern may be given for this temporary member. Longitudinal battens are then sprung over the framework spanning beyond the last frame forward of the transom to the false temporary frame beyond the transom. The location and inclination of the transom (if applicable) can then be plotted by projecting to the battens and cutting to shape using the "staff-and-feeler" method (see Chapter 27). Some builders build the hull oversize in length, then trim it off at the transom, and install the transom after with this approach.

Another method is to extend the various longitudinal battens beyond the last station frame and the aft end of the boat, allowing them to "run wild". Usually this distance will not be excessive and the battens will be

fair enough to plot the transom contours directly. This contour can also be plotted by the "staff-and-feeler" method sticking out to contact the battens.

In either method using the staff assembly, it is removed from position and the contour marked directly to the transom material, then cut to shape. Since both sides of the boat are symmetrical, only one half of the transom need be fitted. A sliding T-bevel can be used to transfer or plot the bevels required along the plywood transom edge to eliminate most fairing along the edge. Then the transom form is erected in place, and the battens trimmed off flush with the transom. This method is good where the transom inclination is severe since it lets you determine the bevels (which will be quite excessive) along the edge quite accurately; this can be difficult for the beginner to visualize when working from loftings or patterns.

If building a curved transom, plywood can still be used (as long as the curvature is not too great) by using thin layers laminated to the curvature. However, it is probably easier to make the transom using the same materials as the rest of the hull. For example, if using C-FLEX, it is simple to span the C-FLEX either vertically or horizontally, supporting it with form members as required. Or if using core materials, use battens running vertically and lay the core material against them. In all cases, the forming materials (C-FLEX or core) will stay in the final transom.

In many cases, however, a transom cored with plywood may be highly desirable, and specifically called for by the designer. This is especially true, for example, on inboard boats which use stern-mounted engines with inboard/outdrive units, jets, and other power units that secure directly to the transom (see Fig. 11-9). A plywood cored transom in these cases provides the extra strength and reinforcement as well as backing for bolts that would be difficult to incorporate if the transom were made from single skin fiberglass or incorporated a soft core material. In these cases, it would still be necessary to incorporate solid wood or plywood inserts into areas receiving stresses, and generally it is just as easy to make the entire transom solid plywood encapsulated with fiberglass (more on encapsulating wood in fiberglass is given in Chapter 24.)

The same principle is often applicable to sailboats where outboard rudders may be hung onto the transom, or where an outboard motor bracket may be attached, or where the backstay attaches. In these cases, depending on the design, it is easier and often preferable to make the transom as a solid plywood core.

ALIGNING FRAME MEMBERS

All members located on the building

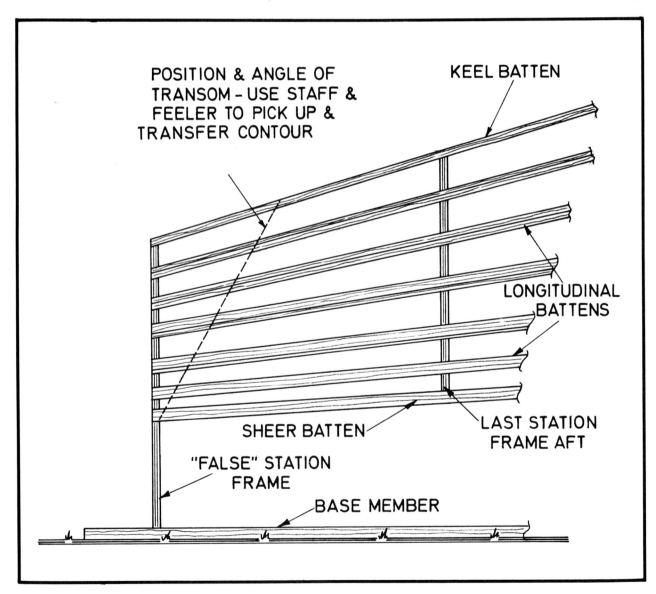

FIG. 11-7 — Sometimes a "false" station beyond the actual end of the boat is given and the transom contour is taken directly from the work using the "staff-and-feeler" method discussed in Chapter 27. In other cases, builders will build the boat longer than need be, and cut it off at the transom, fitting and installing the transom later.

form (as well as the building form itself as has been noted) must be leveled about the horizontal reference plane, or set-up level, both lengthwise and athwartships. The transverse frames must be vertical, at right angles to the centerline, and accurately spaced fore and aft. If there is a transom form, it too must be at right angles to the centerline, and if it is inclined, it must be set at the proper angularity.

Any forming members running lengthwise, or longitudinally, are usually located at the centerline, and should be set exactly in position and vertical. A taut wire or string determines the hull centerline reference, while a plumb bob, builder's level,

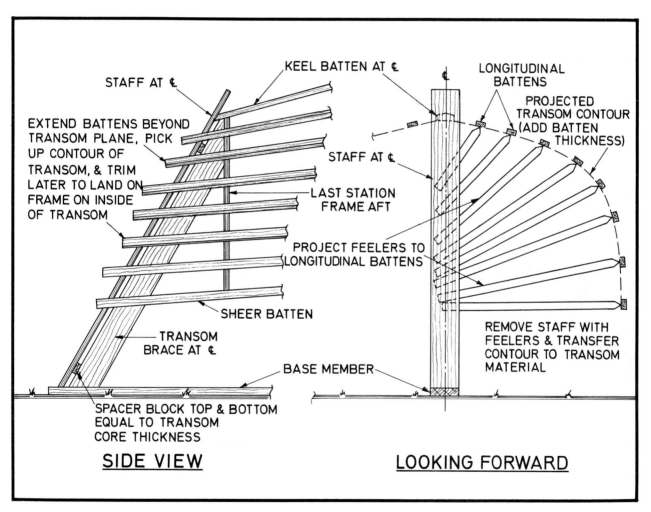

FIG. 11-8 — On some boats with raked transoms and fairly short aft overhangs, another way can be used to pick up the transom contour directly from the work without using a pattern. Let the longitudinal battens extend aft and "run wild" some distance beyond where the actual transom is to be located. (As long as the overhang is not too long, the battens will project fairly some distance if they span several frames forward.) Fit a transom brace at the centerline to match the transom angle. Then use the "staff-and-feeler" method with the staff located against the transom brace to pick up the contour of the angled transom. Only one-half of the transom need be done in this manner since both sides are symmetrical. If bevels are required (such as for the edges of a plywood transom core), these can be picked up with a sliding T-bevel; the angle will be ever-changing in most cases and perhaps severe. Since the plywood transom core will have to be cut oversize to allow for these bevels, this method is more accurate than if working from a pattern which would show just the outer contour. When transferring the contour to the transom member, don't forget to ADD the thickness of the battens and the core thickness (if a cored hull is being built). Use the method shown by Fig. 9-3, but ADD to the contour instead of deducting in this case.

and framing square are used to check for accuracy in aligning the various members. Once all members have been checked for alignment and position, they should be braced with temporary members to the building form and to each other as required to prevent movement.

FAIRING

Before applying any longitudinal battens, the builder should check the framework to assure that it is fair. This can be done by using long, thin battens (like those used for lofting) laid across the framework at many points. If there are any unfair areas which cause the battens to miss certain frames or become deflected from fair lines by frames at other points, the framework must be faired to allow these fairing battens to contact at all points fairly without humps or dips.

Note that fairing is a give-and-take proposition; don't just trim down a member without perhaps shimming up another member in another area where a batten may miss the mark. Material can be added to a frame as required by laying on thin shims, such as with plywood, and sanding the frame contour fair, while perhaps sanding or planing down another frame which is at the same time deflecting the same batten. As far as beveling the frames is concerned, however, this is normally not required other than at the landing point of the battens. Where the battens cross a frame, they must not just rest on corners of a frame member, but rather must mate flat. Hence, the landing point may require some beveling for this to occur.

In addition to fairing battens, in most cases beveling will also be required along certain members, particularly on such members as the stem form and transom form. If these bevels have not been noted or specified, they can be determined directly from the work by plotting the angles at which the battens will mate to these members.

Good tools for fairing purposes include wood rasps, surface forming tools like the patented-type "Surform" planes and rasps, wood planes, and the disc sander. Remember in fairing that it is easy to remove a little material at a time and recheck for fairness, but not so easy to correct when you have removed too much material. So work steadily and progressively, standing back often and rechecking areas that have been faired. While this may all sound a bit tedious, in most cases if you have been careful in the construction up to this point, the work performed in fairing for the fiberglass hull will be minor in nature, and much less than is usually required for boats built from other materials.

FIG. 11-9 — **Fiberglass powerboats are commonly fitted with plywood transom cores. This boat will be fitted with a jet pump unit which passes through the bottom of the hull for the intake and exits through the transom. Notice the plywood transom core showing at the edge of the cutout which helps strengthen and stiffen the transom. This added reinforcement is also necessary for transom-mounted outboards and sterndrive units.**

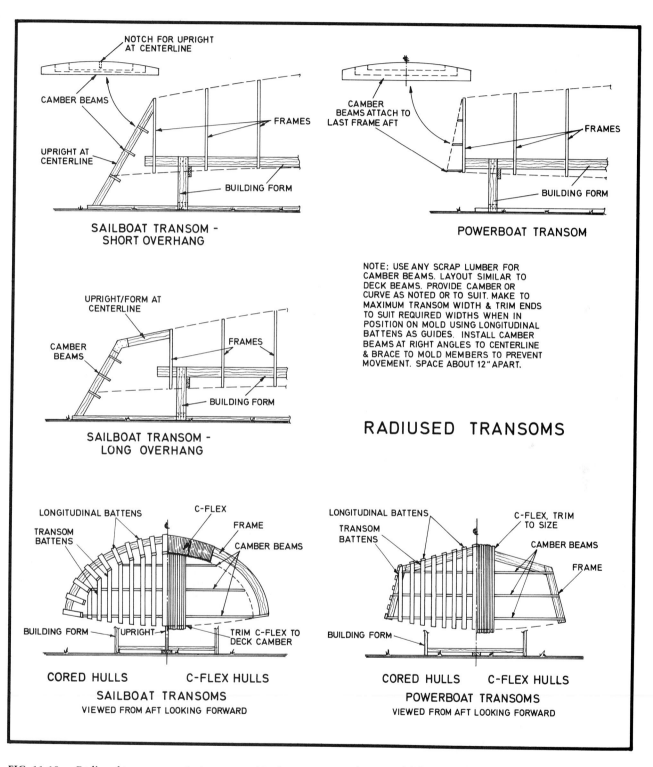

NOTCH FOR UPRIGHT
AT CENTERLINE

CAMBER BEAMS

UPRIGHT AT
CENTERLINE

FRAMES

BUILDING FORM

SAILBOAT TRANSOM -
SHORT OVERHANG

CAMBER
BEAMS ATTACH TO
LAST FRAME AFT

FRAMES

BUILDING FORM

POWERBOAT TRANSOM

UPRIGHT/FORM AT
CENTERLINE

CAMBER
BEAMS

FRAMES

BUILDING FORM

SAILBOAT TRANSOM -
LONG OVERHANG

NOTE: USE ANY SCRAP LUMBER FOR
CAMBER BEAMS. LAYOUT SIMILAR TO
DECK BEAMS. PROVIDE CAMBER OR
CURVE AS NOTED OR TO SUIT. MAKE TO
MAXIMUM TRANSOM WIDTH & TRIM ENDS
TO SUIT REQUIRED WIDTHS WHEN IN
POSITION ON MOLD USING LONGITUDINAL
BATTENS AS GUIDES. INSTALL CAMBER
BEAMS AT RIGHT ANGLES TO CENTERLINE
& BRACE TO MOLD MEMBERS TO PREVENT
MOVEMENT. SPACE ABOUT 12" APART.

RADIUSED TRANSOMS

LONGITUDINAL BATTENS   C-FLEX

TRANSOM   FRAME
BATTENS
                              CAMBER BEAMS

BUILDING FORM   UPRIGHT   TRIM C-FLEX TO
                             DECK CAMBER

CORED HULLS   C-FLEX HULLS
SAILBOAT TRANSOMS
VIEWED FROM AFT LOOKING FORWARD

LONGITUDINAL BATTENS   C-FLEX, TRIM
                             TO SIZE
TRANSOM
BATTENS   CAMBER BEAMS

                              FRAME

BUILDING FORM

CORED HULLS   C-FLEX HULLS
POWERBOAT TRANSOMS
VIEWED FROM AFT LOOKING FORWARD

FIG. 11-10 — Radiused transoms can be incorporated in the male molded hull by using C-FLEX, FERRO-GLASS, or any of the sandwich core materials. Radiused or cambered forming members (similar to deck beams laid horizontally) are located across the transom area and intersect with the other male mold members for support. With C-FLEX, cut and fit the material in vertical strips directly to these members which should support the C-FLEX at about 12" intervals. With the other hull materials, proceed similarly, but install battens vertically to support the mesh or core material. The same laminate used on the hull is then used across the transom with additional laminate at the corners as required.

LONGITUDINAL BATTENS

Once all the transverse frames and longitudinal form members are in place, longitudinal battens will be sprung around the hull, the number and spacing of which will vary with the material and method used to build the hull. More will be discussed about the need for battens with various methods of male mold construction, but the following will provide general information and requirements.

In many cases, longitudinal battens will not be available in lengths that are long enough to reach from stem to stern. However, in all cases, the full length batten that is free from knots or other defects that could lead to unfairness or weakness is preferable. If long lengths are not available, then members of shorter lengths can be joined to form single full-length members. These joints can be either butt joints or scarf joints, but whichever method is used, the joints should not cause the battens to develop flat spots that could lead to an unfair hull.

If battens are butted together, the joints should fall at as flat an area as possible, preferably between frames, with the butt joint backed by a butt block of the same size material as the joining battens. If required to prevent forming a flat spot, the butt block should be shaped to contour to suit. Optionally, laminated members can be used to make full length members, with laminations of thickness to suit.

The longitudinal battens may vary in size depending on the size and shape of the hull, and the spacing of the frames. However, in most cases, the battens can be made from 1" to 2" nominal stock from 1" to 3" in width. In smaller boats in areas of the hull where hull shape changes rapidly, somewhat thinner or lighter battens may be required. Note that as a batten tends to be more "square" in configuration, the easier it will bend compared to one that is wider than it is thick. If a table or radial arm saw is available, you can save considerably on this phase of the proj-

ect by buying large long pieces of lumber and ripping your own battens to size as they are required instead of buying them already milled to size from the lumberyard.

During the application of the battens as well as after they are installed, the builder must make sure that the male mold stays fair and true. Install battens alternating from side to side in order to equalize the stresses transferred to the male mold and building form members. You may find that additional bracing may be required; don't be bashful about putting in these members as required.

Generally it is preferable to apply each batten in full length from stem to stern. Divide the length along each of the frame contours equally for the landing points of each of the battens, as there would be an equal number of battens landing onto each frame in this case. However, as the battens are sprung around the hull, if edge setting (attempting to bend the member in two directions at once) becomes too difficult due to hull shape, then it may be necessary to stop members short and orient battens in a somewhat different sequence. Different approaches to the application of battens is shown by various photos throughout the text. The main point is, however, that the battens be as long as possible in order to keep unfair areas from being formed. Spring a batten in place over as many frames as possible so that there is ample curvature developed to keep from forming flat spots or ridges along any of the battens.

In areas of tight curvature, battens may not always want to lay to the frames; they may want to "twist" and cause an unfair area where everything would otherwise seem to be fair initially. If this happens, use a batten that is more "square" in section, or fit a "strap" of plywood or solid bent wood frame behind the battens, connecting the stubborn batten to several others to make it lay more fairly to the surface (see Fig. 19-26). Check across the battens with thin plywood battens, or thin wood strips, or strips

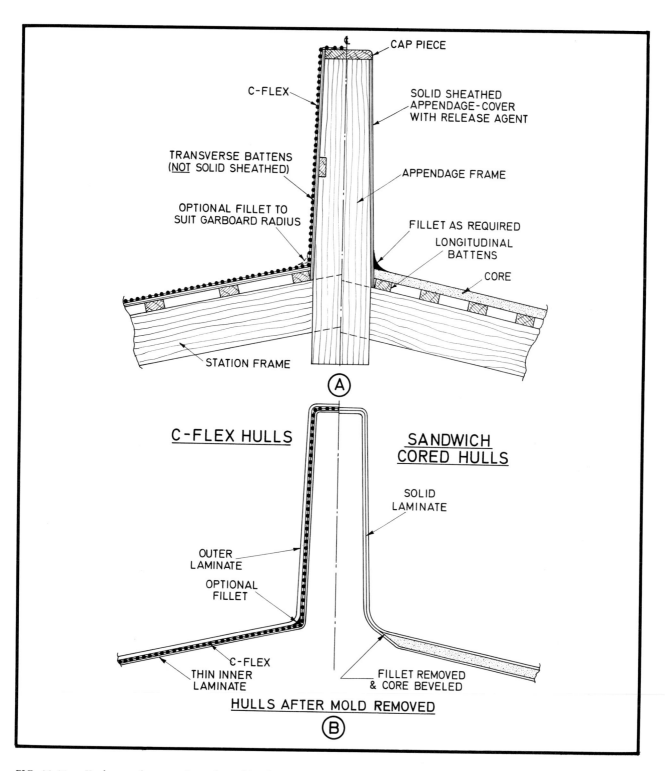

CAP PIECE

C-FLEX

SOLID SHEATHED
APPENDAGE-COVER
WITH RELEASE AGENT

TRANSVERSE BATTENS
(NOT SOLID SHEATHED)

APPENDAGE FRAME

OPTIONAL FILLET TO
SUIT GARBOARD RADIUS

FILLET AS REQUIRED
LONGITUDINAL
BATTENS

CORE

STATION FRAME

Ⓐ

C-FLEX HULLS

SANDWICH
CORED HULLS

SOLID
LAMINATE

OUTER
LAMINATE

OPTIONAL
FILLET

C-FLEX
THIN INNER
LAMINATE

FILLET REMOVED
& CORE BEVELED

HULLS AFTER MOLD REMOVED

Ⓑ

FIG. 11-11 — Keel appendages on the male mold will vary somewhat depending on the construction material as shown by sections of a typical example ('A'). With C-FLEX hulls (left of centerline) using a male mold such as that shown by Fig. 16-3, the C-FLEX is applied to all areas, including the keel appendage. But with sandwich cored hulls (right of centerline), this appendage is often solid fiberglass laminate, requiring a transition from the core material. The area of the mold where the solid laminate is located is sheathed solid with plywood or hardboard, and coated with release agent. The resulting hulls with the molds removed are shown in 'B'.

of foam to assure that none are too high or too low, and adjust them accordingly. The maerial which will be applied over the male mold should mate to all mold surfaces flat and fair.

MALE MOLD VARIATIONS TO SUIT SPECIFIC MATERIALS

In addition to the preceding general information on building an open-battened male mold for fiberglass hull construction, certain specific requirements may be necessary to suit the material or method used to build the hull. For example, if working with C-FLEX or FERRO-GLASS, there are certain variations necessary to suit not only these materials, but also different ways that they can be used. With both these materials, the variations have been included in the chapters where the use of these materials are detailed (see Chapters 16 and 17 respectively). However, all core materials (such as the foams and end-grain balsa) require male mold modifications and requirements that are similar for the most part, and hence can be covered together at this point as a continuation of this chapter.

The open-battened mold used for sandwich core construction is necessary to support the core material while the outer laminate or "skin" is being applied. The spacing of the battens can vary, but in general, they should be spaced approximately 2" to 6" apart depending on the thickness and the type of core material. As noted previously, you will have to make the decision when building the frames to deduct from the contours of these members for the core thickness, plus the thickness of the longitudinal battens, but it is preferable that you do so to maintain the accuracy of the designer's work.

In many sandwich cored hulls there will be portions of the hull that will be built up into solid fiberglass laminates, with the core material being omitted. Common areas (as illustrated in this chapter as well as Chapters 19 and 20) where this may occur are along the sheer and keel centerline areas, where there are through-hull fittings, or as designated on the plans. Where these areas occur, the builder must build up the area on the male mold to the thickness of the core. These areas are usually built up with solid wood members or pieces of plywood. However, this procedure is NOT necessarily mandatory; it just makes for a better, and usually more convenient and less tedious, job (although it takes some forethought on the part of the builder).

If you do NOT build up these solid areas initially and use the core material over all areas instead, the core material will have to be removed from these areas later, AFTER the hull has been righted and the male mold removed. This is a tedious and difficult job, especially over large areas, and is best avoided.

In many cases, solid laminate will be used in such areas as the keel, skeg, or other hull appendages where it is not practical or necessary to use the core material. To form these areas to the required shape, several materials can be used, including wood, resin putty fillers, and non-structural foams such as urethane. These materials can be shaped and faired easily enough to the desired shape, and then covered with a release agent or parting film since they will not remain in the completed hull. The outer laminate is then applied over these areas.

Examples where these areas occur are illustrated. In the sandwich core hull using a solid fiberglass keel appendage, for example, there is a radiused transition between the hull and the keel appendage, and it is often impractical to bring the core material around this rather tight turn. On the male mold this can be handled by building up a fillet using resin putty or wood to make a smooth transition from the hull to the member forming the keel appendage.

With sandwich core construction, forethought must always be given as to what

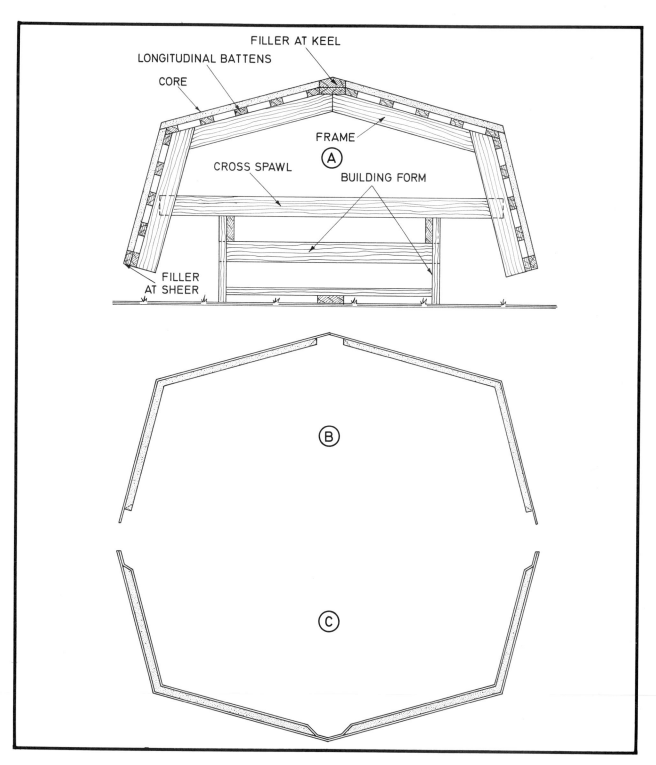

FIG. 11-12 — A hard-chine sandwich cored hull is shown in section view on the male mold, which is in turn mounted to the building form. In sandwich cored hulls, areas along the centerline and sheer are frequently solid fiberglass laminate. These areas are usually built up with fillers (usually of wood or plywood) as shown in 'A', and coated with parting film or release agent. After the outer laminate has been applied and the hull is removed from the male mold, it will appear as in 'B'. The core is thus eliminated at the centerline and sheer areas. Edges of the core are bevelled and then the inner laminate is applied, as in 'C', bonding both skins together where the core is not located.

will remain in the hull and what will not. To make it easy to remove the hull from the male mold, release agent and/or parting film must be used over ANY area of the hull which will come into contact with resin (EXCEPT the area of the core itself that will remain in the hull). Once the hull is righted and the male mold is removed, these areas will all be covered with the inner laminate, plus perhaps additional layers of reinforcement depending on the design.

There are a couple of other considerations that must be made if using a core material. First, you must decide if the male mold will be used again to build another boat. If it will be used again, then care must be taken in planning to assure that it can be removed easily from the completed hull without ruining it. On sailboats, keel appendages will require sufficient draft (angling of the sides) so the mold will slip off of the keel. It is also preferable to remove the male mold in a single piece, although there have been some cases where boats have been built in two-piece molds that have been re-assembled and realigned to build additional hulls, or molds that have been fitted with inserts. But these extra complications may confuse the beginner.

A consideration in removing the male mold is if the hull has any areas of obvious "tumblehome", where the topsides contour up to the sheer and lean toward the inside of the boat so that the sheer is narrower than

some portion below it. In these cases, some fancy modifications may be required to pull the male mold out without tearing it to pieces. Otherwise, if you don't care about the male mold, it can be removed from the hull in any suitable manner, including tearing it to pieces.

Note that if the mold will be used again to build another boat, there may be an obligation to the designer to pay him a royalty for this privilege. It is customary for a designer when he sells plans, or designs a custom design for a client, to allow the rights for the construction of just a single vessel from this transaction. In other words, while the boat may be yours, the design always remains the property of the designer, so it is best to check with him regarding any royalty arrangements.

Another important point in building the male mold for sandwich core materials is that access should be provided to underneath or inside the male mold while it is upsidedown. This is necessary in order to complete the application of the core material, whether sewing it on or fastening it on. Usually raising the building form above the floor sufficiently so that a person can crawl under the sheer will do the job. But conversely, the hull should not be so high that it cannot be worked on conveniently. If this occurs, such as on a very large vessel, then a scaffold will have to be erected around the hull, either supported from the ground or from rafters of the building shed if there is one.

SOLID MALE MOLD

Some variations with core materials allow the use of a solid sheathed male mold as opposed to the open battened male mold. One such variation is detailed in Chapter 22 and uses a vacuum bag technique. The underlying problem with a solid sheathed male mold is that there is no practical way to sew or fasten on the core material, espe-

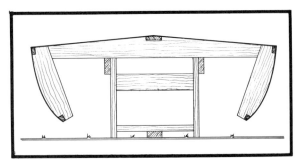

FIG. 11-13 — This section through a male mold shows a hull shape with severe "tumblehome". It will not be possible to pull the hull off of such a shape without dismantling the male mold first.

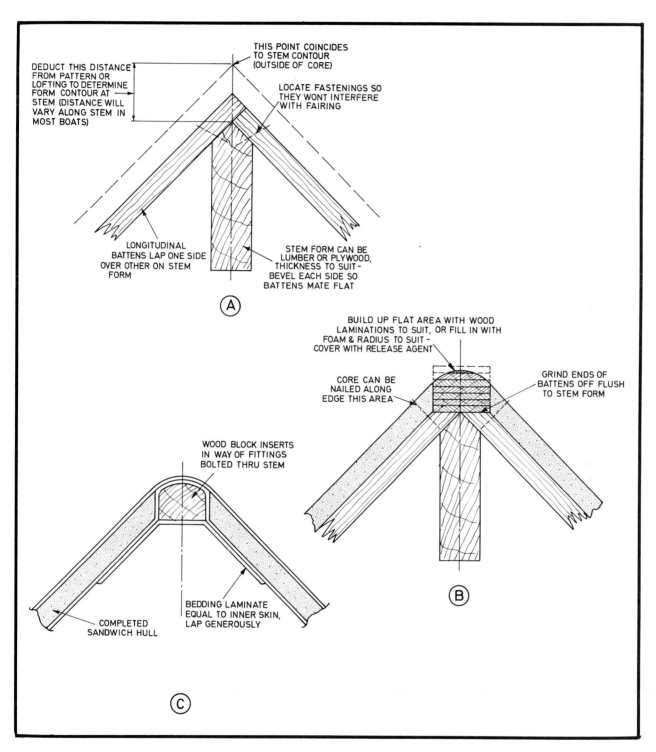

FIG. 11-14 — The area along the stem form of the male mold used for sandwich cored hulls usually requires a deduction from the given stem contour to allow for the core and batten thickness. In most cases, this total thickness can be deducted directly from the contour ('A'). The stem form is then beveled each side of the centerline for the longitudinal battens. The battens can then be trimmed off flat and the area built up with thin wood strips as a filler to suit the core material ('B'). Since this area is usually to be solid fiberglass laminate, cover with release agent or parting film after shaping or radiusing the stem area to suit. After the outer laminate is applied and the male mold removed, the inner laminate is applied ('C'). Photos of a boat being built with this condition are shown by Fig. 19-24 through 19-48.

FIG. 11-15 — Note the forming members being used along the centerline area of this male mold for a sandwich cored hull. The keel appendage (at left) is sheathed over with plywood since the keel appendage will be solid fiberglass. Thin wood strips are being used to form the garboard radius between the hull bottom and keel appendage since fiberglass laminate will be located here also. The contoured member along the centerline forms the profile at the lower edge of the keel appendage and aperture in the aft area. This hull is shown completed in Fig. 14-6.

FIG. 11-16 — The male mold for this AIREX sandwich cored hull has the core material applied around the garboard area and onto the keel appendage surface. The area along the centerline (edge of the keel appendage) is built up with wood to be flush with the core surface, and faired to shape for the solid fiberglass laminate that will be used along this area. Note the orientation of the longitudinal battens, especially those forming the garboard area. Not all core materials will conform to the relatively tight curvature in this area. When this is the case, the method shown by Fig. 11-11 and Fig. 11-15 must be used.

cially if the inner skin is applied first. Some builders, however, have used solid sheathed male molds with balsa core material with some success (because it is "limp" and conforms to contours easily with just contact forming). But using other core materials without vacuum bag application over the initial inner skin is questionable and often impractical.

FIG. 11-17 — Male mold frames set up on a building form. Any scrap lumber can be used to make these frames, pieced and joined as required. Note the bracing on the frames and the cross pawls which are located at a reference point for accuracy of construction.

FIG. 11-18 — This photo shows the inside of an open battened male mold used for building a foam sandwich cored hull. The core material has been applied (see Chapter 19). Note the frame members, frame bracing, and cross pawls spanning across the building form members.

CHAPTER 12   laminating procedures

This chapter will describe the procedures for building up (laying up) fiberglass laminates using conventional materials like mat, woven roving, and cloth. The procedures are similar whether the job is being done inside a female mold or over a male mold using any of the male mold processes such as C-FLEX, FERRO-GLASS, or any of the sandwich core materials. The sequence in which the respective materials are used, and their weights and types, should be specified for the design being built, and this sequence is usually referred to as the laminate schedule.

JOINTS IN MATERIALS

Fiberglass materials come in rolls of limited widths, so each layer in a laminate is made up of many strips or widths of material. Thus, there is the decision as to whether the joints between the strips of materials are to be butted together or whether they should be overlapped. To the novice it would seem that overlapping joints would be stronger, but there is more involved in this choice as will be covered in more detail momentarily.

If the boat is being built in a female mold where the inside appearance is not important, and undulations are acceptable in the layup, then overlapped junctions are satisfactory (except that mat edges should be handled in a manner which will be discussed later in this chapter). However, if the boat is being built over a male mold and the laminate is to be applied over a material like C-FLEX or FERRO-GLASS, or will be the outer skin over one of the sandwich core materials, and there will be three or more layers in the laminate, the layers of fiberglass should be butted together and NOT overlapped. The reason is that overlaps will

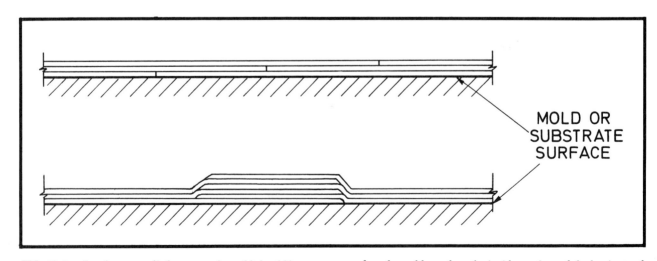

MOLD OR
SUBSTRATE
SURFACE

FIG. 12-1 — Laminates applied over a male mold should be applied with butted joints. Overlapped joints will build up an uneven surface that will be difficult to fair. However, in female molds, and on the inside portions of the laminate of male molded hulls, overlapping joints are acceptable, as long as appearance is not critical.

build up double thicknesses of materials in some areas, making a surface that will be difficult, if not impractical, to fair smooth (see Fig. 12-1). Of course, with the laminate on the INSIDE of sandwich core hulls, or on the inside of C-FLEX and FERRO GLASS hulls, junctions can be either butted (assuming three or more layers) or overlapped if appearance inside does not matter.

While it would seem that lapped joints would be much stronger than butted joints, this is really true only if joints are considered in a SINGLE layer of laminate. But when considered in the TOTAL laminate, there is very little loss of strength in the laminate as long as all butt joints do NOT occur at the same point. Tests show (see Appendix 2) that the difference in strength characteristics between butted and lapped joints in laminates can be discounted for all practical purposes in the majority of most boats that an amateur would be involved in when using conventional materials in the laminate. For example, flexural strength remains virtually the same, as does inner-laminar strength, while tensile strength decreases only about 10% and compressive strength by only about 7%.

When speaking of butting joints in conventional fiberglass materials, the actual butt joint is not quite the same as, for example, butting two hard objects together such as sheets of plywood. In the case of mat, although the widths of the material may have somewhat crisp and distinct edges, and can be butted in this form, it is preferable to tear or "feather" the edges so that the adjoining torn edges can be melded into one another (see Fig. 12-3). This results in a more continuous layer without an obvious discontinuity between strips of mat created by a butt joint. Such a procedure will strengthen butt joints in mat layers, and if carefully done, will form a joint that is virtually indistinguishable.

With woven roving, the edges of the material are usually not selvedged or cut, so there are no distinct edges to the material. Instead, the weft or cross rovings may extend loosely a bit beyond the boundary or edge warp roving. This allows the ends of the cross rovings to be intermingled with those of the adjoining strip of woven roving as the layup progresses, resulting in what

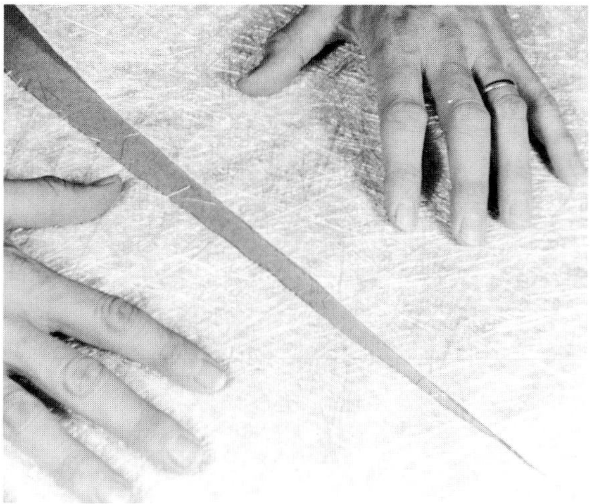

FIG. 12-2 — Widths of mat taken from the roll have a crisp and distinct edge. If butted together, the surface will be smooth, but there will be no strength continuity in this layer of laminate at the butt joint. See Fig. 12-3 for a better method of joining widths of mat.

FIG. 12-3 — Adjoining edges of mat should preferably be torn, leaving a ragged or "feathered" edge. The two widths of material when joined together then meld into each other for better strength continuity. In effect, the joint disappears.

amounts to nearly a continuous, homogenous structural component even though the joints have technically been "butted" together (see Fig. 12-4).

Another reason why butted joints are preferable to overlapping joints, especially with thicker mats, is that there is a chance for building up a resin-rich pocket along the edge of the first layer of mat directly under the overlapping layer, and making a perfect area for air entrapment (see Fig. 12-5).

FIG. 12-4 — The loose ends of woven roving strands should be lapped and intermingled with each other at junctions in the fabric for continuity.

Hence, lapping of layers could actually result in not only a weaker joint, but probably one that is heavier and would use more resin. It will also require more work on the part of the laminator to keep the situation under control as the work proceeds. Consequently, there is no reason NOT to use all-butted joints as long as they are made in the manner recommended, and are in a laminate at least three layers thick.

Another principle that should be emphasized, and which was briefly noted earlier, is that, as a precaution, all butted joints should be well staggered with respect to those in adjoining layers (see Fig. 12-6). This will generally occur automatically if the laminate is applied in a staggered lap or "shingled" manner which will be described. Also, joints in ANY of the laminations of fiberglass materials over structural areas that will be subjected to stress should NOT be permitted. This would include such areas as along the keel and stem at the centerline, along the chine on hard-chine hulls, at transom corners, and similar areas (see Fig. 12-7). Instead, always continue the endings of materials well beyond such areas, and alternate the ending points from layer to layer.

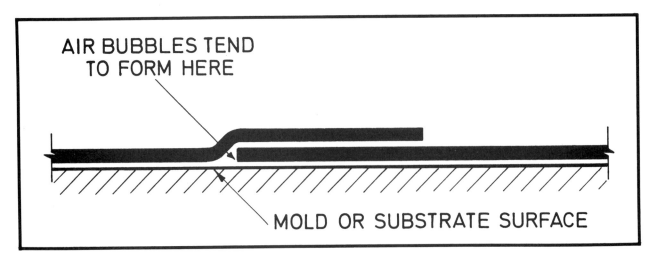

FIG. 12-5 — Overlapping joints in mat, especially in heavier weight materials, may tend to form resin rich pockets and air bubbles at the overlap. One way to prevent this (if an overlap is necessary) would be to taper or "feather" the edge of the cured underlying layer first with a disc sander. However, in conventional laminates, this is seldom necessary since butt joints as described in this chapter are preferable.

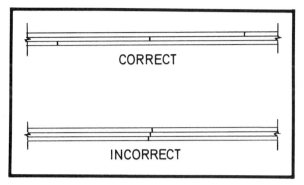

FIG. 12-6 — Butt joints in materials should not align coincidentally with any other adjacent butt joints in a laminate. Instead, they must be well staggered or separated from each other for strength continuity.

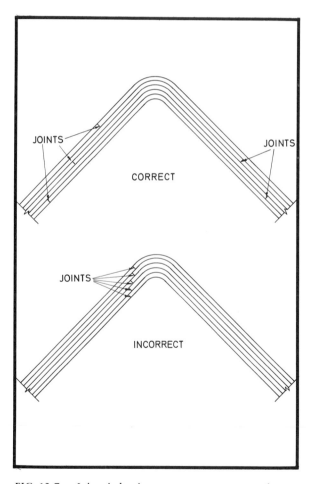

FIG. 12-7 — Joints in laminates over or near structural areas or areas subjected to stress, such as stem, chine, and transom corners, should not be permitted. Instead, junctions should be located well beyond these areas and alternated or staggered with respect of other joints in the laminate. Although not shown, additional laminate is usually applied at these points.

INTERLAMINAR BOND

The manner in which the laminate application is approached will vary depending on several factors. These may include the size of the boat, the length of time available in any working period, the number of people who may be available to help, and personal preferences.

The only REAL problem with varying the manner in which a hull is laid up has to do with those factors which could affect the bonding between layers of material, or the interlaminar bond. Either a bond will be a continuous or "primary" type, or if the resin sets up and cures, and a subsequent layer of the laminate is laid up over this, it will be an interrupted or "secondary" bond.

While a primary bond is always superior and desirable, a secondary bond is not detrimental in CONVENTIONAL laminates as long as only a brief period transpires before the next layer is applied, and the surface is clean and free of dust, moisture, or other elements that could affect the bond. There is a technical definition for a "secondary bond" based on U. S. Navy and Coast Guard specifications. These state that a secondary bond is equal to twice the gel time, or gel time plus two hours, whichever is greater. However, it should be noted that these specifications involve the use of fire-retardant resins which may not bond as well as other types of resins; thus secondary bonds are more critical in this instance. Even if a great deal of time has passed between application of one layer from another, the only requirement would be that the surface should be roughened up by sanding to give the next layer some "tooth", and to clean it up, such as with a wipe down with a solvent wash. So don't worry about being intimidated by what may seem to be an overwhelming project; just try to do the layup as quickly as possible within a reasonable length of time without large time gaps between layers.

It is difficult to state just how long these

time gaps should be if a continuous laminate cannot be built up in one operation. Much depends on local conditions, such as heat and other elements that will speed or protract total cure. As ambient temperatures increase, fiberglass cures faster, which means that the quicker you proceed with the layup the better your bonding conditions will be. Generally, however, it is not unusual for several days or perhaps even a week or more to go by before subsequent work is done over an existing laminate. But anything longer than this is not advisable. In any case, if a surface has cured, it should be properly prepared before subsequent applications of laminate.

SEQUENCE AND DIRECTION OF MATERIALS

In conventional layups, the laminate consists of alternating layers of mat and woven roving or cloth. Usually the first layer of material against the mold surface (in the case of female molded hulls) and against the male mold material (C-FLEX, FERRO-GLASS, or sandwich core) will be mat. This is usually followed by woven roving, and then alternated with mat, woven roving, mat, etc. In very small boats, cloth may be substituted in place of the woven roving.

The final layer for boats built over male molds is usually a layer of mat since this surface provides the finishing base. The mat as the outer surface layer also "waterproofs" the laminate, whether the boat is built in a female mold or over a male mold. With female molded hulls, the layer of mat against the mold surface provides reinforcing and a proper balance of resin for the gel coat, and prevents what is called "print through", the telegraphing of the waffle-like pattern of the woven roving, which would occur if woven roving were used directly against the surface of the mold. However, on the inside of hulls regardless of

the materials used in the construction, the inner exposed fiberglass layer can be either mat or woven roving, or perhaps cloth; it makes little difference.

The mat in a laminate can be run lengthwise, longitudinally, or diagonally, it makes no difference strengthwise. Remember that the mat is an isotropic material with comparable strength in all directions. On the other hand, the fibers in woven roving and cloth have high strength in the warp direction especially, and usually satisfactory strength across the material in the weft direction, but with minimal strength diagonally.

In most boats using conventional laminates, the woven roving is applied across the hull mainly for convenience. However, in multiple-layer laminates, one layer of woven roving could be laid across the boat, with another perhaps laid lengthwise, and maybe another in a diagonal manner to impart strength in several directions. However, in most boats with multi-layers of mat and woven roving applied alternately in the conventional laminate, fiber orientation is usually not so critical. The combination of random fibers in the mat together with the directional fibers in the woven roving provides enough reserve of strength properties.

With C-FLEX hulls, it is mandatory that the woven roving (at least one of the layers) be applied at approximately right angles to the C-FLEX. This is done to reinforce the butt joints between the C-FLEX planks; otherwise it is possible that a butt joint in the woven roving could coincide with a butt joint in the C-FLEX planks, creating a weak spot in the laminate if the woven roving was applied lengthwise.

If the design specifies that materials be applied in certain directions in any of the layers of the laminate, be sure to adhere to this recommendation. But generally, it is easiest to apply woven roving at about right angles to the boat's centerline, or crosswise, especially for the beginner who may be short of time and short of help. If the hull shape makes it practical, apply the mat and woven roving clear across the hull from sheer to sheer.

Keep in mind the reasons for using the various types of reinforcements in a laminate and the reason for alternating materials. In the conventional layup with mat and woven roving or cloth, the mat is used to guarantee a sound interlaminar bond between woven roving layers, and to build up hull thickness to add stiffness. The woven roving is what gives the laminate its strength (tensile and impact strength most importantly).

In all cases, strive for as high a percentage of glass content compared to resin as is possible (about 40% glass being a good target), since the resin merely acts as a glue or binder to hold the reinforcing materials together and make them rigid. This is not meant to discount the role of the resin, however, since without it, the ultimate strengths of the materials in the laminate would not be realized.

LAMINATE APPLICATION

At the outset, one important point must be emphasized, especially for the beginner: DON'T USE TOO MUCH RESIN! Use only that amount of resin which is required to thoroughly wet out the materials. It is a common mistake for the amateur to use more resin than he should. This probably results because the person who is not familiar with wetting out fiberglass thinks that the speed and thoroughness with which the fiberglass is saturated is directly proportional to the amount of resin poured over the reinforcement. Instead, what must be kept in mind is that the resin must be worked thoroughly and constantly, using techniques that will allow the resin to work for you in the process to guarantee a properly wetted out laminate.

Unfortunately, working with fiberglass in the laminating procedure is one of those things that is more difficult to explain and describe in words than it is to physically do. But since in a book there is no other way to go through the procedures, just keep in mind that fiberglass work is basically simple and straightforward, though perhaps a bit messy. An attempt will be made to cover all aspects of the job, what can be expected, and how to avoid problems.

One problem that occurs in most laminates, especially those which include mat, is the tendency to build up high and low areas. This is not much of a consideration in the female molded boat, but is important for hulls built over male molds. Throughout the layup the worker must take care to prevent building up lumps, hills, and valleys in order to keep the amount of final fairing and smoothing work to a minimum. Even if the extra work were not a consideration in fairing, the extra buildup of resin putty filler coats on the outside surfaces makes a brittle, less durable surface, and adds to the weight and cost of the boat.

To prevent or minimize irregularities, use a squeegee and mat roller with as much care as possible (a feel for these tools will come quite quickly), alternating with heavy pressure over high spots, and using less pressure over low areas. At the same time, take care to avoid resin-rich and resin-starved areas by moving resin about as needed; but be careful when adding resin since it is easy to apply more than can be worked or used at a time.

Additionally, as layers are applied, try finishing off the woven roving layers with a large steel drywall-type trowel or putty knife (from 12" to 24" wide), pressing firmly to both even out the surface and to remove excess resin (either push the excess resin to a new, dry area or remove it and throw it away). This practice is shown in several photos in the text. Squeegeeing in this manner helps pull the laminate down tighter if working over a male mold, but cannot be done successfully in a female mold since doing so will pull the laminate away from the mold surface. Incidentally, this is one of the reasons why boats built over male molds can often be structurally stronger, yet lighter in weight, than boats built in female molds; the technique tends to increase glass content ratios.

If in applying the laminate an unfair surface is built up, it is best to correct it before proceeding too far into the laminate so that it will not carry through to the surface. Mix up a filler using milled glass fibers and resin, and apply to these areas as the layup progresses. Such additions should be kept to a minimum in order to keep weight down. By working on fairness throughout the laminating process, much fairing and finish work on the male molded hull will be eliminated.

CONTINUOUS VS: INTERRUPTED APPLICATION

Basically, the laminate will be applied either continuously if there is enough time or enough workers, or it will be applied a portion at a time. If possible, it is desirable to apply the laminate in a single, continuous operation. One important point, however, should be made with a continuous application. It is possible to build up heat due to the exotherm of the resin where thickness is also built up rapidly. This heat build-up, if too great, can cause undue shrinkage and lead to a weakened laminate. Thus, if using a continuous technique where thickness builds quickly, it may be desirable to reduce the amount of catalyst since a concentrated batch of resin cures faster and gives off more heat than one spread out over a broader, thinner area.

One may ask, since resin has such a short period of time before it starts to set up, and only a limited area can be worked at a time to assure a properly saturated laminate, how is it possible to do any type of CONTINUOUS laminating? The required technique is called keeping a "wet edge", much

like in painting. As long as the resin is worked progressively, moving from an area that is almost ready to set up and into one that is still wet, replenishing resin as work proceeds, there is no reason to ever stop the laminating procedure as long as conditions permit. In Fig. 12-8, a worker is shown moving along the length of a hull, working continuously. In this instance, both a layer of mat and a layer of woven roving are being wetted out at once. By keeping a wet edge, the worker can keep wetting out material until he either runs out of material or he reaches the end of the project.

A single, continuous operation usually requires two or more workers (the more the better). One worker applies the mat while another follows immediately with the woven roving, and so on until the laminate has been completed. In this method, the woven roving is easier to apply and wet out because the preceeding layer of wet mat will be soaking into the underside of the successive layer of woven roving, thereby helping wet out the woven roving, which can sometimes be stubborn in accepting the resin, especially in heavier weight materials. Another advantage of this method is that it is possible to squeegee out over the woven roving and remove excess resin more effectively, thereby having a final laminate with better qualities.

If the above continuous method cannot be used (for example if a person is working alone or there is not enough time for a continuous operation), some variations will be required. Each layer of fiberglass material can be applied one layer at a time, completing each before applying the next. However, don't stop intermittently with a layer of mat; instead end off with a layer of woven roving applied over the mat, and let this cure. Then start off later with mat and another layer of woven roving.

Applying the laminate in this sequence insures a positive secondary bond because the wet mat will fill in the interstices of the woven material, and one can more effectively squeegee down the wet woven roving to remove excess resin. However, mat cannot be squeegeed down in this manner since it tends to tear apart. The worker can complete the last layer of a laminate with either a layer of mat or woven roving. However, a better bond to subsequent parts installed on the inside of the hull will result with a final mat layer. Sanding and minor fairing work can be done directly against a mat surface, but woven materials should not be ground excessively as this will cut away reinforcing fibers and take away strength.

STAGGERING JOINTS

Apply all layers in the laminate basically a strip at a time, setting back each subsequent edge from the edge of the layer underneath by 6" or more. However, the first strip in the second layer of the laminate will have to be cut to a narrower width than the layer underneath to allow for the next 6" nominal overlap as shown by Fig. 12-9. Where the laminate application begins, makes little difference, but for convenience of explanation, assume work begins at one end or

FIG. 12-8 — If enough help is available, a continuous laminate application is possible (although not necessary). These workers are applying a layer of mat and a layer of woven roving simultaneously along the length of a C-FLEX hull.

Note the wide trowel being used to force the laminate down and prevent resin-rich areas from forming. The resulting surface will be quite fair and smooth.

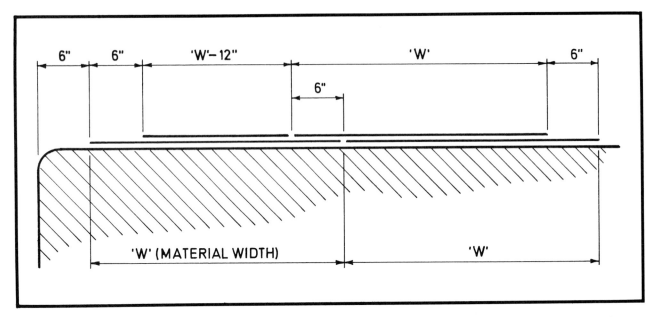

FIG. 12-9 — This illustration shows the method described in the text of building up a laminate by applying a layer of material at a time so that proper overlaps result and joints will not occur at stress areas, such as corners.

another of the boat. For example, set the first strip of the first layer of mat back from the starting end of the boat (stem or transom) by 6″ or so (you can start from the middle or at any other point, however, it is easiest to assure having a proper setback without pre-cutting the materials first). The setback is done to assure that a joint will not fall over the centerline at the stem or at the transom corner.

Then apply the next layer (woven roving) back an additional 6″ from the starting edge of the mat layer. However, cut this strip to be at least 12″ narrower than the underlying mat so you will have space for the 6″ setback on one edge plus 6″ at the other edge for the overlap of the next adjoining layer of woven roving to be applied over the first mat layer. Proceed with the two layers of the laminate so that joints between them are a minimum of 6″ apart.

The above approach is what is called a staggered lap or "shingle" method and it prevents butt joints in materials from falling directly over one another. As the next two laminates (mat and woven roving) are applied, start the mat at least 6″ from the previous woven roving layer so that all starting and ending points will be with butt joints staggered at least 6″ from any others. This same basic principle is used wherever joints should not be allowed, such as at the transom corners, chine corners, along garboard radiuses, and along the centerline or keel. To simplify joints along the centerline, however, if the hull form permits, it may be possible to apply some or all of the strips all the way across the hull from sheer to sheer, effectively eliminating joints in this area.

The non-continuous approach allows the work to be done on limited areas, stopping when required. Work progressively from forward to aft, and vice versa, but also from side to side in order to distribute any possible distortion or shrinkage tendencies that may occur in the laminate. Note, however, that materials at adjoining sections where secondary bonding will occur may require scuff sanding and cleaning before applying adjoining laminates.

A big part in making the laminating process go smoothly and quickly is to be organized BEFORE the work begins. All materials should be pre-measured, pre-cut, labeled, and rolled or folded up and set aside ready for immediate use. Have batches of resin poured into dispensing containers pre-measured, and with the proper amount of catalyst ready to go for each. Keep a container of solvent ready to receive tools, and have all the tools at hand. While the job can be done by one person, a "helper" is always handy to have when the blur of activity gets beyond the point where two hands are enough. With this kind of organization, you will be amazed how much laminate can be built up in a short period of time.

"TIPS" & TECHNIQUES

Part of the secret of speed in laminating involves certain "tips" and techniques like the "pro's" use. We'll discuss a few. For example, when applying mat, an easy way to apply it is to cut a piece somewhat over-size and fold it onto itself in several large folds towards the middle of the piece, so that most of the underside surface (the side which will mate to the mold surface) is exposed. This approach is shown several times in the text. Also cut the piece of woven roving which will coincide with this mat layer and set it aside.

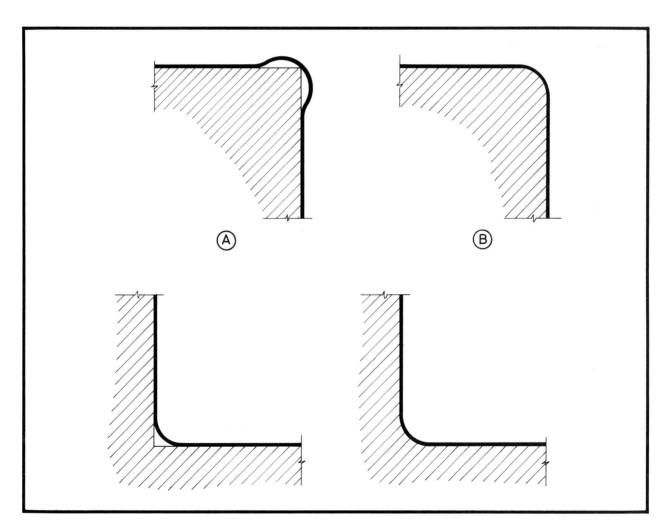

FIG. 12-10 — Fiberglass laminates cannot adhere to hard inside and outside corners as in 'A' without forming voids and air bubbles. When these occur, there is a loss of strength, and in most cases, adequate strength is more important at such points than in flatter areas. Hence, corners must have a sufficient radius, either by rounding outside corners or by building up inside corners, as shown in 'B'.

119

Place the mat on the hull surface in this folded position and use a brush to daub on resin liberally. Unfold the material onto the hull surface as each folded section is coated. Don't be fussy how you daub on the resin; just get it on liberally and quickly. Saturation of the mat at this point is not important. Tug on the mat to smooth out wrinkles and bunched areas, and then brush the exposed surface with more resin, pulling the mat to work out big wrinkles. The principle of this method is that it allows the underside of the mat to be saturated while at the same time saturating from the topside, and provides resin to help saturate the underside of the next woven roving layer which should be applied immediately over the mat. As the woven roving is unrolled over the mat, resin can be applied to the side of the woven roving that will mate to the mat in additional amounts so that less resin will be required over the top surface of the woven roving itself, helping to wet out the woven roving from the back side. Use a squeegee or mat roller to smooth out and saturate the woven roving layer.

On smaller areas such as transoms and other similar vertical surfaces, another technique can be used. Prefit the material and set aside, then coat the surface initially with resin. Lay on the first layer of mat and then apply more resin over it. The initial coat of resin helps hold the mat in place while the balance of the laminate is applied, and helps wet out the layers by working from the backside. Spring clamps or other devices can also be used in many cases to hold materials in place on vertical or inclined surfaces.

As can be seen from both of the foregoing techniques, it is always helpful (especially on heavier weight materials like woven roving) to apply the resin in such a way or sequence that the materials are being wetted out (or at least helped in this regard) from BOTH sides. Otherwise, the wetting out will have to be done from just the exposed or top side. This can slow the process considerably, and with heavier weight woven roving, can be tedious or even impractical.

In laminating with fiberglass materials, note that all layers must be totally saturated and wetted out with resin throughout the construction. All materials should be free of air entrapment and air bubbles. Use a mat roller to force out air bubbles and smooth out mat laminates. While it is almost impossible to get out all the little bubbles (those around $\frac{1}{8}$" or so can be neglected), make sure the big, obvious ones are eliminated. Use the squeegee for this purpose over woven roving or cloth, as well as for removing excess resin. Excess resin should be moved or squeegeed into areas of the laminate which appear white or resin-starved. If there is still more resin than can be used, remove it completely from the surface and discard it. A well-saturated laminate will appear totally transparent (assuming no pigment has been added to the resin).

It should be emphasized that fiberglass materials will not adhere to sharp corners, either inside or outside, without forming air bubbles underneath (see Fig. 12-10). These are caused because the materials lift from the surface, and for this reason, corners must be generously radiused so the material adheres to the surface. Round all outside corners with a disc sander or other suitable tools. On inside corners, these should be built up with resin putty filler fillets trowled and formed to suit and sanded as required, or install cant strips before applying the laminate.

If there is difficulty getting air out of an area, cut through it with a sharp knife and work it out while it is still wet. If the material is lifting around corners and trapping air, it means that the corner is too sharp and should have an easier radius. Or sometimes if not too severe, it can be worked out by continuous squeegeeing and daubing until the resin sets up a little. If the resin keeps draining or running down from upper to lower areas, and the laminate is transparent, it means that there is probably too much resin and the excess should be moved or removed. If a problem occurs in wetting out and moving resin around, and the resin is setting up before an area is fully saturated, try working a smaller area, decreasing the catalyst a bit, cooling the work area, or working in somewhat cooler temperatures.

In wetting out materials, keep fresh resin ahead of the squeegee at all times, pulling the squeegee in long parallel endless sweeps using firm pressure, and ending strokes in a swirl motion so that the squeegee does not leave the surface. Throughout the laminating process, work the materials as long as possible to prevent air bubbles and resin-rich or resin-starved areas from forming. Move the resin around constantly until an area is completely saturated, and on vertical surfaces, work the resin long enough so that it stays put and does not drain from such surfaces before saturation is complete. Make sure that ONLY laminating resin is being used in this process, and at least in the beginning, UNDER-catalyze the resin somewhat for a longer cure to minimize shrinkage and distortion from exothermic build-up, and to allow more working time until some experience has been gained. If you are totally inexperienced, start out on a small area first, such as the transom, and get a feel for the materials and how they handle.

As noted previously, ends of materials should not occur over such areas as the keel centerline, stem, or transom corners, but instead should lap well beyond these areas. For example, at the stem, lap a layer of material applied to one side onto the opposite side by 6″ or so, butting the next strip of material on this opposite side along the 6″ overlap. Then on the next layer, lap to the opposite side from this previous layer in a similar manner. Follow this approach on all subsequent layers, but vary the overlap locations so that butted joints do not occur in line with those below (see Fig. 12-6).

In many boats, extra reinforcement will be required at such areas as along the centerline, keel, stem, and transom corners. These are usually applied on the inside after the hull has been righted and removed from the mold. Here the materials can be overlapped since extra build-ups and appearance are not a problem. However, the ending points of materials should not occur at the same point; they should be staggered to form a tapered setback as shown by Fig. 12-11.

With some experience, it is usually practical to apply multiple layers of mat and woven roving in one operation; that is, apply a second or additional layers BEFORE the first has been allowed to cure. As mentioned in Chapter 5, there are combined mat and woven roving materials available that allow this operation using just a single material, having been specially developed for production situations. Applying multiple layers of mat and woven roving, or using one of these combination materials, is acceptable as long as the heat being generated during curing of the resin does not cause excessive shrinkage, distortion, or a weakness or brittleness in the laminate. This can be observed when the cured resin appears to be a darker brown with prevalent and numerous hairline cracks visible. Therefore, it is recommended that the resin be under catalyzed somewhat for this procedure, and the working conditions not too warm.

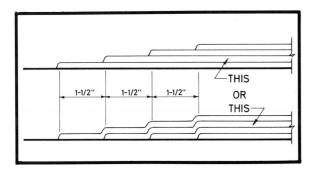

FIG. 12-11. — When additional laminates of multiple layers are subsequently applied, such as on the inside for extra strength or for secondary bonding purposes, the edges of the built-up area should not end abruptly or else a localized stress may be set up. Instead, stagger or offset the endings of layers in the laminate as shown, forming a tapered ending.

While fiberglass materials are somewhat difficult to cut or trim while wet, there is a point in the curing cycle of the resin that overhanging edges of materials can be easily cut with a sharp razor knife. Otherwise, after the resin cures, these will need to be ground with a disc sander or the laminate cut with a saw using either an abrasive cut-off disc or tungsten/carbide blade, since the fiberglass dulls most cutting edges quickly.

For those who have not worked with mat and woven roving, note that woven roving can be biased or worked around rather complex shapes; the material is usually fairly supple. But due to the resin binder holding the strands together, mat will not bias when it is dry. Mat can be cut or "gored" when it will not conform to a given surface in the "dry" state, but it is probably easier to wet the mat first which causes the binders to break down, making the mat more supple. The mat can then be "stretched" somewhat and worked around compound curves

easily, although ridges and wrinkles of excess material will still try to form. The mat can either be cut or gored, or simply torn and feathered in to get rid of any excess build up. The mat roller can then be used to remove entrapped air and wet out the material so it adheres in position properly.

While a long nap roller works well to apply resin over woven roving, it cannot be used repeatedly on mat since the resin will simply pull the mat apart. Daub or pour resin on the mat liberally, then use the mat roller to roll out the mat and get rid of entrapped air. Then immediately place the woven roving over the mat and use all the application tools necessary, making sure that the waffle pattern of the woven roving is well embedded into the cushiony felt of the mat.

If care is taken to prevent unfair build-ups of material, and each coat of resin applied over the woven roving is screeded or troweled off, a fair hull surface will result, mak-

FIG. 12-12 — A layer of mat is being applied over a C-FLEX laminate. The worker behind is coating the cured C-FLEX surface with resin which will help wet out the mat from the backside (note the mat draped back and ready for laying onto the wet surface). The strip of mat in the foreground has already been laid down and the worker here is rolling it out from the topside.

FIG. 12-13 — The mat is rolled out prior to applying the next layer which will be woven roving in this conventional layup. A layer of woven roving has already been applied to the right. Note that the mat is quite smooth (no bubbles or wrinkles) and not overly wet.

FIG. 12-14 — Woven roving is applied over the wet mat, which helps wet out the material from the backside. The worker at the right is applying more resin with a roller to completely wet out the woven roving. Troweling or squeegeeing of the surface will be done next to smooth out the laminate, provide even resin distribution, and adequate pressure for a proper glass content without defects. While the worker is cutting the length of woven roving, final trimming of edges can be done later.

FIG. 12-15 — With most larger boats, laminates are applied across the hull as is being done here over a C-FLEX hull. Note the stiffness of the mat due to the binders in the material. This quickly disappears once resin is applied. Torn edges along the mat would be technically preferable as pointed out in this chapter. However, if there is a sufficient number of layers, and joints are staggered, strength will probably be adequate.

FIG. 12-16 — Woven roving is applied over the mat (the mat can be seen at the bottom of the photo). Note the roller extension which allows the worker to reach all areas of the hull.

FIG. 12-17 — Excess resin is removed and distributed with a wide trowel or drywall knife used over the woven roving. Note that joints in the woven roving are barely noticeable.

ing the final surface finishing much easier. A proper resin-to-glass content in laminates is important since this is what largely determines the final weight and strength characteristics of the hull. That's why as little resin as possible should be used.

Although the foregoing has been referring generally to woven roving, some boats, especially smaller ones, may use cloth in place of woven roving, but the methods for handling it parallel those used for woven roving. Also, as noted, mat is used between layers of woven roving for purposes of interlaminar bonding. While layers of woven roving are best separated by layers of mat, there is no reason why layers of mat cannot be applied directly adjacent to each other if the occasion arises.

However, in some designs where light weight is important, or a higher glass content is desired, the layer of mat between woven roving layers is sometimes omitted

LAMINATING RESIN TROUBLE SHOOTING

Listed below are some of the more common (not all) laminate problems.

PROBLEM	CAUSE	ITEMS TO CHECK
Soft spots	Unmixed catalyst	Was catalyst added and stirred into all resin batches?
Hot spots	Overcatalyzing	Reduce catalyst content.
	Resin-rich areas	Reduce resin content, & work resin more carefully.
	Unbalanced laminate	Check thickness for uniformity.
Dry glass area	Resin too thin.	Use higher thixotrope resin.
	Long gel time	Increase catalyst where allowed, check temperature.
Voids	Entrapped air	Poor rollout, wrong type of glass; resin-starved areas, resin viscosity high; filler level high; resin drainout.
Glass pickup on roller	Rolling near gelation	Adjust gel time.
	Styrene evaporation	Dip rollers in styrene or fresh catalyzed resin.
	Rolling too fast	More deliberate rolling.
	Too high % glass	Increase resin
	Dirty rollers	Change solvent
Resin crack	Too hot	Resin puddles, excessive catalyst; resin too high in exotherm
Warpage of parts	Unbalanced laminate	Use symmetrical lay-up.
		Mix in catalyst well; reduce % catalyst, resin puddles; moist glass.
Delamination	From gel coat	Dust on gel coat; gel coat cured too long; mold release buildup dissolved by gel coat; used enamel instead of gel coat.
	Between laminate	Poor impregnation, resin rich; wax in resin, weak resin, check grade and physicals.
	Cloth from cloth or woven roving from woven roving	Use mat or chopped between
	Uncured	Check % catalyst, temperature.
Poor wetting	Viscosity too high – glass type or wet	Check glass type and for moisture, add up to 3% styrene.
Long gel time		Check % catalyst and type, temperature, laminate too thin.
Slow cure		Check % catalyst and type, temperature, laminate thickness.

in professional practice. In place of the mat, a resin filler paste made up of milled glass fibers is brushed between layers to assure a positive interlaminar bond and make up for the lack of mat. Such a filler must include enough glass fibers to achieve a high enough percentage of glass content necessary for strength, and to keep the resin layer from being overly resin-rich. Yet such a layer should not be overly thick, and because of these rather precise requirements, the amateur is advised to use mat instead in the conventional laminate to assure positive results.

In most cases, the last layer in a laminate over a male mold will be mat, although in some smaller boats, this could be cloth. The mat layer provides a sanding and fairing base or "buffer" that will prevent damaging the structural portion of the laminate (the woven roving directly below the mat) when finish work begins. It also provides a more watertight "seal" or covering for the hull and prevents moisture from "wicking" along the strands of rovings which could occur if the outer layer was woven roving.

The final resin coat in the last layer of laminate on a male mold boat should be a resin containing wax or surfacing agent if the final finish will be fair enough to require little, if any, filling. Otherwise, if a filler coat will be required, use regular laminating resin preferably. Remember, however,

FIG. 12-18 — Note the spring clamps used to hold this length of woven roving in position while the worker wets out the material on the inside of this hull.

that if any sanding or grinding is required at all, it will be difficult to do over laminating resin and will cause the sanding medium to load up quickly. At this point, the hull is ready for finishing.

CHAPTER 13

finishing

Finishing techniques and methods will vary depending on the materials used to build the hull, the manner in which the hull was built, the degree of quality and durability of finish desired, and the care that was exercised in building up the laminate during the construction process. For example, if the boat has been built in a female mold using a gel coat against the mold surface, the hull will be virtually complete. There will be no need for additional finishing work unless you wish to apply a paint coating over the gel coat, or some minor gel coat "touch up" work is necessary.

However, if the hull has been built using one of the male mold methods, there will be some finishing and fairing work required in order to have a hull surface that is equal to that which comes out of the female mold. If you have been careful in the application of your laminate, the work at this point will be minimized to a considerable extent. In most cases, however, a fair amount of work will be required in finishing and fairing to make the hull have a surface free of deviation and distortion; in other words, a "yacht-like" finish.

This finish work is not especially complicated or difficult, but it can be tedious, especially if your hull surfaces are not as fair and smooth as they could be. This is why we have stressed throughout the construction procedures in building with male mold methods to take care in the building process to keep things fair. Although just about any unfairness can be corrected by the addition of mat or filler coats to low areas, this practice should be kept to a minimum since such build-ups just add weight, increase the brittleness of the exterior surface, and add

to the work and expense.

The first question most builders will have is just how fair is fair enough? This is certainly a value judgement, but an easy way to check fairness (other than the obvious humps and dips) is to sight along the hull so that highlights become obvious. Strong sunlight or a portable light source used at night are good ways to highlight the hull and spot irregularities. Fairing battens across the hull surfaces at a variety of points will help pinpoint high and low areas that may not at first be obvious.

With most conventional laminates, you will end off with a lightweight mat, or by what is sometimes called a "surface veil", another name for a very thin mat layer. As noted before, the mat layer provides a good sanding and grinding base to prevent damage to the underlying structural reinforcement, which is usually woven roving. The mat layer also acts as a moisture barrier for the hull, since contrary to common belief, fiberglass itself is hygroscopic; that is, it will absorb some moisture. However, if using high modulus materials for the hull skin, as are discussed in Chapter 21, this mat layer is usually deleted and other techniques are used, which will be covered later.

The final mat layer can be applied using a finish resin (or resin containing wax) if sanding and grinding will be done directly on this layer. Otherwise, a laminating resin is preferable since the filler coat will bond better to laminating resin. Use either a clear or a pigmented resin in this coat as you wish. The main reason to use a pigmented resin is to form a base coat or undercoat of a similar color as that which will be used for the final paint coat. This will make any surface abrasions and wear less noticeable, however, the use of pigment will interfere with your ability to tell how much resin is being applied and how many bubbles or other flaws there are in the mat layer as it is wet out. The choice of using pigment in this coat then is up to the builder. But because the surface may require a fair amount of sanding and grinding, the use of pigment in the final coats is otherwise a waste of time and money, since the final surface will require painting regardless.

MALE MOLD FINISHING TECHNIQUES

The main consideration in preparing the surface for final finish is to provide a surface which can be sanded, smoothed, and finished with a minimum of effort. Building up the surface with straight resin and sanding until the surface is smooth is NOT the easiest method, although it could be done this way if desired. The problem with this approach is that the surface will be more brittle, heavier, and costly. Such a practice also is usually only practical if the underlying

surface is already relatively fair since resin alone cannot effectively fill in and build up low spots.

One finishing technique that can be used is applicable to smaller boats where the final layer in the laminate is a lightweight cloth, say 4 oz. to 10 oz. material, and where surface irregularities have been kept to a minimum. Such a situation is shown in Chapter 19. The cloth is laid up over mat that is still wet with resin. A squeegee is used over the cloth, using considerable pressure over high spots and less pressure over low areas, attempting to get the surface as smooth and even as possible. Working over the cloth in this manner will allow the underlying mat to be smoothed easily without tearing it to shreds, which would be the case if the cloth were not used. As an alternate, a grooved mat roller could be used, but a squeegee gives a better "feel" for the surface. Then a coat of finish resin can be applied to the cloth after this first coat cures.

The surface is lightly sanded to remove the wax, being careful not to cut through the weave of the cloth to any extent. It is not necessary for the weave of the cloth to be

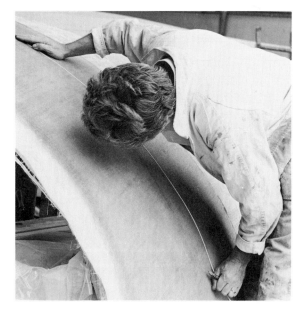

FIG. 13-1 — The builder is checking the surface for fairness by using a single stripped rod of C-FLEX.

FIG. 13-2 — High and low areas can be marked for grinding and filling.

completely concealed since the surface is next built up by spraying a high-build, high-chalk primer or undercoat that can be tinted to match the final paint color to be used. This primer is used to build up the surface and conceal all minor flaws, including the cloth weave. The surface is sanded down just as would be done in any paint primer application prior to the first coat. The whole premise of this method is that it is easier to sand primer than it is to sand resin, and the primer may be cheaper and easier to apply. The final paint coating is then applied after sanding the primer coat smooth and fair.

In the preceding method, a finish resin or laminating resin with wax added is used because the final paint coating will be applied to this resin. While it may be possible to use some paints directly over a surface coated with laminating resin, there have been problems reported which makes this approach questionable. Paint flaking, peeling, and bubbling are some of the results of this practice. The probable reason is that the laminating resin does not completely cure, allowing the resin to "creep" or move. This lack of a stable base under the paint can cause finish problems when the paint is applied over laminating resins that technically do not cure, or at least cure very slowly, unlike finish resins. However, when using finish resin or resin with wax, the surface must be sanded BEFORE applying paint coatings in order to remove the wax so that the paint will adhere.

RESIN PUTTY FILLER COATS

With most boats built by male mold methods, however, a different approach is required to finish off the hull. Since the surface will seldom be perfectly smooth and fair, it will need to be built up with a material that is easy to sand and apply. This is where resin putty filler coats enter the picture. A resin putty filler coat, or "troweling

compound" as it is sometimes called, is much like a thin plaster coating. This material can be made from several additives or fillers such as talc, silica, or microspheres, either separately or in combination in resin as noted in Chapter 7.

Talc or silica by themselves, however, make hard, brittle, dense, and heavy fillers that are not as easy to sand as they could be. Microspheres extends the resin while decreasing its weight and density. They give the resin strength and go a long way to make the surface easier to sand. They are, however, more costly than talc or silica. Where light weight is important, the microspheres should be used alone in the resin. But if weight is not so critical, equal volumes of microspheres and talc can be mixed to a fairly thick, plaster-like consistency. This mix, while somewhat heavy, is easy to trowel on and sand, and does increase the abrasion resistance of the coating, which can be important for some boats, such as commercial types which are often abused in service.

FIG. 13-3 — Obvious high spots (areas of excessive resin buildup) are ground down on the laminate before applying filler coats. Take care NOT to grind into the fiberglass material excessively, especially if of a woven material.

If you have built up your final layer in the laminate with mat and wetted this out with a finish resin, the surface must be sanded PRIOR to applying the resin putty filler coat. If laminating resin has been used, apply the resin putty filler coat directly to the surface. The resin putty filler is used to build up low areas to make the surface fair. If high spots exist in the laminate, it means that the rest of the surface has to be built up to the same level as the high spots to have a fair hull. However, by sanding the high spots in the final mat layer FIRST, you can reduce the discrepancy between the high and low areas, thereby reducing the amount of filler applied, which in turn reduces the cost, effort, and weight to achieve a suitable exterior finish. The only drawback is that grinding directly on the mat/resin surface is harder than on the filler surface, especially if laminating resin has been used in the final coat. After sanding and grinding on this mat layer, the surface should be coated with a flood coat of finish resin to reseal the glass fibers against moisture absorption, and allowed to cure for the application of the resin putty filler coat which can be applied after

light sanding to remove any wax.

The trick with applying resin putty fillers is to apply as thin a coat as possible, and yet get enough on to make for a smooth and even surface once sanded. It is always possible to add more resin putty filler as required, however, thick unreinforced layers can become brittle and crack, and perhaps chip off at a later date. Pigment can be added to fill coats if desired, but this tends to complicate things. However, not all microsphere products lend themselves to pigmentation since some have colors of their own, negating or changing the color of the pigment once it is mixed in.

The consistency of the resin putty filler coat is a hard thing to describe. The filler should be easy to mix. It should be smooth and creamy so that it will trowel on well, but it should not run or sag on vertical or inclined surfaces. Because there are so many different fillers and combinations, try starting off with a batch with 20% filler by weight of resin. If you are not sure of this "mix" and are a beginner, start off on a small area, like the transom, where you can get a "feel" for the mix and yet not get

FIG. 13-4 — A wide trowel or screed can be used to apply the resin putty filler coat.

FIG. 13-5 — The worker is using a "Foamglas" block on the surface after the resin putty filler coat has set up.

yourself into trouble.

As on all areas of the hull, apply the filler coat with a wide trowel, putty knife, or dry-wall knife; in other words, a tool about 6" to 12" wide, or wider once you feel you can handle bigger areas. Some prefer to use a notched trowel like those used to spread linoleum adhesive, or an old saw blade. The reason is that the serrated edge of the tool gives the surface alternating high and low streaks which make it easier to tell just how much material is being removed when sanding, and how much should be removed to get as thin a coat as practical. This tends to make the sanding easier with less guess-work, partly because less material is sanded since you are only hitting the ridges of the streaks. Others advise tinting the putty in alternate applications in different colors. The reason is that this shows how much coating has been sanded away by the change in color. The builder is advised to try these different techniques and judge for himself what he prefers.

In applying the resin putty filler, start at higher areas and work downward in long, sweeping strokes. For example, start at the keel or centerline, and work toward the shear across the hull. It will take a couple of batches of filler before the "right" consistency and resin/catalyst mix are established. Try for a gel time of about 15 to 20 minutes; this will allow you to start sanding and smoothing the surface relatively soon after applying the filler. However, for thick coats, a slower gel time may be preferable to minimize heat build-up and shrinkage. There is a point in the resin cure cycle when the resin has not cured completely (the resin is said to be still "green"), and it is much easier to sand. The sandpaper cuts much faster at this point with less effort than if the resin is allowed to cure completely, and does not tend to clog up the paper as quickly as if the resin had not cured long enough. Instead of coming off as dust, the resin tends to "ball up" instead.

When a batch of resin putty begins to set up, throw it away and start with a fresh mix to prevent dragging around lumps in the resin which will just impede progress. Pre-mix several containers, adding catalyst prior to using them. You'll soon get to the point where you can carefully judge how much resin to mix up and apply at a time to minimize any sort of waste.

SANDING AND FAIRING THE FILLER COAT

Sand and grind the surface as the work progresses, using a disc sander with a #24 to #50 grit disc fitted with a pad and/or flexible disc plate to prevent gouging the surface. Some workers use a plywood disc they make themselves, about 12" in diameter instead of a pad. This is attached to the disc sander (a slow-speed type is preferable), and a sheet of sandpaper bonded to this. The plywood disc prevents gouging of the surface and is easy to handle. Don't try to sand too soon as the paper will clog quickly; yet don't wait too long either since the surface will get too hard. Mark high spots with a pencil or marker, and grind them down. Mark low areas similarly and apply more filler as required. In some areas a belt sander may be preferred by some workers, and this tool can be used alternately. Fill and fair a section at a time rather than applying the resin putty filler to the entire hull at once (except on the smallest of boats); this will make sanding and grinding easier.

Sight along the hull frequently, using highlights from direct sunlight or a portable light fixture to spot unfair areas. Spring a fairing batten over the hull surfaces at several points to find humps and dips in the surface. Sand or add more filler as required, but remember that the filler coat should be kept thin. If you can see that the resin putty filler coat is going to have to be overly thick, an additional layer of lightweight cloth, or mat applied locally, may be required, especially in low areas, in order to reinforce the mixture. However, the filler does not wet out these materials as easily as straight resin, so watch the mixing consistency IF this practice is required. Or you can add mat patches saturated with resin first before applying the resin putty filler coat. Hopefully, your surface will be true enough to avoid this added weight, work, and expense.

One technique for fairing that works well is to sand the filler coat with blocks of "Foamglas". This material makes a self-cleaning abrasive and can be cut into sanding blocks of a convenient size. When used like sanding blocks on the hull, they reduce the high areas without digging into the low areas. An ordinary clothing dye mixed with acetone and sprayed onto the hull before using the blocks allows the high areas to remain obvious as these spots are sanded down.

For final sanding and finishing on the resin putty filler coat, disc and belt sanders can be used, but their sanding areas are so small that it takes exceptional skill to get an extra smooth and fair final surface over a large area without indiscriminately reducing both high and low spots. Instead, hand

FIG. 13-6 — Using a foam-backed sanding disc for fairing is one way to prevent gouging the filler coated surface.

sanding tools, such as long sanding boards, or large pieces of "Foamglas", can be used. Sanding boards can be made by the builder by gluing strips of sandpaper to long boards about 3' to 5' long. The "Foamglas" blocks also work well, with about a 2' piece being good for alternately spanning low spots while taking down high spots. The "Foamglas" has just enough flexibility to shape itself to the contours of the hull. Sanding boards are generally not as flexible and there is always the problem of the sandpaper tending to load up.

In the final sanding, there is the choice of completely sanding the surface to a high degree of smoothness, working gradually to ever-finer grades of sandpaper, and ending off with a wet-or-dry type for the ultimate in a smooth finish. Or the surface can be smoothed out with sanding boards or with "Foamglas", and then sprayed with a high-build, high-chalk type primer undercoat, then sanded to a fairly high degree of smoothness, but letting the final quality of surface be determined by the coating system used; it all depends on the quality of finish desired and the amount of work that one is willing to undertake.

With either method, when sanding, if you penetrate through the filler surface, you should stop. The resin and mat below abrade at different rates than the filler coat, and if sanding is continued, unfair sections would start to be formed, just complicating the task. If there are any remaining low spots, these should be filled and faired as required.

GEL COATS OVER MALE MOLDED HULLS

Many novices are convinced that gel coats are the BEST way to finish their boats no matter how they are built. They have heard that fiberglass boats use gel coats and that this is largely the basis for their low-maintenance requirements. They also want that "popped-out-of-the-mold" look common to boats made in female molds using gel coated surfaces. Thus, the amateur wants these same "benefits" even when the hull is built with male mold methods. However, there are some misconceptions involved.

Probably the most important point is that, unless applied against the surface of a mold, a gel coat resin is basically just another polyester resin. It is the finely polished surface of the mold which gives that smooth, glossy finish to the gel coat, and in the male molded hull, this condition does not exist. In order to develop a smooth high surface sheen like that found in female molded hulls, considerable sanding, buffing, and polishing will have to be done on the gel coated surface. This is more work and effort than other finishes discussed. Gel coat resins have no surface building capabilities such as high-build primers or resin putty filler coats. Hence, they will not smooth out surface discrepancies, which means they would be suitable only over a VERY smooth surface if no filler coats were used.

Furthermore, gel coat resins are generally air-inhibited types that stay tacky, which is necessary in their normal use in female molds. If gel coats are used as the final exterior coating over a male molded hull, surfacing agent must be mixed in to lock out the air in order for the resin to cure completely.

Even if a high quality gel coat surface is produced over the male mold, the gel coated surface will probably not be as durable as some of the modern coatings. As noted elsewhere, some fiberglass boat manufacturers use these paint systems EVEN FOR THOSE BOATS BUILT IN FEMALE MOLDS WITH GEL COATS. Just like all polyester resins (although gel coats are somewhat better than ordinary types), they discolor, fade, chalk, yellow with age, and lose their luster to the point that eventually painting, or at least polishing and waxing will be required to restore their original gloss. They simply don't hold up as well under exposure to the sun and other elements found in the marine environment, although current gel coats have been much improved over the years.

The modern paint systems hold their gloss better, retain their color longer, often have better moisture resistance, and are tougher and more durable. Although perhaps more expensive, the paint systems have built-in gloss without the need of the mold surface. Their resistance to chalking, chemicals, and corrosion is also superior.

Application conditions with gel coats are very critical. Temperature, humidity, and draft control requirements should be strictly adhered to in order to prevent questionable or variable results. A uniform coating to a specified thickness is also important and difficult to maintain in the male mold situation. While modern coating systems may be equally critical in application, the difference is that the coating once applied is finished. But with gel coats, additional finish work will still be required when applied over the male molded hull. Thus, gel coat application over male molded boats, while it can be done, is probably more work and the results not as desirable as other approaches.

PAINTING

In today's technology, the terminology "paint" is virtually out of date. Instead, modern paints are really coating systems that may require a very specific "menu" of products as well as sequence of procedures to complete the final finish. While the more traditional paint systems may still be available (and no doubt probably much improved over the years), the newer paint systems are more like plastic coatings, such as the acrylic, epoxy, and urethane types.

With paint systems, it seems that you get about what you are willing to pay for; the more expensive the product, the better they seem to perform and the longer they last. At this stage of development, the two-part urethane coatings probably offer the best qualities of exceptional gloss retention, durability, absence of fading, chalking, peeling, crazing, and chipping, and resistance to all the adverse elements encountered in a marine environment.

But they ARE expensive, at least in relation to cheaper marine enamel systems, and many cannot be used below the waterline. Yet unlike most enamels, they will probably last for several more years before having to be repainted. Hence, the cost is a relative factor which must be compared to the life of the coating, frequency of application, etc. You should consider all the cost factors which apply to your situation. For example, if your boat is a large size that requires a yard for hauling out, this is a cost that must be considered, and in theory, a paint that lasts longer may require poten-

tially fewer haul-outs than a paint that is less durable.

In applying any paint systems, always follow the instructions provided with the products TO THE LETTER! Do NOT mix products from different manufacturers, including interchanging of thinners and solvents, except on the advice of experts. With many products, ambient conditions with regard to temperature, humidity, and the like are extremely critical. If the manufacturer recommends a spray application, don't attempt to apply with a brush or roller, or vice versa.

Be religious with regard to surface preparation, and after the job is done, don't launch the boat until the manufacturer advises. If problems develop with your paint system, don't be afraid to contact the manufacturer; most paint companies have very competent technical staffs, and because of

FIG. 13-7 — This "one-off" male molded hull was built by an amateur using the FERRO-GLASS system. The high quality of the finish, as shown by the reflection of the trailer frame onto the hull, is every bit as good as that which results from a female mold.

the competition in the business, they are anxious for you to have excellent results so that you'll speak kindly about their products to other potential users. But don't blame them for your mistakes!

As far as what paint system to use, particularly with regard to anti-fouling bottom paints, it is always best to inquire locally in the areas where the boat will be moored in order to tell what product is having the greatest or least success on comparable boats in the same situation. A paint system that works well in one location may not perform so well in another (often in spite of what the paint company says!). If in doubt about being able to do a competent job in painting your boat, then it may be desirable to hire a professional, especially if sophisticated equipment is necessary for the appli-

cation. This could be cheaper in the long run, assuming you do all the preparation work.

Apply the final paint coat only after all exterior appendages, such as rub rails, etc., have been fitted and positioned (although not necessarily fastened in place) to avoid marring the surface. If the deck has not yet been installed, and there will be a deck laminate of fiberglass that will bond to the hull, such as along the sheer, mask a strip a few inches or so below the sheer line in order to keep paint off the fiberglass hull in this area so that the deck laminate can bond to the hull.

The following is a general description of the procedures and system of one of the popular two-part urethane systems to give an idea of what is involved in a coating

FIG. 13-8 — Surface finish quality equal to this male molded "one-off" C-FLEX hull can be achieved by most amateurs as long as the laminating and finishing procedures described in the text are followed. One would be hard-pressed to tell this hull from one built in the factory.

system application as condensed from the manufacturer's literature:

"No finish is any better than the surface to which it is applied. The surface should be clean and dry, with a solvent wipe recommended BEFORE final sanding or painting is done to be sure any waxes, body oils, mold release agents, or hydrocarbons are removed. Don't let these solvents evaporate; wipe them dry with a clean rag. All surfaces should be tack-ragged (specially treated lint-free cloths available in paint stores) with the products recommended by the manufacturer.

"The area surrounding the boat should be clean and dust-free. Working or ambient temperatures should be from 60 to 80 degrees, with 75 degrees ideal. Although high humidity is desirable, but NOT essential to this product, surface moisture in the form of rain, fog, or dew within the first eight hours after application can result in a loss of gloss. Precise mixing of all the products used is critical, so follow the label carefully on each item in the system.

"Application equipment must be clean. Two thin coats of paint are better than a single thick one; attempting to apply too thick a coat can result in runs and sags. Prime the surface with the recommended primer, taking care to see that all pinholes and porous areas are filled. Sand with fine sandpaper and wipe this surface with tack rags, then apply the final finish. Allow seven days for complete cure, and 24 hours before removing masking tape. Recoat within 36 hours without sanding first. If more than 36 hours transpire before recoating, sand the surface lightly between coats."

Hulls that are built over male molds, or upsidedown, must be righted to complete the balance of the construction. Before removing any hull from a male mold, the position of all bulkheads, floors (*), etc., should be marked to the inside of the hull. If possible, locations for shelf tops, cabin soles, berth tops, countertops, seat tops, and especially the horizontal reference plane and centerline, should also be marked. It is easier and more accurate if this is done BEFORE removing the male mold. With open-battened molds, make marks as best you can between the battens, frames, etc., with a permanent marker.

Two variations can be used in righting the hull; either righting the hull together with the male mold (including the building form as well), or removing the hull from the mold and righting it by itself. This latter approach is not preferred, especially in the case of sandwich core hulls where the inner laminate has not been installed, since the hull will be so "floppy" that it may distort out of shape. Also, it will not be possible to use the building form as a reference to re-level the hull when it is right side up.

Whichever way is used, the hull will have to be supported once it is set upright. The hull can be righted and set into a matching cradle, or the cradle can be built onto the outside of the hull and righted with the hull. This latter approach is preferred, especially with sandwich core hulls, since the cradle and mold will help keep the hull from distorting.

Whichever is the case, supporting cradles should be made directly from the hull be-

(*) See Chapter 27 for definition of "floors"

fore righting while it is upsidedown. These supports can be made from any suitable scrap lumber similar to the transverse frames used to build the mold. Use at least two such forms for smaller boats, or more for bigger boats, to prevent movement. Although single skin fiberglass boats may seem to be quite strong at this point, they still should have support.

All fiberglass boats, especially sandwich core boats, tend to be weak before the deck is installed, especially around the sheer area. This area can be reinforced by adding good sized wood battens fastened or clamped along the sheer area. These battens can be made up in laminations to suit the curves and to make the required lengths. Another, or perhaps, additional method is to add spreaders across the sheer from side to side, fitted with blocks at the ends which hook over the sheer corresponding to the widths port and starboard at their respective locations to match the widths taken from the loftings or full size patterns. These spreaders will keep the sheer from springing out of shape until some of the interior bulkheads have been installed. However, to be accurate, the hull must be prevented from distorting BEFORE the spreaders have been fitted.

SUPPORTING CRADLES

In making cradles, use the full size patterns or the body plan loftings, or make templates directly from the hull surface. Whichever method is used, cut them slightly oversize; that is, larger than the respective station contour. Place strips of parting film over the hull where the cradle supports will be positioned. Then use scrap pieces of foam or strips of carpet taped in place over the parting film strips, and saturate the exposed surface (the carpet backing in the case of the carpet strips) with resin and several layers of mat. Place the cradle supports over these strips and use bonding angles of mat and/or woven roving or cloth to secure the cradle supports to the foam or carpet.

The cradle supports should be sized and shaped to support the sheer, chine, and keel areas as required to suit the design, and should be made to allow the hull to be re-leveled once righted. All cradle members should be joined to form a rigid platform for the balance of the project. In the case of boats with long, straight, horizontal lines, the cradle supports can be made lengthwise using the same principles. If the boat is a trailerable type, the best supporting cradle of all will be the actual trailer that will be used to transport the boat. Even still, you may want to add extra temporary cradle supports to keep the hull rigid until the deck and/or cabin has been installed.

RIGHTING METHODS

The methods used to right the hull will vary with the size and weight of the hull, the amount of manpower available, equipment available, and other factors such as space, intruding power lines, etc. On smaller boats, it's just a matter of having enough people to do the job with manpower alone. Boats up to above 25' long can usually be handled in this manner. Note that boats in this size range at this stage of construction are usually not as heavy as they may seem; just bulky, ungainly, and awkward.

On larger hulls, a series of blocks and tackle arrangements, or large "A"-frames, or chain hoists with slings, or a small crane, can be used. The means and devices used to right the hull seem to be limited only by the imaginations of the various builders. Consequently, there is no preferred method or "best" way; only what works for you. Therefore, the methods described in the following should not be considered as the ONLY ways to right a hull. These are merely some of the suggested ways which have

FIG. 14-1 — Righting cradles can be built from any scrap lumber. The carpet padding used to conform to the hull contours is made stiff and bonded to the cradles with mat saturated with resin. The cradles are tied together fore and aft and the corners have been radiused. Chain hoists are attached to the rafters of the building shed.

FIG. 14-2 — Righting the hull shown in Fig. 14-1 has been done virtually within the width of the hull. Note the clamps holding wood members at the sheer and the spreaders across the hull for rigidity. These are a "must" for a sandwich cored hull (such as this AIREX cored boat) if the hull is righted without the male mold.

evolved over past years. They may not be the best or most suitable way for each and every type or size of boat.

In selecting a method to right the hull, always keep in mind that lifting the boat up to turn it is usually the simpler part of the task. It is the lowering of the hull down once it has been flipped over where the most care and effort must be taken. On most boats, there are limited ways of holding onto, or securing the hull as it comes down right side up. Most first-timers are admittedly nervous about this task, but if it will put their minds to rest, MOST boats are righted without problems as long as everything is well planned.

The typical procedures for righting a boat with just manpower alone is to have plenty of room to one side. With the cradles attached, just "roll" the boat over to the upright position, which is easier to do if the cradles have radiused corners. A series of old tires can be used to cushion the load of the boat as it it momentarily supported along the sheer area if contact with the floor or ground seems likely.

Gather together as many people as possible for this "rolling" ceremony, perhaps providing plenty of beer and "eats" to get everyone enthused and to relieve the anxiety. Line everyone up on the side opposite the clear area and lift the boat up to where it is teetering on edge. Then leaving just a few people to stabilize the hull in this position, have everyone run around to the other side and let the hull down slowly and cautiously.

A second, but similar, method can be

FIG. 14-3 — A series of chain hoists are being used to lift and right this AIREX sandwich cored hull. Note the attachment points bonded onto the hull which will later be removed. This is the hull shown under construction in Fig. 19-13 and Fig. 19-14.

used on larger hulls. All elements are similar, but instead of using manpower, a light crane is substituted. The crane controls the lifting and the rolling procedure all along, even though some manpower must be used to properly guide the hull. While the use of a crane may seem extravagant, the time required is only a short period, and the safety and control where a large craft is concerned is usually worth the money, especially if helpers are not available.

As a precautionary note, some sailboat hulls may have ballast installed in or on the hull before it is righted. When righting a hull of this type, considerable care must be taken because of the leverage such ballast will exert. Once such a hull reaches a certain position, the leverage arm of the ballast could quickly "snap" the boat over and cause quite a hazardous situation. Therefore, some means of control, such as check

lines to the keel, or keel bracing, or other shock dampening devices should be provided to restrain this action.

Another method of righting a hull is to use a series of blocks and tackle from a gin pole (see Fig. 14-7). The pole must be long enough for the tackle to reach beyond the beam of the boat when it is on edge. The gin pole is erected approximately at amidships on one side of the hull. The tackle is hooked to a sling around the hull that cannot slip. The pole must be supported with guy wires to the sides so it will not fall. As the hull is gradually lifted, it must be pulled toward the pole to allow it to come down in about the same area as when it was upsidedown. Depending on the size and weight of the boat, several helpers could be required, both to control the tackle, and to guide the hull. The more parts forming the tackle, the easier the tackle will lift the hull, but the

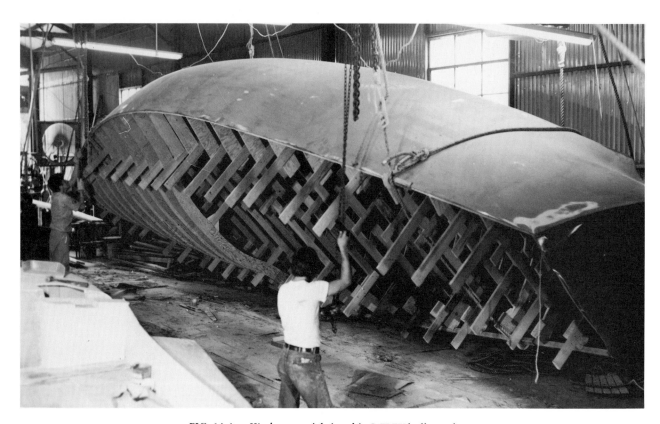

FIG. 14-4 — Workers are righting this C-FLEX hull together with the male mold which will be removed later. Again, the hull can be righted in virtually its own width if necessary.

slower the tackle will travel through the blocks. On heavier boats, it would be possible to use two such arrangements side by side; however, this could take even more manpower.

A method that can be used, especially on a heavier hull where limited manpower is available, is to jack one edge of the hull up progressively. Use braces to hold the boat on edge while shifting the jack up on supports as the limit of each jack is reached. Once the boat is on edge, use guy lines,

FIG. 14-5 — This C-FLEX hull is being righted with a small crane. The male mold members are still in position to keep the hull true and rigid against the force of the slings. Notice the transverse "ribs" or battens showing through the hull that supported the C-FLEX initially.

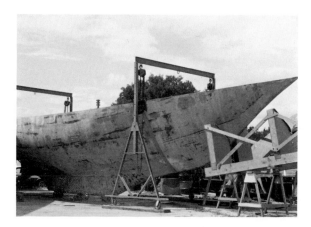

FIG. 14-6 — Gantries with chain hoists can be used to right a hull, and these are often available on a rental basis. Setting the hull onto a supporting cradle with this arrangement for the balance of construction is easy.

preferably from each end of the boat, and connect these to the trailer hitch of a car, or to a good, stout bumper on a pick-up truck.

Locate the vehicle at right angles to the hull approximately amidships so the guy lines form approximate 45 degree angles with the boat's centerline. The guy lines support the hull on edge, and then the vehicle can be slowly backed towards the hull to let the hull down on the right side. Care should be taken to ease the fall of the hull and to prevent it from "scooting out" along the bottom as it is lowered. Obviously, with this method, there must be considerable room to one side for the vehicle to maneuver in.

Finally, a novel method that has been used by some builders is to treat the hull like a hunk of meat on a barbeque rotisserie. Scaffolding is erected at each end of the hull which is somewhat higher than the half-width of the hull. The hull is raised off the ground to a height equal to just slightly more than the half-beam. A length of pipe of robust size is spanned between the scaffolds under the hull from bow to stern, being securely anchored to the hull at several points to form a "spit" about which the hull is then rotated. Lines attached to either side are used to tip the boat and to control the speed of the roll. On heavy hulls, a series of blocks and tackle can be used for greater leverage. After the hull is righted, it is then lowered down for the balance of the construction.

On some sailboats which have external-type ballast keels, the hull and ballast keel unit are built separately. When the hull is righted, it must be set onto the ballast keel unit. When this is the case, the hull can be righted by just about any of the means described. However, it must be raised high enough to be set onto the keel unit. In some cases, this will be complicated by keel bolts that may have to pass through the hull at rather precise points. This will require that the hull be lifted even higher. While it may be possible to jack such a hull to this height, in most cases a light crane is preferable, since aligning the hull exactly in position can be more carefully and easily done, besides being much safer. One way to simplify the problem, however, is to set the ballast keel into a hole dug in the ground, or to even cast the keel in this position at the site, which will save a lot of work in moving the ballast keel around.

Regardless of the manner used to right the hull, it must be releveled once right side up for the balance of construction, and held in this position securely to prevent movement. When this has been done, a standard builder's level and framing square can be used to complete the interior members to assure that they are true and accurate. A

taut line or wire should also be fastened in position to designate the centerline from bow to stern. If the waterline has been struck and is true, this can be used to level the hull using lengths of clear plastic hose filled with water, one in the fore and aft direction, and another athwartships.

One last item concerns whether or not the hull should be completely finished and painted before the righting. This depends on the size of the boat as well as on a few other factors that may vary from boat to boat. For example, it matters little with smaller boats whether they are painted before or after righting, since they can be readily flipped over upsidedown again with relative ease, if necessary. While it is easiest to paint

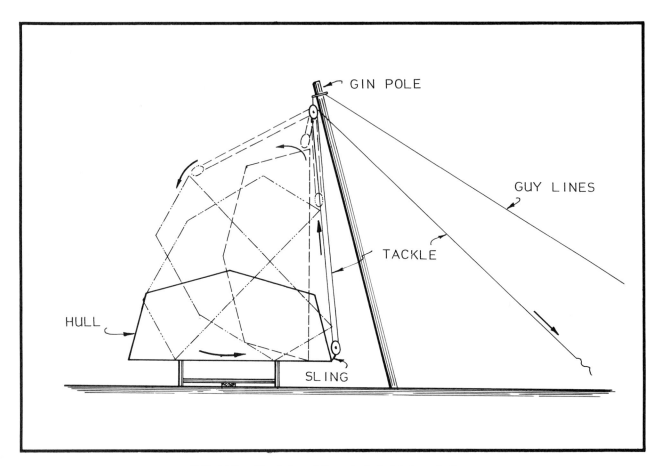

FIG. 14-7 — The "gin pole" method of righting a hull as described in the text using a block and tackle system. A supporting cradle used for the balance of the construction can be built around the hull prior to righting.

boats when they are upsidedown, there is always a chance that something will come up that was forgotten, and interfere with the building sequence. For example, there may be the addition of a through-hull fitting, which could make a "patch-up" job necessary. Then too, there is always the risk of scratching or marring the hull in the process of righting it.

In some cases, while painting of the boat upsidedown can virtually be all but completed, there are designs which may require the planning of a strip or area along the sheer that must remain UNPAINTED in order to receive the overlap of the deck laminate. In this case, if the boat has been painted up to this point, additional painting will no doubt be required on the deck also.

Since boats are re-painted in the boatyard in the right side up position all the time, the choice of when to paint is up to the builder. Generally, painting while upsidedown, and even scribing and painting the boot top, is most convenient. Just make sure the laminate has plenty of time to cure before applying any exterior coating systems.

REMOVING THE MOLD

After the hull has been righted and it is securely chocked and supported in position to prevent movement, the male mold can be removed. On single skin boats, such as those built with C-FLEX, it may be that some bulkheads are already permanently in place. If this is the case and the mold will be used again, hopefully you have planned for this so the mold will come out in one piece, or at least in pieces or sub-assemblies that can readily be re-joined to remake the mold. Otherwise, the mold will have to be ripped apart to get it out if permanent interior members are in place.

Most beginners will prefer removing the mold and then installing internal members AFTER, since considerable interior fiberglass work will be required in most boats. Attempting to fit internal members as a part of the original male mold does take quite a bit of preplanning and forethought.

Before removing the male mold, again make sure that all reference marks, bulkhead locations, etc., are marked to the inside of the hull. If it is possible, lift the mold in one piece from the hull. Otherwise, remove the mold piece-by-piece, in which case it will not be reuseable. If the hull tends to stick to the mold members at any point, give it a couple of solid raps with a mallet onto the sticking areas. Where substantial moldings or portions of the hull have been made over more-or-less solid surfaced forming members, such as a keel or rudder skeg appendage, compressed air or injected water can be forced between the parts, whichever is practical. Remove all nails, screws, stitching, or other protruding fastenings and staples, either by pulling them out or by grinding them down flush. You are now ready to complete the interior and apply the interior laminate if this is required (see Chapter 23).

CHAPTER 15

female molding

In an earlier chapter the concept of female molds and why the technique is usually not adaptable to the amateur who may wish to build just a single boat was discussed. It was noted that a three-step procedure was generally necessary, involving the building of the "plug", then building another part over this called the "mold", and with the third part built inside this mold being the first hull. It was also emphasized that the equipment and methods used in this procedure were usually beyond the skills and budgets of most amateurs, and that these techniques were usually best suited to the production operation. But it was also pointed out that there was at least one method for building female molds cheaply and with relative ease. This type of female mold will be discussed in this chapter.

CHINE HULL MOLD

The type of female mold that lends itself to amateur construction such as will be described must consist of flat or developable surfaces (those which are NOT compounded, but rather generated from segments of cones or cylinders) which lend themselves to making the mold surfaces from sheet materials. Typical hull shapes which often lend themselves to this type of mold are hard-chine or multi-chine hulls (like those often built from sheet material such as plywood, aluminum, and steel). Round bilge hulls having surfaces of compound curvature are NOT adaptable; this type of hull form, if built in a female mold, virtually has to be made using the typical three-step female mold-making process,

without going through an inordinate amount of work that would be more effort in the long run. If a "one-off" round-bilge fiberglass boat is desired, it will be better to select one of the male mold methods and materials described elsewhere in this book. This doesn't mean that a female mold cannot be made from wood strips, veneers, or other materials, and form almost any compound shape. The work and cost of such a mold, however, would exceed that required to build such a hull by conventional "one-off" methods.

However, if the boat is a simple hard-chine or multi-chined form with developable surfaces, there is no reason why it cannot be built in a simply-made female mold that you can make yourself. The system can also be used to build any flat or nearly flat surfaced part, big or small, such as a deck or cabin, a cockpit, control consoles, and numerous other small parts. The beauty of the female mold system, or course, is that the outer final surface requires virtually no additional finish work.

Building such a mold for making a hull is a lot like building the boat inside out. In other words, the mold will be a mirror image of the part to be molded, all without the need for a "plug." The female mold built by this method is also much like building a male mold, except that the frame contours are taken to the OUTSIDE of the hull surfaces. Longitudinal members are notched into these frames at such joints as the chine, keel, and sheer, and as required to provide the necessary rigidity to the sheeting material used to form the mold surfaces (see Fig. 15-1).

As with any mold, this female mold must

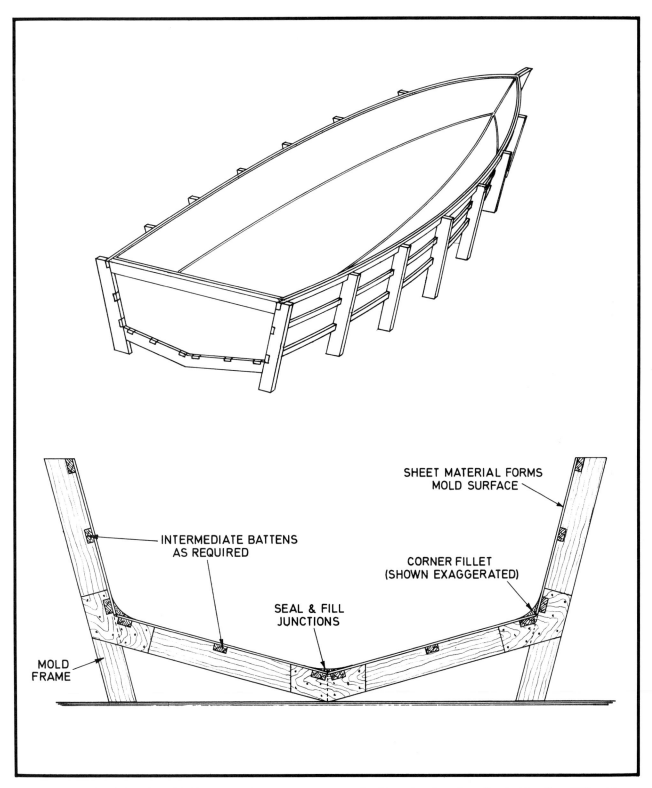

FIG. 15-1 — A simple female mold of hard-chine form using sheet materials is usually simple to build. Hull surfaces must be of the "developable" type for ease of construction. In the section shown through such a mold, the chine and keel junctions have been fitted with radiused fillets (shown exaggerated for clarity) so the laminate will conform at the corners. Such a mold must be strong and should be anchored to the ground to prevent distortion.

Labels in figure:
SHEET MATERIAL FORMS MOLD SURFACE
INTERMEDIATE BATTENS AS REQUIRED
CORNER FILLET (SHOWN EXAGGERATED)
SEAL & FILL JUNCTIONS
MOLD FRAME

be rigid so that it will not move during construction, and it should be true. If possible, anchor the mold in place to prevent movement, or at least make the structure so that it will not distort while it is being built, or while the hull is being molded up inside the mold. Even though the type of mold being discussed is an inexpensive, expendable type, and will probably only be good for making a few parts at most, it still must be structurally sound and not subject to movement.

Several sheet materials can be used to make the surfaces of the mold. These can include plywood, hardboard (such as "Masonite", a brand name) with the smooth side being the mold surface, plastic-coated hardboard (such as the melamine-coated shower and tub enclosure materials frequently seen), and laminated plastic sheeting used on countertops ("Formica", a brand name, is one such product). If using hardboard, the untempered type will be easier to bend, but if surfaces have little shape, either the untempered or tempered type can be used. Materials like plastic sheeting, however, are brittle and not strong without adequate support underneath, and tend to chip and crack fairly easily. However, they are adaptable to certain conditions. Plywood is a suitable material, but the grain pattern of the sheet must be filled in and the surface smoothed carefully if the surface of the molded part is to be smooth and of high quality. This can be done by sheathing with fiberglass cloth just as would be done over a plywood boat hull.

MOLD DESIGN CONSIDERATIONS

Several points should be noted with regard to the mold, regardless of the sheeting material used. First, the shape of the hull or part laid up in the mold must have sufficient draft, or the canting outward from bottom to top of the sides of the part, in order to pull free from the mold after the part has

been made (see Fig. 15-2). If the part being molded is quite shallow, there need be little draft, but as the depth of the part increases, together with complexity of shape, there should be at least a 2 degree angle to this draft. And on parts that are deep and narrow, such as appendage keels and skegs, which are difficult both to lay up and remove, 10 degrees of draft is not too much. If such draft is not incorporated into the "shape" of the desired part, perhaps it should not be made in a one-piece female mold. Also, shapes which have inward canting returns or "tumblehome" present similar problems (see Fig. 15-3).

The problems with "shape" of the molded parts may be solved by using split

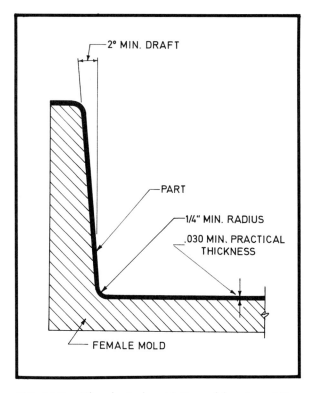

FIG. 15-2 — The physical restrictions of female molding must be considered if the part is to be easily removed from the mold. Greater draft angles at the sides than shown are always preferable, as are more generous corner radiuses. The necessary amount of radius varies with the composition of the materials used in the laminate. Thinner mats can be worked into tighter corners than, for example, heavy woven rovings. A generous radius also makes a more durable part less subject to damage. Hard corners must be avoided.

molds or molds with removable inserts. A split mold is generally made in two halves joined at the centerline of the hull. The two halves are fitted with a husky outer flange all along the edge where they join, and this is bolted together to hold the two halves together while the halves are being molded. Later, the two halves are unbolted, and the hull removed from the mold. An insert is similar, with the insert being set in position while the hull is molded, and then removed so the completed part can be pulled from the mold. However, the use of split molds or those with inserts may complicate things for the amateur, requiring more thought and planning to make a mold that is strong enough for the task and that will result in the making of a successful part. Split molds for production use are shown in Chapters 8 and 19.

Another consideration, especially with larger hulls, is how the hull or part will be pulled from the mold. If the mold is a single-piece type, there must be enough room above the mold (at least twice the height of the hull) to lift the hull completely free of the mold and set aside, or for the mold to be slid out of the way. Lifting gear (often in the form of chain hoists) must also be provided, and these devices are commonly attached to the roof structure of the building shed. If a split mold is used, there must be room on either side of the hull to pull the mold halves away from the hull.

MOLD SHEETING APPLICATION

The mold sheeting material can be fitted, cut, and attached to the female mold framework in a number of ways. Some advocate attaching the sheeting with various adhesives such as contact cement or panel adhesive. The idea here is that fastenings which must be patched over and sanded for a smooth surface can be omitted. This technique no doubt works well in flat areas, but where panels curve a lot, this can be difficult, especially with contact cement. Once the contact cement grabs hold, there is no chance to reposition a sheet if it has not been located properly. Generally, flat head wood screws countersunk slightly are easiest to use, but the screw holes must be filled

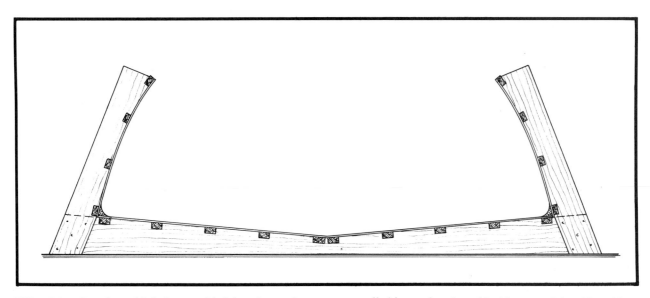

FIG. 15-3 — Female molded shapes with inboard canted surfaces, returns, or "tumblehome" (as shown by the section through a hull in a mold of this form), usually cannot be pulled from a female mold without special mold modifications, such as split molds or mold inserts.

in with putty and then sanded smooth. Nails are not as satisfactory since it is difficult to conceal the heads and they tend to "pop", leaving unsightly dimples in the molded part.

Depending on the size of the hull or part, joints in the mold sheeting will no doubt occur, whether they fall at the chine or keel, or between the panels themselves where they butt join. Regardless of the junction, they must be backed so that there is no flexibility or loss of strength of the mold surface at such points. In flat areas at butt joints, use butt blocks glued and fastened behind the joints. Where junctions occur, such as along the chine or keel, use longitudinal battens to support the edges of the panels all along. Such battens need not back the joint at the exact panel edge, but can be set in from the edge somewhat just as long as there is no movement of the panel at the joint. Later, these joints will be filled and fitted with resin putty fillets on the inside.

At butt joints between panels, there are a couple of ways these can be smoothed over on the surface. Much depends on the degree of quality desired on the mold surface, however. If one is willing to accept minor imperfections, or is willing to do a little finish work on the outside later, then tape butt joints with a wide cellophane tape. This will show slightly on the finished part later, but minor sanding and buffing will take care of most of the blemish.

Otherwise, fill in the butt joints with resin putty and sand smooth for a continuous panel surface. Some may feel that as long as the butt joints between panels fit tight enough, there is no need for treatment and that the minor "ridge" formed on the molded part can be ground smooth later. However, there is a chance that the molded part will hang up at these spots, and this can damage the gel coat at this point and make pulling the part out of the mold more difficult.

All corners of the mold must be fitted with fillets usually made with resin putty

filler. The laminate will not adhere to sharp inside corners without forming air bubbles, and these are not acceptable. Even if hard corners could be molded in the female mold, these would not be durable in use and should be avoided. If the sheeting material used is hardboard or plywood, use ordinary polyester resin for the putty. However, if using a melamine-coated hardboard or plastic sheeting, it is questionable that polyester resin will stick to these surfaces, and hence, an epoxy resin is recommended (although these may not stick too well either). The more generous the radius of the fillet, the easier it will be to lay up the laminate in the mold. There are no hard and fast rules for this radius, but the heavier the material used, and the more layers, the more generous the radius should be.

Once the joints have all been treated, the surfaces must be prepared so that the laminate to be applied will not stick to the mold and will pull free after layup. If plastic sheeting or melamine-coated hardboard has been used for the mold surfaces, no further treatment is required on the surface other than the use of wax and perhaps a release agent, as will be explained later.

However, if hardboard or plywood are used, these will have to be sealed somehow in order to provide a suitable surface. There are many materials that can be used, but some that will not work. For example, plywood and hardboard surfaces can be coated with resin, such as a tooling gel coat often used by production outfits for making plugs and molds. Or the surfaces can be coated with urethane or epoxy coatings. However, other types of coatings such as varnishes and paints may be attacked or softened by the resin and not work. If in doubt, make a small test panel first, using the sheeting material. Cover with the sealer and then apply resin and check the results. In general, ordinary paints will not be suitable. But regardless of the material used to make a smooth, glossy surface against the mold surface, remember that the mold surface quality is equal to the surface quality of the molded part. And the smoother this surface is, the easier it will be to remove the molded part from the mold. Considerable sanding and polishing work on the mold surface is common for a high quality job, so be prepared to give the project some "elbow grease".

When the mold is ready for doing the layup, consider how the job will be done. Some means must be provided in order to reach all areas in a big mold. This can be done by a scaffolding suspended from the ceiling, or it may be possible to rotate the mold as long as it can be held rigid so as not to distort. The mold should be located indoors and out of the elements, and should be clean and free from dirt, dust, oil, and grease. Then pre-fit and pre-cut all the materials. Label and roll them up, setting them aside for immediate use as they become necessary.

MOLD PREPARATION

The mold surfaces must be treated so the molded part will not stick to the mold surfaces and can be pulled free with relative ease. Basically, this consists of waxing the mold surfaces and polishing them to a smooth, glossy, and slippery surface. Several well-applied coats of Carnauba paste wax can be applied to the mold. Apply the wax to a limited area at a time and buff instead of waxing the entire mold first and then attempting to polish later after the wax dries; this can be tedious. Also, do NOT use a power buffer for final polishing as it may burn through the waxed surface causing bare areas; use clean soft cheesecloth.

For an easier job, but perhaps more costly, there are numerous proprietary mold release wax systems. The use of one of these products is highly recommended since they are easier to apply and use. Many fiberglass suppliers carry suitable products. Follow the instructions provided with the product used for best results.

Don't be careless in selecting a wax to use as a mold release. Although there are many types of paste waxes, not all are suitable as a mold release agent. Avoid standard automotive products and waxes. Some contain silicone agents and these can react negatively with the PVA release agent usually applied next, as well as to the gel coat if this is used against the mold. Surface blemishes and beading up of the PVA can result from using the wrong wax. Some automotive buffing compounds contain shellac or similar components that can leave an adhesive layer on the mold, making it difficult to remove the molded part from the mold.

After building up the surface of the mold with wax and thoroughly polishing the surfaces to a high gloss, let the mold set for a number of hours before applying the release agent. This allows time for the solvents from the wax to evaporate. Then apply the second release agent (preferably on the same day that the laminate will be started) which is usually PVA. The PVA is usually sprayed on in the factory, and spraying is highly preferable. It can also be applied to the surface with a brush or a sponge, but this is difficult to do evenly and properly.

If the PVA is applied prior to the solvents of the wax evaporating completely, "fisheyes" may result. Fisheyes are round crater-like discontinuities in the film forming a non-wetted area due to surface tension. These are caused by entrapped solvents, dust, water, oil, or silicone on the surface; a heavy buildup of wax (such as could be caused by improper buffing); a sudden decrease in temperature inhibiting the evaporation of the solvent; or a porous surface on the mold. However, if fisheyes do develop after application, simply wash off the entire PVA film and reapply again later; don't attempt to make local repairs in the PVA film.

If fisheyes develop while applying the PVA film, stop immediately, remove the

PVA entirely with water, buff out those areas where the defects occurred, and wait 2−3 hours before reapplying. Do not dilute the PVA. It takes about 30 minutes for the PVA to dry, however, this can be speeded up if the PVA is heated to about 80 degrees F. by putting the container in warm water (DON'T heat it with electricity or an open flame!). This will shorten the drying time to around 5−10 minutes. In any case, wait until all evidence of wet areas have disappeared before doing further work. Remove any excess PVA from corners and crevices.

If spraying on the PVA, apply a light fog or "tack" coat, then follow with a couple of "wet" coats after the first coat dries. Hold the gun perpendicular to the surface 12" to 20" away. Allow the complete PVA coating to dry and take care not to abrade or scratch the coating. One gallon will cover about 400 sq. ft. In cool or humid weather, warming the mold will accelerate drying. However, externally applied heat is NOT desirable; warm air blown over the wet film may cause the surface to "skin over", while trapping moisture within the film. When dry, the surface should be tack-free, smooth, and glossy. While using PVA, take care to heed the precautionary labels provided with the product. The PVA is flammable, so make sure to extinguish all flames.

Note that in the foregoing mold preparation, it may be adequate to just use wax in several coatings as a mold release, especially if a plastic-covered sheeting has been used for the mold surfaces. The use of PVA together with wax, however, is highly advised if using hardboard or sealed plywood, at least for making the first few parts. In a factory situation, after several parts have been molded, a mold becomes broken in and the application of PVA before molding subsequent parts is not necessary; just a light reapplication of wax and polishing to a high gloss. The exothermic heat from successive molding "conditions" the mold by driving the waxes deeply into the mold surface so that PVA is not required after the first few parts. In fact, some fabricators do not use PVA at all.

TROUBLE SHOOTING − PVA

Air bubbles in the PVA film:
Air pressure too low. Use at least 80 psi at the gun.
Film solution runs:
Film is too thick.
Dull spots in the film caused by PVA overspray:
Spray dried PVA film with water to cause reflow and flow out.
Entire film is dull and hazy, grainy looking:
Film not thick enough. Film not sprayed to a "wet" coat.
Surface on part is rough and dull:
See above two problems.
Film won't wet out evenly:
Non-silicone wax *not* used. Contaminated mold.
Hard, white build-up accumulates on the mold:
PVA film not thick enough, (See PVA etch). Laminate too hot.
PVA Etch:
PVA film too thin, (less than 2 mils).
Part sticking:
Caused by too thin of PVA film.

GEL COATS

A choice must be made as to whether a gel coat will be used against the female mold surface. This is technically optional, and if a gel coat is NOT used, then the part will have to be painted in order to have a color imparted to the surface and for durability. However, if having gone to the trouble of making a female mold, it seems like wasted effort NOT to use a gel coat. Contact one of the gel coat manufacturers listed and obtain their technical manuals if gel coat is to be used (also see Bibliography). The field of gel coat technology is complex, and a successful application of gel coat, as well as pulling the completed part from the mold, can be fraught with complications.

General recommendations and procedures will be discussed, however, this is a rapidly changing field so it is best to check with your sources of supply for the latest technical advice to suit the products being used. In all cases, follow the instructions provided with the products to the letter. Although seldom done, it is possible to use epoxy resins in a female mold laminate, but it is recommended that the gel coat supplier be contacted first if a polyester gel coat is contemplated. It may be better to omit the polyester gel coat in this case, or the gel coat entirely. The surface finish will then be provided by the epoxy resin and any subsequent coating applied.

Some of the general conditions which should be adhered to when using gel coats are as follows. Ambient conditions must be carefully controlled. The work areas AND the mold surfaces must be spotlessly clean and free of dust. Wipe down mold surfaces with soap and water before applying mold release and allow to dry. Use an oil-free tack rag over the mold surfaces to remove dust prior to applying the PVA. Temperatures in the work area and against the mold surface itself should be held within a range of 60 to 85 degrees F, and these conditions should be held throughout the cure of the gel coat. All

work should be done under cover, away from sources of moisture and humidity, and NOT in direct sunlight. The gel coat resin and catalyst proportions must be carefully regulated to achieve proper cure time; too much or too little catalyst can ruin the application.

A common problem with gel coats is finding a source of supply. Gel coats are usually used in production situations, and as a result, the suppliers are used to selling in bulk quantities. Small batches in the precise color wanted may be hard to find. Some therefore attempt to use general purpose resins and mix in their own pigments in an attempt to make their own "gel coat" resin. However, the results are usually less than satisfactory. Not only may the resin be of the wrong formulation to do the job, but it is extremely difficult to mix continuous batches with pigments so that the color is uniform throughout, and the tint of the resin may effect the color. While clear gel coat resins may be available, with pigments added for tinting by the end user, there is still the problem of mixing uniform batches, and is not advised by most gel coat manufacturers.

It is HIGHLY recommended that the gel coat be sprayed on for best results. Brush application of gel coats can be done, but this is only moderately successful for smaller parts. It is difficult to apply a uniformly thick and continuous coating by brushing, and uniformity IS important. The gel coat resin is thick and stiff, and does not level out or apply like ordinary paint. Brush strokes tend to remain, but don't go over the area repeatedly in an attempt to remove them. Brushing over and over will redistribute the release agent, causing the resin to stick to the mold. Allow each coat to cure before reapplying another coat so the styrene of the next coat will not tend to soften the first coat and thus lead to defects.

If applying by brush, use a 3" to 4" wide brush with fairly soft bristles. Several coats may be required to build up to the required thickness. A pound of gel coat will cover an area of about 8 to 10 square feet. If working in sections, allow each section to cure, and do not overlap more than 2″ onto the previously applied section. On vertical surfaces there will be a tendency for the resin to run and sag. However, avoid going over these areas with the brush since the styrene will tend to soften up the release agent. Instead, apply a thin enough coating so that running and sagging will be minimized; a little running and sagging is preferable to rebrushing as long as the total gel coat thickness is uniform.

If spraying equipment is available (consult the gel coat manufacturer for his recommendation of suitable spray guns), the builder may spray his own gel coat, or it may be possible to hire out this task. In most large cities, there are numerous fiberglass fabricators, both large and small, and they may be interested in doing part-time jobs, especially when work is slack. Spray application of gel coat does take a certain technique, but like spray painting, it can be mastered by the amateur.

Schedule the work so that once the gel coat has been applied, there is a time period of not more than 6 to 8 hours before applying the laminate. This will give the gel coat plenty of time to cure and yet form a good bond with successive layers in the laminate. But don't leave it overnight or over a weekend before applying the laminate; a poor bond may result. Once the gel coat has been applied, however, DON'T touch it in any way, and keep the mold under cover and out of the elements.

The thickness of the gel coat will vary somewhat with the type used. Usually a thickness of 15 to 20 mils (mils being thousandths of an inch and 15 mils equal to about 1/64″) is an acceptable range. Use a batch of resin that can be applied in 15 minutes or less. Several passes may be required for a film of sufficient thickness.

If spraying, don't do it outside, as breezes can carry off the material in the form of potentially damaging spray dust. Wear a face mask, goggles, and protective clothing. Use barrier cream on exposed skin and extinguish all flames in the working area — NO SMOKING!

Spray not too fast nor too slow. Move the gun from side to side, overlapping 30 to 50%, or as recommended by the manufacturer. Stop the gun at the ends of the swing to avoid buildup. Watch for runs and sags on vertical surfaces and avoid applying too much gel coat to these areas, however, do make sure they are coated. Have acetone ready to clean the gun once the gel coat starts coming out in "slugs" and starts spitting. This indicates that the resin has started to cure and it will be obvious since the resin will not spray as smoothly as before. It is important to stop and clean the gun at this point or it will be ruined. Clean the parts for several minutes in acetone, however, DON'T get any acetone onto the gel-coated mold.

A black gel coat is often sprayed over the initial gel coat (which is frequently white or other light color). This is done because it is easier to see air bubbles and defects over the darker color in the laminate to be applied. Since most gel coat formulations are opaque, there is no danger of the black showing through to the outside as long as the coating is of the proper uniform thickness. However, the black gel coat need be sprayed only until it is sufficiently "gray", with perhaps more being used in corners because this is where most air bubbles tend to form. In other words, keep this second coat as thin as possible since resin-rich surfaces tend to be brittle.

Although it has been emphasized that mold surfaces should be smooth, there may be certain conditions where some modifications may be desired. For example, for deck surfaces, it is possible to mold in the non-skid surface. One way is to use non-skid compound (such as ground walnut shells or sand) added into the mold finish medium. Other methods include incorporating embossed sheet metal or plastic, or vinyl fabrics of a desired pattern. The rough or patterned surface will be transferred to the surface of the molded part. When using these materials, care must be taken to assure that they are smoothly applied, adhere firmly (especially at the edges), and are thoroughly waxed and coated with PVA for a clean, easy release. It should be pointed out, however, that molded-in non-skid patterns may not be as effective as other methods ADDED to the surface later, such as some of the proprietary products available for this purpose.

GEL COAT PROBLEMS

It should first be noted that ANY defect in a gel coat is purely cosmetic and NOT structural. In other words, the part's structure will be sound even if it does not look too nice. However, gel coat defects can be difficult and costly to correct if appearance is important. Although recommended practices for gel coat applications are well understood and documented in the industry, variations in conditions can still cause problems in the final results. Most problems can be traced to external factors such as temperature variations, catalyzation, and handling techniques. Note, however, that problems with gel coats can occur long after the boat has been in service.

Probably the most common problem is wrinkles or "alligators" in the gel coat skin. This can be caused by the gel coat being too thin. Insufficient thickness causes an incomplete cure in the gel coat that may not be strong enough to resist the wet resin later applied, causing the skin to buckle during cure. More important, the styrene from the layup resin can penetrate and swell the gel coat if too thin, leading to severe wrinkling and lifting.

Wrinkles are also caused by starting the layup before the gel coat cures. Again, the styrene penetrates and wrinkles the under-cured gel coat. Slow cure may result from water or solvent entrapment in the gel coat, not using enough catalyst, cold temperatures, high moisture or humidity, and other conditions that lead to undercuring or lack of cure. Check the spray equipment to make sure it is free of solvents, make sure the mold surface is dry before spraying, and avoid excessive dilution with solvents. Also, if the gel coat contains pinholes, these will permit styrene-resin penetration. Pinholes can have several causes, including water, oil, or solvents in the lines, silicon on the surface, dust in the release agent, poor breakdown due to improper spray pattern, and holding the gun too close to the surface, causing air entrapment.

If the gel coat cures too slowly, check the handling of the resin at all stages. As noted before, temperatures below 60 degrees F. will drastically increase gel time. Also, slow curing can result from containers stored outdoors overnight, high humidity, moisture condensation on mold surfaces, and the like. Check the flow of catalyst in the spray equipment and make sure the nozzle is clear. Note that the grade of catalyst from manufacturer to manufacturer can vary; were catalysts switched in midstream?

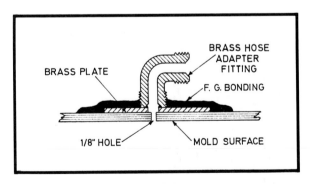

FIG. 15-4 — One or two of these fittings attached to the outside of a female mold will be a big help in pulling a "sticky" part out of the mold. An ordinary garden hose attached to the fitting allows water to be injected between the mold surface and the part, helping the part to "float" free. A piece of cellophane tape is used to cover the hole on the mold surface to keep resin out while the part is laid up. The brass plate is brazed to the brass fitting.

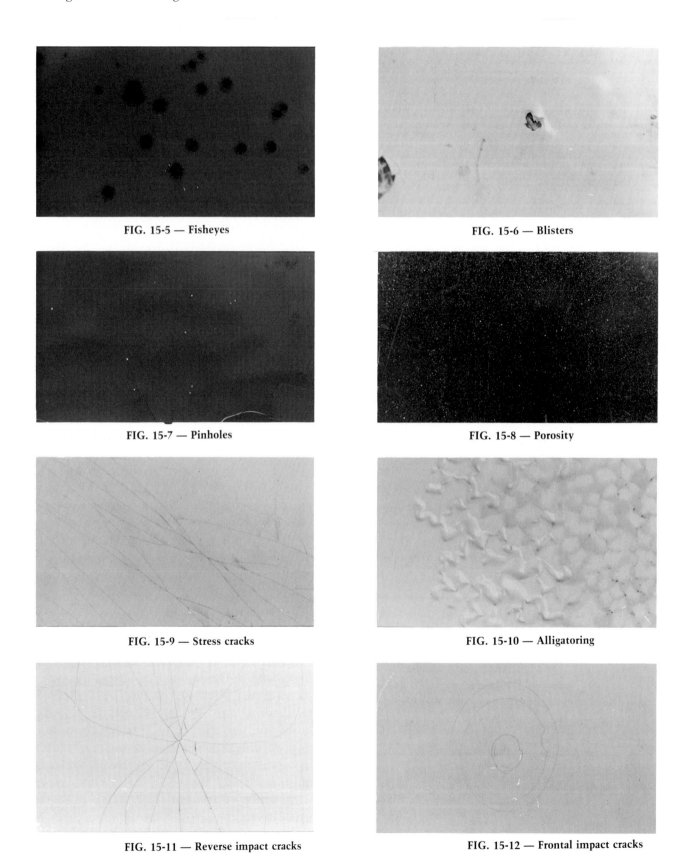

FIG. 15-5 — Fisheyes

FIG. 15-6 — Blisters

FIG. 15-7 — Pinholes

FIG. 15-8 — Porosity

FIG. 15-9 — Stress cracks

FIG. 15-10 — Alligatoring

FIG. 15-11 — Reverse impact cracks

FIG. 15-12 — Frontal impact cracks

COMMON GEL COAT DEFECTS

Porosity in the gel coat is another problem. This is usually caused by trapped air. Check to see that the correct air pressure is being used in the spray equipment. Too much pressure tends to yield fine porosity. Catalyst containing a high percentage of free hydrogen peroxide can break down excessively fast in the gel coat film and form small oxygen bubbles. Spraying too much gel coat or too thick of a film too fast will not allow trapped air to be released. Apply a 5 to 6 mil thickness on the first pass and then build up to the desired thickness in two or three more passes.

Uneven bands of color intensity, or "color float," can occur, most frequently in pastel shades where the tinting color is a small percentage of the white pigment. This color separation is caused by a "floating" of the color and a settling of the white. This can be accentuated by excessive thinning of the gel coat resin. An excessively heavy coating in one pass may result in sagging and runs; spray overlap may cause thick and thin gel coat areas that result in a mottled color float area. Reduce or eliminate the thinning solvent and use proper spraying techniques. First apply a thin "tack" coat of 1 to 3 mils in thickness to the mold, wait a few minutes, and then make a second pass applying a heavier flow coat perpendicular or crosswise to the first pass.

Sagging and running of gel coats that have the proper thixotropic qualities occurs usually when the gel coat has been thinned too much or the gun has been held too close to the mold surface. Most quality formulated thixotropic gel coats can be applied to thicknesses of 15 to 18 mils without sagging. Keep the spray gun 12" to 18" from the mold surface and maintain this distance throughout the pass.

An extremely heavy application in one pass can lead to sagging, especially in corners and confined areas. Avoid aiming the spray fan directly into corners as this will "funnel" a concentration of gel coat into the corner line. Instead, cover the flat wall surface either side of the corner separately; the thin edge of the spray fan pattern will overlap into the corner line in a couple of passes.

Craters and pock marks on the surface inside (not against the mold) are caused by improper atomization, inadequate air pressure, or excessive fluid pressure. As a result, the spray cannot break up into the fine mist needed to obtain a smooth surface. Craters on the face (exposed) surface may be caused by defects or foreign matter on the mold, trapped solvents, or oil from the spray line.

Oil, moisture, and/or dirt on the mold can cause fisheyes on the surface. Use oil-free rags for cleaning and polishing the mold, bleed all air lines to remove water and oil, and keep them clean. Minute particles of silicone oils can also create this condition.

Gloss variation is often related to a poor mold finish and improper polishing. Too much wax or styrene will leave a dull, gummy surface that will transfer to the part. Adding wax and inert extenders to the gel coat resin may also lead to dullness in the finish. This defect may also be caused by pulling the part from the mold before the cure is complete. Catalyst overspray on the mold or a PVA film that is not dry or is rough can also cause a dull finish.

If the gel coat lifts from the mold before the laminate has been applied, check the following conditions. Too fast a cure caused by too much catalyst or high ambient temperatures can cause shrinkage which results in lifting. Prevent the problem by reducing the catalyst level. If too long a time passes before the laminate is applied, shrinkage can occur, causing the gel coat to pull away. The same thing can occur if the resin has been thinned too much with styrene. If thinning is necessary, some gel coat makers advise thinning with equal parts of acetone and styrene, or styrene alone at not more than 10% by weight. Finally, a gel coat not applied in a uniform thickness causes some sections to cure and shrink at different rates than other areas, causing lifting at certain areas.

If the glass reinforcement shows through the gel coat, it means that the gel coat is too thin, or the laminate was started too soon after the gel coat was applied, or that mat against the gel coat was omitted or was too thin, allowing the waffle pattern of the woven roving to print through.

Cracking of gel coats on a new part is usually caused by flexing of the part before a complete cure has occurred or by too weak a laminate. If the bond between the gel coat and the laminate is weak, the gel coat may crack also. Crazing or cracking can also be caused by an uneven application, rapid cure, and air bubbles or voids between the gel coat and the laminate. Finally, excessive pounding against the mold to free a stubborn part can crack and damage the gel coat.

Certain defects in gel coats can be repaired with relative ease. Small, shallow scratches may be sanded down, buffed, and polished. Deeper gouges may be repaired with a patching paste or putty made from matching gel coat mixed with a fine filler such as silica. Apply the filler and cover with cellophane or spray on a coating of PVA. Let the patch cure, then sand, buff, and polish. A slight color variation may occur at these spots due to differences in catalyzation and the state of cure, even though the same gel coat batch may be used. The only way around this is to completely paint the boat afterward.

One of the most common problems with gel coats for hulls is blistering upon immersion in water. There are a number of causes for this, including an incomplete or partial cure. The partially cured gel coat is more readily permeated by water vapor causing the film to "stretch," allowing water to collect internally. This forms a blister at a pinhole, or discontinuity between the gel coat and the backing laminate.

Another cause of blistering is when the backing laminate has not been completely wetted out. This results in a weak area that allows water and/or water vapor to accumu-

late, making a blister. The back of the gel coat can also become contaminated before th laminate has been applied. This results in a poor bond between the gel coat and the laminate, again allowing an area for the water to gather. Trapped air between the gel coat and the laminate leads to a similar situation.

Finally, if the gel coat is too thin, it may be too weak to withstand water immersion. If the water is warm, the blistering problem is accentuated. The resin properties such as heat distortion, cross-linking with other agents, and toughness determine the degree to which a gel coat resin will resist the formation of blisters in addition to the causes noted. This is another reason why specially formulated gel coats should be used instead of making one up from general purpose resins.

COMPLETING THE LAMINATE AND REMOVING FROM THE MOLD

After the gel coat has been allowed to cure properly, the balance of the laminate can be applied. Since gel coats used in female molds are air-inhibited, the gel coat surface will still be tacky to the touch, as it should be. The laminate should start out with at least a layer of mat that is fairly well saturated with resin. This mat should have enough total thickness to avoid showing the pattern of the woven roving to be applied and to provide ample reinforcing to the gel coat. Generally, a 1½ oz. weight mat is a minimum, and a thicker mat layer is desirable.

Certain areas of the part being molded should have extra layers of mat build-up, such as at corners and other areas where there is a distinct change in direction of the mold surface. This can be done by using strips of mat applied to these areas initially before the first mat layer, or by double lapping mat junctions where they occur.

Otherwise, apply the laminate in the

normal manner if it is of the conventional type. The only variation that should be considered is that if a core material will be applied part way through; joints in materials should then probably be butted together, with the butts generously staggered so they do not fall at the same points. This is done so that a double lapped area will not be built up, making it difficult to get the core material to lay flat to the surface at all points. Apply the laminate, no more than a mat and woven roving layer at a time, to prevent non-uniform shrinkage that can lead to distortion of the part and premature lifting from the mold surface. Don't build up the laminate too fast either, since the exothermic heat can not only cause shrinkage and distortion, but make a brittle laminate that may be weak.

If a core is not used, or on the inside laminate or parts with a core, junctions can be overlapped or butted. The last layer in the inner laminate can be either mat or woven roving, or even cloth. Cloth or woven roving is easier to smooth out and get rid of excess resin, but mat provides a better secondary bond to any parts subsequently installed.

It is preferable to install all structural hull members and stiffeners before removing the part from the mold. This means that the final resin coat in the laminate should be a wax-free resin to provide a sound secondary bond to joining members. After this, a fin-ishing coat of resin containing wax can be applied to eliminate all tacky surfaces. Painting is optional, however, it is possible that the paint will not adhere too well to the wax-coated surfaces and it will no doubt be impractical to remove the wax by sanding. Probably a better solution at this point would be to apply an interior gel coat, a special gel coat resin that contains wax and pigment to suit, that requires no additional finish directly over the final fiberglass laminate.

The completed hull or part can now be removed from the mold. Hopefully, the part will pull free easily. But most likely, it will take a little bit of "coaxing", and in some cases, it may be stubborn. Several techniques can be used to free a sticky part. A few raps with a mallet against the mold may be required, but take care not to crack the surfaces. Or compressed air or water can be injected between the mold and the part. Water between the mold and the part will solubilize the PVA mold release and help "float" the part free. Lift the part free of the mold and support as required for the balance of construction. If the gel-coated surface has been damaged, repair it as required. If a gel coat is not used, then finish the surface using coating systems as described before. As a last resort, break up the mold if the part won't pull free; but the mold will not be reuseable in this instance.

GEL COAT TROUBLESHOOTING

Listed below are common gel coat problems and their usual solution:

Problem	Cause	Solution or Items to Check
Part is dull when pulled	Rough mold	Polish mold sufficiently.
	Wax Buildup	Wash and buff with cleaner. In most instances, what is called wax buildup is actually polystyrene buildup and should be treated as such.
	Polystyrene buildup	Sand or scrub with brush and strong solvent. Read precaution on solvent before using.

157

Problem	Cause	Solution or Items to Check For
	Dirt or dust on mold	Clean mold. It is best to clean just prior to gel coating. Time span should be as short as possible between cleaning and gel coating.
	Solvent or Water	Check for.
	Raw catalyst	Start catalyst flow from gun away from mold. Only the catalyzed gel coat should be sprayed into the mold.
	Rough PVA or wet	Check spray technique. Allow longer to dry. (See PVA application procedures)
Part goes dull after being pulled	Insufficiently cured gel coat	Correct excessive or insufficient catalyst level in gel coat and laminate.
		Wait longer before pulling.
		Check for low temperature (minimum of 60°F.)
		Check for contamination, water, oil or solvent.
Fiber pattern in parts	Insufficient cure	Correct excessive or insufficient catalyst level in gel coat and/or laminate.
		Wait longer before pulling.
		Check for low temperature.
		Check for contamination, water, oil or solvent.
	Transferred from mold	Refinish mold.
	Glass cloth	Use a mat skin coat first.
		Wait longer before pulling.
	Woven roving	Use as the last layer of the laminate and as far away from the gel coat as possible.
	Gel coat too thin	Use 18 (±2) mils, wet.
	High exotherm of laminate	Cure laminate slower.
		Apply in stages. Use lower exotherm laminating resin.
Dull or soft spots, at random	Gel coat uneven	Poor breakup, use three passes.
	Catalyst poorly mixed into either gel coat and/or laminate	Mix catalyst thoroughly. Equipment surging (material pump and/or atomizing air).
		Improper catalyst settings (high or low)
		Gun operated too close to mold.
	Trapped solvent can be in gel coat and/or laminate	Check cleaning procedure. Check catalyst level with equipment using solvent reduced catalyst.
	Trapped water can be in gel coat and/or laminate	Drain lines and correct the problem.
Porosity	Entrapped air	Wrong air pressures. Too high tends to yield fine porosity, while low will produce larger, surface porosity.
	Wrong Catalyst	Check material supplier for recommendation.
	Gel coat film thickness	Applied too thick; use 18 (±2) mils, wet.
	Application	Poor spray technique. Apply 5 to 7 mils or thin continuous film, wet, on the first, and make a total of three passes to achieve a total thickness of 18 (±2) mils wet.
	Formulation problem	Improper viscosity and/or resin solids.
	Water or solvent	Check for contamination.
Gel coat pre-release occurring before lamination causing obvious surface distortion	High catalyst level / Uneven and/or too thick gel coat allowed too long to cure	Decrease catalyst. Check millage, not to exceed 25 mils, wet. Gel coat should not be allowed to stay on the mold for more than several hours without laminating at least a skin coat. Varies with temperature—should be laminated within same day.

158

Problem	Cause	Solution or Items to Check For
	Resin solids too low	Check with manufacturer. Do not add styrene without their approval.
	Uneven cure	Improperly dispersed catalyst. Increase catalyst level. If low, use fans for more uniform cure.
	Trapped solvent	Check for contamination, such as acetone, water, oil, . . . etc.
Mold release	Type and amount on the mold.	
Gel Coat pre-release, occurring after lamination. Observed as a spot on the surface with a distinct line.	Laminate curing too fast	Check for proper catalyst level. Check resin to glass ratio. Resin drain out or puddling. Build laminate in stages.
This area is typified by increased fiber pattern and duller surface.	Laminate curing uneven	Uneven laminate thickness. Resin rich areas. Low resin solids
Spider cracks. Cracks radiating out from a central point or in circles.	Impact	Check on handling and demolding procedures. Caution on hammering on parts. Excessive gel coat thickness.
	Mold mark	Defect in the mold; repair defect.
Cracking in parallel lines.	Stress due to flexing	Excessive gel coat thickness. Low glass ratio in laminate. Laminate thickness too thin. Pulled too green; laminate undercured. Demolding or handling procedures. Defect in the mold. Sticking in the mold.
Alligatoring. A wrinkling of the gel coat, pushed up in ridges or Crows feet.	Insufficiently cured gel coat	Wait longer before bringing polyester product in contact with gel coated surface.
(a) Before laminating	Solvent	Do not reduce with solvents, such as acetone.
	Raw Catalyst	Check for leaks or overspray.
(b) After or during lamination, or a second application of gel coat.	Thin gel coat	Use a minimum of 18 (±2) mils, wet.
	Insufficiently cured gel coat	Improper catalyst level: either high or low.
		Low temperature. Long gel time.
		Insufficient time between coats or lamination.
		Moisture or contamination in the mold.
Laminate does not adhere to gel coat. (a) in spots	Contamination	Check for solvent, moisture, catalyst getting onto gel coat surface.
		Excess mold release wax floating through the gel coat surface, creating an area that will not adhere.
(b) Large area	Gel coat too fully cured.	Check for high catalyst level. Letting the gel coat cure too long, such as overnight. Skin coat, rather than leave on the mold for long periods of time.
	Contamination	Excess mold release wax, or wax in the gel coat.
	Unbalanced laminate	Dry fiberglass.
Color Separation	Pigments separate from each other	Check for contaminates such as water or solvent.
		Dirty equipment.
		Overspray.
		Sagging and excessively applied gel coat millages.
		Excessively high delivery rates causing a flooding onto the mold surface.

159

Problem	Cause	Solution or Items to Check For
Pigment darting or specks	Contamination Foreign particles	Clean pump and lines. Strain and keep material covered. Poorly ground pigments.
Resin tearing	Resin separates from pigments	Check for sources of water.
	Formulation	Viscosity and thixotropic properties of the batch.
	Application	Improper spray techniques creating excessive overspray droplets and flooding. Can be aggravated by long gel time and sagging.
Pock marks	Contamination	Check for water, solvent, or improperly mixed catalyst. Overspray. Seedy Resin
	Other	Excess binder on the glass mat. Thin laminate or gel coat. Very dry laminate. Air entrapped in laminate. Post curing of the laminate.
Fading — a bleaching out or loss of color (also see water spotting)	Contact with certain harsh cleaners or chemicals—usually strongly alkaline or acidic types	Check for misuse of cleaners and/or chemicals.
	Poorly cured gel coat	Check for both over and under catalyzation.
	Unstable pigmentation	Check with supplier for proper product selection.
Softness	Soft gel coat film which can be easily marred	Incomplete cure of gel coat upon removal from mold. Check catalyst levels, contaminates, and film thickness.
Chalking	Dry, chalk-like appearance or deposit on surface	Under or over catalyzation giving incomplete cure. Check catalyst level, film thickness, water, solvent. Surface soil picked up from atmosphere. Breakdown of resin on surface from prolonged exposure to weather.
Checking (mud cracking)	Single or groups of independent or crescent shaped cracks	Trapped vapor or incompatible liquid which blows through the gel coat film on aging. Check catalyst level. Check for water, solvent, . . . etc. Chemical attack.
Water Spotting (also see fading)	Usually caused by exposure to a combination of excessive heat and moisture	Use only a product recommended for the particular application.
	Poorly cured gel coat	Check for both over and under catalyzation.
	Certain chemical treatments such as chlorine and/or cleaners	User misuse of these chemicals.
Pinholes and fisheyes	Water, oils, or silicones	Drain air lines. Check mold release wax. Check lubricating materials used within the equipment.
	Gel coat thickness	Use 18 (±2) mils, wet, in 3 passes.
	Low viscosity material	Old material — rotate stock. Batch out of specification. Wrong or improper gel coat formulation.
	Other	Improper atomization.
Pock marks while spraying	Chunks in the batch	Check atomizing air. Dirt in the gun or material. Material old and starting to gel, rotate stock. Strain.
	Other	Clogged gun. Clean. Improper atomizing air setting

Problem	Cause	Solution or Items to Check For
Sags and runs	Excessive gel coat thickness	Apply 18 (±2) mils, wet.
	Spray techniques	Atomizing air is pushing and blowing the gel coat.
	Low viscosity	Check viscosity and thixotropic properties. Over-agitated. Material was reduced, but should not have been.
	Other	Jarring the mold while moving.
Blisters appear shortly after part pulled especially when put in sun	Unreacted catalyst or undercure	Check % catalyst, catalyst overspray Mixing and leaks.
	Solvents, water, or oil	Check air lines, drums, and rollers.
	Air pockets	Check roll out.
Appear after part in field	Unreacted catalyst	Check catalyst levels.
	Solvent, water, or oil	Check lines.
	Air pockets	Check laminate.

This is only a partial list of defects and corrective steps as it is impossible to list every defect or to foresee every and any situation.

CHAPTER 16

C-Flex fiberglass planking

ABOUT THE MATERIAL

This chapter will be devoted to a specialized fiberglass material called C-FLEX fiberglass planking. This proprietary material is more than just another fiberglass material like those mentioned in Chapter 5; it is the basis of a system used to build "one-off" fiberglass boats. C-FLEX fiberglass planking was invented a number of years ago by a very practical, yet technically knowledgeable, individual named William Seemann. Bill had been involved for many years in the construction of boats and knew the problems associated with the amateur builder, especially those who wanted to build boats in fiberglass. His invention of C-FLEX had a radical impact on the fabrication of "one-off" fiberglass structures, not only in the field of boating, but also for the building of such diverse products as storage tanks, automobile bodies, and housing structures. This material, more than any other past development, has made it possible for the amateur to build his own fiberglass boat quickly with a high degree of success at a reasonable cost.

The C-FLEX material consists of parallel lengthwise rods of fiberglass rovings reinforced with cured polyester resin (like little continuous lengths of fishing poles side by side) alternating with bundles of continuous fiberglass rovings that are not saturated with resin. The whole is held together by a layer of lightweight unidirectional fiberglass cloth on each side. The C-FLEX comes in standard continuous lengths of 100' or 250', both 12" in width, rolled into a coil about 3' in diameter for shipping. Two weights are available from stock; one is a lightweight grade called

"CF-39" for smaller boats, and the other is considered a standard grade called "CF-65" used for most other applications, or on larger boats.

The C-FLEX material is commonly used over a male mold framework to build a single-skin fiberglass hull. Although the material is versatile, the basic construction principles are similar for just about all applications in fiberglass boatbuilding. Because the material is unidirectional by nature, it develops considerable strength in the longitudinal direction parallel with the rods, which have a high glass content in relation to the resin which forms them. Furthermore, the loose rovings held by the scrim between the parallel rods add to this strength once they have been saturated with resin during application, and become a part of the laminate that will be built up over the C-FLEX.

Although one can apply the C-FLEX around a male mold in different directions, it makes sense to apply the material in a generally lengthwise orientation to take advantage of the material's longitudinal strength, which is important in most boats, especially for competition powerboats or sailing craft.

For example, one of the important factors aboard racing sailboats is to keep sufficient tension on the headstay so that the headsails present a straight luff for efficiency. But a problem with this tension is that it tends to distort the hull, which may not be able to resist these forces completely. In effect, the tension exerted on the backstay to keep the headstay taught tends to skew up the hull, making it "banana" shaped. Because of the inherent longitudinal orientation of C-FLEX in a laminate, the material is a natural for helping to provide the necessary resistance to these strains, and hence the material has been frequently used to build custom-built "one-off" competition sailboats.

The main function of the C-FLEX, however, is that it provides the base or surface over an open male mold on which to build up a laminate in order to make a fiberglass hull or part. The material is ideal for this use since it has the ability to move on the bias, allowing it to conform to just about any hull contour (including compound curvatures found on round bilge hull forms) without deforming or stretching. This

---

ACTUAL TIME FOR APPLICATION OF C-FLEX

25' LOA Sailboat:
C-FLEX applied and wet out — 7 man hours

32' LOA Powerboat:
Frames set up, C-FLEX applied and wet out, first laminate applied — 18 man hours

37' LOA Sailboat:
C-FLEX applied and wet out — 14 man hours

38' LOA Powerboat:
C-FLEX applied — 18 man hours

42' LOA Sailboat:
C-FLEX and all laminate applied — 108 man hours

44' LOA Sportfisherman:
C-FLEX applied — 20 man hours

48' Trawler:
C-FLEX applied — 36 man hours

FIG. 16-1 — One of the advantages of C-FLEX is the speed that it affords in building a "one-off" fiberglass boat. The examples given are actual records of various boats that have been built with C-FLEX. Although the figures will vary with the design and the worker's tools and abilities, the man-hour figures given are fairly representative of what is possible.

means that no special forming tools or heating ovens (such as those sometimes necessary for shaping the foams used in sandwich core laminates, or vacuum bag techniques sometimes used to bond skins to core materials) are required. Conventional laminating procedures are all that is required to bond C-FLEX into the laminate. The C-FLEX has a natural flexibility in all directions, yet becomes stiff enough when wetted out with resin to provide a reasonably solid foundation over which the rest of the fiberglass hull laminate can be applied.

Another advantage of C-FLEX as opposed to the methods used to build sandwich core hulls is that the majority of the hull laminate is applied on the OUTSIDE of the C-FLEX, as opposed to righting the hull to install the inner laminate skin as is usually required with sandwich core methods. This means that the initial stiffness of the hull is much greater. The need to assure that the hull stays rigid during the righting process is not as critical since the C-FLEX hull will not be nearly as "floppy" at this point in the construction.

Furthermore, the male mold used to build the C-FLEX hull is not quite so elaborate, and therefore easier to build and not as costly. There is usually no need to get under or inside the mold, as is usually the case with sandwich core boats, and applying the C-FLEX to the male mold is much easier and faster than applying core materials. At the current time on a per-square-foot basis, C-FLEX is also somewhat cheaper than the foam core materials that will be discussed in further chapters. However, because C-FLEX makes a single-skin boat, it does have the disadvantage of not having the insulative properties of sandwich core hulls, although how to compensate for this shortcoming will be discussed later.

MALE MOLD VARIATIONS WITH C-FLEX

In Chapter 11, we discussed in general the procedures for making a male mold, and these principles are generally applicable to the C-FLEX mold as well. In this section, however, we will give more specific information and other variations required in making the male mold for the C-FLEX method.

With C-FLEX, there are two primary approaches or variations for building the male mold; however, the principles are similar in both cases. The main requirement for building in C-FLEX is that the C-FLEX strips must be supported at fairly close intervals along the lengths of the strips. Since there are two weights of material in common use, this spacing varies. With the "CF-39" grade, the material should be supported at intervals not exceeding 14". With the heavier "CF-65" grade, the support intervals should not be over 18".

The manufacturers of C-FLEX recommend that the lighter weight material be used on smaller boats up to about 18' overall, with the heavier material being used on all larger boats. However, since the C-FLEX just provides a foundation or base for the subsequent laminate, the author has seen instances where the lighter material has been used on larger boats, with the supports being at the closer interval to give it the recommended support. But, if a laminate calls for the heavier "CF-65" grade, and the builder uses the lighter "CF-39" grade instead, compensation for the loss of strength in the C-FLEX will have to be made by the addition of more mat and woven roving in the balance of the laminate. Whether the

FIG. 16-2 — This type of C-FLEX male mold consists of closely spaced transverse frames made from plywood. Longitudinal battens are used only at the sheer and keel in this instance.

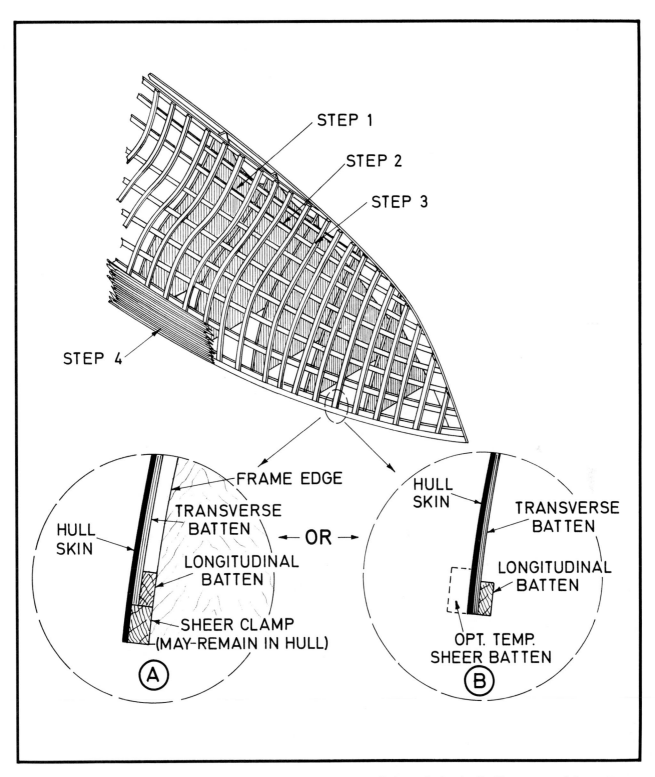

STEP 1

STEP 2

STEP 3

STEP 4

HULL SKIN

FRAME EDGE

TRANSVERSE BATTEN

← OR →

LONGITUDINAL BATTEN

SHEER CLAMP (MAY-REMAIN IN HULL)

(A)

HULL SKIN

TRANSVERSE BATTEN

LONGITUDINAL BATTEN

OPT. TEMP. SHEER BATTEN

(B)

FIG. 16-3 — This alternate "ribband-batten" method of building a male mold for C-FLEX uses transverse frames or bulkheads located at wider intervals, or at stations (STEP 1). Longitudinal battens span across and are notched into these frames or bulkheads (STEP 2). Thin transverse battens are applied over the longitudinal battens spaced about 12″ apart to support the C-FLEX (STEP 3). The C-FLEX is then applied lengthwise over the transverse battens (STEP 4). The sheer area can be handled in a couple of different ways. See FIG. 16-5 if the sheer clamp is to remain in the hull.

difference in cost savings resulting from using the lighter weight C-FLEX and the added cost of the extra laminate is worth it, must be determined by the builder. There would seem to be not much of a savings, and the procedure is not specifically recommended by the manufacturers of the product.

When C-FLEX was first offered, the typical male mold consisted of transverse forms spaced about 12″ to 18″ apart, providing the necessary support for the C-FLEX. In this approach, virtually no longitudinal battens (other than perhaps along the sheer or keel, or along the chine also in hard-chine hulls) were required (such as shown by Fig. 16-2). However, this approach did require a considerable number of transverse frames, even

though these could be made from cheap plywood or particleboard. The problem was the extra lofting work involved, in addition to making the extra frames, since with most boats, at least one, and perhaps two, EXTRA frames could be required BETWEEN those located at stations.

While there is nothing wrong with this previous approach technically, an alternate method was developed which only requires transverse frames at stations (see Fig. 16-3). This type of mold resembles the open-battened mold, such as that used for sandwich core hulls, in that longitudinal battens span across the frames from stem to stern. Although these battens are notched into the transverse frames, the C-FLEX does NOT contact them in the way that the core mate-

FIG. 16-4 — A photo of a "ribband-batten" mold for a C-FLEX hull. Note the widely spaced frames spanned by longitudinal battens which in turn support the closely spaced transverse battens to which the C-FLEX is attached.

rial does in a sandwich method. Instead, transverse battens made from thin, narrow strips of wood or plywood are laid across the longitudinal battens from sheer to keel on round bilge boats, and from sheer to chine, and chine to keel, on hard-chine boats, all spaced about 12" apart. The C-FLEX is supported on these transverse battens (see Fig. 16-4).

With this improved latter method (better known as the "ribband-batten" method), the transverse frames are cut to shape from the loftings or full-size patterns, with a deduction being made from the contour equal to the net thickness of the transverse battens that will be used. The longitudinal battens should not be any thicker or wider than necessary in order to span fairly between the frames (a ¾" net × 1-¼" net wide batten works for most boats, but anything of comparable size is suitable if the battens

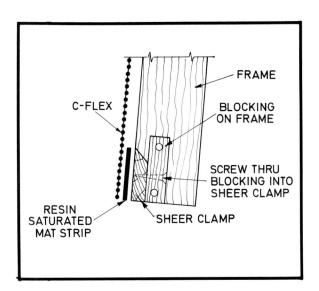

FIG. 16-5 — If the wood sheer clamp member is to remain in the hull, apply a resin-saturated strip of mat between the sheer clamp and the adjoining strip of C-FLEX to bond and wet out the C-FLEX completely in this area. Do not fasten through the sheer clamp into the frame. Instead, attach blocking to the side of the frames and screw fasten through this blocking into the back side of the sheer clamp. Back these screws out to free the frames from the sheer clamp and hull later. One problem with bonding in the sheer clamp at this point is that the mold framework will probably have to be broken apart in order to separate the male mold and the hull.

conform to the hull shape).

The battens are set in place before notching to make sure that the lines are fair by varying the depth of the notches as required. Position the entire length of each batten initially before fastening in place in order to check and vary for fairness. Use only enough battens as necessary to give the proper form or curvature to the transverse battens that will be applied over them. In areas of extreme hull curvature, or where the hull shape changes quickly, more longitudinal battens may be required in order to hold the transverse battens to contour. In flatter, straighter areas, however, the longitudinal battens can be more widely spaced.

The transverse battens can be made from ¼" or thinner plywood, or of solid wood of thickness to conform to the contours, about 1" to 2" wide and spaced about 12" apart as noted.

It is not necessary that the transverse battens be precisely at right angles to the longitudinal battens; they can run angularly or on a diagonal as required to conform to the hull shape. Just make sure that the lines of the mold will be fair, and then fasten the transverse battens at each contact point to each longitudinal batten. If the contours of the hull are too tight so that the transverse wood battens will not make the bends, you can use strips of C-FLEX cut along the rods through the scrim at least 2 or 3 rods wide. These strips are later stapled in place, then coated with resin to make them more rigid. While you will not be able to staple the C-FLEX to these strips, the planks can be wired in place to them instead.

Although the following is perhaps premature (since we have yet to describe the application of the C-FLEX), depending on the design or the desires of the builder, the sheer clamp member can be located on the male mold so that it will remain in the completed boat. This is done by applying a layer of resin-saturated mat to the outer surface of the sheer clamp and immediately applying the C-FLEX directly over it so that the mat will bond the C-FLEX permanently to the wood sheer clamp member all along. Of course, some pre-planning will be required in order to be able to pull the hull off the mold, together with the sheer clamps in place. But this can usually be arranged with some forethought by making the sheer clamp a removable member from the male mold framework. (See Fig. 16-5)

If a sheer clamp will NOT be molded into the hull at this point, then an outer temporary sheer batten should be clamped or otherwise secured to the hull around the sheer at all points after the hull has been built. This is necessary to provide the rigidity required when righting the hull and removing the male mold until the permanent sheer clamp member can be installed.

C-FLEX APPLICATION

Basically, the C-FLEX must be held to the transverse members or mold frames (depending on the method used to make the mold). But before applying the C-FLEX, all surfaces which will be in contact with the hull (those surfaces which the C-FLEX contacts, AND which are NOT to remain in the hull) must be coated with parting film. If these surfaces are the edges of frames or form members, cover with strips of cellophane tape. Alternately, the entire male mold can be covered with plastic sheeting. The main point is that for an easy release of the hull from the mold, the mold members must be treated or covered with something that will not bond to resin.

The C-FLEX strips or "planks" are applied over the form in single, continuous lengths. They should NOT be cut short and butt-joined between at any point as this will result in a loss of strength and cause fairing problems. In most cases, the framework in contact with the C-FLEX need not be beveled, but the builder should take care NOT to pull down the C-FLEX unfairly between frames or transverse battens, thereby causing hollows or "dishing". The stem form, however, which usually runs fore and aft, may require just enough of a bevel to present a flat surface for the C-FLEX to bear

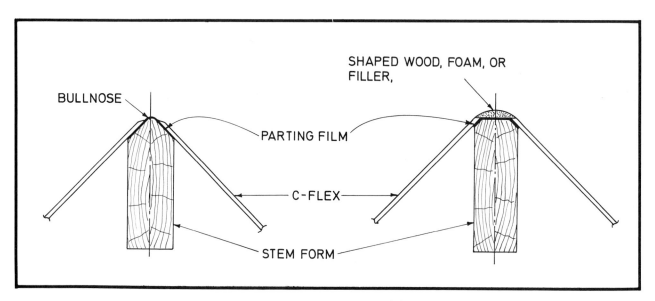

FIG. 16-6 — The C-FLEX usually lands onto a stem form at the bow which is part of the male mold. The stem form must be beveled to some degree for attaching the C-FLEX at this point. The builder can vary the contour or crispness along the stem to some extent by the amount of bevel and thickness of the stem form. The narrower the stem form and the greater the bevel, the sharper the junction will be. However, if the contour is too "crisp," hull damage in use will occur more easily.

on (see Fig. 16-6), but these details may vary with the design.

Where the C-FLEX application begins will vary depending on the type of boat (round bilge vs. hard-chine), hull configuration, etc. Different applications are shown by the photos in this chapter. Generally, on most round bottom boats, it is easiest to start along the keel centerline. It may be possible to start at the sheer and work to the keel; it makes little difference. It is possible to start from both points, coming together at some midpoint and fitting a final strip of

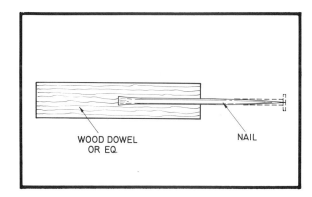

FIG. 16-7 — A cross-section showing "ice-picks" used to hold C-FLEX to the male mold that the builder can make. See the text for instructions.

FIG. 16-8 — C-FLEX application over a round bilge hull form. In this instance, the C-FLEX is being wetted out a strip at a time. Note the translucent quality of the wetted out C-FLEX. Optionally, the entire hull can first be covered with C-FLEX and wetted out after. Note the ice picks used to hold the material in position. Application in this instance began at the sheer.

C-FLEX in by cutting it to shape. On hard-chine hulls, the C-FLEX is best applied starting at the chine, with one length divided equally on the topsides and the bottom, keeping the same two rods in the center of the C-FLEX strip straddling the chine batten corner all along its length for a fair, neat chine edge. As the C-FLEX runs out to the keel or the sheer, it can be trimmed as required before or after it has been wetted out.

With some designs, it will not be obvious as to which way will be easiest to apply the C-FLEX. In this case, cut off a length and try it in different ways to find the easiest orientation. It may be advantageous to mark where each of the plank edges will land and

check with trial strips to see if there will be any problems as the C-FLEX application continues. However, this approach is usually only necessary on a design of unusual shape. Because of the flexible nature of the C-FLEX, it will usually bend enough so that the planks can be butted alongside each other along their lengths. Don't overlap these edges nor butt them too closely, as this will make a bump or ridge that will cause fairing problems later.

Sometimes the C-FLEX will not lay on the bias as it should, due to a tight curvature, for example. In this case, it may require some "help". Two small "C"-clamps (say 1" or 2" size) are clamped tightly to the ends of a single rod on the inside of the

FIG. 16-9 — A simple male mold for a hard-chine C-FLEX hull. Frames in this case were cut from low-grade plywood as is the stem form member. Note the battens only along the sheer, chine, and keel area. The edges of all frame members are covered with cellophane tape so that the resin-coated C-FLEX will not stick to them.

curve and then pulled from both ends. As long as the pull is in line with the rod and kept from twisting or bending the rod, the material can be forced down. However, the C-FLEX will tend to follow the fair lines of the hull and this treatment is rarely necessary.

In some cases, certain hull shapes, such as those with reversed sheers, or with very straight sheers, or on hulls that are wide for their length, the C-FLEX may not easily conform to these curvatures without excessive sideways bending. There are two ways to help in this situation. First, the application of the planks can begin in the middle area, letting the planks "run out" to the sheer and keel.

Or if the builder has already started the application and finds that curvatures are getting too tight, he can stop and wet out a plank that is already in place and allow it to cure. Then he takes another unsaturated plank and places it over the mold, letting it fall naturally in place by butting it along-side the cured plank in the middle length, but allowing it to fall across the cured plank at the ends where the curve is probably tight and causing the problems. The new plank is marked along the edge and cut to form a length of plank that is tapered at the ends, and then applied. The next subsequent plank will then fall in place alongside the plank which has been cut to shape, and the application can proceed easily. Where edges of adjoining planks will not fit closely, sew, stitch, or wire the edges together also, but this is seldom necessary.

To cut the C-FLEX to length, or for trimming purposes, heavy shears, tin snips, or a circular saw with an abrasive cut-off disc can be used, setting the blade of the saw just deep enough to cut the material. Another way is to group the material and cut with a hack saw. For material that has been saturated, the abrasive cut-off disc also works well. For lengthwise cuts before saturation, use a utility knife or shears down between the rods. For long diagonal cuts on unsatu-

FIG. 16-10 — In this application of C-FLEX to a hard-chine hull, the lower strip of material straddles the chine batten underneath (not visible). Ends of the material can be left long for trimming later.

rated planks, place a piece of scrap lumber under the material where the cut will be made for support, and use the circular saw to cut through it. When a cut is necessary along the hull, such as for the sheer line or keel, or at the ends where the material extends over, it is easiest to get a neat edge if the material has been wet out first and allowed to cure.

When applying the C-FLEX, note that the material has a slight "set" when rolled. It is easiest to apply if the side facing to the inside of the roll is placed DOWN to the frames. Check for fairness frequently during the application. Always cut a length longer than necessary and check for fit, as the material has a tendency to "creep" par-

allel with the rods. This distorts any dimensions used beforehand to determine the length of a plank.

At least two workers are best to lay the strips in place, one holding the material at each end and fastening in place where required. It may sound strange, but the recommended way to hold the C-FLEX in place is with ice picks! In addition, staples can be used, and it is desirable to have both available if possible. Both methods are shown in several of the photos. Since it is a little hard to find ice picks, let alone find enough of them, many just use staples alone. The best type have a narrow crown about 3/16" wide by ⅜" long, although other similar sizes also work.

FIG. 16-11 — On this hard-chine hull, the builder began the C-FLEX application at the centerline over the keel and worked out to the chine. One worker holds the end of a strip (but does not stretch it) while the other worker staples the material in place. The ice picks hold the strip in place at other points as stapling progresses.

172

However, you can make your own "ice picks" as shown by Fig. 16-7. Use lengths of wood (either 1" dowel stock like broom handles or 1" × 1" square stock) for handles to suit. Then drive in nails (say 16 penny size) with the points flattened with a hammer so they won't turn in the wood (pre-drill undersize if the wood tends to split). Leave about half the nail exposed and grind

off the head end to form a pointed end like an awl or ice pick. Many of these can be made in a short time.

There is some argument as to whether the staples can be ordinary steel, or whether bronze or Monel staples should be used. If the staples are removed from the C-FLEX just prior to the saturating coat setting up hard, any type of staple is acceptable. But if

FIG. 16-12 — One way to cut the C-FLEX material in the raw state is to bunch the material together and saw with a hack saw.

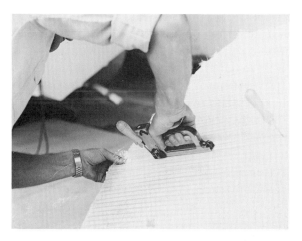

FIG. 16-13 — The ice picks hold the C-FLEX in place while the strips are stapled.

FIG. 16-14 — Overhanging ends of C-FLEX can be wetted out locally, allowed to set, and then sawn off or ground off to size.

FIG. 16-15 — Minor rough spots and high areas which occur after the C-FLEX has been wetted out can be lightly knocked down with a disc sander prior to applying the laminate over the C-FLEX.

you do NOT remove the staples, and instead leave them in place in the laminate (and some will have to be left in to hold the works together until the resin sets up hard), there is the chance that steel staples will rust. However, this seems fairly remote, especially if the interior will be given some additional layers of fiberglass that will, in effect, "seal in" the staples permanently. If the staples are left in, however, any protruding points should at least be ground down. While it may be possible for water or moisture to get to such staples eventually, it seems that the worst that would happen is that rust stains could show up on the surface (interior or exterior) at some later time.

The reason that ice picks AND staples are advised is that the ice picks are easy to shift around, which is helpful in holding the material roughly in place while being fitted. In other words, you will no doubt be moving the planking strips around to some extent, and the ice picks are quick and handy to use in this phase. Staples can then be used to hold the planks in permanent position after, but use only enough fastenings as are required to hold the planks to the frames and formwork. Apply additional fastenings only at areas where the material does not contact a frame all along.

It is often necessary to remove ice picks or staples, reposition a strip, and then refasten in order to keep the material fair. Do not stretch the material or try to get it too taut. Just have enough tension in order to make the C-FLEX contact the frames fairly and evenly. Sight along the hard strands of the material to spot unfair areas before saturating the C-FLEX. Do not allow any gaps between adjoining strips. Push any loose selvedge or edges down under where the planks join each other alongside.

Generally, stapling begins in the middle of the boat, working out to the ends, stapling along the butted edges first and working out to the free edge. One worker can hold the planks while the other staples and fits. Ice picks are ideal to hold the material

temporarily in position at this point. Generally it is only necessary to staple the outermost rods of each plank, but more staples may be required at the ends over the stem, transom, or in areas of concavity.

In concave areas, fastening the C-FLEX in place is a bit more work. It is possible that each rod in each plank could require a staple to hold the planks to the frames in these areas. Another method, instead, is to strip the individual rods from a length of C-FLEX and lay some of these transversely or across the plank being applied to hold the plank in place from the top (much like a frame in reverse; see Chapter 30 where C-FLEX is used for cabins and decks). Staple over these rods and through to the mold frame at the lowest point of the concave area, and this will flex the rods in place. By using a few more staples, this will hold the rod against the concave area and hold the planks in place. A variation on this theme is to use thin wood battens which have been covered with cellophane tape so that resin will not stick to them. But these will not bend as easily as the C-FLEX rods in areas of tight curvature. The rods or wood battens are removed from the surface after the C-FLEX has been coated with resin and allowed to cure. However, don't apply resin directly where the C-FLEX rods are located; just up to them so they won't stick. Then allow the resin to cure, remove the strips, and cover the small areas with resin later.

Once all the planks have been installed, the surface should be carefully checked for fairness and evenness. Any irregularities NOT corrected at this point will just be telegraphed to the outer surface where they will be far more difficult to take care of. So spend some time sighting along the hull areas at all visual angles. Correct all high spots and don't be afraid to readjust planks which seem too low or that have been pulled so tight that they seem to be flat between supports.

While all the foregoing comments concerning the application may seem long-winded and tedious, the builder's confidence should be restored by stating that this is just another example of it taking more effort to explain how to do something than it actually takes to do the job. In actual fact, the application of the C-FLEX proceeds quickly, and even big boats can be planked and ready for coating with resin in a day or two at most. Of course, this DOES assume that the workers are organized and properly equipped.

INITIAL RESIN COATING

Don't be intimidated, but the most CRITICAL part of building with C-FLEX is the initial coat of resin used to wet out the material after it has been applied to the mold. Over the years, I have talked to many people who have worked with C-FLEX, and I'll put in my own two cents worth of personal experience with the material as well. The relatively few people who have expressed reservations about the material, or

FIG. 16-16 — The wrong resin and improper methods were used to wet out the C-FLEX in this application. Note the flattened or "scalloped" effect between frames. While the hull need not be written off, considerable fairing and additional resin putty and/or mat will be necessary to restore the original lines and appearance. This adds considerably to the work, weight, and expense.

who just plain don't like working with C-FLEX, have INVARIABLY made the same mistake: They have used the WRONG resin at this critical stage OR they have applied the resin improperly, or BOTH!

The type of resin to use for the initial coating, while not really anything "special", is NOT ordinary polyester laminating resin as would be used for building up the conventional fiberglass laminate. Instead, the resin used has certain qualities and specifications that are important if the C-FLEX is to perform as it should. I will put this in prominent type so nobody will miss it:

THE TYPE OF RESIN TO USE IS A WAX-FREE, NON-THIXOTROPIC, CLEAR LAMINATING OR CASTING RESIN OF LOW SHRINKAGE WITH A VISCOSITY RANGE OF 600—1000 CPS (*)

This type of resin (which can be an ortho or iso type) does NOT have any fillers, and is frequently used for making artificial marble castings. It is important that the resin be somewhat under-catalyzed so it will cure slower to minimize shrinkage. The viscosity range is also fairly important, since a resin above 1000 cps will be too thick for practical use, while resins below about 600—800 cps will tend to shrink too much as they cure. In the 800—1000 cps range, the C-FLEX gets an acceptable wet-out with little or no shrinkage.

Be warned that if a resin is used that does NOT meet these criteria, you will no doubt have a C-FLEX hull where the planks have "dished", "scalloped", or flattened between transverse supports from undue shrinkage (see Fig. 16-16), making the boat MUCH harder to fair out. While this problem is especially critical with round bilge hulls, it can also occur with flatter hard-chine hulls. It should be emphasized that the boat in

(*) The abbreviation, "cps", means centepois, the standard measurement of viscosity.

this condition is probably NOT ruined. But to correct the problem, you will have to build up the flat spots with mat layers or with resin putty filler on the final coats, or by similar means, resulting in a hull that is MUCH heavier and more expensive than need be. This could also ultimately affect the performance of the boat. But worst of all, a tremendous amount of labor will be required to correct the situation.

So be safe and use the RIGHT resin at this critical point. Don't improvise and use other types of polyester resin, and DON'T use epoxy resins either. Note that this resin specification is ONLY critical for initial coating of the C-FLEX itself; regular laminating resins will be used for the application of the balance of the laminate over the C-FLEX, although the makers of C-FLEX highly recommend that isophthalic resin be used throughout the laminate as opposed to ortho-type resins.

In applying the initial coat of resin, another precaution should be emphasized: DON'T USE TOO MUCH RESIN! It is neither necessary NOR desirable to completely saturate the C-FLEX when upside-down on the mold. While the C-FLEX will require complete saturation eventually, this can be done from the back side after the hull has been righted and the male mold removed. At this stage it is only necessary that the C-FLEX be wetted out enough to provide a rigid base for applying the balance of the laminate. Later, the builder can coat areas that were missed, such as those areas behind the frames and bulkheads.

Resin can be applied to the C-FLEX with

FIG. 16-17 — This C-FLEX hull is being wetted out after all the material has been applied. Note the orientation of the rods along the leading edge of the keel; this was done by slitting a strip of the material lengthwise to the desired width.

brushes, rollers, or even a spray gun. But the simplest and easiest way is probably with a long nap roller. A typical problem with beginners is that they want to use TOO MUCH resin, and this must be avoided on the C-FLEX. Catalyze the resin and dip the roller right into it. Roll a coat over an area and let it soak in for a couple of minutes. Don't try to force the saturation by vigorous rolling as this will not speed saturation, but may instead loosen staples and upset the fairness of the planking. Then recoat areas which are dry and let these soak in, but be sure to remove excess resin with a squeegee, or move it around to other dry areas to avoid resin-rich areas.

Excess resin over and above that required to saturate the C-FLEX can cause a brittle laminate, excess shrinkage, and excess weight. Once the material has been wet through, do NOT apply more resin. It is not necessary to saturate the material so as to appear totally transparent, since this can be done from the inside later.

Once the C-FLEX has been coated and allowed to cure, the surface should be checked again for obvious irregularities, such as protruding bits and humps of material. A light sanding with a disc sander will even out the surface to remove nubs, high spots, or excessive resin build-up. Any obvious resin-rich areas should be sanded

FIG. 16-18 — After wetting out the C-FLEX, the hull is ready for the application of the laminate. Note the fairness of the hull at this point. Scaffolding has been erected for easy access to all areas of the hull surface. The attractive increasing radius along the stem area down to the sheer was made possible by orienting the C-FLEX vertically over this area.

down together with any hard corners and overhanging areas of the C-FLEX. However, take care NOT to cut into the rods of the material.

While slightly unfair areas and other irregularities can be corrected during the application of the laminate, any areas of obvious or severe unfairness should be corrected before applying the laminate. Areas in the rigid C-FLEX which are too low can be shimmed up from the underside, while high areas can be pulled down with wire or line tied from the C-FLEX to the framework. But hopefully your application will be fair enough to begin with so that this procedure is not required. The balance of

FIG. 16-19 — Top hat stiffeners (if required) can be made from C-FLEX and notched into the temporary and permanent bulkheads or frames. Permanent members will be bonded in place after the hull is righted, and all temporary members removed. In the photo, strips of double rods of C-FLEX are laid transversely over the forms and stiffeners to support the C-FLEX.

the laminate can then be applied in the normal fashion as noted in Chapter 12, but read the following section first.

LAMINATING PROCEDURES UNIQUE TO C-FLEX

Before applying the rest of the laminate, let the resin cure overnight first. It is also a good idea to wipe down the hull surfaces with a solvent wash to remove any dirt, dust, or grease. Here are a few points that should also be noted with regard to C-FLEX. A layer of mat is usually recommended directly against the C-FLEX, both on the outside and later on the inside of the hull. This mat layer helps fill in and even out the small hills and valleys along the C-FLEX rods and helps smooth out the surface. The C-FLEX will tend to flex between supports, but this is of no consequence as long as the force is not severe. Generally, woven roving is applied at right angles to the C-FLEX as much as possible (at least one of the layers). But this may vary with the design and should be checked to the plans. Note that when the hull has been righted and the interior of the C-FLEX is to be wetted out completely, it is NOT necessary that you use the special resin used to wet out the C-FLEX initially. Use your regular laminating resin this time because the hull is rigid enough now.

If the C-FLEX hull has been built in the manner previously described, and you plan on righting it WITHOUT the male mold or building form attached, the hull will still be too flexible to NOT require some sort of support, especially along the sheer AND if the boat is relatively large. This has been noted before, but emphasis should be made that additional temporary reinforcing in the form of a sheer batten clamped or fastened around the exterior should be provided to prevent hull distortion if the sheer clamp has not been bonded in permanently. This is why, if at all possible, righting the hull

WITH THE MOLD is preferable to prevent hull distortion.

CONSTRUCTION VARIATIONS WITH C-FLEX

The methods and procedures previously described to build a boat with C-FLEX have been proven over time and are especially suitable for the first-time builder. There are, however, variations and modifications which can be made to this process. For example, one of the advantages of the "ribband-batten" method is that, with some forethought and pre-planning, many (if not all) of the bulkheads, floors, and other permanent transverse hull members can be installed while upsidedown on the building form for permanent positioning into the hull at this time. This is especially applicable to larger designs having more complex interiors. Otherwise, these internal members will have to be installed AFTER the hull has been righted and the male mold removed, requiring a lot of fitting and cutting.

Since most large hulls will have several permanent bulkheads or similar transverse members, these are made in the initial stages of the construction if you wish to incorporate them into the male mold. Then they are set into their respective positions on the building form, along with any temporary intermediate frames required to support the C-FLEX along the length of the planks. When the hull is righted, the temporary frames will be thrown away, leaving the permanent members in place.

The bulkheads which will remain in the hull should not have parting film or tape placed onto their edges since they will be bonded to the inside of the hull skin. But they must be protected on their surfaces against incidental drips and splashes of resin. Conversely, temporary members should be covered with parting film so that the hull does not stick to them. The hull is

then made, and when completed, it is righted together with the male mold which includes the permanent members as well as the temporary members.

With the "ribband-batten" method, because of the thickness of the transverse battens (about ¼" or so in most cases), the bulkheads and other transverse members, if installed while the hull is upsidedown over the male mold, will automatically have the required gap or space between the bulkhead edge and the inner hull to prevent the formation of "hard spots" or stress concentrations (see Chapter 27 for more details). The bulkheads, floors, etc., are bonded in place from the underside; however, this cannot be done completely since the mold battens and other mold members will have to be cut away and dismantled at each permanent member first. Then the members can be completely bonded in place after the male mold framework has been removed.

Large fiberglass boats also usually require what amounts to "framing" in the standard

FIG. 16-20 — Close-up photo of the method of building in top hat stiffeners on a C-FLEX hull. Note the transverse double rods of C-FLEX which support the lengthwise strips of C-FLEX to be applied. Bonding angles will be used later to bond the top hat stiffeners to the inside of the hull (see Chapter 26).

sense, with these frames being what are called "top hat" sections, or channels made from fiberglass (see Chapter 26 for more details). These top hat sections may run athwartships or longitudinally, or both directions. However, especially in the longitudinal format, the C-FLEX is an ideal material from which these stiffening members can be made.

If desired, the top hat sections can be prefabricated and installed over the male mold to build them into the hull (see Fig. 16-19). This takes some pre-planning to know exactly where the bulkheads and frames will be located, and perhaps more lofting skill unless full size patterns are available. The longitudinal stiffeners are not attached to the hull completely until after the hull has been righted. If the top hat sections prove difficult to bend in due to hull shape, they can be cut through the web (not the face) to make them more flexible and later "repaired" with fiberglass bonding angles to restore their strength.

With the hull then righted, any interior laminate required is applied and the bulkheads are first bonded completely in place. Next, temporary members can be removed (the bulkheads now permanently anchored to the hull should provide ample stiffness), and the longitudinal stiffeners bonded in place completely if these are a part of the structure. It is not necessary that the top hat sections contact the hull all along; the slight gap will be taken up by the bonding angle used to bond the top hat sections to the inside of the hull.

While the preceding variations can save a lot of work in fitting and cutting of bulkheads, floors, and similar interior members, as is required when these members are installed AFTER the hull as been righted, the process may be questionable for the beginner. The pre-planning and forethought required may not be applicable to all designs.

For example, with our building form detailed in Chapter 11, it may not be possible to install a full bulkhead since the set-up members may interfere with it. In this case, a modified building form could be used, or perhaps only the portion of the bulkhead ABOVE the set-up members could be installed, or maybe the bulkhead could be "threaded" onto the set-up members beforehand and the holes later patched. As can be seen, complications may arise depending on many variables. In any case, considerable interior fiberglass work will still be required on the inside, and in some cases, this will be easier to do with the hull right side up WITHOUT any of the interior members to cause interference. The builder is advised to follow the plans, or if the option is available, he must make a decision based on his own preferences, keeping in mind the points that have been made.

CORE MATERIALS WITH C-FLEX

One of the disadvantages with C-FLEX hulls (or any single-skin fiberglass hull for that matter) is that there are no sound or thermal insulative qualities. Hence, single-skin fiberglass hulls can be noisy, hot or cold (depending on ambient temperatures), and subject to "sweating" or developing condensation on the inside. All of these problems, however, can be cured by the installation of a layer of foam or balsa core, but at an added expense.

When this is done, note that the core materials are not necessary as a structural component, since the C-FLEX hull should be strong enough on its own. While the core material could be fitted over the outside

(TEXT CONT. PG. 189)

The following group of photos (FIG. 16-21 through FIG. 16-44) show construction procedures required to build the 11' "FEATHER" sailboat illustrated by FIG. 1-1. The boat is built using C-FLEX fiberglass planking over a male mold. While this is a small boat, the procedures are similar to most boats using this material, regardless of size.

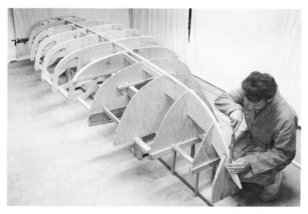

FIG. 16-21 — Frame members are aligned, mounted, and braced to the building form. A bevel is being applied to each side of the stem form so the C-FLEX will mate flat at this point.

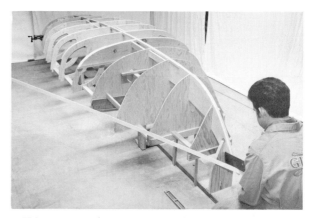

FIG. 16-22 — Sheer clamps fit into notches in the frames and are bevelled to mate flat to the side of the stem form. Use only enough fastenings to hold the members in place.

FIG. 16-23 — Frame members which will NOT remain in the hull are covered with cellophane tape along the edges to keep resin from sticking to them.

FIG. 16-24 — The C-FLEX material comes in a coiled roll. Oversize lengths are cut from the roll and applied over the framework.

FIG. 16-25 — A thin wood batten is laid over the centerline and the contour marked to the C-FLEX to determine the point where the overhanging strips will be trimmed to size.

FIG. 16-26 — A pair of tin snips is one method that can be used to trim the strips of C-FLEX to size after marking and stapling in place.

FIG. 16-27 — Staple the C-FLEX only as required to hold the material in place. Staples may have to be pulled and replaced in order to prevent buckling and unfair areas.

FIG. 16-28 — Notice the smooth curve of the C-FLEX along the sheer. The material should be free of humps and dips, but not overly taut or stretched.

FIG. 16-29 — The C-FLEX will move on a bias to some degree making it easy to apply over compounded or curved surfaces. Note that strips are laid in full lengths without transverse joints.

FIG. 16-30 — Joints between strips of C-FLEX are merely butted; not overlapped. Selvages should be pushed down at joints and protrusions trimmed off. Check for fairness and readjust staples as required.

FIG. 16-31 — The entire C-FLEX surface is wetted out with the initial coat of resin. Use only enough resin to coat the surface. Total saturation can be completed after righting the hull.

FIG. 16-32 — After the initial resin has set, lightly sand to remove any nubs or protrusions. Take care NOT to sand into or through the C-FLEX.

FIG. 16-33 — A layer of mat is normally used next to the C-FLEX. Where the mat bunches, gores can be cut or torn so these areas will overlap when wetted out with resin.

FIG. 16-34 — Fold the mat onto itself to the center of the piece and apply resin to what will be the backside. As the mat is unfolded onto the surface, the resin helps saturate from the backside.

FIG. 16-35 — Additional resin is applied to the surface of the mat once it has been unfolded in place. While a brush is being used here with a stipling action, a mat roller would ordinarily be used also to smooth out and saturate the mat, especially on larger boats.

FIG. 16-36 — The next layer of laminate (in this case cloth) is draped in place over the wet mat and coated with more resin. Apply resin from high areas to low areas, but avoid using too much.

FIG. 16-37 — Squeegeeing over the fabric is done to remove all air bubbles and wrinkles, and to assure even resin distribution. The force on the squeegee should be sufficient to remove any excess resin, yet saturate any resin-starved areas.

FIG. 16-38 — Overhanging edges of material should be trimmed off before the resin sets up hard. Otherwise, once set, the material will have to be ground off since it will be hard.

FIG. 16-39 — The hull is lightly sanded to eliminate any obvious unfair areas after the laminate has been applied. However, take care NOT to grind through any of the reinforcing fiberglass.

FIG. 16-40 — A wide putty knife or trowel can be used to apply the resin putty filler coat. This coat provides a sanding base and corrects for any irregularities.

FIG. 16-41 — The resin putty filler coat covers all areas of the hull. The surface will be rough before sanding, with some minor humps and dips.

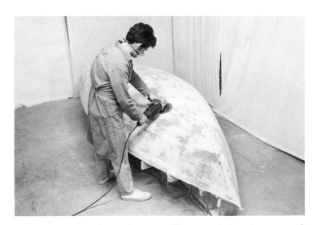

FIG. 16-42 — The resin putty filler coat is largely removed by sanding so the surface is fair and smooth. Notice the white areas indicating filled low spots.

FIG. 16-43 — Temporary forms are used to support the hull when righted and for the balance of construction. Larger boats would be painted and finished at this point, but a small boat such as this can be easily turned again and finished later.

FIG. 16-44 — Temporary members have been removed, but permanent members (sheer clamps, transom core, bulkheads, and partial frames) will remain in the hull. Additional C-FLEX and fiberglass will form the cockpit area and plywood will be used for the foredeck.

The following group of photos (FIG. 16-45 through FIG. 16-60) show construction of a C-FLEX canoe built over a male mold. The application of the C-FLEX is by a somewhat different approach that is not adaptable to all boats.

FIG. 16-45 — The simple male mold is made from plywood frames spanned with small longitudinal battens which in turn support transverse double rods of C-FLEX which support the C-FLEX planking.

FIG. 16-46 — The double transverse rods of C-FLEX are stapled to the longitudinal battens. These support the strips of C-FLEX and provide the hull shape.

FIG. 16-47 — After stapling the transverse double rods to the battens, they are coated with resin for extra stiffness.

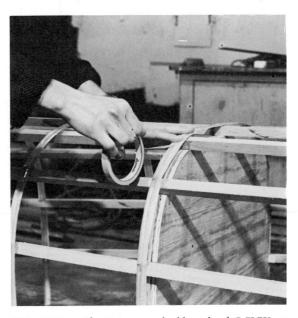

FIG. 16-48 — The transverse double rods of C-FLEX are covered with cellophane tape so the mold can be pulled free after making the hull.

FIG. 16-49 — Lengths of C-FLEX are wired together to form a total "blanket" which is draped over the male mold at once. On larger, more complex hulls, this procedure would not be practical.

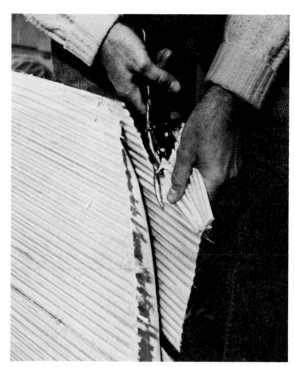

FIG. 16-50 — Tin snips are used to trim the ends of C-FLEX where they lap onto the stem forms.

FIG. 16-51 — At the stems, the ends of C-FLEX and the edge of the plywood stem forms are ground to a smooth radius. Note the temporary batten used to hold the C-FLEX in place.

FIG. 16-52 — After being rounded, the stem form edge is covered with cellophane tape so they can be removed from the hull later.

FIG. 16-53 — The stem junction is reinforced with cloth to join both halves of the C-FLEX together. The temporary batten will be removed after the joint has been coated with resin and allowed to cure.

FIG. 16-54 — The C-FLEX is coated with resin. The wire ties holding the strips together can be removed before the resin sets up hard.

FIG. 16-55 — The laminate has been applied over the C-FLEX and is just about complete. Additional laminate and reinforcing will be applied on the inside later.

FIG. 16-56 — Excess resin is being troweled off and the trowel used against the cloth to force the laminate down. There should be no glossy areas indicating resin richness.

FIG. 16-57 — The resin putty filler coat is being applied using a wide screed. This coat should not be any thicker than required for a fair surface and sanding base.

FIG. 16-58 — "Foamglas" is being used to fair the resin putty fill coat. This material can be cut into blocks of any convenient size.

FIG. 16-59 — The hull is righted and the male mold removed. Note the marks where the transverse double rods were located. The inside of the C-FLEX is now being wetted out. Note the outer sheer batten and wire used to hold the hull in shape temporarily.

FIG. 16-60 — After applying the inner laminate, inner and outer sheer battens of wood are installed, plus interior members. Note that foam is used for the thwarts; these will be encapsulated with fiberglass and bonded in place.

during the laminating sequence at some point, it is easier to put it on the inside wherever it is desired. If the core material is used on the outside in the laminate, it automatically becomes a structural component since it must be a link in the laminate chain, bonding one layer of the laminate to another. Hence, you will have to use one of the more expensive structural types of foam described in Chapter 19. Also, you will have to provide a means of bonding and securing the core in place, and with male mold methods, this could mean resorting to a vacuum bag technique such as shown in Chapter 22.

Regardless of whether the core is placed on the inside or the outside, the contoured type of material is advised since it will conform to contours more readily. However, for interior application, a non-structural core is entirely suitable, and this will not be so costly. When laying the core material on the inside, you will have to either remove any interior framing, such as bulkheads, or work around them. But you will be able to place the material wherever you want it, which would not be the case if the core were placed on the outside; in this instance, it would be difficult (if not impractical) to place the core on the outside in selective areas only because of the discontinuity created in the surface that would cause severe fairing problems. In either case, however, a core material about ¼" in thickness should be enough insulation for most applications to minimize noise and sweating, while giving some thermal insulative qualities as well.

Optionally, foam insulation can be sprayed in place. Sprayed urethane foam makes a tenacious bond to most surfaces. However, this is an operation for a professional, and there is some question regarding the safety of such foam, especially in the event of fire. Perhaps this danger could be overcome if a light laminate is applied over the foam using a fire-retardant resin, but this would add to the weight, cost, and work involved. Such a light, fire-retardant barrier would be advisable over the other insulative materials as well, especially those made from foam.

CHAPTER 17

Ferro-Glass system

"STR-R-ETCH MESH"

The FERRO-GLASS system for building a "one-off" fiberglass boat is relatively little known. The system basically uses fiberglass and resin, together with some proprietary products including a special wire mesh called "STR-R-ETCH MESH" by the inventor of the system, Mr. Platt Monfort. Not only has the system been proven in use as a boatbuilding material, but many professionals find the material ideal for making plugs used to make molds for female mold production work. The products comprising the system have been used to build boats as small as 10' and as large as 60'.

The secret of the FERRO-GLASS system is the "STR-R-ETCH MESH" itself. It's not at all like the ordinary "chicken wire" or typical hardware cloth-type mesh most are familiar with, and you won't find it at your local hardware store or farm implement outlet. The mesh is made up of interwoven 19 gauge wires running at 90 degrees to each other about ½" apart. The wires are NOT bonded or welded at any point except along the edge, which has a welded selvedge. The wires in the mesh are uncoated, bright, hard-drawn steel having a tensile strength of from 100,000 to 120,000 P.S.I. The wire mesh comes in 100' rolls either 3' or 4' wide, weighing about 4 oz. per square foot and .082" in nominal thickness.

A primary advantage of the FERRO-GLASS system using "STR-R-ETCH MESH" is that it is quick and easy, and the mesh is cheap in comparison to most of the materials used in "one-off" fiberglass boatbuilding. In effect, the wire mesh forms a stiff surface base or "armature" over a male mold formwork that allows a laminate to be built up without the need for a female mold. In this respect, the material in principle is much like C-FLEX fiberglass planking.

Because the wire mesh is interwoven and not welded or bonded where the wires cross, it has a unique ability to conform to compounded surfaces and complex shapes that make up boat hulls, especially those of round bilge form. Yet when the formwork is correctly made, the strength of the mesh is such that it provides sufficient rigidity once in place to support the application of the hull laminate. Furthermore, if the wire mesh is left in the hull, as will be discussed, it forms the basis of a wire-reinforced fiberglass laminate that inventor Monfort calls "STEEL-BELTED FERRO-GLASS".

FIG. 17-1 — The FERRO-GLASS system is based on this proprietary wire mesh product called "STR-R-ETCH MESH." The mesh is not bonded or welded except along the edge. This allows it to conform readily to complex shapes and curves.

THE FERRO-GLASS FORMWORK

Setting up the formwork for a hull to be built with the FERRO-GLASS system is much like other methods used to build "one-off" fiberglass hulls, especially C-FLEX, but perhaps even simpler. While one should not be careless in this procedure, the term, "clobbered together", as used by the inventor, is an apt description of the methods used to erect the male formwork over which the hull will be built.

Basically, the male mold consists of the athwartship station forms spaced as far apart as 24" to 30" which are crossed with longitudinal battens. In addition, a stem/keel form (determining the profile of the hull) is also required, and a transom form or stern profile form (if the hull is a double-ender). The longitudinal battens can be 1" × 1" or 1" × 2" members, depending on the hull size, or somewhat larger where station forms may be further apart. The battens are spaced about 6" apart maximum, but need not run full length. The main requirement is that the battens reflect a fair hull form. The orientation of the battens on the formwork matters little as long as they are generally fore and aft. Where they meet the stem form, there is no need for careful fitting since they will be covered by the mesh.

Vertical surfaces, such as those presented by keel appendages on sailboats (which are more or less distinct fins as opposed to the "wine glass" sections of more traditional forms) are best covered with plywood instead of the wire mesh. The fiberglass laminate is then applied directly to the plywood surface after covering with a release agent so that the hull can be easily removed from this portion of the mold. The reason that the mesh is not used on abrupt vertical surfaces is that it is difficult to hang the fiberglass on the mesh surface in this orientation.

In all cases, the formwork should be planned for easy removal once the hull has been righted. In most cases, the formwork will be ripped out of the inside of the hull, which means that it is best to fasten things together with nails as opposed to more permanent types of fastenings.

While the form can be built quickly and simply, this does not mean that it can be unfair. The builder should carefully fair the form members before applying the mesh to assure that unfairness is not "telegraphed" to the hull surface as the laminate is built up. Furthermore, to adhere to the designer's specifications and calculations, there should be a deduction made for the thickness of the battens as well as for the skin and mesh if outer hull dimensions are critical, such as would be the case for boats built to a measurement or class rule.

MESH APPLICATION

The mesh should be applied longitudinally. The builder must determine the width of mesh to be used. On small boats, it will be practical to cover each half with a single width of mesh, or perhaps a single width may cover the entire hull. However, on larger boats, a single width may not span from keel to sheer, and in this case, two or more widths per side will be required. If using two widths per side, butt the two selvedged edges together, letting the free edges run out along the keel and sheer. The butt joint between the two edges of mesh should take place over a batten. It may be necessary to increase the width of the batten used directly under such butt joints because extra stapling will be done in this area.

The mesh is unrolled lengthwise over the battens and stapled in place. The type of stapler makes little difference as long as it is a surface-type such as those used to install insulation, and the points are long enough to hold the mesh in place. Use just enough staples to hold the mesh and no more. Don't drive the staples too deep. Set the pressure of the stapler (if possible) so the staples just touch the wire without embedding it into a batten. Driving the staples too deep can cause an unfair spot to form. Staple alongside a wire where it crosses another so the staples stay low. This will help minimize surface fairing in the long run.

In applying the mesh, it is important NOT to dent the mesh. Such a dent will "telegraph" through the layup and show as an unfair spot. Except on the smallest boats, a helper or two is recommended for mesh application, both to make the job a little easier (since a wide, long roll can be rather unwieldy), and to keep from putting dents in the mesh.

Because of the nature of the mesh, it can conform easily in two directions, or "compound", without crimping. If the selvedge wire causes difficulty in laying on a mesh in any area, it can be snipped every 2" or so until the mesh can be pulled and formed to the contour. The welded selvedge can be cut off, but this can cause the first wire to unravel, and stapling will be more difficult. Don't cut an end off square after fitting, but rather cut an end to contour to match the hull configuration, such as at the stem or keel profile. Allow a 2" overlap at such ends as along the keel and stem when measuring.

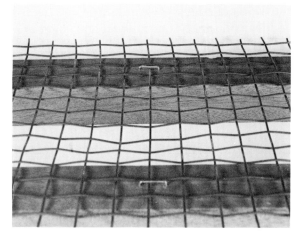

FIG. 17-2 — The "STR-R-ETCH MESH" is stapled to longitudinal battens. The staples are located alongside a wire where it crosses over another so the staples stay low. This helps minimize fairing later.

While the material forms easily to most shapes, it can be pulled or "tweaked" into place by grabbing onto it with a pair of pliers and pulling it into place, and then stapling. On reverse curves or "wine glass" sections, the mesh must be pulled or pushed into shape and stapled in place with enough staples to do the job. Don't over-pull the mesh as this can cause flat spots to form between the battens.

A decision should be made as to whether the mesh will stay in the boat or will be removed after the hull is complete and righted. If you decide to leave the mesh in and "steel belt" the hull (as the inventor calls it), the mesh should be well secured around all edges, and overlaps filled with an epoxy resin filler. Lace butted edges along the selvedge with thin (22 gauge) annealed wire. The mesh is now ready for the application of the hull laminate.

HULL LAMINATE APPLICATION

The approach to applying the laminate may vary both with the size of the boat and the designer's recommendations. A main consideration and advantage of the mesh is that because the laminate will be applied against an open mesh surface instead of against a solid surface, air will not become "trapped" in the laminate. This means that several layers of fiberglass can be applied to the surface and wetted out at once. However, with larger boats using thicker materials, and for beginners with little experience, this may not be advisable, at least without some practice. Another consideration with applying several layers at a time is the element of shrinkage and heat build-up in the resin. Too much resin at once can cause too much heat to build up in the laminate, which can cause problems, and this should not occur in the laminate.

Mat should be applied first against the mesh because the added rigidity of mat initially means that it will not tend to drape in any openings in the mesh. However, the small surface area of the mesh reduces the suction or surface tension that is inherent on a solid mold surface. Therefore on steeply angled or vertical surfaces such as occur when applying layers of mat across a hull, it is necessary to combine a woven roving or cloth layer against the mat to keep it from tearing apart when it is wetted out. In other words, the woven material must be incorporated with the dry layup as a reinforcing layer against the mat while resin is being applied.

Some may question, then, the use of mat against the mesh at all. However, a well wet out layer of mat against the wire prevents the wire from rusting. On larger boats (35' and up) a specialty fiberglass material called "Stitch Mat" can be used for the first layer as it is capable of draping around compound curvatures. This is a unique type of mat that has no starch binder in it, but rather is stitched together with woven roving and thus fulfills the need to reinforce the mat applied against the mesh.

Basically, the fiberglass laminate application is done like any other male mold hull, and final finishing is also the same. However, with the FERRO-GLASS system, technically you need only apply enough lami-

FIG. 17-3 — Open battened male molds ready for application of "STR-R-ETCH MESH." Note the orientation of the longitudinal battens; not all battens need be continuous, but they should span across as many frames as possible for fairness.

nate to make the hull reasonably strong. Once this point has been reached, the hull can be finished and righted, and the formwork removed. Then the balance of the laminate can be applied on the inside without the worry of building up irregularities on the surface, since it is already complete.

In most cases, mat is used as the first layer of laminate against the mesh. This is usually applied transversely, butting the seams and staggering the joints with respect to subsequent layers in the typical fashion. On small boats, the mat may have to be cut into narrower strips where shapes change more quickly in order for the mat to conform to the surface prior to wetting out. On or near areas that are more vertical, you can mechanically attach or otherwise fasten or secure the fiberglass in place as required to get it to lay as fair as possible before wetting it out, and to prevent movement of the materials.

After checking the surface for fairness with the fiberglass in place, wet out the laminate with a slow-curing thixotropic resin of low viscosity for fast wetout, and to minimize heat build-up and shrinkage. Apply resin from top areas to lower areas using just enough resin to make the laminate translucent. This translucency should be just enough to see the crosses of the wires below, but not the full mesh. If this resin application procedure is followed with care, there will be a minimum of resin running over the wood form members below, which will be important in removing the formwork.

Note that while several layers of material may be built up at once over the mesh itself, this is not the case on any vertical areas such as keel appendages covered solid with plywood or hardboard. In these cases, laminate application will be in the typical fashion, a layer at a time. Since such areas will usually be up high with the hull upside-down, start the layup here first. However, continue each layer down onto the mesh area of the hull so that there is plenty of overlap onto the hull surface without a break in the materials right at the transition between the hull and the keel appendage. This will prevent forming a weak spot in the laminate. If such an overlap onto the mesh cannot be conveniently done, then the entire laminate should be applied a layer at a time. After the laminate has been applied, the hull is finished in the standard manner as described in Chapter 13. Then the hull is righted for the balance of the construction.

APPLYING THE INNER LAMINATE

The manner used to finish the hull on the inside will vary if the mesh is to remain a part of the hull, or if the mesh will be removed. In either case, the formwork must be removed; however, don't remove the formwork right away if the mesh will be left in as will be explained shortly. If a large percentage of the laminate has yet to be applied on the inside, then the hull should be adequately supported and chocked in position so as not to distort. Similar methods can be used to support the hull, such as those described for the other "one-off" materials, especially those techniques used for sandwich-cored hulls.

There is some question as to whether or not it is desirable to leave the mesh in the hull or to take it out. The inventor of the

FIG. 17-4 — "STR-R-ETCH MESH" being stapled in place. The worker has the staple gun in position over the butt joint at the selvaged edges between two strips of mesh. Note the spacing of the battens and how the mesh conforms to the hull form.

system feels strongly that the mesh strengthens the hull, making it "shatter-proof" as he calls it. The argument is that the wire mesh has a higher modulus of elasticity than the fiberglass, therefore the hull will be stiffer and stronger. However, there are no known test results at this time to support either position.

Arguments against leaving the mesh in the hull are based primarily on the corrosion factor and rust. Inventor Monfort refutes this based on experience of past boats which have shown no deterioration over the years. He states that this is attributable to the products comprising the system precluding oxygen getting to the mesh (as will be described in more detail shortly), as well as isolating the mesh from contact from any through-hull fittings of dissimilar metals that could lead to corrosion.

If the builder opts to leave the mesh in, he should note that the mesh by itself will not stick to the inside of the hull, at least with any degree of tenacity; it's rather easy to pull it out. If the mesh is to stay in, then there should not be any obvious voids between the fiberglass skin and the mesh. If there are, it may be preferable to remove the mesh instead, since moisture could become trapped next to the wire and the laminate, and lead to corrosion.

If the mesh, however, is a firm, fair fit to the laminate, then another proprietary product in the system comes into play. In order to make a structural bond between the laminate and the wire mesh, a product called "FER-A-LITE" is used, also developed by the system's inventor. The "FER-A-LITE" is a trowelable synthetic aggregate/resin mixture which in effect becomes a "sand-

FIG. 17-5 — This traditional 14' Whitehall was built using the FERRO-GLASS system by an amateur who had never built a boat before.

wich core" (albeit a quite thin one) within the mesh between the inner and outer laminates, bonding them together and locking the mesh in place.

While the first inner layer of laminate should be mat, do not attempt to lay it directly onto the mesh. The mesh must first be filled with the "FER-A-LITE" to bond it in place so the mold can be pulled free without distorting or pulling the mesh out with it. The recommended way to do this is to leave the form battens in place and trowel the mixture between, setting pre-cut strips of mat directly into the wet "FER-A-LITE".

Mix the "FER-A-LITE" on the wet side (fairly thin) so that the resin will readily soak into the mat. Use a small section of metal plasterer's mesh to work the mat into place. When the piece of mesh gets too sticky with resin and tends to pull the mat apart, pour some acetone onto newspaper and rub the tool in it. This will clean off any mat fibers and excess resin, and prevent lifting the mat when tamping it in place. Apply the "FER-A-LITE" in a layer about 1/8" thick, and place the mat in it while it is wet. Gelling occurs in four to eight hours, and it cures to about 90% strength in a week or so.

After the preceding has been done, form members can be removed without pulling the mesh out, and the balance of the areas covered with the "FER-A-LITE" mixture and mat. The balance of the inner laminate can be applied immediately after, just as would be done for a sandwich core boat. Any through-hull fittings can be drilled using a wire-cutting blade in a saber saw, or a suitable hole saw. Fittings should be seated in "FER-A-LITE" so that the wire mesh does not contact any dissimilar metal fittings.

If the decision has been made not to leave the mesh in the hull, simply remove the formwork and the mesh. While the mesh can be removed easily enough, some cutting with snips and "peeling" out sections at a time may be required. After removing the mesh, go over the surfaces with a disc sander and lightly scuff the surface to assure a positive secondary bond for the next succeeding layers. There is no need to use the "FER-A-LITE" mixture in this instance, and the inner laminate is applied the conventional way.

CHAPTER 18   sandwich core materials & principles

WHAT IS A SANDWICH STRUCTURE?

A sandwich structure, such as that used in a boat hull, is a composite consisting of two relatively thin, high-strength, high-density skins or facings, separated by a relatively thick, low-strength, low-density core material. In fiberglass boats, the skins can be made from conventional fiberglass laminates or from the high modulus materials described in Chapter 21. Varying combinations and configurations of materials together with polyester, vinylester, or epoxy resins may be used in the laminate forming the skins, although ordinary polyester resins will suffice with conventional laminates of mat and woven roving or cloth. Several different core materials are available; however, three types have become more or less standard, and they are all in competition with each other as the "ideal" core material. These include END-GRAIN BALSA, non-cross linked PVC foam (such as AIREX), and the cross linked PVC foams (such as KLEGECELL). Each of these materials will be covered in more detail in further chapters, since they all have a place in boats that can be built by the amateur.

SANDWICH CORE PRINCIPLES

Sandwich core construction evolved during World War II as a result of the quest to achieve the highest strength with minimum weight for parts and components used in military service. In sandwich core structures, the skins are bonded to the core material so that there is no movement between the skins when the sandwich panel is subjected to bending and loading. The resulting composite is much stronger and stiffer in most (if not all) respects than if the same materials had been used alone.

Sandwich core construction gains its strength much the same way as an "I"-beam (see Fig. 18-1 and Fig. 18-2). The facing panels or skins are the same in principle as

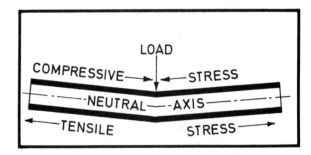

FIG. 18-1 — The facings of a sandwich panel resist the tension/compressive loads, while the core resists the shear stresses and stabilizes the facings against wrinkling and buckling. Because stresses along the neutral axis are minimal, the core material does not require high compressive or tensile strength.

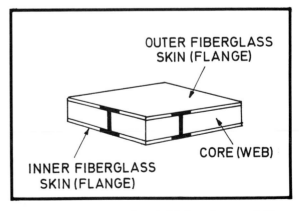

FIG. 18-2 — A structural sandwich functions much like a continuous or infinite "I"-beam. The skins serve as the flanges that carry longitudinal compressive and tension forces, while the core acts as the web carrying the vertical and horizontal shearing forces.

the flanges of the "I"-beam. They carry the longitudinal compressive and tension forces under load while the sandwich core is like the web of the "I"-beam, and carries the vertical and horizontal shearing forces. The core also provides dimensional stability for the relatively thin facings. The structural requirements of the facing panels are tensile, compressive, and yield strengths. In addition, the skins serve other purposes, such as providing toughness, weather resistance, impact and abrasion resistance, and in some cases, decorative value. The basic principle of sandwich construction is that the two facings determine the strength of the panel, while the core material and thickness of the core determines the stiffness of the panel.

One of the main differences between an "I"-beam and a sandwich panel, however, is that the sandwich panel has the ability to absorb damage to a large area, yet still carry a large portion of the original design load. In other words, the sandwich structure functions as an INFINITE or CONTINUOUS "I"-beam; there is no one point which, when damaged by impact or other overloads, would affect the structure's ability to carry the load.

Thus, it is easy to see that the integrity of any sandwich structure is DIRECTLY dependent upon the bond of the skins to the core material, and the ability of the core material to resist deformation and shear (see Fig. 18-3 and Fig. 18-4). The prime function of the core material is to carry shear and compressive loads from one face to the other. Thus, if the core material has a very low shear strength, no matter how strong the skins may be, the sandwich panel will not be able to carry high shear loads. In effect, the core may fail by breaking, crumbling, shearing, or separating, even though still bonded adequately to the skins, thereby allowing the skins to move independently of one another, possibly leading to a loss of structural integrity, and perhaps loss of the vessel. Conversely, a core ma-

terial with high shear strength can withstand high shear loads. Thus, a core material which maintains a sound bond between the skins and will not shear or "break" under load is considered a structural core, even though it may not be particularly strong by itself.

Core shear and the core shear modulus (the term engineers use to measure a core material's resistance to shearing action) are the main considerations in a sandwich core structure and the most important qualities separating a structural core material from one that is classified as a non-structural core, such as urethane foam, mentioned in Chapter 25. A material with low core shear modulus means that the material can bend and deflect, and lacks the necessary stiffness.

The BALTEK Corporation, makers of "CONTOURKORE" END-GRAIN BALSA,

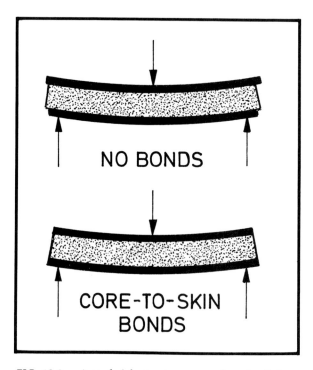

FIG. 18-3 — A sandwich structure cannot function if there are no bonds between the core and the skins. Under load in this situation, the core and the skins will simply slide apart; strength will be inadequate. Core-to-skin bonds must be sufficient to force failure in either the core or the skins at ultimate load; the bonds must NOT fail.

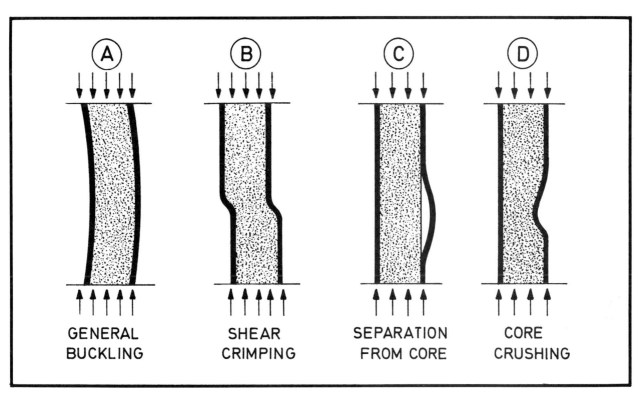

FIG. 18-4 — Several modes of failure that may occur in a sandwich structure under load are shown. General buckling (A) is deflection which may or may not lead to an actual failure, depending on the core material used. While standard sandwich structure design may equate any amount of deflection with failure, an AIREX sandwich, for example, can deflect without damage and virtually return to its original configuration. Shear crimping failure (B) may appear to be a local failure, but is actually a type of general buckling often associated with a core having a low core shear modulus. The crimping of the sandwich usually occurs without warning, causing the core to fail in shear at the crimp. It may also cause shear failure in the bonds between the facings and the core. Wrinkling of the facings may cause local failure such as buckling of the facings either outward (C) or inward (D), which varies with the type of core used and the bond between the core and the facings.

give a good analogy to describe the phenomenon of core shear in their engineering manual. They state that one way to easily understand core shear and core shear modulus is to use a deck of playing cards as an example. Notice that the deck of cards bends quite easily, with each individual card sliding over the other by a very small amount. This is the same as the occurrence of shear in engineering terms. Use a pen and draw a line perpendicular to the face of the cards across the edge of the deck, and the line will distort when the deck of cards is bent, indicating the amount of shear that is occurring within the deck (the deck being analogous to the core material). However, if the deck of cards is glued together and we try to bend them, there will be a tremendous increase in stiffness. The line on the edge of the deck of cards no longer distorts because the cards have been prevented from sliding or shearing; there is a big gain in the stiffness, or shear modulus.

The preceding method using a pen to mark a line along the edge can be used to check the shear modulus characteristics of any material that might be considered for use as a core material. Make a sample of the sandwich and put a series of perpendicular lines on the edge of the panel and then subject it to bending. If the lines remain perpendicular to the faces, this is an indication that the core material has a relatively high shear modulus, or "stiffness", and is not distorting. As the load is increased and the sample is bent, these lines will not remain parallel to one another, indicating further that there is good shear modulus under load. If on the other hand, the lines remain parallel to one another and are no longer perpendicular to the surface under load, this is an indication that there is deflection due to shearing action and the core material has a relatively low core shear modulus (see Fig. 18-5).

As a comparison between two materials often considered for use as a core material, note that END-GRAIN BALSA in standard boatbuilding density has a core shear modulus of 26,000 p.s.i., while urethane foam in a 2 lb. density has a core shear modulus of only 260 p.s.i., or about 1% of that of the END-GRAIN BALSA. In this comparison it is easy to see why a foam material such as urethane, especially in low densities, should not be considered for use as a structural core material in boats. Other physical

characteristics of three popular structural core materials are shown by Fig. 18-6.

Core shear modulus is not the only consideration used for selecting a core material for use in boats. Any core material under consideration should also meet the following criteria (although not listed in order of importance):

a. Lightweight, being preferably buoyant
b. Closed cell structure to prevent the movement or entrapment of moisture or water that may enter the core
c. Resistant to ageing and rot
d. Sufficient compressive and shear strength
e. Resistant to vibration and fatigue
f. Ability to be bonded and stay bonded to the skins
g. Formability to suit hull shapes
h. Good impact resistance
i. Resistant to anticipated ambient temperatures

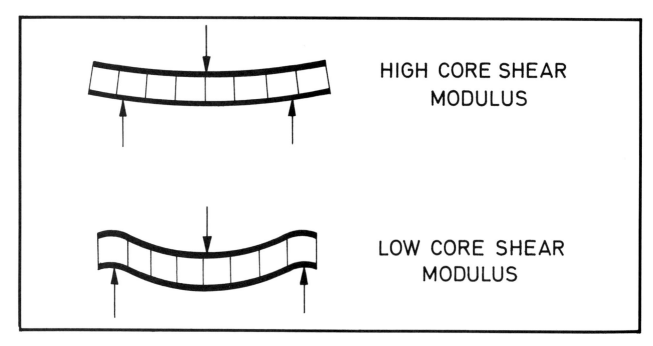

FIG. 18-5 — Core shear modulus measures the resistance of a core material to shearing action or distortion. A core material with low core shear modulus will allow the panel to deflect or distort easily; it will be lacking in stiffness even with strong skins. A core material with high core shear modulus will be stiff and not deflect, thereby allowing the skins to take the compressive and tensile loads in concert. A core material must have a high core shear modulus to be considered as a "structural" core material.

j. Thermal and sound insulative qualities
k. Fire resistant
l. Resistant to salt water, oil, gasoline, etc.
m. Easy to repair
n. Economical to use

Another consideration with core materials and the skin material used in conjunction with them is that they have similar rates of thermal expansion so that there will not be a danger of warping due to temperature changes. They must not swell in the presence of moisture either. The materials previously mentioned (the PVC foams and END-GRAIN BALSA) fulfill most of the foregoing criteria to an acceptable degree.

In all sandwich structures, the skins should have as high a strength as possible. When using fiberglass laminates for the skins, this results from having the glass content as high as possible within practical limits. Hence, with conventional fiberglass laminates, the use of mat should be kept to a minimum, and the higher glass content reinforcements emphasized. Although most core materials require a mat layer directly against the core in conventional fiberglass laminates to assure a positive core-to-skin bond, any other mat layers between layers of woven roving should be as thin as possible.

PHYSICAL PROPERTIES OF COMMON STRUCTURAL CORE MATERIALS [1]

	AIREX [2] TYPE 01/18[3]	AIREX [2] R62.80	KLEGECELL TYPE 75	CONTOURKORE END-GRAIN BALSA	
Density (lbs. cu. ft.)	5 lb.	5 lb.	4.7 lb.	6 lb.	8 lb.
Compressive strength (p.s.i.)[4]	80	125	160	750	1380
Compressive modulus (p.s.i.)		3600	4500	330,000	480,000
Tensile strength (p.s.i.)[4]	200	162	175	1375	1850
Shear strength (p.s.i.)	95	170	94	180	265
Shear modulus (p.s.i.)[5]	1000	1600	1640	14,450	21,400
Flexural strength (p.s.i.)	160	255	195	825	1250
Flexural modulus (p.s.i.)[6]	4400	4000	6200	280,000	425,000
Thermal conductivity (K-factor)	.26	.28	.174@72°	.25	–
Heat stability – max. limit	140°	160°	190°	[7]	[7]

FIG. 18-6

NOTES:
(1) Figures are based on data provided by the manufacturers of the materials. Some variations may occur due to testing procedures, ambient or test temperatures, etc.
(2) Figures for strength based on room temperature; because foams are thermoplastic, figures may vary with ambient temperature.
(3) No longer manufactured; included for comparison purposes to newer R62.80 grade.

(4) Compressive and tensile strengths in effect are opposites; one is pulling apart while the other is pushing together.
(5) Resistance to bending distortion or deflection.
(6) Modulus of elasticity, a measure of stiffness
(7) Not applicable as material does not deflect in presence of heat; will ignite instead at its maximum heat limit point, which is higher than the heat stability limit of the foams.

ADVANTAGES & DISADVANTAGES OF USING SANDWICH STRUCTURES IN BOATS

Why use a sandwich core to build a boat? A comparison can be made with a single-skin solid fiberglass laminate versus a sandwich structure in the load deflection curves shown in Fig. 18-7. Note that the two fiberglass skins of the sandwich structures are comparable to the single fiberglass skin. But with the addition of the core, strength properties in the sandwich structures are increased by wide margins at nearly comparable weights. From a design standpoint, this means that either the boat will be stronger at virtually the same weight, or to obtain the same strength, material usage and weight can be decreased dramatically.

Thus, a sandwich structure increases

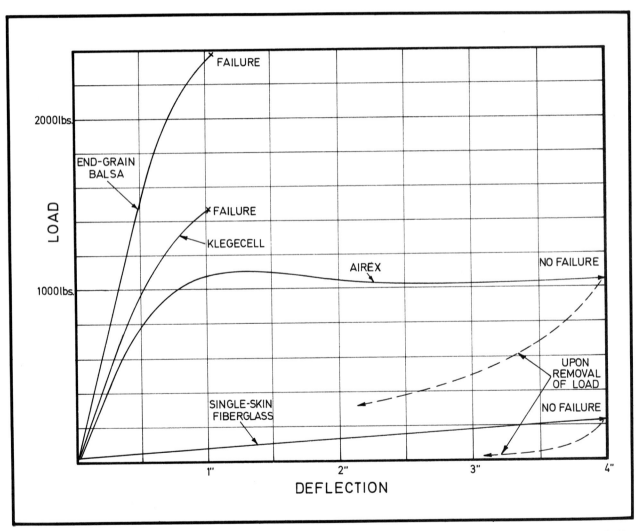

FIG. 18-7 — Typical load deflection curves for several sandwich structures using various structural core materials compared to single skin fiberglass. All cores are of equal thickness, and the fiberglass laminate schedules comparable. Sample panels are supported at the ends while the load is applied at the center. In all sandwich panel samples, the gain in load at low levels of deflection over a single skin fiberglass panel just by the addition of a core is remarkable. The easily deflected single skin fiberglass panels shows why internal stiffening members are necessary for rigidity in the single skin fiberglass hull. However, the curves for sandwich cored panels show the "stiff" nature of this method of construction and why such hulls may need little, if any, internal structure.

both tensile and compressive strengths, as well as impact resistance, while reducing the weight of the boat. This leads to improved and more economical performance, and increased fatigue resistance. Core materials commonly used in boatbuilding also provide acoustical and thermal insulation integral with the hull. The cored hulls and decks are quieter than single-skin fiberglass hulls because the core dampens out hull and machinery-borne noise, as well as slamming-induced noise from the sea. Acoustical properties equal or exceed those noise levels associated with wooden boats. The thermal insulative qualities mean no sweating inside the boat, less heat gain in summer, and less heat loss in winter for a more comfortable accommodation. Core materials also provide built-in buoyancy at the rate of about 55 lbs. per cubic foot of core material, varying somewhat with the core material density. This means that the hull itself could have positive buoyancy and not sink if holed below the waterline (assuming adequate additional flotation material is provided to support non-buoyant items also aboard). But one of the major advantages of using sandwich cores is that very little, if any, internal stiffeners or framing members are required in most cases, other than perhaps a few bulkheads if the boat is decked over.

However, sandwich structures are not without certain drawbacks. First and probably most important to the amateur is cost. Structural core materials are not cheap. In some cases, the core materials alone (without considering the skins) are more costly than some boatbuilding materials which used by themselves will result in a complete hull without the use of any additional materials (e.g. steel, wood, and plywood; see Appendix 3 for a cost analysis). Furthermore, sandwich core materials require extra steps in the building process, and in many cases, add complexity to the vessel's construction procedures and design elements.

Other problems after the boat is in use have been attributed to the use of certain core materials. For example, according to the Marine Survey Manual For Fiberglass Reinforced Plastics (see Bibliography), repetitive impact loads, such as those that may occur during docking, may destroy some cores, leading to progressive failure of the entire sandwich. The facings or skins which may be susceptible to slow leakage, such as through pin holes in the laminate, will lead to water absorption by the sandwich even with some unicellular cores, presumably due to the crushing of the cells at the interface between the core and the skin. This source also adds that cored hulls are more difficult to repair than single skin hulls, especially if any water has migrated into the structure, since all moisture would have to be eliminated before an effectual repair could be made.

However, some knowledgeable people in the field dispute this text, which is somewhat dated and written at a time when inferior core materials were more prevalent. For example, the makers of AIREX stress that repeated impacts do not destroy the cell structure of this type of foam. Because of its rigid-elastic quality, it can be compressed up to 50% of its thickness without crushing the cell structure, which is not the case with urethane or cross-linked PVC foams. They also point out that boats built with AIREX have a lower damage factor, and are actually easier to repair than single skin fiberglass hulls. They contend that there is no skin/core separation and no water absorption with an AIREX core.

It should be emphasized also that core materials like "CONTOURKORE" END-GRAIN BALSA, AIREX foam, and KLEGE-CELL foam, have all been internationally certified for hull and deck construction in fiberglass boats by Lloyd's Register of Shipping of Great Britain, as well as by other similar standards-making agencies in other countries. The fact that these agencies have faith in these various core materials should give confidence as to their value as hull construction materials, since these agencies are the ultimate underwriters of the vessels built with these materials. Because sandwich core hulls offer a unique combination of qualities not available from other boatbuilding materials, and because they can be used in both female and male mold methods, they are well within the realm of consideration by the amateur builder.

DESIGN CONSIDERATIONS & CHOOSING A CORE MATERIAL

The basic problem for the designer in all cases with all materials is, what limits does he design to? Or in simpler terms, how strong is strong enough? This is a big problem, not only because the designer must determine the anticipated stresses and how they will be distributed throughout the structure, but because there are several ways to measure or evaluate strength properties.

The varying physical properties of the various core materials in a boat hull can result in sandwich structures that can react quite differently and distinctly when compared to one another. A designer can make a structure so rigid that there is no allowance for any movement. Or he can design a structure with some degree of flexibility to allow for deflection. This latter approach tends to save weight, which can be important in

COMPARISON OF SANDWICH PANELS WITH VARYING CORE MATERIALS (*)

CORE MATERIAL	CONTOURKORE END-GRAIN BALSA	DOUGLAS FIR PLYWOOD	AIREX (OLD-STYLE 01/18 GRADE)	KLEGECELL (4 LBS.CU.FT.)
Flexural strength at 72° (lbs. rqd. on 20" span to deflect 1")	1272.7	1385.0	318.3	348.3
Shear strength at 72° (p.s.i. rqd. to failure)	491.4	510.0	222.4	59.8
Cleavage strength (bond strength between skins & core) average p.s.i. at 72°	590.9	88.0	230.7	169.3
Cleavage strength after 10 days under water at 8.6 p.s.i.g. pressure	534.7	125.0	229.3	155.0
As above, but with 5 cycles at 12 hour freeze and 12 hour at room temperature	699.1	119.0	266.3	256.3

NOTE: All cores ½" thick with skin facings of two layers 1½ oz. mat each side.

(*) BALTEK CORP.

FIG. 18-8 — Several sandwich panels using several structural core materials are compared. Note that while Douglas fir plywood is heavy, it does perform quite satisfactorily as a core material, except that bond strength is the lowest of the group. However, it surpasses all other core materials in flexural and shear strength, especially the foams. For some unexplained reason, the bond strength of the Douglas fir panel increased after the immersion test, while it decreased for all the other materials. Yet in the cycling test, the foams and balsa increased while the Douglas fir panel decreased. The KLEGECELL panel was much lower in shear strength at room temperature than any other samples, yet increased in value to nearly that of the AIREX sample in the cycling tests. While these tests may be representative, it should be noted that the density of the balsa material, as well as the type and density of the AIREX foam, and the grade and type of plywood are not stated.

many structures, including boats.

For example, examine the load deflection curve again showing curves for various fiberglass structures (see Fig. 18-7). It shows that a single-skin fiberglass laminate gives a curve that is linear with the load. In other words, it does not take much force to deflect the single fiberglass skin, and while deflection increases rather proportionally with increases in load, it does not fail either (within the limits of the graph shown). In other words, the single-skin fiberglass laminate is strong, BUT flexible; it just keeps bending and bending.

On the other hand, consider the curve for the balsa core sandwich, which at the current time is the stiffest of all sandwich structures ordinarily used in boats. The balsa sandwich can withstand a very high load without deflection. But when failure occurs, it comes quickly and with virtually no yield. Yet in a real-life situation, a material that has some degree of yield will provide a warning that the material is about to fail, thus giving time to take remedial actions to perhaps relieve the stresses that could lead to a potential failure.

FIG. 18-9 — **This small sample graphically shows the tremendous gain in stiffness that occurs with the addition of a core material. Notice the flexing of the solid fiberglass portion of the sample at the right. The total composition of the fiberglass laminate is identical on the left side except that a balsa core has been used between to equally divide the laminate into two thinner skins. There is no flexing on this side of the sample. Note the proper taper where the core ends; this prevents stress concentrations from forming at the transition from cored structures to those of solid laminates.**

In the engineering world, the theory is that the engineer knows the limits of the material as well as the forces involved so that the yield point is never reached. However, in naval architecture, knowing what forces will be involved when a vessel is being slammed and banged around in a seaway during a hurricane is still pretty much of a "black art". As a result, a designer literally must "over design" for materials with little or no yield by including a "factor-of-safety" to provide a margin of strength in extreme conditions so that the yield point is never reached.

Looking at the graph further, note that the KLEGECELL sandwich reacts similarly to the balsa sandwich, but will not take quite as much load. The AIREX sandwich, however, reacts quite differently. The curve is similar to that of the KLEGECELL sandwich up to a point, but will not take as much load. However, where the KLEGECELL sandwich fails (albeit at a higher load), the AIREX sandwich starts bending or yielding, but does NOT fail. With the KLEGECELL sandwich, if the load becomes too great, the core will fail through core shear failure. A core material that breaks easily in a simple bending situation does not match the resiliencey exhibited by the fiberglass skins and therefore can delaminate or fail. The brittle behaviour of a foam like KLEGECELL and the "no-warning" failure (albeit at a high load) of a balsa core sandwich contrasts sharply to the rigid elastic properties of a sandwich made from a foam like AIREX, which can bend without failure, but will not sustain as high a load before bending or deflection occurs (accompanying photos show these results in graphic form). It should be emphasized that the comparisons assume equal core thicknesses. Panel stiffness, however, increases by the cube in relation to increases in core thickness. Thus, a small increase in the thickness of an AIREX core, for example, could give stiffness equal to a KLEGECELL core.

Translated to a real-life situation at sea, should a hull suffer an impact, the fiberglass skins may yield without breaking, and absorb the impact energy. But with a core such as KLEGECELL foam or balsa underneath, the impact at a certain point could fracture the core or make it crumble, creating a void and delamination, at least locally. Subsequent flexing or dynamic loadings, and freezing/thawing cycles, could enlarge the delaminated area until it spreads, perhaps leading to an irrepairable situation and possible failure. Because of the brittle nature of the KLEGECELL sandwich and the stiff, unyielding nature of a balsa core sandwich, if an impact load exceeded the anticipated loads for which the sandwich structure was designed, it is likely that BOTH skins on the core would fracture due to the lack of resiliency in the core. This could lead to loss of the vessel. To overcome the problem in the design stage, the designer must use increasing factors of safety so that the ultimate yield or failure point is never reached.

A

B

C

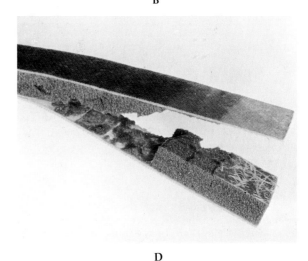

D

FIG. 18-10 — This series of photos shows the mode of failure under simple bending loads between non-cross linked PVC foam (such as AIREX, upper sample in 'A' and 'B') and cross linked PVC foam (such as KLEGECELL, lower sample in 'A' and 'B'). Laminates and core thicknesses are comparable. The non-cross linked PVC foam sample in 'C' shows some core compression and skin damage, but no loss of bond between the skins and the core. The cross linked PVC foam sample in 'D' also shows no loss of bond between the core and skins. However, the core has failed completely and skin damage is more extensive.

A

B

C

FIG. 18-11 — This series of photos shows the results of long beam tests on several core materials using comparable laminates and core thicknesses. In 'A', a balsa core sample shows core shear failure and skins which have delaminated in some areas, but not in other areas. Although the load was much higher than either of the foams (see 'B' and 'C'), failure occurred abruptly at overload and without warning. In 'B', a KLEGECELL foam core sample shows core shear failure. Although the load was higher than with AIREX (see 'C'), failure also occurred abruptly at overload without warning. Note that the core-to-skin bond is largely sound; failure occurred in the foam itself. In 'C', an AIREX foam core sample shows deflection under loads not as great as either the KLEGECELL or balsa sample. But there is no loss of bond and no core shear failure. The core shows only a slight amount of compression; panel integrity is not lost.

With a foam like AIREX, however, the rigid elastic quality allows the skins to move together with large impacts without delamination. Such loads may deform the outer skin as well as the foam core, but once the load has been removed, the foam and outer skin will return to approximately their original configuration, all without damage or failure to the inner skin. In other words, the AIREX hull might bend, but the boat would probably make it back to port. The ability of the AIREX foam to "give" under load, yet return to nearly its original shape and still maintain bonds to the skins, is unique in core materials, and allows the designer to work to lower limits.

However, some qualifications are noted with regard to these "lower limits" by the makers of KLEGECELL foam. While an AIREX core may "give", the KLEGECELL people note that this resiliency may not be suitable in all circumstances, especially in high-performance craft using thin-skinned panels with high-modulus materials like those described in Chapter 21. In these instances, panel stiffness AND lightweight are critical. The makers of KLEGECELL contend that under these conditions, their foam is superior to both AIREX and END-GRAIN BALSA, especially under heavy impact loads, or point loads concentrated over small areas of the hull that can lead to compression of the core and ultimate skin failure. In other words, the configuration of the skins also has a bearing on the performance of the TOTAL sandwich structure, making perhaps one type of core more suitable than another when the type of skin is considered.

The makers of END-GRAIN BALSA state that, in their experience, minute cell structure damage CAN occur in AIREX cored hulls, and that this damage can easily go unnoticed. They contend that this damage can later spread, perhaps leading to serious problems in the future.

The manufacturers of AIREX admit that their foam is inferior in comparison with other foams and cores in certain strength characteristics (see Fig. 18-8). However, they emphasize that in its designed function as a structural core material when used in conjunction with the proper skin facings, the material has not been surpassed by any other product in respect to suitability and performance. They further point out that even if an outer skin were punctured in an AIREX hull, and water did freeze in a void in the sandwich, the AIREX foam would probably have enough flexibility to absorb most of the expansion. However, the KLEGE-CELL people state that this is also the case for their foam (even though this does not seem as likely due to the rigid nature of the

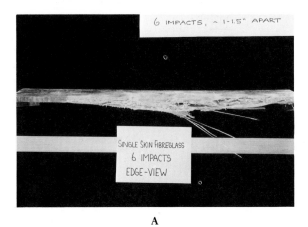

A

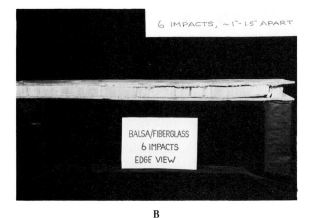

B

FIG. 18-12 — This series of photos shows the results of impact tests on several fiberglass structures. Glass fiber content and laminate compositions are comparable in all samples, although cores have been used in 'B' and 'C'. A single skin fiberglass laminate is shown in 'A'. The plies have delaminated and the laminate has failed, showing extensive damage on the side OPPOSITE the impacts. Structural integrity has been lost. A sandwich core laminate using a balsa core is shown in 'B'. Although the skins are virtually sound, the bond between the skins and the core has failed, as well as the core in limited areas. This indicates that the shock of the impacts has passed through the core to the inner skin. Another sandwich core laminate is shown in 'C' using an AIREX core. Although the top skin receiving the impacts and portions of the core have been somewhat deformed, bonds between the skins and the core remain sound. The inner (lower) skin is not deformed and the somewhat compressed core at the points of impact will recover to a high degree due to the rigid elastic nature of the core. The AIREX foam has absorbed the shock and isolated it from the inner skin.

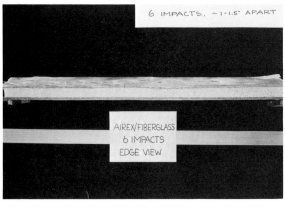

C

foam). And BOTH the makers of KLEGE-CELL and END-GRAIN BALSA dispute that AIREX is any more suitable than their products as a structural core material.

All of the foregoing has been included NOT to prove that one structural core material is better or superior than another. The main point is that there are many possible core materials that may be suitable for sandwich structures in boats. But for any one of them to perform suitably, the sandwich must be designed and engineered with knowledge of the characteristics of each. When designed properly, sandwich structures made from cores using END-GRAIN BALSA, AIREX, or KLEGECELL can result in boats that are more than strong enough for most uses.

THE "CLUB SANDWICH" APPROACH TO SANDWICH STRUCTURES

In some boats using sandwich cored hull structures, especially in the larger sizes, a core material may be used in layers or laminations, with fiberglass laminates on the outer skins as well as between the layers of core material. From a pure engineering point of view, this "club sandwich" approach, as it has become known, is difficult to defend from a strength standpoint. Remember that in the "I"-beam theory, it is the outer flanges of the "I"-beam (the flanges being analogous to the outer skins of the sandwich) that take the tension and compression loads, while the web portion of the "I"-beam (which compares to the core material in the sandwich structure) is in the center with no load taking place at this point, the center of the core being known as the "neutral axis". Thus, in the "club sandwich" approach where two core layers might be used, being separated by a fiberglass laminate, the middle laminate would be serving no useful purpose strengthwise as it is in the neutral axis. If this is the case, why is the "club sandwich"

approach used?

There are several reasons. First, thicker core materials may not be available, and this means that if the determination is made requiring a core of greater thickness than what is available, the designer can make up the required thickness by laminating thinner layers together. Secondly, even if thick enough core material is available, certain hull shapes might make application of the thicker core difficult, if not impossible or impractical. Thick sheet foams, for example, can be very difficult to bend, and hence may not conform to all hull contours, plus they can be harder to work with in certain situations. The answer, then, may be to use two thinner layers.

While it is argued that the additional laminate between layers is an unnecessary use of materials, plus an addition of undesirable weight, the inner layer need be nothing more than a thin, inexpensive mat. A discussion of the actual procedures for making a "club sandwich" appears in Chapter 19.

Currently there is no test data available to support the "club sandwich" approach under performance conditions compared to the standard sandwich. However, many believe that the practice does increase stiffness in the structure as well as the shear qualities of the core material itself due to the laminate skins. Also, it is a simple way to eliminate the need for frames (due to the thicker core) and the addition of complex interior structures, while at the same time increasing insulative qualities. This latter quality could be important, for example, on fishing boats for fish holds resulting in more useable hold volume.

SOME TYPICAL CORE MATERIALS USED IN BOAT STRUCTURES:

The following describes the general types of structural cores used in sandwich construction in boats. More details on how

FIG. 18-13 — A sample of non-cross linked PVC contoured foam (AIREX) where the material is die-cut into partially connected squares to conform to the curved surfaces of female molds.

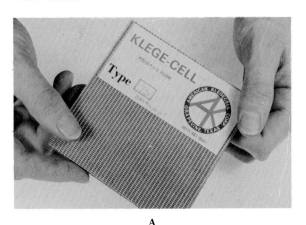

A

B

FIG. 18-14 — A sample of contoured cross linked PVC foam (KLEGECELL) where the material is die cut and held together by a scrim backing. The scrim must not be removed.

these products are used will be given in following chapters, together with related technical data.

TYPE: NON-CROSS LINKED PVC FOAM

A common marine-grade for boat hulls is AIREX. A medium density (5 lbs. per cubic foot) material is available in either a plain sheet or in contoured form which is die-cut into small interconnected squares primarily for use against the surfaces of female

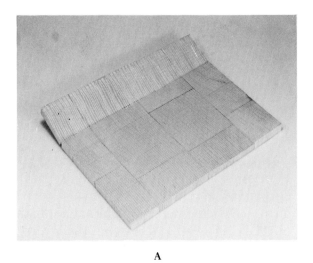

A

B

FIG. 18-15 — A sample of "CONTOURKORE" end-grain balsa core. The balsa is die cut into small blocks held together with a scrim backing that must not be removed.

molds (see Fig. 18-13). Thicknesses include ¼" (7mm), ⅜" (10mm), ½" (12mm), ⅝" (15mm), ¾" (20mm), and 1" (25mm).

TYPE: CROSS LINKED PVC FOAM

A common marine grade for boat hulls is KLEGECELL, usually available in varying densities. One type is available in a lower density of 3 lbs. per cubic foot for use on decks and bulkheads of smaller, lighter hulls. A regular type is used for most boat hulls and decks, and has an average density of 4.7 lbs. per cubic foot. The materials are available in four configurations: Plain flat sheet, a contoured type which consists of smaller squares on a fiberglass scrim backing (*), another similar contoured type which consists of larger squares on a fiberglass scrim (*), and a third contoured type which consists of squares with NO scrim,

but partially cut top and bottom so the squares stay interconnected (similar to Fig. 18-13). Thicknesses include ¼" (6mm), ⅜" (9mm), ½" (12mm) ⅝" (15mm), ¾" (19mm), 1" (25mm), and in contoured types, up to 1½" (38mm). Thicker material is available to order.

TYPE: END-GRAIN BALSA

A common marine grade for boat hulls and decks is BALTEK "CONTOURKORE" in 6 lbs. and 9 lbs. per cubic foot densities. The balsa is die-cut into small blocks held in place on an open weave fiberglass scrim (*). Thicknesses include ³⁄₁₆", ¼", ⅜", ⁷⁄₁₆", ½", ⅝", ¹¹⁄₁₆", ¾", 1", 1¼", 1½", 1¾", and 2". For most pleasure boat hulls, the range of from ⅜" to 1" is sufficient.

(*) Do NOT remove these scrims; they hold the blocks together and are compatible with resin.

CHAPTER 19

Synthetic foam materials of the rigid type are commonly used in fiberglass boatbuilding for several purposes in addition to their use as cores in structural sandwiches. While rigid foams are basically weak materials, they can still be categorized as either "structural" or "non-structural" types using the criteria discussed in Chapter 18 which separates the two. When foam is used as the core material in a structural sandwich core, it must be of a structural type.

However, for other uses of a non-structural nature, ample strength and other physical properties in the foam are not critical. Such uses can include foams used for flotation purposes such as those described in Chapter 25. Another use for non-structural foams is for formers over which fiberglass laminates can be built up into a given shape or configuration.

A common example of this practice is the use of long forming strips of rigid foam used to make the "top hat" sections from fiberglass laminates that serve as stringers or hull stiffeners on the inside of many fiberglass hulls. These types of stiffeners are described in more detail in Chapter 26. Although the foam formers used to make these stiffeners may remain in the hull after the stiffener is formed over the foam, the foam is still considered as a non-structural material since it's primary function is to provide the necessary "shape" required by the stiffener. In other words, the foam former in this case is considered expendable even though it may stay permanently in place.

Although there are several types of non-structural foams available, the two most common are the styrene and urethane types. However, as has been discussed elsewhere, the styrene type (better known as "Styrofoam", a brand name) is attacked by polyester resins without further treatment

A

B

FIG. 19-1 — These two samples of urethane foam may look similar to other types of structural foams. But because they are brittle, fracture easily, and crumble, they must be considered as non-structural types when used in a structural sandwich.

being done to the foam before the application of the resin. Thus, the majority of the non-structural foam used in boatbuilding currently is the urethane type, but this could change in the future, what with the rapid advances taking place in plastic technology.

The urethane foams are available in many densities, but for non-structural forming purposes, the density usually makes little difference. This type of foam can be purchased in sheets and blocks, and can be cut very easily with ordinary woodworking tools, making it ideal to use for forming members. This type of foam glues easily with a wide variety of glues, and can be bonded with resin putty fillers also. However, it should never be expected to stay bonded permanently. The reason is that rigid urethane foams are very friable; that is, they crumble easily and tend to breakdown with vibration and movement. It is this very quality (plus the fact that they absorb water) that makes typical urethanes ineligible for use as a structural core material.

STRUCTURAL FOAMS

There are two types of rigid foams that are frequently advised for use as cores in structural sandwiches used to build fiberglass boats. While both are commonly referred to as "PVC" (polyvinylchloride) foams, and both are manufactured under processes invented by the same person (a Professor Lindeman in Europe many years ago), they are NOT the same foam, and are NOT made with the same ingredients or by the same methods. Hence, they have different properties and characteristics. These have been discussed to some extent in Chapter 18.

One of the foams is generically referred to as a non-cross linked foam made from PVC compounds. An example of this foam is AIREX, a registered trademark of AIREX, A.G., Switzerland. The other foam is a cross linked polyvinyl aromatic polyamid foam consisting of a blend of approximately 60% PVC and 20% diisocyanates (a component used in the manufacture of urethane foams), plus chemical blowing agents. Thus, it is somewhat of a misnomer to refer to this foam as a PVC type. An example of this foam is KLEGECELL, a registered trademark of American Klegecell Corporation.

For simplicity and to avoid confusion, we'll use the brand names of AIREX and KLEGECELL throughout to distinguish between the two types. However, it should be noted in particular that other cross linked foams similar to KLEGECELL may be available in this country or in other countries. Some of these foams go under the brand names of "Divinycell", "Plasticell", and "Termanto", but have similar characteristics for the most part.

Both AIREX and KLEGECELL have been around since the 1950's, however, major market acceptance and use did not occur until the 1970's. While both foams are suitable for boatbuilding, and both have been approved for use in boat hulls by the major classification and underwriting agencies such as Lloyd's, each has different physical properties, advantages, and disadvantages that may be difficult for the novice to sort through. Thousands of large and small boats have been successfully built with either type of foam, and there are plenty of advocates for each type of product, both at the professional and the amateur level.

PHYSICAL PROPERTIES

We have stated that AIREX is a non-cross linked foam, while KLEGECELL is a cross linked foam, but what exactly does this mean? First off, AIREX is referred to as a thermoplastic material; that is, it will bend or form with the application of heat. On the other hand, a thermoset material is one that will NOT bend or form with heat, but instead will burn or melt. A rigid urethane foam is an example of such a foam. In a non-cross linked thermoplastic foam like AIREX, the PVC has molecules which are all "sticking" together when the material is cold, but not connected or "linked" together. In a urethane foam, although there are similar molecules, they are all connected or "cross linked". When the thermoplastic PVC foam is heated, the molecules start to "slide" by one another because they are not cross linked, allowing the material to bend and deform. However, in the thermoset urethane foam, if heat is applied, the foam will simply burn and/or melt because the molecules are connected or "cross linked", and can't move apart.

In KLEGECELL foam and other foams of this type, which is not 100% PVC, the other components "cross link" to the PVC portion, at least partially, forming "bonds" and making what is called a "cross linked" PVC foam. The resulting foam is a different type of thermoplastic material, behaving somewhat like a thermoset urethane foam, but still having thermoforming qualities. Compared to the non-cross linked PVC foam such as AIREX, the thermoforming quality differs to some extent as a consequence of the chemical difference, and this will be discussed later.

The chemical difference between the AIREX type and the KLEGECELL type foams is their most obvious differences (other than color), and is what accounts for the different characteristics of each type. The AIREX foam has a "rigid elastic" property that allows the foam to be slowly bent to virtually 180 degrees at room temperature without breaking. Yet it will return to nearly its original shape after a short period of time. It should be noted, however, that this ability to bend without breaking does diminish with decreasing temperatures. The terminology, "elastic", should not be misconstrued to infer that the foam is flexible like a rubber band; it is still considered a rigid type of foam.

On the other hand, the chemical nature of a foam like KLEGECELL gives the foam a certain brittleness, and if the same sort of bending were to occur, the foam would "snap" and break in two. However, this same sort of rigidity created by its chemical cross linkage increases the flexural and compressive strength over AIREX, resulting in increased stiffness and resistance to flexural (fatigue) failure according to the makers of KLEGECELL. It is this contrast between the two foam types that has caused an ongoing argument regarding the suitability of use of one material over the other as a core in structural sandwichs for boats, and one that will probably not be resolved in the near future.

Both types of foam are classified as "non-friable"; that is, they do not crumble like the typical urethane foam, and they are both closed cell. This closed cell structure is an important quality in core materials used in boats, and is one reason why some types of foam, such as urethane, should NOT be used in hulls for cores in structural sandwiches. A closed cell structure will NOT absorb water or other fluids. A foam core that could absorb water could lead to severe problems if used in a hull. For example, if there was a fracture in the outer skin, water could migrate throughout the core. This would not only add weight, but there could be failure of the sandwich (especially in the case of freezing), a loss of flotation value, a loss of insulative value, etc.

One past potential problem area with regard to AIREX should be clarified at this point, and this has to do with what is referred to as "styrene migration". What this means can best be shown by explaining the basic premise in sandwich construction, which is, the structural integrity of any sandwich structure is purely dependent on the soundness of the bond between the core material and the outer skins. If this bond is interrupted at any point in the structure, there is theoretically a weak spot at that point and the potential for trouble.

With the styrene migration "problem",

214

the styrene (the primary constituent of polyester resin and a solvent) had a softening effect on early types of AIREX. The foam acted somewhat like a "sponge", drawing the solvent from the skins and into the core, causing the resin to undercure in cases of severe styrene absorption and thereby possibly affecting the quality of the bond where this occurred. This phenomenon could occur even though the foam was a closed cell type. Although the foam would eventually harden, there was still a question as to whether the bond was as sound as it should have been. However, no severe consequences have ever been reported to date attributable to this condition, according to the manufacturers, and the conditions making such an occurrence possible no longer exist.

To prevent this softening action from occurring to the early types of AIREX, the ultimate user of the foam had to apply what was called a "seal coat" or "hot coat" of resin. This was either a thin coat of resin somewhat over-catalyzed in order to set up quickly, or a thin layer of promotor (cobalt napthanate) applied to the foam surface. This nuisance was later alleviated by the manufacturer by "pre-sealing" the foam with the cobalt coating at the factory. However, the problem was not completely solved because when working with AIREX as a core material, there is usually at least one of more areas on the hull where the builder sands the foam (such as for fairing purposes), effectively removing the seal coat, if only from a limited area. These "bare" areas then had to be sealed by the builder, again either with the cobalt or with a "hot coat" of resin to prevent styrene migration in these areas.

To put a stop to the problem entirely once and for all, the formulation used to make the foam was modified by the factory by mixing in the cobalt during the manufacturing process. All such foam now available is made in this manner so that seal coats can be dispensed with even if some sanding is required on the foam. The cobalt is now present throughout the foam. However, some long-time builders using AIREX still insist on applying seal coats of resin, but this is probably more out of habit than out of necessity.

Although the styrene migration problem is a thing of the past as far as polyester resins are concerned, there is still a remote occasion where a builder can have problems if he is using some vinylester resins. Under severe circumstances with certain vinylester resins having very high styrene contents of around 50% or more, high temperatures and high humidity common to some areas in the summertime cause the styrene to become more "aggressive", tending to make the foam soften initially. The cause of this effect is not known at this time, and the problem is extremely unusual, but has been known to occur.

The cross-linked PVC foams such as KLEGECELL, however, do not have any tendency for styrene migration or softening effects from polyester or vinylester resins. While iso resins are preferable because of improved physical properties, the less expensive ortho resins are acceptable with KLEGECELL or AIREX. However, bisphenol polyesters (not usually used by the amateur anyway) should not be used with foams because of high exothermic heat. If an epoxy resin is used against KLEGECELL, it should be of a low-solvent or solvent-free type; those which have high solvent concentrations may affect the foam. Hence, the reader is advised to contact the manufacturer of KLEGECELL or his local representative for specific brands and formulations of resin to use or avoid when considering epoxies for best results.

Another past problem with AIREX that has been blown out of proportion according to the AIREX people is the so-called "hot deck" problem. Early grades of AIREX, because of their thermoplastic properties, would start to become flexible at about 140 degrees F. In certain cases, given the right conditions, it could become possible for an AIREX sandwich to come close to these temperatures and become somewhat flexible.

The conditions necessary for this to occur included an AIREX sandwich with thinner-than-normal skins used for decks and cabin tops, by having the surfaces painted with dark or intense colors which absorbed heat readily, by using the boat where ambient temperatures are high (such as in the tropics), and by continued exposure to such conditions over a long period of time. While such an ideal set of negative conditions is rare, there were a few problems of this type in the past. However, the latest formulations of AIREX require over 160 degrees F. for any deflection to occur, and there are no shrinkage problems with the foam at these higher temperatures. Some long-time builders who prefer to use AIREX for hulls, however, still prefer KLEGECELL for decks and cabins. But part of this may be because AIREX is somewhat more expensive.

Other than the foregoing qualities, both the non-cross linked PVC and the cross linked PVC foams have similar physical properties. Both are non-ageing and will not rot, mold, mildew, or support flame. Both are impervious to sea or salt water, as well as dilute acids and alkalies, and resistant to gasoline and diesel fuel oils. However, neither is too compatible with ketones such as acetone, esters, and some chlorinated or aromatic hydrocarbons. Both foams are excellent insulation materials. Although both foams are easy to cut and sand, the cross linked PVC foam has a slight advantage when it comes to sanding and fairing.

THERMOFORMING

The plain rigid sheets of foam material (non-contoured type) may, in some cases, require the application of heat in order to conform to certain contours. This is called thermoforming, and can be done by local application of heat, such as with a portable heat blower, or in an "oven" which can be made by the builder where it is necessary to heat an entire sheet for forming. Generally on larger boats where hull shapes do not change abruptly, little if any thermoforming is necessary; the sheets are usually flexible enough to be held in position without thermoforming.

If thermoforming is required, the methods required and the characteristics of the foam during thermoforming vary between the non-cross linked PVC foams like AIREX and the cross-linked PVC foams like KLEGECELL. The AIREX foam, for example, requires less heat than the KLEGECELL foam. With AIREX, the foam will start to become formable at about 175–180 degrees F. KLEGECELL foam is heat stable to 190 degrees F. and requires 220–230 degrees F. for about one to three minutes before becoming formable.

However, in the author's experience, the AIREX type foam is easier to heat-form than KLEGECELL. Less heat is required to make the foam flexible, and an even application of heat is easier to accomplish without damaging the foam. In addition, the foam stays

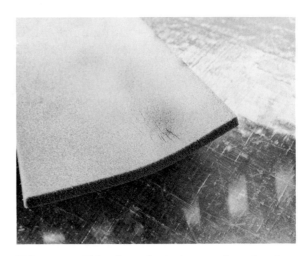

FIG. 19-2 — This piece of KLEGECELL foam has been scorched and deformed by too much heat applied for too long a time. Notice the cracks in one area of the surface. The piece should not be used in this condition.

supple for a longer period of time, making it easier to work and position before the sheet gets hard again.

With KLEGECELL, it is easy to burn or "overcook" the foam (see Fig. 19-2), especially when applying localized heat, tending to make the foam brittle, especially around the edges, and it tends to craze, crack, and develop a "glazed" appearance on the surface more easily. Furthermore, there is usually not enough time to get the foam from the heat source to the work area before the foam becomes unworkable.

Probably the differences between the foams with respect to thermoforming has to do with the fact that AIREX is a thermoplastic, while KLEGECELL is only partially so. However, as noted, thermoforming is seldom necessary, but if a lot of this activity will be required, the AIREX type of foam is easier to work with, partly because it bends easier in the first place without failure.

GLUING FOAMS

In fiberglass boatbuilding there may be occasions where it is necessary to glue foam

FIG. 19-3 — Production builders sometimes use split female molds to make it easier to build the hull and remove from the mold. An AIREX foam core is being applied inside this hull, the halves of which will be joined together later.

materials such as AIREX or KLEGECELL. Generally, most adhesives that can be used to glue other plastic foams such as styrene and urethane, can be used. These glues would include resorcinol, urea formaldehyde (plastic resin), aliphatic resin, epoxy, and water-base contact cements. Adhesives containing solvents such as ketones, esters, and/or aromatic hydrocarbons should normally be avoided. The latter is especially important where foam may be glued to itself in large areas or to an impervious surface where the solvents could be "trapped" and perhaps degrade the foam.

Although a laminating resin can be used for an adhesive, it differs from an adhesive since it is intended to encapsulate a reinforcing material such as fiberglass. Adhesives, however, will generally not encapsulate a reinforcing material, and should not be used for the purpose of reinforcing fibers in the manner that resin is used for a fiberglass structure. An exception to this rule would be most epoxy resin formulations that also make excellent adhesives as well as bonding and wetting-out agents in a reinforcing laminate.

When using any adhesive, follow the instructions to the letter, especially with regard to temperature and moisture restrictions, surface preparation, application methods, and clamping requirements. Note that any adhesive that is not waterproof or highly water resistant should only be used for non-structural or temporary purposes. If you want something to stick permanently in place in the boat, only waterproof or highly water resistant glues should be used.

USING FOAM CORES IN FEMALE MOLDS

Either AIREX or KLEGECELL type foams can be used in female molds to build sandwich cored hulls. However, the contoured type of foam is recommended in order for the foam to conform to the surfaces of the

mold. The contoured foam is also used in this situation in order for air to pass through the slits in the foam to prevent air entrapment between the outer skin and the foam. This usually precludes the need to apply pressure constantly against the surface of the foam by hand, weights, or with a vacuum bag as the resin cures, requiring only

FIG. 19-4 — Contoured-type foam is usually used inside female molds in order to conform to hull contours easily. Note the small blocks of these AIREX sheets are only partially cut. Numbers on the foam sheets designate the positions of the respective sheets in the hull.

FIG. 19-5 — When laying contoured foam in a female mold, pressure against the foam must be uniform, but not excessive. Note the resin coming through the slits in this AIREX core, indicating a sound bond.

that the worker firmly press the foam in place against the surface.

The procedures for building a hull with a foam core in a female mold are the same as for a single-skin hull built in a female mold except that core material is placed into the mold about half-way through the layup. The fiberglass applied against the female mold to this point will be the outer skin, and the fiberglass next applied over the surface of the foam core will make the inner second skin.

Regardless of the configuration of the layup, if it is of the conventional type, the foam core should be placed into a bedding layer of 1½ oz. mat well saturated with resin. Do this by letting the last woven roving layer of the outer skin set up first and grind off lightly any protruding high spots that might

interfere with a smooth mat and foam application. The laminate at this point is allowed to set up also to eliminate any chance for exothermic heat to effect the foam because the foam is a good insulator that may tend to "trap" this heat between the mold surface and the foam. This can have a negative effect on the laminate as well as the gel coat. Then fit the foam core sheets in place, marking them if required so they can be set into their proper positions later.

It is not necessary that the foam sheets be fitted too closely. Where sheets will not fit and butt readily due to hull contours and tend to leave pie-shaped or triangular gaps, fill these in with pieces cut to shape from plain sheets (see Fig. 19-6). Cut slits in one side of these pieces to make them bend easier if required. Any other gaps can later

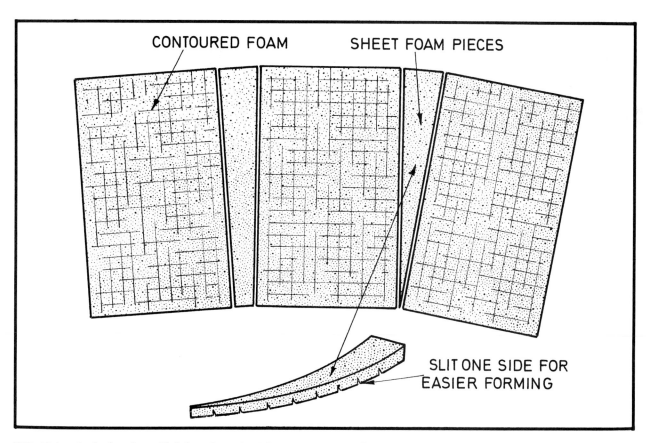

FIG. 19-6 — In the female mold, it is easier and quicker to cut pie-shaped pieces of plain sheet foam to fill in the spaces between contoured sheets rather than cutting contoured pieces to a precise fit. Slit one side of the pie-shaped pieces so they will conform to the mold surface.

be filled in with foam scraps prior to applying the inner laminate. Then apply resin to the surface of each sheet of foam to the side that will face down to the mold surface prior to putting them in position.

Wet out and apply the 1½ oz. mat against the woven roving layer in the first skin with resin catalyzed to gel in 30 to 45 minutes. Roll out the mat with a mat roller just enough to eliminate any air entrapment, and then immediately position the foam sheets in place. Press down on the foam sheets either with paint rollers or hands until resin begins to show between the slits of foam. However, it is not absolutely necessary that the resin becomes visible between EVERY slit; a good bond can still be achieved if the resin does not come up between the slits. When the inner skin is applied, the resin from this layer will be worked down into the foam and pass through any slits where there may be minor resin-free voids. Use weights to hold down

FIG. 19-8 — This type of knife is ideal for cutting, trimming, and bevelling edges of core materials.

the core in any stubborn areas, but these are seldom necessary, at least over extensive areas.

A simple test is used to determine the quality of the bond made under the foam core. Use the edge of a coin and scrape it along all areas of the foam. At areas where there will be a void under the foam (indicating an unbonded area), the sound will be distinctly different from the sound made in most areas; it will give off a "hollow" sound. Such an area can be re-bonded by cutting out or lifting the unbonded squares, applying more resin, and re-bonding the core, or resin can be injected with a hyperdermic syringe. However, there should be few such voids, especially when the contoured type foams are used and a proper, careful application has been done.

Once the foam is in place, and all gaps have been filled in with foam scraps and bonded in place, the surface can be prepared for the application of the inner laminate. Some builders prefer to fill all gaps with a resin putty filler, however, this is more work (requiring careful sanding on the foam which can cause problems) and expense. Pieces of foam bonded in with resin are entirely adequate.

In areas of the hull which are to be solid fiberglass laminate, remove any foam that may be in the way. At the boundaries of these areas, the edges of the foam must be bevelled at least to 45 degree angles or preferably to a 3:1 taper to eliminate the formation of "hard spots" that would other-

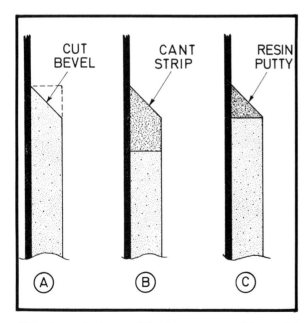

FIG. 19-7 — At the transition from core materials to solid fiberglass laminates, the edges of the core must be bevelled to prevent stress concentrations from forming. Several methods can be used. In 'A', the edge is cut to a bevel. In 'B', a separate pre-bevelled cant strip has been fitted against the square edge of the core. In 'C', a bevel has been built up with resin putty against the square edge of the core.

wise be formed at the transition from the core to the solid fiberglass areas (see Fig. 19-7). Use a sharp knife to cut these bevels (see Fig. 19-8) or a disc sander. Clean up all loose scraps of foam from the surface and preferably vacuum all surfaces to be free of dust prior to applying the inner laminate.

The inner laminate is applied in the conventional manner, using a layer of mat first against the core. However, this layer of mat need be only a light ¾ oz. or 1 oz. maximum weight because the foam is not being "pushed" into the mat as it was against the outer mat laminate. In applying the mat, do make sure there is ample resin. First coat the foam with resin, then the mat after it is fitted, applying the resin to the back side by folding the mat as was noted in Chapter 12. This will assure plenty of resin in this layer and enough to help wet out the next layer of woven roving from the back side which should also be applied immediately after the mat. If a "club sandwich" laminate is required (a double layer of foam), apply another bedding layer of mat against the first layer of foam and repeat with another layer of foam prior to applying the inner laminate.

As with all sandwich structures, the inner and outer skins should be about the same thickness, with perhaps the outer skin being somewhat thicker for practical reasons. Once the inner laminate has been applied, work can be done to the inside of the boat as required. The hull, however, can be removed from the mold prior to this time if necessary, and set into a receiving cradle.

BUILDING A MALE MOLD FOAM CORED HULL

The general procedures (see Fig. 19-9) for building a foam cored hull over a male mold consist of making an open battened male mold over which the foam core is applied, then covering this with the outer fiberglass skin and finishing it off. The hull at this

point is then righted, together with the male mold (and perhaps the building form as well), with a supporting cradle used to hold the hull while the male mold is removed. After the male mold is removed, the inner fiberglass laminate is applied, and then any interior members. This basic sequence is the same regardless of the type of foam used. The methods used to build up the fiberglass portions of the sandwich structure are similar to that of any fiberglass boat. The prime area which requires elucidation is the actual application of the foam core to the male mold.

The male mold is built in the manner previously described in Chapter 11 after considerations have been made for the deduction from the loftings or patterns for the thickness of the core and the longitudinal battens, etc. Areas of the hull that will be solid fiberglass must be built up with solid wood or other suitable filler materials to be flush with the outer foam surface. All such areas of the male mold which will not be bonded to the inside of the hull must be covered with parting agent or release film. Some builders cover the entire male mold with sheet plastic, however, this is technically only required under the joints in the foam sheets (where resin may leak through) and at areas of solid fiberglass laminate.

Plain sheet foam material as opposed to the contour types is usually used over the open battened male mold. There are several reasons for this. First, there is a chance that the small blocks of the contoured type of foam will tend to droop and fall below the surface of the mold, especially if battens are too far apart and the contoured materials held together with a scrim backing are used. Secondly, depending on the hull shape, the small blocks in the sheets of contoured foam tend to present slight raised edges or corners as the sheets are wrapped around the hull contours, making it more difficult to fair the outer surface. This tendency of the contoured foam sheets increases as hull

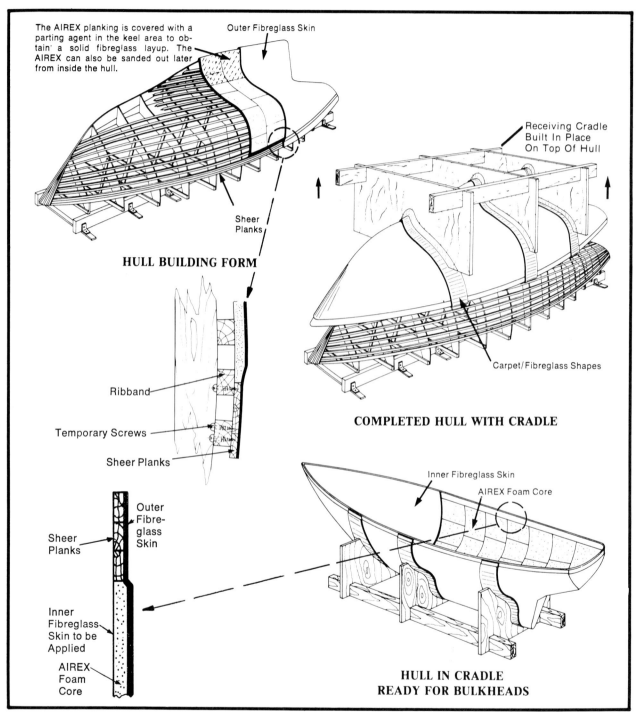

The AIREX planking is covered with a parting agent in the keel area to obtain a solid fibreglass layup. The AIREX can also be sanded out later from inside the hull.

Outer Fibreglass Skin

Sheer Planks

HULL BUILDING FORM

Ribband

Temporary Screws

Sheer Planks

Outer Fibre-glass Skin

Sheer Planks

Inner Fibreglass Skin to be Applied

AIREX Foam Core

Receiving Cradle Built In Place On Top Of Hull

Carpet/Fibreglass Shapes

COMPLETED HULL WITH CRADLE

Inner Fibreglass Skin

AIREX Foam Core

HULL IN CRADLE READY FOR BULKHEADS

FIG. 19-9 — This series of illustrations show the general procedures of building a male molded AIREX foam sandwich cored hull. Other types of foam materials are handled similarly. The core material may or may not be applied along the centerline, depending on the design. In this example, the foam core is initially applied over the mold in the keel area, but removed later to form a solid fiberglass laminate here. This is somewhat a waste of foam and creates additional work on the inside after the hull is righted and the male mold removed. Instead, solid areas can be built up as shown in some of the other illustrations in this chapter so that no foam is required in these areas. Note the details showing the sheer area. The wood sheer clamp members are somewhat thinner than the foam core to provide an indentation or offset along the sheer that will be filled in by the deck laminate where it will later lap over onto the hull surface.

contours become more severe. While the core can be sanded to smooth down such abrupt changes on the surface, this tends to reduce the thickness of the core, reducing the strength properties of the sandwich. Finally, it is more tedious to attach contoured foam sheets to the hull because of all the partially cut or individual small blocks.

The foam sheets can be fastened to the male mold by several methods or combination of methods (see Fig. 19-12). The foam can be nailed to the battens with small-headed nails (like finish nails) of lengths to protrude through the battens on the inside of the mold. These nails can be pulled through the foam later when the male mold is removed. Another method is to use screws from the back side through the battens and into the foam. Screws work well with thicker foams because the screws will have enough thread length to get a hold onto the foam, but not so well with thinner foams of around ⅜" thick or less. Screws should not be so long that the points protrude through the surface of the foam. An excellent screw to use is the pan head or hex head sheet metal screw which has a coarse, open thread for a tight hold onto the foam. However, using screws can be tedious since many will be required.

Probably the easiest way to fasten the foam to the mold is to sew or stitch it on. This is a two-person job, with one worker passing the needle through the core to a

FIG. 19-10 — A section through the male mold shown in Fig. 19-9 showing the progressive steps of building up a foam sandwich cored hull. In this instance, since the foam will be applied across the keel area, battens will be required at this point. Note that the battens in the garboard area (junction at the hull and keel appendage), and at the centerline, are square-shaped and more closely spaced together due to the tight turns. To save work, pre-drill the battens every 6" or so for the screws that will be used to fasten the foam in place. Note the solid wood sheer clamps that will be located between the inner and outer skins. The outer fiberglass skin is then applied. While an additional layup is shown on the outside at the keel, it is also possible to make this extra thickness on the inside laminate later after the foam has been removed from this area; this will save fairing.

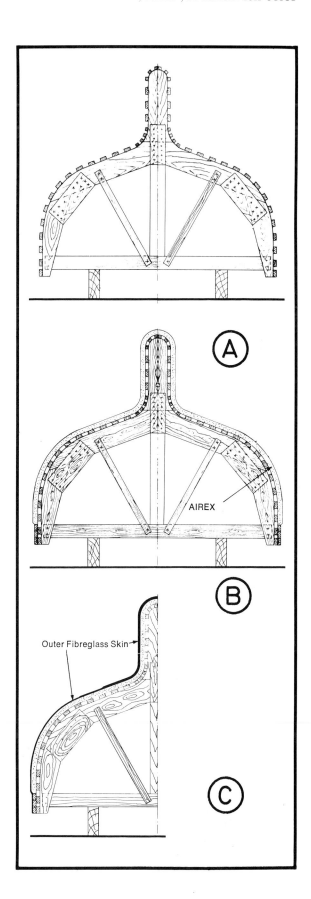

223

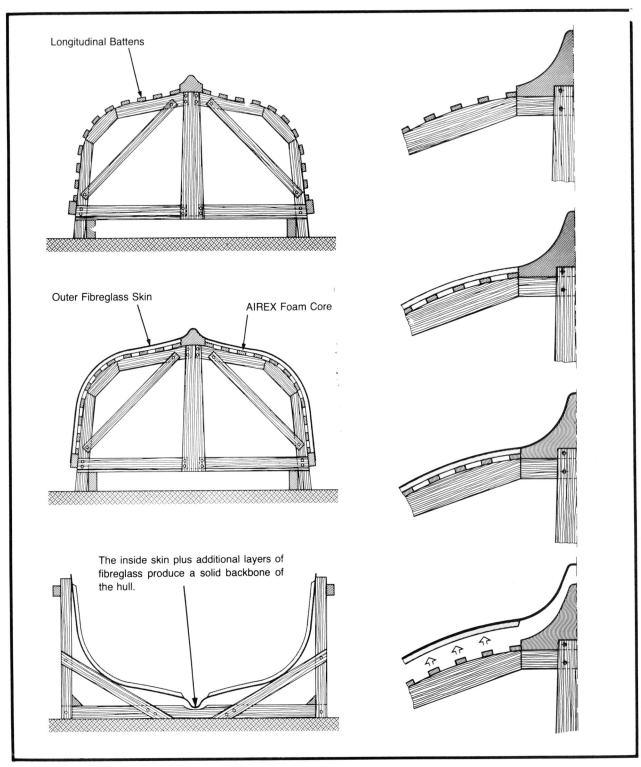

Longitudinal Battens

Outer Fibreglass Skin

AIREX Foam Core

The inside skin plus additional layers of fibreglass produce a solid backbone of the hull.

FIG. 19-11 — This series of illustrations also show the general construction sequence of building a male molded AIREX foam sandwich cored hull. However, in this case, the keel area has been built up on the mold to be solid fibreglass laminate, as have the areas along the sheer. The sheer clamp members will be installed later after the inner fiberglass laminate. Basically, the foam core is applied over the male mold. An outer fiberglass laminate is built up over the foam. After finishing the surface, the hull is righted, the mold removed, and the inner laminate applied.

person on the inside who ties the line around the battens and passes the needle back through (this is one reason why it is necessary to have access inside the male mold). A strong nylon monofilament or polypropylene fishing line about 1/32" in diameter can be used, with a fairly large needle such as the curved-type used in upholstery.

The person on the inside directs the person on the outside where to pass the needle through, taking about a 3" stitch before passing the needle back again. Stitch along all areas and edges of the foam as is required to get it to conform to the mold battens. Pull the line taut enough to slightly indent the foam, but avoid excessive crushing or cutting into the foam with the line. Some workers will actually make a slight slit in the foam on the surface so that the line is just recessed below the surface, the idea being that the line otherwise would make an abrupt surface unfairness that could be transferred to the outer surface of the laminate. However, this practice with most laminates using a moderate sized line is not necessary as the line can be pulled taut and flush with the foam surface. Resin or resin putty can be used at the needle holes where the line passes through to glue or "lock" the stitching to help maintain tension. After the hull is righted, the line is cut at all points prior to removing the male mold.

The makers of KLEGECELL state that their foam can be stapled to the battens in thicknesses up to ½", with the staples being pulled through the foam after the hull is righted. However, this should be done with care since it is easy to pull out bits and pieces of the foam. If this occurs, the damaged areas should be filled. Another problem with stapling is that there is a tendency to indent the foam at each staple, making fairing potentially more difficult.

Instead of physically holding the foam in place against the male mold while fastening the foam, use nails fitted with thin plywood washer blocks as shown in some of the pho-

tos. The plywood washer blocks prevent denting the foam with the hammer and also prevent setting the nail too deeply into or through the foam. They also make it easier to remove the nails once the foam has been fastened in place by stitching or screwing. In many cases, it is not uncommon to use all of the foregoing methods to hold and fasten the foam to the male mold, depending on the type of boat.

THERMOFORMING TECHNIQUES

Where foam sheets will not conform to

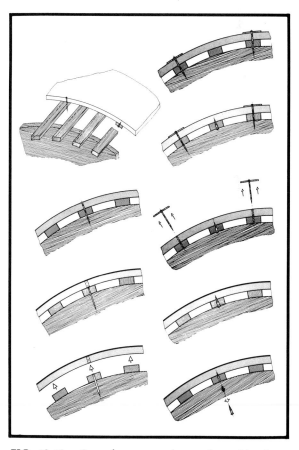

FIG. 19-12 — Several ways are shown of attaching foam cores to the longitudinal battens of the male mold. These include using finish nails which are pulled through the foam when the hull is removed from the mold, screws driven through the battens into the foam from the underside which are backed out before the hull is removed from the mold, and nails fitted with washer blocks to hold the foam in place while it is being fastened or sewn on.

FIG. 19-13 — An AIREX foam sandwich cored hull being built over a male mold. Note the area along the keel that will be solid fiberglass laminate has been built up and shaped accordingly. The workers are applying the foam and holding the sheets in place with nails and washer blocks that prevent hammer indentations against the foam. The foam will later be sewn or fastened on from the underside, and the washer blocks removed prior to applying the outer laminate.

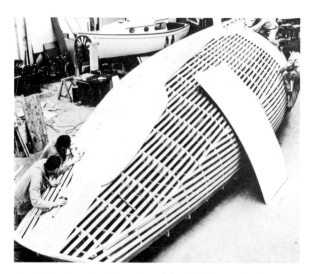

FIG. 19-14 — Another view of the hull shown in Fig. 19-13. Note the orientation and spacing of the longitudinal battens. Not all battens must be full length fore and aft, but they should span as far as necessary to form fair lines. The main requirement for spacing of battens is that they adequately support the core and provide enough attachment points for firm contact against the mold surface.

the mold contours, it may be necessary to heat or thermoform the foam as was discussed earlier. Or it may be possible to cut a sheet into more manageable sizes or shapes that will conform more easily. It is even possible to score or kerf sheets partially (no more than half the thickness of the foam) on the compression side to make them more limber, but take care not to cut them completely through.

There are several approaches and techniques used in thermoforming, and as was noted before, the PVC type foams like AIREX are more adaptable to thermoforming techniques. While the following is applicable to AIREX PVC foam sheets, the same techniques may not work as well with foams like KLEGECELL.

For heating big sheets, a simple oven can be made from plywood which is basically a box. A calrod unit or other type of small electric heating element is used to heat the foam in the box, with the foam setting on a rack made from hardware cloth or

FIG. 19-15 — AIREX foam being applied over an open batten male mold. The large sheets need not be fitted closely since smaller shaped pieces can be cut and fitted between the full sheets later. This will save time and work.

226

"chicken" wire. AIREX foam placed in such an oven will become limber in a minute or so, while KLEGECELL foam may take a minute or two longer. The foam should be removed and applied immediately once it becomes flexible enough. A thermostatic control is recommended to limit the heat range in the oven to no more than about 200 degrees F. for AIREX, and about 230 degrees F. for KLEGECELL type foams.

For localized bending in limited areas, a hand-held industrial blower heater can be used. These are also handy for removing indentations that may occur on the surface. However, take care not to apply too much heat and melt or burn the foam.

Another method for limbering up smaller sheets of foam is to hold the foam in front of an electric heater (make sure no volatile products are in the vicinity), moving the foam back and forth to evenly spread the heat until the sheet softens up. Again take care not to scorch the foam, and do apply it in place as quickly as possible once it becomes limber.

Position the sheet initially against the mold surface before heating to approximate the contour that will be required. Then hold the foam in this approximate shape while it is being heated; this will help it conform to shape more easily once it becomes limber. Because the foam will again harden rapidly once removed from the heat source, this practice will make fitting easier and quicker. However, this works best with AIREX foam over areas of extreme curvature because this foam can be bent severely without breaking.

Foams like KLEGECELL can break easily if bent too much. Pre-bending the foam in this manner and then heating is especially helpful if screws are being used to hold the foam. If the sheet was not pre-bent, there would always be a tendency for the screws to pull out of the sheet due to the tension caused when cold bending it in place. It is also possible to locate the sheet and take the portable heater to the hull and form the

FIG. 19-16 — This open battened male mold for a hard-chined foam cored hull will have all surfaces covered with core material, including the transom.

FIG. 19-17 — Applying AIREX foam to the male mold shown in Fig. 19-16. Note the battens in the transom area; these can run either vertically or horizontally. Some prefer plywood cores in lieu of the foam in this area for attaching sterndrive, outboards, etc., especially on smaller powerboat hulls.

FIG. 19-18 — The worker is using "Foamglas" to smooth down seams between AIREX foam which have been filled with resin putty. This type of filling between sheets is optional and not absolutely necessary if there are no major gaps at joints. Sanding with machines in this case is questionable since it is easy to gouge the foam core.

A

B

C

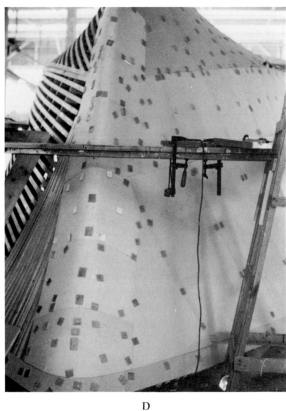

D

FIG. 19-19 — This series of photos shows a method for building up a rounded flared bow over an open battened male mold using AIREX foam sandwich core. Notice the orientation of the battens over the stem area ('A'). A piece of foam over the stem area is being fitted in 'B'. The rigid elastic quality of the AIREX allows it to be "cold formed" over the contour without breaking. As the pieces are cut and fitted, heat is applied locally by a heat lamp ('C') to limber up the foam sheet. After a few minutes of heat, the foam will stay in position. The completed foam application over the stem area is shown in 'D'.

FIG. 19-20 — This photo shows the hull being made in Fig. 19-17 after righting and removing the male mold. The inner laminate can now be installed. This large yacht was built using the "club sandwich" approach.

sheet in place. However, heating should be kept to a minimum. Not only is it easy to damage a sheet, but there is a tendency for the sheet to shrink which can affect the fit to a slight degree afterward.

FOAM APPLICATION TIPS

In most cases, the foam can be applied to the hull in any sequence. It is not necessary to fasten or glue the edges at joints, and in fact, this should not be done. The edges of the sheets need only be butted together and not fitted tightly or "jammed" together.

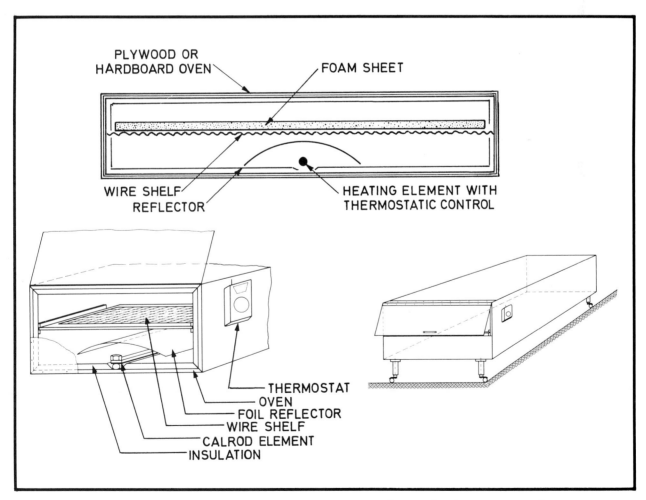

FIG. 19-21 — These details show a simple oven that the builder can make himself for thermoforming sheet foam core materials. The oven should be equipped with casters so it can be moved to the area where the foam is being applied since the foam stays limber for only a brief period.

Some builders do not even bother to butt the foam sheets together, but rather apply them in an almost random pattern determined primarily by the ease of bending of each sheet. Where large gaps then exist, they cut pieces of foam and then fit these in between. Small gaps (those about 1/16" wide) can be overlooked or filled with a resin putty filler for a neat job. However, if using resin putty filler, note that it will have to be sanded, so take care not to sand into the foam surface adjacent to such filler areas. Sanding a large area with soft spots (the foam) and hard spots (the putty filler) without getting an unfair surface can be difficult. Apply only enough putty to do the job, and avoid spreading it around unnecessarily.

A problem which sometimes occurs with foam sheet is that they are not always consistently the exact same thickness; they can vary plus or minus a small fraction of an inch. When this occurs, a ridge may develop at the joints between sheets, and sometimes this can be quite prominent, making it difficult to achieve a fair surface. To avoid

or minimize this problem, check the thicknesses of each sheet beforehand and try using those of similar thickness next to each other as much as possible.

Throughout the application of the foam, it is very important that the hull surfaces be fair, true, and smooth, with the foam contacting all points of the mold (which we already assume to be fair and true). Check the entire surface of the foam for unfair areas, humps, dips, and indentations. All such areas should be corrected prior to applying the outer laminate. Any indentation should either be heated locally so the foam will return to shape or filled with a resin putty filler. While some may argue that certain irregularities can be taken care of on the final layer in the finishing process, it is far easier to correct these defects at this point. Minor sanding, grinding, and fairing can be done directly on the foam, but take care not to decrease the foam core thickness at any point severely or cut through any stitching holding the foam to the male mold. Also take care with power sanders to not gouge the foam, especially adjacent to filled areas which are harder than the foam surface. Do not leave the foam exposed for a lengthy period before applying the outer laminate, especially if working outside.

The outer fiberglass laminate is then applied in the typical fashion, starting the laminate with a layer of mat against the foam. After the hull has been finished using methods described in Chapter 13, the hull is righted using methods given in Chapter 14. At this stage, the foam-cored hull without the inner laminate applied is VERY flexible and "floppy". Thus, it is almost mandatory to right the hull with the male mold in place, and NOT by first removing the hull and righting it separately. Furthermore, the cradle that will be used to support the hull for the balance of construction should also be rigid and true, and give ample support to the hull once it is right side up.

Before removing the male mold, be sure

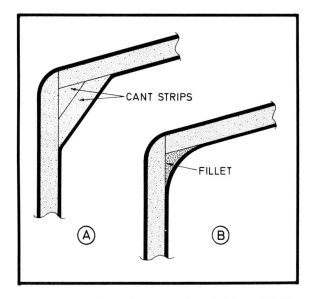

FIG. 19-22 — The inside corners of sandwich cored hulls, such as occur at transom corners and chine junctions on hard-chine hulls, should be built up with foam cant strips ('A') or a radiused resin putty filler fillet ('B') so the inner laminate will adhere without forming air bubbles and voids.

that all reference marks such as those noting bulkhead locations, sole levels, the reference plane, and centerline as required, have been marked to the inside surface of the foam core. A permanent black marker will make lines that are visible through the inner laminate for easy reference later when interior members are installed. Then bevel all edges where the foam adjoins to areas of the hull that will be solid fiberglass laminate, and apply the inner laminate using methods as previously described, with a layer of mat first against the core. However, avoid walking around on the inside of the hull or any other concentrated loads or weights before the inner laminate has been applied, especially if foams like KLEGE-CELL are used. It is possible to distort the hull, fracture or compress the foam, and possibly crack the outer hull laminate.

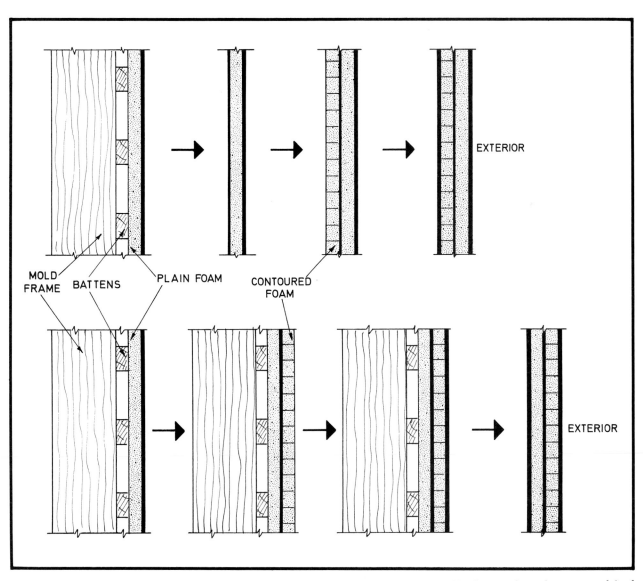

FIG. 19-23 — The illustration shows two ways of making a "club sandwich" (using a double thickness of core material) hull over a male mold. The procedures shown are explained in the text.

THE "CLUB SANDWICH" METHOD

Using a double layer of foam in a process better known as the "club sandwich" method was discussed earlier. In the case of boats built over male molds, there are two ways that a double layer of foam can be applied. In both cases, the hull is built in basically the same way as described in the foregoing. But then the builder can deviate, using one of two approaches to apply the second layer of foam core (see Fig. 19-23).

In the first approach, after the first layer of foam has been applied, this is covered with a bedding coat of mat saturated generously with resin. Then a second layer of foam is immediately applied over this, using contoured type foam by contact methods. After this second layer of foam has been applied, the outer fiberglass skin follows in the typical fashion. The disadvantage of this method is that it is more difficult to keep the laminate fair and true, and requires more work fairing on the contoured foam, especially if contours are severe.

In the second approach, the hull is built in identically the same way as if the boat were going to have a single core thickness up to the point where the hull has been righted and the mold has been removed. But instead of applying the inner laminate as would be done with a single core thickness, the inside surface of the hull is covered with a resin-saturated coat of mat and the second foam layer using contoured material is laid up against the surface of the first layer. The inner laminate is then applied over this second inner layer of foam. The advantage of this method is that the hull is basically finished and fairing is easier. Because the contoured foam is on the inside, irregularities on the surface are not critical.

Regardless of which approach is used, the initial foam surface should be coated with resin first before applying the bedding mat. Then apply the bedding mat layer using a fairly heavy thickness (say 1½ oz. weight)

since this layer will be used for bonding purposes in much the same way as if the foam were being applied inside a female mold. The mating surfaces of the second layer of foam sheets should also be coated with resin and placed immediately into the wet bedding layer. See the previous section on using foam in female molds for procedures which are basically the same. Note that whichever approach is used in the "club sandwich" method, there will be one layer of plain sheet foam and one layer of contoured foam. The contoured foam, being the second layer applied in both cases, is necessary in order to conform easily to the surface since it is not mechanically fastened like the first layer, and because the slits between the blocks prevent air entrapment between the inner and outer layers.

The following group of photos (FIG. 19-24 through FIG. 19-48) show construction procedures required to build the 9' "FOAMEE" sailing dinghy illustrated in Fig. 2-1. The one-off male molded hull uses an AIREX foam cored sandwich structure. The procedures would be similar for most boats using this system, regardless of size.

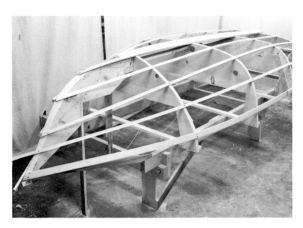

FIG. 19-24 — The male mold members are erected onto the building form. The keel batten protrudes above the surface of the battens and is tapered so the adjacent battens sweep in fairly. Members are bevelled so battens mate flat; notice the bevel on the stem each side.

FIG. 19-25 — The area along the centerline, stem, and sheer is built up to match the thickness of the foam. The battens landing on the stem have been faired off flat and the stem area built up with thin laminations such as that shown by Fig. 11-14.

FIG. 19-26 — Areas of the mold where the hull will be solid laminate and should not stick are covered with clear plastic parting film, such as along the centerline and sheer. Note the transverse "strap" frame forward to keep the battens in proper alignment.

FIG. 19-27 — A piece of foam is being fitted. In this case, a mallet is used to indent the foam and transfer the required contour to the foam sheet. Note how the foam rests against the sheer clamp. Holes have been drilled through the battens for the screws that will hold the foam in place.

FIG. 19-28 — Heating the foam makes it easy to form to the contours. The foam here is being rapidly moved back and forth in front of a portable heater until it is somewhat flexible, then immediately placed in position.

FIG. 19-29 — The first piece of foam has been cut and fitted. Note that the surface of the foam is flush to the stem and sheer area which will be covered by the outer fiberglass laminate.

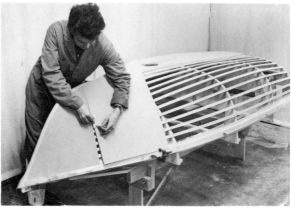

FIG. 19-30 — The next piece of foam has been cut roughly oversize and is being fitted. A marking block is used to transfer the required contour set back from the edge so the piece will fit flush to the first piece.

FIG. 19-31 — After cutting, the second piece is butted next to the first piece. Subsequent pieces of foam are cut and fitted in a similar manner and screw fastened in place from the underside.

FIG. 19-32 — Widths of pieces and their orientation on the mold are not critical as long as the pieces conform to the mold surfaces. Thermoforming will help maintain the shape of the pieces if required.

FIG. 19-33 — Resin putty filler can be used to fill gaps and indentations, but should be kept to a minimum. Take care with belt or disc sanders as the foam can easily be gouged.

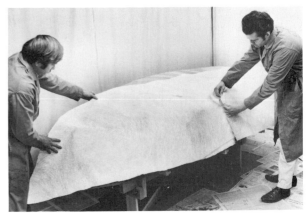

FIG. 19-34 — Mat is usually used against the core. Here a piece is fitted oversize on each side with a lap at the center-line. A gore has been torn where the mat bunches and wrinkles; this will be feathered to blend in fairly.

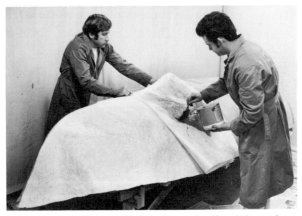

FIG. 19-35 — The mat is folded onto itself and the underside coated with resin to help wet it out from the backside. It is then folded back into position and more resin is applied on top.

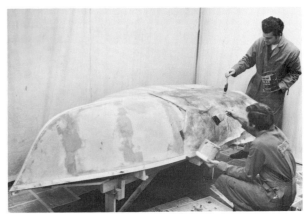

FIG. 19-36 — The previously applied underside has been folded onto the hull and the other portion is now coated with resin. The resin thus saturates from BOTH sides and helps keep the mat in place.

FIG. 19-37 — The next layer of reinforcement (in this case cloth) is draped over the wet mat. Pulling along the edges will help remove major wrinkles and air bubbles.

FIG. 19-38 — More resin is applied and squeegeed well, from upper to lower areas. The opposite hand can be used to help determine the consistency of the laminate application and resin content.

FIG. 19-39 — Once the laminate has been wetted out, additional resin can be rolled on as required to cover the weave of the fabric. On larger boats using woven roving, this can also be done with filler coats.

FIG. 19-40 — Cradles are made to support the righted hull. Use strips of carpet or foam over parting film and resin saturated mat to duplicate the hull shape at the cradle locations. In larger boats, the hull would be finished first. But with this small boat, it can be done later since it is easily reinverted.

FIG. 19-41 — The hull and building form have been righted together and a spirit level is used to level the structure for the balance of work. The building form and male mold can then be removed.

FIG. 19-42 — In this hull, the building form has been removed from the male mold, and the male mold is now being removed separately so it can be reused. The cradles are used to hold the hull in position.

FIG. 19-43 — Edges of the foam where the laminate will be solid are cut at a bevel. Note the plywood insert at the transom for the motor and rudder fittings. The hull is almost ready for the inner laminate.

FIG. 19-44 — A wood beam is bonded inside the transom for rigidity and a resin putty filler fillet applied at the inside transom corner so the inner laminate will conform without air bubbles forming.

FIG. 19-45 — The mat pieces of the inner laminate used against the foam are cut to rough oversize. Binders in the mat make it somewhat unyieldy at this point, but once the resin is applied, the mat becomes limp and conforms readily.

FIG. 19-46 — The mat layer is coated with resin as was done on the outside. Note the lapping of the material onto the transom, and over the centerline and sheer areas. Additional laminate will be applied onto the inside of the transom.

FIG. 19-47 — The next layer of the inner laminate (cloth in this case) is applied immediately over the wet mat. In this boat, this layer also laps onto the transom, as well as at the centerline and sheer areas, joining the inner and outer skins.

FIG. 19-48 — The laminate is smoothed out by squeegeeing, keeping wet resin ahead of the squeegee. Resin will tend to settle to the bottom of the hull, so it is important to keep working the resin up to higher areas to prevent resin-rich areas from forming.

CHAPTER 20

A core material commonly used for sandwich structures in boats is END-GRAIN BALSA, such as "CONTOURKORE", the brand name of the product produced by the BALTEK Corporation. The END-GRAIN BALSA material consists of small, close-fitting end-grain blocks of balsa held together in sheet form by a light, open scrim of fiberglass fabric on one side. In this configuration, the material is much like the contoured types of sheet foam, except that each block is completely independent and not attached in any way to another block other than its attachment on the scrim backing.

Thousands of pleasure and commercial boats ranging from canoes to 90' workboats have been built using END-GRAIN BALSA cores for decks, hulls, cabin tops, and bulkheads, by numerous builders worldwide. END-GRAIN BALSA is approved as a hull material by such major classification agencies as Lloyd's Register, and specified by the U. S. Navy and U. S. Coast Guard for hulls and decks.

However, from the standpoint of the amateur builder using "one-off" methods, END-GRAIN BALSA has not been as widely promoted or used compared to such materials as C-FLEX or the various foam cores. The reason is partly because of the inherent quality of the core material which makes it so well-suited to female mold production methods. The nature of the sheet of balsa is such that it forms a drapable core "blanket" that readily conforms to the contoured surfaces presented in just about any type of female mold. There is no built-in "memory" with balsa core as there is with the foam cores. The material once laid in place against the mold surface depends on surface tension to keep it in place, with little additional force required on the part of the worker.

While this easy drapeability of the balsa is good for the builder working in a female mold, it is not so good when laying the material OVER a male mold, especially on a mold that is more or less open, such as the open-battened type (see Fig. 20-1). It is important to assure that the balsa core is pulled down to the mold surface in all areas. Because the balsa core is in effect "flimsy", more attachment points are required along the mold surface than may be required with other core materials, especially the foams. In order to give adequate support to the balsa and provide enough points for attachment, the form should have battens which are fairly closely spaced, or a solid male mold should be used for support at all points. Either way, a somewhat more elaborate mold is required than with other male

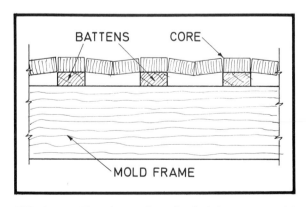

FIG. 20-1 — There is a tendency for the balsa core material to droop between battens over open battened male molds unless the battens are spaced closely enough together. Applying the core in a diagonal manner will also minimize this problem.

mold materials, and hence more work and expense, but only marginally so compared to foam cores.

TECHNICAL PROPERTIES

Tests indicate that the bond between the skins and the END-GRAIN BALSA core is stronger than any competitive core material. Results show that the bond will fail in the resin-glass interface (the actual lines of bonding between layers in the skin laminate) rather than in either the balsa core itself or in the core-resin interface (the bonding line between the first layer against and the core). The reason for this tenacious bond between the skins and the core is because the resin penetrates at least 1/16″ into the cellular structure of the END-GRAIN BALSA, resulting in high-strength bonds. However, this same advantage does require that the worker applying the laminate use enough resin to allow for the extra absorption of the resin by the core. This extra resin tends to make the total laminate somewhat heavier than foam core laminates, and does add to the cost because of the extra resin used, although the foams absorb some resin also.

Builders sometimes use balsa core only in the sides of a boat, or only in the bottom. Some builders still believe that the balsa core may eventually rot, yet want the added stiffness for the topsides, and hence, leave the material out of the bottom. Others feel that the added strength is needed on the bottom, and to save money, will leave it out of the topsides. Both of these practices are really idiosyncrasies on the part of the builders, however, since there is no reason why the material should not be used throughout the hull, other than perhaps for the added cost and work of installation.

Balsa core has a very high compressive strength, being many times higher than any of the foams, plus a relatively higher shear strength compared to the structural foams.

These qualities make balsa an ideal material to compliment the strength properties of the high modulus materials discussed in Chapter 21. The balsa core also has a high shear modulus (explained in Chapter 18) which results in negligible core shear deflection. However, in designing balsa core sandwiches, the designer must design to the ultimate expected load since the material does not yield like other materials, such as an AIREX foam core or a single skin fiberglass laminate. Hence, if the expected load is exceeded, the balsa core sandwich may fail, and because of this, a factor of safety must be added to the calculation to allow for possible overload conditions.

Although the compressive strength of balsa is much higher than that of the foams, this property is not necessarily an advantage under impact loads. The balsa sandwich shows lower shock absorbing properties than a sandwich core using, for example AIREX, which has a much lower compressive strength. Due to the low elasticity and lack of resilience on impact of balsa core, an impact load could be transmitted by the core from one skin to the other more readily. Thus the area of damage and delamination as a result of the impact may be more serious on the opposite side (inside of the vessel) from the impact side. An example is tests made on both balsa core and AIREX core panels for impact resistance (see photos in Chapter 18). Whereas the AIREX cored panel showed a damaged outer skin and core compression, there was no failure because of delamination, but delamination did occur with the balsa cored sample. However, the makers of END-GRAIN BALSA question the results since there is some doubt that recommended laminating procedures were followed in making the test samples. Like the foam cores, balsa sandwich structures provide good acoustical and thermal insulative properties that reduce noise and sweating within the hull, and also provide reserve buoyancy. A balsa cored hull also requires little, if any, internal framing or stiffening structure.

THE POTENTIAL FOR ROT AND DAMAGE

One of the primary concerns with the use of balsa core (at least for the uninformed) is that, since balsa is wood, and wood in water can rot, balsa core structures must be subject to rot. The problem, it would seem, could manifest itself due to water entering the core. This water could become entrapped in the core, and eventually lead to rot as well as delamination of the skins from the core, swelling, and related consequences. However, let's examine the situation in some detail before passing judgement.

When balsa was first marketed many years ago as a core material in boatbuilding, initially only the flat grain lumber was available. Although sandwich cored vessels were built with cores using this lumber configuration, there were problems with some, and this is where balsa core picked up a questionable reputation with regard to water absorption within the core.

However, the breakthrough came in 1964 when "CONTOURKORE" END GRAIN BALSA was developed. A series of tests were conducted by Lloyd's used END-GRAIN BALSA core samples over a period of two years in order to test water absorption characteristics of end-grain balsa by placing the sandwich samples in a water tank at 10 p.s.i. The intent of this test was to simulate an accident at sea by drilling holes completely through the samples. One of the basic premises with a balsa core, in order for it to work to its optimum, is that a high degree of integrity of the bonds must exist between the core and the skins. If there is a leak in the skin, the core can be soaked and lose strength; there is no argument with this.

In the tests, it was found that wherever there was a good laminate bond, water would travel with the grain (which is crosswise from facing to facing in the core), but would NOT travel through the core PARALLEL with the skins as was the case in some earlier boats made from balsa NOT in the end-grain configuration. The reason why the water would not travel across the core is that balsa is basically a natural "honeycomb" structure. Any water which enters the core travels only along the cells that have been exposed to the water source (see Fig. 20-2). Hence, if any water does somehow enter the core (assuming good bonds to the core by the skins), it will not travel beyond the damaged area. In other words, the effects will be localized.

Other tests have shown that under various forms of loading or impacts leading to failure of one or both of the sandwich skins, there was no water migration or penetration beyond the damaged areas. However, the wet core and damaged areas must be repaired. This involves first removing the skins in the damaged area, replacing wet and damaged core material, and then replacing with new skins, but only in the localized area.

FIG. 20-2 — Laboratory test samples show that water will not travel across the grain of the core even when both skins and the core are punctured, as is shown by the tracer dye along the edges and at the hole in the center of the sample which was cut in two after the test.

As far as rot is concerned, it should again be emphasized that not only is the material approved for use in hulls by Lloyd's, but the mills in South America where the balsa material comes from are further certified by Lloyd's as well as the factories where the core sheet material is actually made. In other words, from the cutting of the trees to the making of the end-grain sheets, very strict quality control is exercised.

The lumber is not only kiln-dried (which kills rot spores that are necessary to create rot in the first place), but the material is shipped from the mills to the plants in this country in closed containers. After manufacture, the cartons of END-GRAIN BALSA are "shrink-packed" to virtually eliminate any chance of rot spores entering the material, at least until opened by the ultimate user. Furthermore, rot spores simply cannot live in the core once the sandwich is made, because the chemicals used in the resin kill any surviving spores. All these factors and safety precautions virtually preclude the formation of rot at least until the boat is in service.

But what happens after the boat is in service? Rot could conceivably develop under certain conditions. For example, in a deck using a balsa core, a through-deck fitting like a cleat could work and loosen with time, letting fresh water (such as rain water since rot spores cannot live in salt water) leak into the core. However, experience shows that problems such as this are extremely remote and rare. Usually if water does enter the core, the problem manifests itself with just a wet core. If the bonds are sound, the damage will be localized, although any such problem areas should be repaired.

USING BALSA CORE IN A FEMALE MOLD

The following outlines the procedures for using END-GRAIN BALSA core inside a female mold as summarized from recommendations provided by the BALTEK Corporation. While the basic principles will also be applicable for use in boats built over male molds, there will be certain modifications and variations for these applications which will be noted in the following as well as in the next section of this chapter.

1. In building the boat in the female mold, be sure to use the proper layup schedule regarding core thickness, glass type, glass thickness, laminate configuration, and layup technique. If in doubt about the proper laminate or questions arise on procedures not answered here, the balsa manufacturer should be consulted. They have many years of practical experience and feedback, as well as computer programs that can be used to arrive at a specific type of structure for optimum design.

2. In applying the END-GRAIN BALSA material, bed it in at least a $1\frac{1}{2}$ oz. mat or equivalent layup against the mold surface or gel coat. The glass-to-resin ratio should be within 20–80% to 25–75% which is classified as "resin-rich". Roll out this bedding coat before applying the balsa. The bedding coat provides a certain amount of cushioning or "bedding resiliency", and if less material is used than the above recommendation, the integrity of the bond will be compromised.

3. Pre-wet the core material sheets prior to application, but count the pre-wetting resin in with the total resin weight used to determine the bedding coat resin ratio. Note that sufficient resin is required in the bedding coat to provide the necessary resiliency and also the adhesive medium for bonding the core to the bedding coat. This can be achieved by putting the dry core into the wet laminate, but pre-wetting the core material gives added insurance that enough resin will be soaked up by the core.

4. Note that the resin should not be allowed to cure before the core is placed in position. Adjust the catalyst rate so that the bedding coat resin gels in 20–40 minutes,

FIG. 20-3 — Production workers are fitting balsa core sheets into this female molded hull. The inner laminate has been applied except for the bedding layer used under the core.

FIG. 20-4 — The balsa core has been installed in the hull shown in Fig. 20-3, and the workers are applying the inner laminate. Note that the mold has been tilted for easy access, and will be rotated later for installing the opposite side.

and check a batch of resin first to assure this proper gel time.

5. When placing the core, avoid excessive pressure against the core (such as walking on it). This can squeeze out the resin underneath, leaving voids and resin-starved areas which will lead to no bond or a poor bond in that area. Use only hand pressure, roller, or vacuum bag to push the core into the bedding coat. Slit the scrim backing if necessary in spots to insure that the core remains against the bedding coat, but don't remove it.

6. Allow the bedding coat and core to cure before applying the inner skin to avoid the possibility of expanding air generated by exotherm in the resin, creating possible air bubbles or "pockets" in the laminate. After the bedding coat cures, check for adhesion and bonding qualities before applying the inner skin. Test for adhesion by tapping the core at all points. Where the core is NOT properly bonded, there will be a change in sound, generally a "hollowness" from the average sound. Inject more resin with a hypodermic syringe into such areas if the

FIG. 20-5 — The balsa core is usually bedded into a layer of resin saturated mat as is being done in this round bilge female molded hull. One worker is applying the mat while another is installing the core.

resin has cured, but there should be few, if any, such areas if the application has been done properly.

7. At edges or endings of the core, make the change gradual along the margin by using a canted filler strip, or grind and cut a bevel edge on the core, or taper with a resin putty filler. As with all core materials, this is done to eliminate hard spots or stress concentrations resulting from the difference between the stiffness of the areas covered by the core and the more flexible areas where the core is omitted. This practice also eliminates air pockets and resin concentrations under the inner skin to be applied.

8. Begin the inner skin layup with a minimum of ¾ oz. mat or equivalent against the core. Since the core is not being bedded into the inner skin like it was on the outer skin, the mat can be thinner since the added resiliency is not required.

Note that the sequence of STEP #2 and STEP #8 apply to boats being built in FEMALE molds; for MALE mold application, these two steps would be reversed, although the other procedures would be similar.

For the best laminates, the skins should be the same thickness plus or minus only a slight variation. However, in marine applications, normal practice is for the outer skin to be somewhat thicker for added strength, increased impact and abrasion resistance, and a better finish (the thicker mat, for example, prevents "print-through" of the woven material on the outside of female molded hulls, and gives a better fin-

FIG. 20-6 — The balsa core material conforms easily to complex curvatures as in this round bilge hull. Note the area in the bottom (shown by the "X" at the lower left) where the core will be deleted either for a solid backing block or additional laminate buildup for the rudder port.

ishing surface on male molded hulls). Nevertheless, a reasonable balance should be maintained in skin thickness equality in order for the sandwich to develop optimum structural characteristics.

Note that all materials going into a polyester laminate are sensitive to moisture. Thus care must be taken to insure that moisture is NOT introduced into the laminate by any of the reinforcements. The balsa core material itself should be especially protected from moisture. Store ALL materials in a dry place and avoid high humidity both in the storage area and at the work site.

BUILDING A MALE MOLD BALSA CORED HULL

Building an END-GRAIN BALSA cored hull over a male mold is very similar to the procedures used to build a foam cored hull. In general, the same type of open battened male mold is used, but the battens must be spaced close enough to support the balsa

FIG. 20-7 — After the balsa core is installed, a bedding layer of mat is usually used as the first layer of the inner laminate against the core. A coat of resin is applied to the core first.

core adequately so that there are no blocks within a sheet that tend to droop below the battens. It is possible to use a solid sheathed male mold as discussed later in this chapter, but in this instance, certain methods (such as sewing or wire ties) could not be practically used to attach the core. The mold is also covered with plastic sheeting completely so that resin (and there will be plenty passing through with balsa) will not stick to the mold.

Because of the flimsy quality of the END-GRAIN BALSA sheets, they apply somewhat differently than do the foam core materials. As with foam, there is no special method or configuration for laying on the sheets, but each sheet should be butted as close to the next as is possible for a mini-mum of gaps. The sheets can be laid vertically, horizontally, or at angles; whichever is the most convenient for the boat in question.

It makes no difference in the laminate if the scrim of the balsa sheet is laid up or down. However, in areas of a hull where a convex curve exists, the scrim is usually placed down to the mold. In other areas where there is a concave or reverse curve, the scrim can be placed up so that the blocks in the core will conform more readily. But if sanding will be required over a large area to fair the balsa core surface prior to applying the laminate, it is preferable in all cases to place the scrim against the mold so that it will not be sanded away leaving loose blocks. Note that the sheets can take

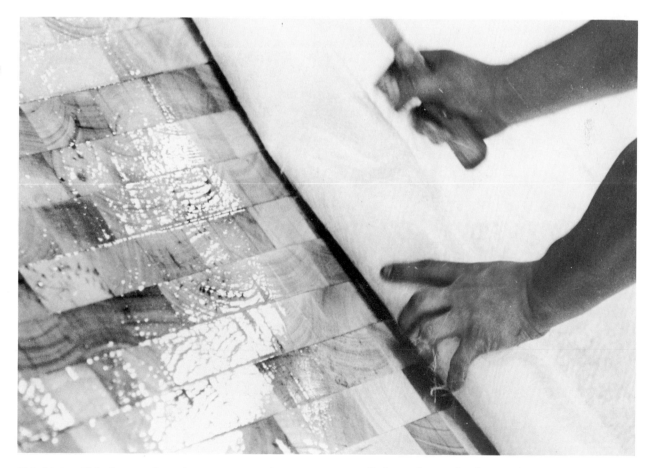

FIG. 20-8 — This close-up photo shows a wet coat of resin against the balsa core and the mat bedding layer being applied over the core for the inner laminate. Woven roving is then applied over the mat in the conventional laminate.

some degree of compound curvature.

There are a number of methods that can be used for holding the balsa core in place against the male mold of the open battened type. One way is to stitch and sew the core in place. In thicker sizes, the core can be screwed from the underside with large threaded sheet metal screws just like foam cores. Small finish nails can also be used to hold the balsa core against the mold temporarily, with the heads protruding so they can be removed prior to the laminate set-

ting up hard in a given area. It is possible that a combination of methods will be desirable.

Stitching and sewing the core in place is done virtually the same way as with the foam cores. Use a strong string or synthetic line and a long large needle. With one person applying the sheet on the outside, another on the inside ties off the line to the mold battens and pushes the needle back to the person on the outside, laying on a stitch 3″ or so before pushing the needle through

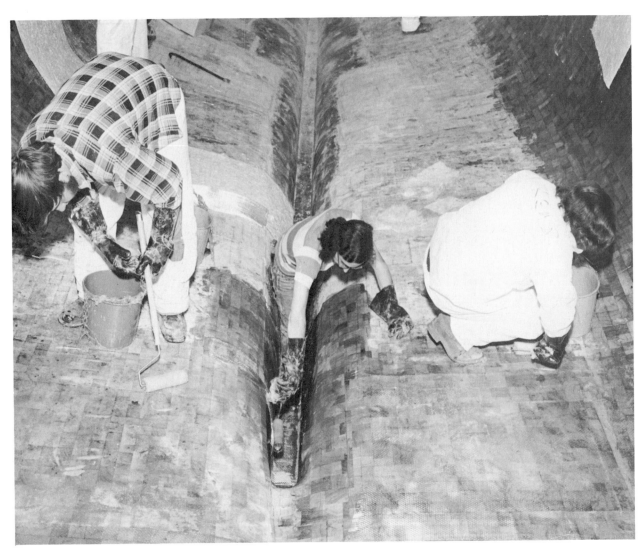

FIG. 20-9 — The inner laminate is being installed in this balsa cored hull using a conventional mat-woven roving laminate. Note the plastic bucket used for the resin, the rollers used for resin application, and the gloves the workers are wearing.

again. The person on the inside directs the person on the outside where to pass the needle through in order to miss the battens and to tie off the line (note that this is a two-person job).

In applying the END-GRAIN BALSA core, the person on the outside also exerts enough pressure against the core material to assure that it contacts fairly to the mold. The stitching should be taut, but not so much so that the core is damaged or the line pulled through the core. Keep the stitching away from any areas where later fairing or sanding will be required since this will just cut the line loose, causing the core to be released from the mold.

If the line being used is fairly husky, a decision may have to be made as to whether the line will make a lump or high spot on the surface that will be "telegraphed" through to the final surface and make fairing more difficult. With ordinary monofilament lines and outer skins made from conventional laminates, the build-up of lami-

nate will cover most irregularities of this type. But for larger diameter line with thinner skins (such as might be the case if using high modulus materials) it may be desirable to recess the line into the core by making a score into the core on the outer surface so that the line will lay flush. Ordinarily, however, if the line is pulled tight enough, it will cut into the core enough to be below the surface to prevent any problems. It is also easy to just tie through the core with short lengths of wire, twisting them around the battens. If copper wire is used, these can be snipped off later and left to remain in the hull.

Although the balsa sheets should be fitted as closely as possible, minor gaps can be filled with small pieces of core material so that a minimum of resin will be used to fill the slits between core blocks. On the other hand, if the sheets tend to overlap during fitting, just trim off the excess as required to make a close fit. The balsa material cuts easily with either a utility

FIG. 20-10 — Balsa core used in a male mold situation can be applied over a solid sheathed mold or an open battened mold, depending on the design. In the latter case, the balsa core must be sewn and/or fastened to the mold battens.

FIG. 20-11 — The scaffolding used around this large hull provides easy worker access to all surfaces. Note the area of solid laminate along the stem/keel area.

knife or fine-toothed saw.

As with foam cores, there may be areas where the core material will be omitted to provide solid fiberglass areas in the laminate. These areas on the mold can be built up with solid wood, plywood, or foam pieces to be flush to the balsa core surface where required. Then they are covered with plastic sheeting or release agent so that the laminate will not stick where no core is desired.

In some areas on certain boats, the blocks of the core may tend to separate, such as at hard corners or on tight convex curves. Some builders fill in such gaps while others do not, and the builder will have to decide just how big a gap is too big. Large gaps should be filled in with the balsa material as noted. However, smaller gaps can be filled in with standard resin putty filler, but this should not be done over extensive areas as will be explained shortly.

On foam cored boats where fittings will be located, proper practice is to remove the core and fill in with a blocking of solid wood or other material of higher compressive strength where high loadings will be concentrated. But on balsa cored hulls, this practice is optional and often not necessary. Because of the high compressive strength of END-GRAIN BALSA, which may be as high as wood inserts often used in foam cores, the need is not so critical (especially with balsa core in higher densities). In other words, wood core inserts are only necessary if the loading on the attached fitting will exceed that of the core material itself. Core inserts should be used, however, or at least considered, for propeller shaft struts, rudder ports, stern bearings, and the like. Metal backing plates should still be used in all cases, or at least large, flat washers backing up all through-hull fittings, together with suitable bedding compounds under the fittings, whether bolt inserts are used or not.

Surface fairing of the balsa core should generally not be necessary, but if required in any area, use sanding blocks, the patented "Surform" tools, and similar tools. The surfaces of the balsa mold must be fair and true, without any protruding edges or corners of end-grain blocks sticking up that would lead to an unfair laminate. If necessary, sand all surfaces, but avoid cutting through any sewing used to hold the core in place. Keep sanding on the core to a bare minimum to avoid decreasing the core thickness by any appreciable amount. If too much sanding appears to be required, then the core has probably not been applied properly, or the mold is unfair.

Some builders will apply resin putty fillers in those areas of the core which are unfair, or where gaps exist. However, this indicates that the hull may not be fair in the first place, and more care and work should be done to make the core surface fair and true. Covering the balsa core surface with resin filler coats should be avoided, however, especially over large areas, since the advantage of using balsa core is the positive bond resulting from the interface between the bedding coats and the core itself. Adding resin filler coats that are later sanded and faired, seals the vessels of the core and creates a secondary bonding situation, negating the prime advantage of using balsa core in the hull in the first place. So make sure the balsa cored hull is fair BEFORE applying any laminate. Not only does this make a better bond possible, but less resin will be used, making a laminate that is both lighter in weight and lower in cost.

The outer hull laminate is applied in the manner described in Chapter 12 if using conventional fiberglass laminates for the skins. As with any core material, one must be careful with air entrapment and resin starvation. But with balsa, air entrapment is not much of a problem, first because the slits between the blocks allow air to escape during laminating, and second, because about 3% of the balsa core consists of vessels or holes which go right through the core from top to bottom to let air pass.

As has been noted, the type of material to

use against the core is mat of at least ¾ oz., but not more than 1½ oz., weight; and the resin-to-glass ratio should be high against the core. Coat the core material first with resin to insure a good saturating coat that will preclude resin starvation, and then apply the bedding mat layer just as soon as possible in order to assure a positive bond. Don't let the first coat of resin against the core cure completely or set an inordinate amount of time resulting in a questionable secondary bonding situation. After the bedding coat has been applied, apply the balance of the laminate in the normal manner.

The hull can be righted after completing the outer laminate and finishing as described in Chapter 13. Then the inner laminate can be applied, all in the same manner as if the boat had a foam core. Again, along the edges of the core where portions of the hull will be solid fiberglass, these should be chamfered or beveled for an easy transition in the laminate so that hard spots are not built into the hull, and to make the application of the inner laminate easier.

SOLID SHEATHED MALE MOLDS

It is possible to build a balsa cored hull over a solid sheathed male mold, applying the inner laminate first and the core over this by using either contact molding or vacuum bag methods like those described in Chapter 22. With contact molding, surface tension between the core and the resin holds the core in place just the same as when used in a female mold. However, it is easy to build up unfair surfaces. This is minimized by avoiding overlaps in BOTH laminates. Additional build-ups of laminate, if required, are applied on the inside of the hull later.

If vacuum bag methods are used, note that this can be tricky and may not be suitable for all amateurs. Vacuum bag methods are recommended only for the more experimental types. The following briefly describes certain considerations that apply to the use of balsa over male molds, however, Chapter 22 should be followed for more complete information regarding vacuum bag methods.

Because the balsa absorbs more resin than the foam core materials, and because the builder will be applying balsa against a wet laminate just as if he were using the balsa core in a female mold, it can be difficult to assure that a sound bond is being made at the interface of the inner laminate and the core. To overcome this potential problem, pre-coat the core with a thin coat of resin somewhat over-catalyzed. This "hot coat" helps partially seal the core to minimize resin absorption. If using a vacuum bag, the vacuum pressure against the core material should not be as great as that used with foam materials in order to keep from forcing resin out of the bedding mat layer. Foam cores can stand higher pressures because they don't soak up as much resin. Yet enough resin must be applied to assure a positive bond. Again, a thin "hot coat" is advised over the core when using vacuum bag techniques with balsa core. Otherwise, the method of building up the balsa cored hull over a solid male mold with or without vacuum bag methods is virtually the same as that used for a female mold as previously described. The primary difference is that the builder will be working from the inside to the outside, and since there will be no gel coat, surface finishing techniques described in Chapter 13 will have to be used.

CHAPTER 21

high modulus materials & specialty reinforcements

WHAT ARE HIGH MODULUS MATERIALS?

A "high modulus" material is a material having a high modulus of elasticity, or one that is very stiff. Ordinary steel is such a material, but one that is quite heavy. The newer high modulus materials are quite low in weight, and this quality together with their great strength, allows boats to be built that can be light, stiff, and strong. These qualities of high strength with light weight not only improve the boat's performance, but make it more economical to operate, and perhaps safer. It may even be cheaper to build because less materials on a weight basis are required, although certain high modulus materials are quite expensive.

Some of the more common high modulus materials applicable to boat construction include S-glass, Kevlar, and carbon fibers (also known as graphite). These materials are sometimes used alone or in combination with more conventional fiberglass materials in laminates. Kevlar, S-glass, and carbon fibers are stronger than steel or aluminum pound for pound (see Fig. 21-1).

The use of these materials in boatbuilding from the standpoint of the amateur, is in its infancy. Generally, these materials have evolved and been perfected in the aircraft and aerospace fields, or other areas of high technology, where costs are often secondary. In these fields, ideal "laboratory" or carefully controlled conditions can be maintained to realize the ultimate properties of these materials. Such conditions in boatbuilding, especially with regard to the amateur building his own boat, however,

are unrealistic and usually impractical to obtain. The use of any of these materials, especially when epoxy resins are used, can be highly effected by ambient environmental conditions, such as high and low temperatures, high humidity, and interruptions in construction procedures.

Tests have shown that laboratory-prepared samples, as opposed to samples prepared under "shop" conditions have yielded results in tensile strength that may vary up to 50%, depending on the material. Hence, test samples should be made under

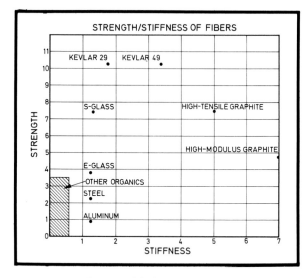

FIG. 21-1 — This simplified graph compares the relative strength and stiffness of several materials (including the high modulus materials) used in boatbuilding. Strength refers to the tensile strength divided by the density of the material, while stiffness refers to the tensile modulus divided by the density of the material. Note that Kevlar is much stronger than any of the materials, but not nearly as stiff as graphite. S-glass also is much stronger than E-glass, steel, or aluminum, but has about the same stiffness. This graph helps explain why certain materials may be combined into "hybrid" materials or combined in laminates for improved overall strength properties.

the actual conditions in which the materials will be used, and then submitted to testing procedures in order to determine if optimum strength properties are being realized. If the results are not up to expectations, it may be advisable for the builder to use a material or method of fabrication, or combination of materials, that is more forgiving.

Because the high modulus materials can be used to make laminates that are quite thin and light in weight with high strength, there is not as much room for error in the laminating procedures as there is in a thicker laminate using conventional fiberglass materials. This is why high quality control is important. Optimum bonding characteristics of the resin are also important, and this means that premium types of resin (other than general purpose ortho-type polyesters) are highly advisable. Also, the techniques used during fabrication must be carefully done to prevent defects such as air bubbles and voids, and to maintain proper fiber orientation. For these reasons, the use of these materials may be considered "experimental" for the first-time builder. Many of the high modulus materials can only be recommended for the builder who is willing to take a chance with the results of the project.

The following will discuss some of the high modulus materials and how they are used in boatbuilding. Because this is a new field, however, the long-term effects are not precisely known, although much information and data are available. Also, this is a rapidly changing area of boatbuilding, and even for the professional builder, much which may be "correct" in the way of information or knowledge may become outdated or invalid in a short period of time.

S-GLASS

The type of fiberglass most often used to make fiberglass materials for boatbuilding

is designated by the letter "E" as noted in Chapter 5. Another type of glass goes by the letter designation "S". This type, while looking just like the "E" type is considerably stronger. For example, in monofilament fibers, E-glass has a tensile strength of 500,000 p.s.i., but S-glass has a tensile strength of 625,000 p.s.i. Each type is made by a somewhat different process, with the S-glass having a premium multi-stage finish. Both work equally well with resin. Although S-glass is about 20% stronger than E-glass and has a higher modulus, it is more expensive than E-glass.

Thus, there is some argument as to whether the extra cost is worth the slight gain in strength, especially where unidirectional, biaxial, and triaxial fabrics are used, since either E-glass or S-glass can be used in making these specialty fabrics which will be discussed later. One important quality of S-glass is that it has the highest impact resistance of all common boatbuilding fibers.

KEVLAR

Kevlar is a registered trademark of the Du Pont Corporation for its family of high strength, high modulus aramid fibers. Aramid is technically an aromatic polyamide, which is a complex hydrocarbon, and a distant cousin of Nylon. Kevlar is lightweight, about five times stronger than steel, and about ten times stronger than aluminum on a weight basis. Kevlar has been used to make bulletproof vests, tire cords for radial tires, and as a substitute for asbestos, since it is flame resistant and will not melt. It is up to 2½ times as strong, and up to three times stiffer than E-glass per weight, and only 43% of the density of fiberglass. Kevlar is resistant to corrosion, is nonconductive, and more durable than fiberglass regarding resistance to damage, vibration, and crack propagation.

The lightweight, high strength properties of Kevlar have the potential to make lighter boats that help reduce operating costs, operate more quietly, are more resistant to impacts, have lower thermal conductivity, and resist temperatures better than fiberglass. Kevlar has good chemical resistance except to strong acids and alkalies. It is dimensionally and temperature stable. Kevlar fibers have the highest specific tensile strength of any continuous fiber commercially available. The specific tensile modulus is three times that of E-glass and 75% that of carbon fiber.

However, in spite of all these sometimes incredible qualities, Kevlar does have certain drawbacks, some of which are important, and therefore must be considered when used as a structural material in boatbuilding. Kevlar is hygroscopic; that is, it will absorb moisture. It must be kept dry and away from moisture, or else questionable bonds will result in the laminate. Kevlar is sensitive to ultra violet (UV) light and should not be used in direct sunlight without the surface being protected by resin containing pigments, or by other protective coatings such as paint. Although Kevlar laminates are much stronger in tension than fiberglass laminates, they are not as strong in compression and bending. The compressive strength of Kevlar is perhaps its weakest point, being about half that of fiberglass composites. Hence, to overcome this weakness, the Kevlar must be used in combination with other materials, thereby forming a composite. Du Pont recommends that carbon fiber (in its pure form or as a "hybrid" material mixed with Kevlar) be used in Kevlar laminates if they are carrying bending and compression loads. This type of "hybrid" or "composite" technology can be considered truly "experimental" since performance results are difficult to predict.

Another caution with Kevlar is that it can abrade with a consequent loss of strength. It should not be the outer ply of a laminate in a boat as it will not hold up well in service due to collisions with docks, running aground, or running the boat up onto the beach. Furthermore, in the male molded boat, sanding against a Kevlar laminate surface is not practical. In the raw state, a Kevlar fabric should never be folded so that hard creases will form that then abrade easily and damage the fibers. Kevlar laminates will not crack like fiberglass, but instead will dent like metal. However, to realize this high potential impact resistance, most experts state that the higher grade (and more costly) resins such as vinylesters and epoxies should be used to provide for higher elongation strength, especially in competition craft.

Although Kevlar is 7 to 9 times as expensive as fiberglass, this does NOT mean that the hull or part would cost that much more. The cost difference would only apply to the material that would be replaced by the Kevlar, plus a consideration for the amount of resin used which would vary depending on the laminate, but would probably be less for the Kevlar portion.

Basically, Kevlar is a fabric that was never really intended to be bonded to itself or to other materials. This means that bonding problems can occur between layers of Kevlar fabrics. Consequently, the fabrics are treated with finishes which are compatible with both polyester and epoxy resins to improve flex and shear strength retention, and is another reason why resins with better bonding characteristics should be used with Kevlar laminates. Interlaminar bonding problems are also overcome in laminates by using alternate layers of fiberglass mat between layers of woven Kevlar materials just the same as is done in an all-fiberglass conventional laminate using mat and woven roving. However, this mat should only be a minimum layer such as a ¾ oz. weight.

Some may ask, why not use a mat layer made from Kevlar? Even if a mat material were available made from Kevlar, this would make little sense. Because mats absorb a high percentage of resin, there would be little weight savings regardless of whether the mat was of Kevlar or fiberglass, since the amount of resin used would be the same in either case. Because of the non-directional orientation of the mat, there is little strength benefit in a mat made from Kevlar. And if the mat were made from Kevlar, it would be much more costly than fiberglass. So in this application, the fiberglass mat does the job just as well and it is low in cost.

Hence, Kevlar is available in yarns, rovings, and woven fabrics. Kevlar is an easy material to wet out with resin and it is non-irritating. However, it should be pointed out that Kevlar does not wet out like fiberglass; it does not become translucent. Instead, it retains its golden color, and this can make it difficult for the novice to know how much resin to use for a proper job of bonding and wetting out. Because of the toughness of the material, it can be difficult to work with regarding machining and sanding, such as for trimming overhanging edges in a laminate or cutting through for fittings, etc.

Kevlar has been used in conventional hand layup situations using only Kevlar. However, this has usually been relegated to smaller craft such as kayaks, canoes, and racing sculls. Generally, even in these types of boats, the material is usually used in a composite with fiberglass or other materials in either epoxy or polyester matrices. All-Kevlar boats are not common because of the extra expense. A composite which contains other materials is necessary to make up for the shortcomings of the Kevlar to provide all the strength and service properties necessary in use.

In fact, many boatbuilders feel that just as good a strength can be obtained by using fiberglass materials alone without the added cost and trouble of using Kevlar. Although an all-Kevlar laminate in a small boat like a canoe or kayak may result in a craft 25% to 40% lighter than a comparable boat in fiberglass, the weight savings would not be so dramatic where the material is used in combination with fiberglass in larger boats. The following illustrates some of the physical properties of resin-impregnated reinforcing fibers comparing Kevlar to conventional fiberglass and high modulus graphite:

	KEVLAR 49	E-GLASS	GRAPHITE
Tensile strength p.s.i.	525,000	350,000	450,000
Tensile modulus p.s.i.	19,000,000	10,000,000	32,000,000
Elongation to break (%)	2.3	4.0	1.25
Density (lbs. per cu. in.)	.053	.093	.063

SANDWICH CORE TESTS USING KEVLAR

Sandwich core tests have been made to test the stiffness, strength, weight, and impact resistance of Kevlar (see Fig. 21-2). The data provided by Du Pont shows all samples used polyester resin catalyzed with MEK peroxide catalyst (although many experts advise against using ortho general purpose polyester resins with Kevlar). Core type was not stipulated, but this makes little difference in the tests since all samples used the same core.

SAMPLE 1 consisted of all fiberglass (for comparison purposes), with mat and cloth on each side and no gel coat. SAMPLE 2 consisted of one ply of Kevlar 49 Style 281 fabric plus one ply of mat on each side. SAMPLE 3 consisted of one ply of Kevlar 49 Style 281 plus a light fiberglass surface veil on each side. SAMPLE 4 consisted of one ply of Kevlar 49 Style 328 plus a light fiberglass surface veil on each side.

A summary of the results showed that SAMPLE 2 weighed the same as SAMPLE 1, but was 60% higher in stiffness, had over twice the strength, and had superior impact resistance. SAMPLES 3 and 4 were 18% and

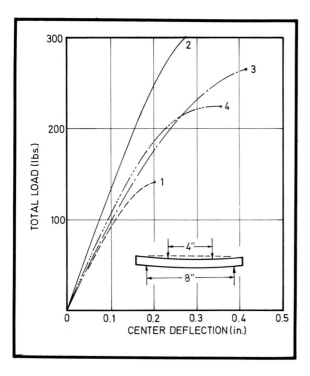

FIG. 21-2 — The graph showing the sandwich core tests using Kevlar as discussed in the text.

15% lighter in weight respectively, and had similar impact resistance as SAMPLE 2. However, SAMPLES 3 and 4 were not nearly as stiff, nor quite as strong as SAMPLE 2 which had fiberglass mat on each side. Thus, it can be concluded that ultimate strength results with a combination of Kevlar and fiberglass, or perhaps other reinforcements, even though impact strength is comparable in all cases where the laminate included Kevlar. In the case of SAMPLE 2, the addition of the mat gives thickness to the skins, thereby increasing stiffness and prolonging failure of the core as well.

CARBON FIBERS

Carbon or graphite fibers are made from a precursor material that is passed through a number of heat treatment processes that converts the precursor material into a resin. This resin is then pulled into strands which

are heated further to form the carbon fiber filaments that are about 6 to 10 microns in diameter, much like fine black hair.

The tensile strength of carbon fibers is three times, and the specific tensile modulus five times greater than steel. While Kevlar is stronger in specific tensile strength than carbon fiber, it is not as stiff. Hence, Kevlar and carbon fiber are often used together or in the form of "hybrid" materials in a laminate to compensate for the weaknesses and improve the physical properties of each. Few boats are made entirely from carbon fibers simply because the material is too expensive and cannot stand up to abuse without help from other materials in the laminate, such as Kevlar and fiberglass. The main function of carbon fiber is for local reinforcement.

While carbon fibers are incredibly stiff and strong in tension relative to weight versus metals, the shear strength for both carbon fiber and fiberglass is relatively low. Metals are likely to take a permanent set or deformation (dent) at overloading, while carbon fibers and fiberglass are more apt to "snap" when values are exceeded. These same qualities, however, allow fiberglass and carbon fiber to be less subject to fatigue under repeated loads not exceeding maximum yield limits. However, because carbon fibers are weak in shear strength and impact resistance, they should not be used on the outside of laminates of hulls; they must be shielded from abrasion. Some experts advise using carbon fibers only on the inner skin of sandwich structures for these reasons, especially where thin high modulus skins are being used.

While carbon fibers can be woven, the fibers will lose a certain degree of strength when woven just as all fibers will. For ultimate strength, carbon fibers must be kept straight with no wrinkles or kinks. There is disagreement among experts as to whether ortho or iso polyester resins are suitable for use with carbon fibers for bonding and laminating purposes. Some manufacturers of carbon fiber products state that polyester resins are entirely suitable for making laminates with carbon fiber materials. Some fabricators feel that vinylester resins are preferable over regular polyesters for use with carbon fibers, while others feel that only epoxy resins offer suitable properties of strength and bonding to realize the potentials of the carbon fibers. Furthermore, some experts feel that carbon fibers require MORE than just contact molding; pressure or vacuum bag techniques are said to be necessary to eliminate air bubbles and for thorough wet-out so that defects that can lead to failures are not allowed to form in the laminate.

Failures of items made with carbon fibers are often attributed to porosity, improper fiber orientation, and hand layup techniques. When using carbon fibers in layers, thin multiple layers should be used, applying one layer at a time. Also, resin bond lines between layers should be kept as thin as possible. Because of the difficulty of working with carbon fibers in their "raw" state, which is in the form of "tows" or strands of fine hair-like bundles, most prefer to use one of the proprietary fabrics available for easier handling.

It is possible to buy shaped parts in long lengths made from carbon fiber, such as thin, narrow flat bars. The flat bars are made using an epoxy matrix laminated and cured under pressure or vacuum in controlled conditions for uniformity. These parts can be added into laminates for increased strength at given areas much the same way that lumber members are added into the hull framework of wood boats. In these instances, it is possible to use polyester resins for the bonding by bedding the carbon fiber members within the laminate, although some question the ability of polyester resins to bond to room temperature-cured epoxies. The surfaces of the flat bars are provided with peel plies for good secondary bonding, and the builder need not worry about building in defects with the carbon fibers. The manufacturers of the parts should be contacted for their recommendations for proper use and application.

Some precautions should be noted with regard to carbon fibers. There is a slight danger to breathing carbon in the air. Unattached fibers can become airborn easily, so wear a filter mask when cutting and fabricating the material, just as would be

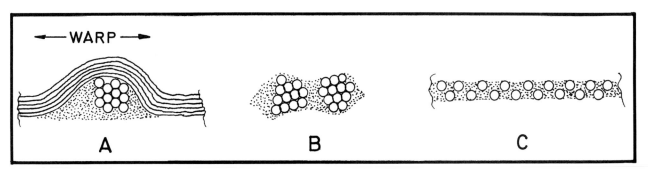

FIG. 21-3 — A comparison of resin dispersion is shown in exaggerated form in three types of reinforcements. In 'A', a cross-section of a typical woven roving material impregnated with resin is shown. Note the resin-rich areas that can form under the crimp of the warp roving, and the dry strands that may form in the center area above the weft roving. The crimp makes the layer thicker and decreases strength in the warp direction fibers since they have been distorted by the intersection. Extra resin is required which increases weight and cost. In 'B', a cross-section is shown through a typical unidirectional material. While an improvement over 'A', there are still potential resin-rich areas in the gaps between strands, and possible dry areas in the center of these strands. However, because the warp fibers are straight, there is a gain in strength in this direction. In 'C', a cross-section through a unidirectional material of aerospace quality (such as ORCOWEB as described in Chapter 22) is shown. The fibers are spread to allow almost 100% encapsulation of each by the resin, resulting in a more homogeneous laminate. This results in a much stronger laminate in the direction of the strand than in 'A', and one that is thinner and lighter in weight, requiring less material than either 'A' or 'B'.

done with fiberglass. Metals in contact with graphite in salt water are highly susceptible to corrosion due to the difference in electrolytic potential; contact must be avoided because such corrosion of the metal is rapid.

SPECIALTY REINFORCEMENTS

Unlike conventional fiberglass materials like mat, woven roving, and cloth, there are several non-woven materials available that will be classified as specialty reinforcements. The primary difference in these materials, other than the fact that they are non-woven, has to do with the directional orientation of the fibers in the material. As has been pointed out before, in order to realize the ultimate strength in a material, the fiber must be kept as straight as possible and reasonably taut. The resin matrix is then used to hold or bond the fibers in this orientation.

However, in the weaving process of conventional materials using the standard "waffle" pattern of the cross weave, the fibers go up and down in the weave where they cross (see Fig. 21-3) and this allows for resin-rich pockets that detract somewhat from the strength of the fibers. In the conventional laminate this is little problem, but with high modulus materials where thin skins are used, and which may include carbon fibers where the fibers must be kept straight to work, the strength loss can be critical if the fibers are not kept as straight and flat as possible.

The specialty reinforcements that make this possible are the unidirectional (often abbreviated as "UDR"), the biaxial, and the triaxial fabrics. The unidirectionals are simple, with all the strength fibers going in virtually one direction, usually along the warp of the fabric, but sometimes across the weft. In general, there are two types of unidirectional fabrics; those that are of the conventional type, and those that are of aerospace quality and make much thinner

laminates.

The biaxial fabrics usually have the fibers going with the warp and the weft, but they are different from woven roving in that they are not woven; the fibers are in flat strands laid over each other and stitched, knitted, or bonded together to make a material much thinner than woven roving of the same weight. The triaxial fabrics have the fibers going in three directions. One group of fibers goes in the direction of the warp, while the other two go on the bias or diagonally in each direction, or in other words, they are "double" biased. Instead of being woven, the strands are knitted together as in the biaxial material.

Just about any of the specialty materials can be had in the various high modulus materials previously discussed, and sometimes in combination. These materials are much more expensive than the conventional fiberglass materials, at least on a weight basis, and not as readily available to the amateur builder. Their prime function is to make laminates that are stronger, lighter, and thinner than would be possible with conventional laminates, but their use may not be as straightforward for the amateur, and they may require more expensive resins, especially if made from other than fiberglass materials.

ARE HIGH MODULUS MATERIALS AND SPECIALTY REINFORCEMENTS WORTH IT?

There is considerable disagreement among boatbuilders and other knowledgeable people as to the value of high modulus reinforcements and specialty materials. Some feel that the weight savings of these so-called "exotic" materials come nowhere near offsetting their increased costs and handling difficulties. They feel that equally high-strength laminates can be made at lower cost using more conventional reinforcements without the inherent problems.

FIG. 21-4 — Examples of aerospace-quality unidirectional materials. The lighter material is S-500 ("S-2 Fiberglas") ORCOWEB, while the darker material is graphite fiber ORCOWEB. Note the bonded cross-ties used to hold the fibers in line.

For example, some feel that a laminate using conventional E-glass combinations and iso polyester resins results in a lighter, cheaper boat than, for example, laminates using more expensive S-glass and vinylester resins. They feel that any gain in strength of the S-glass laminate would be marginal and not worth the added cost or difficulties of working with vinylester resins.

Others consider materials like Kevlar to be a waste of money and effort, stating that a boat made with S-glass and iso polyester resins is just as strong. For example, potential bonding problems with Kevlar have been noted and the need to add mat layers between, thereby negating, at least partially, the weight savings. It can be argued

	CONVENTIONAL FIBERGLASS	FIBERGLASS TYPE S-500 ORCOWEB	GRAPHITE ORCOWEB
Construction of Skin	1½ oz. mat. 24 oz. woven roving 1½ oz. mat. 24 oz. woven roving 1½ oz. mat. against core	4 plies 0°-90°-0°-90° +¾ oz. mat. against core	3 plies 0°-90°-0° +¾ oz. mat. against core
Skin Weight - psf	1.79	0.64	0.44
Skin thickness - inches	0.237	0.086	0.057
Core thickness - inches	0.35	0.59	0.59
Core density - pcf	4.5	4.5	4.5
Total Laminate Weight - psf	3.71	1.51	1.10
Total Laminate Thickness - inches	0.824	0.762	0.704
Fiber Content			
% by Weight	35	48	40
% by Volume*	19	29	29
Relative Tensile Strength - 0°	100	111	92
Relative Tensile Modulus - 0°	1	2.5	4.6
Relative Compressive Strength - 0°	100	95	105
Relative Flexural Stiffness	1	1	1

*Glass Density = .09 pci, Graphite Density = .064 pci, Resin Density = .04 pci

NOTE: Relation of mechanical properties between laminates as shown is virtually the same for polyester, vinyl ester, or epoxy resins. Relations are likewise very similar for cores of different densities.

FIG. 21-5 — Comparison data of sandwich laminates using hand layup techniques with conventional fiberglass, ORCOWEB Type S-500 Fiberglass, and graphite ORCOWEB. Note the dramatic decrease in weight over the conventional laminate and much higher fiber contents of the ORCOWEB laminates while maintaining relatively similar tensile strengths, compressive strengths, and flexural stiffnesses. The gains in tensile modulus in the direction of the fibers for the ORCOWEB laminates is impressive.

that while higher strength or lighter weight may be desirable, it is more practical to obtain these results by using more compatible unidirectional fiberglass materials in place of Kevlar.

While every ounce of weight saved, together with each gain in strength, may be necessary or desirable in certain types of boats, such as competition craft, it may not be worth the added cost in more conventional boats, nor worth the added complexity and difficulty for the person building his own boat. Not only are there numerous combinations of materials available such as E-glass, S-glass, Kevlar, and carbon fibers, but also several types of resin, including the ortho's, iso's, vinylesters, and the epoxies. This makes a mind-boggling combination of possible "ingredients" that is difficult, to say the least, for the amateur builder to sort through and evaluate. The picture may be further complicated by the fact that core materials can also be used, as will be discussed next.

USING HIGH MODULUS MATERIALS IN SANDWICH CORE CONSTRUCTION

The exceptional high strength properties of the high modulus materials make it possible to build hulls with very thin skins compared to conventional fiberglass materials. However, while these thin skins may have enough strength technically, they lack stiffness and other properties resulting from thickness necessary for service requirements if used alone in a single skin configuration. While the skin could be made thicker, this would defeat the purpose and be too costly. Hence, it is desirable to use one of the core materials such as foam or balsa in order to have a practical hull structure. In fact, the use of a core is virtually a necessity as high-strength skins become thinner.

In order to match the high tensile properties of the high modulus materials, a core material must be selected to have strength properties to work in concert with the strong, but thin, skins. One of the most important qualities in this regard is the compressive strength of the core material. Of the two structural marine grade density foams (for example, AIREX and KLEGE-CELL), the AIREX foam has the lowest compressive strength, being about 75% of that of KLEGECELL.

From a practical standpoint, the high modulus materials with thin skins using an AIREX core can present a potential problem due to its lower compressive strength. For example, when the boat is on a cradle or trailer where point loadings may occur, the thin skins which are strong yet flexible, may not keep the foam from compressing.

While KLEGECELL is no doubt better with regard to compressive strength than AIREX, END-GRAIN BALSA core is far superior to either since its compressive strength is several times higher yet. Of course, compressive strength in any core does depend on the density of the core, but denser cores do cost more and they add weight to the boat. With foams, increasing density also makes it potentially more difficult to build the boat.

However, compressive strength is only one factor. The KLEGECELL people state that their foam is the ultimate core for use with high modulus materials, mainly because of the stiffness of the foam. Their contention is that the core should be as stiff as possible, because if it is not, the core could possibly deflect under the skins. This may elongate the skins beyond their elastic (stretching) limits, leading to rupture. Furthermore, in this situation, the potential for delamination and/or buckling under stress loadings is increased. Assuming equal skin properties and core thickness, the KLEGE-CELL people claim that their foam is potentially the stiffest and strongest foam core material.

While the preceding may be true, the state of the art in the use of high modulus materials with cores is in its infancy. Because so little evidence exists (both in the way of testing and records over time of existing boats), it is difficult to state categorically whether a foam such as AIREX can be suitably used with high modulus skins or not.

The latest AIREX formulation has much improved properties over early types (see Chapter 18), and as can be seen, END-GRAIN BALSA core has much higher properties than either of the foams. Yet balsa should be partially sealed with a "hot coat" of thin resin when used with high modulus skins or else it will soak up more resin than either of the foams. A layer of mat (a minimal ¾ oz. weight has been used successfully with high modulus skins) should be used against the core to assure a positive interlaminar bond. This relatively heavy mat layer on either side, plus the added

weight of the balsa itself, does negate the reason for using high modulus skins in the first place, at least to some degree, although the lighter density (6 lb. grade) balsa is only slightly heavier than the foams. There have been some competition boats that have used high modulus skins with balsa core without the use of mat, but this practice may not be suitable for the amateur. It is recommended that the builder who wants to use balsa core with high modulus skins contact the BALTEK Corp. for their specific recommendations regarding laminate schedules and layup procedures, unless specifically called out on the plans.

With AIREX and KLEGECELL foam, the fine closed cell structure only absorbs resin along the thin surface of open cells. This not only cuts down on weight, but also on costs, since less resin is required. On KLEGECELL hulls, high modulus materials can be

 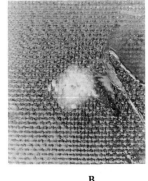  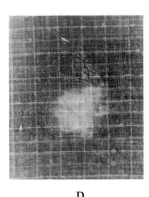

| A | B | C | D |

FIG. 21-6 — This series of photos compares the impact resistance of several laminates. Particular attention should be given to the weights per square foot of the various samples. All samples feature sandwich construction except 'A', which is solid fiberglass.

('A') — Consists of six plies woven roving and five layers of mat, solid fiberglass conventional laminate weighing 4 lbs. 10 ozs. per sq. ft.

('B') — Consists of two plies woven roving and two layers of mat each side of a 5/8" KLEGECELL core, weighing 2 lbs. 10 ozs. per sq. ft.

('C') — Consists of three plies woven Kevlar and three layers of mat each side of a 5/8" KLEGECELL core, weighing 2 lbs. 3 ozs. per sq. ft.

('D') — Consists of four layers S-500 ORCOWEB on exposed side, three layers graphite ORCOWEB on other side, with 5/8" KLEGECELL core between, 1 lb. 1 oz. per sq. ft.

While difficult to show by photos, the intensity of the white areas indicates the extent of damage to the samples. Note that the conventional solid fiberglass laminate ('A') suffered the most extensive damage. Yet, the use of a core material with thinner conventional fiberglass skins ('B') shows much less damage. While Kevlar is reputed to have high impact resistance ('C'), some indentation of the core did occur, indicating core damage. The ORCOWEB sample ('D') is superior, showing virtually no damage or indentation of the core material, yet is less than one-half the weight of the next heaviest sample.

applied directly against the foam without the need for mat, making construction faster and easier. Compared to standard END-GRAIN BALSA, KLEGECELL (as well as AIREX) is lighter in weight. This means that when used for decks and cabins, the center of gravity of the boat will be lower. In high performance craft, especially with sailboats, this can be an important factor. However, if the lighter weight 6 lb. density balsa is used, this narrows the core weights to a negligible difference.

It should be noted that balsa advocates feel it is a waste of money to use high modulus skins without considering core shear properties and using a suitable core having high core shear strength like END-GRAIN BALSA. Their argument is that with the lower core shear properties (such as those which a KLEGECELL sandwich would have), if the core is taken to ultimate loading, the skins will probably not come anywhere near to the ultimate loading, but the core will fracture regardless. With END-GRAIN BALSA, they state that balsa cores can be designed into very efficient structures that take advantage of the very high compressive and shear strengths of the material.

ARE HIGH MODULUS SKINS PRACTICAL FOR THE AMATEUR?

In making a determination on whether to build a boat with high modulus materials using thin skins and core materials, as opposed to using more conventional materials with thicker skins and the same core materials, one must remember that fiberglass is a very forgiving material when using conventional reinforcements and general purpose resins. The builder can make a lot of little mistakes, and yet the boat will probaby hold together indefinitely.

Consider the conditions under which the typical boat is built by an amateur. In many cases, the boat may sit out in the open exposed to the elements of sun, heat, moisture, freezing, and worse. A secondary bond, for example, may not occur for months, and may be made under the worst of conditions with little quality control. Past experience shows that amateur builders may sometimes be careless (although it should be added that production fiberglass boatbuilders are also often careless, and in some cases, more so than amateurs). Of course, this should not be taken as an excuse, and the builder should maintain strict quality control as much as possible, following the recommendations that have been set forth. The amateur should select materials and methods that will allow proper quality control under the conditions that will prevail as the boat is being built.

For example, a core material such as AIREX may be a preferable core material for use with conventional laminates because it will allow for a lot of minor errors or defects under less than ideal building conditions without disastrous consequences, mainly due to the elasticity of the foam. If there was a lack of bond between the core and the skin in a certain area, which would allow the core to move or "creep" around, the foam would still very likely not break as would other cores. And if water did enter the core, it would not travel as far as it would, for example, in a balsa core. Generally, with conventional fiberglass materials, there is enough latitude to permit a fair amount of indiscretion in their use. It is this quality that makes conventional laminates ideal both for the production builder (because he can then use basically unskilled, lower-priced labor), and the amateur, who must learn skills quickly and easily.

However, such is not the case when the project calls for increasingly higher technology in materials and fabricating techniques, such as are required with high modulus skins in sandwich structures. Using these materials often requires standards of quality control and building skills that can approach aircraft industry tolerances. There is less chance for error. Where perhaps a single worker could build an entire fiberglass boat using conventional laminates, an operation using high technology materials could demand a crew of several workers to insure that a certain aspect of the job was done properly without interruption.

Defects in a laminate using high modulus materials can become critical both from a strength standpoint as well as with durability and longevity. This is why there are many professional designers and builders who feel that, while certain high tech-nology materials and methods may be suitable for certain types of amateurs building certain types of boats (especially competition craft that may not be intended for long-term durability), they are not suitable for the builder who may not have the skills or abilities necessary to control quality AND who wants a boat to last a lifetime under the most extreme seagoing conditions. If the latter fits your situation, then perhaps you should stick to building with conventional materials and use methods which have more latitude for errors.

CHAPTER 22   vacuum bag methods with sandwich cored hulls

The following vacuum bag method using a male mold describes a boatbuilding procedure that may not be suitable for all amateurs, especially beginners. Yet it has enough appealing aspects that many may want to give it a try. The method has been promoted by the makers of KLEGECELL foam, who have dubbed it appropriately as the "3-STAGE" system, because the inner laminate is applied first in Stage One, the core material is applied next in Stage Two, and the outer laminate applied last in Stage Three (see Fig. 22-1). In effect, the "3-STAGE" vacuum bag technique sort of bridges the gap between those cored hulls built in female molds and those "one-off" cored hulls built over open battened male molds.

The vacuum bag method to be described, however, does not refer to the type of large vacuum bag sometimes used in the production situation, which is used to make an entire hull or part in one operation. This procedure is not practical for the amateur. Instead, the method shown uses a smaller vacuum bag procedure that is used to fabricate one section of the hull at a time. Because of this segmented approach, the method becomes adaptable to the amateur who is willing to experiment.

While the photos show a boat being built using high modulus unidirectional layers of S-glass material for the skins, the same vacuum bag techniques and features are equally applicable to skins made up from more conventional laminates as well as other high modulus materials and specialty reinforcements. Some specifics regarding the use of the high modulus S-glass as they relate to this example will be discussed later in this section.

Also, while a cross-linked PVC foam (KLEGECELL) is used in this description, it is possible that other foams and balsa core materials could be used, although experience with any of the products at this point is limited. It is recommended that if the builder wants to deviate from the materials shown (particularly in regard to the core), representatives of the firms making the materials that will be used should be contacted for their advice. These techniques are not time-proven, and there are some aspects which are somewhat "tricky" and experimental.

WHY A VACUUM BAG?

Building a hull over a solid male mold as opposed to building on the inside of a female mold has several appealing points for the amateur or even the professional builder who wants to build one or a few hulls. The typical open battened male mold ordinarily used for foam and balsa cores does involve a special sequence of building operations, some of which must be carefully and conscientiously performed. These include righting the partially completed hull without distorting it, and applying the interior laminate without crushing the core, yet assuring an even dispersion of resin to all inner areas.

With the vacuum bag system, all layup of the skins and the core takes place on the outside of the male mold. Instead of using an open battened male mold, the male mold is a closed surfaced male mold with the vacuum bag method. The male mold in this situation is actually like a "plug" as would be used in female mold boatbuilding, yet no elaborate or costly female mold is required. In fact, the sequence of layup is exactly the reverse of that used for a female mold, with perhaps some minor exceptions. Core "attachment" is really done in the form of bonding by the use of a vacuum bag, which is more of a sheet than an actual bag.

The advantages of the vacuum bag method compared to using an open battened male mold using core materials are:

1. No need to turn the hull over until it is completed.
2. No need for an elaborate receiving cradle to hold the hull rigidly until an inner laminate is applied.
3. No resin drainage problems on the inside.
4. No chance for hull distortion to occur.
5. No thermoforming of plain sheet core materials since contoured types are used.
6. Smooth interior surface (looks better and is easier to maintain).
7. Vacuum bag improves chances for a more efficient, defect-free laminate with less resin usage.
8. Mold can more easily be used again.
9. Most major fairing can take place on the core instead of on the outer skin.
10. Because contoured foam is used, resin passing through the slits between the blocks will form "resin ties" between

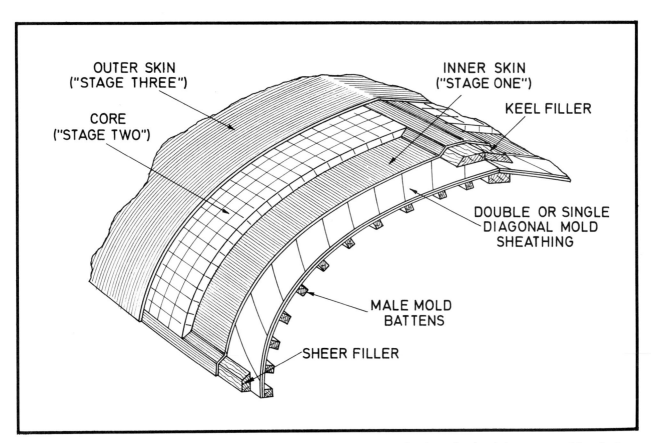

FIG. 22-1 — The "3-STAGE" system for building a hull as described in the text is shown. A solid sheathed male mold is first built, and this is covered with the inner laminate (stage one). The core material is applied next (stage two) and this is covered with the outer laminate (stage three). The vacuum bag is used to bond the core material to the inner skin. Note in this example that the inner skin is joined to the outer skin at the keel and at the sheer (see Fig. 22-2 for variations).

the skins for increased strength, which is not the case when plain sheet foam is used.

MAKING THE MALE MOLD

There are several ways that a solid male mold or "plug" can be made for the vacuum bag method. First, an actual boat hull can be used as long as it is properly prepared and the completed hull has a shape that allows easy removal. However, from a design standpoint, this practice is questionable and could be a violation of the law.

If the hull form of the design is composed of developable surfaces (from segments of cones or cylinders), the mold can be made from sheet plywood, Masonite, or similar sheet materials. If the hull form consists of compounded or double curvature surfaces, it can be planked with diagonally applied strips of thin plywood such as that used for door skins, or thin, narrow strips of Masonite. In the photos, the builder made a mold using just a single layer of plywood door skins cut up into narrow strips laid diagonally. However, on a large boat hull where the builder may have to climb onto the mold, there may be too much deflection with a single thin skin. Hence, a double layer as a minimum is recommended, even though a single layer of materials may be enough to give the required hull form.

As far as the framework for the male mold is concerned, this can be of any suitable

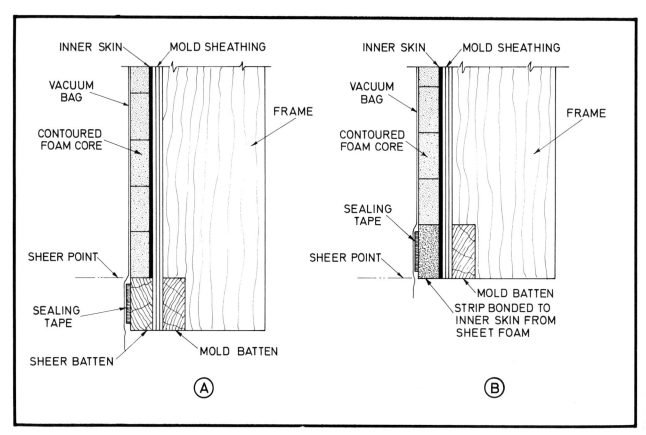

FIG. 22-2 — Two sections at the sheer of a hull built using the "3-STAGE" system are shown. In these cases, the sheer clamp or sheer reinforcement will be applied later, and the inner and outer skins are not joined at the sheer as in Fig. 22-1. Because of this, a means must be provided for sealing the vacuum bag along the sheer. This is done either with a wood batten bordering just below the sheer to which the sealing tape for the bag is applied (as in 'A'), or a width of sheet core material is bonded all around the sheer area to which the sealing tape is applied (as in 'B').

material including plywood, lumber, particleboard, etc., for athwartship members. Wood longitudinal battens are placed over these, spaced apart as necessary to support the mold skin. Although cheap scrap material can be used to build the mold, it must be strong and rigid to prevent movement, and securely anchored in place, even if only one hull will be built from the mold.

Surface quality of the mold is not critical, but the degree of quality desired on the inside hull surface is directly dependent upon the quality of this surface. Furthermore, the mold surfaces must still be fair and smooth enough so that unfairness is not telegraphed through the hull laminate, making it difficult to finish the hull or apply the core material. While resin putty fillers can be used to smooth out and fair the mold surfaces, there is no reason why cheap materials such as plaster patch compounds can't be used as well.

One consideration with the vacuum bag method is that the entire hull will be built and then removed from the mold. With fiberglass and resin, there is bound to be some shrinkage upon curing, causing the hull to decrease in size somewhat. This can make it more difficult to remove the hull from the mold upon completion. If only one boat will be built, the mold can be destroyed and broken apart to free the hull. But if the mold is to be used again, another approach can be used similar to that used in female molds noted previously. Simply drill some small holes through the mold skin to suit the size of an air gun jet and seal these with cellophane tape from the outside. It is then easy to use compressed air to "demold" the hull.

MOLD SURFACE PREPARATION

Since the hull will have the inner skin laminate made directly on the mold surface, it must not stick to the mold when it is time to remove the hull from the mold.

There are several ways to treat the mold surface so that the hull will not stick, with much of the choice depending on the quality of inner surface of the hull that is desired. The mold can be coated with tooling gel coat, sanded and faired, and then coated with wax and mold release for the ultimate in a high quality inner finish. Or the mold surface can be covered with parting film such as thin Mylar or other plastic sheeting. Or it is possible just to build up the mold surfaces with resin-compatible sealers and apply generous coatings of wax. The mold used for the hull in the photos was covered with strips of 12" wide red cellophane tape, and as an added step, was coated with a layer of paste wax. Whichever method is used, the mold is now ready for the application of the inner laminate, or "Stage One".

APPLYING THE INNER LAMINATE

The inner skin laminate is applied to suit the design specifications, stopping short of the final layer of material next to the core. With conventional laminates, this final layer next to the core will usually be mat. The type of resin used may vary; however, when using KLEGECELL, an iso polyester is preferred over the ortho type. In certain cases with competition boats using high modulus materials, vinylester resin or perhaps epoxies may be called for.

In the initial layer of the inner skin, the fabric can be taped in place if it can be wetted out from the topside (this is also known as the "dry method" for wetting out a layer of reinforcement). Or the resin can be applied to the surface of the mold and the material set in it to help wet it out from the underside (this is referred to as the "wet method"). All through the application of the inner laminate, care should be taken to assure an even and fair surface. This surface quality and care is important since it will be transferred to the forthcoming layers of

FIG. 22-3 — In the "3-STAGE" system, the core material is applied after the inner skin. Here the contoured-type foam core panels (KLEGECELL in this vessel) are being fitted. Note how the panel conforms to the hull surface.

FIG. 22-5 — A double sided "bubble gum" sealing tape is used to hold the plastic sheet vacuum bag in place against the hull.

The following photos (FIG. 22-3 through FIG. 22-30) illustrate the procedures of building a hull using the "3-STAGE" system with vacuum bag techniques, and thin, high modulus skins on either side of a core material. Similar vacuum bag procedures would be used with skins composed of conventional laminates.

FIG. 22-4 — The foam core is coated with a thin coat of laminating resin to minimize resin absorption of the foam. The procedure may be optional or vary depending on the type of core used.

FIG. 22-6 — The vacuum bag has been applied and pulled back for the application of the core. Note the sheet foam strip at the sheer with the sealing tape applied (see Fig. 22-2). Also note the vacuum equipment in the foreground showing the various fittings and gauges.

materials, including the core material.

The application of the laminate should be done just the same as would be done over the core when using an open battened male mold; junctions in the materials used for the inner skin laminate should be butted and not overlapped. Once the inner laminate is complete (short of the final layer that will be next to the core), carefully sand it fair to insure a smooth bonding surface, but take care not to grind or cut into the fiberglass reinforcement material excessively, especially if using high modulus materials. A laminating resin should be used, even though it will be more difficult to sand and grind. However, if a good job has been done building up the laminate, this smoothing and fairing work will be minimal.

INSTALLING THE CORE WITH THE VACUUM BAG

The reason that the final layer of laminate of the inner skin is not applied is that it acts as a bedding layer for the core material. Because of this, it cannot be allowed to set up first. If the mat is still wet when the core is applied, a much better bond wil result.

A wood batten or board can be used all around the hull just BELOW the sheer line, as the hull is upsidedown (see Fig. 22-2). The tape which is used to attach and seal the vacuum bag is attached to this batten. Or cut a strip of foam about 2″ to 3″ wide all around the sheer to serve the same purpose, using the same thickness of foam that will be used for the core. With the foam, however, it can be placed ABOVE the sheer (as the boat is viewed when inverted), since it can remain in place in the completed hull. Contoured foam should not be used for this strip since the vacuum will suck in air through the slits in the contoured material and not allow sufficient vacuum to be pulled by the vacuum pump. If using the foam strip, clamp and bond it in place to the inner laminate with strips of resin saturated

mat. Or apply the sealing tape to the inner skin if foam is deleted at the sheer, as is the case in Fig. 22-1.

The core material to be used should be the contoured type except that on hulls having very straight or boxy contours with flat surfaces, plain sheet material can be used. It is easier for the contoured type of material to conform to hull contours, however, because the slits between the blocks keep air from becoming trapped on the underside, causing a void and lack of bonding at such areas. The slits in the contoured material act as pathways for the air to travel out as well as for the resin to fill in. This increases the strength of the final sandwich once the outer skin has been applied.

If plain sheet foam material is used for the core, holes should be punched through each sheet no more than 4″ apart. This can be done easily by making a nail board with nails hammered through at 4″ intervals. Simply press the board against the sheet and all the holes will be punched through in one quick step. However, a problem that can occur with plain sheet core material so punched is that the resin tends to be sucked up through the holes and against the vacuum bag. This tends to cancel out any further suction that may be necessary to pull the sheets down as firmly as they should be.

Dry-fit the core (cutting it to shape as necessary) using a marking pen around the perimeter of each sheet onto the inner laminate. Number each space AND each corresponding core sheet. Use a dark permanent marker and you will have no trouble seeing the marks through the mat layer to be applied once it is wet out. Note, as shown in the photos, the sheets need not necessarily be fitted closely; it is always possible to fill in any gaps that may exist between sheets with narrow strips. However, sheets can be butted if desired, but the areas near the edge will have to be filled with resin putty filler to seal the slits in the

FIG. 22-7 — The inner laminate is coated with a resin putty bonding coat which bonds the core to the inner laminate. This coat should be fairly thin, but not so runny that it drains to lower areas.

FIG. 22-8 — The pre-fitted sheets of core material are placed onto the inner laminate after the resin bonding coat has been applied. Note the gap between adjoining panels where the sealing tape is located. This gap will be filled with foam scraps later.

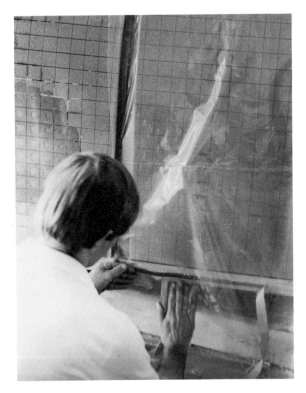

FIG. 22-9 — After the foam is in position, the vacuum bag is draped back into place over the core material, and the edges sealed with the tape. The vacuum is being pulled at the same time.

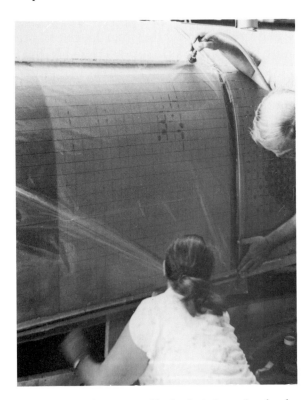

FIG. 22-10 — The vacuum bleed tube is located under the vacuum bag as it is draped over onto the foam and the vacuum is pulled. Some resin can already be seen coming through the slits in the core.

contour material in order to prevent air leaks through the slits once the bag is in place and the vacuum is pulled.

In general, there is no particular preference or sequence for fitting the core sheets. However, it is usually easiest to start along the sheer and work towards the centerline on round bottom boats. On hard-chine hulls, it makes little difference where the fitting of the core begins. The same applies to the actual core application. However, some prefer to start at the centerline and get a feel for the procedure in a flatter area so that handling the resin will not be as difficult. If the resin DOES run in this situation, it will do so from a higher area to a lower area where the excess can be more easily removed, which would not be the case if core material had already been installed along a lower area first.

With the core sheets fitted and removed, fit the vacuum bag around the perimeter of the sheets to be applied. Most workers will be able to handle an area about 4' × 5' with two or three people working. Note that this vacuum bag process is NOT advised for the single worker; too many things will be taking place too quickly for the lone worker to handle. The vacuum bag is actually nothing more than a sheet plastic material that is sealed down all around the perimeter of the foam. The vacuum bag can be made from clear poly sheeting (about 4 to 10 mil thickness is usually good), or any other comparable material such as Mylar or nylon-reinforced plastic sheeting.

The plastic sheeting used for the vacuum bag is stuck to the hull surface and sealed around the edges of the core sheet by duct tape or with a special double-sided thick mastic tape often called "bubble gum tape" or "Tacky-Tape", a brand name. This type of tape is available from fiberglass supply houses and sometimes through glaziers. The tape is applied about 2" to 3" out from the edge of the core sheet perimeter all around to form a tight seal. The double-sided tape has a peel strip that allows the

worker to put the tape in place and later apply the vacuum bag sheet to it. Remove the peel strip along the top or highest point and stick the vacuum bag to it along this area. At the same time, fold the bag back toward the centerline, or if working along the centerline, fold the sheet to the opposite side of the hull.

First make sure that all surfaces are clean and free of dust. Then check all vacuum equipment so that everything is ready for immediate use. This leads into a discussion regarding the type of vacuum equipment required. The type of vacuum pump can vary, and some have even used a shop vacuum cleaner to do the job. But the use of a "shop vac" is questionable as to whether sufficient vacuum levels can be pulled to assure a sound bond, and if it has the necessary endurance. Ideally, the type of vacuum pump to use should be capable of pulling a large volume of air, but not necessarily at a high vacuum. The types ordinarily used, for example, in refrigeration work or for scientific purposes which pull down a high vacuum, but not much volume, are not as good, since removing the last bit of air is not really critical.

The measurement of pulling a vacuum is given in inches of mercury, and is written frequently as, for example, 6″ Hg, or 6″ of mercury (divide by 2 for p.s.i.). A pump that can pull a vacuum in the range of from 10″ to 18″ Hg maximum, and is capable of holding this vacuum for at least an hour (and preferably longer) should be used.

With the vacuum equipment ready for use, apply a layer of mat to the inner laminate surface after it has been saturated with resin. The pre-coated wet face of the core material is applied to this mat immediately and vacuumed in position.

The vacuum pump is connected to a manifold or bleed tube that is located under the vacuum bag by a hose. The bleed tube and fittings can be ordinary plastic pipe and fittings. About a 1″ size pipe will suit most conditions. The manifold bleed tube is

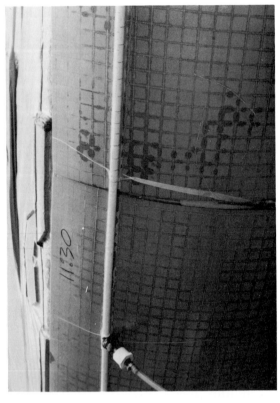

FIG. 22-12 — The vacuum tube (plastic pipe) has slits or holes to distribute the vacuum evenly. Note the time marked onto the bag to gauge the length of cure.

FIG. 22-14 — Various sections of the hull have been covered with the core material a section at a time. The gaps between sections are filled in later.

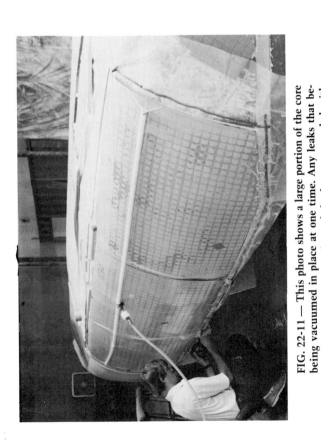

FIG. 22-11 — This photo shows a large portion of the core being vacuumed in place at one time. Any leaks that become apparent at the edges of the bag are resealed with additional tape as required.

FIG. 22-13 — After the resin cures, the vacuum bag and bleed tube are removed from the hull. Notice the resin between the slits of the foam. Resin which has set up around the bleed tube can be easily sanded or ground down later when the core is faired for the outer laminate.

simply a length of pipe that is slit with saw kerfs about an inch apart just deep enough to keep from weakening the pipe, alternating from one side to the other, or with holes drilled, similarly spaced and positioned. The pipe is as long as is required to pull the vacuum over the given area being worked on at the time.

For best results, the manifold is located about ¼ to ⅓ down from the upper edge (or edge nearest the centerline). For some unexplained reason, the vacuum often sucks up more thoroughly from the bottom or lower areas than it does from upper areas. The manifold is positioned on top of the core and taped in place to the underside of the vacuum bag. The end of the manifold pipe is fitted with a 90 degree elbow and short nipple which passes through the vacuum bag sheet. This connects to the hose leading to the vacuum pump. Where the nipple passes through the vacuum bag, use plenty of sealing tape so that air will not leak through the opening in the sheet. Then reposition the vacuum bag and tape the sheet in place all around the perimeter while drawing the vacuum at the same time. If any air leaks are heard, apply more tape to these areas. It makes little difference what type of tape is used as long as the sticking power is sufficient to provide a tight air seal and resist the vacuum level being pulled.

The pump system must have a vacuum gauge (preferably at the manifold where it can be easily seen) to monitor what is happening, and a bleeder valve to control the amount of vacuum. The vacuum gauge will quickly tell if the proper vacuum is being pulled; if it is not, then there are probably leaks. By listening carefully around the perimeter of the bag, leaks can be readiy detected and plugged. Vacuum gauges may be available from auto supply stores.

As the vacuum is pulled, resin will begin to appear in the slits between the squares of the core, assuming that enough resin has been applied. Check the position of the core as work proceeds to make sure that the sheet has not moved.

In applying the mat between the inner hull surface and the core, a 1 oz. or 1½ oz. weight will usually suffice. A lighter mat may not provide sufficient cushioning for the core, and heavier mats add unnecessary weight. In addition to coating the inner laminate surface with mat, also coat the back side of the core material (the surface that will mate to the mat) with resin. This can be done with a roller for speed so that the core and mat are applied while the resin is wet on both sides. If the core used has a scrim backing, this side of the sheet is ordinarily coated and laid against the surface. Position the core sheet, applying hand pressure initially.

Although ample resin should be applied to the bedding mat and to the back side of the core sheet, there should not be so much resin that it will be sucked into the pump. Some pumps have provisions to prevent this from occurring, and these are desirable, but not necessary if care is taken. Experiment with a small section first to get a "feel" for the work. If the resin has been properly applied, there will be resin pulled up through the slits between the blocks, but there will be very little resin on the surface of the core.

As the resin begins to cure while pulling the vacuum, press against the core, especially in the areas where the resin passes through, to check the curing progress as well as the bond. If the vacuum sheet seems to be preventing the air from being bled out from all areas because it is compressing too tightly against the core, lay polyethylene ropes between the sheet and the core to create air passages for the air to escape through to the pump. The distribution of the vacuum pressure must be even and the gauge will not necessarily indicate that this is occurring even if vacuum pressure is at the prescribed point.

After a section has cured (maintaining the vacuum until cure takes place), remove

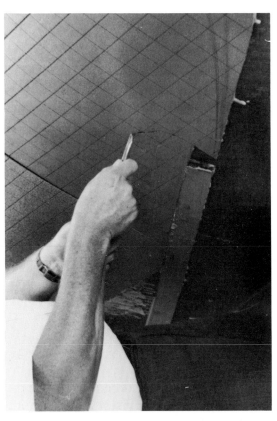

FIG. 22-16 — If void areas are found under the core (using methods described in the text to locate these), the foam covering the area can be cut away and removed. Additional resin is then applied and the piece reinserted.

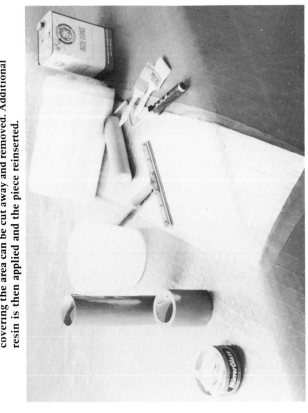

FIG. 22-18 — These are most of the tools used to make a laminate using a sandwich core with high modulus aerospace-quality reinforcements. Application tools include brushes, rollers, and squeegees. The wax and mold release film were used on the mold so the inner skin would not stick

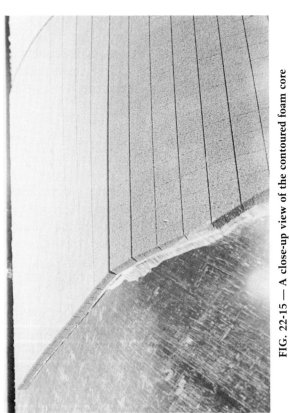

FIG. 22-15 — A close-up view of the contoured foam core after bonding in place with the vacuum bag. Note how this type of foam readily conforms to the hull contours. Resin from the outer laminate will fill in the slits which have not been completely filled in with the bonding resin.

FIG. 22-17 — An incomplete unsatisfactory bond is shown by the photo which was caused because the sheet foam used in this area (instead of the contoured type) did not conform well to the contours. Contoured foam is preferable for this reason.

the vacuum bag and check to see that there are no voids under the core. This is done with the coin-on-edge method scraped along the surface, with voids being corrected as for any cored hull (as has been noted previously). However, such voids should be minimal if everything has been done properly.

FAIRING THE CORE

After all panels have cured, and the surface has been checked for voids, with the voids being corrected, the entire surface can be faired. Minor gaps should be filled with resin putty filler, but larger gaps should be fitted with slivers or pieces of core material fairly closely fitted. Sand lightly only, using a long sanding board or "Foamglas", and do NOT remove core material to any great extent.

Some builders apply a filler coat over the entire core surface in order to fill in all the slits in the contoured core. This is probably acceptable (but usually not necessary) as long as most of the filler is squeegeed off and the surface cells are not filled. If the core surfaces are filled, this will interfere with fairing because the core surface is much softer than the cured resin filler, and the tendency will be to develop prominent high and low spots if sanding is not done with care. The filler, if it fills the core surface, will also set up a secondary bonding situation since the first layer of the outer laminate will then be applied to the cured filled surface instead of to the open-celled surface of the core.

If the surface of the core is too smooth with filler, it should be roughened up with coarse sandpaper or a "Surform" tool. There should be no areas of the hull where core blocks have protruding corners and edges. In areas of concaved curved sections (especially in areas of tight contours), the core blocks should not be flat, as this would indicate a void under the core. In other words,

the core surface should be as fair as is expected in the final hull, since any imperfections at this stage will be "telegraphed" to the outer skin, resulting in an eyesore.

The outer laminate can now be applied just as if the hull had been built over an open battened mold, finished the same way, and righted (see Chapters 12, 13, and 14). Since the hull is virtually complete at this time, it will be rigid. However, as with any boat, until the deck is in place, there will still be the possibility of distortion occurring, so don't be careless and assume that the hull is totally self-supporting at this point.

VARIATIONS TO VACUUM BAG METHOD IF USING HIGH MODULUS MATERIALS

Certain variations in the foregoing procedures may be required if other than conventional fiberglass materials are used for the skins, and instead specialty fabrics made with the high modulus materials are used. The following will describe the use of one such high modulus material in a specialty fabric form in actual use in an amateur boatbuilding project. The procedures and recommendations apply to this specific material, however, and if other materials are used, the builder is advised to contact the manufacturer of the material in question for specific advice, or at least confirm the methods discussed to determine their suitability to the materials in question. The principles, however, should be similar with most.

The material described in the following is classified as an aerospace-quality unidirectional fabric. The difference between aerospace-quality unidirectional fabrics and conventional woven rovings, as well as conventional unidirectional materials, was shown in Chapter 21. The obvious difference is that the aerospace-quality unidirectional material has an even dispersion

FIG. 22-19 — The reinforcement material (in this case aerospace-quality ORCOWEB S-500 fiberglass) is applied a layer at a time. The various layers in each skin (three per skin in this boat) are oriented in different directions as required.

FIG. 22-20 — The ORCOWEBS are easy to apply because the tackiness of the underlying cured resin surface helps hold the material in place.

FIG. 22-21 — Widths of ORCOWEB are butted and not overlapped. Tape can be used to hold the material in place as needed, being removed as the resin is applied.

FIG. 22-22 — Lengths of ORCOWEB can be trimmed to rough oversize and left for final trimming after the resin has been applied. Shears are used to cut the material in the dry state.

of resin and reinforcing fibers resulting in a thinner, but stronger, laminate, layer per layer. This form of unidirectional material offers an outstanding strength-to-weight ratio, excellent glass-resin ratio control, ease of handling without distorting the fibers, elimination of gaps associated with other types of unidirectional materials, virtual elimination of resin-rich or resin-starved areas associated with conventional fabrics, and exceptionally high impact resistance.

The aerospace-quality unidirectional material being used is "ORCOWEB" made by the ORCON Corporation. The ORCOWEB is made with a process that locks the unidirectional fibers in place with no crimps so that maximum fiber strength is realized. The integrity of the ORCOWEB is maintained by very fine, adhesive-coated weft yarns that are bonded (not interwoven) to the unidirectional fibers. The adhesive used for bonding is compatible with virtually all types of resins used in boats, including polyesters, vinylesters, and epoxies. The material comes in 12" wide roles up to 300' in length, with a polyethylene interliner to keep the material clean during handling. Because of the configuration of ORCOWEB and the manner in which it is made, it is ideally suited to hand layup application, and it is this quality which makes it suitable for the amateur building his own boat. There is very little waste involved.

ORCOWEB is available in either "S-2 Fiberglas" (S-glass), E-glass, graphite (carbon fiber), or a combination material of "S-2 Fiberglas" with Kevlar. The "S-2 Fiberglas" ORCOWEB is used where high physical properties are desired with minimum weight and nominal cost. Two layers of this material laid crosswise are often substituted for one layer of 24 oz. woven roving, resulting in almost equivalent strength with better stiffness when used in a sandwich structure. The "S-2 Fiberglas" ORCOWEB, when used for skins in sandwich panels, has far greater impact strength than

with skins made with any other type of fiber, including E-glass, carbon fiber, or Kevlar. This latter comparison is surprising since Kevlar supposedly has greater impact strength by itself. However, in the sandwich configuration, "S-2 Fiberglas" samples show less damage and indentation than do the all-Kevlar samples.

The graphic (carbon fiber) ORCOWEB is used where maximum stiffness, extremely high tensile and compressive strengths, and low weight are critical requirements. The material is seldom used for an entire overall laminate, mainly because of high cost and the fact that carbon fibers lack certain other qualities necessary in boats for general purpose laminates as noted before. The primary use of the material is for local reinforcement where needed in a laminate.

The ORCOWEB material which combines Kevlar with "S-2 Fiberglas" offers superior resistance to fatigue and better fiber-resin ratios than would an all-Kevlar ORCOWEB. The combination provides a high modulus of stiffness and good tensile strength combined with improved compressive strength, low weight, and low density. The combination also improves wet-out behavior, bondability, and impact strength when used in hand layup situations. The presence of "S-2 Fiberglas" enables the worker to visually determine when the material is properly wetted out, and the bond is superior to an all-Kevlar product. However, only vinylester or epoxy resins are advised.

For some unknown reason, the small amount of "S-2 Fiberglas" combined with the Kevlar increases the impact strength of a laminate made with this combination ORCOWEB, as has been confirmed by physical tests. Because the Kevlar does not make a good sanding surface (it is very tough, making it difficult to work on, as was noted previously), an outer ply in the form of a thin glass cloth, surfacing veil, or "S-2 Fiberglas" ORCOWEB should be used over this material if finish work will be neces-

FIG. 22-24 — After applying a layer of material, it is wetted out with resin. A brush is being used here initially to get the resin onto the surface.

FIG. 22-26 — A squeegee is used to force the laminate down and remove any excess resin or entrapped air. With the ORCOWEB, the squeegee is pulled along the warp of the material so it is not distorted and pulled out of shape.

FIG. 22-23 — Where a length of material runs short, join with another length with a slight lap for continuity. The material is so thin that an unfair build-up will not be noticeable.

FIG. 22-25 — After applying the resin, a foam roller is used to distribute the resin and wet out all areas evenly.

sary. One benefit of the Kevlar ORCOWEB is that laminates containing this material tend to be quieter and less sensitive to engine vibration than with either fiberglass or carbon fiber materials.

Materials like ORCOWEB can be used in both single skin and sandwich-type construction. This type of material lends itself ideally to use with a core and thin outer skins and has been used extensively with cores such as KLEGECELL. Even with very thin skins, impact energy is absorbed quickly and rapidly disseminated so that the core is less apt to suffer damage and the integrity of the skins is maintained.

An important quality of materials like ORCOWEB is that when used with other reinforcing fibers, the ORCOWEB will take the load first. For example, if a layer of ORCOWEB is applied over woven roving, the only contribution of the woven roving is to increase the stiffness due to its thickness. The ORCOWEB will take all the loading forces. Thus, in a single-skin laminate, a reinforced "core" can be made from mat and resin, and the "skin" would then be the desired number of ORCOWEB plies. Such a laminate would be heavier than if a foam or balsa core material is used instead, but possibly cheaper.

There is no doubt that materials like ORCOWEB are expensive, at least on a weight or square-foot basis. However, all factors must be looked at to see just how much more expensive these materials are in the TOTAL cost of the boatbuilding project. For example, less material will be required, and this means less resin will be used. Because a stronger laminate will result, fewer internal hull members will be required, especially if used with a core material. The boat can be lighter for a given length, and this means lighter rigging, a smaller mast, a smaller engine, smaller winches, and so forth. A cost analysis of various laminate combinations in Appendix 3 gives a better idea of true hull costs.

With several types of high modulus mate-

rials available, the novice may be confused about which one to use or what combination is suitable. Even the experts can't decide on this one. It is generally impractical to make laminates ENTIRELY out of either Kevlar or carbon fiber; these are best combined with fiberglass materials, with carbon fiber used at localized areas for reinforcement. Some experts feel that Kevlar and carbon fiber ORCOWEB have little justification in most boats; they contend that an all-S-glass laminate over a core on each side is strong enough.

The hull being built in the photos incorporates this approach, using a ⅝" thick KLEGECELL core with outer skins of "S-2 Fiberglas" ORCOWEB. The ORCOWEB consist of three layers on each side, with the fibers oriented diagonally each way (−45° and +45°), and lengthwise, or at 0°. Although the skins are actually less than ¹⁄₁₆" thick, the laminate is incredibly strong. It should be emphasized that this type of boat is intended for pure competition use where light weight takes precedence over durability. A carbon fiber ORCOWEB could have been incorporated for even greater stiffness, but the S-glass provides ample strength with light weight, excellent impact resistance, and toughness.

USING AEROSPACE-QUALITY UNIDIRECTIONAL MATERIALS

Using a material like ORCOWEB requires additional care on the part of the builder. First, because the skins may be quite thin, the configuration of the laminate (number of layers, direction of fiber orientation, etc.) as specified should be strictly adhered to. Don't add a layer "just to be safe" or change direction because it's easier that way.

As a general rule, each layer in a high modulus laminate should be wetted out and allowed to cure before applying another when working over a male mold. With cores

FIG. 22-28 — A completed laminate using ORCOWEB. Notice how fair this hull is as shown by the highlights. Finish work will be kept to a minimum, reducing building time, effort, weight, and costs.

FIG. 22-30 — Note the fair, smooth hull surfaces. The urethane coating makes this "one-off" hull look as though it were build in a female mold.

FIG. 22-27 — A layer of ORCOWEB is being applied over an underlying layer which has cured. It is easy for two workers to apply a layer of laminate in a brief period of time using this type of material.

FIG. 22-29 — The completed 40' craft before installation of the ballast keel is incredibly lightweight, weighing LESS than 700 lbs. (hull, deck, and cabin).

and high modulus materials, the layer of mat next to the core is usually omitted. This means that the entire inner laminate can be built up without stopping short of the final layer before applying the core as was done in the conventional laminate. Then fair the inner laminate surface that will bond to the core, but be careful NOT to sand or grind excessively, cutting into the reinforcement material, and thereby weakening the skin. This is VERY important in high modulus skins because they are quite thin in the first place. If the skins have been applied properly, this fairing will be minimal. Again, the importance of starting with a fair mold should be stressed at this point in order for a fair hull to result.

Instead of bedding the core into a wet mat layer, the core is bedded in a thin resin putty filler mixture applied to the surface of the inner skin before applying the core. With balsa core, it may still be advisable, however, to use a light weight (¾ oz.) mat against the core, or at least apply a coat of resin to the core before putting it in place, since the balsa does absorb more resin than do the foam cores. This resin should not be allowed to set up before the core is in place.

The resin putty filler coat is made from resin and microspheres (the phenolic type are not preferred according to the KLEGECELL people in this instance) to a consistency of thin pancake batter. It can be applied with a brush, or notched trowel; but apply the mix as smoothly, evenly, and rapidly as possible. Mix up a batch about ½ gallon at a time, mixing in the catalyst AFTER the resin and microspheres have been thoroughly mixed. Use a mechanical or power mixer preferably, but one of a low-shear type that is not so vigorous that the spheres collapse or fracture. The mix will begin to change color when the catalyst has been evenly dispersed (a small amount of dye mixed with the catalyst may also be used to check for thorough mixing). Once this color variation is even, apply the mix quickly. Silica or talc fillers are not as good

for this mix because they are heavier and more brittle, and could diminish the bonding qualities.

To make the first layer of ORCOWEB stick to the mold surface, apply a very thin layer of resin to the mold surface, and then apply the ORCOWEB over this. The resin will help wet out the ORCOWEB from the back side and help it stay in place. Or tape the strips in place and wet out from the topside. Apply the first layer with the cross ties up; not against the mold. If the strips of ORCOWEB are running athwartships or diagonally, they should preferably go entirely across the hull. If this is not possible, then lap them well across the centerline so that no endings occur at this point, and stagger or alternate the endings from side to side. This same principle applies at the stem areas, at transom corners, and similar junctions. If a length of ORCOWEB runs out at some point on the hull surface (like at the end of the roll), lap another new roll over it a few inches. At these joints, cut the ORCOWEB BETWEEN the cross ties so the loose fiber ends can be blended in with one another. The parallel strips are otherwise edge-butted; however, very minor gaps or overlaps in these parallel butt joints will do no harm.

When applying resin, the worker must watch out for resin richness. While the ORCON brochure says that resin can be poured, sprayed, or brushed on, better control probably results with a brush application. Don't dump the resin onto the material since it is too easy to get too much resin on the surface and it will be difficult to distribute around evenly. The same thing can happen by spraying if one is not careful.

Once the resin is on the ORCOWEB surface, roll it out with a roller to distribute it evenly, and then use a squeegee to remove any excess and to get the material firmly in position. A foam roller seems to work best; however, some types disintegrate rather quickly when used in resin. Watch out for dry spots and air bubbles, but small air bubbles, such as those that may tend to form against the cross ties can be ignored. In fact, these air bubbles may not be air bubbles at all. The adhesive binder used at the cross ties may be softened by the resin and flow slightly. The adhesive shows up as milky areas on both sides of the fabric within the finished laminate, but will not show after the hull has been finished and painted.

The ORCOWEB material wets out quite quickly with very little resin. A properly wetted out layer will look dry but translucent. Since the material is 12" wide, a wide window-cleaning squeegee works well for laminating. Squeegee in the warp direction first to get the material down, using light pressure to remove excess resin. Do not squeegee crosswise, at least initially, as there is a chance of distorting the fibers. The material should be taut without wrinkles or changes in direction. With these techniques, it is easy to maintain a 40% fiber content, and as more experience is gained, fiber ratios (glass content) of 50% can be obtained.

Bubbles that occur under the ORCOWEB must be removed if they are of any size. A standard mat roller does not do a good job of this, however. Applying the material by the "wet method," that is, coating the surface with resin first, then rolling the ORCOWEB over it, will help minimize the formation of air bubbles, since the resin is helping to wet out the back side.

The sequence in which the ORCOWEB is applied matters little. But DON'T apply multiple layers at once; it is not practical to wet out more than one layer at a time. A layer of ORCOWEB can be laid over the entire surface of the hull and then wet out with resin; this is the "dry method." Or try just a strip at a time. In either case, there is no need to stop applying resin since each strip is progressively wet out before going on to the next, while maintaining a wet edge as work proceeds.

The next layer can be applied right over the initial one immediately after the first cures. The tackiness of the laminating resin will hold the ORCOWEB material in place. When it comes time to apply the layer against the core surface, apply resin to the core so that the ORCOWEB is wet out from the back side, and so that there will be enough resin to assure a sound bond to the core. On the last layer on the outside of the outer skin, place the cross ties of the ORCOWEB down on the surface so they will be inside the laminate. This will make finishing much easier. If the laminate has been applied with care, little finishing or fairing will be required. Often it is possible to simply apply a high-build primer over the surface and omit the use of a resin putty filler coat. This does save weight, money, and work. But otherwise, the surface can be built up with a thin resin putty filler coat such as that described in Chapter 13, and finished. The hull can then be painted just like any other.

It should be noted that one of the advantages of using a "3-STAGE" vacuum bag method with a material such as ORCOWEB is that it is easier to apply the ORCOWEB material OVER a male mold than it is on the INSIDE of a female mold or on the inner laminate of "one-off" cored boats. The reason is that the material applies easier over convex surfaces than into concaved areas. It is easier to squeegee down the material and there is not as much tendency for the resin to run down into the bottom of the boat.

Another point should be brought up. There has been little experience in the use of high modulus skins in powerboats, particularly when used with cores such as KLEGECELL. In fact, most applications have been on sailboats, and then most of these have been for competition craft where long-term durability may not be especially important. Records of use over a period of years simply do not exist because these are new approaches to boatbuilding. Some knowledgeable people and boatbuilders question whether thin skins of high modulus materials used with foams like KLEGE-

CELL will stand up to the continued panting loads that high-speed powerboats are subjected to, especially in boats with flatter bottoms. There is the suspicion that prolonged treatment of this kind may cause the skins to delaminate and/or the core to shear and fail. Time will no doubt be the judge.

CHAPTER 23   completing the hull interior

This brief chapter serves as an introduction to those aspects of the fiberglass boat-building project which take place after the hull has been completed and righted. At this stage, most boats will require the installation of many internal members, such as hull stiffeners, bulkheads, engine stringers, mast steps, chainplates, sheer clamps, cabin soles, tanks, engine, etc. These are all preferably installed before decking the boat over and installing the cabin structure. In addition, however, hulls made over male molds will usually require some additional laminate on the inside, especially with sandwich-cored hulls built over open-battened molds where perhaps the entire inner laminate must be applied, and this will be the first order of business in these cases.

Basically, any interior laminate which must be applied is done in much the same manner as was done on the outside. However, in most cases, there is not as much concern with the appearance. This does NOT mean, however, that the quality control taken during the application of the inner laminate need be any less stringent than the outside, especially where sandwich cored hulls are concerned.

On large hulls, this inside work can be simplified by a scaffold arrangement that can be suspended from spreaders across the hull or hung from the rafters of the building shed structure. Whether or not the builder should walk around on the inside of the hull in the process depends on what materials were used in the construction. Single skin

FIG. 23-1 — After righting sandwich cored hulls and removing the male mold, the hull is prepared for the application of the inner laminate. Sandwich cored hulls are quite flexible at this point until the inner laminate is applied. The edges of the foam core in this AIREX cored hull along the keel and sheer have been bevelled for the inner laminate. Note that the worker is wearing soft soled shoes which help protect the core from indentations.

FIG. 23-2 — Inner laminates of the conventional type are applied just like those on the exterior. Materials are usually run across the hull as is being done in this case. Note the fan aft for air circulation and the spreaders keeping the sheer areas rigid until the inner laminate is applied.

hulls will have no limitation in this regard since they are basically self-supporting at this point. However, in all cases avoid walking around too much just as a matter of cleanliness in order to assure sound secondary bonds for the items that will be bonded in place later.

With cored hulls where the inner laminate is not yet applied, avoid walking on the inner core surfaces. This is especially important where cores such as KLEGECELL-type foams and high-modulus skins are used. This type of core tends to be brittle, while the outer high-modulus skin will be quite flexible at this stage; the weight of a person walking on the structure could cause it to fail.

On cored hulls, all edges around the perimeter of the core where there is to be solid fiberglass laminate, and where the inner and outer skins join, should be bevelled or tapered to prevent hard spots from being built into the boat. These edges should be at least at 45 degree angles, and preferably at a 3-to-1 taper (see Chapter 19). In lieu of tapering such edges, build up a triangular section using resin putty filler troweled and shaped in place, or fit in a triangular cant strip of foam.

The methods for beginning the first layer of the inner laminate are covered with the respective chapters describing the materials and methods used to build the hull. Layers in the interior laminate should be lapped generously over such areas as the keel centerline and along the chine on hard-chined hulls, thereby forming a double thickness of reinforcing in these areas. Again, however, do NOT stop or butt ends of materials over these stress areas; lap them well beyond. Apply extra laminations of materials as specified on the plans where required, taking care NOT to end such build-ups at one point. Instead, endings of materials should be tapered back a generous distance, or with layers extending beyond each layer underneath a comparable amount to prevent stress concentrations.

In cored hulls, there will probably be areas where solid fiberglass laminate is required, such as at chainplates, rudder ports, through-hull fittings, stemhead plates, stern bearings, struts, and the like. Such areas are shown in several photos in

FIG. 23-3 — In this AIREX cored hull, note the sheer clamp members which are in place to stiffen up the hull. When the hull is in this position, there is a tendency for the resin to run to the bottom of the hull. Thus, it is important to keep working the resin from lower areas to upper areas until it begins to set up.

FIG. 23-4 — Workers are using rollers with extensions in order to reach all areas conveniently when applying the inner laminate. In this case, the spreaders at the sheer also support a scaffold for easier access along the sheer area.

the text. The core material should be cut away in these areas and fitted with extra layers of fiberglass or solid wood backing blocks bonded in place. Sand such areas where the core has been removed before applying any additional laminate or backing block in order to assure a sound bond and to remove the core material completely.

While the final resin coat on the inside can be a finish resin, or resin containing wax, do not use this resin until all the hull structural members have been installed, along with their respective bonding angles, laminate build-ups, and reinforcements. A proper secondary bond cannot be made to such a resin without sanding, and preferably wiping down the surface with solvent

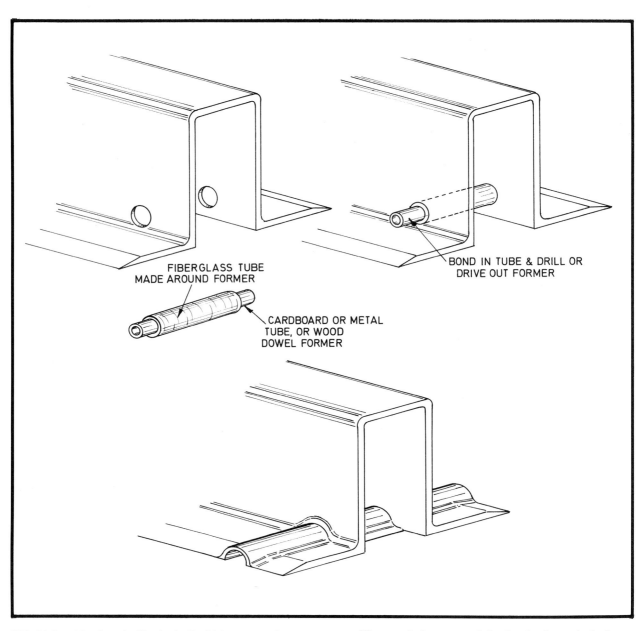

FIG. 23-5 — Members inside the hull which may restrict bilge water from draining to the sump should be fitted with limbers, such as these examples shown through top hat stiffeners. Limbers are made in place by the methods shown and described in the text.

also; this can be inconvenient and tedious on the inside of a hull. In lieu of using a finish resin on the inside, there are special interior gel coat resins which can be used to finish off the interior later. These are available in various colors that give a neat "finished" look to the inside, and are a type of resin that will cure tack-free.

Note that several points should be kept in mind regarding the work done on the hull from this point on until the cabin and deck are installed. First, certain details will vary depending on the type of deck and cabin superstructure that will be used. Although some details will be illustrated in the text, these may be superseded by the details provided on the plans, and are merely shown for explanation purposes. The function of the text is NOT to show design details, but many of the methods described make some detailing necessary. The details shown are not necessarily a preferred or "better" method; in fiberglass boatbuilding there are many ways to do things, and when possible, the amateur is advised to stick to the plans.

Second, keep in mind how the sequence of events in the construction procedures will occur. Especially critical is the installation of the engine and related items such as tanks and auxiliary systems that may interfere with the cabin, deck, and joinery. Generally, as much of these systems as possible should be installed before the cabin, deck, and joinery.

Finally, consider hull drainage throughout the installation of the interior structure. Any water that may come aboard should be allowed to drain to the bottom of the boat or to the sump, where it can be pumped overboard. Drainage is accomplished by limbers (drain holes) through any members that would restrict or trap this water. These limbers should NOT be drilled through cored members such as top-hat stiffeners, but rather molded in place. This can be done by molding over polyethylene plastic pipe stubs which can be driven out later, or made over half-sections of mail tubes. Limbers should be large enough so they don't clog with debris, yet they should not be so large that they would tend to weaken a member where they pass through (see Fig. 23-5).

CHAPTER 24

wood in the fiberglass boat

In most fiberglass boatbuilding, more lumber and plywood may be used than might first be imagined. Wood members are shown in various applications throughout the text, and are discussed as the occasion arises. However, the following serves as a general specification of how to select lumber and how it should be used in the fiberglass boat.

All lumber should be first grade, free from defects such as warping, splits, checks, loose knots, and the like. Lumber should be dried to the proper moisture content, which is usually 12% for most woods in most areas. Although air-dried lumber is often recommended for boat use, it is seldom available today and not that critical for our uses.

A designer may specify a certain type of lumber for some part of the structure. This can usually be deviated from in order to use other woods more readily available or lower in cost. This practice is usually acceptable as long as the woods selected have been proven in use in similar type boats located in the general locale, and are of similar weight and strength characteristics.

With plywood, the Marine grade is highly desirable, but the most expensive. Exterior grades can be used with certain qualifications. While the glues used for bonding veneers in either the Marine or the Exterior grade panel are usually the same waterproof type, the core lumbers can vary in the Exterior panel, along with the quality of the core, which can include voids, joints, and junctions. In the Marine grade panel, core veneers are of the same wood as the face veneers, and are solid. If using Exterior grade panels, try to examine such panels

BEFORE purchase to assure that they are of reasonably good quality, free from obvious voids. Interior grade plywood has no place in boats and should not be used. The Douglas fir type of plywood is most common, however, other types of plywoods are usually suitable as long as quality equals the foregoing description.

ENCAPSULATING WOOD WITH FIBERGLASS

After all the years that fiberglass boats have been built, the jury is still out regarding encapsulating wood in fiberglass, or otherwise using it as a core material. Even the opinions of experts are mixed. For example, take this quote from a copy of the "Rules For Building and Classing Reinforced Plastic Vessels" as set forth by the American Bureau of Shipping (ABS), a major classifying agency in the United States:

"With the exception of balsa, hardwoods are not to be used as core materials. Softwoods encapsulated in FRP (fiberglass) are considered to be effective structural materials where used above the waterline. Softwoods used below the waterline should not be encapsulated; where softwoods below the waterline are encapsulated, they are considered to be ineffective, nonstructural materials."

On the other hand, the ABS feels that the situation is different with the use of plywood, since the rules further state:

"Plywood encapsulated in FRP is considered to be an effective structural material."

Note that in this last statement, there is

no proviso whether the plywood is used above or below the waterline. On the other hand, a technical report[1] written by two experts in the field of designing large fiberglass vessels had this to say about the construction of fiberglass shrimp trawlers in the 70′ to 80′ range:

"Bottom stiffening is generally wood (pine or plywood) encapsulated in FRP. There is some question as to the validity of this practice, due to the possible rotting of the wood if the FRP encapsulation is porous, but this method of construction has been used successfully in commercial boats for years. . . ."

What all these sources seem to be saying is that there MAY be problems with encapsulating wood in fiberglass, but they're not quite sure if problems will occur 100% of the time. So what's the problem? Should wood be encapsulated or not? And if it is, how should it be done?

WHY USE WOOD IN A FIBERGLASS BOAT?

The "purists" will say to eliminate wood entirely from the fiberglass boat; this will stop any purported problems at the outset. Numerous "sea stories" are recited to the effect that the wood will swell and "burst" the hull if it is totally enclosed with fiberglass. Or that the wood will rot and cause gases to build up to a pressure that will blow the laminate to pieces! I have never seen either of these two common stories substantiated; however, water incursion can occur.

While it is entirely feasible to have a 100% fiberglass boat, and eliminate the use of wood, the main reason against this approach is, quite simply, cost and weight. Wood is cheap compared to fiberglass, and in most fiberglass boats of any size, there will be many situations where it's use, if not actually mandatory, will certainly be the most practical alternative.

While the advantages far outweigh the disadvantages of using wood with fiberglass, consider some of the disadvantages at the practical level. First, it is often stated that wood or plywood are heavy materials. However, this is only true in comparison to the thin, high modulus skins used with certain core materials in sandwich construction. The cost to achieve such strength with light weight, however, exceeds several times the cost of wood or plywood cores.

Secondly, fiberglass is a heavy material. For the purist who would build up a single skin, all-fiberglass laminate to the same strength as that which could be achieved by a wood or plywood core encapsulated in a laminate, not only would such a laminate be expensive, but the weight would be staggering compared to the laminate made with the wood. This is not an attempt to advocate the use of wood cores, but merely to illustrate a point. Contrary to popular opinion, fiberglass for COMPARABLE strength is FAR heavier than most woods. This can be proven by throwing a slab of fiberglass into the pond along with a chunk of wood and seeing which one heads for the bottom.

The fact of the matter is that fiberglass and wood have a modulus of elasticity (which indicates the stiffness of the material) that is quite similar. However, wood weighs considerably less. Because of this, sheets of plywood are commonly encapsulated into the bottoms and transoms of boats, especially those with flat surfaces that need strength without excessive weight. Not only is the plywood cheaper, but nearly as strong and much lighter in weight.

WHAT ABOUT ROT?

Finally, there's the old bugaboo, rot! This is the subject that scares the pants off any boatowner, especially one who has never experienced it. Some people are so paranoid about rot and know so little about it that they find it hard to believe that men actually built boats from wood in the past and are still doing so. It's even more incredible for them to realize that many of these boats are still around after 50 years or more, and in good condition.

While no fiberglass boat can boast this kind of longevity at this time, there is no reason to doubt that a good fiberglass boat will last as long. And when one does, she will probably have wood encapsulated in her structure. Similarly, in the fiberglass boat built by the amateur, there is no reason why the builder cannot work in some wood members, goop them in place with resin and fiberglass, and hope for equal longevity. It is generally agreed upon by knowledgeable people that if certain precautions are taken, there is no reason NOT to use the economy, ease of workability, ready availability, and convenience of wood which is so familiar to most.

ENCAPSULATING TECHNIQUES AND RECOMMENDATIONS

The following will provide some guidelines to follow when encapsulating wood in fiberglass hulls. Note that encapsulating wood with fiberglass requires much the same treatment and care as bonding fiberglass to wood, such as applying only onto a clean, bare wood surface. And if the wood surface is quite smooth, it should be roughened up a bit so the resin will get some "tooth" into the wood.

What about the use of wood preservatives? In a word, DON'T! Polyester resins just don't adhere well with most types commonly available. Besides, the polyester resin has some preservative effect of its own. The preceding may be dogmatic, and no doubt there are certain preservatives that are compatible with resin. The problem is, however, that experience shows that the

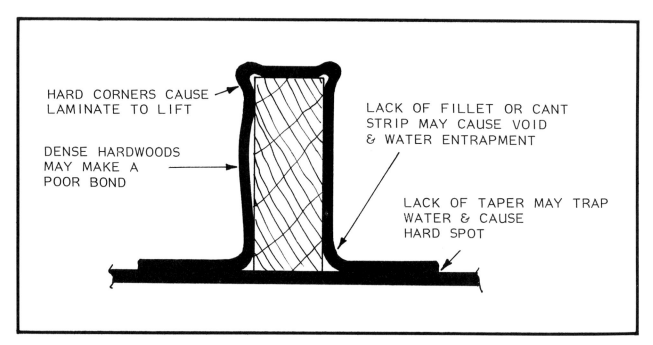

HARD CORNERS CAUSE LAMINATE TO LIFT

DENSE HARDWOODS MAY MAKE A POOR BOND

LACK OF FILLET OR CANT STRIP MAY CAUSE VOID & WATER ENTRAPMENT

LACK OF TAPER MAY TRAP WATER & CAUSE HARD SPOT

FIG. 24-1 — The "wrong" way to encapsulate wood members. The fiberglass laminate surrounding this wood stringer is delaminating on one side because a dense, oily hardwood was used. At the inside corners against the hull, no fillet or cant strip was applied, causing the laminate to lift and form air bubbles and voids. Water may penetrate these voids, possibly freeze and displace the structure, and perhaps eventually lead to rotting of the wood. The top corners of the member have not been radiused and the laminate has lifted, leading to similar problems. Finally, there is no taper at the endings of the encapsulating laminate. The lack of taper tends to trap water and forms a potential stress concentration.

average amateur is bewildered by the wide array of chemical concoctions available as preservatives at the local paint store. The fine print listing the ingredients is rarely read, and even if one looks at the listing of ingredients, who knows what they mean let alone how to pronounce them. This is further complicated by the fact that the guy behind the counter probably knows little about the product, especially for use in boats. Perhaps the ABS in their manual previously quoted from will define this position better:

"Wood encapsulated in FRP is not to be treated with a preservative of a type that will prevent adhesion of polyester resin."

Woods which will be encapsulated should be first grade, free from defects (which excludes wood where rot has already started or which has termites!), and at the proper moisture content. Don't use wood that is obviously green or wet, or is structurally unsound in the first place (a rule which applies to any wood used in any boat, by the way). If using plywood, make sure it is either an Exterior or Marine grade; Interior grades are not acceptable.

HARDWOOD VS: SOFTWOODS

It was noted earlier that the ABS stated that hardwoods (other than balsa, since it is used as a core material) should not be encapsulated, but softwoods are OK, at least ABOVE the waterline. This requires more explanation. First, the difference between hardwoods and softwoods should be explained. The terms "softwood" and "hardwood" DON'T mean woods which are actually soft or hard, but their true botanical differences.

Softwoods are generally those woods from trees having needles, and with the seeds exposed, usually in cones. These trees are called conifers, or cone-bearing, and botanically known as Gymnosperms. For the most part, these trees are green all year,

or evergreen. Such woods include the pines, firs, spruces, cedars, and redwoods.

Hardwoods are those woods ordinarily from trees which shed their leaves each season. These are called deciduous trees and include such woods as the oaks, maples, and ashes. Hardwood trees are botanically known as Angiosperms, and usually have true flowers and broad leaves, with the seeds enclosed in a fruit of some type. While this all seems to be a neat, ordered division, as with any rule, there are always exceptions to complicate things.

Unfortunately, the rule of using ONLY softwoods is not hard-and-fast. Perhaps some explanation will help. As a generalization, woods used in encapsulation should be dimensionally stable so that they will not expand and contract too much and exceed the limits of the fiberglass covering. If this occurs, the fiberglass will crack and fail, thereby allowing a passage where water may enter. Because of the cross-ply construction of plywood, it is quite dimensionally stable. That's why the rules state that plywood is acceptable for encapsulation under just about all conditions.

But with most hardwoods, it's a different story. The heavy, dense types (such as ash, oak, and teak) absorb water slowly enough, but as they do, they can exert tremendous pressures upon expansion, which can be far greater than the fiberglass can withstand. Complicating this is the fact that resins do not bond as well to these dense, heavy woods. On the other hand, softwoods (such as pine and Douglas fir in particular) DO tend to bond better with resin. Although they too expand in the presence of moisture, the better bond and less dense quality of the wood gives more latitude for expansion, offering far superior results.

Here's where the exceptions to the rule enter the picture. Bonding problems do occur with certain woods, namely hardwoods. But these problems also occur with certain softwoods, such as redwood and Western red cedar. These woods (in addition to oily hardwoods like teak) give off substances not compatible with polyester resin, and hence will make for a questionable bond. Oak is also guilty in this regard. The acid content of oaks can cause a breakdown and staining of the laminate if the laminate cracks and water gets to it. However, all the various types of mahogany (the true American and African types as well as the Philippine types), which are hardwoods, seem to bond quite well to fiberglass, as long as good quality, properly dried material is used. In summary, there are certain woods which lend themselves to encapsulation in fiberglass, while others do not. While softwoods are generally preferable in this regard, there are certain softwoods AND hardwoods that should be avoided.

While a poor bond resulting from an improper choice of woods in an encapsulated situation may certainly be "out-of-sight, out-of-mind", a void can not only form a perfect moisture trap where rot can form, but can lead to structural failures as well (see Fig. 24-1). The condition is worsened if the boat is subjected to freezing conditions which can cause further expansion and damage. Thus, select woods which are compatible to avoid problems.

USING PLYWOOD

It would appear that plywood is the best choice whenever possible. But, plywood can be made from softwoods like Douglas fir (the standard variety in this country) as well as from hardwoods like mahogany in its various forms. Experience shows that either of these types is suitable for encapsulation, however, do avoid using teak-faced plywood.

Some builders will substitute plywood members in place of members specified for solid wood. For example, the engine girders in a boat may be specified of solid wood members encapsulated with fiberglass and a builder wants to substitute plywood.

While it can be argued that the fiberglass provides all the strength, and the lumber might be considered "non-structural", to make a point, assume that the lumber is structural. If plywood is substituted for solid lumber to make structural members, it must be increased in size over the solid wood member. Why?

Assume a standard nominal 2" member was specified in Douglas fir, which yields a member that is actually about 1½" thick (see Fig. 24-2). If the member is made from two layers of ¾" plywood, the thickness is also 1½" thick. But will it be the same strength as the solid member of the same thickness? No, because only those plies running lengthwise contribute to the longitudinal strength that is needed. The vertical cross plies add little or nothing to the longitudinal strength. Thus, the plywood member will have to be nearly double in thickness to be comparable in longitudinal strength to the solid member.

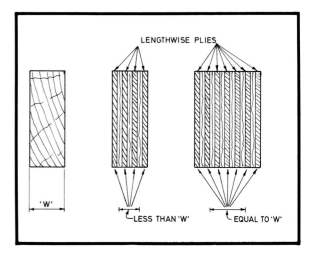

FIG. 24-2 — A section (left) is shown through a solid wood strength member of a given thickness ('W') which may be encapsulated with fiberglass. If plywood of the same overall thickness is substituted for this member, the plywood member will not be as strong since the cross plies NOT running lengthwise will have little strength in the longitudinal direction. The total thickness of the lengthwise plies will be less than the solid wood member (center). To compensate for this loss of strength due to the cross plies, a thicker plywood member having enough lengthwise plies to equal the thickness of the solid wood member will be required (as at right).

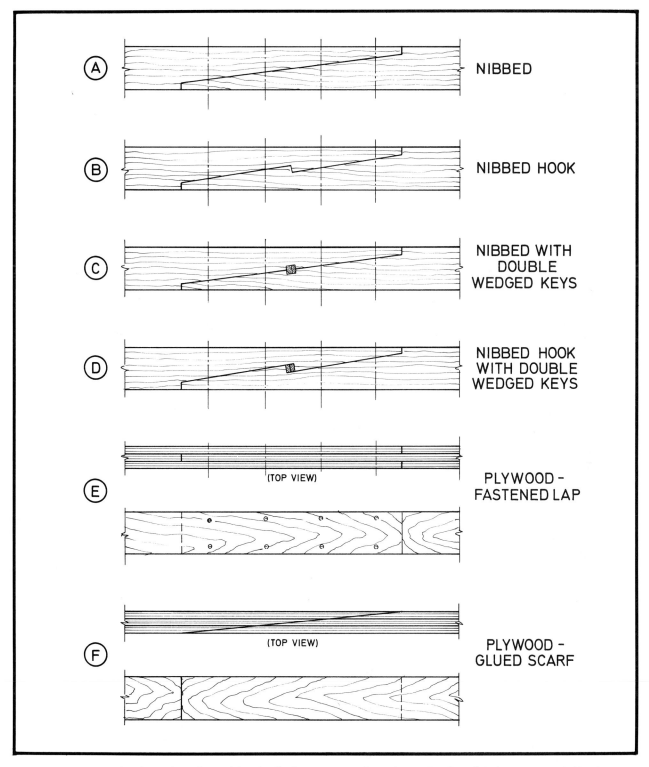

FIG. 24-3 — Encapsulated wood or plywood longitudinal strength members which must be joined should be done in the same ways as in proper wood boatbuilding practice. Simple butt joints are not advised. With solid wood members, various types of nibbed scarf joints can be used, as shown in 'A', 'B', 'C', and 'D' (as recommended by the A.B.S. rules). Double wedged wood keys are driven crosswise through the joint in 'C' and 'D'. With plywood members, multiple layers of plywood should be joined with staggered laps as in 'E' or with long glued scarfs as in 'F'.

JOINING METHODS

Another consideration should be given when making long members from wood or plywood. If single full-length members are not available, then proper joining methods must be used for strength continuity, even if the members are encapsulated (see Fig. 24-3). Solid wood members should be scarf-joined as in good wood boatbuilding practice. Plywood longitudinals should be treated similarly, or by using multiple laminations with long overlaps between butt joints in the respective layers. Under no circumstances should solid wood or plywood structural longitudinals be merely butted together and then covered with fiberglass. This practice will make a discontinuity leading to a stress concentration that could cause the fiberglass to fail.

KEEPING MOISTURE OUT

As can readily be seen, the goal of encapsulating wood with fiberglass is to keep the water out. All fiberglass work with wood should be carefully done to assure that moisture will not become trapped where it shouldn't be. Since rot needs air, moisture, rot spores, and suitable temperatures to occur, remove any one of these elements and the formation of rot is stopped. So encapsulate with care. Shape all wood members so they are easy to mold over, especially on outside corners. Build up inside corners with generous fillets, cant strips, or radiuses. On wood backing blocks or flat members, apply gently sloped bevels along the edges.

The point is to avoid any areas where air bubbles can be formed in the laminate by not conforming to the surface. These air bubbles or pockets can form passages for water that can become entrapped, or lead to a "wicking" effect through the exposed fiberglass strands that will allow the water to travel into wood-encased members.

If a hole must be drilled through a laminate with an encapsulated wood member, don't just leave the edges bare. Apply resin-saturated mat if possible, or at least apply a generous coating of resin (see Fig. 24-4). If a fitting will be attached, do the same where the fastenings pass through and always use bedding compound under the fitting.

As a further precaution, always start off with mat against wood since it bonds better and can be worked into corners more easily. The mat tends to be more resin-rich and this helps keep moisture out of these areas where water tends to settle. Remember that even the best fiberglass laminates are at least slightly permeable. No matter how slowly, some moisture is bound to be absorbed by the laminate. But if the job is properly done with care and the right woods, there's no reason why the boat should not have a long, trouble-free life.

As a final "editorial" comment, if one tries to abide by the recommendation of NOT using wood BELOW the waterline, this certainly can complicate things, both for the builder and the designer. For example, what happens to sailboats which when underway may heel along at 20 degrees or more, perhaps for weeks on end? To abide by the rule, and to conform to the theory,

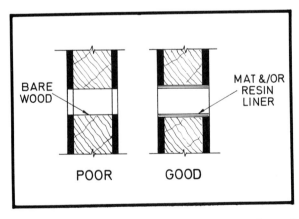

FIG. 24-4 — Holes drilled through encapsulated wood members should NOT be left bare. The hole should preferably be covered with a layer of resin saturated mat, or at least a coat of resin to seal the wood.

one should plot the normal heeling angle to determine the heeled waterline and keep wood above this heeled waterline point!

This concern for rot below the waterline seems to be a mis-directed concern. The bilges in fiberglass boats are not difficult to keep virtually dry in normal operation, making it very unlikely for any substantial damage to occur, at least for a very long period of time. It would seem that more concern would be directed at emphasizing watertight integrity at deck level where fresh rain water and moisture have a habit of trickling down the tiniest crevices to wreak havoc. In wood boats, rot has always been most prevalent at the weatherdeck, especially in the ends of the boat, and the factors leading to this are the same for the fiberglass boat. Hence, particular care should be taken at these areas, such as with the installation of decks, cabins, and deck fittings, as well as assuring sound maintenance practices and good ventilation at all times.

[1] "FRP TRAWLER DESIGN AND FABRICATION IN THE UNITED STATES" by R. J. Scott and J. H. Sommella – 1971

CHAPTER 25 flotation

Everyone knows that wood floats, and as a result, wood boats by themselves cannot sink. However, such is not the case with fiberglass. A solid single-skin fiberglass boat if punctured below the waterline will head for the bottom, unless provisions are made to keep it from doing so. The simple reason is that fiberglass weighs MORE per volume than does an equivalent amount of water; hence it will sink in water. Wood, on the other hand, weighs less than a comparable volume of water (although to be completely fair, there ARE certain woods that DO weigh more than a comparable volume of water, but these are seldom found in boatbuilding).

The desire to prevent the fiberglass boat from sinking if hull integrity is lost can be fulfilled in several different ways. For example, you could build in air chambers. These have been used in the past, being built integrally with the hull. However, these are not recommended since an impact puncture making a hole into one of these chambers would cause an immediate loss of flotation value. Another approach has been to use buoyancy bags filled with air ("air bags"). These must be well secured in the boat so that they can't move, especially in an emergency or if there is some damage done to the boat, and they should be made of a material that will not puncture easily and not leak. Probaby the most popular method, however, is to provide flotation material in the form of plastic foams.

First, let's consider some aspects of adding flotation materials. Everyone must admit that having positive flotation value aboard a boat is a good quality, and in theory, enough flotation material or devices can conceivably make a boat that is IMPOSSIBLE to sink. Yet for every cubic foot of flotation value added, we must also give up that amount of space in our boat that could be used for something else. If water weighs something over 60 lbs. per cubic foot, then each cubic foot of flotation volume will support almost an equal amount of that weight in our boat.

But if our boat is big and heavy, and includes things like engines, tanks, ballast, batteries, generators, and other items that have virtually no flotation value, or negative flotation value, it is easy to see that it will take a lot of flotation volume to support these items in the event that our hull is flooded. Hence, this is why as the boat gets larger and more complex, the addition of flotation material may become less practical. If one were to add enough flotation material to do the job, there could be a substantial loss of accommodation and storage space, perhaps even making the boat impractical to use.

Thus, in the larger boat, especially those having many items of dense, heavy materials, other approaches to preventing sinking are resorted to. These may include the use of watertight doors that subdivide the vessel into watertight compartments, more-than-adequate bilge pumping systems, and proper equipment to deal with abandon-ship conditions such as life rafts, emergency provisions, etc. In other words, as the vessel grows in size, the approach changes from preventing flooding to controlling it and coping with the possible loss of the vessel.

FLOTATION FOAM

In the smaller fiberglass boat, it is common to add flotation material, usually in the form of a non-structural plastic foam. There are several types of foam that can be used. The main criteria is that the material should be able to withstand the combined effects of petroleum products like gasoline, bilge solvents, and fresh and salt water.

The plastic foam materials are usually available in different densities and different forms. The density refers to the weight of the foam per cubic foot of material. In order to determine the net value for flotation purposes, the weight of the foam per cubic foot must be deducted from the weight of the water per cubic foot. For example, salt water weighs about 64 lbs. per cubic foot, and fresh water about 62½ lbs. per cubic foot.

If the foam being used weighs 2 lbs. per cubic foot, this will leave a net flotation value of 62 lbs. per cubic foot if the boat is used in salt water, and a net flotation value of 60½ lbs. per cubic foot when the boat is used in fresh water. It can readily be seen that the lighter the density of foam used, the higher the flotation value per cubic foot of volume.

A common type of foam most people are familiar with is foamed polystyrene (a typical example being "Styrofoam", a registered tradename of Dow Chemical). This foam is cheap (at least in relation to other plastic foams) and readily available. However, it is not suitable as a flotation material, at least in its natural state. Without additional treatment, this type of foam is attacked on contact by polyester resins, and its resistance to gasoline is poor. It can, however, be sealed with epoxy resins first, but this adds to the work and does drive up the cost substantially, perhaps making it more economical to consider a more expensive, but better suited foam in the first place. Another consideration is that this type of foam is extremely flam-

mable. However, there are special formulations that are solvent-resistant and self-extinguishing. An improved type of foam that is similar to foamed polystyrene is called styrene acrylonitrile. This foam has negligible water absorption and reasonable solvent resistance, but the styrene base would still make it incompatible with polyester resins.

The most common type of plastic foam used for flotation purposes is the urethane type, available in blocks or sheets, or in "pour-in-place" kits. In production boatbuilding, boatbuilders use rather elaborate and costly foam-in-place machines not readily available to the amateur. However, this same material is being used in many cases for home and building insulation, and it may be possible to contract with a firm that specializes in this process to install the foam directly into the boat if desired.

Urethane foams in sheets and blocks are easily cut and shaped before installation using ordinary woodworking tools, and readily glued in place with most glues. They are not attacked by resins and are resistant to gasoline and oil, which affect the foam only by a slight swelling after several hours

FIG. 25-1 — Pour-in-place foam can be used in void areas of the hull for flotation purposes. An irregularly shaped area, such as shown, is ideal for this type of material. Several pourings should be made instead of a single pour in order to assure that all areas of the void are filled.

of complete immersion when low density (1.5 to 2.0 lbs. per cubic foot) types are used.

However, this quality of the low-density variety does allow it to absorb large quantities of water over a long period of time. Because of this, the foam in low densities is not recommended for use below the waterline. Therefore, for applications below the waterline, use urethane foams of 4.0 lbs. per cubic foot density or greater. At this density there is also no discernable impact on the foam from hydrocarbon solvents such as gasoline or oil. While urethane foam is combustible, I have been told that it can be made self-extinguishing, so you might want to discuss this quality with your supplier. Both the sheet or block type, and the pour-in-place type have similar characteristics in the final form. Both are quite friable and crumble easily, which causes a loss in bond and breakdown of the foam in high vibration situations such as those found in powerboats.

If using a pour-in-place type foam, these should be considered as VERY hazardous products when in use. Follow the label precautions and instructions to the letter. Experience shows that the volume of foam that results from one of these products can vary somewhat. The rate of expansion also varies with ambient temperatures; the hotter it is, the faster the reaction and the more the foam tends to expand.

Since most are a two-part concoction, they must be carefully and accurately mixed, and once mixed, there will be little time to get the product into the areas where it is wanted. Mixing by hand is usually not complete enough nor quick enough; a power mixer such as a paint mixer attachment on a power drill is preferable. Do NOT apply the foam mix into restricted spaces except in several smaller pourings as opposed to a single batch, and allow about 20 minutes between batches. The expanding gases created by the foam can be so great that it can burst out members that may be restricting it. Provide vent holes about 1″ in diameter to prevent this from happening. Don't rush the job; make a small test batch to observe the reaction, rate of expansion, and mixing time. If possible, have a helper available. Trying to mix, stir, and pour can get tricky. Make sure everything is ready to receive the pouring since pot life is usually LESS than a minute. Wear gloves to avoid skin contact and don't breathe the fumes.

For flotation purposes, distribute the foam as much as possible so the boat will float nearly level if holed. If all the foam were placed forward, for example, the stern would sink and the bow would stick up, perhaps nearly vertically. However, flotation should be concentrated near items of negative buoyancy, such as engines, batteries, etc.

Other types of plastic foams that can be used for flotation purposes do exist, but they are not as common for one reason or another. For example, there are epoxy foams with properties quite like urethanes. They are resistant to solvents and absorb practically no water. Some types can be foamed in place, or cut from pre-cast blocks or slabs. But their high cost rules them out for extensive use.

Another type is extruded polyethylene which is suitable as a flotation material, but it does swell slightly in gasoline and does absorb a very small amount of water. Although this foam is combustible, it is slow burning. However, it is not as readily available as the urethane type.

In addition to the above foams, those foams used in structural cores, such as AIREX and KLEGECELL, or even balsa core material as described in other chapters, make excellent flotation materials when installed properly. Usually when they are used as a core material in sandwich structures, they will provide enough flotation value to support the hull itself. This means that additional flotation foam would only need to be provided for those items aboard that had little or negative flotation value. The cost for these materials for flotation purposes other than as a core material, however, is usually much higher than for the urethane type. A consideration may be that while PVC foams do not burn, as such, they WILL melt.

No doubt other types of foams are available that are suitable, and there is little doubt that new foams will be developed in the future which may prove suitable for flotation purposes. If you discover such foams that we have not listed here, there is a simple check that can be made to see if the foam may be suitable for flotation purposes. Take a small cube of the foam (say a 1″), weigh and measure it accurately (you will need a VERY accurate scale!), then submerge it completely in gasoline for 24 hours. Recheck the dimensions and the weight. If there is no appreciable gain in either size or weight, and the material does not soften substantially, the foam should be compatible for boat flotation use if it can be secured in place to prevent movement. Also check for combustibility characteristics.

Locating sources for plastic foam flotation products is often difficult for the amateur builder. In most larger cities, however, the Yellow Page directories will usually have a listing under the heading, "Plastics, Foam", or other similar heading. Other sources are insulation contractors and suppliers as noted previously, as well as firms which manufacture large commercial refrigeration systems and ice boxes, such as those used in markets, which require insulation materials in the walls. Many of these insulation materials are suitable for boat flotation purposes.

HOW TO FIGURE FOAM FLOTATION VOLUME

A simple series of calculations or the use of a pocket calculator can determine the volume of foam flotation required to provide flotation capabilities to an object. The terms used for these calculations are as follows:

W = Weight in lbs. of object in air
S = Specific gravity of object
PB = Portion of weight in lbs. with positive buoyancy
NB = Portion of weight in lbs. with negative buoyancy
F = Flotation value of foam in lbs. per cubic foot

STEP 1: Determine the weight and specific gravity (*) of the boat and the items inside (see chart for specific gravity of common materials, or use any engineering handbook).

(*) Specific gravity means the ratio of mass of an object to that of an equal volume of water. For example, a cubic foot of solid fiberglass weighs about 115 lbs., while a cubic foot of salt water weighs about 64 lbs. Thus, 115 lbs. ÷ 64 = 1.8 Specific Gravity. In other words, the fiberglass is 1.8 times HEAVIER than salt water. Any object with a specific gravity OVER 1.0 will NOT float; it will have negative buoyancy. Any object with a specific gravity LESS than 1.0 will float, while an object having a specific gravity of 1.0 will float awash, or have neutral buoyancy.

STEP 2: Figure the weight of the object when totally immersed in water (this provides the quantity PB, or that portion of the object that has flotation capabilities). For example:

W ÷ S = PB

(If PB equals or exceeds W, the object will float. Subtracting W from PB will indicate the amount of POSITIVE flotation value in lbs. which the object contains; no flotation material is required for this object in theory).

STEP 3: If PB is LESS than W, determine the negative buoyancy (NB) of the object, or:

W − PB = NB

STEP 4: Determine the volume of flotation material required, or:

NB ÷ F = Volume of foam flotation material in cubic feet.

Note: As a factor of safety (call it "FS"), it is common to multiply the result by 1.33, and use this total for the actual amount of foam used.

If a pocket calculator is available, these steps can be transposed into the following algebraic key steps, or:

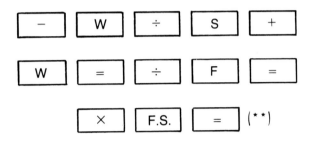

Note that the letter-designated keys refer to variables which must be entered; not actual keys.

(**) If the total is a MINUS number, this shows a reserve of flotation volume over and above that required for flotation purposes. If the total is ZERO, it means that buoyancy will be neutral.

EXAMPLE: Assume a 1500 lb. hull made from solid fiberglass. A foam will be considered for flotation purposes capable of supporting 60 lbs. per cubic foot. Thus, using a calculator:

−1500 ÷ 1.8 + 1500 = 667 ÷ 60 = 11.11 cu. ft. × 1.33 (factor of safety; applies in ALL cases) = 14.78 cu. ft. of foam required to support the hull only.

SPECIFIC GRAVITY OF SOME COMMON MATERIALS

(Approximate values in salt water. For calculations in fresh water, increase values by about 2½%.)

Aluminum	2.6
Bronze	8.0
Concrete	2.25
Fiberglass	1.5/1.8
Fir	.5
Gasoline	.72
Glass	2.5
Iron (cast)	7.0
Lead	11.0
Mahogany	.6
Man	1.1 (‡)
Oak	.8
Oil	.83
Spruce	.42
Steel	7.8
Teak	.83

(‡) For people, it is common to provide 1/3 cubic foot of foam assuming 150–200 lbs. person when they are immersed to keep them afloat.

CHAPTER 26

Whether or not a fiberglass hull will require supplemental hull stiffening members on the inside varies with the size of the boat, its configuration, and the materials and methods used in the construction. If stiffeners are required, these should be noted on the plans. Generally, sandwich-cored hulls will require little, if any, additional hull stiffeners, other than perhaps some bulkheads and floors; the sandwich-cored hull is usually stiff enough once it is decked over. If stiffening is required, methods shown in Fig. 26-1 can often be used in the foam cored hull.

Single-skin fiberglass structures, however, are a different story. While a panel of solid fiberglass may be quite strong, it is usually not very stiff, especially over a broad area. A relatively thin fiberglass panel will tend to bend and flex under load, or vibrate under mechanical cyclings, perhaps leading to fatigue and ultimate failure if stresses exceed the strength of the panel. Thus, stiffeners are added to reduce the span of unsupported fiberglass panels to increase their rigidity. There are many ways to add the necessary stiffness, including making the laminate thicker, molding in shapes in the panel (such as ridges, corrugations, and curvature), adding sandwich structures, adding bulkheads and floors, and adding stiffeners of various configurations. It is this latter method that is of most concern at this point.

In the single-skin fiberglass boat, sandwich structures for stiffnesss are not appli-

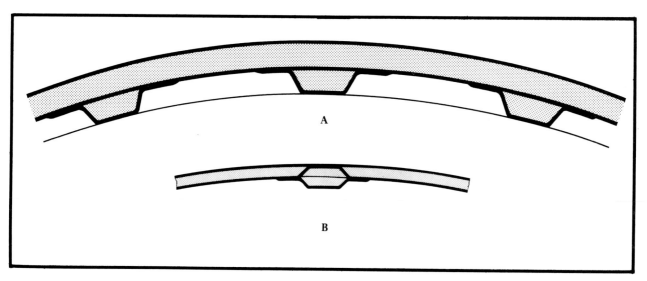

FIG. 26-1 — These two types of stiffeners can be used in the foam cored hull if necessary for added panel stiffness, such as for decks and other flat areas. The stiffeners are made using the same foam as is used in the sandwich, and encapsulated with fiberglass. The encapsulating laminate is usu- ally equal to the composition of the inner laminate when using conventional layups. The method shown in 'B' can be used in any area that requires a considerable increase in stiffness.

cable, nor is it practical to mold in shapes in the hull skin other than the normal hull contours and curvatures. While making a solid fiberglass panel thicker may make it stronger, this also adds to the weight and expense. Bulkheads may be a part of the structure, and these are covered in Chapter 27, but hull stiffeners must be installed first. Hull stiffeners can be of many different shapes made by several different methods, but the most common configuration for stiffening hulls is what is called the "top hat" section shown by Fig. 26-2. Another common configuration which is not quite as strong is the half-circle section shown by Fig. 26-3. Several variations are also shown in Fig. 26-4.

These hull stiffeners can be oriented in any direction as required. For example, the stiffeners can be athwartship (across the boat) much like frames in traditional wood boats. Or they can run longitudinally fore and aft along the hull. Because most boats will have at least some bulkheads and floors (providing stiffness in the athwartship plane), hull stiffeners are often oriented in the longitudinal direction. The stiffeners do not interfere with the accommodations as drastically this way, they are somewhat easier to install fore and aft, and in general additional longitudinal strength is more important in pleasure boats.

MAKING STIFFENERS

Hull stiffeners can be made up in place in the hull or fabricated outside of the hull and later bonded in place. The half-circle type stiffener (also known as the "mail tube" stiffener) is usually made up in place for lighter duty stiffening purposes. Although a split cardboard mailing tube can be used, any other similarly shaped molding former not attacked by resin can be used, including plastic garden hoses, wood moldings, and metal shapes. It should be emphasized that the strength of the stiffeners does NOT

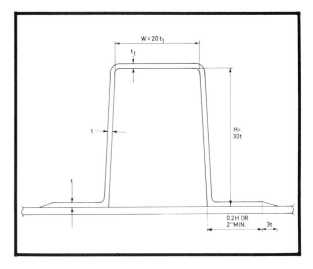

FIG. 26-2 — A section through the typical top hat stiffener is shown. The proportions per the recommendations of the A.B.S. rules can be used as guidelines. Note that the height of the stiffener is equal to 30 times the thickness, but this is variable and taller stiffeners are possible as long as they have adequate lateral support. Stiffener thickness is often increased at the top. Hence, the top or crown width is equal to 20 times this thickness. Note the flange which mates to the hull each side. On pre-molded stiffeners without these flanges, the bonding angles would be of comparable proportions.

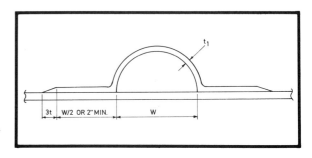

FIG. 26-3 — Another common stiffener is the half-round type. Proportions based on A.B.S. rules are given for reference. If flanges are not used, bonding angles should be of comparable proportions. This type of stiffener is not as strong as the top hat configuration.

come from the forming material, but ONLY from the resulting stiffener (engineers refer to this as adding to the "section modulus," which is accomplished partly by the distance from the hull skin to the top of the stiffener).

The former member is taped or otherwise held in place, and the stiffener laminate laid up over the former, encapsulating it permanently in position. The former can be considered as "sacrificial"; it makes no difference what happens to it. The former will always be there even though it could possibly deteriorate over time. It is also possible to prefabricate this type of stiffener over similar formers covered with wax or parting film so that the stiffener can be pulled free after fabrication. The stiffeners are then bonded in place. However, this type of stiffener is usually for lighter duty use over flatter areas since bending them in place to extreme contours is difficult if not impractical.

Top hat stiffeners are made somewhat differently. When made up in place, urethane foam formers are usually cut to the required shape and bonded in place inside the hull (see Fig. 26-5). These formers need not be in continuous lengths; shorter pieces can be butted together as required to conform to the hull surface. Anything that will bond the foam formers to the hull can be

used, including resin putty, mat strips saturated with resin, and even glue. A sound permanent bond of the foam former is not critical; once the stiffener has been made, it is inconsequential what becomes of the foam former since it is non-structural in this application.

Mark the positions of the stiffeners inside the hull, bond in the foam formers, and then coat the foam surfaces with a thin coat of resin; this will minimize resin soaking into the foam as the stiffener laminate is laid up over the form. Pre-cut strips of mat and woven roving (or whatever other materials are specified for the stiffener laminate) of widths to cover the formers and lap onto the hull the required distance. Mat should be used as the first layer in the stiffener laminate for a sound secondary bond to the hull surface. Roughen up the bonding surface on the hull. Pre-wet the mat strips over wax paper or other parting film, applying resin to both sides prior to laying them over the

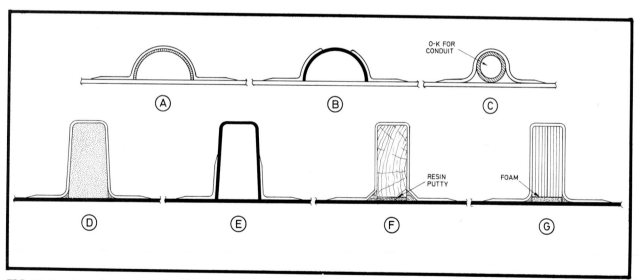

FIG. 26-4 — Several variations of stiffeners are shown. The half-round stiffener shown in 'A' is laminated in place over a split cardboard mailing tube or comparable former which stays in place, but is sacrificial and non-structural. The half-round stiffener shown in 'B' is pre-formed over just about any round or half-round object, such as a metal or plastic tube, pipe, wood dowel, etc. Bonding angles are used to hold the stiffener in place. When a pipe or tube is used as in 'C', and bonded in place, some builders run wiring in the conduit former which stays in place. The top hat stiffener shown in 'D' is made up in place over a foam former. The foam can be a non-structural type. The top hat stiffener in 'E' is a pre-formed type held in place with bonding angles. The stiffener in 'F' is made from solid wood encapsulated with fiberglass. In 'G', a similar stiffener is shown, however, this one is made from plywood. Note the inside corners in both 'F' and 'G', as well as the foam spacers between the hull skin and stiffener. These foam spacers are optional, but advisable to minimize stress concentrations, especially when used for engine girders.

FIG. 26-5 — Foam formers have been cut to shape and bonded to the inside of this hull ready for the application of the stiffener laminate and glassing in place. The forward ends, while appearing to end abruptly, will terminate at a structural bulkhead not yet installed. This will prevent the formation of a "hard spot".

FIG. 26-6 — The bottom hull stiffeners in this twin-screw yacht will also form engine girders. Additional support will be provided laterally, such as by bulkheads.

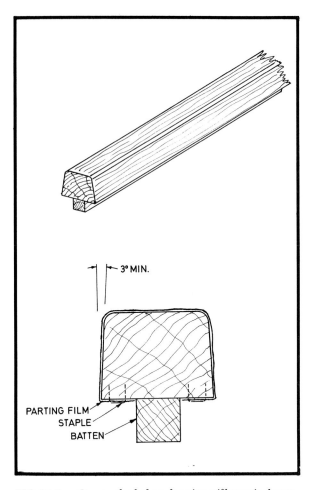

FIG. 26-7 — One method of pre-forming stiffeners is shown. Many types of fiberglass materials can be used to make these stiffeners, including conventional mat and woven rovings, unidirectional materials, and C-FLEX laminates. The stiffeners are bonded in the hull as shown by Fig. 26-9.

foam formers. Joints in the stiffener laminate should be well staggered.

Prefabricated stiffeners can be made up over a solid former such as shown by Fig. 26-7. The former is a length of wood run through a saw to provide the proper taper at the edges. The length of wood should equal that of the longest stiffener required. Shorter wood form members can be butt joined and held together with the cleat on the underside. Then parting film is stapled over the former and it is clamped or fastened to a bench or saw horses, and the laminate applied.

An ideal material for making prefabricated stiffeners is C-FLEX. Either the solid former just described or an open former such as that shown in Fig. 26-8 can be used for making a C-FLEX stiffener. This material already has built-in longitudinal strength by virtue of the rods, and it drapes easily over the former in a continuous length. Other unidirectional materials are also suitable.

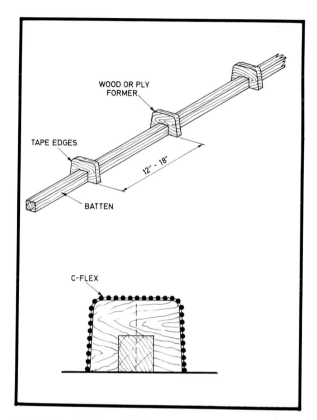

FIG. 26-8 — This method shows one way to make stiffeners with C-FLEX as a base material over which additional laminate can be applied to build up the required stiffener thickness.

If C-FLEX is used, cut the material lengthwise to drape completely over the three surfaces or edges of the former. Wet out the C-FLEX from both sides and lay over the former. Then apply the balance of the laminate with mat against the C-FLEX. Any overhanging edges should be trimmed prior to the resin setting up hard; otherwise trimming will be more difficult.

After the stiffener has been made, remove it from the mold and position it in the hull (see Fig. 26-9). There are several ways to make the stiffener conform to the hull contours. First, shoring or bracing members can be used to hold the stiffeners in place, bracing these to the building shed, scaffolding, etc. For gentle bends, use duct tape to hold the stiffeners in position and release the tape progressively as the bonding angles are

applied and cured. The sides of the stiffeners can also be cut or kerfed to make bending easier. The bonding angles in this case must be of sufficient thickness to restore the strength of the stiffener. Such cuts should be kept of a minimum number and a minimum depth; do NOT cut into the top surface of any stiffeners.

A couple of final points should be made with regard to stiffeners. At some point the stiffeners may end, and such ends should be gradually made, using gently sloped tapers to the hull surface (see Fig. 26-12 and Fig. 26-13). At the bow, stiffeners on one side are frequently joined together to those of the other side via a floor or bulkhead or at the stem for strength continuity. Abrupt endings should be avoided to prevent hard spots from forming.

Another point is that stiffeners may restrict water from flowing to the lowest point of the hull. Where this occurs, limbers

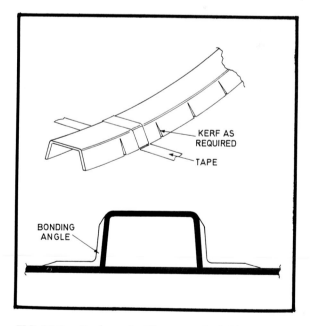

FIG. 26-9 — Pre-formed stiffeners can be held to the hull surface in several ways, including strong tape. If hull contours prevent bending in the stiffeners, kerf the sides to make them more limber. The bonding angles are then used to restore the strength of the stiffener. Remove the tape progressively as the bonding angles are applied.

FIG. 26-10 — These workers are using strips of woven roving for bonding in the stiffeners on this C-FLEX hull.

FIG. 26-11 — Note that the longitudinal stiffeners in this C-FLEX hull pass through the bulkhead which has been notched over them. The worker is completing the bonding laminate over the stiffeners.

(as shown in Chapter 23) should be molded in place under the stiffeners in such a manner that water will not enter into the enclosed void. Under no circumstances should a limber be merely drilled through a stiffener without molding in some laminate to prevent water from entering under the stiffeners or into the stiffener laminate by "wicking".

WOOD STIFFENERS

Stiffeners are frequently made with fiberglass over wood or plywood in place in the hull which are often used for engine girders or motor stringers. The merits of using wood or solid wood and encapsulating it in fiberglass were discussed in Chapter 24. There are certain recommendations which should be followed, especially when the members will be used to support an engine.

For example, if using a KLEGECELL foam core, the firm states that motor stringers can be mounted directly on the inner fiberglass skin IF the engine is light, small, and vibration-dampened. However, if the en-

gine is a rough-running type (such as many single-cylinder types) or large, then the foam should be removed where the motor stringers will be located and filled in with the inner skin, plus perhaps some additional laminate for strength. Another approach may be to fit in a solid core insert. The problem for the amateur, however, is defining what a light and small engine is, and "rough running" is a rather subjective opinion. Also, if the hull is made with high modulus skins, best practice would be to avoid any stress concentrations directly against the thin inner skin. Thus, prudence might be the best in this matter, using the stronger treatment for ANY engine. Or it may be better to suspend engine stringers free of the hull, spanning across from bulkhead to bulkhead, plus perhaps making some connections with floors.

Motor stringers may be the actual top hat section stiffeners also, with wood or plywood inserts at the points where the engine is mounted. While some builders mount the engine directly on top of the motor stringers, it is better to mount it to beds which side to the stringers (see Fig. 26-14).

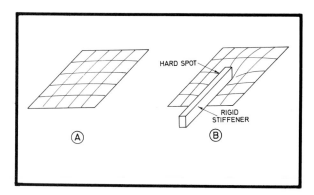

FIG. 26-12 — Stress concentrations or "hard spots" will cause a hull or fiberglass laminate to be unfairly distorted. This can lead to a visual unfairness, impaired performance, and possibly ultimate failure. In 'A', a flexible fiberglass panel is shown deflecting under a uniformly distributed load without a stiffener; there is no "hard spot". In 'B', the same panel is shown with an abrupt ending of a rigid stiffener causing a high stress concentration that deflects unfairly against the fiberglass panel under load.

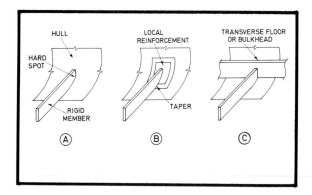

FIG. 26-13 — Rigid longitudinal stiffeners should not end against the hull skin at an unsupported area; a "hard spot" will result as in 'A'. A better method results when the member is tapered to reduce its stiffness as in 'B'. Additional laminate is used locally for reinforcement under the ending point of the stiffener in this case. An even better method, however, is to end rigid longitudinal stiffeners at an athwartships bulkhead or floor (as in 'C'); this transfers the loads to other members and prevents localized stresses.

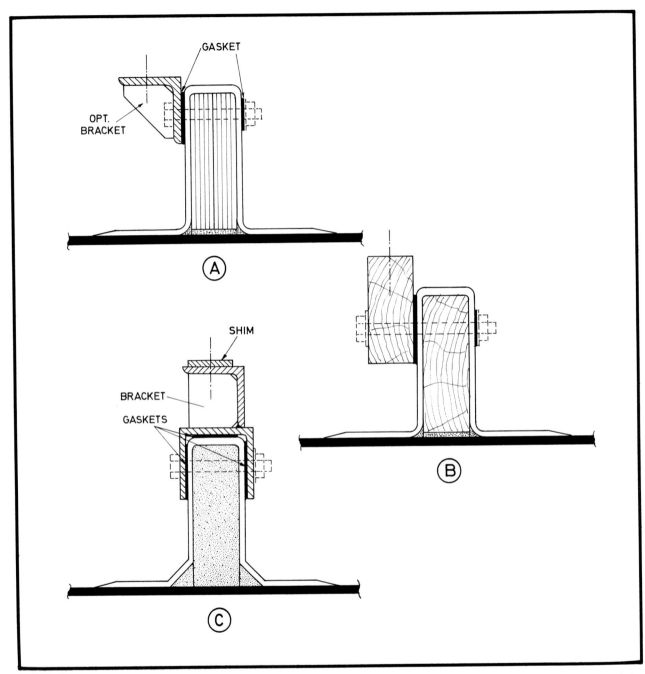

FIG. 26-14 — Sections through several types of motor stringers or engine girders are shown. The stringers are variations on top hat stiffeners, and include those made over plywood, solid wood, and foam core formers. Note that in 'A' and 'B' the engine mounts to beds which in turn side to the motor stringers. This makes alignment and changing motors easy. In 'A', metal angle brackets serve as motor mounts, bolted through the motor stringers. In larger installations with angles having wide legs, brackets may be used to provide adequate rigidity to the metal angle. In 'B', the motor bed is made from solid wood which can be sized and shaped to suit. A more elaborate arrangement is shown by 'C'. Here a metal channel is mounted over the top of the stringer to prevent crushing the member as the bolts are taken up. Metal angles can be welded to this channel for receiving the motor mounts. Brackets are advisable for larger installations for strength. In all cases, note the gaskets (which should be "Neoprene" or equivalent material) between the stringer laminates and the unyielding motor mounts. The gaskets offer some resiliency and cushioning, spread the loads more evenly, and protect the laminate (which will no doubt be somewhat uneven) from crushing as the bolts are taken up.

FIG. 26-15 — These wood motor stringers are encapsulated with fiberglass and support a small auxiliary engine in a sailboat. Notice how the stringers terminate with a floor member forward and taper toward the hull aft so that stresses are well distributed to the hull.

The beds can be made from solid wood or metal angles which are, in turn, bolted through the stringers to which they side. Provide solid blocking inserts for bolts or backing plates if foam or hollow section stiffeners are used.

With this mounting method, it is easier to align the motor since it can first be fastened in place to the beds and shifted as required until it is in alignment; it is easier to change the engine and vary the mount spacing at a later date; better, more secure mounting results since through bolts pass through the beds and stringers, with both ends of the bolts accessible; and finally, there is no precise shaping or molding required to suit the engine that will be used.

Regardless of the type of motor beds used, the mounting surfaces of the fiberglass-covered stiffeners or stringers should be as smooth as possible. A Neoprene-type gasket material should be used between the beds and stringers, and the stringers and the nut washers, to take up any discrepancies, to prevent crushing the laminate, and to prevent vibration damage. Best practice would call for adequately sized metal backing plates, plus a gasket under the head and nut end of all through bolts.

In some cases, some engine manufacturers make powerplant systems in which a fiberglass or other type mounting grid is supplied with the engines. These may be different from the preceding mounting method, but should be used if available. Certain modifications in the design may be required to adapt the unit, so follow the manufacturer's instruction for installation.

CHAPTER 27

In a boat, the bulkheads are like the walls in a house; they divide and separate the empty space of the hull to form the boat's accommodations. And like the walls in a house, they generally are structural members which strengthen the hull and help make it rigid. Because of this, they must be installed properly. Bulkheads may extend the full width and full height of the hull, or they may extend only for a limited way above the bottom of the boat or across it; these latter bulkheads are called partial bulkheads.

Bulkheads can be made from several materials or combinations of materials, but ordinarily they are made from panels of plywood. Plywood bulkheads are low in cost, strong, readily available, durable, and easy to install. Where light weight is important, other types of bulkheads can be made from

FIG. 27-1 — Bulkheads are usually made from plywood. However, lighter weight alternatives are possible, such as this balsa cored sandwich product having thin hardwood skins on either side. This product is available from the BALTEK, Corp.

sandwich-cored panels that consist of thin outer skins of veneers or plywood over cores of honeycomb material or even balsa or foam cores (see Fig 27-1). These latter types may be more work and expense. The weight savings is usually only critical in competition craft. Installation and fitting is similar for all types of bulkheads.

In the traditional wood boats of the past, each half of a frame is joined together across the middle of the boat low down in the hull with wood members called floor timbers. The floor timbers have nothing to do with the floor in the conventional sense; aboard the boat, the surface that is walked on is called the sole, NOT a floor. These floor timbers may also serve other functions, such as supporting the ballast and strengthening the keel. In fiberglass boats, however, the traditional floor timber is not required since there will be few, if any, frames in the traditional sense. Yet it is still necessary to "hold" both halves of the boat together, and perhaps strengthen and support the ballast. This is done with partial bulkhead-like members called "floors" located across the boat low down in the hull.

Floors may be independent members or they may tie in with other structural members such as bulkheads, engine girders, and mast steps. They may be made from solid fiberglass, or with cores of plywood, foam, balsa, or hardboard ("Masonite") (see Fig. 27-2). Fitting of floors is done similarly to that of bulkheads. Floors and bulkheads are generally installed after all hull stiffeners, but before the cabin and deck. Although it is possible to install these AFTER the cabin and deck have been fitted, it is much easier

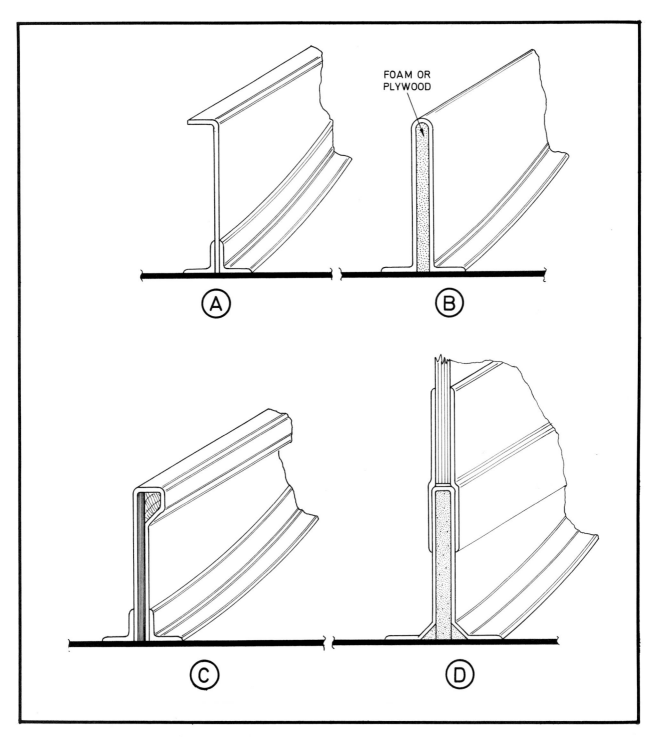

FOAM OR PLYWOOD

Ⓐ Ⓑ

Ⓒ Ⓓ

FIG. 27-2 — Several types of floors are shown. A solid pre-fabricated fiberglass floor joined to the hull with bonding angles is shown in 'A'. The flange at the top helps stiffen the member. In 'B', a floor is made in place by laying up fiber-glass over a core forming material which can be sheet foam, balsa core, plywood, etc. A plywood or hardboard floor covered with fiberglass and bonded into place with bonding angles is shown by 'C'. The cleat across the top stiffens the floor and also provides support for adjoining bulkheads and cabin soles. If wood below the waterline is not desired, a fiberglass floor using a foam core can be made in place up to a certain point above the waterline. Then a plywood bulkhead can be joined to the top edge with fiberglass strips to form an integral member as shown in 'D'. This integrity depends on a sound secondary bond; mechanical fastening through the bulkhead is optional.

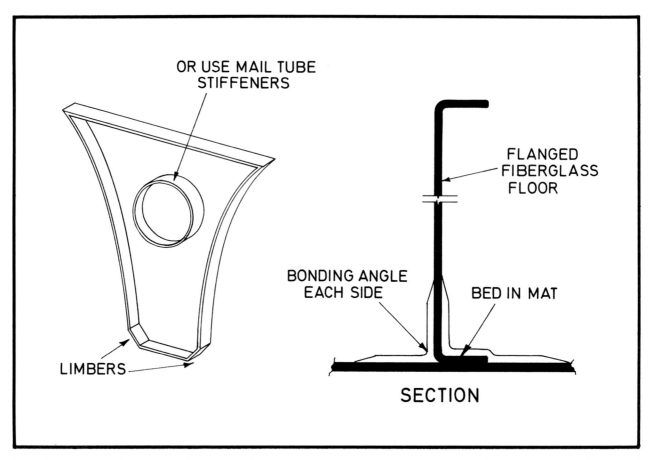

FIG. 27-3 — An all-fiberglass floor is easy to make as explained in the text. The flange stiffens the member, and for larger panels, a flanged hole or other stiffening devices (such as half-round stiffeners) can be used for additional rigidity.

Note the molding in of the limbers. Bed the floor in a layer of mat and bond in place with bonding angles on each side as shown in the section (right).

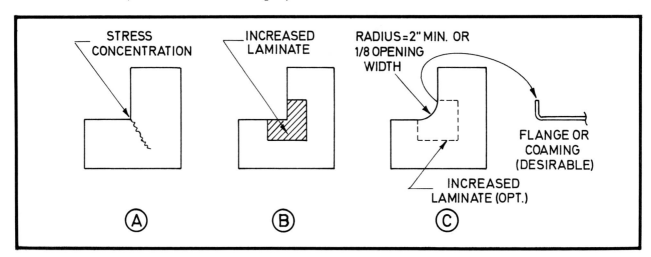

FIG. 27-4 — Openings in fiberglass laminates can lead to stress concentrations if not built correctly. In 'A', a hard inside corner at an opening will cause a weak spot that may lead to a failure in the laminate at this point. A better method in this case is to build up the laminate locally for additional strength, as in 'B'. The preferred method, however, is to radius the corner as in 'C'. An even more desirable structure results if a flange or coaming is built into the corner; additional laminate applied locally is optional.

310

to fit, cut, trim, and maneuver the members without interference from a constricting cabin and deck structure.

MAKING FLOORS

There are several ways to make floors; however, the method shown on your plans should be adhered to if specific recommendations are given. The following will show some methods that can otherwise be used.

The all-fiberglass floor can be laid up over a flat well-waxed surface (such as "Formica", "Masonite", strong glass, or sealed plywood) using alternating layers of mat and woven roving to the required thickness. However, because a flat, thin sheet of fiberglass may be quite flexible, some form of stiffening may be necessary. This should first be provided with an angle flange all around the edge of the floor which not only adds to stiffness, but makes it easier to install. This type of floor is shown by Fig. 27-3. Note that a hole has been located in the floor with a similar flange at the edge for stiffness. While shown as a round hole, this opening can be of any shape as long as the corners are radiused to prevent stress concentrations (see Fig. 27-4). This type of floor can also be stiffened with mail tube stiffeners or similar methods as shown in Chapter 26. Note the limbers at the bottom; these allow any bilge water to drain to the sump or lowest portion of the bilge for pumping overboard. Limbers should be provided through all floors and any bulkheads which may land on the bottom of the hull at the lowest point (except, of course, those bulkheads which are specifically intended to be watertight).

Other methods for making floors consist of laying up fiberglass laminates over core materials such as plywood, foam, balsa, or hardboard like "Masonite". In other words, the core materials are encapsulated with fiberglass. The core may be considered a "former", with the ultimate strength of the

floor coming from the fiberglass laminate on either side. However, a structural core material such as plywood, foam, or balsa does add significant rigidity to the member as long as moisture does not enter the core.

Making a floor from plywood is simply a matter of fitting the plywood and laying up fiberglass laminate over the surfaces (see Fig. 27-5). Mat is used against the plywood, with alternating woven roving and mat layers to the required thickness. Such a floor can be prefabricated outside the boat or made up in place. A floor member made from sheet foam is done similarly. However, if using a contoured core material like END-GRAIN BALSA, the floor is prefabricated over a flat surface just like with the solid fiberglass floor and then set in place. This would be accomplished by applying the necessary laminates against the flat surface, then bedding the core in resin-saturated mat, and applying the other outer layer of fiberglass laminates over the core, making sure the core is totally encapsulated.

Another way to make floors is to use a hardboard former such as "Masonite"

FIG. 27-5 — The floors in this sailboat are plywood covered over and bonded in place with fiberglass. These floors help support the ballast keel below and distribute the forces to a larger area of the hull. Note the limbers through the floors.

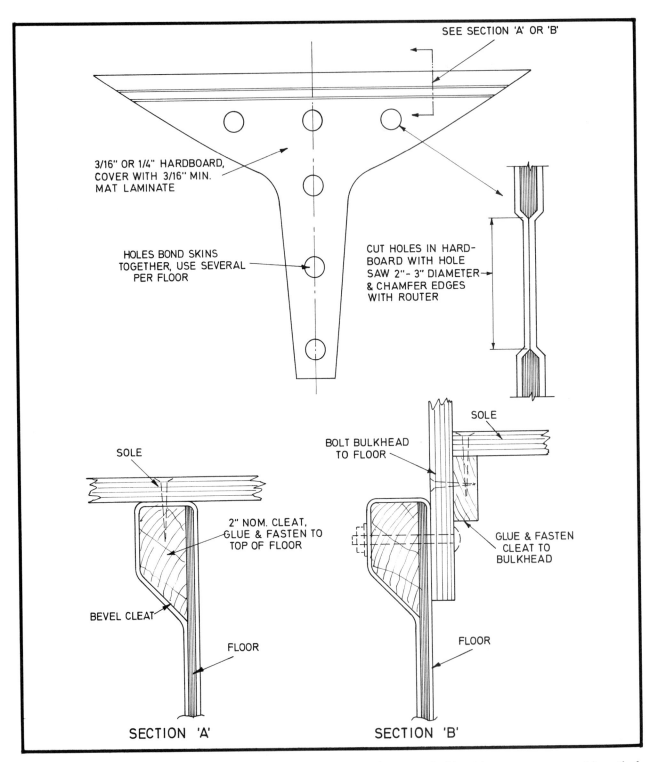

SEE SECTION 'A' OR 'B'

3/16" OR 1/4" HARDBOARD, COVER WITH 3/16" MIN. MAT LAMINATE

HOLES BOND SKINS TOGETHER, USE SEVERAL PER FLOOR

CUT HOLES IN HARD- BOARD WITH HOLE SAW 2"- 3" DIAMETER & CHAMFER EDGES WITH ROUTER

SOLE

2" NOM. CLEAT, GLUE & FASTEN TO TOP OF FLOOR

BEVEL CLEAT

FLOOR

SECTION 'A'

SOLE

BOLT BULKHEAD TO FLOOR

GLUE & FASTEN CLEAT TO BULKHEAD

FLOOR

SECTION 'B'

FIG. 27-6 — A floor made from 3/16" or 1/4" thick hardboard is shown, although comparable plywood could also be used. Fit and cut the hardboard to shape, glue and fasten a 2" nominal bevelled wood cleat across the top edge, and round the top edge corners. Use a hole saw to cut out several holes 2" to 3" in diameter. Bevel the edges of these holes at 45 degrees each side with a router or comparable method. Apply fiberglass mat to both surfaces at least 3/16" thick, making sure the skins on both sides join to each other at the holes. The completed floor is then installed in the hull using bonding angles. Cabin soles and bulkheads can be supported and fastened to the floor at the top through the cleat.

(about ¼" thick) with fiberglass laid up over it. Fit the hardboard and cut to shape. Then with a hole saw, cut several holes through the hardboard and chamfer the edges as shown by Fig. 27-6. Since the hardboard should be considered as "non-structural" material, the holes let the laminate on either side bond together at several points for added strength. Although the hardboard former gives stiffness, the laminate should be to the total thickness as used in a solid fiberglass floor. For extra rigidity at the top, a solid wood former is installed with a chamfer on the lower edge to make it easier to apply the laminate. This wood member also provides fastening blocking material for any bulkheads or soles that may be adjoining. The principles and methods for fitting and installing floors are similar to those used for bulkheads, which are discussed later.

INSTALLING BULKHEADS

In most pleasure boats, bulkheads are usually made of thick enough plywood to be self-supporting without additional stiffening members. Usually there are enough interior joinery members attached to the bulkheads for adequate strength except on the largest boats or along the edges at openings. In these cases, additional framing may be required to prevent the bulkheads from moving or "buckling". Thus, while much joinerywork is usually considered as "non-structural", the various soles, shelves, cabinet facings, berth fronts, and similar members can do a lot in the way of stiffening bulkheads where they adjoin; joinery members should be well-fastened and joined to bulkheads wherever possible.

There are several principles to keep in mind when installing bulkheads in fiberglass hulls. First and foremost is to prevent the formation of stress concentrations or "hard spots" that could press unfairly against the hull, leading to a deformation

and perhaps ultimate failure. Bulkheads located under masts, or adjacent to shroud attachments, or that support motor stringers will be subjected to considerable stresses, and these stresses must be transferred to the hull over as generous an area as possible free from stress concentrations.

Thus, a close, tight fit of a bulkhead is NOT necessary nor desirable. This makes cutting and fitting somewhat easier than in the case of boats built from other materials; however, one should not construe that the work can be sloppy. For deep bulkheads, it is probably easier to fit a floor first and then attach a bulkhead to it later; this will be easier to fit than handling a single tall bulkhead, especially with complex hull shapes.

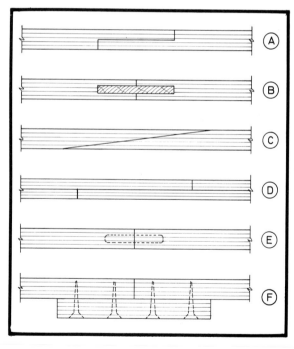

FIG. 27-7 — Plywood bulkheads can be pieced and joined by several methods. A simple lap joint is shown by 'A', while a spline joint using a wood spline is shown by 'B'. A scarf joint is shown by 'C', and in 'D', a lap joint is formed by using a double thickness of plywood, offsetting or staggering the butt joints between the two layers. Dowels are used in 'E', and in 'F', a butt joint backed with a butt block is shown. In 'A', 'B', 'D', and 'F', the plywood should be at least ¾" thick for a practical joint. All such joints should be glued. The joints in 'C' and 'F' are recommended for structural bulkheads.

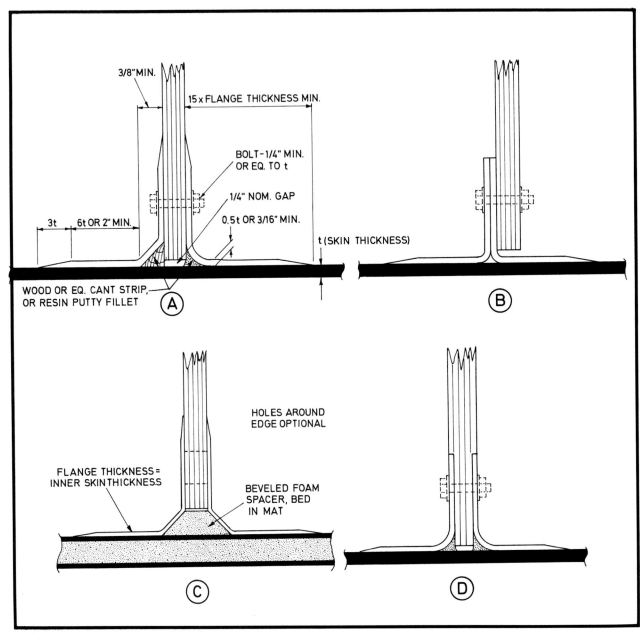

FIG. 27-8 — Several recommended methods of installing bulkheads are shown. Requirements as advised by the ABS rules are shown in 'A' which can be used as guidelines. The minimum width of bonding angles is listed below. This organization recommends that bulkheads also be bolted in place, with bolts spaced as follows:

It should be pointed out that mechanical fastening of bulkheads in pleasure boats is not standard practice, and other methods as described in the text can result in adequate junctions. Bulkheads installed in sandwich cored hulls should be done as in 'C', with a foam spacer between the bulkhead edge and the inner laminate. In 'D', the bulkhead has been relieved around the edges each side so the bonding angles will fit flush to the bulkhead surface. Note the gap shown between the hull skin and the bulkhead edge in all cases with single skin hulls, and radiused fillets or cant strips used at the junctions to the hull. Foam spacers between the bulkhead and hull can also be used on single skin hulls.

BOLT SPACING

VESSEL LENGTH	FLANGE WIDTH	UNRESTRICTED SERVICE	LIMITED SERVICE
30'	2.5"	6.0"	9.0"
40'	3.0"	6.5"	9.5"
50'	3.5"	7.0"	10.0"
60'	4.0"	7.5"	10.5"

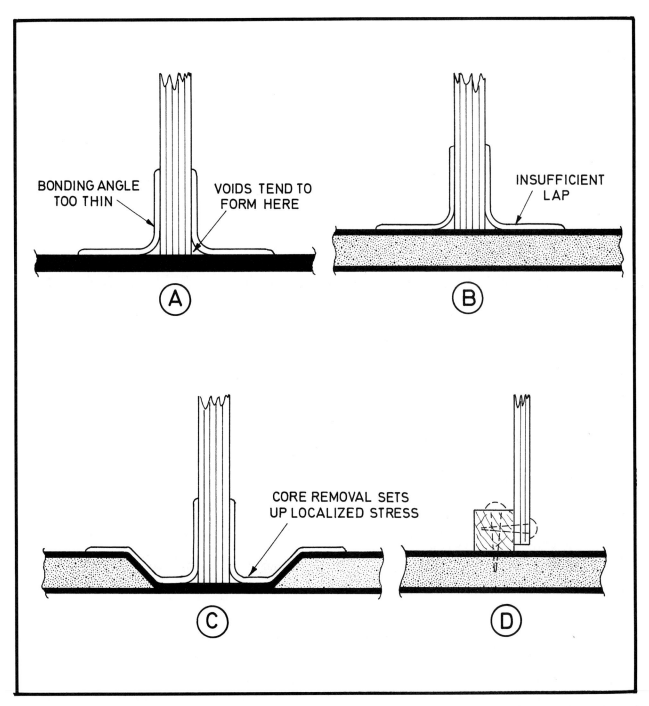

FIG. 27-9 — Incorrect methods of installing bulkheads are shown. Bulkheads should never contact against the hull; always leave a gap or fit a foam spacer between. The junctions should always be fitted with a radiused filler fillet or cant strip to prevent voids from forming under the bonding angle. The bonding angles must be of sufficient thickness with generous laps (as shown in Fig. 27-8). The cores of sandwich cored hulls should NOT be removed at bulkhead junctions. A conditionally acceptable situation is shown in 'D' for sandwich cored hulls. In this example, the bulkhead is a light non-structural member, such as would be used only for unstressed joinery work, and located above the waterline using a conventional laminate. Hulls with thin high modulus skins, for example, should NOT include this method. The wood cleat is bonded or glued to the inner skin and fastened with a large threaded screw through the inner laminate and only partially into the core. The bulkhead is then screwed to this cleat. It should be emphasized that this junction is only acceptable in a light duty non-structural application.

It is a good idea to leave all bulkheads tall or overside at the top, and later trim to fit to suit the cabin and/or deck camber.

In smaller boats, it may be possible for a single standard plywood sheet to make an entire bulkhead without joints. However, in larger boats, two or more panels may be required that will require joining. The bulkhead joining method will depend partly on the thickness of the plywood. Several joining methods are shown by Fig. 27-7, including a simple lap, spline, scarf, laminating two or more thickness, or a simple butt block. Note that bulkheads joined with a lap, dowels, spline, or by laminations should be done only with thicker plywood, such as ¾" or more.

As noted in Chapter 24, there is some disagreement about the use of wood or plywood located below the waterline. In many cases, bulkheads will be located below the waterline. For those who do not want any wood below the waterline, one way to solve the problem is shown by the floor/bulkhead junction in Fig. 27-2(D). In this case, the lower portion of the bulkhead below the waterline is made from a foam sheet material encapsulated with fiberglass, with the plywood bulkhead bonded to the top above the waterline.

Bulkheads are installed in the fiberglass hull with bonding angles made from fiberglass as shown by Fig. 27-8(A). These bonding angles must be applied against a clean, dry, oil-free, bare wood surface for an adequate bond to the bulkhead. If the bulkhead is teak-faced, the surface should be wiped with acetone or similar solvent or the teak veneers can be removed in the area of the bonding angle, such as with a router (see Fig. 27-8(D)). If the teak remains, then the bulkhead should also be bolted through the bonding angles. The bulkhead surface at the bonding angle should not be smooth; if it is, roughen the surface with coarse sandpaper. Bulkhead edges (those against the hull)

FIG. 27-10 — Numerous very small holes have been drilled into this bulkhead all around the edge at the bonding angle. Larger holes would be preferable. These provide a better "grip" for the bonding angles since the mat against the bulkhead in this area will tend to fill into the holes somewhat. Note the resin putty fillets along the bulkhead edge and the stiffeners which pass through the bulkhead.

FIG. 27-11 — An AIREX foam cant strip is being used in this bulkhead installation under the bonding angle. Note how easily it conforms to the contour.

should also be coated with resin to seal the end grain against moisture and possible rot. The surface of the bulkhead should also be primed with a thin layer of laminating resin prior to applying the bonding angle.

Although many production boatbuilders depend on the bonding angles to hold the bulkheads in position, additional security can be provided by bolting the bulkheads through the bonding angles or by drilling a series of holes into (but not necessarily through) the bulkhead around the perimeter under the bonding angles (see Fig. 27-10). The idea here is that the bonding angle laminate (which should consist of mat as the initial layer) will work down into the

holes and form a better "grip" once set. The bonding angle should not just consist of mat; there should also be a strength material such as woven roving or cloth as well, applied in alternating layers. The bonding angle should run all around the perimeter of the bulkhead and lap generously onto the hull as well as the bulkhead. How much should this lap be? The more the better; however, a 4" nominal lap is considered excellent. How thick should the bonding angle be? This may be given on your plans, or as a rule of thumb, about half the hull thickness will suffice for most single-skin hulls, or for sandwich-cored boats, at least equal to the inner skin thickness. The de-

FIG. 27-12 — Bulkheads are best installed before the super-structure. These bulkheads have been trimmed to size and shape at the top for the deck and cabin installation. Note the pre-cut strips of fiberglass draped over a bulkhead ready for use as bonding angles.

tails show the proper methods to keep the bulkhead from contacting unfairly against the inner hull.

FITTING BULKHEADS

There are so many methods that boat-builders use to fit bulkheads and floors that it is not practical to cover them all. Several methods are well suited to the amateur, and these will be described. With any of these methods, the first requisite is that the bulkhead be fitted true and aligned accurately. In other words, the bulkhead must be at right angles to the centerline (in most

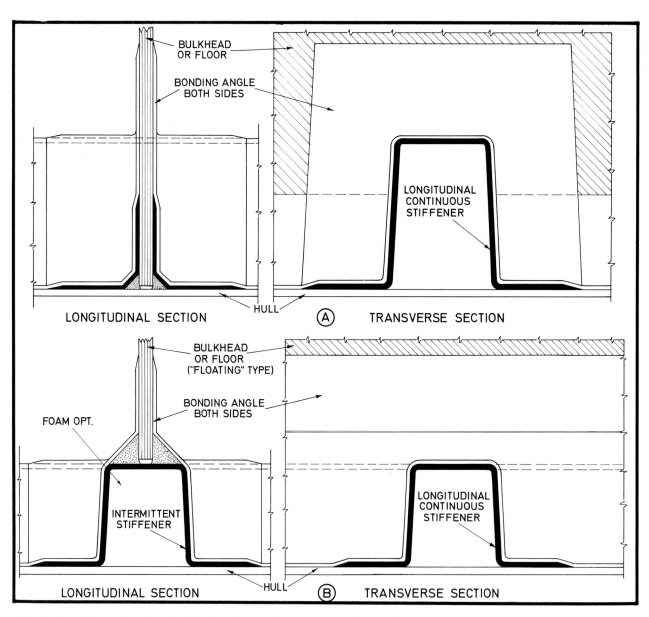

FIG. 27-13 — The sections show bulkheads or floors which can be fitted around longitudinal stiffeners as in 'A', or that rest on the stiffeners as in 'B'. This latter method is referred to as a "floating" bulkhead, and in this case, intermittent stiffeners are fitted under the bulkhead between longitu-dinal stiffeners. Also in 'B', the bonding angle will lap onto a larger area of the bulkhead, which may be objectionable from an appearance standpoint in some cases. Note the bonding angle orientation in both cases.

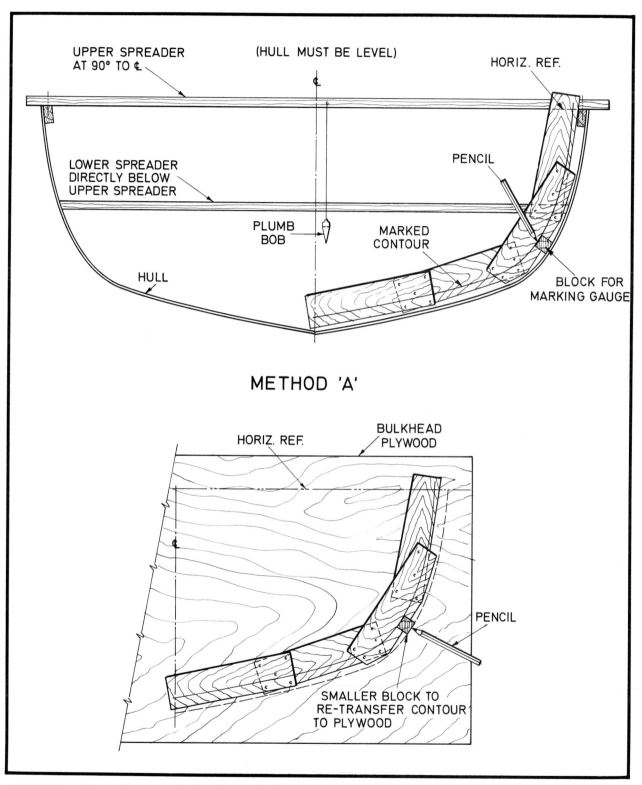

UPPER SPREADER
AT 90° TO ₵

(HULL MUST BE LEVEL)

HORIZ. REF.

LOWER SPREADER
DIRECTLY BELOW
UPPER SPREADER

PENCIL

PLUMB
BOB

MARKED
CONTOUR

HULL

BLOCK FOR
MARKING GAUGE

METHOD 'A'

HORIZ. REF.

BULKHEAD
PLYWOOD

PENCIL

SMALLER BLOCK TO
RE-TRANSFER CONTOUR
TO PLYWOOD

FIG. 27-14 — Fitting and cutting a bulkhead using Method "A" is shown. The spreaders accurately position the bulkhead. The marking block is used to transfer the contour to the mock-up. But to provide for the proper gap that should exist between the bulkhead and the hull, a somewhat smaller block is used to re-transfer the contour onto the bulkhead material.

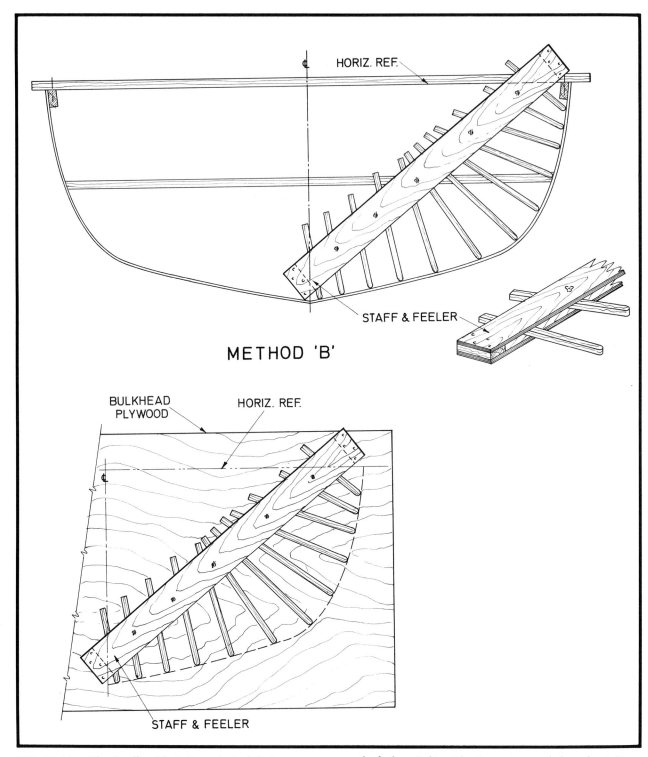

HORIZ. REF.

STAFF & FEELER

METHOD 'B'

BULKHEAD
PLYWOOD

HORIZ. REF.

STAFF & FEELER

FIG. 27-15 — The "staff-and-feeler" method of fitting a bulkhead (or Method "B") is shown. The orientation or position of the staff can be in any direction (such as vertically or at any other angle) to suit the hull shape. The staff shown consists of two lengths of wood or plywood joined and separated by blocks at the ends of the same thickness as the feelers. Bolts with wing nuts spaced along the staff are tightened down to clamp the feelers in place. After determining the contour, the assembly is placed onto the bulkhead material and the contour marked around with a spline (don't forget the deduction for the gap along the edge of the bulkhead).

cases), exactly vertical, and not skewed or warped. Accuracy in the bulkhead installation will pay off later when the balance of the joinery is installed, since everything will be easier to cut and fit in place.

First, determine the location of the bulkhead (this may have been marked to the hull before the formwork was removed). Then place a wood spreader (a 2″ × 4″ will do) flatwise and horizontally across the hull. If the sheer clamps are in place, temporarily fasten or clamp the member to the sheer clamps. Or use a member wider than the hull at this point with blocks fitted at the ends to hook over the sheer each side. In either case, set the wood piece at right angles (90 degrees) to the centerline of the hull.

Then it is preferable to put another 2″ × 4″ spreader directly below by a foot or two, and parallel to the first one. This piece will have to be cut to length and wedged to the hull or stiffeners. If this is not practical, it can be omitted (although this will make fitting somewhat more difficult, as will be shown). Use a plumb bob to locate this second flatwise member DIRECTLY below the one above. This will establish an accurate visible athwartships vertical plane for fitting the bulkhead (the centerline of the hull should also be indicated by a taut wire in place from bow to stern for reference purposes).

Now the bulkhead can be fitted, and three methods will be described. In all cases, it is necessary to duplicate the contours of the inside of the hull and transfer these to the bulkhead material. The methods that are used to do this may vary with the builder's preferences as well as with the shape of the hull; simpler shaped hulls, such as those having straight, flat surfaces, are easier to fit to than those having more complex curves and shapes.

As noted before, the bulkhead should NOT protrude directly against the hull and should have a gap (between ¼″ and ½″ is acceptable). If a foam block is used, the gap should match the thickness of the foam block. The precise fit required with other boatbuilding methods is not necessary; minor discrepancies can be taken up by the bonding angles. Also, if the boat has any longitudinal hull stiffeners that will interfere with the fitting of the bulkhead, the builder has two options; he can fit and cut the bulkhead around all these members (which can be tedious), or he can fit to the inside of the stiffeners and let the bulkhead rest on the stiffeners (Fig. 27-13 illustrates both conditions).

In Method "A" (see Fig. 27-14) mock up some pieces of scrap wood or plywood to approximate the inside hull contour for one-half the bulkhead at the bulkhead point. Then clamp this mock-up to the two athwartship spreaders; this will be the position of the bulkhead. If the lower spreader was not installed, then use the plumb bob from the upper spreader to determine the lower ending point where the bulkhead will land at the centerline on the bottom of the hull. The mock-up will have to be held in position somehow at the bottom, using a clamp to the upper spreader. Then use a level to make sure that the mock-up is vertical (this isn't necessary if two spreaders are used, since they will already be in alignment).

Regardless of the procedure used up to this point, use a small block of wood as a marking gauge to mark points to the mock-up as it is moved along the surface of the hull from top to bottom (the block of wood must be larger than the largest gap between the mock-up and the hull at any point). Also mark the position of the spreader and the centerline, along with any other pertinent members, such as the sheer clamp notch, etc. If it is assumed that the hull is IDENTICAL on both halves, there is no need to repeat this procedure for the opposite side. However, if both sides are NOT symmetrical, repeat for the opposite side of the hull.

With the mock-up marked, remove the assembly and lay it on the bulkhead mate-

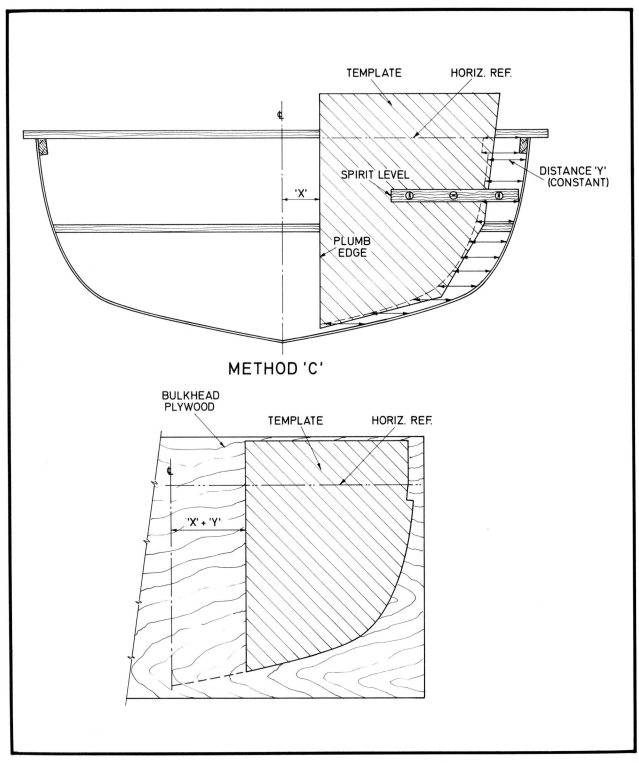

FIG. 27-16 — Method "C" is shown for fitting a bulkhead. The level must be held horizontally at all points using a fixed distance which can be taped or marked to the edge of the level. After marking the points to the template, it is sawn to contour and laid onto the bulkhead material which is then cut to match. The distance 'X' plus 'Y' must be added each side in the case of a full-width bulkhead due to the offset caused by the 'Y' dimension. With a partial bulkhead, distance 'Y' must be added to the plumb edge to obtain the net bulkhead width.

rial. Strike a horizontal reference plane onto the bulkhead at the level of the spreader, and also the centerline, which should be at right angles to this plane. Then re-transfer the line on the mock-up onto the bulkhead material. But this time DON'T use the same block used first; instead use a block of a thickness that is smaller, to allow for the depth of the gap that will exist between the hull and the bulkhead, or to match the thickness of the strip of foam used between the bulkhead and the hull. Or mark with the original block, but after re-transfering the line, use another block to the required deduction around the contour to make a new second line INSIDE the first one.

Method "B" (see Fig. 27-15) is sometimes called the "staff-and-feeler" method. The bulkhead contour jig (the "staff") shown

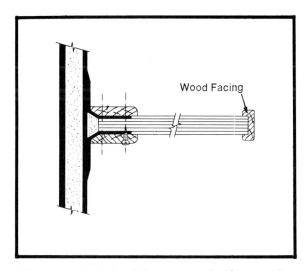

FIG. 27-17 — This detail shows one method for concealing the bonding angle where appearance is important. The bonding angle has been let into a relieved area (a rabbet) all around the edge equal in thickness to the bonding angle. Wood trim is then used over the bonding angle, screwed in place through the bonding angle and into the bulkhead.

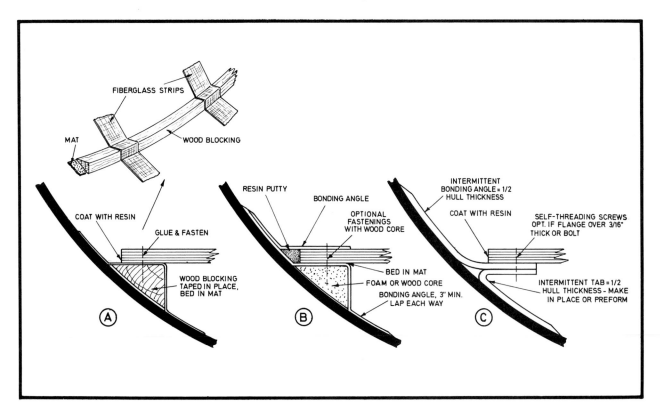

FIG. 27-18 — Soles and flats (such as berth tops, shelves, etc.) are somewhat like horizontal bulkheads. Several methods of joining these members to the hull are shown. An embedded continuous wood or foam shaped blocking as in 'B' is neat and sound. However, exposed continuous or intermittent wood blocking as in 'A', or tabs made from fiberglass as in 'C' are also acceptable. Edges of plywood should be coated with resin in all cases. Be sure to make traps or access holes through any soles or tops which are permanently bonded in place for maintenance and inspection purposes.

uses two strips of wood or plywood fitted with blocks at the ends. Then wood fingers equal in thickness to the blocks form the "feelers". Several carriage bolts fitted with wing nuts along the length of the "staff" can be used to hold the fingers in position. A less elaborate variation on this theme uses just a length of wood for the "staff" with fingers nailed or clamped in place once their positions are determined. In either case, the device is clamped to the spreaders, and the fingers (which must be of lengths to suit) are positioned to pick up the hull contours. However, leave the required distance for the gap between the ends of the fingers. Then remove the jig to the bulkhead material, with the horizontal level and centerline marked to the surface. Use a spline or batten (long, thin strip of wood) to mark the contour to the bulkhead.

The third method is shown by Method "C" (see Fig. 27-16). With this method, use a piece of scrap wood, or a mock-up like that used in Method "A", or use a portion of the actual bulkhead clamped to the spreaders (it is easy to make a rough approximation of the contour in some cases and make a preliminary cut to rough size). Clamp to the spreader and use a level to transfer a fixed horizontal distance at numerous points along the piece being fitted. A simple way to do this is to tape a rule on the edge of the level, or use a piece of masking tape on the edge marked to suit, or use a square that has a level bubble built in. Whatever is used, be sure that the tool is held level at all points marked.

Note that if the actual bulkhead is fitted in place, it must be somewhat taller than will need be to allow for the material which will be cut off. After fitting, remove the piece, join the points with a batten (again allowing for the gap between the bulkhead and the inside surface of the hull), and saw to shape. Note that the distance marked must be ADDED to make the required bulkhead width. If camber is required at the top of the bulkheads, use a template taken from the deck or cabin pattern, or from the loftings, and transfer to the bulkhead if the exact height of the bulkhead can be determined at this time. If the bulkhead goes across the centerline, make a small hole for the wire used for the centerline and plug this later. With the bulkhead made and ready for installation, temporarily nail or clamp it in place to the spreaders and then bond it in place.

CHAPTER 28

ballast

Ballast is used for stability purposes mainly aboard monohulled sailboats, but sometimes in powerboats also. Generally this ballast is located as low in the hull as possible to keep the vertical center of gravity low enough to overpower any heeling tendencies that could upset or capsize the vessel. In sailboats, the ballast is located within a keel appendage on the bottom of the boat, in which case it is referred to as internal ballast. Or the ballast may be formed as a separate part suspended from the bottom of the boat, in which case it is referred to as external ballast.

The various attributes of either approach will not be covered in detail since this text is not concerned primarily with design aspects. Either method does have good and bad features, and there are advocates of both methods. However, the amateur should understand a couple of points which are directly related to the construction.

With internal ballast, a potential problem is that the keel appendage may be punctured due to a collision or running aground. If this happens, water may enter into any voids that may exist in the ballast, leading to perhaps serious problems, especially if the water becomes trapped and freezes. Or the water may leak into the hull, perhaps leading to the loss of the vessel. Also, if the ballast is not correctly installed, it could tear loose in a seaway, leading to catastrophic results in a knockdown. Thus, internal ballast must be securely bonded to the hull, free of voids (especially between the inner hull skin and the ballast), AND soundly encapsulated within the keel appendage.

With external ballast, the main potential for problems is with the attachment method of the ballast to the hull. The exterior ballast is usually bolted through the bottom of the hull. Because of the weight of the ballast (which can sometimes equal 50% or more of the boat's total displacement) there are tremendous forces at work which must be transferred to the boat's structure. Thus, the structure at these attachment points must be strong enough not only to take these loads, but also to prevent working and movement of the connections when the boat is underway (see Chapter 8 for reinforcing guidelines). If there is any movement at these points, leaks and worse may result. Also, there is always the potential for corrosion at the bolts, which must always be monitored, leading to increased maintenance.

The ballast configuration of the boat being built should be specified by the designer. Also, the type of ballast material to be used, together with the required weight, should be noted. There are several methods and materials possible, but because of their density, lead and steel or iron are commonly used. These materials combine high density at low volume and they are commonly available. Other materials such as concrete, sand, and rock require too much volume in most boats to provide sufficient weight for ballast purposes, although they are sometimes combined with heavier materials to reduce costs.

EXTERNAL BALLAST

Usually external ballast is in the form of a casting or a prefabricated part welded up from steel in the form of a "can" or container into which ballast material is inserted. Casting from lead is sometimes practical for the amateur, but this can be an involved operation which increases in difficulty as the size and weight of the casting increases. Hence, the task is often subcontracted to a foundry specializing in lead castings. Nevertheless, handling, maneuvering, and attaching a heavy casting to the bottom of a boat can be a formidable task for the amateur, especially if he is working shorthanded. Numerous texts describe the procedures for casting in lead, and some of these are noted in the Bibliography if the builder wants to attempt casting his own external ballast.

If the option is given for fabricating the unit from steel in the form of a can, the details and information should be provided on the plans. This component can be built by the amateur if he is capable of welding operations, or any local welder should be able to do the job. The steel can be metalized or hot-dipped galvanized after fabrication, or covered with a light fiberglass sheathing for protection from corrosion using an epoxy resin for a sound bond.

The external ballast must fit tightly to the hull at the point of attachment in order to prevent leaks and movement. Some advocate bedding the ballast against the hull is a "cushion" layer of resin-saturated mat of sufficient thickness to fill in minor discrepancies as the bolts are taken up. However, as the mat sets up, it tends to shrink, harden, and crack, leading to leaks. Epoxy fillers would form perhaps a better bond in this situation, however, these too tend to be hard and brittle.

A better method is to bed the junction liberally in an elastomeric compound such as a silicon or polysulphide sealant. There are numerous varieties of these products, and one should be selected that sets up to moderate hardness (neither too soft nor too hard) that is permanently elastic.

Hopefully the top of the external ballast,

as well as the bottom of the hull where the ballast mates, will be true without humps, dips, or other deviations that will interfere with a tight, firm fit. Layers of mat or a thick resin putty filler can be applied to the hull and then ground flat and true, but this build-up should not be overly thick. If the external ballast is a lead casting, ordinary woodworking tools can be used to true-up the top to conform to the joining area on the hull.

Take care when attaching the external ballast to the hull. Alignment is important, especially if the external ballast is also a fin keel appendage, providing lateral resistance and lift for windward performance. In this case, the ballast fin must be accurately centered along the centerline and vertical. If the hull has been leveled true, the ballast can be trued vertically with a plumb bob. Another way is to check measurements from known points on either side of the boat to the bottom center of the appendage, but this assumes that the hull is EXACTLY symmetrical, which may not be the case.

The keel bolts on the inside of the hull should be fitted with large metal backing plates or at least oversize washers three times the bolt diameter in size and 25% of the bolt diameter in thickness. Some believe that these bolts should be covered with a laminate of fiberglass to protect them from corrosion by bilge water. However, this is not wise since corrosion may still occur below the laminate due to electrolytic action. Thus, the bolts should best be exposed and accessible to check their condition. If a casting is used, the bolts should also be replaceable.

INTERNAL BALLAST

Internal ballast is ideal for the amateur because it is a job that can be done by one person. In some production boats, the internal ballast is a casting that is set down into the keel appendage; this no doubt is quicker and saves time in the production situation where numerous boats of a given type may be built. However, with the amateur-built boat, just about any type of scrap lead, steel, or iron can be placed into the keel to form the ballast.

Whether lead, steel, or iron, or a combination of these, can be used should be stipulated on the plans. Lead has traditionally been more expensive than steel, but it tends to be favored by designers because it is higher in weight for a given volume than steel or iron (about 700 lbs. per cubic foot as opposed to about 450 to 500 lbs. per cubic foot for iron or steel). This means that the center of gravity can be lower with less volume devoted to the ballast, and this helps increase both the performance and the safety of the vessel. If a builder wants to substitute steel or iron for lead, he should always contact the designer first for his advice; not only could there be an impact on the stability of the boat, but there is a chance that there may not be sufficient volume provided in the keel appendage for a less dense material.

There are any number of forms of lead, iron, and steel that can be used for internal ballast installed by the amateur. Both new and scrap materials can be used, including metal shot, pigs, ball bearings, boiler punchings, old lead wheel weights used in alignment shops, scrap lead from batteries, typesetters, and plumbers, scrap steel, and so forth. The scrounger-type who will require a large amount of ballast materials will start collecting ballast material early in the project wherever he can; this will save considerably on the cost of the ballast, especially if lead is required.

The metal ballast material once collected is not merely dumped into the keel cavity. Instead it should be mixed with a material that will fill in any voids and bond the ballast in place to the inside of the hull. In order to maintain as high a density as possible, the percentage of ballast material should be as high as possible, using a minimum amount of the mixing material.

Several materials come to mind for this mixing material, including concrete, pitch (bituminous tar), resin, or resin putty filler. While concrete and pitch are cheap, polyester resin is an ideal material. A thin resin putty filler will reduce the volume of resin required, however, it may decrease the density too much for practical use.

A problem with concrete is that even after it sets, if it gets wet, it can attack glass fibers. If concrete is used, because of the potential for moisture, it is poor practice to glass over it; leave it exposed. The concrete tends to crack and shrink down at the edges in many situations, leaving places where bilge water may tend to settle and get between the hull skin and the ballast. Such joints must be well sealed with mastic. Another problem with concrete is that it is more difficult to mix and eliminate voids since it is not free-flowing. The concrete ballast must also be prevented from falling out in the event of a capsize.

Pitch also has some of the same problems as those associated with concrete. The bond over time to the fiberglass hull is questionable and there is very little strength in the material itself to hold things together. If one tries to bond over the ballast with a fiberglass laminate to hold the ballast in position, the pitch will interfere with the bond.

In the fiberglass boat, a slurry of polyester resin mixed with the ballast is really the ideal material. It will bond the ballast tenaciously in position and it is easy to install a fiberglass laminate over the top to anchor and seal the ballast in place. This fiberglass covering over the ballast also makes it unlikely that the hull will flood if the keel appendage is ever holed; in other words, it forms a "double bottom".

The ballast should be mixed with resin in small increments and poured into the cavity in consecutive pourings. Each batch of ballast should be carefully weighed and recorded, and if a certain proportion of ballast-to-resin is required, this should be adhered to. While the metal ballast material will absorb much of the heat of exotherm in the resin, smaller pourings will prevent any excessive heat build-up that could damage the hull laminate. Do not use more resin than is required; this just reduces the ballast density. Any contaminants or oil on the ballast can be ignored for the most part. Oil will tend to float to the top and can be removed with a solvent wipe. Ideally, the ballast should be poured in a reasonably continuous operation if possible.

Regardless of the mixing material, the ballast should be tamped and preferably mechanically vibrated in place to eliminate any major voids. These voids provide water traps and decrease the density of the ballast, and may raise the center of gravity if care is not taken. For reinforcement, steel re-bar is sometimes worked into the ballast where steel ballast is used to help tie the mass together and increase the strength of the hull. This works especially well where resin is used in the mix, and a firm bond results to the hull skin. However, because lead and steel have different potentials electrically, they should not come into contact with one another since corrosion may eventually occur if water enters the ballast.

With internal ballast, it is a good idea to form waterways in the top so that bilge water will drain to the lowest portion of the hull for pumping overboard. In some cases, a sump can be molded into the top of the ballast for this purpose. It may also be a good idea to not pour all the required ballast, especially if there have been major changes in the locations of weights that could upset the trim or balance of the boat. In this case, save out a portion of the ballast (say 10 to 25%) and launch the boat with all items aboard and positioned as they will be in normal use. If the boat is then out of trim, the extra portion of ballast can be located in the proper location to level out the boat. The top of the ballast, however, should be smooth and arranged so that bilge water will not become trapped. After installation, it should be covered over with a fiberglass laminate that is at least half the total skin thickness for single-skin boats, or at least equal in thickness to the outer skin in sandwich cored hulls. This covering should lap up onto the hull sides by at least several inches and be tied to all adjoining structural members.

CHAPTER 29

tanks

Tanks are mainly used aboard boats for the storage of fuel, water, and waste. Many sizes and types of stock tanks are available from numerous manufacturers made from a variety of materials. Tank materials include steel, aluminum, stainless steel, various copper-bearing alloyed metals, and various types of plastics including fiberglass. In addition, custom-made tanks can be made from most, if not all, of these materials by firms which specialize in the manufacture of tanks. However, manufactured tanks (especially those which are custom made) can be expensive. Because of this, the amateur builder often desires to build his own tanks. Fiberglass thus becomes a natural choice, especially for the builder already working with fiberglass and who is not capable of building his own metal tanks. Fiberglass tanks are lightweight, corrosion-free, and virtually one piece.

Some may question the practice of amateur-built tanks, especially for the storage of fuels such as gasoline. It cannot be over-emphasized that the correct and proper fabrication and installation of fuel tanks and fuel systems is probably the most important safety element aboard a boat, especially where gasoline is used for fuel. Boats are often subjected to conditions which are extreme and hazardous. Thus, tanks and their system components must be able to withstand the exposure of marine service, including the effects of pressure, vibration, shock, and hull movement, as well as attack by oil, gasoline, solvents, grease, corrosion, water, heat, cold, and other adverse elements.

While it may be of questionable practice for the rank amateur who has little or no experience with fiberglass to build fiberglass tanks (especially for gasoline), if one is well along with the fiberglass boatbuilding project BEFORE tanks are tackled, there is little reason NOT to build fiberglass tanks as long as it is done properly. Using the skills already learned and the information provided in this chapter, there is no reason why high-quality, long-lasting tanks cannot be made by the amateur.

GENERAL TANK RECOMMENDATIONS

The approach to tank construction depends somewhat on what will be stored in the tank. Obviously, tanks used for water are not as critical from a safety standpoint as those which contain fuel, especially gasoline. However, just because gasoline is more volatile than diesel fuel does NOT mean that one can be more careless in the fabrication and installation of tanks for diesel use. Diesel fuel tanks need to be equally sound and secure, but there are somewhat less stringent requirements in their specification and design, as will be pointed out.

Although the information presented here is as up to date as possible, the builder should check with local governing authorities (such as the U. S. Coast Guard) for the latest information regarding tanks and fuel systems since requirements can change from time to time. This can save possible headaches later in the project when it might be discovered that something was not done up to par and costly or difficult changes will be called for.

When building a new boat, the locations

of tanks and their sizes or capacities are usually given on the plans or noted by the designer. Capacities and tank locations should be adhered to as closely as possible. If the builder wants to change the capacity or the tank locations, he should first contact the designer for his advice. In most boats, the weight of tanks and their contents is a considerable portion of the total boat weight. Any significant change in location or capacity of tanks can alter not only the weight of the boat, but the balance and perhaps the stability. This can lead to questionable results regarding performance and safety.

Although often seen on boats, especially in the smaller sizes, avoid locating tanks in the forward portion of the boat, especially directly in the bow. Shock loadings and motion are much more pronounced here, and consequently, tanks will be subjected to much greater stresses. Hence, these tanks will require stronger structures, which further aggravates balance problems that arise due to the tank being empty or full. Since a boat is like a teeter-totter with the hull balanced over the center of buoyancy (usually near the center of the boat), tanks are best located as close to the middle of the boat as

possible to negate balance problems caused by varying loads in the tanks. When tanks must be located nearer to the ends of the boat, then some means should be provided for transferring the contents of the tanks from one tank to another to help trim or balance out the boat as fluids are consumed.

All tanks of any size should be fitted with baffles or "slosh plates" between the ends and/or sides. The baffles prevent the surge of the contents from making noise. But more important, they prevent the movement of perhaps a tremendous amount of weight, which could alter the stability and safety of the vessel. Such baffles also provide strength to the tank and keep the sides, top, and bottom from bulging out when loaded. Baffles should be fitted where any distance exceeds about 30″ so that tank intervals will not exceed 20″ maximum, or no more than about three cubic feet in volume between baffles. Limbers or drain passages should be fitted at all corners in baffles for

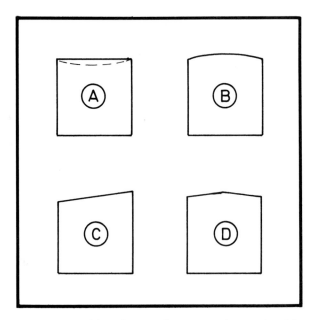

FIG. 29-2 — Although some illustrations show tanks with flat tops for simplicity (as in 'A'), such tanks may droop slightly and tend to trap moisture which can damage tank fittings. Therefore, tank tops should be cambered ('B'), canted ('C'), or domed ('D') so that water, such as from condensation, will drain off.

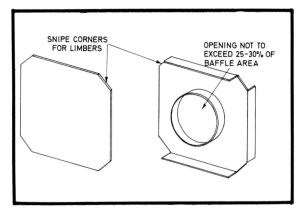

FIG. 29-1 — Baffles prevent surging of the tank contents for safety and minimize noise. Baffles of fiberglass can be solid or open. The open-type shown is stronger unless stiffening is built into the solid baffle. The opening should not exceed 25 to 30% of the baffle area. Baffle thickness should match that of the tank sides.

the passage of air and fluids in the tank. Baffles can be solid or open (see Fig. 29-1), however, open baffles should not have an open area larger than 25% to 30% of the baffle area. Generally, baffles should be of the same thickness and structural specification as the tank sides.

No exterior part of a tank should hold or trap moisture, especially on the top around fittings. Tops should be domed or have cambers, or be canted so that moisture will drain off (see Fig. 29-2). Curved, corrugated, or surfaces that are otherwise NOT flat will

make for a stronger fiberglass tank; however, this may add complexity for the amateur. Fiberglass tanks can be made with flat surfaces, but they must be made thick enough, or be fitted with stiffening members to prevent bulging when full. The American Boat and Yacht Council (ABYC) recommends the following thicknesses as a minimum for solid fiberglass fuel tanks:

TANK CAPACITY

To 60 Gals.	.187″ Thick
60 – 120 Gals.	.250″ Thick
Over 120 Gals.	.300″ Thick

It should be noted, however, that no specific laminate in the above thicknesses is prescribed other than to state that the glass content should be between 30 and 50%. This means that an all-mat laminate may be acceptable; however, for added strength, some other materials having greater tensile strength should be a part of tank laminates. Also, no distinction is noted for surfaces which may be flat or contoured.

Tanks are preferably shaped so that sediment (or water in fuel tanks) will not collect or become trapped at the bottom. One way to eliminate this problem is shown by Fig. 29-3. This detail shows a sediment trap that can be removed from the top of the tank through the fill. Another way to help prevent trapped sediment is to avoid sharply "vee'd" corners at the base of the tank. Instead, make at least a small flat area at the bottom of all tanks.

All tanks should be individually vented. Tank vents are important as they prevent pressure from building up due to expansion with temperature increases and during filling, and allow for pressure equalization as the contents are used.

All tanks should be planned and arranged for future maintenance so that a minimum of the boat's structure is effected. Non-integral tanks should allow for removal and re-

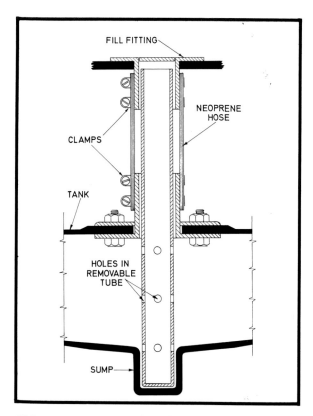

FIG. 29-3 — A sump such as this can be molded into the bottom of many fiberglass fuel tanks where water and dirt can settle. The detail shown (modified from the 1973 edition of Skene's Elements of Yacht Design by Francis Kinney) features a removable tube within the fuel fill that is closed at the bottom. Simply lift the tube out, together with accumulated water and dirt, for cleaning. If the tube is made from fiberglass, it will be easier on the fiberglass tank. Extra laminate thickness at this area is desirable, especially if a metal tube is used; a synthetic rubber pad at the lower end of the tube will protect the tank laminate from damage in this case.

placement. Stress concentrations in mountings should not be allowed at any portion of tanks. Support non-integral tanks on bearers or chocks to prevent movement and to allow air movement around all tank surfaces (see Fig. 29-4). Non-integral tanks should be supported in such a manner that the stresses imparted to the hull are transferred over as broad an area as possible. Hold-down straps are preferable to molded-in mounting lugs or angles in non-integral fiberglass tanks to prevent stress concentrations. These straps should be located near tank ends and baffles, but NOT directly at these points. Hold-down straps should be fitted with "Neoprene"-type cushioning strips between the straps and the tank.

Similar non-abrasive, non-absorbent material should be used between the tank and all chocks.

All tanks should be water or air pressure tested to detect leaks. Fuel tanks should be air pressure tested to at least 3 p.s.i. However, the tank should be allowed to cure for at least 48 hours prior to testing.

SHOULD TANKS BE BUILT IN?

The idea of building tanks integrally with the hull, or "built-in", is an attractive one in the fiberglass boat. Valuable space can be saved and devoted to the accommodations, and the volume of tanks can be increased

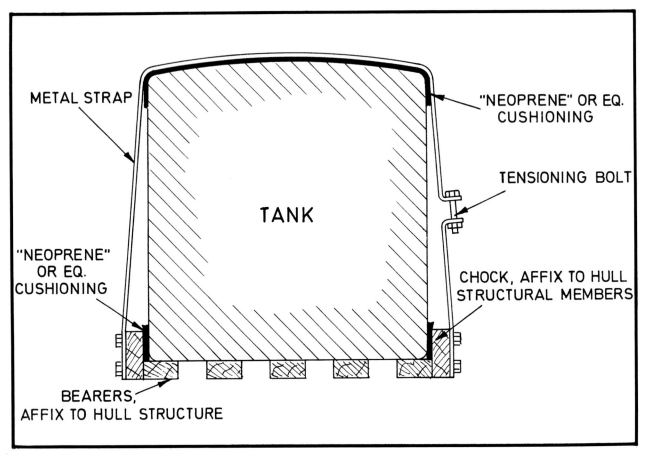

FIG. 29-4 — The general principles for securing and supporting a non-integral tank are shown. Metal straps securing fuel tanks, as well as all metal fuel tank fittings, should be connected to a common ground. Tension on the straps should only be enough to securely hold the tank in place. Note the position of cushioning to relieve the tank from stress concentrations.

over tanks which are non-integral. Whether or not tanks should or can be built in depends on several variables. The choice is not always a simple one, and if integral tanks are used, there are certain precautions and recommendations that should be followed.

What's wrong with integral tanks? First, the presumption is that the fiberglass skin of the hull which will form a surface of the tank is watertight. All fiberglass laminates are hygroscopic at least to a very slight degree; that is, they absorb moisture to a

certain extent, although a good resin-rich surface can keep this within practical limits. If there is a defect of any sort where water could migrate by "wicking" in the laminate, there is a chance for water to enter, and if not contaminate the tank, perhaps taint the contents to some degree. Conversely, there is a chance that the tank will leak, and with gasoline tanks, this could be extremely hazardous.

Another problem is damage to the hull. Given a sufficient collision that could puncture the hull at a vulnerable area, it is

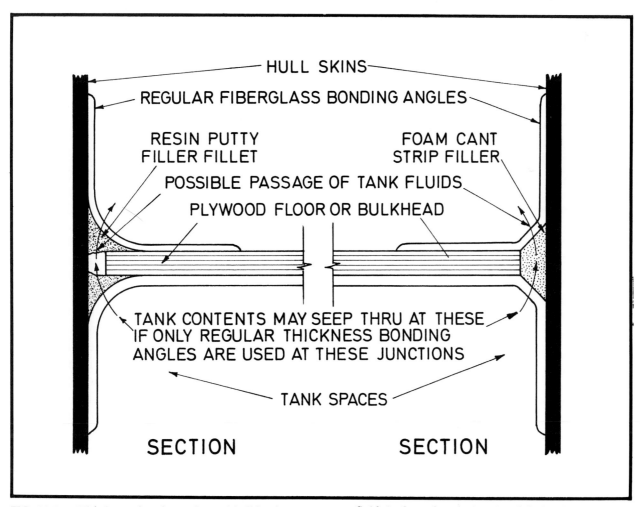

FIG. 29-5 — With integral tanks, a plywood bulkhead or floor may form a tank boundary that is quite strong. However, since the bulkhead or floor should not contact the hull directly in order to prevent forming a "hard spot", there is a possibility for seepage due to the added pressure from the fluids in the tank at the junction if the bonding angle is not thick enough. Therefore, the fiberglass lining of the tank should be that specified to suit the capacity of the tank, AT LEAST IN THE AREA OF THE BONDING ANGLE, so that the tank has the uniform minimum strength at all points.

possible that all fuel could be lost, even though the vessel may not be sink. But worse, if a collision causes a failure at the wrong spot, puncturing or rupturing the tank surface exposed in the bilge, it is possible to flood the bilges with fuel. Obviously this would be an extremely dangerous situation, especially if the engine or other heat-producing appliances were in operation. Furthermore, integral tanks cannot be replaced if there is a defect, and correcting such defects may be impractical. Correcting damage can also be difficult, especially where fuel tanks are concerned, since tank surfaces will be contaminated with products that do not bond to resin. Hence, repairs may not be effectual unless careful procedures are followed and the tank again tested after repairing.

Because of the preceding, integral tanks for gasoline should never be used. Most standards-making organizations simply do not allow the practice. Building in gasoline tanks may make buying insurance impos-

sible and it would surely detract from resale value. Integral tanks for diesel fuel, water, and waste are used, but some still question the practice in light of the preceding points.

While integral tanks may seem to be a simple solution, there are certain technicalities that add to their complexity. For example, if the hull has a sandwich core, integral tanks should not be used. If there is any seepage at all in the tank, the fluids in the tank will tend to migrate into the core. This is especially critical with fuel since prolonged exposure may damage the core and/or the bond to the skins, as well as making repairs difficult and costly.

Another complication with integral tanks is with stiffeners that may pass through the tanks. The general recommendation is that no stiffeners should penetrate tank boundaries so that the tank contents will not find a path out of the tank via the enclosed "tunnel" created by the stiffeners. This is especially important, for example, where a stiffener may pass through a fuel tank and a water tank, or through a water tank and a waste holding tank. There is also a problem at tank ends and baffles which may also form floors and bulkheads. Since these structural members should not be hard-pressed against the hull in order to avoid "hard spots", there is a minor gap (see Fig. 29-5) forming a void here as well as a thinner laminate at the bonding angle that could cause problems if there was a leak through the tank surface (unless additional fiberglass is applied). Furthermore, a foam cant strip at this point should also be avoided for the same reason that sandwich cored hulls should not be used with integral tanks.

If integral tanks are used, they must be separated by void spaces (called "cofferdams") between tanks containing dissimilar fluids (see Fig. 29-6). Such tanks should never share a common boundary since contamination will always be a danger. With a cofferdam, if there is a leak, it will be easier to detect and there will be no chance of

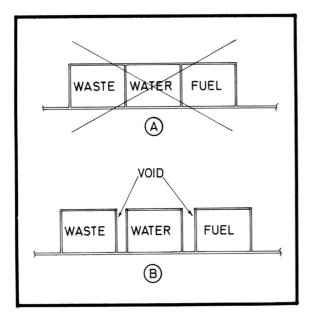

FIG. 29-6 — Integral tanks containing different fluids should not share common boundaries as in 'A'. If there is any seepage at all, the contents of the adjoining tank will become contaminated or tainted. Therefore, such tanks should be separated by void spaces as shown in 'B'.

contamination. Another problem with built-in tanks is that it is more difficult to post-cure the tank. This will be discussed later, but tanks which are not post-cured sufficiently will effect the taste and odor of drinking water. Because of these added complexities, many elect to install separate tanks and avoid integral tanks. The choice is up to the builder.

TANK SPECIFICATIONS

Fiberglass tanks for fuel will vary somewhat depending on whether they are for diesel fuel or gasoline. As noted, diesel tanks can be integral with the hull or separate; however, gasoline tanks should never be integral. In either case, the entire fuel system should be able to withstand fire from an external source for at least several minutes, and the entire fuel system should be liquid and vapor-tight. For TOTAL fire protection, this means that fire-retardant resins should be used throughout the construction of fiberglass tanks. Some builders try to short-cut this requirement by just coating the outside of fuel tanks with fire-retardant resin, paints, or other similar products. But the effectiveness of this practice, especially in machinery spaces, is questionable, although better than no protection at all. While either ortho or iso resins can be used to make tanks, the iso type is advised because of its higher corrosion resistance (this applies to BOTH fuel and water tanks; resin suppliers state that polyester resins once cured are non-toxic).

Tanks used for gasoline should have no openings or fittings in the bottom, sides, or ends. Clean-out plates of metal or fiberglass can be installed in tanks for diesel fuel, but these are preferably installed on top of the tank (see Fig. 29-7). Such clean-out plates or access holes should be provided for each baffled space and be at least 5″ in diameter, or a larger plate can be centered over a baffle to allow access to the space on either side. Some prefer to make the entire tank top removable (see Fig. 29-8); this is recommended only for smaller tanks not used for gasoline. While clean-out plates are not specifically recommended for gasoline tanks (which means that there is no practical way to gain access to the inside), it is always possible to cut an opening through the top and later remold and repair with fiberglass to restore the tank's integrity.

It is important that the inside surfaces of fiberglass tanks be resin-rich. This is best done by having a sufficient thickness of mat in the laminate adjacent to the inside surface. For example, the ABS recommends that the inside of fuel tanks shall be a minimum of 2 oz. mat total IN ADDITION to the tank skin thickness used for strength purposes alone. Lloyd's also specifies a 2 oz. mat layer thickness as the first inside layer, and some builders apply additional resin after the tank has been built as added insurance that all pinholes and voids are completely filled and covered with resin. The ABYC states that the interior resin coating should be not less than 20 mils (.020″) thick. Furthermore, any fiberglass used inside the tank, such as for bonding angles at baffles, must be equally covered and saturated with resin.

Fittings for fuel tanks should be located on top of the tank. However, tanks for diesel use are sometimes fitted with drain cocks at the bottom as well as with sight glass tubes with cocks, but these practices may be frowned upon by some authorities and underwriters. Because fiberglass is translucent, such sight glasses or fuel gauges may not be necessary to check the fuel level in fiberglass tanks. For additional information on fuel systems, vents, fills, and fittings, see the Bibliography for texts which discuss these subjects.

Exposed edges of the tank laminate at any openings made for fittings must be sealed and coated with resin. Metal fittings should be mechanically fastened to tanks and NOT merely bonded (see Fig. 29-9). Such bonds,

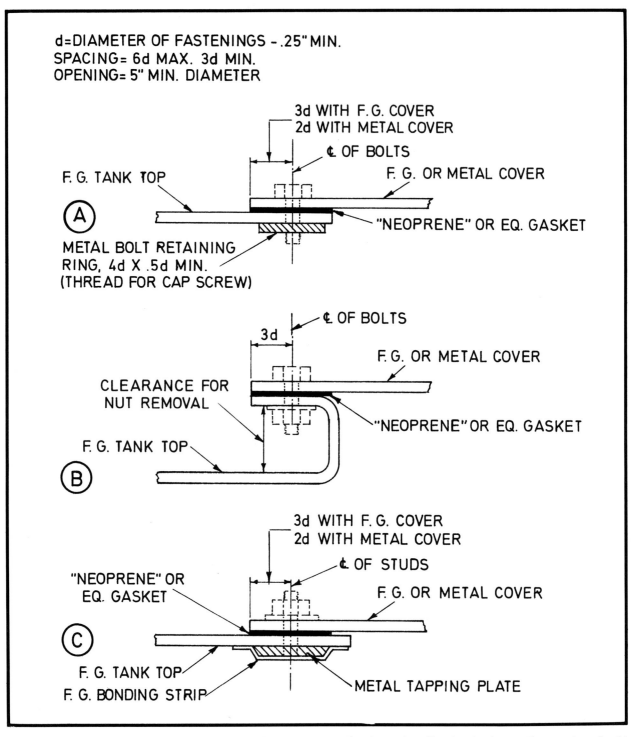

d=DIAMETER OF FASTENINGS – .25" MIN.
SPACING= 6d MAX. 3d MIN.
OPENING= 5" MIN. DIAMETER

3d WITH F.G. COVER
2d WITH METAL COVER
¢ OF BOLTS
F. G. OR METAL COVER
F. G. TANK TOP
"NEOPRENE" OR EQ. GASKET
(A)
METAL BOLT RETAINING
RING, 4d X .5d MIN.
(THREAD FOR CAP SCREW)

¢ OF BOLTS
3d
F. G. OR METAL COVER
CLEARANCE FOR
NUT REMOVAL
"NEOPRENE" OR EQ. GASKET
F. G. TANK TOP
(B)

3d WITH F.G. COVER
2d WITH METAL COVER
¢ OF STUDS
"NEOPRENE" OR
EQ. GASKET
F. G. OR METAL COVER
(C)
F. G. TANK TOP
F. G. BONDING STRIP
METAL TAPPING PLATE

FIG. 29-7 — There are several ways to make access holes in fiberglass tanks. The details show recommendations of the ABS. Several points should be noted. Screws and bolts bearing against fiberglass should NOT be countersunk. The diameter of bolts or machine screws should NOT be less than the thinner of the joined fiberglass parts (¼" minimum). Washers are advisable under bolt heads and nuts bearing against fiberglass laminates. These washers should be at least 2.25 × 'd' in diameter and .10 × 'd' in thickness. In 'A', a hex head cap screw threads into a metal retaining ring. In 'B', the plate is bolted in place. In 'C', studs fit into a metal tapping plate with nuts being used to secure the plate. Locking nuts or washers are recommended in all cases.

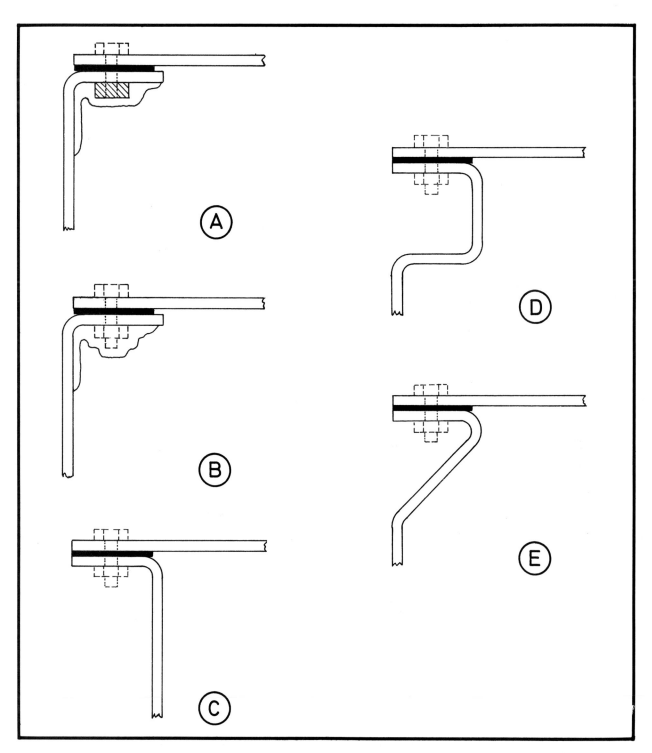

FIG. 29-8 — Several methods of making removable tank tops are shown. A "Neoprene" or equivalent gasket is used between the top and flange. The flange in all cases should be about 2″ to 3″ in width. Fastening size and spacing can be the same as that specified for access plates. Removable tank tops, however, are NOT recommended for gasoline tanks. In 'A', a tapped metal strip is bonded under the flange with fiberglass mat. A simpler method uses nuts bonded in place under the flange as shown in 'B'. The outside flange in 'C' gives easy access to the nuts, however, it does take up some added space. To save space, either 'D' or 'E' can be used, however, these will require a somewhat more elaborate mold to allow for the recess.

even with epoxy resins, are questionable and bonding may make replacement of such fittings difficult or impractical. While the builder may make his own fittings, complete fuel fittings assemblies may be available from tank manufacturers as "replace-ment" fittings for their stock tanks. These can usually be adapted in most cases to fiberglass tanks (see Fig. 29-10).

Tanks that are rectangular or have specially shaped contours should have rounded corners. While the ABYC recommends at least a 1" inside radius, this is not always practical with all building methods described. However, the builder should strive to make the corners as gentle in radius as possible; this makes the tank stronger, easier to maintain, and minimizes chances for leaks. Tank tops should lap onto the tank shell with a minimum of 2" overlap. If flanges are used to receive the tank top, these should also be 2" wide. Any areas of secondary bonding should be clean and rough sanded. Bonded lapped joints should be bedded in strips of resin-saturated mat at least 2" wide if parts are to be permanently bonded. For removable parts, such as clean-out plates, bed these in mastic that will not taint the contents of water tanks, or use "Neoprene"-type gaskets for fuel tanks. Ordinary rubber gaskets should not be used

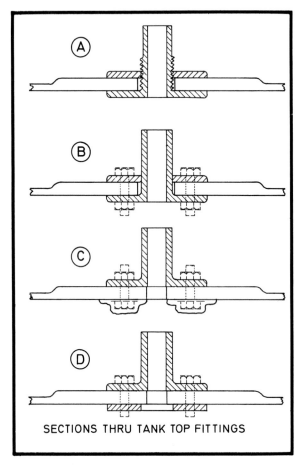

SECTIONS THRU TANK TOP FITTINGS

FIG. 29-9 — Several methods for installing fittings on fiber-glass tanks are shown. Such fittings may be installed through fiberglass tank tops or access plates. In either case, the laminate should be doubled in thickness in the area equal to twice the diameter of the fitting. Fittings which are only bonded in place (even with epoxy resin) are NOT rec-ommended; they should be mechanically secured. Fittings should be bedded in mastic or with "Neoprene" or equiva-lent gaskets between the laminate surfaces and the fittings for fuel tanks. The edges of the openings through the lami-nate should be well coated with resin. A threaded compres-sion fitting is shown by 'A', while 'B' shows a bolted type of compression fitting. In 'C', cap screws are bonded with fiberglass to the underside to form studs that are used to bolt the fitting. In 'D', a threaded retaining ring bonded to the underside receives cap screws that hold the fitting. For gasoline tanks with no openings and non-removable tops, either 'C' or 'D' will allow easy replacement of the fitting.

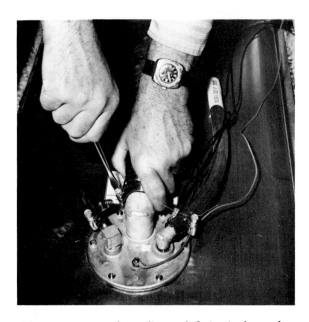

FIG. 29-10 — A stock gasoline tank fitting is shown that includes the fill, vent, ground, fuel gauge sender, and supply lines all in one. Such fittings are available on a parts basis and are adaptable to a fiberglass tank made by the builder.

for fuel tanks as they will deteriorate.

Fiberglass tanks should be thoroughly cured after fabrication, or "post-cured". This is especially important in the case of fresh water tanks for odor and taste protection. It is the volatization of the resin (especially the styrene portion) that makes fresh water become tainted, and this diminishes with curing. Several methods can be used to speed this curing process, and this is what "post-curing" means. While some builders do not post-cure tanks (letting time do the job), it is easy to speed the process. One way is to set the tank in the sun for a few days. Another way is to apply heat to about 145 degrees for about 3 hours. Some use steam inside the tank, and if the clean-out plate in the tank is large enough, an electric kettle or coffee pot filled with water set to boiling can accelerate curing in a matter of hours (however, make sure that the water does not boil away and create a fire hazard). If taste and odors persist, there are any number of "cures", ranging from products that can be bought, to filling the tank and draining with solutions of water mixed with chlorine bleach or baking soda.

MAKING FIBERGLASS TANKS

Fiberglass tanks can be all-fiberglass or fiberglass-covered plywood. In this latter instance, the plywood may be totally encapsulated with fiberglass, but some builders have left the plywood bare on the outside, with fiberglass used only on the inside of the tank. In either case, the plywood portions become the strength members and fiberglass laminates need not be as thick as previously noted. This type of tank is literally a plywood tank that has a fiberglass lining. Although plywood will make strong tanks, and the flat surfaces will be stiffer and lighter than all-fiberglass tanks, this practice is not advised for fuel tanks, since the plywood becomes more like a core material and possibly susceptible to the

problems discussed earlier when cores are used in tank structures. Such tanks are appealing to the amateur because they are cheap and easy to make.

All-fiberglass tanks can be made OVER a male mold former or INSIDE a female mold (see Chapter 31). The male mold method is recommended whenever it is suitable since it is easier to get a smooth, resin-rich inner surface. Other than this quality, there is little preference between the two methods. Baffles are placed in the tanks after the basic "box" has been made in either method.

Another way to make tanks is to prefabricate sheets of solid fiberglass laminate to form the sides, tops, ends, and baffles. The fiberglass sheets are composed of pieces of mat laid up over flat sheet material such as sealed plywood, "Masonite", melamine-coated hardboard, "Formica", or even strong glass. The surfaces should be coated with several layers of wax first. Then apply several layers of mat against the sheet surface and wet out with resin. The pieces of mat can be cut to the size required. Once the resin is applied and worked in with a mat roller, the pieces will expand in size a slight amount and this will provide enough material extra for trimming to the net size required. It is not necessary to make the sheets to the total required thickness initially; additional layers of the laminate can be applied on the outside of the tank after it has been assembled enough to form a "box" without the lid.

Fig. 29-11 shows the construction of a tank using prefabricated sheets and bonding angles. Prefabricated bonding angles can be made from mat layers using a light metal angle as a former (see Fig. 29-12). The chart shown in Chapter 8 giving thicknesses for various materials can be used to determine what combination of material will make a laminate of suitable thickness for the tank sides. This thickness can be made up from alternating layers of mat and woven roving or cloth; however, use enough mat against the initial surface to meet the requirements

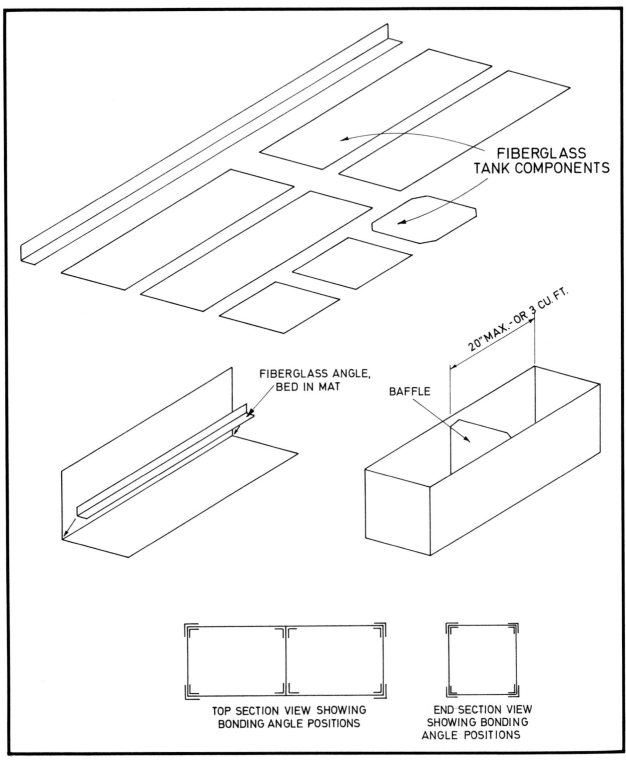

FIBERGLASS
TANK COMPONENTS

20" MAX.- OR 3 CU. FT.

FIBERGLASS ANGLE,
BED IN MAT

BAFFLE

TOP SECTION VIEW SHOWING
BONDING ANGLE POSITIONS

END SECTION VIEW
SHOWING BONDING
ANGLE POSITIONS

FIG. 29-11 — Construction of a simple rectangular tank using prefabricated sheets and bonding angles made from fiberglass. The prefabricated bonding angles (see Fig. 29-12) bedded in mat are used to join the components together. Additional bonding angles made up in place over the outside are applied later. The sections show the positions of all the bonding angle members. Alternately, the bonding angles can be made up in place using layers of resin-saturated mat. Methods for installing the top of this tank are shown in Fig. 29-13, while baffles are installed as shown in Fig. 29-14.

noted previously (mat layers are ALWAYS used inside before any other type of reinforcement). Apply resin to the mold sheet surface first, then the mat, and wet out. Two or three layers of mat can be saturated this way in one shot.

After the tank components have been built up sufficiently thick for rigidity, the pieces can be lifted from the mold surface (use a putty knife if they tend to stick), trimmed, and cut to size. The pieces are then ready for assembly. For tanks with squared sides and corners, set one piece flat and hold in place. Then erect an adjoining side along the edge at 90 degrees. Use a couple of framing squares or wood "jigs" clamped in place to check and maintain angularity. Then use the prefabricated bonding angles or strips of mat about 4″ wide for bonding angles made in place to join the two pieces (the mating areas should be rough-sanded beforehand to assure a sound bond). This procedure is followed for

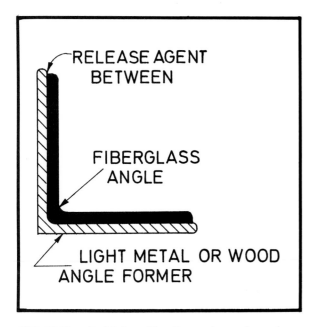

FIG. 29-12 — Prefabricated bonding angles can be made up of resin-saturated mat layers using a wood or light metal angle about 2″ × 2″ of length to suit. Apply wax to the angle as a release agent first. Such angles are suitable for joining flat sheet tank components at the inside corners of fiberglass tanks having square corners.

all the sides until a somewhat flimsy "box" is formed. Note that prefabricated bonding angle are bedded in resin-saturated mat.

Technically, the inside corners should be filleted or radiused. However, the lack of an inner radius will be compensated for partly on the outside, since the outside corners are radiused instead. Then apply a couple of strips of mat around the outside corners. Next build up the exterior of the tank with additional laminate, which should include some woven materials for added strength.

The drawings show two ways that angle flanges can be made on the tank for securing the tank top (see Fig. 29-13). Outwardly turned flanges are best if bolts are used to secure the tank tops, since the fastenings are easy to get at. However, the inward flange takes up less room.

The baffles and tank top can be made the same way as the other tank components. Baffles can be bonded in with bonding angles or fitted with flanges that are bedded in mat and then bonded in (see Fig. 29-14). In either case, baffles should have bonding angles on both sides. Tank tops can be bonded in place or bolted to be removable (except for gasoline tanks). Note that wherever secondary bonding will occur, the surfaces should be sanded to roughen them up a bit, and then wiped clean with a solvent wash.

Before applying the tank top, clean out the tank. Then install the tank top, preferably with the fittings pre-installed. Some builders pour a nominal amount of resin into the tank after completion as insurance against any pinholes or voids; this is optional. If clean-out plates are required in lieu of a removable top, these can be made per the detail shown by Fig. 29-9. Where fittings will be located, double the thickness of the laminate in way of the fitting and make this double thickness area about twice the diameter of the fitting in size to relieve any stress loads. With fittings as well as clean-out plates, use take-up washers or fastenings which compress the fiber-

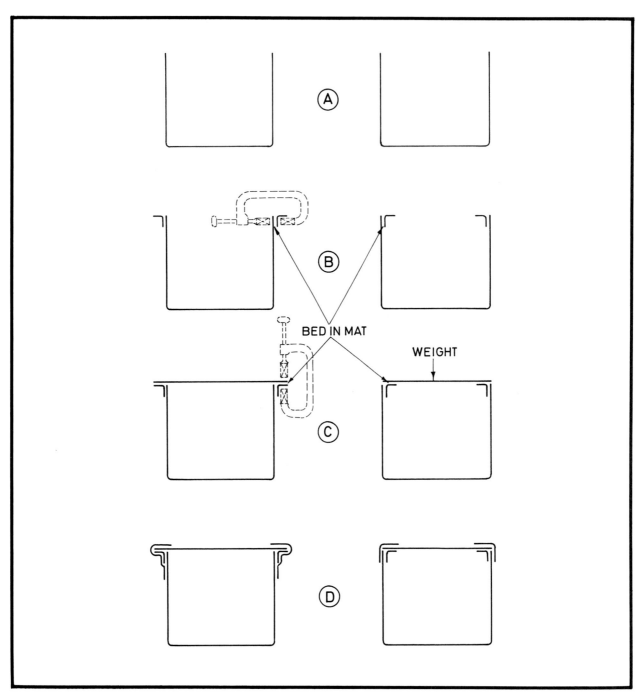

FIG. 29-13. — Two variations are shown for attaching tops to fiberglass tanks. The basic tank as shown in 'A' can be made from fiberglass sheet components, molded IN a female mold, or molded OVER a male mold to form the basic open "box". Prefabricated bonding angles forming flanges are located at the top, facing either inside or outside the tank to suit ('B'). These are bedded in mat and clamped in place. A couple of lengths of wood on edge and several "C"-clamps are used to provide a positive secondary bond for the bonding angle flange. If the tank will have a removable top, attach the top per Fig. 29-8, A, B, or C. The prefabricated fiberglass sheet tank top can then be bonded in place (if of the non-removable type) after the baffles have been installed using clamps or weights until the resin sets ('C'). If access holes are not provided (to allow access for applying molded-in bonding angles joining the top to the baffles), the baffles should preferably have flanges at the top so that resin-saturated mat strips can be used to bond the top to the baffles. After the top has been applied, additional bonding angles of resin-saturated mat are used on the outside to complete the job. Extra care should be given at the top corners to assure a tight tank that won't leak.

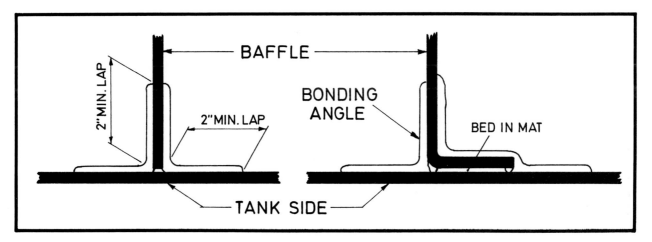

FIG. 29-14 — The joining of two types of baffles to fiberglass tanks is shown. The fiberglass bonding angles (which may be made up in place or of the prefabricated type) should be located on BOTH sides of the baffles. Their combined thickness should be equal to that of the tank sides. If prefabri- cated bonding angles are used, these should be bedded in resin-saturated mat. Don't worry about using too much resin on the inside of tanks; plenty of resin should be used at these junctions to assure a positive bond, seal the fiberglass material, and assure a leak-proof tank.

glass laminate from BOTH sides and do not depend on fastenings just in the laminate. Bed these fittings in mastic or "Neoprene"-type gaskets for fuel tanks.

Throughout the tank-making procedures, laminating resin is used. Care must be exercised to eliminate any bubbles in any part of the tank. Although some sanding will be required in certain areas, finish resin (which contains wax) is not advised because of potential bonding problems and because it may not be possible to remove the wax from inside the tank before use. Finish resin, however, can be used on the final coating on the EXTERIOR surfaces if desired; but if the tank is post-cured, the resin will eventually set up virtually tack-free regardless.

Integral tanks can be made similarly to the preceding. The only difference is that templates will have to be made to determine the contours of the tank surfaces which adjoin the hull. The required parts are made that same way, but they are installed in place in the hull. Cardboard or hardboard templates can be used to determine the shapes of the required parts, and these are then cut to shape and marked around the perimeter directly onto the flat molding surface; this shows the boundaries of the tank part that will be required. A precise fit is not absolutely critical; any discrepancies can be taken up with the bonding angles. With tank sides and ends for integral tanks, however, the bonding angles should be built up in thickness to equal that used for the sides and ends.

Non-integral tanks built over or inside molds are made using simple laminating procedures once a mold is made up. Simple straight-surfaced molds are shown in Chapter 31. More complex shapes are possible, but take more effort. While a female mold is acceptable, the inside corners should be built up with radiused fillets. This is more work than rounding corners over a male mold, and the surface of the tank on the inside will be smoother with the male mold. In either case, flanges can be molded into the tank as shown. Baffles and tank tops are made the same way as noted before. If sufficient draft is not incorporated into the mold, it may be necessary to break up the mold in either case. This won't usually matter unless several tanks of the same configuration are required.

There are numerous ways to make deck and cabin structures using several different materials. Fiberglass decks and cabins can be made from solid laminates or with sandwich cores. Deck and cabin structures using fiberglass can be made over male molds, in female molds, and directly in place in the hull using temporary mold or forming members. It is also possible to build cabins using prefabricated fiberglass components which are later assembled in place on the boat. Finally, conventional wood and plywood structures are commonly used for deck and cabin structures on hulls built in fiberglass. Although there are all these dif-ferent approaches for building the hull superstructure, the plans being used no doubt will show a certain method. This probably does not mean that deviations are not possible, but the builder may wish to contact the designer first if any major changes are contemplated.

It should be emphasized that the deck and cabin are important strength members in the boat, and therefore their construction should not be compromised. The superstructure gives considerable stiffness and strength to the hull and can be subjected to considerable forces. Such loads include the weight of crew members jumping onto the

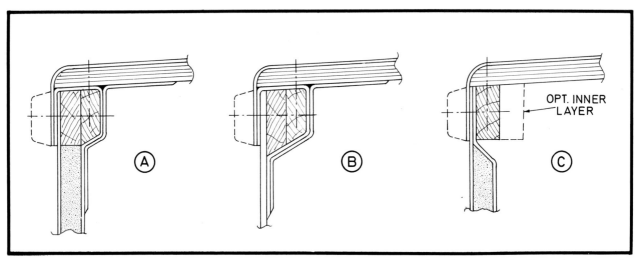

FIG. 30-1 — Several sections through hull-to-deck joints are shown using plywood decks and wood sheer clamps. In 'A', a sandwich cored hull is shown, with the layer of the wood sheer clamp against the outer skin installed when the hull is built. The second layer can be installed after the hull is righted, and the whole encapsulated in place. 'B' is similar, but the hull is single skin fiberglass; the members can be installed before or after the hull is righted. In both cases, note the bonding angle applied later, joining the hull to the deck on the inside. The deck is bedded in wet mat or resin putty after grinding the mating edge flat, and mechanically fastened to the sheer clamp. The rub rail is then bolted in place, securing the deck mechanically to the hull. See Fig. 30-4 for bolt size and spacing, and bonding angle overlap recommendations. In 'C', the sheer clamp is installed after the hull is righted; an additional sheer clamp lamination may be optional. In this case, the deck is glued and fastened to the sheer clamp. Although a sandwich core is shown, this detail would be similar with a single skin hull.

deck from the dock; loads from the shrouds, sheets, and halyards; anchor loads from the windlass; loads transferred from mooring cleats; and the tremendous potential forces imposed by seas breaking onto decks and cabins. The latter should not be underestimated if the boat is intended for open water use. Hence, the structure and all junctions in the deck and cabin, and the connections to the hull and bulkheads, should be carefully made for strength and watertight integrity.

SHEER CLAMPS

The foundation member often used for attaching the deck to the fiberglass hull is the sheer clamp (sometimes referred to as the "shelf clamp," "deck clamp," or "deck shelf"). The sheer clamp is usually made from wood and is located on the inside of the hull at the sheer (for discussion purposes, the sheer is the point where the deck joins the hull, although this is not always technically the case).

The sheer clamp can be made from a single layer of wood or laminated in two or more layers depending on the curvature of the hull, the mass required, etc. In many cases, the sheer clamp will be laminated in place as the hull is built. In other cases, it can be installed permanently after the hull has been righted and the mold removed. In this latter instance, a temporary stiffener will probably have to be installed either in-

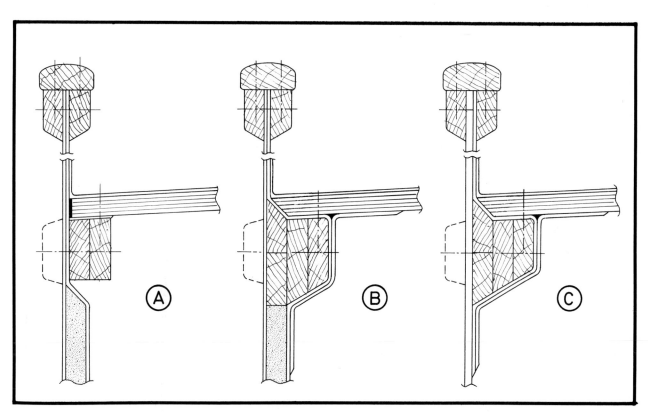

FIG. 30-2 — Several sections through hull-to-deck joints are shown on hulls having raised bulwarks using plywood decks and wood sheer clamps. 'A' is different from 'B' and 'C' because the sheer clamp layers are not encapsulated with fiberglass; the plywood deck is glued and fastened in place instead of being bonded in place with fiberglass or resin putty, and fastened. The sheer clamp in 'A' is installed after the hull is righted, but in 'B', the sheer clamp layer against the outer skin is applied when the hull is upside-down. In 'C', the sheer clamp can be installed before or after the hull is righted.

side or outside, or on both sides of the hull, clamped or temporarily fastened along the sheer for rigidity until the permanent sheer clamp is installed.

The wood sheer clamp (or first layer of the laminated sheer clamp member) can be bonded in place to the inside of the hull in a resin-saturated mat layer or generous bedding of resin putty or epoxy glue. Use clamps to clamp the member in place if numerous clamps are available, or screws driven through the hull from the outside into the sheer clamp member. Note that these screws are not structural; they are used to hold the sheer clamp in place with suitable pressure until the resin sets. Thus, they can be a flat-head type slightly countersunk, or a round or pan-head type that can be removed later, if an outer rub rail is bolted through the sheer clamp.

If the member will be laminated, subsequent laminations can be glued and fastened to the first layer. In some cases, a sheer clamp can be laminated from layers of

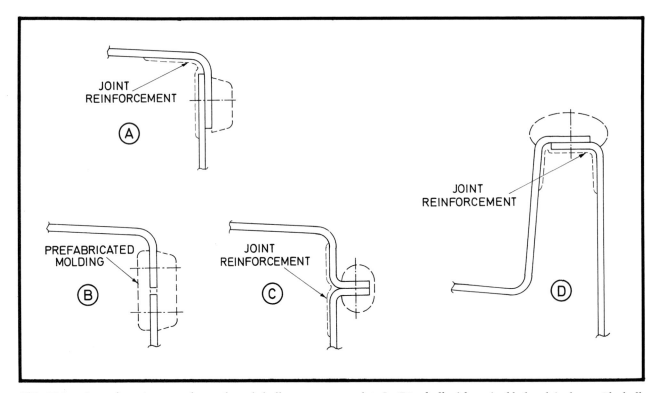

FIG. 30-3 — Several sections are shown through hull-to-deck joints on single skin hulls using pre-molded decks. Most of these junctions are best adapted to female moldings due to the rather precise fits required for a quality junction. In 'A', a simple "shoe box" lid method is shown. A rub rail is added on the outside for protection and sometimes serves as part of the mechanical joining method for joining the two parts. In 'B', the hull and deck are joined with a special metal rub rail extrusion that mechanically joins the two parts together; this method may best be done in the factory situation with the smaller boat since repairing or replacing the extrusion may not be practical without endangering the integrity of the junction. A positive seal using elastomeric sealant is a necessity. In 'C', the hull and deck are joined wtih mating flanges which are protected by a rub rail mold- **ing. In 'D', a hull with a raised bulwark is shown. The hull and deck have a lapped flanged similar to the joint in 'A'. The return flange on the hull molding may add to the difficulty of making a female mold, possibly requiring the use of a split mold to remove the hull. After joining the parts together, the junction at the top of the bulwark can be capped with a wood rail. In all cases except 'B', note the fiberglass joint reinforcement on the inside of the hull. Ideally, any protective rails at hull-to-deck junctions should be removable for repair or replacement without endangering the integrity of the junction. Elastomeric marine sealants are usually generously applied at all such junctions. See Fig. 30-4 for bolt sizes and spacing, and bonding angle overlap recommendations.**

plywood. The plywood sheer clamp technically should be nearly double the thickness of a solid wood member or laminated member to compensate for the loss of strength created by the cross plies. One advantage of plywood is that the member will have better dimensional stability once encapsulated. But if plywood decks will be fastened into the plywood sheer clamp, the screws will be going into the edge grain of the plywood, and there will be very little holding power in this situation.

The top edge of the sheer clamp will usually have to be faired for flat mating to the underside of the deck. The sheer clamp can then be covered over on the inside with fiberglass. Usually the underside of encapsulated sheer clamps are bevelled, with the corners radiused so the fiberglass will conform easily around the contours. The sheer clamp is then bonded and encapsulated with fiberglass lapping generously onto the inside of the hull. If the deck structure joining the sheer clamp will be fiberglass, the sheer clamp can be totally encapsulated with fiberglass. If plywood decks will be used, the top surface of the wood sheer clamp can be bare wood for gluing the deck to the sheer clamp, or the sheer clamp can be encapsulated with fiberglass as noted previously. In this latter case the mating surface between the encapsulated sheer clamp and deck should be ground smooth for a firm fit to the deck. Bed the deck in mat or resin putty and fasten to the sheer clamp.

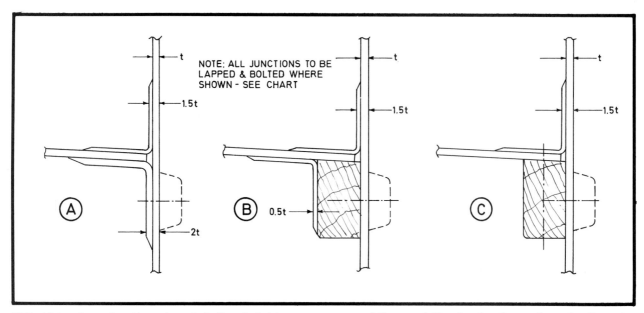

FIG. 30-4 — Several sections through hull-to-deck joints are shown with single skin hulls having raised bulwarks and fiberglass decks. The proportions and following recommendations are based on ABS rules and can be used as guidelines. In 'A', the deck is bonded in place with bonding angles only. In 'B', the deck is also bonded in place, but to a wood sheer clamp. In 'C', the deck is mechanically fastened as well as bonded to a wood clamp. Such joints should be protected on the outside by a protective rail. The joining surfaces of deck moldings to hulls should be set in elastomeric bedding compound, resin putty, or equivalent material for a tight fit. Below are recommendations for bolt spacings, diameters, and the minimum widths of overlaps and flanges of fiberglass bonding angles or bonding reinforcements at hull-to-deck joints. The proportions at junctions should be to the minimum shown in this illustration for female molded single skin hulls.

| | MAX. BOLT SPACING | | | MIN. OVERLAP OR |
LENGTH	Unrestricted Service	Limited Service	MIN. BOLT DIA.	FLANGE WIDTH
30'	6"	9"	.25"	2.5"
40'	6.5"	9.5"	.30"	3"
50'	7"	10"	.35"	3.5"
60'	7.5"	10.5"	.40"	4"

DECK BEAMS

Athwartship deck beams may be required to support the deck, especially if wood decks are used. These can be joined at the sheer clamps by several methods which are shown by Fig. 30-5. One way is to make a beveled notch into the sheer clamp, apply glue, and drive a screw in angularly through the deck beam and into the sheer clamp. However, such notches into the sheer clamp will tend to weaken the sheer member, so it should be thick enough (or have enough laminations) to overcome this weakening. If plywood is used for the deck, considerable strength will be regained along the sheer after the deck has been applied, perhaps compensating for any weakening of the sheer clamp that may occur by notching.

On smaller, lighter boats, deck beams are sometimes butted to the sheer clamps and bonded in place with layers of fiberglass mat and/or cloth. In other cases of light duty use, the deck beams are blocked to the sheer clamp. In this method, wood blocking is glued and fastened against the sheer clamp, and the ends of the deck beams fastened to these. A third way to join deck beams to fiberglass boats is to install a plywood or wood bracket bonded and encapsulated in position to the hull. The deck beam then laps to this bracket and can be bolted or screwed in place. The camber (top curva-

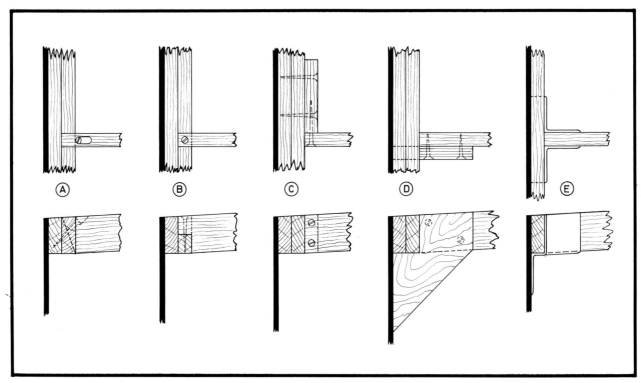

FIG. 30-5 — Several methods are shown for joining wood deck beams to fiberglass hulls. All examples use wood sheer clamps. In 'A', using a laminated sheer clamp, the inner layer of the sheer clamp is bevel-notched for the deck beam and screwed as shown. In 'B', the inner layer of the sheer clamp and the end of the deck beam are joined in a half-notch and screwed as shown. In 'C', blocking is fastened to the inside of the sheer clamp and the deck beam is fastened to this. In 'D', a wood bracket or gusset has been bonded to the hull with fiberglass bonding angles similar to that shown in Fig. 30-6, with the deck beam lapping and fastening to this bracket. In 'E', the deck beam has been butted to the sheer clamp and bonded in place using fiberglass bonding angles. This latter method and that shown in 'A' are best suited to smaller boats subjected to light-duty use. All junctions joining wood-to-wood should also be glued as well as fastened.

ture) of the deck beams (as well as for the cabin top) may be given by a full-size pattern or can be determined from the loftings. The method for developing a deck beam is illustrated by Fig. 30-9 and Fig. 30-10.

LAID DECKS

Many builders want the beauty and practicality of wood decks, such as teak, even aboard fiberglass boats, and are willing to bear the additional cost. However, unless the deck is framed by traditional wood methods and planked with thick, solid planks (expensive and heavy), or laid in the form of a "veneer" over a plywood sub-deck, the results are often less than satisfactory and sometimes impractical. The problems of attempting to lay a wood-veneered deck (particularly teak) over a fiberglass substructure are numerous and complex.

First, the fiberglass deck and wood are rather hard, unyielding materials. The fiberglass deck may not be completely true and flat, yet the bond between the two must

FIG. 30-6 — A plywood bracket has been bonded to the inside of this fiberglass hull. Such a bracket can be used to support a deck beam or chainplates in a sailboat. Note the bevel on the lower edge of the sheer clamp which has not yet been encapsulated in place.

FIG. 30-7 — These deck beams lap to wood brackets which have been bonded to the inside of the hull. Note the sheer clamp which has been encapsulated in place to receive the plywood deck.

FIG. 30-8 — Another view of the hull shown in Fig. 30-7. Note the beams and deck battens which will support the plywood deck and cabin structure.

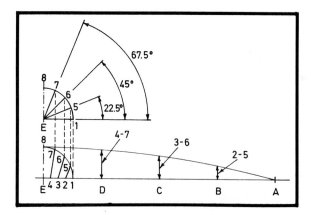

FIG. 30-9 — If a full size pattern is not given for the deck or cabin camber, or if working from lofted lines, this method can be used to develope the camber as follows:

A—E = Distance from sheer to centerline.

8—E = Height of deck crown

A—E is divided into 4 equal parts so that AB = BC = CD = DE. Erect perpendiculars along line A—E at points E, D, C, and B.

Draw arc 1—8 with 8—E as the radius.

Divide arc 1—8 into 4 equal segments so that 1—5 = 5—6 = 6—7 = 7—8.

Divide 1—E into 4 equal parts so that 1—2 = 2—3 = 3—4 = 4—E.

Layout distance 4—7 on perpendicular at D; 3—6 at C, and 2—5 to B.

Use batten to fair in arc 8—A.

Using same distances between E, D, C, B, and A, layout other side of beam or camber.

be as firm and tight as possible. Second, to make a practical join, BOTH a bonding adhesive and mechanical fastenings are required. If the fiberglass deck is not a true flat surface, either the deck will attempt to flex to conform to the wood (assuming that thick stock is used), or the wood will attempt to conform to the perhaps "wavy" surface of the deck (assuming a thin veneer is used that will not overcome the stiffness of the fiberglass deck). Either way, a poor bond may result, the deck may work and eventually leak, and the job may not look good. Furthermore, if there is any chance of working or flexing at all, only an elastomeric adhesive should be used for bonding and at the joints between the planks. A rigid adhesive (even many epoxies) may crack and fail, particularly with teak since it is one of the most difficult woods for bonding. If the wood deck is fastened through the fiberglass subsurface, and there is working at the bond between the teak and the fiberglass, the fastening holes through the fiber-

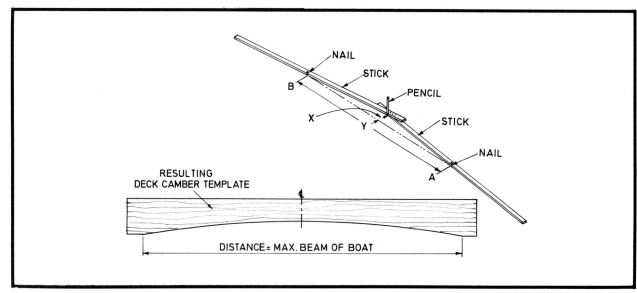

FIG. 30-10 — A method for striking an arc for a deck or cabin beam is shown as follows:

1. Draw line A—B to distance 'Y' which is the width of the beam required.
2. At midpoint of 'Y', erect a perpendicular 'X'. Height of 'X' is amount of crown required.

3. Drive nails at points 'A' and 'B'. Use two sticks sufficiently longer than 'Y'. Fasten sticks securely together where shown.
4. Move sticks along nails using pencil held at vertex of sticks to draw the required arc as the sticks are moved around.

FIG. 30-12 — This deck/cabin structure is being built up directly in place onto a fiberglass hull using C-FLEX. The C-FLEX is used just as it would be used to build the hull. In this case, athwartship beams fairly closely spaced support the C-FLEX.

FIG. 30-14 — Additional laminate is being applied to this C-FLEX deck/cabin structure. The C-FLEX does adapt well to the various contours in this situation.

FIG. 30-11 — C-FLEX is being used here over an open inverted mold to form a separate deck/cabin molding which will later be joined to a hull. Note the cross strips made from double rods of C-FLEX to hold the C-FLEX planking in place against the framework until it is wetted out with resin. After this surface has been covered with laminate, the molding can be removed from the mold, set in place on the hull, and the outer laminate applied and finished.

Fig. 30-13 — Workers are wetting out the C-FLEX after it has been applied over the framework. Not all superstructure configurations are equally adaptable to this method. Disadvantages include the difficulty in removing the framework once the cabin is enclosed, and applying additional laminate on the underside in an enclosed space.

glass may enlarge, leading to leaks if the bonding material cracks.

Fastening of wood to fiberglass sandwich decks cored with balsa or foam should be avoided. Through-bolts will tend to crush the core, while screw fastenings passing through just one skin must be avoided to prevent pulling the skin away from the core.

Some builders have attempted to lay wood decks down with the bonding adhesive alone. However, most adhesives require a certain amount of uniformly applied clamping or bonding pressure over a specified period of time; this can be a difficult task yielding questionable results.

Assuming a flat, true fiberglass surface, others have bonded and fastened wood decks in place, using screws driven through the solid fiberglass deck from the underside. This method may be reasonably satisfactory if the wood is thick enough for the screws to get a grip, the bond is sound, and the fiberglass portion of the deck is stiff. However, driving screws through fiberglass tends to crush the laminate locally, and if there is any working, the fastening will tend to enlarge the hole and become less secure in the future. Also consider the large number of screws required, all peppered along the underside of such a deck. At the very least, washers should be fitted under the screws to minimize crushing the laminate.

With the preceding points in mind, probably the most successful method for the amateur who wants a laid wood deck is to apply it over a well-sealed plywood base. In this method, the plywood deck can be thick enough by itself for strength purposes. This way, a thin, non-structural wood veneer will be practical and help lower the cost and weight. A teak veneer from ⅛" to ³⁄₁₆" will be thick enough to provide a durable, long-wearing deck surface, although thicker material is optional, depending on how the veneer is applied.

The plywood can be sealed with epoxy resin, or covered with a single layer of fiber-glass cloth and polyester resin, carefully applied to keep the surface smooth, or otherwise sealed on the surface. Because the plywood is dimensionally stable, there will be little, if any, movement from contraction and expansion in the deck, so that leaks are unlikely, regardless of the adhesive used. However, an epoxy or an elastomeric product like polysulphide is superior over the long run.

As this is not a book on wood boatbuilding, the reader is referred to books in the Bibliography that cover laid wood decks in more detail. Approaches may vary; however, it should be pointed out that thick teak decks can be heavy and perhaps detract from the stability of the boat. Contact the designer if in doubt about the effects of such a deck if the method chosen adds a significant amount of weight over the original structure.

USING FEMALE MOLDS

A deck and cabin structure can be built up inside a female mold, using similar procedures as outlined in Chapter 15, as long as the surfaces are not of complex shapes and contours. Such a structure can be either solid fiberglass or a cored sandwich. The advantage of such a structure is that the outer surface will be smooth and require little, if any, additional work. With some forethought, the builder can mold in all sorts of features, such as raised pads for the mounting of fittings, drip rails, gutters, hatch and window openings, etc. However, a large molding may be difficult to handle, and the junction of the deck to the hull is critical regarding strength and a watertight seal. Some hull-to-deck junctions are shown in this chapter; however there are numerous methods and styles that have evolved, and hopefully the designer has shown the type he prefers if this type of structure is specified on the plans.

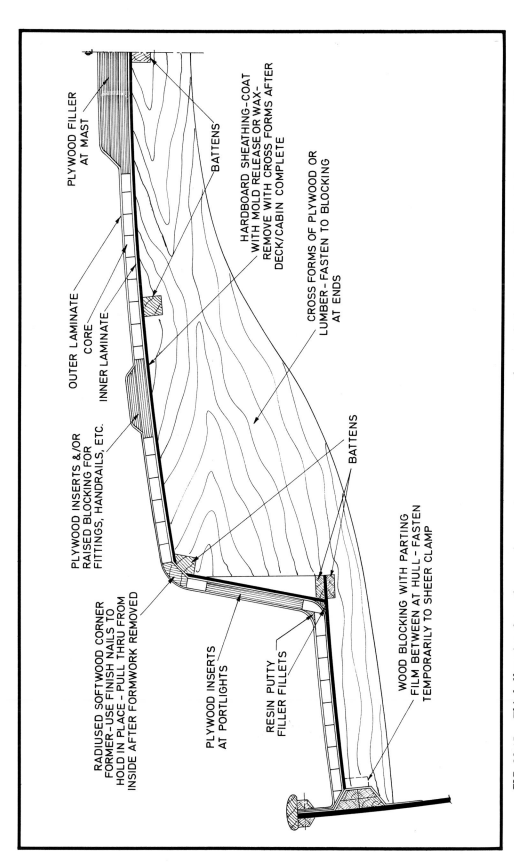

PLYWOOD FILLER AT MAST

BATTENS

HARDBOARD SHEATHING-COAT WITH MOLD RELEASE OR WAX-REMOVE WITH CROSS FORMS AFTER DECK/CABIN COMPLETE

CROSS FORMS OF PLYWOOD OR LUMBER-FASTEN TO BLOCKING AT ENDS

OUTER LAMINATE

CORE

INNER LAMINATE

PLYWOOD INSERTS &/OR RAISED BLOCKING FOR FITTINGS, HANDRAILS, ETC.

RADIUSED SOFTWOOD CORNER FORMER - USE FINISH NAILS TO HOLD IN PLACE - PULL THRU FROM INSIDE AFTER FORMWORK REMOVED

BATTENS

PLYWOOD INSERTS AT PORTLIGHTS

RESIN PUTTY FILLER FILLETS

WOOD BLOCKING WITH PARTING FILM BETWEEN AT HULL - FASTEN TEMPORARILY TO SHEER CLAMP

FIG. 30-15 — This half-section shows the procedures used to build a solid surfaced male mold sandwich cored deck/cabin structure directly in place in a fiberglass hull. Beams or cross forms similar to those shown in Fig. 30-12 can be made from lumber or plywood cut to the required contours, spanning between the sheer clamps where they are temporarily blocked in position. Additional longitudinal battens for support and to form surfaces or contours are notched into the beams as required. Hardboard sheathing is applied over this framework and coated with wax. The inner laminate is then applied over the sheathing and the core material applied over this. Plywood or wood inserts can be located to suit for such items as hatch and portlight openings, winches, handrails, etc. The outer laminate is applied after and the surface is finished just as would be done for a male molded hull. The supporting framework is then ripped out, leaving a smooth interior surface on the overhead in the cabin. At bulkheads, the superstructure is joined in a similar method as at the hull.

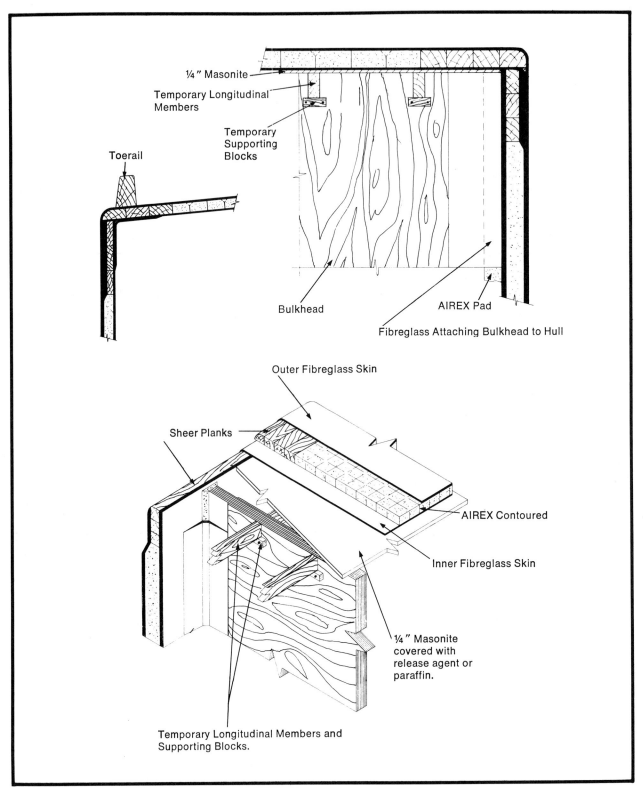

FIG. 30-16 — The details show a variation on the method shown in Fig. 30-15 for building a sandwich cored deck over a solid sheathed male mold. The main difference is that **cross forms are not used. Instead, the bulkheads serve this purpose, with longitudinal members blocked to the bulkheads to support the solid sheathing material.**

USING MALE MOLDS

A deck and cabin structure can also be built over a male mold, either as a separate molding, or directly in place on the hull. A male mold can be an open mold or the molding can be done against a solid surface. With the open-type mold, C-FLEX is often used just as it is used to build a hull. If the molding is done separately from the hull, the completed molding must be placed onto the hull the same way as if the part had been made in a female mold. The main advantage of this method is that the mold members are simple to make and low in cost, and making the deck will not interfere with other phases of the construction that can go on concurrently.

A solid surfaced male mold can be made in place on the hull using temporary framing members to support sheet materials such as waxed hardboard or melamine-coated hardboard (see Fig. 30-15). These can be nailed, screwed, or glued to the framing, although fastenings will show slight marks on the inner fiberglass surface that will be laid up over these sheets later. Some builders use contact-type adhesives for this reason. The deck cabin is then built up over this temporary structure, which is later ripped out after the deck/cabin is completed. Although the structure can be solid fiberglass laminate, contoured type cores of foam or balsa are ideal for stiffness, strength, light weight, and insulative qualities. An advantage with having a smooth surface is that it will look neat in the cabin, and there are numerous fabric materials that can be glued to this surface for decorative effects. As with all cored structures, the

FIG. 30-17 — This photo shows the sandwich core being installed over an inner fiberglass skin in the method of building the deck/cabin shown by Fig. 30-15 and Fig. 30-16.

The outer laminate will be applied after the core. Note the raised area for the mast.

FIG. 30-18 — This AIREX foam cored deck and cabin structure is just about ready for the application of the outer laminate.

builder will have to consider where solid core inserts will be required in advance. Adding deck-mounted fittings later that were not planned for may not be possible in the future without extensive modifications of the deck adjacent to the fitting.

On larger boats having substantial deckhouses, it is possible to prefabricate fiberglass components or "walls" for the outside cabin structure. Fiberglass sheets to a desired thickness can be laid up over a flat surface coated with wax to make the cabin sides. Then a wood framework (much like the framing used in a house) is bonded to the fiberglass sheet. This is all covered with plywood, which will form the inside of the "wall" or cabin side, and can be of a decorative type since it will be visible. All the components are then assembled in place in

the boat, with the result being that the cabin side is all-fiberglass, yet the interior will have a decorative look. While considerable forethought and planning of such a structure will be required, there are many advantages for those willing to overcome the technicalities. For example, wiring, plumbing and insulating material can be run in the furred space between the panels.

WOOD & PLYWOOD SUPERSTRUCTURES

Finally, decks and cabins can be made with traditional wood methods or of plywood sheathed with fiberglass. These materials have much to recommend them. They are low in cost compared to most fiberglass methods. Wood is easy to work and familiar to most. Wood is also a traditional material which may be the only choice from an aesthetic point of view with certain designs. Plywood decks and cabins are easy to make, and they are strong, light in weight, and generally watertight. When the plywood superstructure is sheathed with fiberglass on the outside, it offers most, if not all, the advantages of an all-fiberglass structure, without certain disadvantages, and it is easy to maintain. One major advantage of plywood and wood structures is that fittings can be located and installed at will without special considerations. Details for wood and plywood superstructures may be given on your plans or in several of the texts noted in the Bibliography.

CHAPTER 31   outfitting the fiberglass boat

This final chapter covers several items that relate specifically to the fiberglass hull and superstructure when fitting out and completing the amateur-built vessel. These items include the proper use of fastenings, the correct installation of hull, deck, and underwater fittings, and making the propeller aperture. Also included is a section on making parts from fiberglass. The chapter does not include information such as selecting hardware, rigging, equipment, engines, and auxiliary systems. These items are not discussed since they are not specifically related to fiberglass boats and are basically the same on any craft regardless of the hull construction material used. Other texts are available on these subjects and should be consulted for additional information.

FASTENINGS

Although there may be little need for structural fastenings in the fiberglass boat,

no doubt some will still be used. The following is included to serve as a general guide in the selection and use of fastenings as they relate to the amateur building his own fiberglass boat.

The fastenings that may be used, even though they may not be exposed directly to the elements, should still be of a marine-type such as bronze, hot dipped galvanized steel, or stainless steel. Brass, which is quite low in strength, and the cheap electroplated steel fastenings commonly found in domestic hardware stores, have no place in boatbuilding, other than perhaps for use with incidental non-structural joinerywork.

Many people think that stainless steel fastenings are the ultimate marine material for fastenings. However, there are many grades or types, some of which are quite susceptible to corrosion in a salt water environment by a process known as "crevice corrosion". This insidious type of corrosion starts as a small, perhaps invisible, pit or pockmark and corrodes from the inside out

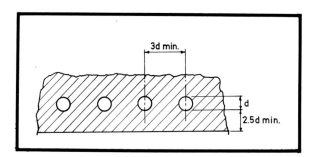

FIG. 31-1 — Any fastenings used through fiberglass laminates should be carefully located to minimize localized stresses since holes weaken a laminate. No fastening holes should be located closer to the edge of a laminate, nor closer together in a series, than noted.

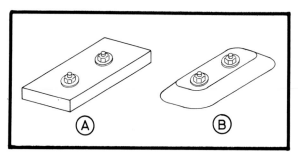

FIG. 31-2 — Backing blocks or plates, such as those used under deck fittings, should preferably be tapered at the edges with radiused corners as shown in 'B'. The type of block with hard corners as in 'A' can set up localized stresses in the adjoining laminate as the fitting works. This may crush the laminate to the point where it may fail.

so that the fastening is virtually disintegrated. Failure of such a fastening can then occur suddenly without warning. The same situation exists with stainless steel fittings.

To minimize the chances of crevice corrosion occurring, exposed stainless steel (such as at fittings) should be kept clean, polished, and free from oil or grease that could trap moisture between the surface of the fitting and the oily coating. If a stainless steel fitting is located underwater (such as a propeller shaft), the water should not be stagnant, but rather well aerated or moving. If stainless steel fastenings are desired, try to use the Type 316 which is more resistant to corrosion than lesser grades.

The mixing of metal material types, that is, combining different or dissimilar metals, as least below the waterline, should be avoided since corrosion may result, especially in salt water. For example, bronze and steel fastenings should not be used in combination. When joined by an electrolyte (such as salt water or even contaminated water), a battery effect can occur and dissipate the less-noble material (in this case, the steel).

There are some fastening specifications which should be followed when fastening into fiberglass components. For example, don't countersink fastenings into fiberglass that will be used for structural purposes. If

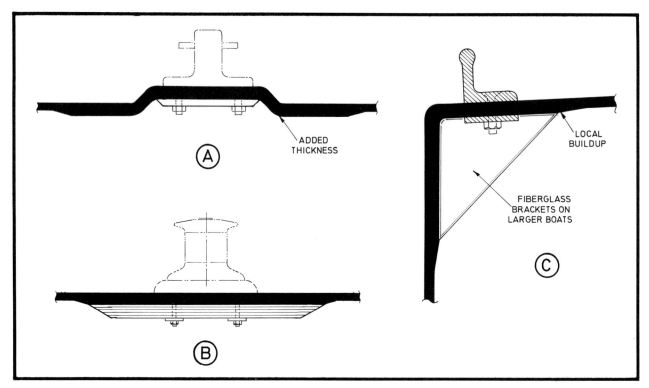

FIG. 31-3 — These details illustrate the principles of attaching fittings to solid fiberglass laminates. In 'A', the bitt has been located on a raised portion of the laminate and the laminate has also been increased in thickness by at least 25% for added strength and stiffening. Finally, the fitting has been bolted through and backed with a metal plate having tapered edges. In 'B', a winch has been bolted onto a wood base block which helps transfer the load better over the surface of the laminate. In this case, a plywood backing block of generous size having tapered edges is located on the underside, and the laminate has been increased the recommended amount over a large area. Ideally, because winches can be subjected to tremendous stresses, a structural member such as a bulkhead would be located at or adjacent to this area. In 'C', a section through a metal extruded toe rail (a sail track would be done similarly) is shown along the deck edge. Again, the laminate thickness has been increased and the fitting backed up with a metal plate. On larger boats, fiberglass brackets can be spaced at intervals along the fitting for added reinforcement.

self-tapping screws are used, they should be of the thread-cutting variety as opposed to the thread-forming type. The thickness of the fiberglass laminate should be at least 1½ times the diameter of such screws. However, this type of screw is not advised where high stresses will be encountered.

Fastenings into a fiberglass laminate should be spaced no closer than 3 times the fastening diameter apart, with the fastenings located in from edges at least 2½ times the fastening diameter. Self-tapping screws should be used only into the inner skin of sandwich cored hulls, and only for use with incidental non-structural purposes since there is a danger of pulling the inner skin away from the core if the items fastened are subjected to stress.

Rivets and self-tapping screws should generally not be used for structural junctions because of working which can increase the holes and lead to leaks and failure

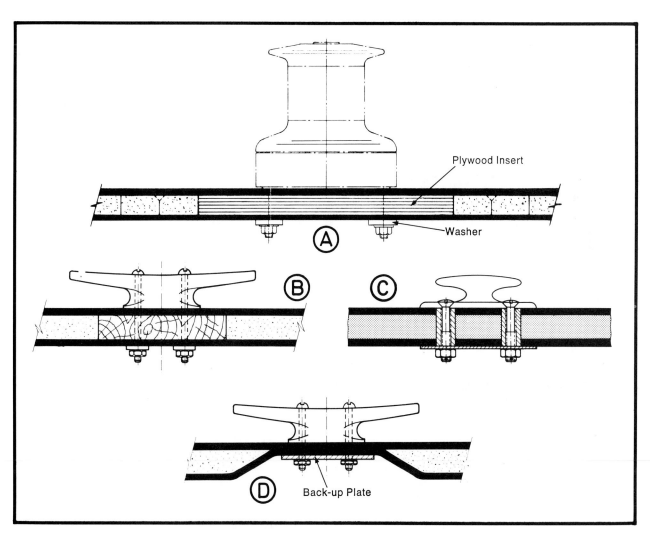

FIG. 31-4 — These details illustrate the principles of attaching fittings to sandwich core laminates, especially those using foam cores. In 'A', a plywood core insert has been used to back up a winch. Note that the insert is much larger than the base area of the winch for strength. In 'B', a solid wood insert has been used to back up a cleat. In 'C', compressive sleeves or ferrules have been used at the bolts, along with a plate under the nuts on the underside, in order to prevent crushing of the core. In 'D', the core has been removed and the inner and outer skins brought together. In this case, the fitting is installed as in a solid fiberglass laminate.

of the fitting. Nuts should be backed with washers sized at least 2¼ times the bolt diameter, and be 0.10 times the diameter in thickness. Use locking nuts or washers, or peen the threads to prevent nuts from unthreading from bolts. If a fitting is backed only with washers, ALWAYS increase the adjoining laminate thickness by at least 25%.

HULL & DECK FITTINGS

Just about any boat requires numerous fittings which must be attached to the boat at various locations. These fittings include cleats, chainplates, winches, padeyes, through-hull fittings, and other similar items that may be subjected to tremendous loads. In the fiberglass boat, it is important that items such as these be installed properly, especially with sandwich cored structures.

As a general rule, fittings should be through-bolted so that the stresses are carried by as large an area of the fiberglass part as possible. The fitting should be attached in such a manner so that the fiberglass structure does NOT fail. While resins will stick to metals, they do not adhere well enough for structural purposes; fastenings are required for

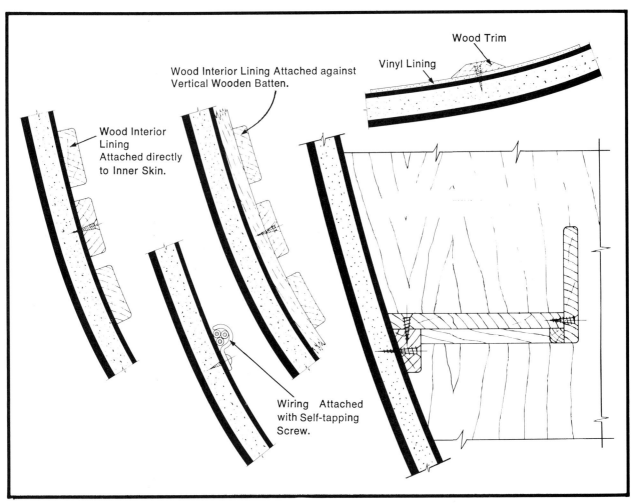

FIG. 31-5 — These details show ways of attaching NON-STRUCTURAL, NON-STRESSED items to sandwich cored hulls, such as AIREX. Self-tapping screws are used in these instances, but ideally the laminate should be at least ³/₁₆″ thick for a positive hold, and the fastening must NOT come near contacting the outer skin.

Labels within figure:
Wood Trim
Vinyl Lining
Wood Interior Lining Attached against Vertical Wooden Batten.
Wood Interior Lining Attached directly to Inner Skin.
Wiring Attached with Self-tapping Screw.

attached fittings. Yet fiberglass laminates do not hold metal fastenings well, such as rivets and bolts. Vibration and working can cause fasteners to enlarge their holes, and fastenings which are cinched up too tightly can crush a laminate, eventually leading to failure.

Hence, fittings should be backed with backing blocks, large backing plates, or at least large diameter washers. This practice prevents crushing of the laminate and transfers the loads so that localized stresses do not develop. It is prudent to always increase laminate thickness at all fittings (25% additional is a good rule-of-thumb as a

minimum), and to taper endings of materials at these thicker areas.

With sandwich cored structures, especially foam cores, solid wood or plywood inserts must be used in place of the core material under the fitting. Alternately, the core must be removed and the inner laminate joined to the outer laminate using supplemental backing methods as if the laminate were a solid fiberglass laminate. In lieu of these methods, inserts or ferrules set in mastic must be used between the skins around the bolts so that the core is not crushed.

Backing blocks on the inside can be made

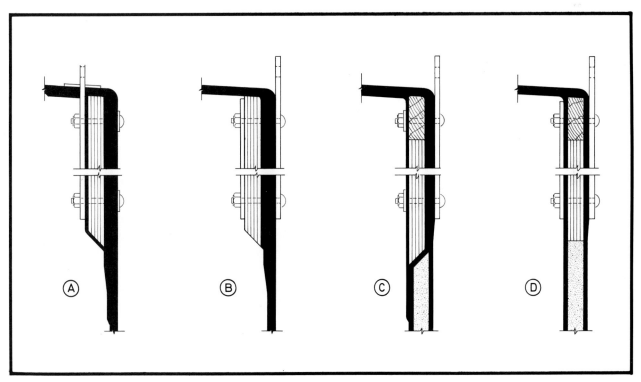

FIG. 31-6 — Several sections are shown at chainplates attached to fiberglass hulls. In 'A', the chainplate is located on the inside of a single skin fiberglass hull. The laminate has been generously increased, with the chainplate backed by an encapsulated plywood block much larger in size than the chainplate. The bolts should be of a hex head or round head type, with large washers under the heads outside. In one-off hulls, a wood sheer clamp would be shown at the hull/deck junction. In 'B', the chainplate is located on the outside of the hull. The plywood backing block in this case is bedded in mat and the nuts on the inside are backed with a metal plate. Optionally, the block could be encapsulated. 'C' and 'D' show chainplates in sandwich cored hulls. In 'C', the inner and outer skins have been joined at the sheer and filler blocking used on the inside, encapsulated in place. Large washers have been used under the nuts. In 'D', the filler block has been inserted between the outer and inner skins, and the nuts backed up with a metal plate. Note the increased laminate on the outer skin in both cases. In all cases, backing blocks, chainplates, and backing plates mating against laminates should be bedded in mat for a firm fit, and also in mastic for a watertight seal.

from solid wood or plywood with tapered edges and rounded corners preferably. It is not absolutely necessary that they be totally encapsulated with fiberglass. But if they are, the laminate should be substantial enough to prevent the fitting from working in order to keep water out. Otherwise, leave the bedding block exposed, but bed it generously in mat and resin to prevent movement, and use plenty of mastic under the fitting and fastening washers. The raw edges of the holes through the laminate, core structures, wood, and plywood should be sealed with resin and mat, or at least coated with resin.

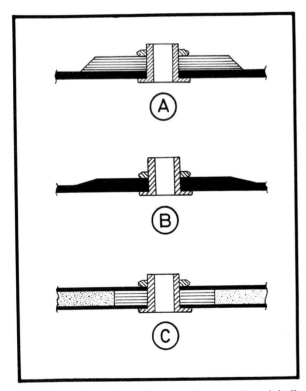

FIG. 31-7 — Several sections are shown at through-hull fittings, such as at sea cocks, drains, etc. Compression ring fittings are shown, however, the principles would be the same if the fittings were through-bolted. In 'A', a plywood backing block bedded in mat in a single skin hull is shown. In 'B', the single skin laminate has been increased in thickness over a generous area in way of the fitting. In 'C' with a sandwich cored hull, a plywood insert of generous size has been fitted between the skins.

CHAINPLATES

Chainplates are of particular concern in sailboats. There are numerous types and details for making these. Attempts have been made to embed chainplates within the laminate, but this is not recommended. The practice makes them difficult (if not impossible) to replace. Furthermore, there will be a poor bond between the metal chainplate and the laminate, which will lead to working and perhaps failure. It is also difficult to spread the load over a large part of the hull with such a chainplate.

It is always preferable to connect the chainplate to a bulkhead or to a solid fiberglass or plywood bracket bonded to the hull (see Chapter 30). However, chainplates are often connected to the hull, either on the inside or the outside.

With chainplates fastened directly to the hull, the hull laminate should be increased in the general area and the fastenings backed up with large metal plates. Oversize wood blocking or plywood backing blocks bonded and encapsulated with fiberglass are also advisable. Bolt holes should be VERY tight with plenty of mastic used under the fitting and bolt washers. With sandwich cored hulls, solid core inserts such as plywood can be used in the areas of the chainplates.

The skin that is against the chainplate should be increased in thickness by at least 25% of the single skin laminate, or of the external skin thickness of a cored hull. One standards-making organization recommends that this additional thickness should be along at least a distance equal to the beam of the boat at the mast, fore and aft of the chainplate. Chainplates can be set in wet mat to correct for any discrepancies in the adjoining laminate, but a layer of mastic is still recommended since the mat will form a brittle junction once the resin sets.

THROUGH-HULL FITTINGS

Many boats will require holes through the hull for the propeller shaft, rudder shaft, and various through-hull fittings. In most cases, these can be drilled through the fiberglass laminate after the hull is complete. However, this can be hard on tools, and some therefore prefer to mold in the hole as the hull is being built.

In some cases, this is advisable, especially when using the FERRO-GLASS system using "STR-R-ETCH MESH". The wire mesh could interfere with the drilling of the hole. In these cases, the builder can mold in an oversize waxed wood plug where the hole is desired, and this can easily be knocked out after the hull has been built.

At all such holes made through the hull, such as for rudder or propeller shafts, an embedded plywood backing block on the inside at least ¾" thick, or an increase in the hull laminate thickness, should be provided over a generous area around the hole. This will take the compression stresses of the fittings attached at these points, as well as the stresses set up by the rudder and propeller shafts, or adjoining fittings.

There is some disagreement as to whether this precaution needs to be taken at through-hull fittings where sea cocks are attached, since little stress is ordinarily taken at such a fitting. However, there is always a chance that something or someone will slam against such a fitting, subjecting it to an abnormal loading. A failure at this point could lead to disastrous results. As noted before, where a hole passes through the hull, be sure it gets a generous lining with fiberglass and resin, or at least a coating with resin. Also back the fitting with mastic, and if the adjoining laminate is uneven, bed the fitting in mat first to form a firm fit, and then re-bed it in mastic later

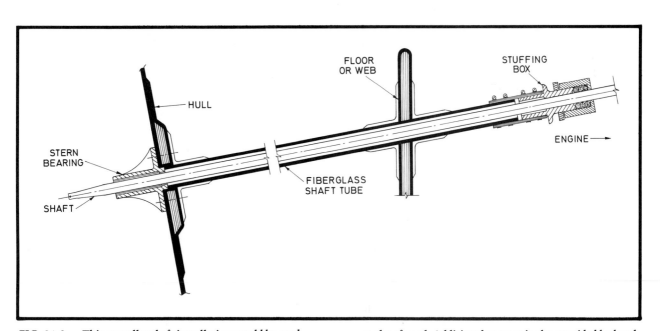

FIG. 31-8 — This propeller shaft installation would be used on a boat with a deep skeg or keel appendage, with or without a propeller aperture (see Fig. 31-9). A fiberglass shaft tube is used which keeps water out of the boat and allows the stuffing box to be located at a convenient point inside the hull. The tube can be purchased ready-made or made by the builder over a mandrel. It is bonded to the hull at the aft end. Additional support is also provided by bonding to intersecting bulkheads and floors, or at specially-made webs located as required. Note the blocking encapsulated on the inside of the hull at the aft end for the stern bearing bolts and to distribute the stresses over a larger area. A generous increase in the laminate at this area can be usd alternately.

after the mat sets up hard.

UNDERWATER FITTINGS

This section, is primarily concerned not with the actual underwater fittings as such (the propeller, rudder, shaft, etc.), but with the means of connecting these items

through the hull in a sound fashion that will not leak or fail. In the traditional wood boat, the propeller shaft often passed through a hole bored through the wood backbone structure of the hull, with this shaft bore being commonly lined with a metal tube, such as copper or lead.

In the fiberglass boat, this configuration is not required. Instead, the shaft will often

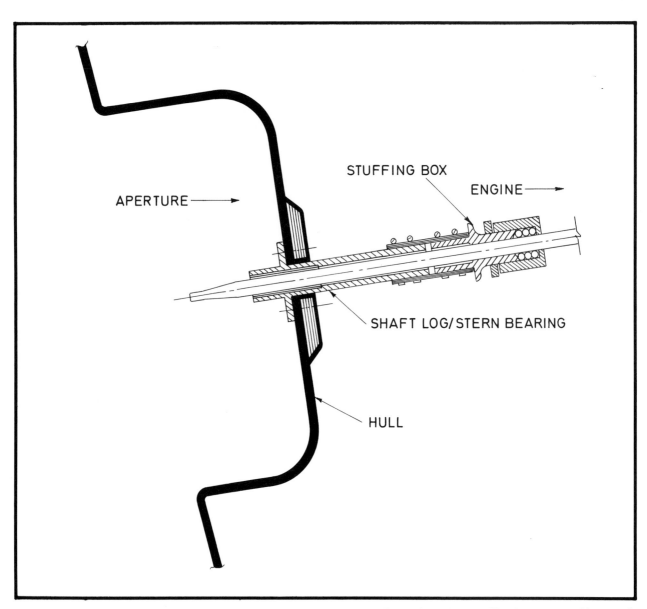

FIG. 31-9 — This propeller installation uses an aperture cut or molded into the skeg or keel appendage. In this case, if the engine is located a short distance forward (allowing a short propeller shaft) and the stuffing box is accessible, a stock combination shaft log/stern bearing fitting can be used; a shaft tube is then not required.

pass through a tube having a stuffing box on the inside of the boat to keep the water out. The length of the tube varies with the length of unsupported shaft allowable to suit the shaft material used, and as required to provide convenient access to the stuffing box on the inside of the hull. While a metal tube could be used for the shaft tube aboard the fiberglass boat, a tube made from fiberglass is usually ideal for several reasons.

First, the fiberglass shaft tube can be readily bonded to the fiberglass hull structure at any point, in effect becoming an integral leak-proof member. Secondly, the shaft tube is resistant to corrosion, rot, worms, and other problems associated with more traditional shaft tube linings. Third, although stock fiberglass tubes can be purchased ready-made, the builder can make his own. Thus, fiberglass shaft tubes can be much more economical, especially compared to certain metals that might be used in other types of boats.

Any round cylindrical object (wood dowel, shafting, pipe, tube, etc.) can serve as a mandrel over which the tube can be laid up with a fiberglass laminate. While the fiberglass laminate will theoretically not stick to the surface of the mandrel, as long as it is coated well with wax or parting film, there is a tendency for the laminate to shrink with cure, making it a very tight fit over the mandrel and difficult to remove. For this reason, it is a good idea to wrap the mandrel with numerous layers of newspaper, then a final layer of waxed paper or plastic film, to act as a "cushion" to permit this shrinkage to occur, yet still allow for easy removal of the mandrel.

Stock fiberglass tubes are excellent and easy to use, with a wide variety of sizes and wall thicknesses available. However, a source of supply may not always be readily available. Many types are filament wound by machine, which offer good strength with uniform wall thickness. However, a shaft

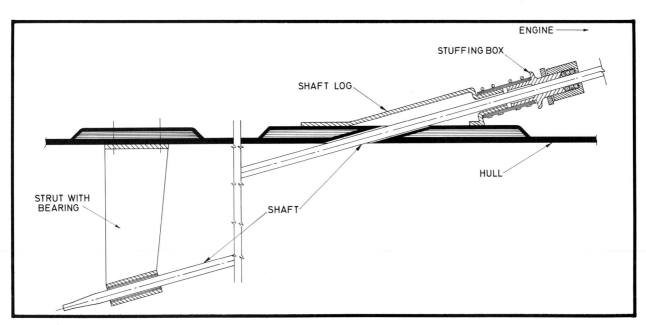

FIG. 31-10 — A propeller installation in a typical powerboat of the planing-type. The shaft is supported aft by a strut bolted through the hull at an area which should be heavily reinforced, either by a backing block, or an increase in laminate thickness, or by internal structural members. The shaft passes through a hole in the hull. A backing block on the inside can be used for fastening the shaft log in place. A standard stuffing box and mastic under the shaft log prevent leaks, although a fiberglass tube as shown in Fig. 31-8 could be used in lieu of this fitting.

tube is not under severe stress and is thus not a critical strength member; it's primary purpose is to keep water out of the boat and to allow the stuffing box to be conveniently located.

Thus, the laminate used to make the shaft tube can be of several materials or combinations. However, the inside surface should be resin rich, and hence a good thickness of mat should be used first against the mandrel. Strips of material about 6" wide can be wrapped in a spiral fashion over the mandrel, going in both directions for uniformity of strength and to prevent unfair build-ups of material, until the desired thickness is reached. The tube is ordinarily made oversize and trimmed to the desired length. Be sure to make the wall thickness so that the tube diameter will correspond to any fittings which must be attached to either end. One way to do this is to vary the thickness of the laminate at the ends to suit.

In the fiberglass boat, the rudder shaft can pass through the hull to the inside by several means. A common method, which is used on boats built from other materials, uses a standard rudder port fitting (a type of stuffing box) bolted to the bottom of the boat. This type of fitting keeps water out of the boat and serves as one of the rudder shaft bearings.

Another method uses a fiberglass shaft tube in much the same way as a fiberglass propeller shaft tube is used. If the fiberglass shaft tube is a tight fit to the rudder shaft, this will serve as a bearing, especially at the point where it passes through the hull. A stuffing box like that used on a propeller shaft can be used inside the boat to keep water out. However, if the end of the tube is well above the waterline (at least 12" should be considered a minimum), the stuffing box can be omitted. Some builders install a grease fitting onto the fiberglass shaft tube, but friction here is usually minimal.

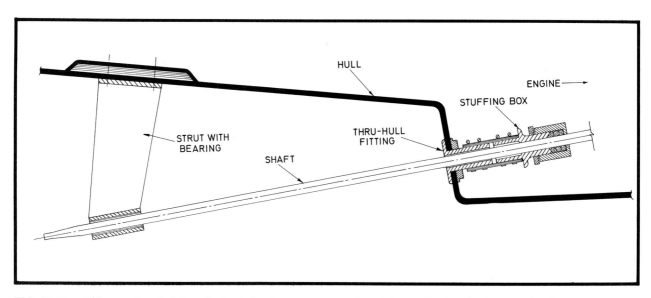

FIG. 31-11 — This propeller shaft installation is in a boat where the shaft passes through a shallow, abbreviated skeg. The shaft is supported at the aft end as in Fig. 31-10, but passes through the hull via a stock through-hull fitting which connects to a stuffing box. In this case, the shaft length is usually short (unless extra bearing support is provided within the hull as required to suit the longer shaft), and the stuffing box should be readily accessible. Laminate thickness should be ample at the through-hull fitting.

PROPELLER APERTURES

Some boats require an opening or special space in the hull keel appendage for the propeller called the propeller aperture. In the fiberglass boat, this aperture is usually made in one of two ways, depending on the hull, builder preferences, etc. One way is to mold in a removable filler block or insert when the hull is being built. Coat the insert with wax or cover with parting film so it can be knocked out later. The other way is to build the hull first and then cut away the area after for the aperture.

Some build up the propeller aperture with foam and fair and embed the stern bearing or housing in this for a smoother flow of water to the propeller. If this is done, the stern bearing must be rigidly anchored to the hull structure, or bonded to the hull laminate directly; NOT just to the foam filler material, even though it too will be bonded to the hull. The foam filler will not have enough strength to resist the forces of the turning shaft and propeller, and will probably break free eventually, possibly allowing a dangerous leak to develop.

In this installation, a means must be provided for replacing the shaft bearing, such as an access hole through the embedding laminate for the bearing set screw. Water tubes must also be provided, being built in

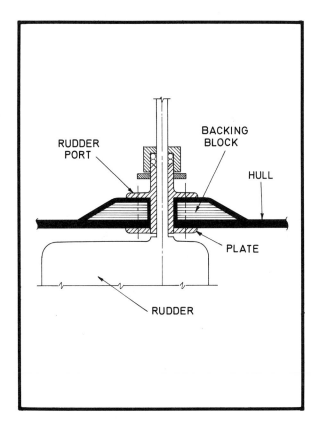

FIG. 31-12 — This section where the rudder shaft passes through the hull is typical of powerboats. A standard rudder port stuffing box fitting is used to prevent leaks and provide a rudder bearing (additional bearing can be provided at the top and/or bottom of the shaft, depending on the design). Note the backing block under the fitting.

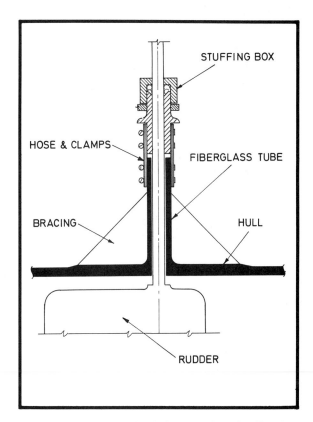

FIG. 31-13 — This rudder shaft passes through a fiberglass rudder shaft tube. If the tube fits fairly tightly, it can serve as a bearing. If the tube ends well above the waterline, a stuffing box is not mandatory. Additional bearing support is usually provided for the rudder shaft at the top beyond the shaft tube, and the top of the tube is usually braced to the hull structure by some means.

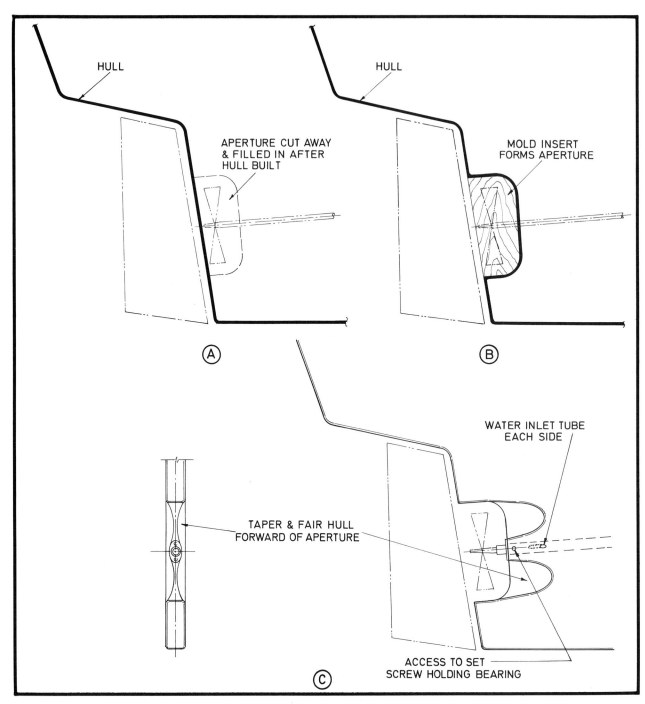

FIG. 31-14 — Propeller apertures that may be required in fiberglass hulls can either be cut to size (as in 'A') or molded in place using a mold insert (as in 'B'). In either case, a shaft layout should be made for accuracy and clearances must be known (see Bibliography for texts which discuss motor installations). Ideally, the aperture should be faired and contoured for a smooth flow of water to the propeller located in the aperture for powering efficiency, as in 'C'. In this case, the aperature can be molded or cut larger in size. The shaft is then rigidly supported to the prescribed angle, and then foam filler material is built up and shaped approximately to the contours shown. Fiberglass laminate is then applied over the area (as well as on the inside) to encapsulate the foam. As shown, the stern bearing fitting has also been encapsulated. In this case, a hole has been provided for access to the set screw to allow bearing replacement, and water inlet holes have been located on either side so that the shaft bearing will be lubricated. Alternately, water could be injected on the inside of the boat into the shaft tube for the same purpose, using the engine cooling water.

through the embedding laminate on each side of the skeg with openings to the sea forward of the bearing and into the shaft tube for proper lubrication of the fitting.

Alternately, water can be injected at some point along the shaft tube. Preferably, the injection point should be near the forward end of the tube so the water will also cool and lubricate the stuffing box. In some cases, such fittings are a part of standard stuffing boxes; in other cases it is easy to fit a stuffing box with a grease cup or Zerk fitting by tapping threads into the stuffing box housing. Whether or not a stuffing box requires lubrication and cooling varies with the installation. Cooling and lubrication become necessary as shaft speeds and tube lengths increase.

PARTS YOU CAN MAKE

By the time the reader reaches this point in the book and has followed through with this project, he will no doubt realize the

FIG. 31-15 — This photo shows a faired propeller aperture as described in Fig. 31-14C. Note the stern bearing.

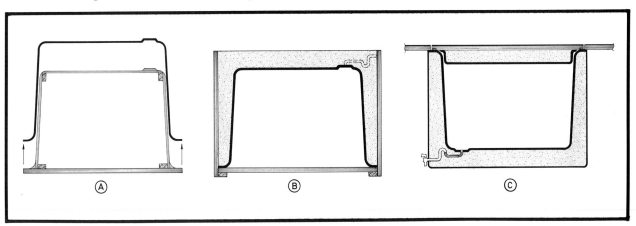

FIG. 31-16 — The builder can make many smaller parts using either male mold or female mold principles. In this example, an ice box (or ice box liner to be exact) is being made over a simple male mold (notice the draft angle) so that the smooth surface will be on the inside of the ice box when completed. It is easy to build in details, such as the relieved area for a drain in this instance (see 'A'). After the part is removed from the mold, it can be set into a forming box which is then filled with pour-in-place foam that will serve as insulation. Note the drain tube which can be fitted at this time. After the foam has been poured, the box is broken free. The outside of the unit is then covered with fiberglass laminate and positioned into the cabinet. The lid, which is usually made from plywood, can be insulated with foam glued to the underside. Fiberglass can be laminated over this, or a shallow female mold can be made to form the liner on the underside of the lid.

vast potential that exists for making innumerable items from fiberglass, using both female and male molding methods. The principles explained and the data provided can be used as guidelines for building many parts from fiberglass that would otherwise be built from other materials, such as wood or metal.

Common items which can be prefabricated from fiberglass include engine oil drip pans, trunks for daggerboards and centerboards used on sailboats, tubes used for shafts and mast supports, battery boxes, ice boxes, bait tanks, cockpit wells, control consoles, hatches and hatch boxes, ventilation boxes and trunks, tanks, seat foundations, etc.

A simple mold is all that is usually required for most of these items, or mandrels of a suitable size or configuration. With some items, a female mold will be ideal, such as for parts where the smooth side will be exposed. In other cases, the smooth side might be on the inside, such as with ice boxes or drip pans. In these cases, a male mold will be desired. With a little forethought and planning (now that you've acquired the necessary knowledge and skills), the possibilities are endless. Happy molding!

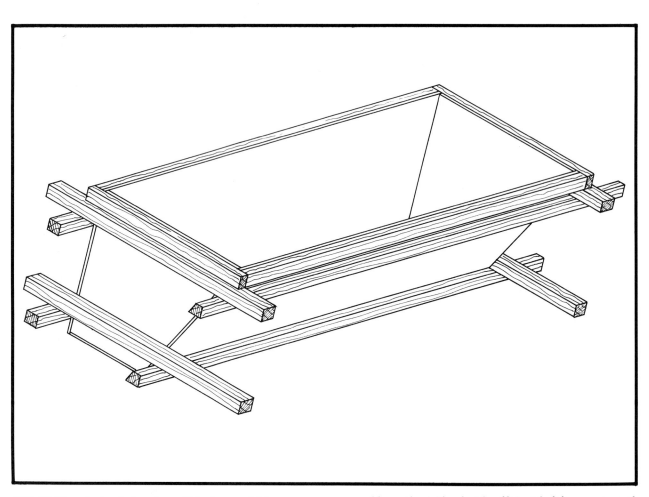

FIG. 31-17 — A simple female mold is shown which can also be used to make numerous parts. In this instance, the mold is used to form a tank, with the sides of the mold being hardboard, plywood, or comparable sheeting material. The mold must be rigid and with sufficient draft for easy removal if the mold is to be saved. Inside corners should be built up with fillets also.

The following series of photos shows various components made from fiberglass that are used in the "FOAMEE" dinghy shown under construction in Chapter 19. These photos show some of the principles discussed in the text for making parts which may be applicable to a wide variety of situation in the fiberglass boatbuilding project.

FIG. 31-20 — The laminate is built up over the daggerboard mold. In this case, mat and cloth are used simultaneously, wrapping the materials around until the desired laminate is built up.

FIG. 31-18 — In the "FOAMEE" design, a daggerboard is used which passes through the hull inside a daggerboard trunk or sheath which supports the daggerboard and keeps water out of the boat. The daggerboard itself thus makes a perfect mold for making this trunk. In the photo, the daggerboard has been wrapped with several layers of newspaper for "cushioning" and waxed paper is being used over this as a release agent.

Fig. 31-19 — The waxed paper is coated with resin preparatory to applying the fiberglass laminate around the daggerboard. This will help wet out the material from the underside and form the desired resin-rich inner surface.

FIG. 31-22 — The "FOAMEE" design uses a free-standing mast which is supported in place by a tube. The mast serves as a mandrel for making this tube in the same way that the daggerboard was used to form the trunk. Here, fiberglass material laid on waxed paper is being wetted out with resin.

FIG. 31-24 — The worker is using his hands to smooth out the laminate and remove excess resin since the shape is not conducive to the use of a squeegee in all directions. After the resin sets up, the part can be pulled off the mandrel.

FIG. 31-21 — Final squeegeeing over the cloth is done to smooth out the laminate and remove excess resin. After the resin sets up, the daggerboard is pulled from the part and installed in the boat (see Fig. 31-26).

FIG. 31-23 — The mast (or section of it) is wrapped with waxed paper and the fiberglass is rolled onto it to form the laminate. Additional resin can be applied as the mandrel is rolled onto the laminate.

FIG. 31-26 — The previously molded daggerboard trunk is being installed into the "FOAMEE" hull. The adjoining seat and the daggerboard are used to check alignment and position.

FIG. 31-28 — A foredeck made from AIREX foam has been installed, and when covered with laminate, will permanently bond the mast tube in place and provide the necessary support to the free-standing mast. The hull interior is nearly ready for finishing.

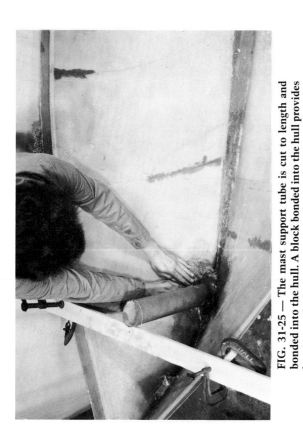

FIG. 31-25 — The mast support tube is cut to length and bonded into the hull. A block bonded into the hull provides bearing at the bottom. The board across the sheer is used to hold the tube in alignment.

FIG. 31-27 — After aligning the assembly, the daggerboard is fixed in place using fiberglass bonding angles around the base. Resin or resin putty will also be used on the exterior to prevent leaks. Note the mast tube which is now in place.

Tests have been made regarding joint configurations and the effects of surface preparation on bonds at such joints, such as at the attachment of bulkheads and stiffeners to the inside of the hull (*).

With regard to top hat section stiffener installations in static rupture tests, there was very little difference in strength between a primary versus a secondary bonding situation. And when the bonding surface was wiped down with an acetone wash first, the gain in strength was less than 10%.

On the other hand, when the bonding surfaces were sanded first, there was a 15−20% gain in joint strength over both the primary AND secondary bonding situations having no bonding preparation at all. But in addition, when the bonding surfaces were not only sanded, but fitted with fillets as well, strength increased on the order of 50% over primary or secondary bonding situations which had no bonding preparation.

Thus, when bonding in top hat section stiffeners, best practice for ULTIMATE strength shows that bonding preparation should include BOTH roughening of the bonding surface by sanding, and fitting fillets along the inner corner junctions of the stiffener. It is also prudent to wipe the surfaces down first with acetone or similar solvent to assure a clean secondary bond. In addition (as mentioned further in the study), mat layers should be used against the hull surface as the first layer in the bonding laminate.

In the same group of tests regarding bulkhead attachments (using ¾" "A-C" Exterior-grade Douglas fir plywood in all samples), the study emphasized that the strongest bonds resulted when the plywood bulkheads were actually bolted or mechanically fastened through the bonding angles, something that is not universally done in production yachts, incidentally. The reason why bulkheads should be so fastened (according to the study) is that when test samples secured only with fiberglass bonding angles were subjected to stress, the peel strength of the plywood cores was such that the plies tended to fail in the plywood panels, or at the plywood/bond angle interface. On the other hand, in those samples which were bolted, strength was increased to the point that when failure did occur, it occured at the shell or hull laminate. In other words, the bolted junction was strong enough to transfer the stresses to the hull where they belonged.

It should be added, however, that the grade of plywood used in the test could be part of the failure in my opinion. The typical "A-C" Exterior-grade Douglas fir plywood panel, while probably glued with the same waterproof glue between the plies as is used in the better quality Marine-grade panel, may not necessarily consist of good quality wood in the inner plies. In the Marine-grade panel, Douglas fir solid cores are used throughout. However, in the Exterior-grade Douglas fir panel, woods OTHER than Douglas fir can be used for the inner cores, and these may not be of as strong a wood or of as sound a quality. Furthermore, the "C" grade outer ply of the typical "A-C" panel is a poor choice in boat work because of the exposed voids. However, this lower grade panel is commonly used in production work to cut costs.

A panel of at least a "B" face is always preferable, since at least the knot holes and other defects must be plugged according to

(*) "Joint Configuration and Surface Preparation Effect on Bond Joint Fatigue in Marine Application" by Eugene Gray, Jr., Earl M. Zion, and C. Stephen Richter, Owens-Corning Fiberglass Corp., Jan. 2, 1973.

grading standards. Also, experience shows that quality does vary from one mill to another, even though the same grading standards are supposed to apply. Perhaps the test results would have been different had a higher quality Marine-grade panel with "A-A" or "A-B" faces been used. While this could be an argument for the builder who cares about quality to buy the better grade materials, I have never heard of a boat failing structurally because "A-C" panels were used.

Like the stiffener bonding samples, the bulkhead joint strengths increased dramatically when bonding surfaces were sanded and fillets were fitted. A worthwhile gain in strength was also shown at the junction with an initial acetone wipe, as opposed to installation without these additional steps in a primary or secondary bonding situation alone. Likewise, such a bond should be made against a mat surface, using the mat as the initial layer of the bonding angle laminate.

A most important point in the tests was that top hat section stiffeners and bolted plywood bulkhead joint failures were most likely to occur NOT at the bond interface, but rather in the hull laminate itself! Almost every joint failure was confined to the test sample base laminate (representing the inner hull surface), with the resin pulling off the top woven roving layer. The method suggested to prevent this failure is that the final ply of reinforcement IN THE AREA OF THE BOND LINE should be chopped strand mat, with secondary layup of the bonding angles also being mat as the first ply. In other words, secondary bonds should be made mat-to-mat, NOT mat-to-woven roving or woven roving-to-woven roving.

Furthermore, under dynamic tests (fatigue tests to failure after a given number of cycles), filleted joints showed improved performance 2 to 3 times that of non-filleted joints used in top hat section stiffener installations. This is due to the stress concentrations at the inside corners of non-filleted junctions. Again, failure occured at

the inner hull laminate, either in the form of resin delamination from the last woven roving layer, or from fracture and peel of the last woven roving layer. This further points out the need for mat layers in way of the bond line on the hull and for the first layer of the bonding angle.

A suggestion made by the study in lieu of mat-to-mat secondary bonding was the use of a peel ply. The peel ply, for example, can be a layer of fiberglass cloth laid in the final coat of resin, and pulled free prior to the resin setting up. The idea here is to protect the surface from contamination, leaving a rough or "primed" surface that will "grip" better to the secondary bonding material. However, it seems doubtful that the average amateur will want to go through this trouble and added expense, especially when good results can be had by the methods previously noted.

While bulkheads have sometimes popped loose in earlier production fiberglass boats (probably due to a lack of knowledge of proper installation, a too-flexible hull, careless labor, imprudent skipper operation, or any combination of these causes), such failures are NOT common. This section should not be reacted to by alarm on the part of the prospective builder. In the amateur-built boat, the person building a boat for his own use will tend to take greater care than the typical factory worker whose performance may be judged on the number of hulls that can be turned out in a certain time. Hence, the advantage in a quality-built boat lies again with the amateur, especially if he knows how and why to do the job properly.

While bolting bulkheads in place through the bonding angles is ideal, the method shown in Chapter 27 of drilling holes either through or partially into the bulkhead around the perimeter so that bonding angles on either side get a better "grip" onto the plywood works well in use, although this is not substantiated by any test results. These methods make it extremely unlikely that the bulkhead will ever peel away from the bonding angle.

APPENDIX 2   layup configurations

The U.S. Navy has investigated several types of layup procedures to determine the properties and advantages of each. The results of the tests were published in the Naval Engineers Journal, October, 1971, and have been included here.

Several points should be made. First, the laminates were ALL woven roving without the use of mat between, tending to make a laminate having a higher glass content than a mat/woven roving layup. Second, laminate samples were made under laboratory conditions. Finally, laminates were made using fire-retardant resins in the Navy tradition. Thus, the results cannot be compared to laminates having alternating mat and woven roving layers, or those made with regular polyester resins, nor can the builder expect similar results under normal working conditions.

However, this is not the point for including the test results. The main reason for citing the test is to show the effects on various layup procedures only as they effect strength properties in comparable laminates. A similar trend in deviations should occur between mat/woven roving laminates even though the figures may vary in totals. It is possible that results with mat/woven roving laminates could match or exceed those figures shown. This could occur since there is generally a better interlaminar bond between mat/woven roving laminates (at least under shop conditions), probably better compressive strength by virtue of the thicker mat layers, and perhaps better bonding by virtue of regular polyester resins over the fire-retardant type.

The laminates used in the tests are shown by Fig. A 2-1. The parallel layup is the "ideal" laminate in theory, with all layers applied in a continuous "one-shot" method without junctions or laps; such a laminate is seldom practical under shop conditions.

The continuous-shingle layup is similar to the preceding, but allows the practicality of limited widths of materials, with laps at junctions for compensation of these theoretically "weak" spots.

The interrupted-shingle layup is similar, but includes the condition where work must stop for a prolonged period, leading to a secondary bonding condition that would be common under shop conditions.

The lapped layup approach is another method for handling joints in layers to overcome any weaknesses caused by these joints. It should be noted that this type of laminate will build up uneven areas quickly.

The butted layup is the type largely specified in this text, especially where a male mold is being used in order to keep the laminate fair and smooth. Note that butt

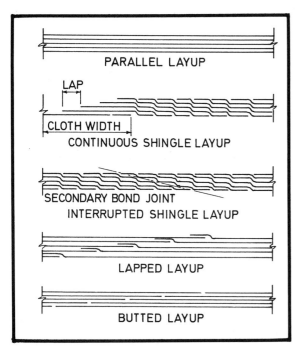

FIG. A2-1

joints are staggered a nominal amount.

The results of the test are amazingly similar in almost all areas. Generally, the deviation is about 10% or less in most categories, certainly not enough to rule out any one approach, especially when practical limitations are considered. Although the parallel laminate is superior in most respects, this laminate should only be considered as a point of reference, since this method cannot be practically used, at least by the amateur builder. It should be noted that the interrupted-shingle layup actually gained strength over the other laminates in several instances, indicating that potential secondary bonding problems can be overcome if practically handled. While the butted laminate was weakest, it was virtually comparable to the lapped layup, indicating that lapped joints do little if anything in the way of increasing strength properties by themselves in this configuration. The continuous-shingle or interrupted-shingle layups show the best results of laminates that can be practically used; however, because they don't build up as evenly as the butted layup, they are usually used only in female mold situations.

VARIABLE LAYUP METHODS—WOVEN ROVING, FIRE RESISTANT POLYESTER LAMINATES
(LAB SAMPLES)

PROPERTY	PARALLEL[1]	CONTINUOUS[1] SHINGLE	INTERRUPTED[1] SHINGLE	LAPPED[1]	BUTTED[1]
Flexural Strength (p.s.i.)	39,600	38,190	40,980	36,230	36,300
Flexural Modulus (p.s.i. $\times$ 10⁶)	2.66	2.60	2.76	2.67	2.41
Tensile Strength (p.s.i.)	51,200	45,460	41,770	42,420	38,650
Tensile Modulus (p.s.i. $\times$ 10⁶)	2.73	2.77	2.91	2.39	2.06
Inner-Laminar Shear (p.s.i.)	1,730	2,300	1,780	1,920	1,910
Compressive Strength (p.s.i.)	35,300	35,550	35,820	34,240	31,920
Compressive Modulus (p.s.i. $\times$ 10⁶)	2.93	3.52	3.15	3.15	2.79
Glass Content (% weight)	55.94	55.56	55.81	55.55	53.18
Thickness (inches) 16 ply	0.485	0.490	0.544	0.535	0.516

[1]See Figure A2-1 for types of reinforcement lay-up procedures

APPENDIX 3 cost factors

The following compares cost factors as a percentage or ratio of a base material (plywood) for several materials commonly used to build boat hulls. Actual costs are not given because of possible fluctuations over time. Instead, the base material is given the factor of 100(%) and the other materials are expressed as a number in relation to this base number. For example, if the plywood base material was priced at $1.00 per square foot at a factor of 100, and another material being compared had a factor of 150, the cost of this second material would be $1.50 per square foot, or 150% of the base material.

The data and comparisons were determined from costs available at the retail level in the Southern California area at the time of printing. The ratios are based on the cost of a square foot of hull surface material or laminate composition that could be used to build the hull of a typical pleasureboat in the 30' to 35' range. The scantlings noted (the sizes, thicknesses, or composition of materials in the laminates) are not necessarily comparable in strength properties, but are representative of what could be used in a hull within the size range noted. The scantlings are not necessarily adaptable without modification to any and all boats in this size range.

Scantlings are based on hull surface material only and no consideration has been given to internal structure, framing, local reinforcement, etc., which will vary from design to design, and with hull construction methods and materials. For example, little internal structure may be required in a sandwich cored hull, thereby perhaps reducing its relative overall hull cost compared to a hull built using another material even though having a higher cost factor. On the other hand, a single skin fiberglass hull may require much more in the way of internal structure which could offset its lower cost factor. Other costs not reflected in the data would include the costs for the plug and mold, form members, welding rods used for steel and aluminum hulls, fastenings and glue used in wood hulls, sandblasting and priming, gel coats, filler coats, and finishing. The goal of the data is to illustrate current trends and differentials between materials to give the builder an idea of what is potentially a "cheap" or "expensive" hull construction material.

It should be noted that any differentials do NOT reflect the TOTAL cost differential of the boat, but only in the hull material itself. For example, assume that a boat is built for a total cost of $10,000 using the plywood base material. If hull cost is assumed to be 10% of total cost (a rule-of-thumb says that hull costs are usually 10−15% of overall cost, however, this does vary with equipment, materials, etc.), it will cost $1000 to build the hull. If it is assumed that the planking cost is 75% of the total hull cost, then this portion would be $750.00.

How much MORE it would cost to build the hull in the example using another material can be easily determined using the factors provided. For example, if a C-FLEX hull was desired instead of plywood, multiply the hull planking cost by the factor given for C-FLEX (183% × $750.00 = $1372.50, or $622.50 MORE for the C-FLEX hull covering portion). It is VERY important to consider one point: In the example, while the C-FLEX may cost 183% more than the plywood base material, the additional TOTAL boat cost is MUCH less than this differential. With plywood, the TOTAL boat cost is $10,000. With C-FLEX, the total boat cost would INCREASE to $10,622, or only a little more than 6% in TOTAL overall boat cost even though the material is actually 183% more than plywood as a hull material. The same applies in ALL cases, although the range of possible variations may be more or less depending on boat size (smaller boats would have a higher percentage of their cost in the hull than would larger boats with extensive superstructures, added equipment, etc.).

It should be emphasized that costs will vary considerably depending on many elements and the ratios can only apply at a given time. Inflation, world-wide supply and demand, raw material costs, technological advances, and other elements in the marketplace may change these ratios at any moment. Costs will also vary with locale, quantity purchased, how and when the materials are bought, shipping costs, and charges for extra services that may be related to buying certain materials.

Weights and thicknesses of materials are given per square foot and based on listed figures. Fiberglass laminates use average resin/glass ratios found in normal shop conditions with the materials noted. Weights are nominal and not absolute, and are given for comparison purposes only.

COST COMPARISON FACTORS FOR BOATBUILDING MATERIALS — 30' − 35' PLEASUREBOAT

PLYWOOD — ¾" Marine Douglas Fir Plywood with one layer of fiberglass cloth and polyester resin. Weight: 2.61 lbs.
FACTOR: 100% (BASE FACTOR)

PLYWOOD — As above but with epoxy resin
FACTOR: 127%

COLD MOLDED WOOD EPOXY – Four layers 1/8" Douglas fir veneer epoxy glued and sealed, with one layer of fiberglass cloth on exterior. Weight: 1.82 lbs.
FACTOR: 149%

STEEL – Mild 10GA. plate. Weight: 5.625 lbs.
FACTOR: 117%

ALUMINUM – ¼" Alloy 5086-H116 Weight: 3.44 lbs.
FACTOR: 380%

CONVENTIONAL SINGLE SKIN FIBERGLASS LAMINATE (Mold and plug cost not included) – Alternated layers of mat and woven roving, 5 layers 18 oz. WR and 6 layers 1 oz. CSM using ortho resin. Thickness: .325"
Weight: 2.49 lbs.
FACTOR: 114%

CONVENTIONAL SINGLE SKIN FIBERGLASS LAMINATE – As above but using iso resin.
FACTOR: 117%

C-FLEX SINGLE SKIN FIBERGLASS LAMINATE – Includes C-FLEX type CF-65 with 1 oz. CSM each side, plus alternating mat and woven roving on outside, 3 layers each 18 oz. WR and 1 oz. CSM. Thickness: .362" Weight: 2.7 lbs.
FACTOR: 183%

C-FLEX SINGLE SKIN FIBERGLASS LAMINATE – As above but using iso resin.
FACTOR: 189%

FERRO-GLASS SINGLE SKIN FIBERGLASS LAMINATE WITH "STR-R-ETCH MESH" – Includes wire mesh with 1½ oz. CSM each side, plus alternating layers of 1 oz. CSM and 18 oz. WR, 2 layers each side of mesh (4 of each total), plus final 1 oz. CSM on exterior. Thickness: .378" Weight: 2.47 lbs.
FACTOR: 143%

FERRO-GLASS SINGLE SKIN FIBERGLASS LAMINATE – As above but with iso resin.
FACTOR: 150%

CONVENTIONAL SANDWICH CORE LAMINATE – Using ortho resin and ½" thick core material of type noted by factor. Skins on either side of core consist of alternating layers of 1 oz. CSM and 18 oz. WR, 2 layers each side, plus final 1 oz. CSM on outer skin. Thickness: .148" outer skin, .118" inner skin. Weight: Varies with core material; see factor below.
FACTOR:

End-Grain Balsa Core:	173%	Weight: 2.41 lbs.
KLEGECELL Foam Core:	208%	Weight: 2.22 lbs.
AIREX Foam Core:	222%	Weight: 2.25 lbs.

KEVLAR SANDWICH CORE LAMINATE – As above but using Kevlar K-49 13 oz. WR in place of the 18 oz. fiberglass WR (NOTE: This laminate is included to illustrate why high-content Kevlar laminates are seldom used currently due to high cost).
FACTOR:

End-Grain Balsa Core:	445%
KLEGECELL Foam Core:	480%
AIREX Foam Core:	494%

HIGH MODULUS LAMINATE USING AEROSPACE-QUALITY UNIDIRECTIONAL S-GLASS ("ORCOWEB") – Consists of 3 layers each side of ⅝" KLEGECELL foam core using iso resin. Thickness of skins: .048" each side. Weight: .91 lbs. total.
FACTOR: 347%

HIGH MODULUS LAMINATE – As above, but substituting one layer of S-glass each for one of graphite ORCOWEB and one of Kevlar ORCOWEB – Thickness of skins: .046" each side. Weight: .84 lbs. total.
FACTOR: 449%

RELATIVE VALUES OF INDIVIDUAL GROUPS OF MATERIALS USED IN FIBERGLASS BOATBUILDING.

RESINS (Factor per lb.):

Ortho	100%
Iso	110%
Vinylester	178%
Epoxy	340%

CORE MATERIALS (Factor per sq. ft.):

END-GRAIN BALSA	100%
KLEGECELL	147%
AIREX	167%

REINFORCEMENTS (Factor per lb.):

Chopped Strand Mat	100%
Woven Roving	100%
Unidirectional E-Glass	135%
Cloth	264%
C-FLEX	268%
Kevlar K-49 Woven Roving	1446%
S-Glass ORCOWEB	1008%
Kevlar ORCOWEB	2462%
Graphite ORCOWEB	5414%

ACCELERATOR – Material used in conjunction with a catalyst to produce internal heat to reduce the gel and curing time of a thermosetting resin. Cobalt napthanate and DMA are two such materials.

ACETONE – A highly flammable cleaning fluid solvent used to remove uncured plastic resin from tools and clothing. Will attack rayon and Dacron.

ACTIVATOR – See **ACCELERATOR**

ADDITIVE – Substance added to resin to impart special characteristics such as fire-retardancy.

AIR BUBBLES – Entrapment of air particles in resin or in a fiberglass laminate caused by improper mixing of the resin, improper laminating practices, attempting to laminate around abrupt corners, etc.

"AIREX" – Proprietary non-cross linked PVC structural foam.

AIR-INHIBITED RESIN – See **LAMINATING RESIN**

BIAS – In a diagonal direction across a fabric

BI-AXIAL – See **BI-DIRECTIONAL**

BI-DIRECTIONAL – Fiber orientation in a fabric or laminate in two directions.

BINDER – A bonding agent used to adhere fibers in the manufacturing of fiberglass material, especially mat.

BOND – The adhesion between two materials. Also, to attach materials together by means of an adhesive agent.

BUILDING BERTH – See **BUILDING FORM**

BUILDING FORM – The supporting foundation or base structure over which a framework or male mold is erected for building a hull.

BULKHEAD – An upright partition in a boat.

BUTT JOINT – A joint made by positioning materials together end-to-end or side-by-side without any overlap.

CARBON FIBER – A fine high modulus reinforcing fiber material with superior strength-to-weight characteristics.

CATALYST – Material added to polyester resin to make it cure rapidly by oxidizing an accelerator. The common catalyst is MEK peroxide.

CAVITY MOLD – See **FEMALE MOLD**

"C-FLEX" – Proprietary fiberglass material used as a substrate over a male mold to form a hull, while also becoming a part of the laminate.

CHOPPED STRAND MAT (C.S.M.) – See **MAT**

CHOPPER GUN – A special spray gun used for sprayup laminates which chops predetermined lengths of fiberglass rovings or strands, and deposits them together with catalyzed resin at the same time onto a mold surface.

CLOTH — A woven fabric made from fine yarns of fiberglass.

COBALT NAPTHANATE — An accelerator used in polyester resin. Also an additive that will allow resin to be used at lower temperatures.

COLOR PIGMENTS — See **PIGMENTS**

COMPOSITE — A type of construction using two or more different materials as primary structural components.

CONTACT MOLDING — Low-pressure laminating process where reinforcing materials are built up on the surface of an open mold by hand layup techniques.

CONVENTIONAL LAYUP — Laminate consisting of mat and woven roving, usually in alternating layers.

CORE — The central material in sandwich construction encapsulated between skins.

CRAZING — Hairline cracks in the resin, either within or on the surface of a fiberglass laminate, caused by internal stresses generated by excessive heat during cure, improper removal from the mold, impact, or flexing.

CROSS LINKED FOAM — A foam material where the chemical molecules of the material link together, creating a thermoset material. Urethane is such a foam.

"CSM" — See **MAT**

CURE — The total polymerization of a liquid resin to a solid state of maximum hardness.

CURE TIME — The time required for the liquid resin to reach a fully polymerized state after the catalyst has been added. From a practical standpoint, cure time refers to the point where the resin is hard enough to have other processes performed on it, such as sanding or finishing.

DELAMINATION — Separation or failure of the bond in laminate layers or skins from a core material.

DIMENSIONAL STABILITY — The ability to retain constant shape and size, as opposed to stretching or shrinking.

"DMA" — Dimethylanaline, a promotor used in resins.

DRAFT — The degree of taper on the sides of a female mold to allow the molded part to be pulled from the mold.

DRAPEABILITY — The ability of a fiberglass material to conform to contours, corners, and shapes when saturated with resin.

DRY SPOT — See **RESIN-STARVED**

E-GLASS — Type of electrical-grade fiberglass base material commonly used for boatbuilding reinforcements.

EPOXY RESIN — Thermosetting resins of a two-part type, consisting of a resin and a hardener combined in varying proportions, resulting in improved bonding strength and physical properties compared to polyester resins.

EXOTHERMIC HEAT — Heat given off during polymerization due to the chemical reaction of the accelerator and catalyst when mixed in a polyester resin.

FEMALE MOLD — The type of mold commonly used in production fiberglass boatbuilding where the outer surface of the molded part contacts, and is formed by, the surface of the female mold.

"FERRO-GLASS" — A proprietary method of one-off fiberglass hull construction using a substrate material known as "STR-R-ETCH MESH".

FIBERGLASS — Fibers similar to those of other fabrics, but made from glass. Also, the materials made from these fibers. Loosely defines the plastic laminates made with fiberglass and resins.

FILAMENT — A single thread-like fiber, or a number of these fibers put together in virtually an endless length.

FILL — See **WEFT**

FILLER — Relatively inert materials added to resin primarily to extend the volume, lower the cost of the resin, or improve certain properties.

FILLET — A concave junction where two surfaces meet so that air bubbles are not formed in the adjoining laminate.

FINISH — The surface treatment given to fibers or filaments after they are made into strands, yarns, or woven fabrics to allow resins to flow freely around and adhere to them. The finish determines the quality of the adhesion between the glass and the resin.

FINISHING RESIN — A polyester resin containing surfacing agent which floats to the surface to exclude the air from the resin surface thereby allowing it to cure or "set up".

FIRE-RETARDENT RESIN — A resin containing additives to reduce or eliminate its tendency to burn once cured, or that will self-extinguish when the flame source has been removed.

FLEXIBILITY — A qualitative term used to describe the degree of rigidity of a resin after it cures.

FLOOR — An athwartship member in the bottom of a hull across the centerline used to reinforce the keel area, support the ballast, and tie each half of the hull together.

FLOW COAT — See **GEL COAT**

FOAM — Generic name of lightweight plastic materials used for cores, formers, and flotation purposes.

FORM — See **BUILDING FORM.** Also, loosely referred to as a frame, support, or other member used to impart a given shape or contour to a molded part.

FRAMES — The contoured athwartship members that form the basic backbone of a mold or hull and give it its shape and form. The frames are usually mounted onto the building form.

"FRP" — Fiberglass reinforced plastic, or "fiberglass" as it is commonly known.

GEL/GELATION — The partial cure of polyester resin to a semi-solid, jelly-like state.

GEL COAT — A thin surface coat of specifically formulated polyester resin used as the surface covering on hulls made in female molds. The gel coat is decorative and also protects the underlying laminate.

GEL TIME — The time required to change the liquid resin to a non-flowing gel. Also, the time available for working the resin once applied.

GLASS CONTENT/GLASS-RESIN RATIO — The amount of fiberglass reinforcing material in a laminate compared to the amount of resin. Glass content assumes that sufficient resin exists to convert the materials into a stiff, structural laminate.

GRAPHITE – See **CARBON FIBER**

"GRP" – Glass reinforced plastic. See **"FRP"**.

HAND LAYUP – The building up of fiberglass laminates by hand over or in a mold using low pressure techniques. See CONTACT MOLDING.

HARDENER – See **CATALYST**

HIGH MODULUS MATERIAL – A material that has a high modulus of elasticity, or that is very "stiff" when used in a laminate.

INHIBITOR – An additive that retards, slows down, or prevents a chemical reaction. In resins, an inhibiter usually increases the shelf life of the resin or retards curing.

INTERLAMINAR BOND – The bond between layers of materials in a laminate.

ISOPHTHALIC ("ISO") RESIN – Isophthalic acid based polyester resin which has somewhat higher physical properties than orthophthalic resins, but also considered a "general purpose" resin.

ISOTROPIC – The arrangement of reinforcing fibers in a material in a random manner so that equal strength properties result in all directions.

JIG – See **BUILDING FORM**

"KEVLAR" – A proprietary Aramid fiber made by Du Pont Chemical for making reinforcing materials.

"KLEGECELL" – A proprietary cross-linked PVC structural foam.

LAMINATE – A material or composition made from successive layers of fiberglass or other reinforcing products bonded together and saturated with resin.

LAMINATE SCHEDULE – The order or composition of layers of reinforcing materials and their orientation in a laminate.

LAMINATING RESIN – A polyester resin that will not completely cure tack-free in the presence of air.

LAMINATION – A layer of material in a laminate.

LAP JOINT – A joint made by positioning one material over another end-to-end or side-by-side as opposed to a butt joint. The joint consists of two layers of material.

LAYUP – The placing of fiberglass reinforcing materials in or over a mold and applying resin to form the completed laminate. Sometimes used interchangeably with the term, laminate.

LOFTING – Redrawing and fairing the lines of the hull to full size in order to determine the actual contours used to build the boat.

MALE MOLD – The type of mold where a part is made up over the mold instead of inside the mold, with the inner surface of the molded part against the mold surface.

MAT – A felt-like material of randomly oriented strands of glass fibers held together with a binder.

"MEK" – Methylethyl ketone, a solvent sometimes used for clean-up purposes.

MEK PEROXIDE – Methylethyl ketone peroxide, the catalyst commonly used for curing polyester resin.

"MICROBALLOONS" – Proprietary name for a brand of microspheres.

MICROSPHERES – Generic name for filler materials consisting of minute hollow gas-filled spheres used to make syntactic foams.

MIL – A unit of measurement used to measure fiber diameter or coating thickness (.001").

MOLD – An appliance or device used to shape and/or duplicate a part.

MOLD FRAME – See **FRAMES.**

MOLD RELEASE – See **RELEASE AGENT.**

MOLDING – The molded part or the act of forming materials into a given shape or form until the materials cure into a rigid part.

MONOFILAMENT – A single filament of indefinite length.

MONOMER – A simple compound capable of polymerization with itself or a compatible resin, while acting as a diluting agent. Styrene is the common monomer used in polyester resins.

"NEO" – Neopentyl glycol, a base used for certain gel coats.

NON-AIR INHIBITED RESIN – See **FINISHING RESIN.**

NON-CROSS LINKED FOAM – A foam material where the chemical molecules of the material are not linked together, making a thermoformable material.

ONE-OFF – The construction of a single boat or part, i.e. a "custom built" or "limited production" boat.

ORTHOPHTHALIC ("ORTHO") RESIN – Orthophthalic acid based polyester resin. Considered a "general purpose" resin.

ORTHOTROPIC – The arrangement of reinforcing fibers in a material so that different strength properties result in various directions. Strength is highest along the directions of fiber orientation.

PARTING FILM – See **RELEASE AGENT**

PIGMENTS – Coloring additives used to give color to resin much like the addition of pigments to paints.

PLUG – The appliance or device which is identical in shape to the finished object over which a female mold is built.

POLYESTER RESIN – Thermosetting resins which require the addition of a catalyst and accelerator to effect the cure. This is the common type of resin used in fiberglass boat construction.

POLYMER – The technical word for the end product produced from a monomer.

POLYMERIZATION – The chemical crosslinking reaction of the molecules in a resin or monomer, changing it from a liquid state to a solid state.

POROSITY – The formation of undesirable clusters of air bubbles in the surface or body of a laminate.

POST-CURE – Exposure of the cured resin to higher temperatures than during curing in order to obtain a more complete cure or more rapid cure.

POT LIFE – The length of time that a catalyzed resin remains workable while in a container until it must be discarded. Similar to GEL TIME except that this refers to the working time once the resin has been applied to the surface.

PREPREG — Reinforcing material impregnated with catalyzed resin ready for use, but retarded (such as by refrigeration) from premature curing.

PRIMARY BOND — Subsequent bonding of materials where the initial laminate has not yet cured.

PRINT-THROUGH — The weave or pattern of reinforcing material showing through the exterior surface or gel coat of a laminate.

PROMOTED RESIN — Polyester resin to which an accelerator has been added. Resin which does not have accelerator is said to be "unpromoted". Resin which has the promoter added before the user adds the catalyst is said to be "pre-promoted".

PROMOTOR — See **ACCELERATOR.**

"PVC" FOAM — Polyvinylchloride foam, a rigid structural foam.

"PVA" — Polyvinyl alcohol, a clear water soluble release agent.

RELEASE AGENT — Any material used to coat a mold to prevent a molded part from sticking to the mold, or a material used to keep the resin from sticking to any part of the work.

RESIN — A liquid plastic substance used to bond and saturate reinforcing materials which polymerizes to form a structural laminate.

RESIN-RICH — An area in a laminate where too much resin exists in relation to the reinforcing material.

RESIN-STARVED — An area in a laminate where too little resin exists in relation to the reinforcing material.

ROVING — Continuous strands of glass or other fibers grouped together to form an untwisted yarn or rope.

SANDWICH CONSTRUCTION — A type of laminate consisting of a core material bonded to skins on either side.

SECONDARY BOND — Subsequent bonding of materials where the initial laminate has cured.

SET UP — Resin which cures and hardens is said to have "set up", or polymerized.

SHELF LIFE — The length of time an uncatalyzed resin remains usable while stored in a sealed container.

S-GLASS — A type of fiberglass base material having higher strength properties than E-GLASS.

SILICON DIOXIDE — Common filler used to make a resin with thixotropic properties.

SIZING — The surface treatment of glass fibers during fiber forming operations which aids in machine manufacturer as well as aiding resin compatibility.

SOLE — The "floor" aboard boats.

SPECIFIC GRAVITY — The ratio of weight of any volume of a substance to the weight of an equal volume of water.

SPLASH — The questionable practice of making a female mold from an existing hull or part which serves as a plug to side-step the work of making a plug.

SPRAYUP — The method of building up fiberglass laminates using a chopper gun to simultaneously deposit fibers and resin onto a mold surface.

SQUEEGEE – Any tool used to wet out a laminate with a smoothing, spreading, or wiping action in order to eliminate wrinkles and air entrapment.

STRAND – A bundle of continuous fiberglass filaments.

"STR-R-ETCH MESH" – A proprietary woven steel wire mesh product used as a substrate in the FERRO-GLASS system.

STRONGBACK – See **BUILDING FORM.**

STYRENE – The primary monomer ingredient and diluting agent used in polyester resins.

SUBSTRATE – A material that provides a supporting surface for other materials.

SURFACING AGENT – Material added to polyester resin or used with it to prevent air from reaching the surface so that the resin will cure tack-free. Paraffin wax in a solution of styrene is a common type. PVA also serves this purpose, but it is not mixed with the resin.

SURFACING MAT OR VEIL – A thin mat layer usually used against the surface of a female mold or as the surface layer in a laminate to prevent print-through, water absorption, and damage to the reinforcing portion of the laminate.

SYNTACTIC FOAM – Resin which has been made lower in density, lighter in weight, higher in viscosity, and generally "stretched out" for filling purposes.

TABLE OF OFFSETS – The table or listing of dimensions used in lofting.

TACK – Stickiness of a cured resin or other surface.

TAPE – A narrow type of fiberglass cloth.

THERMOPLASTIC – A type of plastic or resin which can be repeatedly softened or reformed by the application of heat, and can be hardened by cooling.

THERMOSET – A type of plastic or resin which will undergo a chemical change to a solid state from a liquid as the result of the heat induced by the addition of certain materials. Once it becomes solid, it cannot be reformed by heating. Polyester and epoxy resins are examples of this type.

THICKENER – Material added to resin to thicken or increase the viscosity so it will not flow as readily. See FILLER.

THINNER – Material such as styrene added to resin in order to thin it or lower the viscosity.

THIXOTROPIC – A quality of some resins to thicken at rest, but become fluid again on agitation and stirring.

TRI-AXIAL – Fiber orientation in a fabric or laminate in three directions.

UNIDIRECTIONAL – Fiber orientation in a fabric or laminate in one direction.

VACUUM BAG MOLDING – The process of eliminating voids and forcing out entrapped air and excess resin from laminates, while providing laminating pressure, by drawing a vacuum into a plastic bag draped over the part.

VINYLESTER RESIN – A type of polyester resin with improved physical properties, especially at elevated temperatures, over either ortho or iso polyesters.

VISCOSITY – The quality of a liquid's resistance to flow. A more viscous liquid will not flow as easily as one that has less viscosity.

WARP – Along the length of fabric or material.

WEFT – Across the width of fabric or material.

WET OUT – A material which is saturated with resin is said to be "wet out". Also the quality of a material to absorb resin.

WICKING – The travel of moisture or water through fibers in a laminate not totally wetted out or encapsulated with resin.

WOOF – See **WEFT**.

WOVEN ROVING (W.R.) – Rovings of fiberglass or other materials woven into a coarse, heavy fabric.

"WR" – See **WOVEN ROVING**.

YARN – Twisted strands or strands of glass fibers which can be woven, braided, served, and processed on conventional textile equipment.

suppliers & manufacturers

BALTEK CORP.
P.O. Box 195
Northvale, NJ 07647
201/767-1400
Manufacturers of CONTOURKORE end-grain balsa and distributers of AIREX foam

COOK COMPOSITES & POLYMERS
P.O. Box 419389
Kansas City, MO 64141-3689
Manufacturers of gel coat resins

DIAB GROUP/KLEGECELL
204 N. Dooley St.
Grapevine, TX 76051
817/481-3547
Manufacturers of KLEGECELL foam and PRO-BALSA

DIAB GROUP/DIVINYCELL
315 Seahawk Dr.
Desoto, TX 75115
972/228 7600
Manufacturers of DIVINYCELL foam

GLEN-L MARINE DESIGNS
9152 Rosecrans Ave.
Bellflower, CA 90706-2138
562/630-6258
Suppliers of fiberglass boatbuilding supplies

ORCON CORP.
1570 Atlantic St.
Union City, CA 94587
510/489-8100
Manufacturers of ORCOWEB specialty and high modulus reinforcements

RAM PRODUCTS
210 E. Alondra Blvd.
Gardena, CA 90248
213/321-0710
Manufacturers of gel coat resins

SEEMANN FIBERGLASS
6117 River Rd.
Harahan, LA 70123
504/738-6035
Manufacturers of C-FLEX fiberglass planking

bibliography & selected reading

The following listing includes books on subjects directly or indirectly related to fiberglass boat design and construction, and completing or outfitting boats in general. No single text can be expected to cover all aspects of every boatbuilding project; there are too many types and sizes of boats for this to be practical. Hence, a brief description of each text has been made so that the reader will have an idea if the book noted is applicable to his needs. The listing is not meant to be all inclusive, however, the books listed are highly recommended by the author with respect to their subject areas.

APPLICATIONS MANUAL FOR COOK'S POLYCOR POLYESTER RESINS & GEL COATS — Fifth Edition. Cook Paint & Varnish Co., Kansas City, MO

Although oriented to the factory situation, it covers tooling and fabrication with polyesters in detail, including gel coats and fabrication equipment, with an emphasis on trouble shooting.

BOATBUILDING — Howard I. Chapelle, 1994. W.W. Norton & Co., New York, NY

This classic text is a good orientation to boatbuilding even though it is concerned with traditional wood construction. The sections of lofting, joinery, and outfitting are timeless.

BOATBUILDING MANUAL, FOURTH EDITION- Robert M. Steward, 1994.

International Marine, Camden, ME

A good general introductory text on boatbuilding emphasizing wood boat construction, but with details and information applicable to all types of boat construction, including lofting.

BOATBUILDING WITH BALTEK DURACORE — David G. Brown, 1994.

This book details the use of DURACORE.

BOATBUILDING WITH PLYWOOD - THIRD EDITION — Glen L. Witt, 1989. GLEN-L Marine Designs, Bellflower, CA

A valuable text where plywood will be included in the project, whether or not the boat is built from fiberglass. Also covers lofting and joinerywork.

C-FLEX CONSTRUCTION MANUAL FOR CUSTOM GRP FABRICATION WITH C-FLEX FIBERGLASS PLANKING — Barry Kennedy, 1991. Seemann Fiberglass, New Orleans, LA

Technical manual published by the manufacturer's of C-FLEX Fiberglass Planking. Covers all aspects of the use of this material.

FIBERGLASS BOAT DESIGN & CONSTRUCTION — Robert J. Scott, 1973. John de Graff, Inc., Clinton Corners, NY

Professional design and engineering manual oriented to female mold series production. Some good construction details.

HOW TO FIBERGLASS BOATS, 2nd Edition — Ken Hankinson, 1986. GLEN-L Marine Designs, Bellflower, CA

A concise introductory "how-to" text on working with fiberglass and resin, and related materials, although oriented primarily to the sheathing of wood boats.

INBOARD MOTOR INSTALLATIONS — Glen L. Witt & Ken Hankinson, 1978. GLEN-L Marine Designs, Bellflower, CA

Covers all aspects of installing any type of motor in any type of boat, including fuel systems, exhaust and cooling systems, ventilation, steering, controls, propellers, and transmissions.

RULES FOR BUILDING AND CLASSING REINFORCED PLASTIC VESSELS — 1978. American Bureau of Shipping, New York, NY

Technical "building code" manual covering scantlings and other aspects of classified fiberglass boats. Much information applies to the larger commercial-type craft; not for the novice.

SAFETY STANDARDS FOR SMALL CRAFT — American Boat & Yacht Council, New York, NY

Manual covering recommended practices and standards of design, construction, equipment, and fitting out of all types of pleasure boats. An industry "bible" that's suitable for the amateur builder involved in larger projects.

YOUR BOAT'S ELECTRICAL SYSTEM — Conrad Miller & Elbert S. Maloney, 1988. Hearst Books, New York, NY

Covers all aspects of electrical systems and equipment, installation, trouble shooting, and maintenance. While not related specifically to fiberglass boatbuilding, the book is recommended to anyone installing any sort of electrical system aboard any boat.

illustration credits

Aladdin Products — Fig. 13-7, 17-2 through 17-5.

Baltek Corp. — Fig. 8-3, 8-4, 20-3 through 20-11.

Berkeley Pump Co. — Fig. 11-9.

Brewer, Ted; 217 Edith Point Rd., Anacortes, WA 98221 — Fig. 11-15, 14-5, 14-6, 23-3, 30-18.

Conboy, Joseph; West Urbanna Wharf, Route 615, Urbanna, VA 23175 — Fig. 19-9, 19-10, 30-16, 31-4, 31-5.

Cook Paint & Varnish Co. — Fig. 15-5 through 15-12.

Cross, Norman; 4326 Ashton, San Diego, CA 92110 — Fig. 12-18, 27-11, 30-6.

Orcon Corp. — Fig. 21-4, 21-6, 22-4, 22-6, 22-11 through 22-14.

Owens-Corning Corp. — Fig. 5-1, 5-3, 5-4, 5-5.

PPG Industries — Fig. 5-2.

Seemann Fiberglass — Fig. 12-8, 12-12 through 12-17, 13-1 through 13-6, 14-4, 16-2, 16-4, 16-8 through 16-20, 16-45 through 16-60, 26-10, 26-11, 27-10, 27-12, 30-11 through 30-14.

Steward, Robert; 4335 Lucera Rd., Jacksonville, FL 32244 — Fig. 19-16 through 19-20, 26-5, 26-6.

Torin, Inc. — Fig. 8-1, 11-16, 11-17, 11-18, 14-1, 14-2, 14-3, 18-11, 18-12, 19-3, 19-4, 19-5, 19-8, 19-11 through 19-18, 23-1, 23-2, 23-4, 26-1, 27-17, 30-17.

Touchberry, Andy; — Fig. 10-2.